Legal Research

Second Edition

DELMAR CENGAGE L[...]

Options.

Over 300 products in every area of the law: textbooks, online courses, CD-ROMs, reference books, companion websites, and more – helping you succeed in the classroom and on the job.

Support.

We offer unparalleled, practical support: robust instructor and student supplements to ensure the best learning experience, custom publishing to meet your unique needs, and other benefits such as Delmar Cengage Learning's Student Achievement Award. And our sales representatives are always ready to provide you with dependable service.

Feedback.

As always, we want to hear from you! Your feedback is our best resource for improving the quality of our products. Contact your sales representative or write us at the address below if you have any comments about our materials or if you have a product proposal.

Accounting and Financials for the Law Office • Administrative Law • Alternative Dispute Resolution • Bankruptcy Business Organizations/Corporations • Careers and Employment • Civil Litigation and Procedure • CLA Exam Preparation • Computer Applications in the Law Office • Constitutional Law • Contract Law • Court Reporting Criminal Law and Procedure • Document Preparation • Elder Law • Employment Law • Environmental Law • Ethics Evidence Law • Family Law • Health Care Law • Immigration Law • Intellectual Property • Internships Interviewing and Investigation • Introduction to Law • Introduction to Paralegalism • Juvenile Law • Law Office Management • Law Office Procedures • Legal Nurse Consulting • Legal Research, Writing, and Analysis • Legal Terminology • Legal Transcription • Media and Entertainment Law • Medical Malpractice Law Product Liability • Real Estate Law • Reference Materials • Social Security • Sports Law • Torts and Personal Injury Law • Wills, Trusts, and Estate Administration • Workers' Compensation Law

---

DELMAR CENGAGE Learning
5 Maxwell Drive
Clifton Park, New York 12065-2919

For additional information, find us online at:
www.delmar.cengage.com

DELMAR CENGAGE Learning™

Legal Research

Second Edition

William H. Putman

DELMAR
CENGAGE Learning™

Australia • Brazil • Japan • Korea • Mexico • Singapore • Spain • United Kingdom • United States

Legal Research, Second Edition
William H. Putman

Vice President, Career and Professional Editorial: Dave Garza

Director of Learning Solutions: Sandy Clark

Senior Acquisitions Editor: Shelley Esposito

Managing Editor: Larry Main

Senior Product Manager: Melissa Riveglia

Editorial Assistant: Danielle Klahr

Vice President, Career and Professional Marketing: Jennifer McAvey

Marketing Director: Deborah Yarnell

Marketing Manager: Erin Brennan

Marketing Coordinator: Jonathan Sheehan

Production Director: Wendy Troeger

Production Manager: Mark Bernard

Senior Art Director: Joy Kocsis

Manufacturing Buyer: Charlene Taylor

Content Project Manager: Karunakaran Gunasekaran

Compositor: PrePress PMG

For product information and technology assistance, contact us at
Cengage Learning Customer & Sales Support, 1-800-354-9706

For permission to use material from this text or product,
submit all requests online at **cengage.com/permissions**
Further permissions questions can be e-mailed to
permissionrequest@cengage.com

Library of Congress Control Number: 2009929662

ISBN-13: 978-1-4283-5701-3

ISBN-10: 1-4283-5701-7

Delmar
5 Maxwell Drive
Clifton Park, NY 12065-2919
USA

Cengage Learning is a leading provider of customized learning solutions with office locations around the globe, including Singapore, the United Kingdom, Australia, Mexico, Brazil, and Japan. Locate your local office at:
international.cengage.com/region

Cengage Learning products are represented in Canada by Nelson Education, Ltd.

To learn more about Delmar, visit **www.cengage.com/delmar**

Purchase any of our products at your local college store or at our preferred online store **www.ichapters.com**

Notice to the Reader

Publisher does not warrant or guarantee any of the products described herein or perform any independent analysis in connection with any of the product information contained herein. Publisher does not assume, and expressly disclaims, any obligation to obtain and include information other than that provided to it by the manufacturer. The reader is expressly warned to consider and adopt all safety precautions that might be indicated by the activities described herein and to avoid all potential hazards. By following the instructions contained herein, the reader willingly assumes all risks in connection with such instructions. The reader is notified that this text is an educational tool, not a practice book. Since the law is in constant change, no rule or statement of law of this book should be relied upon for any service to any client. The reader should always refer to standard legal sources for the current rule or law. If legal advice or other expert assistance is required, the services of the appropriate professional should be sought. The publisher makes no representations or warranties of any kind, including but not limited to, the warranties of fitness for particular purpose or merchantability, nor are any such representations implied with respect to the material set forth herein, and the publisher takes no responsibility with respect to such material. The publisher shall not be liable for any special, consequential, or exemplary damages resulting, in whole or part, from the readers' use of, or reliance upon, this material.

Printed in the United States of America
2 3 4 5 6 7 13 12 11 10

DEDICATION

This book is dedicated to P. Y., whose love,
inspiration, and guidance made this text possible.
Thank you.

Brief Contents

Contents

CHAPTER 4 Constitutions, Statutes, Administrative Law, and Court Rules—Research and Analysis · 73

CHAPTER 5 Case Law—Research and Briefing · 122

CHAPTER 9 Computer and Internet Research   266

CHAPTER 10 Commercial Internet Research   285

CHAPTER 11 Legal Citation   312

CHAPTER 12 Counteranalysis   352

CHAPTER 13 The Research Process for Effective Legal Research   371

Preface

Paralegals and law clerks are increasingly called upon to perform substantive legal research tasks. The purpose of this book is to provide instructors with a textbook that focuses on legal research. Currently, few texts are limited solely to the topic of legal research. Most of the texts include both legal research and legal writing. In those texts, often either the research or the writing component is not covered in depth. If you are interested in a text that covers research, analysis, and writing, consider using *Legal Research, Analysis, and Writing*, 2E, Delmar Cengage Learning, © 2010. If you are interested in a text that focuses on legal analysis and writing, see *Legal Analysis and Writing*, 3E, Delmar Cengage Learning, © 2009.

The text is designed for use in legal research classes. It can be useful in schools that have separate research and writing courses, where the first course focuses primarily on research with an introduction to writing, and the second course focuses on writing with research as a secondary component.

The goal of the text is to provide the student with in-depth knowledge of the fundamentals of legal research, the operation of the elements of these fundamentals in the research process, and the manner in which the process guides and assists the student in performing a research assignment.

The impetus for this book came from student requests for comprehensive information regarding many of the difficult areas of legal research and analysis, such as:

+ How to identify the key facts in a case
+ How to identify the issue
+ How to conduct statutory research and analysis
+ How to conduct case law research
+ How to brief cases
+ How to determine whether a case is on point
+ How to research secondary authority
+ How to conduct electronic research
+ How to cite authority
+ How to conduct counteranalysis

The book begins with an introductory chapter covering sources of law, definitions of key legal research terms such as *precedent*, an introduction to legal analyses and the research process, and fundamental approaches to legal research.

The second section includes two chapters that focus on how to determine what to research. One chapter addresses key facts and key terms, their importance and use in legal research and analysis, and how to identify key facts and key terms. The next chapter discusses the importance and role of identifying the issue in legal research, the elements of an issue, and how to find the issue (spot the issue).

The next section consists of eight chapters that provide in-depth coverage of the primary and secondary research sources (four chapters on what the sources are, and how to find and use them), Internet and computer research (two chapters), citation format, and case law analysis (determining whether a case is on point).

The text concludes with a chapter on counteranalysis and a chapter on how to conduct legal research in an efficient manner to avoid wasted time and duplication of effort. The last chapter includes a discussion of what to look for when researching, what to do with research after it is found, and how to organize research.

Each chapter includes examples of each concept or principle discussed and a hypothetical fact situation through which the application of the concepts and principles is illustrated.

CHAPTER FEATURES

Each chapter is designed to help students completely understand and apply the concepts presented in the chapter. Chapters include the following features.

Hypothetical

Each chapter begins with a hypothetical that raises a question or questions involving the subject matter of the chapter. Following the hypothetical is a presentation of the principles, concepts, guidelines, and information concerning the subject matter. After the discussion of the subject matter, the principles and information discussed in the chapter are applied to answer the question or questions raised in the hypothetical. In addition, the hypotheticals presented at the beginning of Chapters 1 and 2 are discussed in the application section of each chapter to allow students to see how the principles and guidelines presented throughout the text apply in two different fact situations.

The use of the hypothetical at the beginning of the chapter creates student interest in the subject matter of the chapter. The answer to the hypothetical toward the end of the chapter allows the student to see how the subject matter ties together and is applied.

Key Points

Each chapter has a list of key points that may be used as a quick reference and checklist when applying the concepts presented in the chapter. This checklist allows both the instructor and the student to make sure nothing is missed when reviewing or applying the principles presented in the chapter.

In-Depth Coverage of Topics

The greatest advantage of this text for both teachers and students is the comprehensive and in-depth coverage of topics that are not thoroughly covered in most texts. These topics include the following:

- Step-by-step approach to researching primary and secondary authority with multiple examples
- Issue identification (issue spotting)
- Statutory analysis
- Case law analysis (is a case on point?)
- Counteranalysis
- How to use a research process to conduct legal research in an efficient manner to avoid wasted time and duplication of effort

Examples

A major advantage of the text is that every principle, concept, and so on is followed by an example that illustrates it. One of my students requested that there be "plenty of examples." This text has plenty of examples. These examples help the instructor teach principles and concepts and help the student understand them.

Internet Resources

Each chapter contains a list of Internet resources related to the chapter topic. This allows access to additional information on chapter topics from the Internet.

Assignments

There are assignments at the end of each chapter that range in difficulty. The assignments require students to apply the principles and techniques presented in the text. For example, among other assignments, there are eight case brief assignments in Chapter 5 (the cases are presented in Appendix C). The answers to all the assignments are presented in the Instructor's Manual.

Chapter References

Each chapter will have a list of key terms used in the chapter and the page number in the chapter where the term is introduced, allowing students quick reference to terms used in the chapter. Please note that these "Chapter References" are not like traditional "Key Terms" in that not all of them are defined in the Glossary.

Sample Citations

At the end of each chapter introducing primary and secondary authority are examples of citations to the various authorities discussed in the text.

Appendices

The text has three appendices and a glossary of terms. Appendix A presents a sample memorandum based upon the Chapter 2 hypothetical. Appendix B is a chart listing various research resources and their use. Appendix C consists of court opinions that are used in conjunction with chapter assignments.

Readability

The text is written in a manner that a layperson can understand. Legalese is avoided, concepts are illustrated with examples, and the subject matter is presented simply and clearly.

NEW FEATURES—SECOND EDITION

Chapter 10 was restructured to simplify the discussion of Westlaw and LexisNexis and expand the coverage of nonfee-based Internet resources. Chapter 11 is updated using the 18th edition (2005) of *The Bluebook: A Uniform System of Citation* and the 3rd edition (2006) of the *ALWD Citation Manual: A Professional System of Citation*.

A major addition to the second edition is the inclusion of a CD with each text. The CD provides additional assignments, chapter outline, and study questions for each chapter.

The first edition included repeated references to other chapters and definitions of key terms and concepts throughout the text. One of my goals in doing this was to save students from having to refer to other chapters for the definitions of concepts and terms used in other chapters. From the feedback I have received, it is apparent that these repeated references served more to interrupt the flow of the text rather than help the students. Most of these references have been removed from the second edition. In addition, I have added new material and condensed other sections.

SUPPORT MATERIAL

The text is accompanied by the following support material, which is designed to assist students in learning and instructors in teaching.

Student CD-ROM

The new accompanying CD-ROM provides additional material to help students master the important concepts in the course. The CD-ROM includes additional assignments, chapter outline, and study questions for each chapter.

Instructor's Manual

Each chapter has several exercises ranging in difficulty. The Instructor's Manual provides complete answers to each exercise, general guides for the instructors, lesson plan/ lecture outlines, teaching tips, suggested additional assignments, and answers to Online Companion and Student CD-ROM assignments.

　　The Instructor's Manual also includes True/False and Multiple Choice test questions and answers for each chapter.

INSTRUCTOR
RESOURCES

Instructor Resources CD-ROM

Spend Less Time Planning and More Time Teaching. With Delmar, Cengage Learning's Instructor Resources to Accompany Legal Research, preparing for class and evaluating students has never been easier!

　　This invaluable instructor CD-ROM allows you anywhere, anytime access to all of your resources:

- ✦ The **Instructor's Manual** contains various resources and answers for each chapter of the book.
- ✦ The **Computerized Testbank** in ExamView makes generating tests and quizzes a snap. With many questions and different styles to choose from, you can create customized assessments for your students with the click of a button. Add your own unique questions and print rationales for easy class preparation.
- ✦ Customizable **PowerPoint® Presentations** focus on key points for each chapter.

PowerPoint® is a registered trademark of the Microsoft Corporation.

　　All of these Instructor materials are also posted on our Web site, in the Online Resources section.

Online Companion™

The text has a corresponding online companion that, among other things, has a section for each chapter that includes the following:

- ✦ Additional assignments that allow the students the convenience of being able to obtain assignments through the computer
- ✦ Links to Web sites that provide additional information related to the chapter topic
- ✦ A chapter summary and outline

The Online Companion™ can be found at www.paralegal.delmar.cengage.com in the Online Companion™ section of the Web site.

Web Page

Come visit our Web site at www.paralegal.delmar.cengage.com, where you will find valuable information such as hot links and sample materials to download, as well as other Delmar Cengage Learning products.

Please note that the Internet resources are of a time-sensitive nature and URL addresses may often change or be deleted.

ACKNOWLEDGMENTS

I wish to gratefully acknowledge and express my deep appreciation to a number of individuals who took time and effort to assist in the development of this book. Without their expertise, suggestions, and support, this text would not have been remotely possible. I am particularly indebted to the following individuals:

Pamela A. Lambert, Esquire, who reviewed the text for intellectual and legal content and consistency. Her legal expertise, analytical skills, and input were invaluable. Pam's encouragement and positive attitude helped me through the rough spots.

Kate Arsenault, who reviewed the text for general readability. Kate's patient support and encouragement helped ensure the text would be completed.

Dai Nguyen, Esquire, for her encouragement and assistance with hypotheticals.

Sharon Parmer, a paralegal, whose review and comments were helpful in the development of the text.

Sheila McGlothlin, a paralegal, for her support in the overall development of the text.

West, a Thomson Reuters business, for permission to publish all the cases in this text.

Shelley Esposito, Melissa Riveglia, Melissa Zaza, Danielle Klahr, Mark Bernard, and all the individuals at Delmar Cengage Learning who helped with the development of the second edition. Their encouragement, suggestions, patience, and support were essential to its completion. Finally, I would like to thank the reviewers who provided very valuable comments and suggestions for the text:

Regina Dowling
Bradford Hall Career Institute
Windsor, CT

Scott Myers
Marist College
Poughkeepsie, NY

Patricia Ellis-Griggs
San Jacinto Community College
Houston, TX

Diane Pevar
Manor College
Jenkintown, PA

Janice Kazmier
Tulane University
Jefferson, LA

Derek Thomson
Bryant and Stratton College
Rochester, NY

ABOUT THE AUTHOR

William Putman received his Juris Doctor degree from the University of New Mexico School of Law and has been a member of the New Mexico Bar since 1975. For ten years he was an instructor in the Paralegal Studies Program at Central New Mexico Community College in Albuquerque, New Mexico, and the Paralegal Studies Program at Santa Fe Community College, in Santa Fe, New Mexico.

He is the author of the *Pocket Guide to Legal Writing*, the *Pocket Guide to Legal Research*, and the textbooks *Legal Research, Analysis and Writing*; *Legal Analysis and Writing*; and *Legal Research*. He also authored the legal writing column in *Legal Assistant Today*, James Publishing Co, for two years, and published several articles on legal analysis and writing in the magazine.

Table of Cases

CHAPTER 1

Introduction to Legal Principles and Authorities and the Research Process

Outline

I. Introduction
II. Sources of Law
III. Hierarchy of the Law
IV. Authority
V. Legal Research and Analysis Process
VI. Key Points Checklist: *Researching the Law*
VII. Application

Learning Objectives

After completing this chapter, you should understand:

✦ The main sources and types of law
✦ The basic structure of the state and federal court systems
✦ The hierarchy of the various sources of law
✦ The types of legal authority
✦ When and how legal authority apply
✦ The elements of the legal research and analysis process

Vanessa works in a clerical position at the Addison law firm. She is an excellent employee. Last fall she entered the paralegal program offered by the local community college. The firm, in support of her continuing education, pays her tuition and allows her to leave work early so that she can attend a late afternoon class. The firm recently reassigned her to work in the paralegal division and directed that she be assigned some substantive legal research and analysis tasks.

Her first assignment is to locate the law in a case involving a client, Frank Reins. A year and a half ago, Mr. Reins loaned $2,000 to a coworker, Larry Stewart. Mr. Stewart promised to repay the loan in 60 days. He did not repay it. Every time Mr. Reins asked Mr. Stewart when he was going to pay, he would say, "I'll pay at the end of the month." This occurred for several months and finally Mr. Reins went to Mr. Stewart's house and demanded payment. Mr. Stewart wrote a check and gave it to Mr. Reins. When Mr. Reins went to Mr. Stewart's bank to cash the check, there were insufficient funds to cover the check. Mr. Reins, now angry, returned to Mr. Stewart's house. Mr. Stewart's 20-year-old son accompanied Mr. Stewart when he opened the door. A shouting match ensued and the son attacked Mr. Reins. Once the attack started, Mr. Stewart encouraged his son, yelling, "Hit him again, beat him." Mr. Stewart's only action in the fight was to encourage his son. Mr. Reins suffered a broken jaw as a result of the beating. The son was charged with assault and

battery. The district attorney said that Mr. Stewart could not be charged under the criminal statute. Mr. Reins wants to know if he can sue Mr. Stewart. Vanessa's supervisor instructs her to focus on battery as a possible cause of action.

Vanessa's assignment is to locate and summarize the law governing the liability, if any, of Mr. Stewart. Vanessa's research revealed that the federal law does not apply because the fight did not take place in an area governed by federal law, such as a military base, and it did not involve a federal question. She also found that the state criminal battery statute does not apply to a bystander in a situation such as this. Her research revealed that Mr. Reins could sue Mr. Stewart in a civil tort action for battery. She determined that the state legislature had not passed a law addressing the subject and the matter was governed by the case law (court-made law). She also found that there was an *American Law Reports* (ALR) annotation and a *Restatement of the Law* on the subject.

When summarizing the law, Vanessa realizes that she must determine which research applies and how. If a complaint is filed in state court, which statutes and court opinions, if any, must the state court follow? Why? General guidelines that assist you in determining when and how legal authorities apply are presented in this chapter. The application of the guidelines to Vanessa's questions is presented in the Application section of this chapter.

Vanessa's assignment will be referred to as the *Reins v. Stewart* hypothetical throughout the text.

I. INTRODUCTION

As attorneys become more aware of the abilities of paralegals and legal researchers, paralegals and legal assistants are increasingly being assigned substantive legal research and analysis tasks. **Legal research** is the process of finding the law that applies to a client's problem. **Legal analysis** is the process of determining how the law applies to the problem. Research skills are important because they are necessary for solving legal problems. Inadequate or incompetent legal research may cause the legal question to be answered incorrectly and result in the researcher being fired or the attorney being disciplined or disbarred.

The goal of this text is to provide comprehensive coverage of legal research. Emphasis is placed on many of the difficult areas of legal research and legal analysis such as:

- ✦ Approaching a research assignment
- ✦ Identifying issues and key facts
- ✦ Locating statutory and case law
- ✦ Locating secondary authorities
- ✦ Analyzing statutory and case law
- ✦ Using counteranalysis
- ✦ Conducting legal research effectively and efficiently

Before considering these areas in subsequent chapters of the text, it is necessary to have a general understanding of the law, the legal system, and some of the basic doctrines and principles that apply to legal research and analysis. This is essential because legal research and analysis involve determining how the law applies to a client's facts, which in turn requires knowledge of what the law is, how to find it, and the general principles that govern its application. This chapter presents an overview of the legal system and fundamental principles that guide its operation. The definitions, concepts, doctrines, and principles addressed are referred to and applied in the subsequent chapters of the text. A familiarity with them is essential when studying those chapters.

There are various definitions of the term *law*, depending on the philosophy and point of view of the individual defining it. **Law** can be defined from a political, moral, or ethical perspective. *For the purposes of this text, law is defined as the enforceable rules that govern individual and group conduct in a society. The law establishes standards of conduct, the procedures governing that conduct, and the remedies available when the rules of conduct are not adhered to.* The purpose of the law is to establish standards that allow individuals to interact with the greatest efficiency and the least amount of conflict. When conflicts or disputes occur, law provides a mechanism for a resolution that is predictable and peaceful.

The following sections focus on the various sources of law and the principles and concepts that impact the analysis of these sources.

Note: The hypothetical situation presented at the beginning of this chapter and in Chapter 2 is discussed in the Application section of each chapter to allow you to see how the principles and guidelines presented throughout the text apply in two specific fact situations.

II. SOURCES OF LAW

The legal system of the United States, like the legal systems of most countries, is based upon history and has evolved with the passage of time. When the United States was settled, English law governed most of the colonies. As a result, the foundation of the U.S. legal system is the English model, with influences from other European countries.

In England, after the Norman Conquest under William the Conqueror in 1066, a body of law called the common law developed. The common law consisted of the law created by the courts established by the king. When colonization of the United States took place, the law of England consisted primarily of the common law and the laws enacted by Parliament. At the time of the Revolution, the English model was adopted and firmly established in the colonies.

After the Revolution, the legal system of the colonies remained largely intact and remains so to the present time. It consists of two main categories of law:

✦ Enacted law

✦ Common law/case law

A. Enacted Law

As used in this text, the term **enacted law** is the body of law adopted by the people or legislative bodies. It includes:

✦ *Constitutions*—adopted by the people

✦ *Statutes, ordinances*—laws passed by legislative bodies

✦ *Regulations–Administrative Law*—actions of administrative bodies that have the force of law

In the United States, society is governed by laws established by two governing authorities: the federal government and the state governments. Local governments are components of state governments and have the authority to govern local affairs. Each governing authority has the power to enact legislation affecting the rights and duties of members of society. It is necessary to keep this in mind when analyzing a problem, because the problem may be governed by more than one law. The categories of enacted law are addressed in the following text.

1. Constitutions

A **constitution** is a governing document adopted by the people. It establishes the framework for the operation of government, defines the powers of government, and guarantees the fundamental rights of the people. Both the federal and state governments have constitutions.

U.S. CONSTITUTION. The U.S. Constitution:

✦ Establishes and defines the powers of the three branches of federal government: executive (president), legislative (Congress), and judicial (courts)

✦ Establishes the broad powers of the federal and state governments and defines the relationship between the federal and state governments

✦ Defines in broad terms the rights of the members of society

STATE CONSTITUTIONS. Each state has adopted a constitution that establishes the structure of the state government. In addition, each state constitution defines the powers and limits of the authority of the state government and the fundamental rights of the citizens of the state.

2. Statutes

Statutes are laws passed by legislative bodies. Statutes declare rights and duties, or command or prohibit certain conduct. As used here, statute includes any law passed by any legislative body: federal (Congress), state (state legislature), or local (e.g, city council). Such laws are referred to by various terms, such as *acts, codes, statutes,* or *ordinances.* The term *ordinance* usually refers to a law passed by a local government. Statutory law has assumed an increasing role in the United States because many matters once governed by the common law are now governed by statutory law.

> **FOR EXAMPLE** Criminal law was once governed almost exclusively by the common law. Now statutory law governs a large part of criminal law, such as the definition of crimes.

Since statutes are usually designed to cover a broad range of present and future situations, they are written in general terms.

> **FOR EXAMPLE** Section 335-1-4 of a state's Uniform Owner Resident Relations Act provides, "If a court, as a matter of law, finds that any provision of a rental agreement was inequitable when made, the court may limit the application of such inequitable provision to avoid an inequitable result." The statute is written in general terms so that it covers a broad range of landlord/tenant rental situations and rental provisions. It is designed to cover all provisions of all rental agreements that may prove to be inequitable. The general terms of the statute allow a court a great deal of flexibility when addressing an issue involving an alleged inequitable lease provision. The court "may limit the application . . . to avoid an equitable result." How and to what degree the court limits the application of the lease provision is left to the court to decide.

3. Administrative Law

A third type of enacted law is **administrative law**. Legislative bodies are involved in determining what the law should be and enacting the appropriate legislation. They do not have the time and are not equipped to oversee the day-to-day running of the government and implementation of the laws. Legislatures delegate the task of administering the laws to administrative agencies. The agencies are usually under the supervision of the executive branch of the government.

When a law is passed, the legislature includes enabling legislation that establishes and authorizes administrative agencies to carry out the intent of the legislature. This enabling legislation usually includes a grant of authority to create rules and regulations necessary to carry out the law. These rules and regulations have the authority of law. The body of law that results is called *administrative law.* It is composed of the rules, regulations, orders, and decisions promulgated by the administrative agencies when carrying out their duties.

Administrative law is usually more specific than statutory law because it deals with the details of implementing the law.

> **FOR EXAMPLE** To implement the Clean Air Act, the Environmental Protection Agency (EPA) has adopted various regulations setting air quality standards. Many of these regulations establish specific numerical standards for the amount of pollutants that may be emitted by manufacturing plants. The Clean Air Act is written in broad terms, but the regulations enforcing it are specific. For example, the statute defines the exact amount of pollutants a new automobile may emit.

Enacted law covers a broad spectrum of the law. The process of analyzing enacted law is covered in detail in Chapter 4.

B. Common Law/Case Law

In a narrow sense, the term **common law** refers to the law created by courts in the absence of enacted law. Technically the term includes only the body of law created by courts when the legislative authority has not acted.

> **FOR EXAMPLE** The courts have created most of the law of torts. *Tort law* allows a victim to obtain compensation from the perpetrator for harm suffered as a result of the perpetrator's wrongful conduct. From the days of early England to the present, legislative bodies have not passed legislation establishing or defining most torts. In the absence of legislation, the courts have created and defined most torts and the rules and principles governing tort law.

The term **case law** refers to a broader range of law than *common law* does. Case law includes not only the law created by courts in the absence of enacted law, but also the law created when courts *interpret* or *apply* enacted law.

Often the term *common law* is used in a broad sense to encompass all law other than enacted law (i.e., law enacted by legislatures or adopted by the people). This text uses the term *common law* in the broadest sense to include case law (often called judge-made law). Throughout the remainder of text, the term *case law* is used primarily instead of the terms *common law* or *judge-made law* and should be interpreted to include all law other than enacted law.

As mentioned earlier, the case law system in the United States is based on the English common law, and much of the English common law has been adopted by the states. William the Conqueror established a king's court (Curia Regia) to unify the country through the establishment of a uniform set of rules and principles to govern social conduct throughout the country. The courts, in dealing with specific disputes, developed legal principles that could apply to similar disputes.

With the passage of time, these legal principles came to embody the case law. The case law process continues to the present day in both England and the United States, with courts continuously developing new rules, doctrines, and principles.

> **FOR EXAMPLE** One hundred and fifty years ago, there was no remedy in tort law for strict products liability (liability of manufacturers and sellers for harmful/dangerous defective products). The tort was developed by the courts in the twentieth century to address the needs of a modern industrial society.

The ability to research and analyze case law is an essential skill for a legal researcher. Court opinions are usually required to determine how a law is interpreted and how it applies to specific fact situations and problems such as those of the client's case.

1. Role of the Courts

Disputes in our society arise from specific fact situations. The courts are designed to resolve these disputes. When a dispute is before a court, it is called a case. The role of the court is to resolve the dispute in a peaceful manner through the application of the law to the facts of the case. To accomplish this resolution, the court must identify the law that controls the resolution of the dispute and apply that law to the facts of the case.

When there is no enacted or case law that governs a dispute, the court may be called upon to create new law. Where the meaning or application of an existing law is unclear or ambiguous, it may be necessary for the court to interpret the law. In interpreting and applying existing law, courts often announce new legal rules and principles. The creation of new law and the interpretation and application of existing law become law itself.

The result reached by a court is usually called a decision. The court's written decision, which includes how it ruled in a case and the reasons for the decision, is called an **opinion**. The case law is composed of the general legal rules, doctrines, and principles contained in court opinions.

2. Court Systems

A basic understanding of court systems is necessary for anyone analyzing a legal problem. The approach to a problem and the direction of research may depend upon whether relief is available in federal or state court, or both. This section presents a brief overview of the court systems.

There are two parallel court systems: the federal court system and the state court system. A concept that is common to both systems is jurisdiction. An understanding of this concept is essential to an understanding of the operation of both systems.

a. Jurisdiction

The types of cases that can come before a court of either system are determined by the jurisdiction of the court. **Jurisdiction** is the extent of a court's authority to hear and resolve specific disputes. A court's jurisdiction is usually limited to two main areas:

✦ Over persons by geographic area—personal jurisdiction

✦ Over subject matter by types of cases—subject matter jurisdiction

(1) Personal Jurisdiction.   **Personal jurisdiction** is the authority of the court over the parties to resolve a legal dispute involving the parties. The jurisdiction of state courts is limited to the geographic boundaries of the state or to matters that have some connection with the state.

> **FOR EXAMPLE**   New York state courts do not have authority to decide matters that take place in the state of Ohio. Their authority is limited to the geographic boundaries of the state of New York. A New York state court does have jurisdiction over an Ohio resident if the resident is involved in an automobile accident in the state of New York.

In addition, personal jurisdiction requires that the plaintiff and defendant be properly before the court. Assuming the correct court is chosen, a plaintiff is considered to be properly before the court by filing the pleading that starts the lawsuit (the complaint in a civil case or an indictment/information/complaint in a criminal case). A defendant is properly before the court when the defendant has been notified of the lawsuit, that is, has been correctly served with a copy of the complaint (service of process).

(2) Subject Matter Jurisdiction.   **Subject matter jurisdiction** is the court's authority over the types and kinds of cases it may hear and decide. In regard to subject matter jurisdiction, there are basically two types of courts in both the federal and state court systems:

✦ Courts of general jurisdiction

✦ Courts of limited jurisdiction

Courts of general jurisdiction have the authority to hear and decide any matter brought before them with some limitations. The U.S. district courts are the courts of general jurisdiction in the federal system. They have the authority to hear and decide all matters with federal questions (involving the U.S. Constitution or federal law) and cases where the parties are citizens of different states and the amount in controversy exceeds $75,000. All states have state courts of general jurisdiction that have authority over state matters.

Courts of limited jurisdiction are limited in the types of cases they can hear and decide. There are courts of limited jurisdiction in both the federal and state court systems.

FOR EXAMPLE	1. The U.S. Tax Court's authority is limited to matters involving federal tax law. 2. Most state court systems have courts whose authority is limited by dollar amount. Such courts are limited to hearing and deciding matters where the amount in controversy does not exceed a certain amount, such as $10,000. These courts are called by various names: small claims, magistrate, and so on. Some state courts are limited to hearing specific types of cases, such as matters involving domestic relations or probate.

(3) Concurrent Jurisdiction. **Concurrent jurisdiction** exists when more than one court has the authority to deal with the same subject matter. In such cases, the plaintiff may choose the court in which to file the case.

FOR EXAMPLE	In diversity of citizenship cases (disputes between citizens of different states) where the amount in controversy exceeds $75,000, the matter may be tried in either federal court or the state court of general jurisdiction. Both the federal and state courts have authority to try the case; they have concurrent jurisdiction.

Jurisdiction is a complex subject. Many texts provide an exhaustive and detailed treatment of jurisdiction, and the topic is properly addressed in a separate course of study. The brief discussion here is designed to acquaint you with the fundamentals.

b. Federal Court System

The federal court system is composed of three basic levels of courts.

(1) Trial Courts. The **trial court** is where the matter is heard and decided. It is where the testimony is taken, other evidence is presented, and the decision is reached. The role of the trial court is to determine the facts and how the law applies to those facts. A trial is presided over by a judge and may include a jury. If the trial is conducted by a judge and a jury, the judge decides **questions of law** such as what the law is or how it applies. The jury decides **questions of fact** such as whether a person performed a certain act. If the trial is conducted without a jury, the judge decides both questions of law and fact.

The U.S. **District Court** is the main trial court in the federal system. The court has jurisdiction over cases involving federal questions. This includes matters involving the U.S. Constitution, federal laws, U.S. treaties, and so on. The District Court also has the authority to try diversity cases. These are cases involving disputes between citizens of different states where the amount in controversy exceeds $75,000. Each state has at least one U.S. District Court (see Exhibit 1–1).

In addition to the U.S. District Court, there are other federal courts whose authority is limited to specific matters, for example, the U.S. Tax Court, the U.S. Court of International Trade, the Untied States Court of Federal Claims, and the U.S. Bankruptcy Court.

(2) Court of Appeals. A party aggrieved by the decision of a trial court has the right to appeal the decision to a **court of appeals** (also referred to as an appellate court). The primary function of a court of appeals is to review the decision of a trial court to determine and correct any error that may have been made. A court of appeals only reviews what took place in the trial court. It does not hear new testimony, retry the case, or reconsider the evidence. A court of appeals reviews the record of the lower court

Exhibit 1–1
United States Circuit
Courts of Appeals and
United States District
Courts.
Administrative office of the
United States Supreme Court
1988.

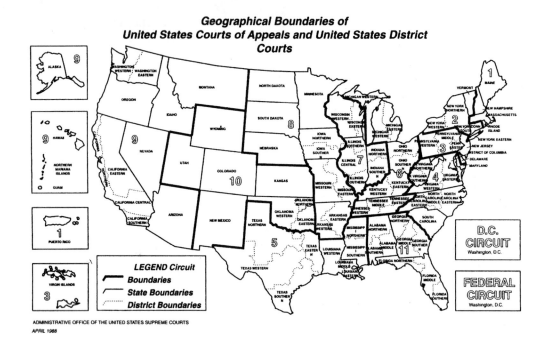

Geographical Boundaries of
United States Courts of Appeals and United States District
Courts

ADMINISTRATIVE OFFICE OF THE UNITED STATES SUPREME COURTS

APRIL 1988

and takes appropriate action to correct any errors made, such as ordering a new trial or reversing a decision of the trial court. The court of appeals in the federal system is called the U.S. Court of Appeals. These courts are also called circuit courts. There are 13 federal courts of appeals (see Exhibit 1–1).

(3) U.S. Supreme Court. The U.S. Supreme Court is the highest court in the land and the final court of appeals in the federal system. With few exceptions, an individual does not have an absolute right to have a matter reviewed by the Supreme Court. A party who disagrees with the decision of a court of appeals must request (petition) the Supreme Court to review it. The request is called a **petition for writ of certiorari**. The Supreme Court has discretion to review or not review a decision of a court of appeals. If the Court denies the petition, the decision of the court of appeals stands. If the Court decides that the matter involves important constitutional issues, if the challenged decision conflicts with federal court decisions, or if a conflict exists between the opinions of the Court of Appeals, the Supreme Court may grant the petition and review the decision of the lower court.

The organization of the federal court system and the various federal courts is presented in Exhibit 1–2.

c. State Court System

Every state has its own state court system, with unique features and variations. The names of the courts vary from state to state.

> **FOR EXAMPLE** The highest court in many states is called the supreme court. In New York, however, the highest court is called the court of appeals.

Because of the unique features of each state system, it is essential that you become familiar with the court system in your state. Like the federal court system, most state court systems are composed of three basic levels of courts.

(1) Trial Courts. All states have trial courts where the evidence is presented, testimony is taken, and a decision is reached. Usually there are trial courts of general jurisdiction and trial courts of limited jurisdiction. The court of general jurisdiction is often called

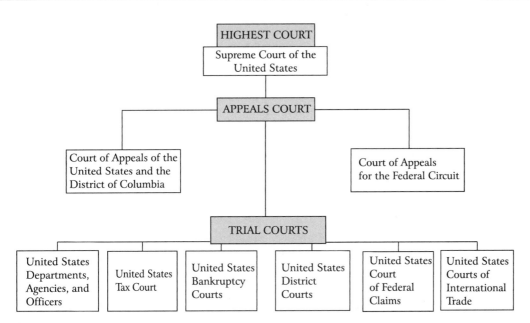

Exhibit 1–2
Organization of the
Federal Court System.

a district court. There are various courts of limited jurisdiction, such as probate courts, small claims courts, domestic relations courts, magistrate courts, and county courts.

(2) Courts of Appeals.   Many states have intermediary courts of appeals that function in the same manner and play the same role in the state court system as the federal court of appeals does in the federal system.

(3) State Supreme Court.   Every state has a highest appellate court, usually called the **supreme court**. This court is the highest court in the state, and its decisions are final on all questions involving state law. In states that have intermediary courts of appeals, the state supreme court often operates like the U.S. Supreme Court in that there is no automatic right of appeal. Like the federal Supreme Court, the state supreme court grants leave to appeal only in cases involving important questions of state law. In those states where there is no intermediary court of appeals, a party who disagrees with a trial court's decision has a right to appeal to the highest court. In either system, state or federal, all individuals have at least one opportunity to appeal the decision of a trial court to a higher court.

3. Precedent and Stare Decisis

It is apparent, when you consider the number of courts in the state and federal court systems, that an immense number of legal questions and problems are being addressed by the courts. Often, similar legal questions and similar fact situations arise in the same court system or in different court systems. If a court in an earlier case has developed a legal doctrine, principle, or rule that helps resolve a legal question, later courts addressing the same or a substantially similar question should be able to look to the earlier decision for guidance. Why should a court go through the process of determining how a matter should be decided if an earlier court has already gone through the process and developed a principle or rule that applies? The efficiency of the court system is greatly enhanced because courts do not have to "reinvent the wheel" in every case—they may rely on legal doctrines, principles, or rules developed in previous cases.

Reliance on doctrines, principles, or rules to guide the resolution of similar disputes in the future also makes the legal system more stable, predictable, and consistent. If the law governing a specific subject or legal question is established in an earlier case, individuals may rely on a court addressing the same or a similar question to base its decision on the principles established in the earlier case. Outcomes can be predicted to some extent, and stability and consistency become part of the court system.

Two complementary doctrines have been developed to provide stability, predictability, and consistency to the case law. These doctrines are precedent and stare decisis.

a. Precedent

Precedent is an earlier court decision on an issue that applies to govern or guide a subsequent court in its determination of an identical or similar issue based upon identical or similar facts.

> **FOR EXAMPLE** The state's highest court, in the case of *State v. Ahrens,* held that bail must be set in all criminal cases except where a court determines that the defendant poses a clear and present threat to the public at large or to an individual member or members of the public. If a case before a subsequent court involves a situation where the defendant has made threats against the life of a witness, *Ahrens* applies as precedent and can serve as a guide for the court's determination of the question of whether bail must be set.

A case that is precedent is often called **on point**. Chapter 6 discusses the process and steps to follow when determining if a court opinion may apply or be relied upon as precedent.

b. Stare Decisis

The doctrine of **stare decisis** is a basic principle of the case law system that requires a court to follow a previous decision of that court or a higher court when the current decision involves issues and facts similar to those involved in the previous decision. In other words, similar cases will be decided in similar ways. Under the doctrine, when the court has established a principle that governs a particular set of facts or a specific legal question, the court will follow that principle and apply it in all future cases with similar facts and legal questions. In essence, stare decisis is the doctrine that provides that precedent should be followed.

> **FOR EXAMPLE** A statute of state X prohibits employment discrimination on the basis of gender. In the case of *Ellen v. Employer, Inc.,* an employee was fired because the employee was homosexual. The supreme court of state X interpreted "discrimination on the basis of gender" as used in the statute to include discrimination based on an individual's sexual preference. The doctrine of stare decisis requires that in subsequent cases, the supreme court of state X and all the lower courts of state X must follow the interpretation of the statute given in *Ellen v. Employer, Inc.* In other words, the lower courts must follow the precedent set in *Ellen v. Employer, Inc.*

The doctrine of stare decisis, however, does not require rigid adherence to the rules or principles established in prior decisions. The doctrine does not apply if there is a good reason not to follow it. Some of these reasons include:

1. The earlier decision has become outdated because of changed conditions or policies.

> **FOR EXAMPLE** In *Plessy v. Ferguson,* 163 U.S. 537, 16 S. Ct. 1138, 41 L. Ed. 256 (1896), the Supreme Court adopted the "separate but equal doctrine" that allowed segregation on the basis of race. In *Brown v. Board of Education of Topeka,* 347 U.S. 483, 74 S. Ct. 686, 98 L. Ed. 873 (1954), the court refused to follow *Plessy* and overruled it, holding that separate educational facilities were inherently unequal and denied equal protection of the law.

2. The legislature has enacted legislation that has, in effect, overruled the decision of an earlier court.

> **FOR EXAMPLE** The state supreme court, in *Stevens v. Soro, Inc.,* ruled that the phrase "on the job" in the Workers' Compensation Act means that an employee is "on the job" from the moment the employee leaves for work until he or she arrives home. After the decision, the state legislature amended the act, defining "on the job" to include only the time the employee is on the premises of the employer. The amendment in effect overrules the prior court decision, and subsequent courts are not required to follow it.

3. The earlier decision was poorly reasoned or has produced undesirable results.

> **FOR EXAMPLE** Review the gender discrimination example presented at the beginning of this subsection. Suppose the supreme court of state X, in a later case, decides that the reasoning in the court's decision in *Ellen v. Employer, Inc.,* was incorrect and that the term *gender discrimination* should not be interpreted to include discrimination on the basis of sexual preference. The court can overrule *Ellen* and is not bound to follow it.

When a court follows the doctrines of precedent and stare decisis, the court can be relied on to reach the same decision on an issue as an earlier court when the cases are sufficiently similar. Without these doctrines, a similar case could be decided in an entirely different manner based upon the unique beliefs of the individual judge and jury. The result would be little or no consistency in the case law, and chaos would reign. When a decision of an earlier court may or must be relied on by a subsequent court is discussed later in this chapter in the sections addressing authority.

III. HIERARCHY OF THE LAW

A hierarchy of authority exists between the two primary sources of law, enacted law and case law. When a question arises concerning which source applies in a case or there is a conflict between sources, a hierarchy governs which source will apply.

In general, within each jurisdiction, the constitution is the highest authority, followed by the other enacted law (legislative and administrative law), and then the case law. This means that legislative acts and court decisions must not conflict with the provisions of the constitution. A court decision may interpret a legislative act, but it cannot overrule an act unless it is determined that the act violates the constitution.

The U.S. Constitution separates the powers to govern between the federal and state governments. This separation of powers is called **federalism**. The **supremacy clause** of the Constitution (Article VI) provides that between federal and state law, federal law is supreme. If an enacted law or court decision of a state conflicts with a federal law or court decision, the state law or decision is invalid to the extent it conflicts with the federal law or decision.

> **FOR EXAMPLE** A state passes a law declaring that it is illegal to burn the American flag. The state supreme court upholds the statute. Both the state statute and the state supreme court decisions are invalid because they conflict with the Constitution of the United States. The U.S. Supreme Court has ruled that the freedom of speech provisions of the Constitution include the right to burn the flag. The federal law is supreme, and the state law is invalid to the extent it conflicts with federal law.

IV. AUTHORITY

To analyze the law, in addition to knowing the sources of law, you must become familiar with the concept of authority, principles relating to authority, and the various types of authority. **Authority** is anything a court may rely on when deciding an issue. It includes not only the law, but also any other nonlaw source that a court may look to in reaching a decision.

This section discusses the two types of authority and the two roles that authority plays in the decision-making process. The two types of authority are:

- *Primary authority*—the law itself
- *Secondary authority*—nonlaw sources a court may rely on

Authority may play two possible roles:

- *Mandatory authority*—the authority a court must rely on and follow when deciding an issue
- *Persuasive authority*—the authority a court may rely on and follow, but is not bound to rely on or follow

The following subsections first address the two types of authority (primary and secondary), followed by a discussion of the role of authority, that is, the value or weight a court must or may give to authority (mandatory and persuasive authority; see Exhibit 1–3, "Types and Role of Authority").

Exhibit 1–3
Types and Role of
Authority.

Types of Authority	
Primary Authority	The law itself, such as constitutions, statutes, ordinances, administrative agency rules and regulations, and court opinions.
Secondary Authority	A source a court may rely on that is not the law, such as legal encyclopedias, ALR, Restatements of the Law, treatises, and law review articles.
Role of Authority	
Mandatory Authority	A source of law a court must rely on when reaching a decision, such as an enacted law (statute, ordinance, and so on) that governs the legal question being addressed, or an opinion of a higher court in the jurisdiction that addressed the same or a similar legal question and facts.
Persuasive Authority	Any authority a court is not bound to consider or follow but may consider or follow when reaching a decision, such as an opinion of a court in another state on the same or a similar issue, or a secondary authority source (encyclopedia article, legal dictionary definition, and so on).

A. Types of Authority

1. Primary Authority

Primary authority is the law itself. It is composed of the two main categories of law: enacted law and case law (discussed earlier in detail in Section II, "Sources of Law").

> **FOR EXAMPLE** Primary authority includes constitutions, statutes, ordinances, regulations, court opinions, and so on.

Courts refer to and rely on primary authority first when resolving legal problems.

2. Secondary Authority

Secondary authority is any source a court may rely on that is not the law, that is, not primary authority. Secondary authority consists of legal resources that summarize, compile, explain, comment on, interpret, or in some other way address the law.

Secondary authority can be used in several ways:

✦ To obtain a background or overall understanding of a specific area of the law. Legal encyclopedias, treatises, and periodicals are useful for this purpose.

> **FOR EXAMPLE** If the researcher is unfamiliar with a specific area of law—for example, defamation—a treatise on tort law will provide an overview of the area. The treatise will also include references to key court cases and enacted law (primary authority) concerning defamation.

✦ To locate primary authority (the law) on a question being researched. ALR, digests, and *Shepard*'s are particularly useful in this regard. All secondary authority sources include references to primary authority.

✦ To be relied on by the court when reaching a decision, which usually occurs only when there is no primary authority governing a legal question or it is unclear how the primary authority applies to the question. Treatises, law reviews, and *Restatements of the Law* are relied on for this purpose.

There are literally hundreds of secondary sources. An in-depth discussion of all of them is beyond the scope of this text, and therefore, only some of the major secondary sources are summarized here.

ANNOTATIONS. Annotations are notes and comments on the law. One of the well-known annotations is the *American Law Reports* (ALR). The ALR is a series of books that contains the complete text of selected court opinions, along with scholarly commentaries explaining and discussing issues raised in the case. The commentaries also include an overview of how the issues are treated nationally, focusing on the majority and minority views, and a list of cases from other jurisdictions dealing with the same issues. The ALR is useful for obtaining an in-depth overview of the courts' treatment of specific questions and issues. These annotations are also useful as an aid in locating court decisions dealing with specific issues.

LAW DICTIONARIES. Legal dictionaries include definitions of legal terms (and usually a citation to the authority for the definitions) and guides to pronunciation. The two major legal dictionaries are *Black's Law Dictionary*, published by West, a Thomson Reuters business, and *Oran's Dictionary of the Law*, published by Delmar Cengage Learning.

LAW REVIEWS. Law reviews are scholarly publications usually published by law schools. They contain articles written by professors, judges, and practitioners and include commentaries written by law students. The articles usually discuss specific topics and legal questions in great depth and include references to key cases on the subjects. These reviews are useful as a source of comprehensive information on specific topics.

LEGAL ENCYCLOPEDIAS. A legal encyclopedia is a multivolume set of books that provides a summary of the law. The topics are arranged in alphabetical order, and the set includes an index and cross-references. The two major legal encyclopedias are *Corpus Juris Secundum* (CJS) and *American Jurisprudence* (now *American Jurisprudence Second*; Am. Jur. or Am. Jur. 2d) both published by West, a Thomson Reuters business. An encyclopedia is a valuable source when seeking an overview of a legal topic.

RESTATEMENTS OF THE LAW. *Restatements of the Law*, published by the American Law Institute, presents a variety of topics and discusses what the law is on each topic, or what it should be. Following a presentation of the law is a "Comment" that explains the rule of law presented, discusses why the rule was adopted, and gives examples of how the rule applies. The *Restatements* are drafted by authorities and experts in specific areas and are often relied on and adopted by legislatures and courts.

TREATISES. A treatise is a single or multivolume work written by an expert in an area that covers that entire area of law. A treatise is often referred to as a *horn book*. It is a valuable resource because it provides a comprehensive treatment of a specific area of law, reference to statutes and key cases in the area, and commentaries on the law.

B. Role of Authority

After the types of authority have been identified, it is important to understand the role these sources play in the decision-making process. Not all authority referred to or relied on by a court when deciding an issue is given equal weight. Authority is divided into two categories for the purpose of determining its authoritative value, or the extent to which it must be relied on or followed by a court: mandatory authority and persuasive authority (see Exhibit 1–3, "Types and Role of Authority").

1. Mandatory Authority

Mandatory authority is any source that a court must rely on or follow when reaching a decision, for example, a decision of a higher court in the jurisdiction on the same or a similar issue. Primary authority can be mandatory authority because courts are required to follow the law itself. As discussed earlier, primary authority is composed of enacted law and case law. Secondary authority can never be mandatory authority. A court is never bound to follow secondary authority because it is not the law.

Not all primary authority, however, is mandatory authority. Not all law must be followed by a court when reaching a decision. Primary authority becomes mandatory authority only when it governs the legal question or issue being decided by the court. The factors involved in deciding when enacted law and case law may be mandatory authority are briefly discussed here.

a. Enacted Law

Chapter 4 addresses in detail the process for determining whether an enacted law applies to govern a legal question or issue before a court. The three-step process presented in that chapter is summarized here.

STEP 1: Identify all the laws that may govern the question. This requires locating all statutes or laws that possibly govern the legal question.

> **FOR EXAMPLE** Some legal questions and fact situations such as gender discrimination are governed by both state and federal law, and occasionally by more than one state or federal law.

After you identify the laws that may govern the question, determine which of these laws applies to the specific legal area involved in the dispute. This requires an analysis of the law.

> **FOR EXAMPLE** In the preceding example, an analysis of the law may reveal that even though both federal and state law govern the question of gender discrimination, the federal law requires that the matter be tried in state court before being pursued in federal court. The federal law, therefore, does not apply until the remedies available under state law have been pursued in the state courts.

STEP 2: Identify the elements of the law or statute. After you determine the specific law or laws govern the question, identify the elements of the law or statute, that is, the specific requirements that must be met for the law or statute to apply. It is necessary to identify the elements before moving on to step 3 to determine whether the requirements of the law or statute are met by the facts of the case.

> **FOR EXAMPLE** Mary bought a toaster at a local store. It did not work when she plugged it in. The store owner refused to replace the toaster or give her a refund when she returned it. The legal question is whether Mary can get a new toaster or her money back.
>
> Assume that after performing the first step, it is determined that article 2 of the state's commercial code is mandatory authority because article 2 applies to the sale of goods and a toaster is considered goods. Article 2 provides that a warranty is created if:
>
> + The transaction involves the sale of goods
> + The seller of the goods is a merchant
>
> These are the elements of the statute. These elements must be identified to determine what the section requires for the warranty to exist. It is necessary to identify these requirements before determining how the section applies to the client's facts. The statute further provides that the seller must replace the item or refund the purchase price if the item doesn't work.

STEP 3: Apply the facts of the case to the elements. The final step is to apply the facts of the client's case to the elements to determine how the law or statute applies. If the elements match the facts raised by the legal issue, the law applies and governs the outcome. Even if some of the elements are not met, the law still applies, but the outcome may be different.

> **FOR EXAMPLE** Step 3 requires matching the elements with the facts of the case. Referring to the previous example, the warranty exists if the two elements are met. In this case the first element is met because a toaster is considered goods. The second element is met because the store owner is considered a merchant because he routinely sells toasters. The elements are met and Mary is entitled to a new toaster or a refund.
>
> If the transaction does not involve the sale of goods, such as the sale of land, or the seller is not a merchant (e.g., the toaster was purchased at a yard sale), the elements of article 2 are not met, there is no warranty, and Mary is not entitled to a new toaster or a refund.

After you determine that an enacted law governs a legal question, the law is mandatory authority, and a court must apply the law unless the court rules that the law is unconstitutional.

b. Case Law

For a court opinion to be mandatory authority (often referred to as mandatory precedent) that binds another court to follow the rule or principle of law established in the opinion, two conditions must be met:

+ The court opinion must be on point.
+ The court opinion must be written by a higher court in that jurisdiction.

FOR EXAMPLE If the highest court in state A defines malice as used in the state's murder statute, then all the lower courts in state A (intermediary and trial courts) are bound to follow the highest court and apply the highest court's interpretation of the term in cases involving the statute.

In regard to the preceding example, is the highest court in state A, in later cases, bound to follow the earlier court's definition of malice? No. The highest court is always free to overturn the opinion and change the definition. The court will follow the earlier decision unless it overturns it or in some way amends it. The lower courts do not have this option.

What if the decision of the highest state court is different from the decision of a federal court? If a state court decision conflicts with the U.S. Constitution or federal law, the state court must follow the dictates of the federal law. State courts usually have the final say over interpretations of state law. If a federal court is addressing an issue involving state law, the federal court usually follows the interpretation of the state law rendered by the state's highest court.

Chapter 6 presents an in-depth discussion of case law analysis and the process involved in determining whether a case is on point.

2. Persuasive Authority

Persuasive authority is any authority a court is not bound to consider or follow, but may consider or follow when reaching a decision. Where there is mandatory authority, persuasive authority is not necessary, although its use is not prohibited. Persuasive authority consists of both primary authority and secondary authority.

a. Primary Authority as Persuasive Authority

On occasion, courts look to enacted law as persuasive authority.

FOR EXAMPLE A court, when interpreting a term not defined in an act, may apply the definition of the term that is given in another act. Suppose the term *gender discrimination* is not defined in the state's fair housing act but is defined in the state's fair loan act. The state's fair loan act is not mandatory authority for questions involving its fair housing act because the fair loan act does not govern housing. It can, however, be persuasive authority. The court may follow or be persuaded to apply the definition given in the fair loan act.

Primary authority represented by case law is often used as persuasive authority (often referred to as persuasive precedent). Even though case law is primary authority, it may not be mandatory authority in a specific situation if it does not apply to govern the situation. The court is not required to follow the authority. A court may, however, be guided by and persuaded to adopt the rule or principle established in another court opinion.

FOR EXAMPLE
1. The courts in state *A* have not addressed a legal issue. Therefore, no mandatory authority exists that state A courts must follow. State A courts may consider and adopt the rules and reasoning of federal or other state courts that have addressed the issue. It is not mandatory that state A follow the primary authority of the other federal or state courts, but state A may be persuaded to adopt the primary authority of these courts.
2. A trial court in state A has written an opinion on a legal issue. A higher court in state A is not bound by the lower court opinion (it is not mandatory authority), but it may consider and adopt the rule and reasoning of the lower court.

When no mandatory authority exists that a court is bound to follow, as in the preceding examples, the court may look to and rely on other primary authority as persuasive authority.

b. Secondary Authority as Persuasive Authority

As discussed earlier, secondary authority is not the law and, therefore, can never be mandatory authority. Where there is mandatory authority on an issue, it is not necessary to support it with secondary authority, although it is permissible. Secondary authority should not be relied upon when there is mandatory authority. In such situations, the mandatory authority governs. If no mandatory authority exists and there is persuasive primary authority, the secondary authority may be used in support of the primary authority.

> **FOR EXAMPLE** The courts in state *A* have never addressed a particular issue. The courts of state B have addressed the issue. The rule of law established by the state B courts can be persuasive primary authority for state A courts. Secondary sources, such as ALR commentaries and law review articles, may be submitted to a state A court in support of the persuasive primary authority from state B. Secondary authority also may be submitted to the court for the purpose of opposing the adoption of the persuasive authority from state B.

Secondary authority is most valuable when there is no primary authority, either mandatory or persuasive. This situation is rare, however. Few matters have never been addressed by either some legislature or court. As noted earlier, secondary authority is also valuable because it is useful in locating primary authority.

Some secondary authority is given greater weight or considered to have greater authoritative value than other secondary authority.

> **FOR EXAMPLE** A court will more likely rely on and give greater weight to a *Restatements of the Law* drafted by experts in the field than to a law review article written by a local practitioner in the field.

Always locate the available primary authority and exhaust all avenues of research in this direction before turning to the location of secondary authority. There are two reasons for this:

✦ Courts look to and consider primary authority before considering secondary authority.

✦ Primary authority often leads to key secondary authority sources.

> **FOR EXAMPLE**
> 1. A court opinion addressing an issue may include references to key secondary sources, such as ALR (*American Law Reports*) citations.
> 2. State statutes are often annotated, and the annotations include references to ALR and legal encyclopedia citations that address the area of law covered in the statute. The annotations also include references to law review articles that address specific issues related to the statute.

V. LEGAL RESEARCH AND ANALYSIS PROCESS

The focus of this text is on legal research and the legal research process. However, legal analysis must be considered when discussing legal research because legal research and legal analysis are integrally related. Legal research is the part of the legal analysis process that involves finding the law that applies to the legal question raised by the facts of a client's case.

A **legal research and analysis process** is a systematic approach to legal research and analysis. This organized approach helps you develop research skills, makes legal research easier, and saves time. There are many approaches to conducting legal research and analysis; there is no magic formula. A two-part legal research and analysis process is recommended. A summary of the process follows. Chapter 13 presents a comprehensive discussion of the process and guidelines to follow when engaging in legal research.

Part A—Analyze the Assignment

Part A requires identifying the type and purpose of the assignment; identifying the constraints on the performance of the assignment (such as time); and preparing an outline for the organization of the research.

Part B—Conduct Research

The second part of the process consists of five steps:

STEP 1: *Preliminary Preparation.* Gathering all information necessary to research and analyze the assignment, identify the key facts, and perform preliminary research if necessary.

STEP 2: Issue. Identify the issue (legal question) or issues raised by the facts of the client's case.

STEP 3: Rule. Identify the law that governs the issue, including the authority that interprets how the law applies to the issue.

STEP 4: Analysis/Application. Determine how the rule of law applies to the issue.

STEP 5: Conclusion. Create a summary of the results of the legal analysis.

An acronym commonly used in reference to steps 2 through 5 is **IRAC**, from the first letter of the descriptive term for these steps. IRAC is an easy way to remember the process—issue, rule, analysis/application, and conclusion. The research component of this process involves steps 1 through 3. These research steps are the focus of this text. Steps 4 and 5 of the process are not concerned with research, rather the analysis after the research is complete. A chart listing research sources and their primary use as research tools is presented in Appendix B.

VI. KEY POINTS CHECKLIST: *Researching the law*

■ When analyzing a legal question or issue, always identify the primary authority (the law) that governs the question. First, consider primary authority, then look to secondary authority. As a general rule, courts rely on primary authority before considering secondary authority.

■ When you are searching for the law that governs a topic, always consider all the possible sources of law:

✦ *Enacted law*—constitutions, statutes, ordinances, regulations, and so on

✦ *Case law*—law created by courts in the absence of enacted law

- Remember that two court systems are operating in every jurisdiction: state and federal. A legal problem may be governed by federal law, state law, or both. Both sources of law and both court systems must be considered when analyzing a problem.

- Remember the hierarchy of primary authority. Constitutions are the highest authority, followed by other enacted law, then by case law. When there is a conflict between federal and state law, federal law governs.

- The doctrines of stare decisis and precedent provide that doctrines, rules, or principles established in earlier court decisions should be followed by later courts in the same court system when addressing similar issues and facts. Therefore, when researching a question, always look for and consider earlier cases that are on point. Chapter 6 presents in-depth coverage of case law analysis.

- Courts are required to follow mandatory authority; therefore, always attempt to locate mandatory authority before searching for persuasive authority.

- Do not rely on persuasive authority if mandatory authority exists. No matter how strong the persuasive authority, the court will apply mandatory authority before persuasive authority.

Secondary authority is never mandatory authority.

VII. APPLICATION

The following example illustrates some of the principles discussed in this chapter. The example addresses the questions raised in the hypothetical presented at the beginning of the chapter. Vanessa's research on the subject of a possible battery claim identified the following authority that might apply to the issues raised in the client's case:

- ✦ Federal law does not apply because the fight did not take place in an area governed by federal law, such as a military base, and it did not involve a federal question.

- ✦ The state criminal battery statute does not apply to a bystander in a situation such as this.

- ✦ The state legislature had not passed a law addressing the matter and it is governed by the case law.

- ✦ A state supreme court case that discusses what must be proved to prevail in a civil action for battery.

- ✦ A state court of appeal case with facts almost identical to those presented in Mr. Reins's case held that an individual who verbally encourages the perpetrator of a battery may be liable for battery.

- ✦ A supreme court case from a neighboring state with facts similar to the facts in the Reins case held that a bystander who verbally encourages the perpetrator of a battery may be liable for battery.

- ✦ An ALR annotation on the topic.

- ✦ A *Restatement of the Law* on the subject.

Vanessa's assignment is to locate and summarize the applicable law. After reviewing the principles and concepts presented in this chapter, she proceeds with the following steps:

STEP 1: Identify and separate primary authority and secondary authority. This is important because the court will rely on and consider primary authority before referring to secondary authority.

1. Primary authority:
   + *Enacted law*—Federal law does not apply to this matter. The state criminal statute does not apply. The state legislature has not passed a civil battery statute.
   + *Case law*—The state supreme court and court of appeals cases and the neighboring state's supreme court case.

2. Secondary authority: The ALR annotation and the *Restatement of the Law* citation.

STEP 2: Organize the presentation of the primary authority. Because the highest authority in the hierarchy of primary authority is the enacted law, followed by the case law, Vanessa organizes her summary of the law with a presentation of the enacted law first. (She did not locate any applicable constitutional law.)

1. *Enacted Law.* In regard to the enacted law, Vanessa determines that there is no enacted law that applies. In her summary, she would explain why the federal law does not apply. She also discusses the state criminal statute and why it does not apply to bystanders. Next she discusses the fact that the state legislature has not passed a civil battery statute and that the matter is governed by the case law.

2. *Case Law.* Vanessa next addresses the relevant case law. She first determines whether the cases are on point. A case is on point if there is a sufficient similarity between the key facts and legal issue addressed in the court opinion and the client's case for the court opinion to apply as precedent. If a case is on point, it provides the court guidance when resolving a legal question or issue.

   If the enacted law is clear and there is no question about how the enacted law applies to the facts of the client's case, there is usually no need to refer to case law. However, enacted law does not apply in this case.

> **FOR EXAMPLE** A client is ticketed for driving 90 mph in a 60 mph zone. The statute establishing the speed limit at 60 mph is clear, and there is no need for case law to interpret the statute. A speed of 90 mph is clearly in violation of the statute.

Even if there appears to be no question about how the statute applies, always be sure to check the case law for possible interpretations of the statute.

After Vanessa has analyzed the case law, she includes a summary of her case analysis, discussing whether each case applies and how. She should include with her summary a brief of the relevant cases. Chapter 5 addresses how to brief a case.

Although Vanessa's summary may include the supreme court case from the neighboring state, it would be used only to support the state court of appeals decision that found the bystander liable. Although the neighboring state decision is precedent (an earlier court decision that serves to guide a subsequent court), it is not mandatory precedent. The state courts of Vanessa's state are not required to follow the decisions of the neighboring state court. They may, however, look to the neighboring state court for guidance.

STEP 3: Organize the presentation of the secondary authority. The secondary authority is included last in her summary because it has the least authoritative value. In this client's case, there is primary authority, so the secondary authority will be used, if at all, in support or opposition to arguments based on the primary authority. Vanessa includes a summary of each authority, emphasizing those aspects that focus on questions and issues similar to those in the client's case. Even if the authorities are not going to be used in court as secondary authority, a summary is included because it may provide Vanessa's supervising attorney with information that proves helpful in the case.

Vanessa's understanding of the primary and secondary sources of law, and the hierarchy of the sources, serves as an essential aid in her organization of the research and preparation of the summary.

SUMMARY

The process of legal analysis and legal writing requires determining which law applies to a legal question and how it applies. To engage in the process, you must understand the law and the basic doctrines and principles that govern and guide the analysis of the law.

There are primarily two sources of law in the United States:

 ✦ Enacted law

 ✦ Case law

Enacted law, as used in this text, consists of constitutions, laws passed by legislative bodies, and regulations adopted by administrative bodies to aid in the enforcement and application of legislative mandates. Case law is composed of the law created by the courts in two situations:

 ✦ When there is no law governing a topic

 ✦ Through interpretation of enacted law where the meaning or application of the enacted law is unclear

There are two court systems in the United States: the federal court system and the state court system. Although there are differences in each system, they have basic similarities. Both systems have trial courts where matters are initially heard, trials are held, and judgments are rendered; both also have courts of appeals where the judgments of trial courts are reviewed and possible errors corrected.

To provide consistency and stability to the case law, two doctrines have evolved:

 ✦ Precedent

 ✦ Stare decisis

Precedent is an earlier court decision on an issue that applies to govern or guide a subsequent court in its determination of identical or similar issues based on identical or similar facts. The doctrine of stare decisis provides that a court must follow a previous decision of a higher court in the jurisdiction when the current decision involves issues and facts similar to those involved in the previous decision.

The two sources of law, enacted and case law, are called primary authority. Primary authority is the law itself. Any other authoritative source a court may rely on in reaching a decision is called secondary authority. Secondary authority is not the law, but consists of authoritative sources that interpret, analyze, or compile the law, such as legal encyclopedias and treatises. Courts always rely on and look to primary authority first when resolving legal issues.

If primary authority governs the resolution of a legal question, it must be followed by the court. This type of primary authority is called mandatory authority. Secondary authority can never be mandatory authority. Any authority the court is not bound to follow, but that it may follow or consider when reaching a decision is called persuasive authority. Both primary authority and secondary authority can be persuasive authority.

A legal research and analysis process is a systematic approach to legal research and analysis. This organized approach makes legal research easier, saves time, and helps develop research skills. A two-part legal research and analysis process is recommended. The first part involves analyzing the assignment and preparing to research and the second part is the research component.

The remaining chapters of this text address the application of the basic concepts and principles presented in this chapter. Each concept and principle plays a critical role in legal analysis and writing.

CHAPTER REFERENCES

INTERNET RESOURCES

<http://www.findlaw.com>
   Considered one of the best sites for finding legal resources in general.

<http://www.uscourts.gov>
   This site offers information about federal court justices, statutes, state laws, and links to other sites.

<http://www.law.indiana.edu>
   Indiana University Law School library.

<http://www.law.cornell.edu/>
   Cornell University Law School Library.

<http://law.vill.edu/>
   This site is a state court locator.

<http://www.access.gpo.gov>
   The official site for the Government Printing Office.

<http://gsulaw.gsu.edu/>
    This site provides an index to legal sites on the Web, including links.

 For additional materials, please go to the CD accompanying this book

 For additional resources, visit our Web site at www.paralegal.delmar.cengage.com

EXERCISES

Additional exercises are located on the Student CD-ROM accompanying the text and Online Companion.

ASSIGNMENT 1

What is the name of the court of general jurisdiction in your state? What is the name of a limited jurisdiction court in your state? What is the subject matter jurisdiction of this court? This information is available in your state statutes.

ASSIGNMENT 2

Describe the differences between a trial court and a court of appeals.

ASSIGNMENT 3

When is a court opinion considered precedent?

ASSIGNMENT 4

Facts: The researcher is analyzing a problem involving the sale of goods on credit in state A.

Authority: The following authority has been located concerning the problem:

1. State A's Uniform Commercial Code Act
2. State A's Consumer Credit Act
3. State B's Uniform Commercial Code Act
4. A federal statute—Consumer Credit Act
5. *Iron v. Supply Co.*—a decision of the highest court in state A
6. *Milk v. Best Buy, Inc.*—a decision of the highest court in state B
7. *Control Co. v. Martin*—a decision of an intermediary court of appeals in state A
8. *Lesley v. Karl Co.*—a decision of a trial court in state A
9. *Irene v. City Co.*—a federal case involving the federal Consumer Credit Act
10. Regulations adopted by state A's Corporation Commission that apply to consumer credit and the sale of goods

11. *Restatements of the Law* defining sales, consumer credit, and other terms related to the problem
12. An ALR reference that directly addresses the issues in the case.

Assume that all the cases are on point, that is, they are sufficiently similar to the facts and issues involved in the problem to apply as precedent.

Questions

A. Which authority is primary authority, and which is secondary authority?

B. Which authority can be mandatory authority, and why? What would be required for any of the sources to be mandatory authority?

C. Which authority can be persuasive authority? Why?

D. Assuming that all the primary authority applies to the issues raised by the facts of the client's case, list the authority in the hierarchical order of its value as precedent, that is, authority with greatest authoritative value will be listed first, followed by other authority in the order it will be looked to by the court.

ASSIGNMENT 5

Facts: Your client is the plaintiff in a workers' compensation case. She was injured in 1993 in state A. In 1995, her employer destroyed all the business records relating to the client. The destruction of the records was apparently accidental, not intentional. They were destroyed, however, while the client's workers' compensation claim was pending.

Authority: You have located the following authority, all of which is directly related to the issues raised by the facts of the client's case:

1. *Idle v. City Co.*—a 1980 decision by the highest court of state A where the court created a cause of action in tort for the wrongful destruction of business records. The court ruled that a cause of action exists if the records were destroyed in anticipation of or

while a workers' compensation claim was pending. The court also held that a cause of action exists if the destruction was intentional or negligent.

2. A 1989 state A statute—a law passed by the legislature of state A that created a cause of action in tort for the intentional destruction of business records. The statute provides that a cause of action exists if the destruction occurs in anticipation of or while a workers' compensation claim is pending.

3. *Merrick v. Taylor*—a 1990 decision of the court of appeals of state A. The court of appeals is a lower court than the state's highest court. The court held that intentional, within the meaning of the 1989 statute, includes either the intentional destruction of records or the destruction of records as a result of gross negligence.

4. *Davees v. Contractor*—a decision of the highest court of state B interpreting a state B statute identical to the 1989 state A statute. The court held that intentional, as used in the statute, includes gross negligence only when the gross negligence is accompanied by a "reckless and wanton" disregard for the preservation of the business records.

5. A 1991 federal statute—the statute is identical to the 1989 state statute but applies only to contractors with federal contracts.

6. An ALR reference—addresses specific questions similar to those raised in the client's case.

Questions

A. Which authority is primary authority, and which is secondary authority? Why?

B. Which authority can be mandatory authority, and why? What would be required for any of the sources to be mandatory authority?

C. Which authority can be persuasive authority? Why?

D. Can *Idle v. City Co.* be authority at all? Why or why not?

E. If *Idle v. City Co.* is authority, to what extent?

F. Discuss the impact of *Merrick v. Taylor* in regard to the 1989 state A statute.

G. Discuss the authoritative value of *Davees v. Contractor*.

H. Assuming that all the primary authority applies to the issues raised by the facts of the client's case, list the authority in the hierarchical order of its value as precedent, that is, authority with greatest authoritative value will be listed first, followed by other authority in the order it will be looked to and relied on by the court.

CHAPTER 2

The Role of Key Terms and Key Facts in Legal Research

Outline

Learning Objectives

After completing this chapter, you should understand:

✦ What are key terms and key facts

✦ What are background and irrelevant facts

✦ The role and importance of key facts

✦ How to identify key facts in a client's case

✦ How to identify key facts in a court opinion

Dustin was recently hired by the Kinsey law firm and was placed under the guidance and supervision of Karen, a 15-year veteran paralegal. They just finished the initial interview with a client, Mr. Eldon Canter. The firm has been appointed to represent Mr. Canter, who is charged in federal court with one count of armed bank robbery, in violation of 18 U.S.C. § 2113 (a) and (d).

Dustin sat in on the interview to observe the process and gain experience. After the interview, Karen told Dustin, "I'm going to prepare a summary of the interview and the case file. I want you to identify the key facts that should be included in the statement of the issues, the issue, research the applicable law, and prepare a legal research memo summarizing your research. The main question we are looking at is whether there is sufficient evidence to support the charge that Mr. Canter used a dangerous weapon when he robbed the bank."

Dustin's notes on the interview and the case file indicate that on January 5 of this year, Mr. Canter robbed the First State Bank. After he entered the bank, he approached a teller, pulled from his pocket a crudely carved wooden replica of a 9mm Beretta handgun, and demanded money. He had carved the replica from a block of pine wood and stained it with dark walnut wood stain to make it look black. He drilled a hole in the barrel end in an attempt to make it look like a real Beretta.

The teller was so frightened that he only glanced at the wooden gun. He believed it was real. The teller at the next window looked at the replica and afterward stated that she was fairly certain at the time that it was a fake. No one else noticed whether the wooden replica was real. The teller handed Mr. Canter the money and Mr. Canter fled.

The Application section of this chapter addresses how Dustin performs the assignment. This hypothetical will be referred to as the *United States v. Canter* hypothetical throughout the text.

Note: The legal research memorandum that Dustin prepares is presented in Appendix A.

I. INTRODUCTION

Most attorney-client relationships begin with the initial interview with the client. During the interview, the client presents information concerning a situation the client believes requires a legal solution. If a lawsuit is ultimately filed, the process begins here. The role of the attorney, often performed by the paralegal or law clerk, is to sift through the facts presented in the initial interview and determine what relief, if any, the law may provide for the problem raised by the facts. Any legal solution to a client's problem involves the application of the law to the facts of the case.

As mentioned in Chapter 1, the first step of the legal research and analysis process is preliminary preparation. That is, gathering information about the case from the case file. At the heart of the first step is the process of sifting through the file to identify key terms and key facts. Key facts are used in the identification and formulation of the issue. The issue guides the researcher to the specific law that governs the client's factual situation. This chapter addresses key terms and facts in general, and emphasizes the critical role of the key facts in a case.

II. KEY TERMS

Most legal research sources such as statutory codes, legal encyclopedias, legal treatises, and digests contain one or more indexes. These indexes list terms that help to locate information. To effectively use an index, you must identify the relevant terms in the client's case. These are the **key terms** that help guide the researcher in the area being researched. If you are researching electronically such as via the Internet, searches are conducted using key terms.

Key terms are identified by reviewing the case file and listing all the terms relevant to the legal questions raised by the facts of the case. When preparing this list, keep in mind the following:

* Parties involved, for example, private citizen, corporation, public official
* Place, for example, public or private property
* Actions or omissions that form the basis of the case, for example, negligence, intentional acts
* Defenses available, for example, self defense
* Relief sought, for example, money, injunction

Key terms may be broad terms you use as a guide to perform preliminary research to become familiar with the area of law governing the client's case, or narrow terms if you are already familiar with the area of law and want to focus your research on a specific aspect.

> **FOR EXAMPLE** The client's case involves a child custody question and the researcher is unfamiliar with this area of law. The researcher decides to read about the topic in a legal encyclopedia. The first step is to list all the terms child custody may be indexed under, such as *divorce, marriage, custody, parent and child, child custody, children,* and *domestic relations.* By listing the terms, you focus the search in the index and avoid having to scan the entire index. The topic will be found under at least one of the search terms.

Because the key term may not be indexed in the way you think it should be, it is important to think of all the terms or categories that might apply. One of the roles of legal education is to teach key terms and what categories they fit in.

Key terms may include key facts from the client's case. This often occurs when one is familiar with the general area of law and is seeking the specific law that governs the client's fact situation.

> **FOR EXAMPLE** The assignment is to locate the federal law the client may be charged with. The client placed a bomb made of nitroglycerin under a bridge. Assume these are the key facts. The researcher, based on her legal education and previous experience, knows that the general research topic is "federal criminal law" and the sub-topic is "explosives." By identifying the key search terms as *nitroglycerin* and *bridges*, the researcher is guided to the specific law within the general area of "federal criminal law" and "explosives."

You should develop a list of key terms while you are reviewing the case and identifying the key facts. If you are unfamiliar with the area of law, use a list of terms related to the general topic of the case to perform general research and obtain a familiarity with the area of law. See the first example provided earlier in this chapter. After you are familiar with the area of law, identify the key facts and the legal issue before conducting research.

III. FACTS—IN GENERAL

Usually some of the factual information the client provides in an interview is not relevant to the outcome of the case. Sometimes important factual information is left out. Before a legal solution to the client's problem can be found or a determination made concerning whether a lawsuit should be filed, it is necessary to identify the facts that are critical to the outcome of the case—the key facts. To ensure that all the key facts are identified and none are missed, all the factual information concerning the problem must be identified at the outset. This is accomplished through a comprehensive review of the entire file.

Often the importance of certain facts may not be determined until the legal issues and the governing law are identified.

> **FOR EXAMPLE** A trespasser enters property owned by one individual (landlord) and leased to another (tenant) and burns a fence. Assume the researcher, based on experience, concludes that the burning of the fence may give rise to a cause of action for conversion (an improper act that deprives an individual of the rightful possession of the individual's property). Upon conducting subsequent research, the researcher learns that conversion requires that the person suing must be in possession of the property.
>
> It is an important fact, therefore, that the person suing must be the person in possession—the tenant, not the landlord. The tenant, being the person in possession of the land, would have the right to sue for conversion. The landlord would not be in possession of the land and, therefore, would not have a right to sue for conversion. The importance of this fact may not become apparent until the legal question and governing law are identified.

This example illustrates another important point concerning facts. When a lawsuit proceeds to trial, the facts presented at trial are those facts identified and considered important prior to trial. Identifying and gathering these facts depends entirely on the thoroughness and quality of the pretrial preparation. If a sloppy job is done, that is, the facts are not thoroughly gathered and researched, a poor outcome may be the result. The case may be lost.

> **FOR EXAMPLE** Referring to the previous example, assume the land was leased. The landlord did not reveal this fact during the interview because, being the owner of the land, he did not think it mattered who was in possession. The interview was not thorough because the landlord was not asked who was in possession of the land. Assume, also, that the researcher believed that the "possession" requirement of conversion is met if the party suing owned the property. The researcher did a sloppy job of research and did not thoroughly research what constitutes "possession" under the law.
>
> If a lawsuit alleging conversion went to trial and this key fact was not identified, the landlord would lose because he was not in possession of the land and did not have a right to sue. The key fact of who was in possession of the land was not identified prior to trial and, therefore, was not presented at trial. The poor quality of the interview and subsequent research resulted in a poor outcome.

Ethics. This may appear to be an extreme example, but it illustrates an important point: the facts presented at trial and often the outcome of the trial are entirely dependent on the quality of work prior to trial. Rule 1.1 of the American Bar Association's *Model Rules of Professional Conduct* requires that a client be provided competent representation. A failure to conduct a proper interview and identify the key facts denies the client competent representation.

The focus of this chapter, and the task assigned to many paralegals and law clerks, is the identification of those facts that give rise to the legal dispute in either a client's case or a court opinion. The facts that give rise to the legal dispute are often referred to as significant, material, or key facts. In this chapter and throughout the text, these facts will be referred to as key facts.

Many of the concepts and principles introduced in this chapter are also addressed in Chapter 3. As noted in that chapter, key facts and issues are integrally related. The key facts are an essential element of the issue. They are essential in the identification and statement of the issue because they give rise to the legal dispute. Disputes arise and take place in the context of facts.

IV. FACTS—DEFINITION

A **fact** is something that is real, that actually exists, an actual event as opposed to an opinion or someone's interpretation of what took place. In a lawsuit, a fact is information present in a case concerning some thing, action, event, or circumstance.

> **FOR EXAMPLE** In the *United States v. Canter* hypothetical at the beginning of the chapter, Mr. Canter's actions of entering the bank, approaching a teller, pulling from his pocket a crudely carved wooden replica of a 9mm Beretta handgun, and demanding money are all facts.

Facts should not be confused with a rule of law. A **rule of law** is a standard, established by a governing authority that prescribes or directs action or forbearance. It may be a constitutional provision, statute, ordinance, regulation, or case law doctrine. Its application determines the outcome of the question raised by the facts of a dispute.

> **FOR EXAMPLE** Title 23, section 1991, of the state statutes provides that the maximum speed limit in a school zone is 10 mph while school is in session. When an individual proceeds through a school zone at 12 mph, this statute governs the question of whether the individual is speeding, that is, the outcome of the question raised by the facts.

Before defining and discussing key facts, it is helpful to consider the importance of facts in general and to identify and distinguish the various types of facts present in a client's case and a court opinion.

V. IMPORTANCE OF FACTS

The importance of giving due consideration to the facts of a dispute cannot be overemphasized.

Facts play a crucial role in each step of the legal research process. Often minimal attention is given to the facts. This is surprising, because our legal system revolves around resolving disputes by applying the rules of law to the facts of a case. Notice the two major factors here—*rules of law* and *facts of the case*. Both are equally important. Novice researchers, however, often focus primarily on the rules of law.

The issue is the precise question raised by the specific facts of the client's case. Therefore, the facts are an essential element of the issue. Rules of law are general principles designed to apply to multiple fact situations and a determination of which law governs the issue is primarily governed by the facts of the client's case. Consequently, the role they play in determining what is in dispute in a case and which law applies is of primary importance. Clients often have little knowledge or concern about general legal principles, but they are concerned with how the law applies to the facts of their case.

Facts are also important because determining how or if a law applies to the client's case often depends upon the presence or absence of certain facts.

> **FOR EXAMPLE** Tom is stopped at a light at a four-way intersection in the city, waiting for the light to change. Mary, stopped behind him, accidentally lets her foot slip off the brake, and her vehicle bumps into Tom's vehicle. After exiting their vehicles and examining them, they discover no visible damage to either vehicle and Tom states he is not injured.
>
> Tom sues Mary for negligence for hitting his vehicle. The researcher working for Mary's attorney knows that the elements of negligence are duty, breach of duty, proximate cause, and damages. Based on her research and education, she also knows that to state a claim, Tom must present facts that establish each of the elements of negligence. Although there are facts to support the first three elements, because there was no damage to the vehicle or injury to Tom, there are no facts that establish the element of damages. This hypothetical is referred to as the minor impact example throughout this chapter.

In the preceding example, as in every case, there are two equally important factors—the law and the facts. The law establishes the conditions that must be met to state a claim for negligence, that is, the elements of negligence. The outcome of the application of the law depends upon the existence of facts, and on two facts in particular in the case—was Tom injured by the impact or his vehicle damaged? Like this example, all legal problems are fact-sensitive; that is, the outcome depends on the existence or nonexistence of a particular fact or facts.

In addition, facts are important because determining whether a court opinion is on point is largely governed by the similarity between the facts of the court opinion and the facts of the client's case. There must be a sufficient similarity between the key facts of the court opinion and those of the client's case before the court opinion can be considered on point and apply as precedent in the client's case.

VI. TYPES OF FACTS

In either a client's case or a court opinion, there may be hundreds of facts, some of which are critically important, some of which are not. To identify the legal issue, the researcher must sort through the facts and determine which facts give rise to the legal question and are essential to its resolution. Helpful to this process is an understanding of the basic categories of facts present in a case. The facts of a case may be placed within the three broad categories presented in Exhibit 2–1.

Exhibit 2–1
Types of Facts.

✦ Irrelevant Facts	Facts coincidental to the event, but not of significant legal importance in the case.
✦ Background Facts	Facts presented in a court opinion, case brief, or legal memorandum that put the key facts in context. Facts that give an overview of a factual event and provide the reader with the overall context within which the facts occurred.
✦ Key Facts	The legally significant facts of a case that raise the legal question of how or whether the law governing the dispute applies. The facts that establish or satisfy the elements of a cause of action and are necessary to prove or disprove a claim. A fact so essential that, if it were changed, the outcome of the case would be affected or changed.

A. Irrelevant Facts

Irrelevant facts are coincidental to the event, but are not of significant legal importance in the case.

FOR EXAMPLE In the minor impact example, the race and gender of the parties are irrelevant facts. They are irrelevant because they are facts that are not necessary to establish or satisfy the elements of the cause of action in the case. They are not necessary to prove or disprove the claim. The race and gender of the parties are irrelevant to the question of whether Mary was negligent.

Beware that certain facts may be relevant in one situation and not relevant in another.

FOR EXAMPLE In the minor impact example, whether it was snowing is probably not a relevant fact. Both vehicles were stopped at a light, and the existence of snow should not affect Mary's duty to keep her foot from slipping off the brake pedal. If the facts, however, were that she was approaching the stoplight and failed to apply the brakes in a timely fashion, the existence of snow conditions becomes a relevant fact. The nature of her duty to exercise care while driving varies with the weather conditions, and the existence of snow conditions requires her to exercise greater care when braking.

B. Background Facts

Background facts are those irrelevant facts that put the key facts in context. They give an overview of the factual event and provide the reader with the overall context within which the key facts occurred. They are not key facts because they are not essential to a determination of the issues in the case, but they are usually necessary and often helpful because they provide information that helps the reader have an overall picture of the environment within which the key facts occurred.

> **FOR EXAMPLE** In the minor impact example, the location and type of intersection are background facts that provide the reader with an overview of the context and scene of the collision. The reader is aware that the impact took place at an intersection in the city, rather than in the country. This information is not essential, but it may be helpful for many reasons. The reader, for example, may want to visit the scene at a later date to investigate and determine whether individuals working in the area witnessed the accident.

C. Key Facts

Key facts are often referred to as significant, material, or ultimate facts. The following section discusses the definition and types of key facts.

VII. KEY FACTS—DEFINITION AND TYPES

A. Definition

Key facts are the legally significant facts of a case that raise the legal question of how or whether the law governing the dispute applies. They are those facts upon which the outcome of the case is determined: the facts that establish or satisfy the elements of a cause of action and are necessary to prove or disprove a claim. A key fact is so essential that, if it were changed, the outcome of the case would probably change. In fact, a useful test in determining whether a fact is key is to ask this question: "If this fact is changed, would the outcome of the application of the law be affected or changed?"

> **FOR EXAMPLE** Consider a fact situation where law enforcement officers are sued for battery based on the following facts. Law enforcement officers pursued a suspect on foot for five blocks after observing him snatch a woman's purse. While making the arrest, the officers encountered resistance, used force to overcome that resistance, and continued to use force for more than a minute after the resistance ceased. The law provides that law enforcement officers may use the amount of force necessary to overcome resistance when making a legal arrest. This hypothetical is referred to in this chapter as the resisting arrest example.

What are the key facts in the preceding example? Which of the facts, if changed, would change the outcome in this case? If the suspect never resisted, the use of force would have been clearly improper. If the suspect never ceased resisting, the officers' continued use of force would have been proper. If the officers stopped using force when the resistance ceased, the use of force probably would have been proper. If the arrest was illegal, the use of force would have been improper. The key facts are the following:

+ A lawful arrest was being made.
+ There was resistance to the arrest.
+ Force was used to overcome the resistance.
+ The resistance ceased.
+ The use of force continued for more than a minute after the resistance ceased.

Each of these facts is a key fact. Each fact, if changed, would affect the outcome of the case.

Other facts, however, are not key facts. How far the officers pursued the suspect or the fact that the pursuit was on foot are not key facts. These facts, if changed, would not change the outcome of the case.

B. Types of Key Facts

There are two categories of key facts:

- ✦ **Individual key facts**
- ✦ Facts considered as a group—**groups of facts**

1. Individual Key Facts

Often an individual fact or several individual facts are key facts in a case. A key fact is an individual key fact if it meets the following test: *if the fact is changed, the outcome of the case is affected or changed.*

> **FOR EXAMPLE** In the resisting arrest example, all the facts identified as key facts are individual key facts: a lawful arrest was being made, there was resistance to the arrest, force was used to overcome the resistance, resistance ceased, and the use of force continued after the resistance ceased. Each of these individual facts, if changed, would change or affect the outcome of the case.

2. Groups of Facts

In some fact situations, no individual fact standing alone is a key fact—that is, no single fact is so significant that, if changed, it would change the outcome.

> **FOR EXAMPLE** An inmate is challenging the conditions of his confinement as cruel and unusual punishment. He alleges the following: there are cockroaches in his jail cell, the recreational periods are too short, his mail is improperly censored, his visitation rights are too restricted, and the temperature in his cell is too low in the winter and too high in the summer. It may be that no single fact by itself meets the test of a key fact, that is, no single fact is so critical that, if changed, the outcome of the case would change. The fact that there are cockroaches in his cell may not be sufficient, by itself, to constitute cruel and unusual punishment; the fact that the recreational periods are too short, by itself, may not constitute cruel and unusual punishment; and so on.
>
> All the individual facts, however, when considered as a group, may determine the outcome of the case and, if changed as a group, would change the outcome. This may be observed in a court opinion when the court states, "No single fact of plaintiff's allegations constitutes cruel and unusual punishment. When taken as a whole, however, the individual allegations combine to establish a violation of the Eighth Amendment's prohibition against cruel and unusual punishment."

Recognizing groups of facts is important because, when analyzing a case, you must be aware that individual facts that seem to be insignificant may be key facts when considered and weighed as a group. When addressing a problem that involves key facts as a group, first review the facts individually to determine whether any individual fact, standing alone, is a key fact. If there is no individual fact that, if changed, would change the outcome of the case, look to the facts as a group.

There is no magic formula for determining how many or what types of facts are required for facts to be considered as a group, or what is necessary for a group of facts to be considered a "key fact." Usually it is necessary to consult case law and locate a case where the court addressed a similar legal problem involving a group of facts.

The next step, after defining and categorizing key facts, is to determine how to locate them in both a client's case and a court opinion. Because the key facts are an element of the issue, the steps involved in identifying and stating the issue necessarily include, in part, some of the steps necessary for locating key facts. Therefore, there is some overlap between Chapters 2 and 3 regarding the identification of key facts.

VIII. KEY FACTS IDENTIFICATION—CLIENT'S CASE

A client's fact situation usually includes a mix of facts—some irrelevant, some background, and some key. A researcher's assignment may be to identify the key facts in the case. The four-step process presented in Exhibit 2–2 is recommended for determining which of the client's facts are key facts.

Step 1	Identify each cause of action possibly raised by the facts.
Step 2	Determine the elements of each cause of action identified in step 1.
Step 3	List all the facts possibly related to the elements of the causes of action identified in step 2.
Step 4	Determine which of the client's facts apply to establish or satisfy the elements of each cause of action—the key facts.

Exhibit 2–2
Steps in Key Fact Identification—Client's Case.

The following example is referred to in this section when discussing the operation of this four-step process.

> **FOR EXAMPLE** The researcher is assigned the task of identifying the key facts in a case. A review of the file reveals the following facts. Jerry and Ann are neighbors. They have lived on adjoining one-half acre lots in a rural subdivision for the past 15 years. Their children are close friends and ride the school bus together. Four years ago, Jerry put in a hedge and planted several trees along his property line with Ann. Every year since then, Jerry rakes the leaves from the hedge and trees into a big pile close to the shared property line and burns it. The prevailing wind carries the smoke and soot across Ann's property, preventing her from working in her garden and usually soiling the clothes that are drying on her clothesline. Every year she asks him to not burn the leaves, and every year he ignores her request and burns the leaves.
>
> Ann wants Jerry to stop burning the leaves and pay her for the clothes that have been "ruined" by the smoke. When used in this chapter, this hypothetical is referred to as the trespass example.

A. Step 1: Identify Each Cause of Action

Identify each cause of action possibly raised by the facts. This step requires determining the possible cause(s) raised by the facts. Depending on the education and legal experience of the researcher, this initial step may not require any research.

In the trespass example, upon reviewing the facts, the researcher may come to a preliminary conclusion that the possible causes of action include trespass to land, private nuisance, and negligence.

B. Step 2: Determine the Elements

Determine the elements of each cause of action identified in step 1. This step usually requires some research. Research may be necessary either to determine the elements of the possible cause of action or to ensure that the law has not changed since the last time research was conducted. This step is necessary because, to state a claim and thereby obtain relief, the plaintiff must present facts that establish or prove the existence of each element of the cause of action. These facts are the key facts of the case.

> **FOR EXAMPLE** The assistant's research reveals that the elements of trespass to land are as follows:

✦ An act

✦ Intrusion on land

✦ In possession of another

✦ Intent to intrude

✦ Causation of the intrusion

The researcher also would identify the elements of each of the other potential causes of action identified in step 1.

C. Step 3: List All Facts Related to the Elements

List all the facts possibly related to the elements of the causes of action identified in step 2. This includes gathering the facts from the client interview and any interviews that have been conducted with witnesses, and reviewing any documents in the case file that may contain factual information. The client files must be checked to ensure they are complete. At the initial stages of a case, the client interview may be the only available source of information.

When listing the facts, include all facts that may possibly be related to any of the causes of action. Err on the side of listing too many facts. You want to have all possibly related facts at hand when you proceed to step 4, where the irrelevant facts are eliminated and the key facts are identified.

> **FOR EXAMPLE** The fact that the children ride the school bus together probably is not related to any of the potential causes of action. The nature of what is being burned may be related. The number of years Jerry has burned the leaves may be related. The weather conditions when the leaves are burned may be related.

Consider the elements of each cause of action individually when performing this task.

> **FOR EXAMPLE** Using trespass to land as a cause of action, take each element and determine what facts from the client's case possibly establish or are related to that element. Which of the facts relate to intrusion? Which of the facts relate to "in possession of another"? Which of the facts relate to the intent to intrude? Which of the facts relate to causation of the intrusion?

After completing this process for the elements of trespass, do the same for each potential cause of action identified in the previous steps.

Note that some facts may establish or relate to more than one cause of action. Some causes of action overlap. Therefore, all the facts must be reviewed when considering the elements of each cause of action.

> **FOR EXAMPLE** The fact that the smoke from the burning leaves crosses on to Ann's property may establish or relate to both trespass to land and private nuisance. The smoke crossing to Ann's land may be the act of trespass, and the crossing coupled with the interference to Ann's enjoyment of her gardening may relate to nuisance. The fact that smoke crosses the property relates to elements of both of these causes of action.

D. Step 4: Determine Which Facts Apply

Determine which of the client's facts apply to establish or satisfy the elements of each cause of action—the key facts. The facts identified in this step are the key facts. Be sure to consider each fact listed in step 3 and determine whether it is essential to establish or satisfy an element of any potential cause of action. It is important to consider all the facts identified in step 3. Step 4 primarily is the process of eliminating those facts listed in step 3 that are not essential or key facts. This is accomplished by taking each element of each cause of action and identifying the fact(s) that are essential to establish or satisfy that element.

> **FOR EXAMPLE** Referring to the trespass to land cause of action, the key facts are as follows:
>
> 1. *Act*—the burning of the leaves produces smoke
> 2. *Intrusion on land*—the smoke crossing over Ann's land
> 3. *In possession of another*—Ann owns and lives on the land
> 4. *Intent to intrude*—Jerry built the fires (they were not caused by lightning or the acts of another), and he continued to build fires after he was notified of the problem
> 5. *Causation of the intrusion*—the fire produced the smoke that passed over Ann's property, and there is no evidence that it came from another source

When determining which facts identified in step 3 establish or satisfy an element, apply the following test:

✦ "Which of these facts, if changed, would change the outcome of the application of that element?"

Or, in other words,

✦ "Which of these facts, if changed, would affect the determination of whether there is present a fact or facts that establishes or satisfies that element?"

> **FOR EXAMPLE** Referring to the trespass to land cause of action, if the smoke did not pass over Ann's land, there would be no facts to support the element of intrusion. If the smoke crossing her land came from a source other than Jerry's land, Jerry would not be responsible for the causation of the trespass.

Other facts identified in step 3 as related to an element that do not establish or satisfy an element are not key facts.

> **FOR EXAMPLE** In step 3, the facts of what was being burned, the weather conditions when the burning took place, and the number of years Jerry had burned the leaves were considered as possibly related to the trespass cause of action. If it is determined that these facts, if changed, would not tend to establish or satisfy an element of trespass, they are not key facts and are eliminated from further consideration.

All the facts identified in step 4 are the key facts. They are essential to the outcome of the case.

E. Multiple Issues

Steps 2 through 4 should be applied to each potential cause of action identified in step 1. Some causes of action can be eliminated because there are no facts present that support the existence of an element.

> **FOR EXAMPLE** If the smoke harmlessly passes over Ann's land and does not interfere with her use or enjoyment of the land, there may be no cause of action for private nuisance.

Additional causes of action may be identified as research and investigation take place. Be sure to address each element of each possible cause of action and determine whether there is any fact in the case that tends to establish or satisfy the element.

CAVEAT. These steps are useful tools and helpful guides when identifying key facts. They will usually help you quickly identify the key facts. Nothing, however, is foolproof. You may not be certain that a fact meets the required standard necessary to support the existence of an element. In some instances that determination may not take place until trial.

> **FOR EXAMPLE** The court may rule that the smoke crossing Ann's land is not a sufficient intrusion to constitute trespass.

Just make sure that there is some fact that arguably meets the requirements of each element of the cause of action.

IX. KEY FACTS IDENTIFICATION—CASE LAW

Every court opinion involves the court's application of the law to the facts of the case. The key facts are those facts in the case that the law applies to and that are essential to the decision reached by the court. If the key facts had been different, the outcome of the case probably would have been different.

Those situations where the court clearly points out the key facts are not addressed in this chapter.

> **FOR EXAMPLE** The court states, "The critical facts in the resolution of this dispute are that the defendant signed the deed and delivered it for filing."

The focus here is on those situations where the key facts are not so easily determined, such as in cases where the court opinion intersperses many irrelevant and background facts with the key facts.

As with determining the key facts in a client's case, there is no magic formula for identifying key facts in a court opinion. The three-step process presented in Exhibit 2–3 is recommended, however, and may prove helpful.

In this section, the following example is referred to when discussing the application of these steps. Notice that the example is factually similar to the case of *Rael v. Cadena*, presented in Exhibit 5–1 in Chapter 5.

Exhibit 2–3
Steps in Key Fact Identification—Case Law.

Step 1	Read the entire case with the following general question in mind: "What was decided about which facts?"
Step 2	Look to the holding. What is the court's answer to the legal question? How does the court apply the rule of law to the legal question raised?
Step 3	Identify the facts necessary to the holding—the key facts. Part 1 List all facts in any way related to the holding. Part 2 Identify which of the listed facts are key facts—determine the key facts.

> **FOR EXAMPLE** In the case of *Joins v. Stevens,* the court summarized the facts as follows:
> Jason Stevens and his nephew Allen Stevens knew Mark Joins for several years. The three occasionally engaged in recreational activities, such as attending baseball games and going on fishing trips. On these outings, they usually drank alcoholic beverages, often to excess. On some occasions, their spouses joined in the activities.
>
> On one of the fishing trips on a Sunday afternoon in July, they were standing under a tree, drinking beer, and waiting for the rain to stop so that they could resume fishing. They had been drinking since morning and were a little drunk. Earlier in the day Mark was the only one who caught any fish. Jason and Allen became increasingly angry as Mark claimed that he was the only "real fisherman" of the group. He continued bragging for an irritatingly long period. When he claimed that he was actually the "only real man" of the three, Allen lost control and beat him up. While the beating was going on, Jason yelled to Allen, "Hit him harder! Kick him! Kick him!"
>
> Mark suffered two broken ribs and was hospitalized. He sued Jason and Allen for the tort of battery. In deciding that Jason had committed a battery, the court stated, "Although liability cannot be based upon one's mere presence at a battery, a person may be held liable for the tort of battery if he encourages or incites by words the act of the direct perpetrator. Because he yelled encouragement to his nephew while the latter was beating Mark Joins, Jason Stevens is jointly liable with his nephew for the battery."

A. Step 1: Read the Entire Case

Read the entire case with the following general question in mind: "What was decided about which facts?" Because key facts in a court opinion are those facts necessary to the decision reached by the court, you must have a general overview of the case before you can focus on determining which of the facts are key facts. You must read the entire case to determine the legal question addressed and the decision reached by the court, keeping in mind the question: "What was decided about which facts in this case?"

- ✦ *"What was decided . . ."* keeps the mind focused on the holding or decision reached.
- ✦ *"About which facts . . ."* keeps the mind focused on specific facts, those specific facts necessary to the resolution of the legal question—the key facts.

By the time you finish reading the entire case, you usually realize that the decision rests on only some of the facts presented in the opinion. If at this point you have not clearly identified which of the facts are the key facts, proceed to step 2.

B. Step 2: Look to the Holding

The holding is the court's application of the rule of law to the legal question raised by the facts of the case. It is the court's answer to the legal question. Ask the following questions to help identify the holding:

- ✦ "What is the court's answer to the legal question?"
- ✦ "How does the court apply the rule of law to the legal question raised?"

In this example, the last two sentences are the court's presentation of the rule of law and the holding—the application of the rule of law to the facts:

- ✦ *Rule of law*—"Although liability cannot be based upon one's mere presence at a battery, a person may be held liable for the tort of battery if he encourages or incites by words the act of the direct perpetrator."

◆ *Holding*—"Because he yelled encouragement to his nephew while the latter was beating Mark Joins, Jason Stevens is jointly liable with his nephew for the battery."

C. Step 3: Identify the Key Facts

Identify the facts necessary to the holding—the key facts. This step is composed of two parts:

   ◆ Part 1—List all facts in any way related to the holding.
   ◆ Part 2—Identify which of the listed facts are key facts—determine the key facts.

Part 1: List All Facts Related to the Holding

List all the facts presented in the case related to the holding. This may require going through the case and listing all the facts presented by the court. The court may present a multitude of background and irrelevant facts that in no way affect the outcome of the case. If that is the situation, identify and list only the facts that are possibly related or necessary to the decision reached.

In the preceding example, it is not necessary to list all the facts presented by the court. Some facts, such as the fact that the spouses sometimes accompanied the men, clearly are not relevant. Some facts—for example, it was a Sunday in July—are merely background facts that provide the reader with the time context of the event. All the facts relating to the argument should be included, such as the location of the argument, the fact they had been drinking, and what was said.

Part 2: Determine the Key Facts

From the facts listed, determine the key facts by identifying those facts necessary or essential to the decision reached. Which facts determine the outcome of the case? There are several ways to identify these facts:

   ◆ One test is to ask yourself whether the decision would have been the same if a fact had not occurred, or if the fact had occurred differently. If Jason had merely stood by and watched, would he be liable for battery? Apply this test to each fact listed.
   ◆ If this test is applied to each fact and no single fact, when changed or omitted, would affect or change the decision, ask whether the decision was governed by the court's consideration of the facts as a group.

> **FOR EXAMPLE** The court may state, "No single act of the defendant is sufficient to constitute breach of contract. The defendant's various acts, however, when taken as a whole are sufficient to establish breach."

   ◆ Where the court lists in its reasoning the elements of a cause of action, ask yourself which of the facts apply to establish the elements. In the battery example, the court stated that an individual may be liable if that individual "incites by words" the acts of the perpetrator. Jason's inciting words are the facts that relate to this element.
   ◆ Ask yourself whether the court indicates that a certain fact is a key fact:
     a. Does the court describe a fact as "essential," "key," or "important"?
     b. Is a fact repeated throughout the opinion, especially in the reasoning supporting the decision?
     c. Does the court agree with a party's description of a fact as critical or key?

> **FOR EXAMPLE** The court may state, "We agree with plaintiff's position that the words used by the defendant were key in inciting the nephew's attack on the plaintiff."

✦ Does a concurring or dissenting opinion identify the key facts? Be aware, however, that the concurring or dissenting judge may have a different view of which facts are key facts, and may identify as key facts, facts that the majority did not consider key.

D. Multiple Issues

The foregoing discussion focuses upon locating the key facts related to a single issue and holding in a case. Often there are several issues and holdings in a court opinion. Apply the steps presented to determine the key facts related to each issue and holding. Follow each step completely for each issue and holding.

CAVEAT. The steps presented in this section are useful tools and guidelines. Following them helps you identify the key facts of a case. There are instances where the court may omit key facts. Also, as you read more cases and become more familiar with case law, you may automatically focus in on the key facts without using any of the steps presented here.

X. KEY POINTS CHECKLIST: *Identifying Key Terms and Key Facts*

■ After you are familiar with the area of law you are considering, identify the key facts and the legal issue before conducting research. A well-crafted issue includes the key facts and will help you identify the key terms that must be researched to answer the specific question raised by the facts.

■ Do not overlook the importance of the facts. Facts give rise to the legal dispute and, therefore, are an integral part of it. Disputes have little meaning outside the context of the facts. How many court opinions have you read that did not have any facts?

■ Key facts are those facts that establish or satisfy the elements of a cause of action and are necessary to prove or disprove a claim. Therefore, the nature and presence or absence of certain facts determine the outcome of a case.

■ A useful test to use when determining whether a fact is a key fact is to ask the question, "If this fact is changed or omitted, would the outcome of the application of the law be changed?"

■ Follow the steps recommended for determining key facts in a client's case. Be aware that the importance of certain facts may not become apparent until legal research is conducted and the elements of a cause of action are determined.

■ When identifying key facts in a court opinion, keep in mind the question, "What was decided about which facts in this case?"

■ Do not get discouraged. The process of identifying key facts becomes easier with practice, and parts of the process become intuitive.

XI. APPLICATION

This section presents examples of key fact identification in a client's case and in a court opinion. Each example illustrates the application of the principles discussed in this chapter.

A. Client's Fact Situation

The following example illustrates the application of the principles to the *United States v. Canter* hypothetical presented at the beginning of the chapter.

STEP 1: Identify Each Cause of Action. *Identify each cause of action possibly raised by the facts.* In this case, the cause of action and area of law are identified in the assignment. The area of law is the federal criminal law and the cause of action is bank robbery with a dangerous weapon.

Step 1 provides a starting point for the identification of the key facts in the case.

STEP 2: Determine the Elements. *Determine the elements of each cause of action identified in step 1.* For each potential cause of action, identify the elements necessary to state a claim. Research is usually required to determine the elements. Facts must be presented that establish or satisfy each element of each cause of action. These facts are the key facts of the case. The statute is 18 U.S.C. § 2113 (a) and (d). The statute requires that the following elements be established:

Section (a)

◆ Element 1: A person by force, violence, or intimidation

◆ Element 2: Takes or attempts to take property or money

◆ Element 3: In the care or possession of a bank.

Section (d)

◆ Element 4: A person committing an offense defined in subsection (a) assaults any person or puts in jeopardy the life of any person by use of a dangerous weapon or device.

STEP 3: List All Facts Related to the Elements. *List all the facts possibly related to the elements of the causes of action identified in step 2.* List all facts potentially related to each of the elements of each cause of action. In this fact situation, these facts include:

1. Mr. Canter entered the bank.
2. He approached a teller and pulled from his pocket a crudely carved wooden replica of a 9mm Beretta handgun and demanded money.
3. The replica was carved from a block of pine wood and stained with dark walnut wood stain to look black.
4. A hole was drilled in the barrel end to make it look like a gun.
5. The teller was so frightened that he only glanced at the wooden gun.
6. The teller believed the replica was real.
7. The teller at the next window looked at the replica and was fairly certain it was fake.
8. No one else noticed whether the replica was real.
9. The teller gave Mr. Canter money and Mr. Canter fled.

Note that some of the facts included may not be related to any element, such as the fact that the replica was carved of pine wood rather than another kind of wood. In this step, however, it is better to include all potentially related facts rather than omit them. Later, research may demonstrate the importance of a fact thought to be insignificant.

STEP 4: Determine Which Facts Apply. Determine which of the client's facts apply to establish or satisfy the elements of each cause of action—the key facts. The facts identified in this step are the key facts. The key facts are as follows:

+ Element 1: A person by force, violence, or intimidation—Mr. Canter approached the teller, displayed the gun replica, and demanded money.

+ Element 2: Takes or attempts to take property or money—Mr. Canter took the money and fled the bank.

+ Element 3: In the care or possession of a bank—the money belonged to the bank.

Section (d)

+ Element 4: A person committing an offense defined in subsection (a) assaults any person or puts in jeopardy the life of any person by use of a dangerous weapon or device—Mr. Canter displayed the crudely carved replica of a 9mm Beretta handgun. The teller he approached believed it was a real handgun. The only other witness was fairly certain it was not real.

Note that this step results in the identification of those facts actually related to the elements of the cause of action and the elimination of all facts that are not necessary to establish a claim. You must apply this step to identify the key facts for each potential cause of action identified in step 1. After this is done, all the key facts for each claim are identified. Note that the relationship between key facts and issue identification is discussed in the next chapter.

B. Chapter 1 Hypothetical *Reins v. Stewart*

The following example requires the application of the principles to the *Reins v. Stewart* hypothetical presented at the beginning of Chapter 1.

STEP 1: Identify each possible cause of action and area of law involved. Based on the instructions in her assignment, Vanessa focuses on civil battery as a cause of action. She does not address criminal battery because the district attorney has stated that Mr. Stewart cannot be charged under the state's criminal battery statute.

Based upon her training and paralegal education, Vanessa knows that the applicable area of civil law is tort. The tort of battery is an act with the intent to cause harmful or offensive contact that causes harmful or offensive contact with the plaintiff's person. Step 1 may require no research. Vanessa may arrive at this point based solely on her education and experience. If she is unfamiliar with this area of law, she would consult a secondary authority, such as a legal encyclopedia, to obtain general information on the law of battery.

Vanessa's assignment is to focus on a possible battery claim. If she identifies another possible cause of action, such as intentional infliction of emotional distress, she should inform her supervisor. If instructed by her supervisor, she would follow steps 2 through 4 for the emotional distress claim.

STEP 2: Determine the elements of the cause of action identified in step 1. Vanessa's research reveals that battery is a common law doctrine developed in case law. How she researches the statutory and case law to determine this is discussed in the application sections of Chapters 4 and 5. The case law requires that the following elements be established to state a battery claim:

✦ Element 1: Act—The defendant must commit an act.

✦ Element 2: Intent—There must be a desire to bring about the consequences of the act or a substantially certain knowledge that the consequences will follow the act.

✦ Element 3: Harmful or offensive—There must be harmful or offensive contact with the plaintiff's person.

✦ Element 4: Causation—The defendant's actions must have caused the consequences to occur or were a substantial factor in their occurrence.

STEP 3: List all facts related to the elements of the cause of action identified in step 2. All facts potentially related to the cause of action include:

1. Mr. Stewart owed Mr. Reins money.
2. Mr. Stewart did not repay.
3. Mr. Reins went to Mr. Stewart's house and demanded payment.
4. Mr. Stewart wrote a check that bounced.
5. Mr. Reins angrily returned to Mr. Stewart's house and demanded payment.
6. Mr. Stewart's 20-year-old son accompanied Mr. Stewart when he opened the door.
7. A shouting match ensued.
8. The son attacked Mr. Reins.
9. After the attack started, Mr. Stewart encouraged his son, yelling, "Hit him again, beat him."
10. Mr. Stewart's only action in the fight was to encourage his son.
11. Mr. Reins suffered a broken jaw as a result of the beating.

STEP 4: Determine which of the facts of the client's case apply to establish or satisfy the elements of each cause of action—the key facts.

✦ Element 1: Mr. Stewart was present at the fight and encouraged his son by yelling, "Hit him again, beat him." He did not otherwise participate. The son attacked Mr. Reins.

✦ Element 2: The nature of the words said, the manner in which they were said, and the fact that they were said during the attack may evidence the requisite intent.

✦ Element 3: Mr. Reins suffered a broken jaw as a result of the beating.

✦ Element 4: Mr. Stewart said the words after the son started to attack Mr. Reins. It is not clear whether this element is met. It is not clear without further research whether words alone can be considered a substantial factor in causing the consequences.

You may not be certain whether a fact meets the established standard for an element. Often that determination may not take place until trial. Just make sure there is some fact that arguably meets the requirements of each of the elements of the cause of action.

C. Court Opinion

This example illustrates the operation of the principles for identifying the key facts in a court opinion. Read the *Flowers v. Campbell* case presented in the following text and apply the steps presented in this chapter to determine the key facts of the collateral estoppel issue.

Note that the doctrine of collateral estoppel is discussed in the case. The doctrine of collateral estoppel prevents a party in a lawsuit from relitigating an issue that was decided in a previous lawsuit. In the case, the trial court ruled that the question of whether the defendant, Campbell, used excessive force in resisting the assault of Flowers was already litigated in an earlier criminal case. Based upon this ruling, the trial court determined that the doctrine of collateral estoppel applied and dismissed Flowers's claim that Campbell used excessive force. The appeal in *Flowers v. Campbell* is from this ruling by the trial court.

CASE

FLOWERS

v.

CAMPBELL

725 P.2D 1295 (OR. CT. APP. 1986)

ROSSMAN, Judge.

Plaintiff brought this assault and battery action to recover damages for injuries allegedly sustained in a skirmish with defendant Campbell (defendant), who was, at the time, an employee of defendant Montgomery Ward & Company. Plaintiff alleges that defendant used excessive force to repel his own aggressive behavior, for which plaintiff was convicted of assault in the fourth degree and harassment. The trial court dismissed the action after ruling, on defendant's motion for a directed verdict, that all material issues of fact were decided against plaintiff at his criminal trial and that he was precluded from relitigating those issues. We reverse.

The violence erupted after plaintiff accused defendant of charging him $12.99 for a lock that had been advertised for $9.97.[1] Plaintiff admits that he became involved in a verbal exchange with defendant immediately before

the fight and that he "threw the first punch." He also concedes both that the jury at his criminal trial necessarily found that his use of force was not justified and that he is collaterally estopped from relitigating that issue. See *Roshak v. Leathers*, 277 Or. 207, 560 P.2d 275 (1977). He contends, however, that the dispositive issue in this civil action is whether defendant responded to his own admitted aggression with excessive force. He contends that that issue was not litigated at his criminal trial.

Under the doctrine of collateral estoppel, a party to an action may be prevented from relitigating issues that were actually decided and necessary to the judgment in a previous action. *State Farm v. Century Home*, 275 Or. 97, 550 P.2d 1185 (1976); *Bahler v. Fletcher*, 257 Or. 1, 474 P.2d 329 (1970). Plaintiff was convicted in the criminal action of assault and harassment. The victim's use of more force than was justified to repel the attacker's criminal acts is not a defense to either of those crimes. It follows that defendant's response to plaintiff's actions could not have been an issue that was necessarily decided in plaintiff's criminal trial. Accordingly, because an aggressor may recover in an action for battery if he proves that the defendant used more force than was justified in repelling the aggression, *Linkhart v. Savely*, 190 Or. 484, 497, 227 P.2d 187 (1951), the trial court erred in holding that plaintiff was precluded from litigating all issues "essential" to his recovery by reason of the judgment entered in his criminal trial.

REVERSED AND REMANDED.

***

[1] Plaintiff was 62 years old at fight time; defendant was 33. Plaintiff allegedly sustained a broken arm and a detached retina. Defendant's jaw was broken.

STEP 1: *Read the Entire Case.* *Read the entire case with the following general question in mind: "What was decided about which facts?"* This step helps you keep the facts in mind while obtaining an overview of what legal questions were addressed and answered.

STEP 2: *Look to the Holding.* The holding is the application of the rule of law to the legal question raised by the facts of the case. *"What is the court's answer to the legal question? How did the court apply the rule of law to the legal question(s) raised?"* These are questions to ask when looking to the holding.

In this case, the court stated that the doctrine of collateral estoppel prevents a party from relitigating issues that were actually decided in a previous action. The court noted that the victim's use of more force than was justified to repel the attacker's criminal acts is not a defense to assault or harassment. Therefore, the issue of the victim's use of excessive force to repel the plaintiff's attack was not litigated in the plaintiff's criminal trial. The court concluded that the trial court erred in applying the doctrine of collateral estoppel to preclude the plaintiff from litigating the question of the victim's use of excessive force to repel the plaintiff's aggression.

STEP 3: *Identify the Key Facts.* *Identify the facts necessary to the holding—the key facts.*

Part 1: List All Facts Related to the Holding. What facts are possibly related to the holding? Plaintiff filed an assault and battery civil action against defendant to recover damages for injuries sustained in a skirmish with defendant. Plaintiff and defendant became involved in a fight as a result of a dispute over an amount plaintiff was charged for an item. Plaintiff threw the first punch.

He claims that defendant responded with excessive force to plaintiff's aggression. Plaintiff was tried in a separate criminal action and convicted of assaulting and harassing defendant. The trial court ruled that "all material issues of fact were decided against plaintiff at his criminal trial and he was precluded from relitigating those issues." All of these facts are possibly related to the holding. Some of the facts of the case, such as what they were fighting about, are clearly not related and are eliminated in this part of step 3.

The trial court in this action ruled that the plaintiff was precluded from relitigating his claim in this action because the issues of fact regarding the fight were decided in the criminal action. The trial court, therefore, dismissed his claim.

Part 2: Determine the Key Facts. Which of the facts listed in part 1 are necessary or essential to the decision reached? Which of the facts, if changed, would change the outcome of the case?

+ The trial court's ruling that the issue of the victim's response was litigated in the criminal case is clearly a key fact. Had the trial court ruled otherwise, the case would not have been dismissed and the appeal filed. Note that a "fact" in this case is how the trial court ruled.

+ The fact that plaintiff was convicted of assault and harassment in an earlier criminal case is clearly a key fact. Had there been no criminal trial, the civil trial court could not have applied the doctrine of collateral estoppel.

+ The fact that defendant (victim) used force in response to plaintiff's aggression is a key fact. Plaintiff's lawsuit rests upon the nature of the defendant's response.

+ The fact that the victim's alleged use of excessive force to repel an attacker's acts of assault or harassment is not a defense to those acts in a criminal case is also key. Had this been a defense to those acts, the question of the victim's use of excessive force would have been litigated in the criminal case and the trial court's ruling would have been correct.

   Note that in this case, a key fact is a rule of law—the victim's use of force in response to assault and harassment is not a defense to either crime.

+ The fact that the plaintiff threw the first punch in his fight with the defendant is probably not a key fact. It is not necessary to establish or satisfy any element of the collateral estoppel issue.

This case is somewhat different from some other cases because the key facts on appeal involve the facts of what occurred between the plaintiff and the defendant, the actions of the trial court, and the law governing defenses to assault and harassment.

SUMMARY

The first step in part B of the legal research and analysis process is preliminary preparation, which is gathering information about the case from the case file. This is accomplished by sifting through the file to identify key terms and key facts. Key terms are terms that help guide the researcher when performing research. Key facts are those facts in the case that are critical to the outcome of the case.

All lawsuits arise as a result of disputes involving facts. Our legal system revolves around resolving disputes through the application of rules of law to the facts of a case. Therefore, the two major components of the dispute-resolution process are the applicable law and the facts of the dispute. Each component deserves appropriate attention.

Some facts are more important than others, and the most important facts are the key facts—those facts upon which the outcome of the case depends. Key facts are those facts necessary to prove or disprove a claim. A key fact is so essential that if it were changed, the outcome of the case would be different. Key facts are an element of a legal issue, which is discussed in Chapter 3.

There are four recommended steps to follow when determining the key facts of a client's case:

Step 1: Identify each cause of action possibly raised by the facts.

Step 2: Determine the elements of each cause of action identified in step 1.

Step 3: List all the facts possibly related to the elements of the causes of action identified in step 2.

Step 4: Determine which of the client's facts apply to establish or satisfy the elements of each cause of action—the key facts.

There are three recommended steps for identifying the key facts in a court opinion:

Step 1: Read the entire case with the following general question in mind: "What was decided about which facts?"

Step 2: Look to the holding.

Step 3: Identify the facts necessary to the holding—the key facts.

These recommended steps are usually helpful in identifying the key facts. You may develop shortcuts or different methods as you become more proficient in analyzing a client's case or a court opinion.

CHAPTER REFERENCES

Background Facts   30

Ethics   28

Facts   28

Groups of Facts   32

Individual Key Facts   32

Irrelevant Facts   30

Key Facts   31

Key Facts/Case Law   36

Key Facts/Client's Case   33

Key Terms   26

Rule of Law   28

INTERNET RESOURCES

As of the date of the publication of this text, there are no Web sites dedicated specifically to key facts. However, using a search engine such as <http://www.google.com> and "IRAC key facts" or "legal analysis and key facts" as a topic, a wide range of Web sites may be found related to the topic of legal analysis and key facts. Most of these sites provide information without charge. As noted in Chapter 10, the two major fee-based online research services are Westlaw and LexisNexis. The publishers closely monitor these services. Information you obtain free from other sites may not be closely monitored and may not be as accurate or have the same quality of material as that obtained from fee-based services. Therefore, exercise care when using freely obtained material.

For additional materials, please go to the CD accompanying this book

For additional resources, visit our Web site at www.paralegal.delmar.cengage.com

EXERCISES

Additional exercises are located on the Student CD-ROM accompanying the text and Online Companion.

ASSIGNMENT 1

Describe in detail the steps for determining the key facts in a client's case.

ASSIGNMENT 2

Describe in detail the steps for determining the key facts in a court opinion.

ASSIGNMENT 3

Identify the background facts in the following cases.

 ✦ *Flowers v. Campbell* (presented in this chapter)
 ✦ *United States v. Leon* (see Appendix C)

ASSIGNMENT 4

Identify the key facts in Assignment 5 in the Exercises section of Chapter 3.

ASSIGNMENT 5

Identify the key facts in each of the hypotheticals presented at the beginning of Chapters 3 and 6.

ASSIGNMENT 6

Identify the key facts in the cases listed in A, B, C, and E of Assignment 10 in the Exercises section of Chapter 5.

ASSIGNMENT 7

Facts: Holly Dixon, the widow of Thomas Dixon, wants to challenge the probate of the holographic will of Thomas Dixon. Mary Cary, the sister of Thomas Dixon and personal representative of his estate, has submitted for probate a holographic will prepared by Mr. Dixon.

The first half of the will is in the handwriting of Mr. Dixon. The second half is typewritten. It was typed by the next-door neighbor, Edgar Mae. Mr. Mae states that Mr. Dixon asked him to finish the will because Mr. Dixon was too weak to continue. The will is signed by Mr. Dixon. There are no subscribing witnesses to the will, but it includes a self-proving affidavit that meets the requirements of the statute.

Rule of Law: Tex. Prob. Code. Ann. § 59, Requisites of a Will (Vernon 1980), provides: "Every last will and testament . . . shall be in writing . . . , and shall, if not wholly in the handwriting of the testator, be attested by two (2) or more credible witnesses. . . ." Tex. Prob. Code. Ann. § 60, Exception Pertaining to Holographic Wills (Vernon 1980), provides: "Where the will is written wholly in the handwriting of the testator, the attestation of the subscribing witnesses may be dispensed with. Such a will may be made self-proved at any time during the testator's lifetime by the attachment or annexation thereto of an affidavit by the testator to the effect that the instrument is his last will; that he was at least 18 years of age when he executed it . . . ; that he was of sound mind; and that he has not revoked such instrument."

Assignment: Identify the key facts in regard to the question of whether the will is admissible to probate under Texas law.

ASSIGNMENT 8

Facts: Terry, a bill collector, has been attempting to collect a bill from Client. Every other evening for the past two weeks, he has called Client at home after 8:30 p.m. and threatened to call her employer and inform him that she refuses to pay her bills. On every Monday, Wednesday, and Friday during the two-week period, he has called Client at work. She has repeatedly requested that he quit calling her at work. On the past two Saturdays, he has come by her home and threatened to sue her and throw her in jail.

Rule of Law: Infliction of emotional distress—extreme or outrageous conduct that causes severe emotional distress.

Assignment: The researcher's assignment is to determine whether the actions of the bill collector constitute "extreme or outrageous conduct." Discuss the assignment from the perspective of individual key facts and from the perspective of a group of facts.

ASSIGNMENT 9

Part A. Read *Dean v. Dickey* in Appendix C. Identify the validity of the will issue.

Part B. Read *United States v. Martinez-Jimenez* in Appendix C. Identify the key facts concerning whether the weapon was a dangerous weapon.

Part C. Read *Wolcott v. Wolcott* in Appendix C. Identify the key facts concerning the modification of child support due to change of circumstances.

Part D. Read *People v. Sanders* in Appendix C. Identify the key facts concerning the existence of spousal privilege for communications made in the presence of the children.

CHAPTER 3

Issue Identification—Spotting the Issue

Outline

Learning Objectives

After completing this chapter, you should understand:

✦ What a legal issue is and the various types of issues

✦ The elements of an issue

✦ How to identify (spot) the issue in a client's case

✦ How to identify (spot) the issue in a court opinion

It was the late afternoon of an already long day when Kevin realized he still had a lot of work to finish before he could go home. Kevin has been Randi McGuire's paralegal for the past five years. He admires her for her tenacity and appreciates the responsibility and independence she gives him to perform his assignments. Kevin's primary role is to conduct the initial interview with the client, prepare a summary of the interview, and assemble a legal memorandum containing an identification of the legal issues and an analysis of the applicable law.

Identifying the legal issue is often the trickiest part of Kevin's job. It did not seem, however, that it would be too much of a problem in Ida Carry's case. He had just finished his interview with Ms. Carry, whose home is across the street from Roosevelt Elementary School. Ms. Carry's best friend, Karen, lives a block away. Karen's seven-year-old son attends school at Roosevelt.

Last month, on April 14, Ida was in her front yard planting tulips. It was lunchtime, and children were playing at the playground. She heard the crossing guard's whistle blow and tires squealing. She looked up and saw a car approaching a curve in the school zone at a very high rate of speed. It jumped the curb, crashed through the chain-link fence surrounding the playground, and hit

the seesaw. The first thing she recognized was the car—it was Bob Barton's hot-rod Camaro. It looked like he was going too fast, lost control on the curve in the school zone, and crashed through the fence.

Bob, a local teen, continually raced in the neighborhood. Several teachers complained to his parents, who did nothing. Bob had received several speeding tickets.

The second thing Ida noticed was that two children playing on the seesaw were injured. One of them was Karen's son, Tim. When she realized it was Tim, she became extremely upset.

Since the wreck, Ida has had severe insomnia and extreme anxiety. When she can sleep, she has nightmares. Her doctor prescribed medication for her nerves and to help her sleep, and he recently referred her to a psychologist. Ida came to Ms. McGuire's office seeking to recover the expenses she has incurred.

After summarizing the interview, Kevin focuses on the next task and asks himself, "What is the legal issue in this case?" The process of identifying the issue, commonly referred to as "spotting the issue," is the subject of this chapter. The Application section of this chapter discusses the answer to Kevin's question.

I. INTRODUCTION

Before research can begin, you must know what you are researching and what you are looking for. This requires that the issue (legal question) to be researched be clearly identified. Unless the assignment specifically informs you of what is to be researched, such as the supervising attorney telling you to look up a specific statute, identifying the issue is the first step of the legal research and analysis process after the preliminary preparation.

Identifying the legal issue(s) presented by the client's fact situation is the foundation and key to effective legal research and analysis. It is the most important task a researcher faces when engaging in legal research and analysis. It guides the researcher to the specific legal problem raised by the unique facts of the client's case. You must know what the precise legal problem is before you can begin to solve it. Identifying the issue determines which direction the research will take. It is like selecting a road—if you select the wrong road, you will waste a lot of time before you get to your destination, or you may get lost and never get there. Half the battle of legal research and analysis is knowing what you are looking for, that is, what is the issue?

If you misidentify the issue (ask the wrong legal question), you waste time and commit legal error. If you ask the wrong question, you will get the wrong answer to the client's problem.

> **FOR EXAMPLE** If you incorrectly identify the issue as a contract law issue when it is really a corporation law issue, you will waste time researching contract law, and the answer you find will not apply to the client's case.

The client does not retain counsel to find the answer to the wrong question. The client pays to have a problem solved. If the issue is misidentified, the problem remains unsolved, time is wasted, and you are no better off than when you started. If the error is not caught, it may result in malpractice because the client is billed for a service not requested.

Not only is identifying the issue the most important step in the research process, it is often the most difficult. When you ask a professional how to spot an issue, the response often is, "I just know" or "After a while it becomes intuitive." It does become intuitive after reading and working on hundreds of cases. This, however, does not help the beginner. Although no simple rule or magic formula exists, there are techniques and steps that are helpful when identifying the issue in a client's fact situation or a court opinion. The starting point is to know what an issue is, that is, how it is defined.

II. DEFINITION AND TYPES

In the broadest sense, the **issue** is a question—the legal question raised by the dispute. It is the legal question that must be answered before a case can be resolved. It occurs whenever there is disagreement or uncertainty about whether or how a rule of law applies to a client's facts. In a narrower sense, it is the precise legal question raised by the specific facts of a dispute.

Issues can be broken into three broad categories:

✦ A question of which law applies

> **FOR EXAMPLE** Do the traffic code provisions of Municipal Code § 2254 or state statute § 35-6-7-28 apply when an individual is stopped in a municipality for driving under the influence of intoxicants?

+ A question of how a law applies

> **FOR EXAMPLE** Under the provisions of New York battery law, is a battery committed by an individual present at the scene of a battery, who encourages others to commit the battery but does not actively participate in the actual battering of the victim?

+ A question of whether a law applies at all

> **FOR EXAMPLE** Does Municipal Code § 2100, Public Sales/Auctions, govern garage sales held on private property?

Regardless of the type of legal question raised by a dispute, the definition is the same: the issue is the precise legal question raised by the specific facts of the dispute.

Now that you know what an issue is, the next step is to determine what it is composed of—the elements. Every issue is composed of elements, and these elements must be determined to identify the issue. Identifying the elements is the key to the process of identifying the issue. Therefore, it is necessary to identify those elements to identify the issue. In fact, after you have determined the elements, the issue can be easily identified.

III. ELEMENTS

A client enters the law office with a unique fact situation that may or may not have a legal remedy. The role of the attorney is to identify the question raised by the facts and determine whether a legal remedy is available and, if so, what legal remedy is available. A well-crafted issue informs the reader of the relevant law, the key facts of the case, and the legal question raised by the law. The exactness and degree of specificity with which the question is posed determines its usefulness to the reader and researcher.

Because the issue is defined as the precise legal question raised by the specific facts of the client's case, a correctly identified issue is composed of the three elements: the applicable law, the legal question, and key facts (see Exhibit 3–1).

Exhibit 3–1
Elements of an Issue.

Applicable Law	The specific law that governs the dispute. It may be a constitutional provision, statute, regulation ordinance, or common law doctrine, principle, rule, test, or guide.
Legal Question	The question concerning the law governing the dispute raised by the facts of the dispute.
Key Facts	The legally significant facts that raise the legal question of how or whether the law governing the dispute applies. Facts that, if changed, would change or affect the outcome of the application of the law.

A. Applicable Law

Applicable law is the specific law that governs the dispute. This may be a constitutional provision, statute, regulation, or case law doctrine, principle, rule, test, or guide.

> **FOR EXAMPLE** Under Indiana Code § 35-42-3-2, kidnapping . . .
>
> According to Florida's law governing breach of contract, . . .

B. Legal Question

This refers to the **legal question** concerning the law governing the dispute, raised by the facts of the dispute.

> **FOR EXAMPLE** Does kidnapping occur when . . .
>
> Is a contract breached when . . .

C. Key Facts

Key facts are the key or legally significant facts that raise the legal question of how or whether the law governing the dispute applies.

> **FOR EXAMPLE** . . . when the individual is held against her will but is not held for ransom?
>
> . . . when the product delivered is grade A- and the contract calls for grade A?

D. Examples

These three elements of the issue—the applicable law, the legal question concerning the law, and the key facts that raise the legal question—are referred to in this text as a comprehensive, **narrow, or specific statement of the issue**. An issue including these elements is comprehensive because it includes the specific law and key facts. It is a narrow statement of the issue because the more facts included, the more specific (or narrow) the legal question becomes. Identify each element as precisely and completely as possible. The following are examples of statements of issues containing the three elements:

+ Under the holographic will statute, Colo. Rev. Stat. § 15-11-503, is a holographic will valid if it is hand-written by a neighbor at the direction of the testator, but not written in the testator's handwriting? **(Applicable Law)** **(Legal Question)** **(Key Facts)**

+ Under Arizona tort law, does a battery occur when law enforcement officers, while making a lawful arrest, encounter resistance, use force to overcome that resistance, and continue to use force after resistance ceases? **(Applicable Law)** **(Legal Question)** **(Key Facts)**

+ Does Municipal Code § 3362 permit the installation of a sign that is 20 feet high by 40 feet wide, more than 15 feet from the property line, and does not block the view of traffic? **(Applicable Law)** **(Legal Question)** **(Key Facts)**

Each of these examples contains the precise law, legal question, and the key facts essential to the resolution of the dispute. Note that the issue is narrowly focused upon the law and specific facts of the client's case.

Failure to include these elements results in an abstract question, a **broad statement of the issue** that is missing the legal (applicable law) and factual context.

> **FOR EXAMPLE** If the three previous examples were stated broadly, and did not include the specific elements discussed in this section, they would appear respectively as follows:
>
> ✦ Was the will valid?
>
> ✦ Did the police commit a battery?
>
> ✦ Is the sign in violation of the municipal ordinance?

Each broad statement of the issue in this example could apply to a multitude of cases involving wills, batteries, or sign ordinance violations. Each issue fails to inform the researcher of the specific factual context of the dispute, the precise law involved, and the question that must be resolved to determine if, and what, remedy is available to the client. A broadly stated issue is not appropriate in legal research and writing for several reasons:

  ✦ It is not helpful or useful for the reader who is not familiar with the facts of the case. This may be a judge in the case of a brief in support of a motion, or an attorney in the office referring to an old memorandum in the office files.

  ✦ It does not guide the reader to the specific law in question. In the previous examples, what specific wills or battery statutes are we talking about? What municipal ordinance does the sign violate? What is the precise legal context of this dispute?

  ✦ It is not useful to the individual drafting and researching the issue.

> **FOR EXAMPLE** "Did Mr. Smith commit a battery?" is such a broad formulation of the issue that it is of little value.

Stated this way, the issue applies to all battery cases. So stated, it is useless. It fails to focus the researcher's inquiry or guide the researcher to the specific area of battery law in dispute.

In West's digests, used to help locate case law, legal topics are identified by key numbers. There are more than 100 battery key numbers under the topic "Assault and Battery." A broad statement of the issue forces the researcher to scan all the subtopics looking for the one that applies. If research is conducted electronically, such as with Westlaw, the search will locate hundreds if not thousands of cases, too many for the researcher to review. When the issue is stated comprehensively, or narrowly, the inquiry is narrowed.

> **FOR EXAMPLE** "Under California's tort law, is a battery committed when a bystander encourages and convinces a perpetrator to beat another individual, and that individual is beaten as a result of the encouragement?" This narrow statement of the issue focuses the researcher's attention to that specific area of the digest involving individuals liable for battery, that is, Assault and Battery—Key Number 18, Persons Liable. If electronic research is conducted, the search is focused and only those cases involving the liability of individuals encouraging a battery will be located.

As the preceding example illustrates, a comprehensive statement directs the researcher's inquiry to a specific subtopic in the digest, and research time is saved. Also, the question is not abstract. The reader does not have to refer to the facts in some other document or file to understand what is in dispute.

In summary, a shorthand/broad statement of the issue fails to inform. It results in an abstract question that forces the reader to engage in further inquiry to determine what specifically is in dispute in the case. It is useful only in casual conversation or conversations where the participants are familiar with the case. In short, an issue broadly identified is an issue not truly identified at all.

The importance of focusing on the elements of the issue and identifying the issue in terms of the elements is critical. It reduces the chance of misidentifying the question presented by the facts and helps guide the researcher, thereby saving time and effort. The task is to identify these elements as precisely and completely as possible.

Paralegals and attorneys becomes involved in issue identification in two different but related situations:

✦ Identifying the issue(s) in a client's case

✦ Identifying the issue(s) in a court opinion

In each situation, it is necessary to determine the three elements of the issue to correctly identify the issue. The next two sections present recommended steps for identifying the issue in a client's case and in a court opinion.

IV. ISSUE IDENTIFICATION—CLIENT'S CASE

The client's fact situation presents a legal question (issue) or set of questions that must be identified before the case can be resolved. A helpful tool to keep in mind, from the outset of the case, is the question: *"What must be decided about which facts?"* or phrased another way, *"What question concerning which law is raised by these facts?"*

This keeps you focused on the elements of the issue—the law, the question, and the key facts of the case. It helps you avoid being sidetracked by related or interesting questions raised by the facts that are not necessary to resolve the legal question(s) of the case. The value of keeping these questions in mind will be illustrated throughout this section.

Identifying the legal question(s) or issue(s) in a client's case is primarily a four-step process (see Exhibit 3–2).

	Steps in the Identification or Spotting of the Issue in a Client's Case
Step 1	Identify each type of cause of action and area of law possibly involved.
Step 2	Determine the elements of each cause of action identified in step 1.
Step 3	Determine which of the facts of the client's case apply to establish or satisfy the elements of each cause of action—the key facts.
Step 4	Assemble the issue from the law and key facts identified in steps 2 and 3. Follow the format: Rule of Law + Legal Question + Key Facts.

Exhibit 3–2
Issue Identification—Client's Case—Four Steps.

Note: Steps 1 through 3 are essentially the same as steps 1 through 4 of the Key Facts Identification—Client's Case section of Chapter 2. They are summarized here with different examples so that you will not have to refer to that chapter.

A. Step 1: Identify Each Type of Cause of Action

Identify each type of cause of action and area of law possibly involved. The first step is to identify the potential cause(s) of action and area(s) of law raised by the client's fact situation. This includes a broad identification of potential issues, the general areas of law, and the client's facts related to each area of law. This preliminary identification is based upon education and experience and usually does not require any research.

> **FOR EXAMPLE** Mary is stopped at a stoplight waiting for the light to change. She is drinking a soft drink. She has been stopped for about 10 seconds when a pickup, driven by Sam, slams into the back of her vehicle. Her automobile is knocked into the intersection and narrowly misses being struck by a vehicle passing through the intersection. Sam jumps out of his pickup, runs to Mary's vehicle, and screams at her that she should not have been stopped and she caused the wreck. Mary thinks he is either crazy or drugged. She is afraid he might hit her. He yanks open her vehicle door and pulls her out of the automobile, screaming, "It's all your fault, it's all your fault." He pulls out a knife and waves it around. A couple of pedestrians approach and Sam runs back to his pickup.
>
> As a result of the incident, Mary suffered whiplash injuries and bruises on her arm, she experiences anxiety whenever she is stopped at a light, and she has severe insomnia. This hypothetical is referred to as the rear-end collision example throughout this chapter.
>
> Based upon experience and tort classes, the researcher identifies four possible causes of action involving four broad areas of law: Was Sam's failure to stop negligence? Did he commit an assault? Did he commit a battery? Did his actions constitute intentional infliction of emotional distress?

In some situations the assignment may identify the specific cause of action and area of law to be researched and this step will not be necessary.

This initial identification of the broad issues and areas of law may be expanded or reduced after subsequent research is conducted. The purpose of doing so is twofold:

✦ To identify, in general terms, the issues involved

✦ To provide a starting point for the identification and clarification of each specific issue that must be resolved in the case

B. Step 2: Determine the Elements of Each Cause of Action

Determine the elements of each cause of action identified in step 1. Apply steps 2, 3, and 4 separately to each potential issue or cause of action identified in step 1. In other words:

✦ Choose one potential issue identified in step 1.

✦ Apply Steps 2, 3, and 4 to that issue.

✦ Complete the identification of that issue before addressing the next potential issue. That is, address one issue at a time, not all the issues simultaneously.

> **FOR EXAMPLE** In the rear-end collision example, there are four broad issues and areas of law involved: negligence, assault, battery, and emotional distress. Choose one area, such as negligence, and complete steps 2 through 4. Be careful to identify and finish with that issue before addressing the next issue.

Focusing on one issue at a time avoids the confusion that may occur when dealing with multiple causes of action that often have overlapping elements. In this example, some of Sam's conduct may constitute elements of both assault and intentional infliction of emotional distress. Researching both issues at the same time could cause confusion.

Step 2 requires researching the area of law to determine the elements necessary to establish a cause of action. To know whether the law provides relief for the client, it is necessary to determine what the law requires to be established (the elements) to obtain that relief. Locate the elements by researching primary authority such as the statutory or case law. If there is no primary authority in the jurisdiction, refer to secondary authority such as a legal encyclopedia, an ALR annotation, or the *Restatement of the Law* governing the topic.

> **FOR EXAMPLE** Using the rear-end collision example, the researcher begins with the issue involving intentional infliction of emotional distress. Research reveals that the following elements must be established to prevail:
>
> 1. The defendant's conduct must be intentional.
> 2. The conduct must be extreme and outrageous.
> 3. There must be a causal connection between the defendant's conduct and the plaintiff's mental distress.
> 4. The plaintiff's mental distress must be extreme or severe.

Note: To help guide you to locate the law at this stage of the process, you may roughly identify the issue with the facts you think are important.

> **FOR EXAMPLE** The assignment is to determine if a will has been validly revoked when the testator wrote, in pencil, across the top of the first page of the will "I hereby revoke this will." To help guide the research for the relevant statute (primary authority) that applies, a rough formulation of the issue can be drafted: Under the wills statutes, is a will revoked when the testator writes in pencil across the top of the first page of the will, "I hereby revoke this will."? This rough formulation guides the researcher to look for the specific wills statute that addresses revocation. After the statute is located and the requirements of the statute (elements) are identified, the application of step 3 determines which facts are key facts. A complete statement of the issue including the specific rule of law can be made after the law is located and steps 3 and 4 are performed.

After the elements are identified, proceed to step 3.

C. Step 3: Determine the Key Facts

Determine which of the facts of the client's case apply to establish or satisfy the elements of each cause of action—the key facts. Steps 1 and 2 identify the law that must be included in the issue, and step 3 identifies the facts that must be included in the issue—the key facts.

Identify the key facts by determining which facts of the client's case apply to establish or satisfy the requirements of each element of the cause of action. This step is necessary because to state a claim, and thereby obtain relief, facts must be presented that establish or satisfy the requirements of each element.

> **FOR EXAMPLE** Using the rear-end collision example, apply the client's facts to the elements:
>
> 1. *The defendant's conduct must be intentional.* In this case, the defendant's running toward the client screaming, opening her car door, pulling her out, and waving his knife are the facts showing intentional conduct that satisfy or apply to establish this element. This conduct is clearly intentional.
> 2. *The conduct must be extreme and outrageous.* The acts identified in number 1 are the facts showing extreme and outrageous conduct that establish this element.

3. *There must be a causal connection between the defendant's conduct and the plaintiff's mental distress.* Since the accident, the client has been unable to sleep and is anxious when stopped at a light. These facts satisfy the third element.

4. *The plaintiff's distress must be extreme or severe.* Anxiety whenever stopped at a light and severe insomnia are facts showing extreme or severe distress and are the facts that establish the fourth element.

By matching the facts with the required elements, the key facts of the emotional distress issue are identified. Because the question is how the law applies to the facts, these facts become part of the issue and must be included. After step 3 is completed, all the elements necessary to identify the issue are in place. All that is left is to proceed to step 4 and assemble the issue.

Note: You may not be certain whether a fact meets the standard established for an element. Often that determination does not take place until trial. Just make sure there is some fact that arguably meets the requirements of each of the elements of the cause of action.

FOR EXAMPLE A determination of whether Mary's insomnia and anxiety are extreme or severe enough to warrant relief may not be decided until trial. Her symptoms are sufficient to arguably meet the requirement of the fourth element. If research, however, reveals that this harm is not sufficiently extreme for the requirements of emotional distress, then there is no emotional distress issue.

If no facts satisfy or establish an element, there is probably no cause of action or issue. In this example, if Mary did not suffer anxiety or insomnia, no facts would meet the requirements of the fourth element, and most likely there would be no emotional distress issue.

D. Step 4: Assemble the Issue

The last step is the easiest. *Gather and assemble the elements of the issue from the law and key facts identified in steps 2 and 3.* The law is emotional distress, the legal question is whether emotional distress occurred, and the key facts are the facts identified in step 3. Putting it all together, the issue is as follows:

> Under (name of state) law of emotional distress, does emotional distress occur when the driver of the rear vehicle in a rear-end collision runs screaming toward the other driver, opens her car door, pulls her out, and waves a knife, and the other driver suffers anxiety and insomnia as a result of the conduct?

The four steps presented here simplify the issue identification process by breaking it down into workable steps. It may not be necessary to follow all the steps. The issue may be apparent in step 1 or at some other point. This process, however, takes some of the mystery out of issue identification and provides a useful tool when the issues are not clear or easy to identify. It allows you to answer the question of "What question concerning which law is raised by the client's facts?"

The answer to the emotional distress issue identified in the preceding example may be determined by reference to case law. The important thing to remember is that by concisely identifying the issue in the context of the key facts, the key facts are less likely to be overlooked. By including the key facts in the issue, the researcher's focus is narrowed, and the researcher is less likely to omit a critical fact and thereby ignore a crucial line of inquiry or misidentify the issue entirely. In the rear-end collision example, it may be that Sam's actions are not sufficiently outrageous to constitute emotional distress—maybe there is not sufficient evidence to connect the anxiety and insomnia to the acts, or maybe the harm is not the type of harm for which relief is granted in emotional distress cases.

Note: At the outset you may know only the general area of law that applies and not the specific statute. By going through the steps and identifying the key facts or terms and the question components of the issue, your search will be narrowed. A complete statement of the issue, including the specific rule of law, can be made after the law is located.

> **FOR EXAMPLE** An individual is arrested by the FBI while robbing a bank with a toy gun. He is informed that he will be charged with robbing the bank with a deadly weapon. By including the known facts, the issue can be stated as "Under the federal bank robbery statute is there sufficient evidence to support charges of bank robbery with a dangerous weapon when the weapon is a toy gun?" By identifying this much of the issue, a researcher is guided to search for the specific bank robbery statute that addresses bank robbery with a dangerous weapon.

As mentioned in step 2, steps 2 through 4 are applied to each of the issues broadly identified in step 1. It may be that certain issues are eliminated as the other steps are followed, such as when research reveals that there are not sufficient facts present to support a cause of action. It may be that additional issues are identified as research takes place.

> **FOR EXAMPLE** In the rear-end collision example, it may be that emotional distress was not considered until research on another issue, such as assault, revealed a case with similar facts that included a discussion of emotional distress.

E. Multiple Issues

Often there are multiple issues in a case. In the rear-end collision example, there were four possible causes of action, each one involving a separate issue. Be sure to list all the facts in the client's case and examine each one to determine if it relates to any identified issue or in any way gives rise to a new issue. In the rear-end collision example, the fact that Mary was drinking a soda may not be important. The fact that Sam ran from his car rather than walked may be critical. It is important to ensure that all the facts are considered and nothing is overlooked. All potential issues should be identified, and the four-step process helps ensure that nothing is missed.

Also, note that a single issue may have multiple parts or subissues.

> **FOR EXAMPLE** In the rear-end collision example, the intentional infliction of emotional distress issue may have separate subissues:
>
> ✦ Was Sam's conduct sufficiently extreme and outrageous?
> ✦ Are anxiety and severe insomnia "extreme or severe distress" within the meaning of the law?
> ✦ Did Sam's conduct cause the insomnia?

Each part or subissue should be separately considered and addressed.

CAVEAT. The steps presented in this section are useful tools and guides. These steps will usually help you quickly identify the issue. Remember that the process gets easier with experience.

V. ISSUE IDENTIFICATION—CASE LAW

This section focuses on identifying the issue(s) in a court opinion. The issue is the legal question addressed and answered by the court, that is, what the case is about. If you do not know what question the court addressed, it is possible to misunderstand the rule of law applied or adopted in the opinion. As a result, it is likely that you will misunderstand how or if the rule of law applies in your client's case and you may not be able to determine whether the case is on point.

This section does not address those situations where the issue is easily identified because somewhere in the opinion the court clearly states the issue.

> **FOR EXAMPLE** "In this case we decide whether an individual's Fourth Amendment right to be free from unreasonable searches is violated when officers executing a search warrant for a stolen television search the individual's pockets and discover drugs."

This section is concerned with those situations where identifying the issue is difficult because the court does not identify the issue, states the issue in such broad terms that it is not helpful, or states the issue in terms of the procedural context in which the case was brought before the court:

   ◆ *Issue not stated*—In some opinions, the court never clearly identifies what the issue is in the case.

   ◆ *Broad statement of the issue*—"The issue in this case is whether the defendant breached the contract."

COMMENT. This is a broad statement of the issue. It fails to inform the reader what the case is about. In the ultimate sense, the court decided whether the defendant breached the contract; but in reality, it reached that conclusion by making a substantive decision concerning the specific facts of the defendant's conduct.

> **FOR EXAMPLE** "The court may have concluded that the defendant's delivery of the order on time 95 percent of the time was substantial compliance with the contract and, therefore, not a breach."

   ◆ *Issue stated in the **procedural context***—"The issue in this case is whether the trial court erred when it granted the motion to suppress the evidence."

COMMENT. The court stated the issue in the context of how the case came before the court procedurally—an appeal of a trial court order granting a motion to suppress. To answer this question, the court actually addressed a substantive question raised by the facts of the case, and the substantive issue is what the case is actually about.

> **FOR EXAMPLE** The substantive issue decided was, "Under the provisions of the exclusionary rule, should evidence be suppressed when law enforcement officers obtained the evidence as a result of requiring the defendant to allow them to inspect the glove box when they were making a routine stop for speeding?"

Beginning students often make the mistake of identifying the issue in the procedural context stated by the court when, in reality, the issue involves a substantive determination of the application of the law to the facts of the case.

The goal when reading a case should be identifying the substantive issue(s) in the case. Ask yourself when reading the case, *"What was decided about which facts in this case?"* or *"What question concerning which law and key facts was decided by the court?"* Like a client's case, a court case is about a dispute concerning how the law applies to the facts. Had there been no dispute involving how the law applied to the facts, the case would not have gone to trial. If your identification of the issue in a court opinion fails to include the rule of law applied and the key facts, you have failed to identify the issue correctly.

How, then, is issue identification in a court opinion accomplished? Again, there is no magic formula. The three-step process presented in Exhibit 3–3 is suggested as a useful tool.

Steps in Identifying or Spotting the Issue in a Court Opinion	
Step 1 General question	Read the entire opinion before attempting to identify the issue. While reading, keep in mind the question: "What was decided about which facts in this case?"
Step 2 Look to the holding	Focus on the holding and ask the following questions: *To identify the law applied ask:* What statute, rule of law, or principle did the court apply to reach its decision? *To identify the question addressed by the court ask:* What legal question was addressed and answered by the holding? *To identify the key facts ask:* Which of the facts presented in the case, if, changed, would change or affect the question addressed in the holding?
Step 3 Assemble the issue	Assemble the issue from the answers to the questions in Step 2. Rule of Law + Legal Question + Key Facts.

Exhibit 3–3
Issue Identification—
Case Law—Three Steps.

Note: Steps 1 and 2 include the requirements of steps 1 through 3 of the Key Facts Identification—Case Law section discussed in Chapter 2. They are summarized here with a focus on the issue identification aspect of each step.

A. Step 1: General Question

The first part of this step is to *read the entire court opinion before attempting to identify the issue.* Important information concerning an issue may be scattered throughout the opinion. An initial reading of the entire case provides the researcher with an awareness of where information is located in the opinion and an overview of the case. This is helpful when you begin to analyze specific portions of the opinion. Read the entire opinion at the outset, even if the court clearly identifies the issue.

While reading the case, keep in mind this question: "What was decided about which facts in this case?" This question helps keep your mind focused on what you need to look for while reading the case to identify the elements of the issue:

✦ *"What was decided?"* keeps the mind focused on searching for the legal issue that was resolved and the law necessary for its resolution.

✦ *"About which facts?"* keeps the mind focused on looking for the facts essential to the resolution of the legal question.

If you keep this question in mind as you read the case, you will stay focused on the essence of the case: the court's application of a rule of law to the legal question raised by the facts. The facts are usually introduced early in the opinion. You will not know what was decided about them until you reach the holding, usually at the end. Asking this question forces you to keep the facts in mind as you read, because you are aware that you must decide which of the facts relate to the holding. When you get to the end of the opinion, you may realize that the holding relates to only a few of the facts presented.

Do not identify the issue(s) from the Syllabus or Headnotes of the opinion. As noted in Chapter 5, these are prepared by the publisher of the opinion. They are not part of the court opinion and are not intended to be used to identify the issue(s) addressed in the opinion. Headnotes may be relied upon to help you locate the issue in the opinion.

If you have not identified the issue by the time you have finished reading the case, proceed to step 2.

B. Step 2: Look to the Holding

The holding is the court's application of the rule of law to the legal issue raised by the facts of the case. It is the court's answer to the legal issue. In a court opinion, the key facts, legal question, and holding are all related. Finding one will help you find the others. Therefore, often the fastest way to track down the issue is to focus on the holding and ask the following questions:

1. *"What was decided in the holding?"*—In other words, "What legal question or issue was addressed and answered by the holding?" This identifies the second element of the issue, the legal question addressed by the court.

2. *"What statute, rule of law, principle, and so on, did the court apply to reach this holding?"*—This question helps identify the relevant rule of law, the first element of the issue.

3. *"Which of the facts presented in this case are related and necessary to the determination of the question identified as addressed in the holding?"* or *"Which of the facts, if changed, would change the outcome of the holding?"*—These questions help identify the third element of the issue, the key facts.

By answering these questions, the elements of the issue are identified: the rule of law, question, and key facts. You can state the issue by adding the rule of law and key facts to the holding and state the holding in question form. It sounds complicated, but it is not.

FOR EXAMPLE In a workers' compensation case, the court presents several facts concerning the plaintiff before and after she joined a monastery, including the following:

1. Her duties as a monastic
2. Her written application for admission as a volunteer to the service of God
3. The written invitation from the monastery, which included an offer of spiritual guidance and room and board in exchange for volunteer service
4. Information concerning her previous career
5. The fact that she did not receive a paycheck
6. Her spiritual motivation
7. Her daily duties
8. The fact that she was injured while mopping the floor
9. Her family relationships
10. The fact that there was no contract of employment

The plaintiff appealed the decision of the trial court granting the defendant's motion to dismiss for failure to state a claim. The issue is not stated in the opinion. The holding in the case was: "Plaintiff rendered services out of religious devotion as indicated by her application as a volunteer, lack of employment agreement, and lack of a paycheck; therefore, she was not an employee within the meaning of the law, and the trial court's dismissal of the complaint is affirmed." This example is referred to in this chapter as the monastery example.

A quick way to identify the issue in the case in this example is to focus on the holding and keep in mind this question: "What was decided about which facts to reach this holding?" Then, identify the elements of the issue by asking:

1. *"What question was decided in this holding?"*—The question decided is whether the plaintiff was an employee. The answer to this question provides the legal question element of the issue.

2. *"What rule of law or principle did the court apply to reach this holding?"*—The answer to this question provides the rule of law element of the issue. It may be, for example, a statute, case law principle, or doctrine. Assume here that it is the Workers' Compensation Act § 36-9-7.

3. *"Which facts mentioned in the opinion are related and necessary to the determination of the question of whether the plaintiff is an employee?"*—The answer to this question provides the key facts element of the issue. In this case, the court focused on the written application as a volunteer, the absence of an employment agreement, and the lack of a paycheck. These facts, if changed, would probably change the outcome. If treated as a group, the changing of all these facts would change the outcome.

C. Step 3: Assemble the Issue

Assemble the identified elements in the Law + Legal Question + Key Facts format. The rule of law is the Workers' Compensation Act § 36-9-7. The question is whether the plaintiff was an employee. The key facts are the written application for admission to the monastery as a volunteer, the absence of an employment agreement, and the lack of a paycheck. The issue, when assembled, is: "Under the provisions of Workers' Compensation Act § 36-9-7, is an individual an employee when the individual is admitted to a monastery upon a written application as a volunteer, does not receive a paycheck, and does not have an agreement of employment?"

D. Other Aids—Case Law Issue Identification

1. Concurring or Dissenting Opinion

In a concurring or dissenting opinion, the issue may be set out more clearly than in the majority opinion. Therefore, these opinions should not be overlooked when identifying the issue. Be aware, however, that the concurring or dissenting judge may have a different view of what the issue is, especially in the case of a dissent. Even if the formulation is different, the discussion of the issue by the concurring or dissenting judge may be helpful in determining the issue in the majority opinion.

2. Other Opinions

Reading other opinions cited in the case may provide guidance concerning the issue in the case you are researching. Also, reading a later court's discussion of the case may prove helpful because it may summarize and clarify the issue in the case you are reading. *Shepard's Citations* will guide you to subsequent cases.

E. Multiple Issues

The foregoing discussion focuses on locating a single issue. Often there are multiple issues in a court opinion. Apply the steps discussed earlier in this chapter to all the issues in the case. *Be sure to follow all the steps presented in this section completely when identifying an issue before proceeding to identify the next issue.* Remember, for each issue, you must identify the rule of law, specific question, and relevant facts.

You may read a case to find the answer to a single question relevant to your client's fact situation, or you may be looking for a specific legal principle, doctrine, or rule of law addressed by the court.

FOR EXAMPLE You are researching a court opinion that involves several torts, but you are interested only in the court's discussion of the emotional distress issue. Follow the steps mentioned previously to identify the emotional distress issue, but make sure that the court's resolution of the other issues does not in some way impact the emotional distress issue. You can accomplish this by reading the entire opinion and checking for any overlap of the issues or interconnectedness of the reasoning.

CAVEAT. As you did in the Issue Identification—Client's Case section, consider the steps presented in this section as useful tools and helpful guidelines. When followed, they will usually, but not always, help you quickly identify the issue in a court opinion. In some instances, the opinion is so obscure that you may not be able to identify the issue. Also, as you read more and more cases, a sort of intuition develops, and you may immediately spot the issue without the use of any of the steps.

VI. KEY POINTS CHECKLIST: *Spotting the Issue*

- When determining the issue(s) in a client's case, it is helpful to keep in mind this question: "What must be decided about which facts in this case?" This question helps keep the mind focused on the rule of law in conjunction with the facts.

- When identifying the issue(s) in a *court opinion,* as you read, keep asking the question, "What was decided about which facts in this opinion?" All cases are about how the law applies to facts. By keeping focused on the law and facts of the case, you are less likely to be sidetracked by issues and questions that do not need to be addressed.

- Address one issue at a time. For each issue under consideration, follow each of the steps presented in this chapter before proceeding to the next issue. In multiple issue cases, separate the issues and identify one completely before addressing the next one.

- When reading a court opinion or working on a client's case, keep in mind the three elements of the issue: rule of law, question, and key facts. This helps you stay focused on what you need to determine to identify the issue.

- Do not be concerned if you cannot immediately identify the issue or issues in a client's case. Complete identification of the issue may not take place until you conduct research, read laws and cases, and identify the required elements of the cause of action. The existence of additional issues likewise may not be known until research reveals their presence.

- Do not stop when you have identified one issue. Most cases have more than one legal question. Separate areas of law, such as torts and contracts, may occur in one fact situation. Always look for all possible causes of action that may arise from a fact situation.

■ Use any technique that works for you. The steps suggested here are designed as guidelines to assist you. They are not magic formulas cast in stone. Use any or all of them and anything else that works.

VII. APPLICATION

This section presents four examples of issue identification or issue spotting. Each example illustrates the principles discussed throughout this chapter and includes a discussion of the application of those principles.

A. Client's Fact Situation

Notice that steps 1 through 3 in the following three examples are the same steps used to identify the key facts in a client's fact situation discussed in the previous chapter. They are repeated here to illustrate the application of the entire issue identification process.

The following example applies the principles to the hypothetical presented at the beginning of the chapter.

STEP 1: Identify each possible cause of action and area of law involved. The first step is to identify each type of cause of action and area of law that may be raised by the client's fact situation. Kevin, based upon his training, realizes that this is a civil, not a criminal, matter. No crime has been committed against Ms. Carry. He also knows that the applicable area of civil law is tort. By a process of elimination, based upon experience, he focuses on infliction of emotional distress. There is no assault or battery because no act was directly or indirectly aimed at the client. Step 1 may require no research. Kevin may arrive at this point based solely on his education and experience, although he may realize, as he conducts research into the emotional distress issue, that other causes of action also are present. *If more than one claim is identified, steps 2 through 4 are to be followed separately for each.*

> **FOR EXAMPLE** If a part from the car flew off and hit Ms. Carry, there would be potential battery or negligence issues, and Kevin would follow steps 2 through 4 for each issue.

STEP 2: Determine the elements of each cause of action identified in step 1. Kevin's research reveals that emotional distress is a case law doctrine. The legislature has not adopted a statute concerning emotional distress. The state's highest court has recognized the tort of intentional infliction of emotional distress. The court requires that the following elements be established to state a claim:

+ *Element 1*—The defendant's conduct must be either intentional or grossly or recklessly negligent.
+ *Element 2*—The conduct must be extreme and outrageous.
+ *Element 3*—There must be a causal connection between the defendant's conduct and the plaintiff's mental distress.
+ *Element 4*—The plaintiff's mental distress must be extreme or severe.

STEP 3: Determine which of the facts of the client's case apply to establish or satisfy the elements of each cause of action—the key facts.

+ *Element 1*—Defendant's conduct of driving at a very high rate of speed, crashing through the fence, hitting the seesaw, and injuring the plaintiff's friend's son are the facts that apply to satisfy the first element of intentional or grossly negligent conduct.

◆ *Element 2*—Driving through a school zone at an extremely high rate of speed is the fact that satisfies the second element of extreme or outrageous conduct.

◆ *Element 3*—Ms. Carry's insomnia and anxiety immediately after the event are facts that apply to the third element of causation.

◆ *Element 4*—Ms. Carry's anxiety and insomnia are extreme and apply to establish the fourth element.

If Kevin could not find a fact that would arguably apply to each element, there would be no issue involving that area of law, and that cause of action would have to be abandoned as a potential avenue of redress for Ms. Carry.

NOTE: As discussed in the Issue Identification—Client's Case section of this chapter, you may not be certain whether a fact meets the established standard for an element. Often that determination may not take place until trial. Just make sure there is some fact that arguably meets the requirements of each of the elements of the cause of action.

> **FOR EXAMPLE** A determination of whether Ms. Carry's insomnia and anxiety are extreme enough to warrant relief may not be decided until trial. Her symptoms are sufficient to arguably meet the requirements of the fourth element. If research reveals that this harm is not sufficiently extreme to meet the requirements of emotional distress, there is no emotional distress issue.

STEP 4: Assemble the issue. Assemble the elements and state the issue. Kevin now has all the elements necessary to identify and state the issue: the area of law, the legal question, and the key facts. Kevin identifies the issue as: "Under (name of state) tort law, does intentional infliction of emotional distress occur when a person suffers severe insomnia and anxiety as a result of witnessing a friend's child being injured by a vehicle that is out of control due to being driven at a high rate of speed through a school zone?"

By following the four steps, moving from a broad identification of the possible causes of action to the specific elements and facts involved under each cause of action, Kevin has identified an issue. He knows what must be decided about which facts for this cause of action. His research is focused on cases in which the conduct involved accidents in school zones where witnesses suffered harm similar to that of Ms. Carry.

B. Chapter 1 Hypothetical *Reins v. Stewart*

The following example involves the application of the principles to the hypothetical presented at the beginning of Chapter 1.

STEP 1: Identify each possible cause of action and area of law involved. Based upon the instructions in her assignment, Vanessa focuses on civil battery as a cause of action. Based upon her training and paralegal education, Vanessa knows that the applicable area of civil law is tort and that battery is an act with the intent to cause harmful offensive contact that causes harmful offensive contact with the plaintiff's person.

Vanessa's assignment is to focus on the battery claim. If she identifies another possible cause of action, such as intentional infliction of emotional distress, she should inform her supervisor. If instructed by her supervisor, she would follow steps 2 through 4 for the emotional distress claim.

STEP 2: Determine the elements of the cause of action identified in step 1. Vanessa's research reveals that battery is a case law doctrine. How she researches the statutory and case law to determine this is discussed in the Application sections of Chapters 4 and 5. The case law requires that the following elements be established to state a battery claim:

- *Element 1 Act*—The defendant must commit an act.
- *Element 2 Intent*—There must be a desire to bring about the consequences of the act or a substantially certain knowledge that the consequences will follow the act.
- *Element 3 Harmful or offensive*—There must be harmful or offensive contact with the plaintiff's person.
- *Element 4 Causation*—The defendant's actions must have caused the consequences to occur or were a substantial factor in their occurrence.

STEP 3: Determine which of the facts of the client's case apply to establish or satisfy the elements of each cause of action—the key facts.

- *Element 1*—Mr. Stewart was present at the fight and yelled to his son "Hit him again, beat him." He did not otherwise participate.
- *Element 2*—The nature of the words said, the manner in which they were said, and the fact that they took place during the attack may evidence the requisite intent.
- *Element 3*—Mr. Reins was injured as a result of the beating. It is not clear whether Mr. Stewart is liable, because he did not do the actual beating.
- *Element 4*—It is not clear whether this element is met. It is not clear without further research whether words alone can be considered a substantial factor in causing the consequences.

STEP 4: Assemble the issue. Assemble the elements and state the issue. Vanessa has all the elements necessary to identify and state the issue: the area of law, the legal question, and the key facts. Following the format presented in this chapter she identifies the issue as: "Under (name of state) tort law, does a battery occur when an individual, present at a battery, encourages the perpetrator of the battery by yelling, 'Hit him again, beat him' but does not in any other way participate in the battery?"

By following the four steps, moving from a broad identification of the possible causes of action to the specific elements and facts involved under each cause of action, Vanessa has identified an issue. She knows what must be decided about which facts for this cause of action. Her research is focused on cases in which a person encourages the perpetrator of a battery but does not in any other way participate.

C. Chapter 2 Hypothetical *United States v. Canter*

The following example involves applying the principles to the hypothetical presented at the beginning of Chapter 2.

STEP 1: Identify each possible cause of action and area of law involved. In this case, the cause of action and area of law are identified in the assignment. The area is criminal law and the cause of action is bank robbery with a dangerous weapon. Therefore, no research other than to locate the statute is required. To help locate the statute, the issue can be roughly stated based upon the information presented in the assignment: "Under the federal bank robbery statute, is there sufficient evidence to support charges of bank robbery with a dangerous weapon when the weapon is a crudely carved wooden replica of a handgun?"

How to locate the statute is discussed in the Application section of Chapter 4. The application of steps 2 and 3 will reveal whether additional key facts must be included in the issue.

STEP 2: Determine the elements of each cause of action identified in step 1. The statute is 18 U.S.C. § 2113 (a) and (d). Note that this step has been performed when you identify the key facts. It is repeated here for illustration purposes. The statute requires that the following elements be established:

Section (a)

◆ *Element 1*—A person by force, violence, or intimidation

◆ *Element 2*—Takes or attempts to take property or money

◆ *Element 3*—In the care or possession of a bank

Section (d)

◆ *Element 4*—A person committing an offense defined in subsection (a) assaults any person or puts in jeopardy the life of any person by use of a dangerous weapon or device.

STEP 3: Determine which of the facts of the client's case apply to establish or satisfy the elements of the action—the key facts.

Section (a)

◆ *Element 1*—Mr. Canter entered the bank holding a fake gun and demanded money from a teller.

◆ *Element 2*—He took money.

◆ *Element 3*—The money was in possession of the bank.

Section (d)

◆ *Element 4*—When he approached the teller he was holding a crudely carved wooden replica of a 9mm Beretta handgun, the teller he approached believed it was a real handgun, and the only other witness did not believe it was real.

STEP 4: Assemble the issue. Assemble the elements and state the issue. All the elements necessary to identify and state the issue are present: the area of law, the legal question, and the key facts.

Following the format presented in this chapter, the issue can be identified as:

> Under the federal bank robbery statute, 18 U.S.C. § 2113 (a) and (d), is there sufficient evidence to support charges of bank robbery with a dangerous weapon when the weapon is a crudely carved wooden replica of a 9mm Beretta handgun, and the teller approached by the robber believed it was a real handgun, but the only other witness did not believe it was real?

By following the four steps, moving from a broad identification of the possible causes of action to the specific elements and facts involved under each cause of action, the issue is identified. The researcher knows what must be decided about which facts for this cause of action. His research is focused on locating cases where an individual uses a fake weapon to rob a bank.

D. Court Opinion

The following example illustrates the application of the principles to the identification of the issues in a court opinion. There are three steps to follow:

1. *General Question*—While reading the case, keep in mind the general question, "What was decided about which facts in the case?"

2. *Look to the Holding*—Identify the rule of law and key facts relevant to the holding.

3. *Assemble the Issue*—Rule of Law + Legal Question + Key Facts.

   Read Acacia *Mutual Life Insurance Company v. American General Life Insurance Company* in the following text.

CASE

ACACIA MUTUAL LIFE INSURANCE COMPANY

v.

AMERICAN GENERAL LIFE INSURANCE COMPANY, 111 N.M. 106, 802 P.2D 11 (1990) OPINION

BACA, Justice.

Appellant David Silver was the general partner of the Santa Fe Private Equity Fund II, L.P. (SFPEF II), a limited partnership.

He appeals from a court order that affirms a settlement agreement arrived upon by the limited partners through their receiver, John Clark, appellee. The order distributes the assets of the limited partnership in order of priority mandated by the legislature in Section 54-2-23 of the Uniform Limited Partnership Act. See NMSA 1978, §§ 54- 2-1 to -30 (Repl.Pamp. 1988). Silver claims that this order unjustly bars his contractual indemnification claim as set out in the partnership agreement. The right to contract is jealously guarded by this court, but if a contractual clause clearly contravenes a positive rule of law, it cannot be enforced, *General Electric Credit Corp. v. Tidenberg*, 78 N.M. 59, 428 P.2d 33 (1967). The indemnification clause clearly contravenes the order of priority in the distribution of assets of a dissolved limited partnership as set out by the legislature.

We, therefore, affirm.

FACTS

In February 1987 the limited partners unanimously voted to terminate their failing partnership, which had shown a loss from the outset, and filed in district court for a confirmation of the dissolution of SFPEF II. They also voted to remove Silver as general partner, but allowed him to resign. Clark was named as receiver and published a notice of dissolution of the partnership in The Santa Fe New Mexican on March 23, 1987. This notice requested creditors to respond with claims against the partnership within fourteen days. Silver wrote a letter within this time, asserting his claim under the partnership agreement for indemnification and reimbursement from the partnership for any partnership debts he paid.

After the notification of dissolution, Clark began negotiations with known creditors of the limited partnership and a determination of the status of the SFPEF II. In analyzing the assets and liabilities of SFPEF II, Clark determined that the limited partners had contributed in excess of $7 million, but he could document only $2.4 million in investments. The estimated value of SFPEF II was eventually determined to be negative $1.4 million, equaling a loss to the limited partners of $8.4 million. Aside from checks written to the general partners in excess of $1 million, the balance of the limited partners' contributions remains unaccounted for.

Clark determined the amount necessary to settle all creditors' claims and on that basis made a third, partial capital call to limited partners to wind up affairs and terminate the partnership. At this point some of the limited partners refused to pay a third partial capital call, claiming other limited partners had not yet paid on the second call.

Approximately a year after the request for confirmation of dissolution was filed, the dispute finally was settled. Clark arrived upon a global settlement agreement that allowed creditors to be paid and the receivership to be terminated. Under the settlement the limited partners were to contribute a final $1.3 million. The settlement agreement also provided for payment of creditors, distribution of any remaining liquid assets to the limited partners, and assignment of all of the partnership's claims against the general partners to one limited partner. Approval of the settlement by the court would bar all claims of creditors who had not asserted a claim. The motion for confirmation was served on Silver, who objected and asserted his indemnification claim from SFPEF II. This was over a year after notification of dissolution and the letter written by Silver to the receiver in March of 1987—the only notice of Silver's indemnification claim. The district court held that Silver's claim was untimely and approved the settlement that foreclosed Silver's indemnification claim. This appeal is taken from that order.

ISSUES—AND NON-ISSUES

Silver phrases the six points of his appeal in terms of his timely notice of a claim against the partnership and of an improper "bar" to this claim for indemnification, along with related claims of procedural due process, equal protection violations, and laches. We identify the issues differently.

We are dealing here with the time-worn principles underlying limited partnerships that restrict the potential liability of a "limited" partner and hold a "general" partner to general, personal liability. "[L]imited partners * * * take no part in management, share profits and do not share losses beyond their capital contributions to the firm." A. Bromberg, Crane & Bromberg on Partnership, § 26 at 143 (1968) (emphasis added).

Indemnifying a general partner for partnership debts by essentially forcing limited partners to pay for them violates the general public policy of limited partnership law. However, it is not necessary to decide this case on general policy grounds alone because such grounds are incorporated into specific statutory provisions that control the order of priority of distribution of assets in these circumstances, and the general partner is statutorily the last in priority. A court cannot depart from the express language of an act, but can only say what the legislature intended. *Security Escrow Corp. v. Taxation & Revenue Dep't*, 107 N.M. 540, 760 P.2d 1306 (Ct.App.1988); *State v. Michael R.*, 107 N.M. 794, 765 P.2d 767 (Ct.App.1988).

The partnership agreement itself supports our interpretation. Silver argues that in the partnership agreement a clause existed, 13(b), which provides that the "Partnership * * * shall indemnify * * * the General Partner [and] its partners * * * against all claims * * * incurred by them in connection with their activities on behalf of the Partnership * * *." This clause, however, is subject to paragraph 6(f) of the partnership agreement, which deals with liability of limited partners and states in pertinent part: "No limited Partner shall be liable for any debts or obligations of the Partnership, including obligations in respect of indemnification provided in paragraph 13, in excess of its unpaid Capital Contribution * * *."

The partnership was terminated, pursuant to its requirements, when the limited partners unanimously voted to terminate. At this point the partnership, along with potential remaining capital calls, went into receivership and dissolution, and this dissolution came under the New Mexico Limited Partnership Act. NMSA 1978, Section 54-2-23 (Repl.Pamp.1988) sets out the order of priority for the distribution of assets:

A. In settling accounts after dissolution the liabilities of the partnership shall be entitled to payment in the following order:

(1) those to creditors, in the order of priority as provided by law, except those to limited partners on account of their contributions, and to general partners;

(2) those to *limited partners* in respect to their share of the profits and other compensation by way of income on their contributions;

(3) those to *limited partners* in respect to the capital of their contributions;

(4) those to *general partners* other than for capital and profits;

(5) those to general partners in respect to profits;

(6) those to general partners in respect to capital. (Emphasis added.)

The law of New Mexico mandates that in a dissolution of a limited partnership, the limited partners are to be paid off before the general partners. The interpretation of the indemnification clause in the contract urged by Silver would have the general partners paid off by the limited partners. Since there are no assets left in this terminated partnership, to indemnify the general partner would require the limited partners to contribute even more funds to a dead entity. The clear language of a statute must be given its full meaning. *Schoonover v. Caudill*, 65 N.M. 335, 337 P.2d 402 (1959); *Weiser v. Albuquerque Oil & Gasoline Co.*, 64 N.M. 137, 325 P.2d 720 (1958). To indemnify the general partners would contravene this statute and is therefore unenforceable.

WE AFFIRM.

IT IS SO ORDERED.

***

STEP 1: *General Question.* Read the entire case. While reading the case, ask yourself, "What did the court decide about which facts?" To answer this question, it is necessary to keep in mind the elements of the issue—the rule of law, the legal question, and key facts. Keeping this question in mind helps you focus on these elements.

STEP 2: *Look to the Holding.* You probably cannot identify the issue after completing step 1. The court did not specifically state the issue, nor is the issue clear from a simple reading of the case. Follow step 2 and find the holding. Here, the holding is presented in the next to the last sentence: "To indemnify the general partners would contravene this statute and is therefore unenforceable." Once identified, locate the elements of the issue relevant to this holding. Ask the following questions:

1. *"What was decided in the holding?"* In other words, "What legal question or issue was addressed and answered by the court?" Determine the answer to this question by looking to the holding and deciding what question was answered by the holding.

    Here, Silver, a general partner and an appellant in the case, argued that section 13(b) of the partnership agreement allowed him to be reimbursed, by additional contributions from the limited partners, for partnership debts he paid. In other words, section 13(b) would require limited partners to share losses beyond their capital contributions to the partnership and require limited partners to pay off general partners. The court held that the section, so interpreted, would clearly contravene the provisions of the statute. The legal question, then, is whether an interpretation of the section of the agreement that would require such payments by limited partners is enforceable.

    In this case, it is difficult to identify the issue without this step because there is information included in the opinion that tends to mislead the reader.

FOR EXAMPLE The last two sentences in the "Facts" section of the opinion indicate that the appeal was taken from a trial court ruling that Silver's claim was untimely. Based upon those statements, the reader is led to believe the case involves a timeliness issue and looks for the court's discussion of that question. The court, however, never mentions timeliness in the rest of the opinion. By looking to the holding and following this step, the reader is directed to the issue actually decided by the court.

2. *"What statute, rule of law, or principle did the court apply when it reached this holding?"* In this case, the court looked to section 54-2-23 of the New Mexico Limited Partnership Act.

3. *"Which facts mentioned in the opinion are related and necessary to the determination of the question addressed in the holding?"* "Which of the facts, if changed, would change the holding?" In other words, "What are the key facts?" In this case, as in many cases, the court presents several facts that have nothing to do with the holding. Usually these facts are presented to give the reader the background and context of the holding. The presentation of too many background facts, however, may mislead the reader and make it difficult to determine what the case is actually about.

    This is especially true in this case. The opinion contains several paragraphs discussing the financial status of the partnership and the details of the global settlement agreement arranged by the receiver. So much is presented concerning these facts that the reader tends to focus on them, and not on the key facts that involve the provisions of the partnership agreement.

    When the holding, however, is referred to and the question is asked, "Which facts are necessary or related to this holding?," it is clear that the facts relevant to the holding are the facts concerning section 13(b) of the partnership agreement, and Silver's interpretation of that section. The key facts are the section of the partnership agreement that provides that the partnership shall indemnify the general partner against all claims, and Silver's interpretation of that section to require limited partners, upon dissolution of the partnership, to reimburse general partners with contributions beyond their capital contributions.

STEP 3: *Assemble the Issue.* The final step is to assemble the issue. All the elements have been identified in step 2:

+ The rule of law is section 54-2-23 of the New Mexico Limited Partnership Act.

+ The question is whether an indemnification provision of the partnership agreement is enforceable.

+ The key fact is an interpretation of the indemnification provision that requires limited partners, upon dissolution of the partnership, to reimburse general partners with additional contributions beyond their capital contributions.

The assembled issue is: "Under the provisions of § 54-2-23 of the New Mexico Limited Partnership Act, is an indemnification provision of a partnership agreement enforceable when it is interpreted to require limited partners, upon dissolution of the partnership, to reimburse general partners with additional contributions beyond their capital contributions?"

SUMMARY

The most important task in either analyzing a client's case or reading a court opinion is to correctly identify the issue(s). You must identify the problem before it can be solved. A misidentified issue can result not only in wasted time but also in malpractice.

The issue is the precise legal question raised by the facts of the dispute. Therefore, each issue is unique because the facts of each case are different, and each issue must be narrowly stated within the context of the facts of that case. The issue is composed of the applicable law, the legal question relevant to the law, and the facts that raise the question. These elements must be precisely identified to determine the issue.

There is no magic formula. This chapter includes steps that help in issue identification. When working on a client's case, there are four recommended steps:

1. Identify each area of law possibly involved.
2. Identify the elements necessary for a cause of action under each law identified in the first step.
3. Apply the elements of the law to the client's facts to determine the key facts.
4. Assemble the issue from the law, elements, and key facts identified in the first three steps.

There are three steps to follow to identify the issue(s) in a court opinion:

1. While reading the case, keep in mind this question: "What was decided about which facts?"
2. Look to the holding to identify the rule of law, legal question, and key facts of the case.
3. Assemble the issue.

These are the recommended steps. They usually work when followed and are always helpful in focusing the practitioner's attention on that which is essential—the rule of law, the legal question, and facts.

CHAPTER REFERENCES

INTERNET RESOURCES

As of the date of publication of this text, no Web sites are dedicated specifically to issue identification. However, using a search engine and "legal analysis spotting issues" as a topic will result in a wide range of Web sites that address some aspect of legal research, analysis, and issue spotting. Some sites involve identifying legal issues in specific areas of the law such as labor law, whereas others discuss the topic in relation to taking exams. There are numerous related sites.

 For additional materials, please go to the CD accompanying this book

 For additional resources, visit our Web site at www.paralegal.delmar.cengage.com

EXERCISES

Additional exercises are located on the Student CD-ROM accompanying the text and Online Companion.

ASSIGNMENT 1

Describe in detail the steps for identifying the issue(s) in a client's case.

ASSIGNMENT 2

Describe in detail the steps for identifying the issue(s) in a court opinion.

ASSIGNMENT 3

Statutes: *Criminal code section 18-760, Robbery.* A person who knowingly takes anything of value from the person or presence of another by use of force, threats, or intimidation commits robbery.

   Criminal code section 18-773, Larceny. Any person who wrongfully takes, obtains, or withholds, by any means, from the possession of the owner or of any other person any money, personal property, or article of value of any kind, with intent permanently to deprive another person of the use and benefit of property is guilty of larceny.

Facts: Over the years, Larry borrowed several tools from his next-door neighbor. Usually he returned the items, but on occasion he forgot. One of the tools he did not return is a drill. The neighbor goes to Larry's house and tells him that if he doesn't return the drill he will file criminal charges. Larry says, "I'm keeping your drill and if you try to come get it or file charges, I'll beat you up."

Questions

Identify the issue(s) involving criminal law raised by this fact situation.

ASSIGNMENT 4

Perform ASSIGNMENT 3 using your state's larceny and robbery statutes.

ASSIGNMENT 5

Identify the issue in the following two fact situations.

Part A   Beth loaned Allen $5,000. The agreement was oral. Allen commutes to a nearby city to work. Beth needs to go to the city three times in May. Allen told her he would give her three free rides to the city to help repay the loan. On one of the trips, Allen was not paying attention, lost control of the car, and wrecked. Beth suffered severe injuries and wants to sue Allen to recover damages.

   The state automobile guest statute bars suits against drivers by automobile guests. The statute does not apply if the passenger confers a substantial benefit on the driver and that is the reason the driver provided the ride.

Part B   Tom and Alex are next-door neighbors. While arguing with Tom, Alex breaks Tom's lawn chair, and as Alex begins to break more lawn furniture, Tom makes a citizen's arrest of Alex. Tom's sons help Tom, and after Alex is subdued, they continue to hit and kick him for a few moments. Alex wants to sue Tom.

   The state's case law defines battery as unauthorized harmful contact; it also allows a citizen's arrest when the purpose is to prevent the destruction of property.

ASSIGNMENT 6

Part A   Read *Dean v. Dickey* in Appendix C. Identify the validity of the will issue.

Part B   Read *United States v. Martinez-Jimenez* in Appendix C. Identify the issue concerning whether the weapon was a dangerous weapon.

Part C   Read *Wolcott v. Wolcott* in Appendix C. Identify the issue concerning the modification of child support due to change of circumstances.

Part D   Read *People v. Sanders* in Appendix C. Identify the issue concerning the existence of spousal privilege for communications made in the presence of the children.

ASSIGNMENT 7

Read *Metropolitan Life Insurance Company v. Syntek Finance Corporation* in Appendix C. The procedural issue is whether the trial court properly denied Syntek's motion for disqualification of counsel. What is the substantive disqualification of counsel issue raised by the facts of the case?

ASSIGNMENT 8

Read *Morgan v. Greenwaldt* in Appendix C. The procedural issue is whether the trial court properly granted a directed verdict on the false imprisonment claim.

What is the substantive false imprisonment issue raised by the facts of the case?

CHAPTER 4

Constitutions, Statutes, Administrative Law, and Court Rules—Research and Analysis

Outline

Learning Objectives

After completing this chapter, you should understand:

✦ What statutory law is

✦ The components of a statute

✦ How to find constitutional, statutory, and administrative law and court rules

✦ How to analyze a statute and apply it to specific problems

✦ The role of legislative history and canons of construction

Alan attended one year of paralegal classes before being admitted to law school. After his first year, he obtained a part-time job with a law firm. Initially, Alan's assignments had been the preparation of deposition digests. He is good at preparing deposition digests but wants to be involved in projects in the early stages of the litigation process. At his request, he was assigned to work exclusively with Ms. Tilton. Ms. Tilton is a litigation attorney who specializes in corporation and contract law.

His first assignment from Ms. Tilton is to determine if Mrs. Jackson has a cause of action against Beauty Care Beauty Salon for breach of warranty under the sales provisions of the state's Commercial Code. Mrs. Jackson went to her hairdresser, Beauty Care Beauty Salon, to get their "special long-term hold" permanent. Once a year for the past three years she asked for the "special" permanent. Beauty Care made no warranties about the permanent. It did not provide Mrs. Jackson, either orally or in writing, any statements concerning the quality of the permanent.

The receipt she received for the permanent listed a $20 charge for the permanent kit and other products, and an $80 charge for the services of the beautician.

Three days after Mrs. Jackson was given the permanent, her hair, which had been blonde, turned a light green. Five days later, it broke off approximately one inch from the scalp—not a good result.

Alan, based on his paralegal and first-year law school courses, is aware that Mrs. Jackson has a possible tort negligence claim and other possible causes of action against Beauty Care. His assignment, however, is to determine if there is also a possible breach of warranty claim under the state's Commercial Code.

Alan has not worked with statutes since he took a paralegal research course. Several questions occur to him: How do I find the Commercial Code statutes? Does the Commercial Code Sales Act apply? Is this a sale of goods within the meaning of the Act? If this is a sale of goods, which warranty applies? How do you analyze a statute?

I. INTRODUCTION

This chapter focuses on how to research and analyze enacted law and court rules. As discussed in Chapter 1, enacted law includes constitutions (governing documents adopted by the people), laws passed by legislative bodies, and the rules and regulations adopted by administrative agencies.

Laws passed by Congress or state legislatures are generally called acts or statutes. This body of law is commonly referred to as **statutory law**. Ordinances are laws usually passed by local governing bodies, such as city councils and county commissions. Administrative agencies, under the authority granted by legislative bodies, adopt rules and regulations that have the force of law. Courts adopt rules that regulate the conduct of matters brought before the court. For the sake of clarity, throughout this chapter the discussion and examples focus upon laws passed by legislative bodies, that is, statutory law. Note, however, that the principles presented in this chapter apply to the analysis of constitutions, statutes, administrative law, and court rules.

Statutory law is a major source of law that a researcher must become familiar with when researching and analyzing the law. The role of statutory law has been increasing in the United States. With the passage of time, the body of law represented by statutory law has expanded greatly. Many matters once governed by case law are now governed by statutory law.

> **FOR EXAMPLE** | Criminal law was once exclusively established and regulated by case law; today, most criminal law is governed by statutory law.

Because an ever-increasing number of legal problems and issues require the interpretation and application of statutory law, researchers are more frequently called upon to engage in statutory analysis. **Statutory analysis** is the process of determining if a statute applies, how it applies, and the effect of that application.

Because most statutes are designed to cover a broad range of present and future situations, they are written in general terms. As a result, a researcher is required to engage in statutory analysis to determine whether and how a statute applies in a specific fact situation.

The focus of this chapter is the process of statutory research and analysis. It begins with a presentation of the anatomy of a statute, follows with a discussion of the process of statutory research and analysis, and ends with general considerations involving statutory construction and analysis.

II. ANATOMY OF A STATUTE

Before you can analyze a statute, you must be familiar with the basic structure of statutory law, that is, the component parts of statutory law. Assume, for the purposes of illustration, that you are interested in whether a contract for the sale of goods must be in writing, and the governing law is the Indiana Code. Exhibit 4–1 shows selected portions of the Indiana Code concerning commercial law. Following Exhibit 4–1 is Exhibit 4–2 that presents the section of the *United States Code Annotated* (USCA) concerning ransom money. To the left of sections of the codes, in the margins, are terms that describe the components of the codes. The following text discusses each descriptive term and that portion of the statutes referred to by the term.

Not all the statutory components included in the discussion following the Indiana Code and the USCA are included in every statute. Some statutes, for example, may not have a definitions section. It is important, however, to discuss the components so that you will be familiar with them if you encounter them in other statutes.

TITLE 26
COMMERCIAL LAW

Number of title

Number of article

ARTICLE.
1. UNIFORM COMMERCIAL CODE, chs. 1-10.
2. COMMERCIAL TRANSACTIONS, chs. 1-6.

ARTICLE.
3. WAREHOUSES, chs. 1-7.

ARTICLE 1
UNIFORM COMMERCIAL CODE

Number of chapter

CHAPTER.
1. GENERAL PROVISIONS, 26-1-1-101 — 26-1-1-208.
2. SALES, 26-1-2-101 — 26-1-2-725.
2.1. LEASES, 26-1-2.1-101 — 26-1-2.1-532.
3. COMMERCIAL PAPER, 26-1-3-101 — 26-1-3-805.
4. BANK DEPOSITS AND COLLECTIONS, 26-1-4-101 — 26-1-4-504.
4.1. FUND TRANSFERS, 26-1-4.1-101 — 26-1-4.1-507.
5. LETTERS OF CREDIT, 26-1-5-101 — 26-1-5-117.

CHAPTER.
6. BULK TRANSFERS, 26-1-6-101 — 26-1-6-110.
7. [WAREHOUSE RECEIPTS, BILLS OF LADING AND OTHER] DOCUMENTS OF TITLE, 26-1-7-101 — 26-1-7-603.
8. INVESTMENT SECURITIES, 26-1-8-101 — 26-1-8-408.
9. SECURED TRANSACTIONS, 26-1-9-101 — 26-1-9-507.
10. EFFECTIVE DATE, REPEAL, SAVING PROVISION, 26-1-10-101 — 26-1-10-106.

CHAPTER 1
GENERAL PROVISIONS

Number of section

PART 1. SHORT TITLE, CONSTRUCTION, APPLICATION AND SUBJECT-MATTER OF THE ACT

SECTION.
26-1-1-101. Short title.
26-1-1-102. Purposes — Rules of construction — Variation by agreement.
26-1-1-103. Supplementary general principles of law applicable.
26-1-1-104. Construction against implicit repeal.
26-1-1-105. Territorial application of the act — Parties' power to choose applicable law.
26-1-1-106. Remedies to be liberally administered.
26-1-1-107. Waiver or renunciation of claim - or right after breach.
26-1-1-108. Severability.

SECTION.
26-1-1-109. [Repealed.]

PART 2. GENERAL DEFINITIONS AND PRINCIPLES OF INTERPRETATION

26-1-1-201. General definitions.
26-1-1-202. Prima facie evidence by third party documents.
26-1-1-203. Obligation of good faith.
26-1-1-204. Time — Reasonable time — "Seasonably."
26-1-1-205. Course of dealing and usage of trade.
26-1-1-206. Statute of frauds for kinds of personal property not otherwise covered.
26-1-1-207. Performance or acceptance under reservation of rights.
26-1-1-208. Option to accelerate at will.

Number of section

Short title

PART 1. SHORT TITLE, CONSTRUCTION, APPLICATION AND SUBJECT MATTER OF THE ACT

26-1-1-101. Short title. — IC 26-1 shall be known and may be cited as Uniform Commercial Code. [Acts 1963, ch. 317, § 1-101, p. 539; P.L.152-1986, § 110.]

Exhibit 4–1

Indiana Statutes—Commercial Law.
Michie, *Burns Indiana Statutes Annotated* (1990), cited material is from Title 26, 1992 replacement pamphlet. LexisNexis® Screen Captures reprinted with the permission of LexisNexis. LexisNexis and *Shepard's* are registered trademarks and Focus and KWIC are trademarks of Reed Elsevier Properties, Inc., used with the permission of LexisNexis.

Purpose clause —————— **26-1-1-102. Purposes — Rules of construction — Variation by agreement.** — (1) IC 26-1 shall be liberally construed and applied to promote its underlying purposes and policies.

(2) Underlying purposes and policies of IC 26-1 are:

(a) To simplify, clarify, and modernize the law governing commercial transactions;

(b) To permit the continued expansion of commercial practices through custom, usage, and agreement of the parties;

(c) To make uniform the law among the various jurisdictions.

CHAPTER 2

SALES

Number of section ——————

PART 1. SHORT TITLE, GENERAL CONSTRUCTION AND SUBJECT MATTER

Short title —————— **26-1-2-101. Short title.** — IC 26-1-2 shall be known and may be cited as Uniform Commercial Code—Sales. [Acts 1963, ch. 317, § 2-101, p. 539; P.L.152-1986, § 119.]

Cross References. Construction against implicit repeal, IC 26-1-1-104.

Rules of construction, IC 26-1-1-102.

Supplementary general principles of law applicable, IC 26-1-1-103.

Indiana Law Journal. The Uniform Commercial Code and Real Estate Law: Problems for Both the Real Estate Lawyer and the Chattel Security Lawyer, 38 Ind. L.J. 535.

Negligence, Economic Loss, and the U.C.C., 61 Ind. L.J. 593 (1986).

Indiana Law Review. The Flammable Fabrics Act and Strict Liability in Tort, 9 Ind. L. Rev. 395.

Survey of Recent Developments in Business and Commercial Law—Vertical Privity and Damages for Breach of Implied Warranty under the U.C.C.: It's Time for Indiana to

Scope —————— **26-1-2-102. Scope — Certain security and other transactions excluded from this chapter.** — Unless the context otherwise requires, IC 26-1-2 applies to transactions in goods. It does not apply to any transaction which although in the form of an unconditional contract to sell or present sale is intended to operate only as a security transaction, nor does IC 26-1-2 impair or repeal any statute regulating sales to consumers, farmers, or other specified classes of buyers. IC 26-1-2 does not impair or repeal IC 9-14, IC 9-17, or IC 9-22-5. [Acts 1963, ch. 317, § 2-102, p. 539; P.L.152-1986, § 120; P.L.2-1991, § 86.]

Exhibit 4–1
Continued

Definitions —————————————————

26-1-1-201. General definitions. — Subject to additional definitions contained in IC 26-1-2 through IC 26-1-10 which are applicable to specific provisions, and unless the context otherwise requires, in IC 26-1:

(1) "Action" in the sense of a judicial proceeding includes recoupment, counterclaim, setoff, suit in equity, and any other proceedings in which rights are determined.

(2) "Aggrieved party" means a party entitled to resort to a remedy.

(3) "Agreement" means the bargain of the parties in fact as found in their language or by implication from other circumstances including course of dealing or usage of trade or course of performance as provided in IC 26-1-1-205 and IC 26-1-2-208. Whether an agreement has legal

PART 2. FORM, FORMATION AND READJUSTMENT OF CONTRACT

26-1-2-201. Formal requirements — Statute of frauds. — (1) Except as otherwise provided in this section, a contract for the sale of goods for the price of five hundred dollars ($500) or more is not enforceable by way of action or defense unless there is some writing sufficient to indicate that a contract for sale has been made between the parties and signed by the party against whom enforcement is sought or by his authorized agent or broker. A writing is not insufficient because it omits or incorrectly states a term agreed upon, but the contract is not enforceable under this paragraph beyond the quantity of goods shown in such writing.

(2) Between merchants, if within a reasonable time a writing in confirmation of the contract and sufficiently against the sender is received and the party receiving it has reason to know its contents, it satisfies the requirements of subsection (1) against such party unless written notice of objection to its contents is given within ten (10) days after it is received.

Substantive provisions

(3) A contract which does not satisfy the requirements of subsection (1) but which is valid in other respects is enforceable:

(a) If the goods are to be specially manufactured for the buyer and are not suitable for sale to others in the ordinary course of the seller's business and the seller, before notice of repudiation is received and under circumstances which reasonably indicate that the goods are for the buyer, has made either a substantial beginning of their manufacture or commitments for their procurement; or

(b) If the party against whom enforcement is sought admits in his pleading, testimony, or otherwise in court that a contract for sale was made, but the contract is not enforceable under this provision beyond the quantity of goods admitted; or

(c) With respect to goods for which payment has been made and accepted or which have been received and accepted (IC 26-1-2-606).
[Acts 1963, ch. 317, § 2-201, p. 539; P.L.152-1986, § 125.]

Reference information ————————

Cross References. Action, definition, IC 26-1-1-201.
Additional terms in acceptance or confirmation, IC 26-1-2-207.

Between merchants, definition, IC 26-1-2-104.
Buyer and seller, definition, IC 26-1-2-103.
Contract, definition, IC 26-1-1-201.

Exhibit 4–1
Continued

Substantive provisions

26-1-2-315. Implied warranty — Fitness for particular purpose. — Where the seller at the time of contracting has reason to know any particular purpose of which the goods are required and that the buyer is relying on the seller's skill or judgment to select or furnish suitable goods, there is, unless excluded or modified under IC 26-1-2-316, an implied warranty that the good shall be fit for such purpose. [Acts 1963, ch. 317, § 2-315, p. 539; P.L.152-1986, § 136.]

Reference information

Cross References. Buyer and seller, definition, IC 26-1-2-103.

Cumulation and conflict of warranties, IC 26-1-2-317.

Exclusion or modification of warranties, IC 26-1-2-316.

Goods, definition, IC 26-1-2-105.

Implied warranty of merchantability, IC 26-1-2-314.

Product liability actions, IC 33-1-1.5-1 — 33-1-1.5-8.

Indiana Law Journal. Implied and Express Warranties and Disclaimers Under the Uniform Commercial Code, 38 Ind. L.J. 648.

The Private Law Treatment of Defective Products in Sales Situations, 49 Ind. L.J. 8.

Consumer Warranty or Insurance Contract? A View Towards a Rational State Regulatory Policy, 51 Ind. L.J. 1103.

Indiana's Implied Warranty of Fitness for Habitation: Limited Protection for Used Home Buyers, 57 Ind. L.J. 479.

Negligence, Economic Loss, and the U.C.C., 61 Ind. L.J. 593 (1986).

Indiana Law Review. Landlord-Tenant Law: Indiana at the Crossroads, 10 Ind. L. Rev. 591.

and Damages for Breach of Implied Warranty under the U.C.C.: It's Time for Indiana to Abandon the Citadel, 21 Ind. L. Rev. 23 (1988).

Notre Dame Law Review. Economic Institutions and Value Survey — Warranty Representation and Disclaimers, 8 Notre Dame Law. 602.

Merchantability and the Statute of Limitations, 50 Notre Dame Law. 321.

Utility "Services" under the Uniform Commercial Code: Are Public Utilities in for a Shock?, 56 Notre Dame Law. 89.

Lions & Lionesses, Tigers & Tigresses, Bears & ... Other Animals: Sellers' Liability for Dangerous Animals, 58 Notre Dame L. Rev. 537.

Valparaiso University Law Review. An Emerging Concept: Consumer Protection in Statutory Regulation, Products Liability and the Sale of New Homes, 11 Val. U.L. Rev. 335.

Risk of Economic Loss and Implied Warranty Liability in Tripartite Finance Leases, 22 Val. U.L. Rev. 593 (1988).

NOTES TO DECISIONS

. ANALYSIS

In general.
Basis for acceleration.
—Encumbrance.
Evidence.
Good faith.
—Erroneous determination of insecurity.

In General.

Acceleration provisions are valid and enforceable in Indiana. Smith v. Union State Bank, 452 N.E.2d 1059 (Ind. App. 1983).

Basis for Acceleration.

—Encumbrance.

The attachment of a superior lien against property subject to security agreement amounted to an encumbrance and was a basis for acceleration under security agreement which provided for acceleration in case of encumbrance. Van Bibber v. Norris, 419 N.E.2d 115 (Ind. 1981).

Evidence.

Where the maker of the note had incurred other financial obligations, had transferred collateral, and secured equipment in which the holder of the note had no superior security interest, the holder could honestly have believed that its chances of payment had

been diminished. Holmes v. Rushville Prod. Credit Ass'n, 170 Ind. App. 509, 353 N.E.2d 509, 54 Ind. Dec. 395 (1976), vacated, 170 Ind. App. 517, 355 N.E.2d 417, reinstated, 170 Ind. App. 509, 357 N.E.2d 734, 55 Ind. Dec. 468 (1977), transfer denied, 267 Ind. 454, 371 N.E.2d 379, 60 Ind. Dec. 413 (1978).

Good Faith.

Where bank had continuing problem of collecting from purchaser of mobile home and such purchaser was delinquent on current payment due and had been arrested and placed in jail and mobile home park had lien on mobile home for rent due, it could not be said that bank did not act in good faith in accelerating payment. Van Bibber v. Norris, 419 N.E.2d 115 (Ind. 1981).

A good faith belief under this section means at least honesty in fact in the conduct or transaction concerned. Smith v. Union State Bank, 452 N.E.2d 1059 (Ind. App. 1983).

—Erroneous Determination of Insecurity.

Assuming a bank was not insecure, even an erroneous determination of insecurity was not necessarily unreasonable or in bad faith. Smith v. Union State Bank, 452 N.E.2d 1059 (Ind. App. 1983).

Exhibit 4–1
Continued

Title
18 § 1202

Ch. 55 KIDNAPPING

§ 1202. Ransom money

Section number

(a) Whoever receives, possesses, or disposes of any money or other property, or any portion thereof, which has at any time been delivered as ransom or reward in connection with a violation of section 1201 of this title, knowing the same to be money or property which has been at any time delivered as such ransom or reward, shall be fined under this title or imprisoned not more than ten years, or both.

(b) A person who transports, transmits, or transfers in interstate or foreign commerce any proceeds of a kidnapping punishable under State law by imprisonment for more than 1 year, or receives, possesses, conceals, or disposes of any such proceeds after they have crossed a State or United States boundary, knowing the proceeds to have been unlawfully obtained, shall be imprisoned not more than 10 years, fined under this title, or both.

(c) For purposes of this section, the term "State" has the meaning set forth in section 245(d) of this title.

(June 25, 1948, c. 645, 62 Stat. 760; Sept. 13, 1994, Pub.L. 103–322, Title XXXII, § 320601(b), Title XXXIII, § 330016(1)(L), 108 Stat. 2115, 2147.)

History and official comments

HISTORICAL AND STATUTORY NOTES

Revision Notes and Legislative Reports

1948 Acts. Based on Title 18, U.S.C., 1940 ed., § 408c-1 (June 22, 1932, c. 271, § 4, as added Jan. 24, 1936, c. 29, 49 Stat. 1099).

Words "in the penitentiary" after imprisoned were omitted in view of section 4082 of this title committing prisoners to the custody of the Attorney General. (See reviser's note under section 1 of this title.)

Minor changes were made in phraseology.

1994 Acts. House Report Nos. 103–324 and 103–489, and House Conference

Report No. 103–711, see 1994 U.S. Code Cong. and Adm. News, p. 1801.

Amendments

1994 Amendments. Subsec. (a). Pub.L. 103–322, § 320601(b)(1), designated existing provisions as subsec. (a).

Pub.L. 103–322, § 330016)(1)(L), substituted "under this title" for "not more than $10,000".

Subsecs. (b), (c). Pub.L. 102–322 § 320601(b)(2), added subsecs. (b) and (c).

FEDERAL SENTENCING GUIDELINES

See Federal Sentencing Guidelines § 2A4.2, 18 USCA.

AMERICAN LAW REPORTS

What constitutes violation of 18 USCA 1202, prohibiting receipt, possession, or disposition of ransom money, 31 ALR Fed 916.

Exhibit 4–2
18 USCA § 1202 and accompanying annotations.
West, a Thomson Reuters business, *United States Code Annotated*, 18 USCA, 1202 (2000), pp. 66–68. Used with permission of Thomson Reuters/West.

Library references/
research guides

LIBRARY REFERENCES

American Digest System
    Kidnapping ☞ 1.
Encyclopedias
    Kidnapping, see C.J.S. §§ 1, 2.
Texts and Treatises
    Character evidence not admissible, see Wright & Graham: Evidence § 5231 et seq.

WESTLAW ELECTRONIC RESEARCH

See WESTLAW guide following the Explanation pages of this volume.

Notes of Decisions

Topics covered
in notes to decisions

Delivery   1
Indictment or information   3
Instructions   4
Interstate commerce   2

1. Delivery

Case Summary

Where defendant picked up money which was intended as kidnap ransom but had been left in wrong place and, after learning that it was intended to be ransom money, continued to keep it, defendant was guilty of possession of ransom money, notwithstanding contention that there had been no "delivery," in purview of this section which defined offense as possession of money, "which has at any time been delivered as ransom." U. S. v. Ortega, C.A.3 (N.J.) 1975, 517 F.2d 1006.

2. Interstate commerce

To establish violation of this section prohibiting possession of ransom money there was no requirement that defendant be connected with interstate commerce element of primary kidnapping offense under section 1201 of this title. U. S. v. Ortega, C.A.3 (N.J.) 1975, 517 F.2d 1006.

3. Indictment or information

Indictment charging in several counts conspiracy to commit offenses under this section and sections 875 and 1202 of this title and charging substantive offense of kidnapping and three separate offenses of transmitting communications in interstate commerce

demanding ransom money and charging receiving, possessing and disposing of ransom money charged separate offenses and was not duplicitous. Amsler v. U. S., C.A.9 (Cal.) 1967, 381 F.2d 37.

4. Instructions

In prosecution for possession of ransom money and making false statements to grand jury, trial court did not err in refusing to charge that defendant could be acquitted if he had relied upon advice of Federal Bureau of Investigation agents in attempting to return money anonymously, where such advice occurred a week after defendant had made his false statements to grand jury and no attempt was ever made to return money in manner suggested. U. S. v. Ortega, C.A.3 (N.J.) 1975, 517 F.2d 1006.

In prosecution under former section 408c-1 of this title accused could not complain of instruction that receipt of ransom money was criminal offense, where court instructed as to what constituted a conspiracy, and that unless jury found accused became part of conspiracy there should be acquittal, and that if accused entered conspiracy jury should further find that accused accepted ransom money knowing it was such, or aided owners in exchanging it. Laska v. U.S., C.C.A.10 (Okla.) 1936, 82 F.2d 672, certiorari denied 56 S.Ct. 957, 298 U.S. 689, 80 L.Ed. 1407.

Exhibit 4–2
Continued

A. Numbers

Each statute has numbers assigned for each section of the statute. Every legislative authority—local, state, and federal—follows a different numbering system. Therefore, it is not practical to discuss each numbering system separately. Some general similarities, however, can be addressed.

Most laws are usually divided into broad categories, each of which is assigned a number. These broad categories are divided into topics or smaller categories that are also assigned numbers. The topics are further divided into subtopics and assigned a number, and so on. The number of categories and divisions depends upon the statutory scheme of the particular legislative authority.

> **FOR EXAMPLE** The laws of Indiana are divided into broad categories called titles. Commercial Law is assigned the number 26. (See NUMBER OF TITLE at the top of the first page of Exhibit 4–1 and the first page of Exhibit 4–2.) Each Title is divided into areas called articles. Commercial Law in the Indiana Code is divided into three articles numbered 1, 2, and 3. The Uniform Commercial Code article, which governs commercial transactions, is assigned the number 1. The three articles are listed under COMMERCIAL LAW. (See NUMBER OF ARTICLE at the top of the first page of Exhibit 4–1.) Article 1, the Uniform Commercial Code, is divided into 10 chapters. They are listed under UNIFORM COMMERCIAL CODE. (See NUMBER OF CHAPTER on the first page of Exhibit 4–1.) The chapter governing the sale of goods is Chapter 2, Sales. Each chapter is divided into sections and each section is assigned a number. (See NUMBER OF SECTION in Exhibit 4–1 and Exhibit 4–2.) Each section contains the actual law that governs a subject. The section of Chapter 2 (Sales) that establishes when a contract must be in writing is assigned the number 201. This section is called Formal Requirements—Statute of frauds (see § 26-1-2-201 Exhibit 4–1).
>
> Therefore, if you want to read the law in the Indiana Code governing when a contract must be written, you refer to Title 26 (Commercial Law), Article 1 (Uniform Commercial Code), Chapter 2 (Sales), Section 201 (Statute of Frauds). This is usually referred to numerically as § 26-1-2-201, Statute of Frauds.

B. Short Title

The short title is the name by which the statute is known. This name is easy to use when referring to the statute. Included in the example are two short titles: the short title of article 1 of the Indiana Code, Uniform Commercial Code (§ 26-1-1-101) and the short title of Chapter 2, Uniform Commercial Code—Sales (§ 26-1-2-101). (See SHORT TITLE on the first and second pages of Exhibit 4–1.)

C. Purpose Clause

The purpose clause includes the purpose the legislative body intended to accomplish when drafting the statute. It is helpful in determining the legislative intent. (See PURPOSE CLAUSE Exhibit 4–1, § 26-1-1-102.)

D. Scope

Some statutes have sections called scope sections that state what is specifically covered and not covered by the statute. A researcher should first review this section when analyzing a statute, because a review of this section may lead to a determination at the outset of whether the statute applies. (See SCOPE Exhibit 4–1.)

> **FOR EXAMPLE** Assume you are researching a question under Indiana law involving a contract that grants a security interest in goods that are being sold. The scope section of the Uniform Commercial Code, § 26-1-2-102, provides that the section does not apply to such transactions. You know at the outset that the state Uniform Commercial Code does not apply and need not be considered further.

E. Definitions

Some statutes have definition sections that define terms used in the statute. The definitions are helpful in determining the parties and situations covered by the provisions of the statute. (See DEFINITIONS Exhibit 4–1, § 26-1-1-201.)

F. Substantive Provisions

The substantive sections set forth the substance of the law. (See SUBSTANTIVE PROVISIONS Exhibit 4–1.) They establish the rights and duties of those governed by the statute: that which is required, prohibited, or allowed. A substantive section of the Indiana Code addresses the question posed at the beginning of this section, "When must a contract for the sale of goods be in writing?" (See § 26-1-2-201 Exhibit 4–1.)

The substantive sections may include sections that provide remedies, such as fines or imprisonment in criminal cases. There may be sections governing procedure, such as which court has jurisdiction over the matters covered by the statute. The substantive provisions are what you usually refer to when addressing the client's legal problem.

G. Other Provisions

Not included in the example in Exhibit 4–1 are other types of statutory sections which you may encounter.

> **FOR EXAMPLE** There may be statutory provisions that do the following:
>
> ✦ State which administrative agency is responsible for administering the act
> ✦ Incorporate by reference sections of other statutes
> ✦ Limit the application of the statute through exceptions
> ✦ Establish when the statute takes effect
> ✦ Repeal other statutes
> ✦ State that the statute is cumulative to the case law and other remedies still exist

H. Annotations/Reference Information

Following each section of a statute, in small print, are references to various sources of information related to the section. This information is usually referred to as annotations. Some of these are:

   ✦ The history of the section, including dates of amendment. It may also include summaries of the amendments and previous statutory numbers if the section number has changed due to recodification (see the first page of Exhibit 4–2).
   ✦ Official comments on the section (see the first page of Exhibit 4–2).
   ✦ Cross-references to other related statutes (see the last page of Exhibit 4–1).
   ✦ Library references/research guides—references to other sources that may be useful when analyzing the statute, such as books, digest key numbers, law review and other articles, ALR cites, and legal encyclopedia cites that discuss the

section (*Corpus Juris Secundum*, and *American Jurisprudence Second*). (See the last page of Exhibit 4–1 and the first page of Exhibit 4–2.)

✦ Notes to decisions—the name, citation, and summaries of key court decisions that have discussed, analyzed, or interpreted the statute. When a statute has been interpreted or referred to in a large number of cases, the cases are indexed according to subject and each category is assigned a number. If you have a question concerning the interpretation of a statute, you may immediately locate a case on point by scanning the notes. This often saves time spent in locating a case through other means. (See the last pages of Exhibits 4–1 and 4–2.)

Annotations are sources of information and are not part of the statute. They are not the law and do not have legal authority.

It is easier to work with statutes after establishing a familiarity with the component parts. The material presented here will help you gain that familiarity, but the greatest familiarity comes with practice. Choose a subject you are interested in and, in your jurisdiction, read the statute that governs the area.

III. STATUTORY RESEARCH—LOCATING STATUTES

Statutory research is the process of finding the statutory law that applies to a problem. The first two parts of this section discuss statutory research sources, that is, where statutory law can be found. The third part presents research strategies or techniques—how to conduct statutory research. Locating uniform laws and model acts is covered in the next chapter. Note that the U.S. Constitution is included with the *United States Code Annotated* and the *United States Code Service*, the main research sources for federal law, and most state constitutions are included with the state statutes. The research techniques and strategies that apply to statutory research also apply to constitutional research.

A. Federal Law

1. Publication

Each law passed by Congress is assigned a public law number. The number reflects the order in which the law was passed and the session of Congress. For example, Public Law 107-35 was the 35th law passed by the 107th session of Congress. The full text of each law is published separately by the U.S. Government Printing Office and is referred to as a **slip law**. Slip laws are available at most law libraries and many public libraries. The *United States Code Congressional and Administrative News Service* (USCAN) is a publication by West, a Thomson business, which presents the complete text of all public laws passed by Congress. It is available by subscription and through Westlaw. In addition, slip laws may be purchased from the U.S. Government Printing Office, which can be reached by calling (202)512-0000—or through your congressional representative. The Government Printing Office Web site is presented in the Internet Resources section of this chapter. Note that each session of Congress lasts one year. And, because there is a new Congress every two years with the election of the House of Representatives, there are two sessions for each Congress.

At the end of each session of Congress, the slip laws are placed in chronological order, (organized according to the date the law was passed) and published in volumes titled the *United States Statutes at Large*. Because the laws are placed in chronological order, it is difficult, if not impossible, to conduct research using the *Statutes at Large*. For example, if you are assigned the task of locating the laws relating to the distribution of drugs, you may have to research every volume of the more than 100 volumes. A further impediment to research is that each volume has a separate index. There is no single index that would inform you which volumes contain laws relating to the distribution of drugs.

In 1925, Congress authorized the preparation of the *United States Code* (USC). In the *United States Code*, the laws contained in the *United States Statutes at Large* are organized (codified) by subject into 50 categories called "Titles" (see Exhibit 4–3). Each title covers a different area of law (see Exhibit 4–3). A citation to a *United States Code* statute refers to the title number, the name of the code, the section, and the year. Note that the year is the copyright date and not the year the statute was enacted.

FOR EXAMPLE	18	USC	§	1115	(2000)
	Title	Code	Section Symbol	Section No.	Year

A new edition is published every six years and cumulative supplements called pocket parts are published for each volume during intervening years. The *United States Code* is the "official" code of the laws of the United States. A publication of a code of laws is an official code when the government itself publishes the code or arranges for or directs a commercial publisher to publish the code.

TITLES OF UNITED STATES CODE AND UNITED STATES CODE ANNOTATED

1. General Provisions
2. The Congress
3. The President
4. Flag and Seal, Seat of Government, and the States
5. Government Organization and Employees
6. Surety Bonds (*See Title 31, Money and Finance*)
7. Agriculture
8. Aliens and Nationality
9. Arbitration
10. Armed Forces
11. Bankruptcy
12. Banks and Banking
13. Census
14. Coast Guard
15. Commerce and Trade
16. Conservation
17. Copyrights
18. Crimes and Criminal Procedure
19. Customs Duties
20. Education
21. Food and Drugs
22. Foreign Relations and Intercourse
23. Highways
24. Hospitals and Asylums
25. Indians
26. Internal Revenue Code
27. Intoxicating Liquors
28. Judiciary and Judicial Procedure
29. Labor
30. Mineral Land and Mining
31. Money and Finance
32. National Guard
33. Navigation and Navigable waters
34. Navy (*See Title 10, Armed Forces*)
35. Patents
36. Patriotic Societies and National Observances, Ceremonies, and Organizations
37. Pay and Allowances of the Uniformed Services
38. Veterans' Benefits
39. Postal service
40. Public Buildings, Property, and Works
41. Public contracts
42. The Public Health and Welfare
43. Public Lands
44. Public Printing and Documents
45. Railroads
46. Shipping
47. Telegraphs, Telephones, and Radiotelegraphs
48. Territories and Insular Possessions
49. Transportation
50. War and National Defense

Exhibit 4–3
Titles of United States Code and United States Code Annotated.
West, a Thomson Reuters business, *United States Code Annotated*, List of Titles of United States Code and United States Code Annotated, 2000, from title 18 USCA p. II. Used with permission of Thomson Reuters/West.

A drawback of the *United States Code* is that it is not annotated; it merely recites the federal statutes. It does not provide the researcher with the valuable information included in the annotations, such as library references and notes to court decisions that have interpreted the statutes.

There are two privately published annotated codes: *United States Code Annotated* (USCA), published by West, a Thomson business, also available on Westlaw, and *United States Code Service* (USCS), published by the LexisNexis, a division of Reed Elsevier, Inc. (referred to in the remainder of this text as LexisNexis). These are "unofficial codes," that is, they are not published at the direction of the government. A discussion of these annotated codes follows.

2. United States Code Annotated

The *United States Code Annotated* consists of approximately 200 volumes and includes a General Index. In the front of each volume is a list of the 50 titles of the *United States Code* (see Exhibit 4–3). Each volume has a table of contents listing the chapters and features in the volume and a cite page, which lists the citation to use for the volume. The first volumes contain the U.S. Constitution with annotations. The subsequent volumes include the entire text of the 50 titles of the *United States Code* arranged according to the 50 titles of the USC. Most titles include a title index as well as appendix material, and each volume is periodically supplemented with pocket parts that update the main text. The appendix material may include sections of the *Code of Federal Regulations* (CFR), previous code text, and other materials such as international conventions. (See Exhibit 4–2 for an example of a USCA section.)

a. General Index

The *General Index* is a softbound multivolume set that is updated annually. It consists of descriptive words or phrases, arranged alphabetically, with headings and subheadings. Following each topic is the title and section number(s) of the relevant statutory provision. When the reference to a section number is followed by the abbreviation *et seq.*, it means that the reference is to a group of sections beginning with that section. (See Exhibit 4–4 for an example of an index page.)

b. Pocket Parts and Supplementary Pamphlets

The hardcover volumes of the USCA are updated with pocket parts that are placed in a pocket at the back of each volume. The pocket parts include any revisions to a statute and additional annotations such as recent cases interpreting the statute. If a statutory section is not included in the pocket part, the section has not been amended and there are no new annotations. The pocket parts are cumulative—they update the volume from the date of the volume's publication. For example, if the hardbound volume was published in 2007, the 2010 pocket part will include all the changes, updates, and new cases construing the statutes contained in the volume from 2008, 2009, and 2010.

If the pocket part is too large to fit in the back of a volume, the publisher will provide a softbound supplement that sits next to the volume. Occasionally a new hardbound volume will be printed that includes the information contained in the pocket part or supplement. When this occurs, the publisher will place in the pocket a notice that states "This Volume Contains No Pocket Part." If there is no pocket part or a notice that the volume does not contain a pocket part, assume it is missing and check with the librarian. (See Exhibit 4–5 for an example of a portion of a pocket part.)

Pocket parts are published only once a year. To ensure that the information contained in the USCA is current, supplemental pamphlets, called Statutory Supplements, are published every three to four months following the publication of the pocket part.

KEROSENE

KEROSENE—Cont'd
Summer Fill and Fuel Budgeting Programs, 42 § 6283

KERR-MILLS ACT
Medical Assistance, generally, this index

Reference to Title 7 Section 515 and the Sections that follow

KERR-SMITH TOBACOO CONTROL ACT
Generally, 7 § 515 et seq.

—KETOBEMIDONE
Controlled Substance, generally, this index

KETTLE RIVER
Wild and scenic rivers, 16 § 1276

KETTLEHOLES
Ice Age National Scientific Reserve, generally, this index

KEWEENAW NATIONAL HISTORICAL PARK
Generally, 16 § 410yy et seq.

KEY LARGO CORAL REEF PRESERVE
Genarally, 16 § 461, nt, PN 3339

KEY LARGO NATIONAL MARINE SANCTUARY
Designation, 16 § 1433 nt

KEYS

Reference to Title and Section

Defense Department, Security, theft, forgery, fines, penalties and forfeitures, 18 § 1386
Internal Revenue Service, proprietors of distilled spirits plants to furnish to Secretary, 26 § 5203

KHMER REPUBLIC
Kampuchca, generally, this index

KIAVAH WILDERNESS
Generally, 16 § 1132 nt

KICK-BACK RACKET ACT
Generally, 40 § 276c
Public Building, Property, and Works, generally, this index

KICK-BACKS
Anti-Kickback, generally, this index Health insurance for aged and disabled, 42 § 1320a-7b
Income tax, deductions, 26 § 162
Medical assistance programs, grants to States for, criminal penalty, 42 § 1320a-7b
Presidential Election Campaign Fund, 26 § 9012
Presidential primary matching payment account, 26 § 9042
Public works, 18 § 874
Real Estate Settlement Procedures, this index Sentence and punishment, 18 USSG §2B4.1

KICKAPOO INDIANS
Indians, this index

KIDNAPPING
Generally, 18 § 1201 et seq.
Aircraft, jurisdiction, 18 § 1201
Attempts, 18 § 1201
Attorney General, this index

KIDNAPPING—Cont'd
Banks and banking, robbery, 18 § 2113
Cabinet departments, heads and deputies, Interception of wire, oral, or electronic communications, 18 § 2516
Kidnapping, attempts, conspiracy, penalties and forfeitures, 18 § 351
Chief Justice of Supreme Court, kidnapping, attempts, conspiracy, fines, penalties and forfeitures, 18 § 351
Children and Minors, this index
CIA, director, deputy director, fines, penalties and forfeitures, 18 § 351
Congress, this index
Conspiracy,
    Against right of inhabitants, fines, penalties and forfeitures, 18 § 241
    Fines, penalties and forfeitures, 18 § 1201
    Foreign countries, 18 § 956
Deprivation of rights under color of law, fines, penalties and forfeitures, 18 § 242
Domestic violence, parental kidnapping, reports, 28 § 1738A nt
Employee Retirement Income Security Program, protection of employee benefit rights, fiduciary responsibility, 29 § 1111
Evidence, congress, cabinet department heads, knowledge, 18 § 351
Fair housing, sale or rental, intimidation, interference, penalties, 42 § 3631
FBI database, crimes against children, registration, 42 § 14072
Federal officials, fines, penalties and forfeitures, 18 § 1201
Federally protected activities, intimidation, interference, fines, penalties and forfeitures, 18 § 245
Fines, penalties and forfeitures, 18 §1201
    Indian lands and reservations, 18 § 1153
    Ransom money, 18 § 1202
    Transportation, interstate commerce, 18 § 1201
Foreign countries.
    Children and minors, 42 § 11608a
    Conspiracy, 18 § 956
    U.S. citizens, 22 § 2715a
Foreign Diplomatic and Consular Officers, this index
Forfeitures. Fines, penalties and forfeitures, generally, ante
Indians, this index
Interception of wire, oral, or electronic communications, President, congress, 18 § 2516
International Child Abduction Remedies, generally, this index
Interstate and Foreign Commerce, this index
Involuntary servitude, intent to sell, 18 § 1583
Jurisdiction,
    Indian lands and reservations, 18 § 3242
    Internationally protected persons, victims, 18 § 1201

Exhibit 4—4
Excerpt from the USCA General Index.
West, a Thomson Reuters business, *United States Code Annotated*, General Index (2000), p. 787. Used with permission of Thomson Reuters/West.

§511. Liability of States, instrumentalities of States, and State official for infringement of copyright

(a) In General.—Any State, any instrumentality of a States, and any officer for employee of a States or instrumentality of a State acting in his or her official capacity, shall not be immune, under the Eleventh Amendment of the Constitution of the United States or under any other doctrine of sovereign immunity, from suit in Federal court by any person, including any governmental or nongovernmental entity, for a violation of any of the exclusive right of a copyright owner provided by section 106 through 121, for importing copies of phonorecords in violation of section 602, or for any other violation under this title.

Amendment to law

[See main volume for text of (b)]

(As amended Pub L. 106-14, § 1(g)(6), Aug. 5, 1999, 113 Stat. 222.)

HISTORICAL AND STATUORY NOTES

Amendments
1999 Amendments. Subsec. (a). Pub.L. 106-44, § 1(g)(6), substituted "121" for "119."

LIBRARY REFERENCES

Text and Treatises
Business and Commercial Litigation in Federal Courts §§ 65.2, 65.3, 65.4, 65.10, 65.15 (Robert L. Haig ed.) (West Group & ABA 1998)

7A Fed Proc L Ed, Copyrights § 18:187

NOTES OF DECISIONS

New annotations

Constitutionality ½
Immunity 2
Waiver 3

½. Constitutionality
Statute purporting to abrogate states' sovereign immunity in copyright infringement suits was not enacted pursuant to a valid exercise of congressional power to enforce the guarantees of the Fourteenth Amendment's due process clause and thus did not validly waive states' immunity. Rodriguez v. Texas Com'n on the Arts, C.A.5 (Tex.) 2000, 199 F.3d 279, 53 U.S.P.Q.2d 1383.

2. Immunity
Provisions of Copyright Art and Lanham Act that purported to require states to submit to suit in federal court for violation of those statutes exceeded Congress's constitutional powers. Chavez v. Arte Publico Press, C.A.5 (Tex) 1998.157 F.3d

282, rehearing granted, vacated 178 F.3d 601, 53 U.S.P.Q.2d 2009.
University employee who allegedly authorized printing of copies of author's book in violation of Copyright Act was entitled to qualified immunity, where contractual provision relating to duration of university's publishing license was ambiguous and was susceptible of interpretation that permitted employee's actions. Chavez v. Arte Publico Press, C A.5 (Tex.) 1995, 59 F.3d 539, 35 U.S.P.Q.2d 1609, vacated 116 S.Ct. 1667, 517 U.S. 1184, 134 L. Ed.3d 772, on remand 139 F.3d 504, 46 U.S.P.Q.2d 1541, on remand 157 F.3d 282, certiorari denied 116 S.Ct. 1672, 517, U.S. 1187, 134 L.E.d.2d 776.

3.Waiver
University waived its Eleventh Amendment immunity from suit for copyright infringement . . .

Exhibit 4–5
Pocket part update for 17 USCA § 511.
West, a Thomson Reuters business, *United States Code Annotated,* 2001 Cumulative Annual Pocket, Title 17 § 511, p. 27. Used with permission of Thomson Reuters/West.

WESTLAW ELECTRONIC RESEARCH

United States cases: 398k[add key number].

§ 757c.   Work under reimbursable agreements; recording obligations and crediting amounts received

LIBRARY REFERENCES

American Digest System
   United States 🗝 82(1)

Encyclopedias
   United States, see C.J.S. § 122

WESTLAW ELECTRONIC RESEARCH

United States cases: 393k[add key number],

CHAPTER 12—FEDERAL REGULATION AND DEVELOPMENT OF POWER

SUBCHAPTER I—REGULATION OF THE DEVELOPMENT
OF WATER POWER AND RESOURCES

§ 803. Conditions of license generally

NOTES OF DECISIONS

32. Fish and wildlife protection—Generally

Under Federal Power Act section providing for inclusion of recommendations from federal and state fish and wildlife agencies in hydroelectric power licenses, Federal Energy Regulatory Commission (FERC) has discretion to reclassify, reject or modify such recommendations, including power to determine that recommendation does not qualify for treatment under that section, although FERC must afford significant deference to recommendations made for protection, mitigation, and enhancement of fish and wildlife. American Rivers v. F.E.R.C., C.A.9 1999, 187 F.3d 1007.

Exhibit 4–6

Excerpt from Noncumulative Pamphlet Entry for USCA §§ 754c and 803 Supplement Page.
West, a Thomson Reuters business, *United States Code Annotated*, Pamphlet #1, Supplementing Pocket Parts, Laws February 11, 2000 to April 2, 2000 (2001) p. 158. Used with permission of Thomson Reuters/West.

Like pocket parts, they include any revisions to a statute and additional annotations. These pamphlets are not cumulative; each one covers a specific time period. This means that you must check each supplement when updating research. (See Exhibit 4–6 for an example of a portion of a *Statutory Supplement* page.) These supplemental pamphlets are usually located at the end of the USCA set. *You must always check the pocket parts and supplemental pamphlets to ensure that your research is current and that there have not been changes in the law subsequent to the publication of the main volume.*

c. Popular Name Table

Statutes are often referred to by a popular name, such as the Americans with Disabilities Act or the Freedom of Information Act. If you know a statute's popular name but do not know the citation, a quick way to locate the statute is through the Popular Name Table. The table can be found in the last volume of the *General Index*. The table provides you with the public law number, the *Statutes at Large* citation, and the title and section numbers. (See Exhibit 4–7 for a page from the Table.)

d. Conversion Tables

If you know the *Statutes at Large* citation, the public law number, or the year and chapter of a law, the conversion tables allow you to find where the law is classified in the USCA. The conversion tables are located in the Tables volumes. They are published annually and updates are located at the end of each noncumulative supplement. (See Exhibit 4–8 for an example of a Table page.)

POPULAR NAME TABLE

Freedom of Information Act (FOIA)
  Pub.L. 89-487, July 4, 1966, 80 Stat. 250 (See 5 § 552)
  Pub.L. 90-23, § 1, June 5, 1967, 81 Stat. 54 (5 § 552)
  Pub.L. 93-502, §§ 1 to 3, Nov. 21, 1974, 88 Sat. 1561 (5 § 552)

Freedom of Information Reform Act of 1986
  Pub.L. 99-570, Title I, Subtitle N, Oct. 27, 1986, 100 Stat. 3204-48 (5 §§ 552, 552 notes)

FREEDOM Support Act
  See Freedom for Russia and Emerging Eurasian Democracies and Open Markets
    Support Act of 1992

Freedom to E-File Act
  Pub.L. 106-222, June 20, 2000, 114 Stat. 353 (7 §§ 6901 note, 7031 to 7035)

Freedom to Farm Law
  See Emergency Farm Financial Relief Act

French Spoliation Claims Act
  Jan. 20, 1885, ch. 25, 23 Stat 283

Fresh Cut Flowers and Fresh Cut Greens Promotion and Information Act of 1993
  Pub.L. 103-190, Dec. 14, 1993, 107 Stat. 2266 (7 §§ 6801, 6801 note, 6802 to 6814)

FRIENDSHIP Act
  See Act For Reform In Emerging New Democracies and Support and Help for
    Improved Partnership with Russia, Ukraine, and other New Independent States

Public law number

USCA Citation

Statutes at Large citation

FRLA
  See Federal Regulation of Lobbying Act

FRRAPA
  See Forest and Rangeland Renewable Resources Planning Act of 1974

FRRRRA
  See Forest and Rangeland Renewable Resource Research Act of 1978

FRSA
  See Federal Railroad Safety Act of 1970

Frye Acts
  See Shipping Acts

FSC Repeal and Extraterritorial Income Exclusion Act of 200 (Foreign Sales Corporation
  Repeal and Extraterritorial Income Exclusion Act of 2000)
  Pub l. 106-519, Nov. 15, 2000. 114 Stat, 2423 (see Tables for classification)

FSIA
  See Foreign Sovereign Immunities Act of 1976

FSLMRA
  See Federal Service Labour-Management Relations Act

FSPA
  See Uniformed Services Former Spouses Protection Act

FTCA
  See Federal Tort Claims Act

FTCPMA
  See Federal Timber Contact Payment Modification Act

Fuel Distribution Act
  Sept. 22, 1922, ch. 413, 42 Stat. 1025

Fugitive Felon Act
  June 22, 1932, ch. 271, § 1, 47 Stat. 326
  May 18, 1934, ch. 301, 48 Stat. 301 (See 18 § 1073)

Fugitive Slave Laws
  Sept. 18, 1850, ch. 60, 9 Stat. 462
  June 28, 1864, ch. 166, 13 Stat. 200

Exhibit 4–7
USCA Popular Name Table Page.
West, a Thomson Reuters business, *United States Code Annotated*, Popular Name Table (2000), p. 787. Used with permission of Thomson Reuters/West.

106-546   2000

106-546...§ 1	114 Stat 2726	42 §13701
§ 2	114 Stat 2726	42 §14135
§ 3	114 Stat 2728	42 § 14135a
§ 4	114 Stat 2730	42 § 14135b
§ 5(a)(1)	114 Stat 2731	10 § 1565
§ 5(a)(2)	114 Stat 2732	10prec. 1561
§ 5(b)	114 Stat 2733	10 § 1565 nt
§ 5(c)	114 Stat 2733	10 § 1565 nt
§ 6(a)	114 Stat 2733	28 § 531 nt
§ 6(b)(1)	114 Stat 2733	42 § 14132
§ 6(b)(2)	114 Stat 2733	42 § 14132
§ 6(b)(3)	114 Stat 2733	42 § 14132
§ 6(b)(4)	114 Stat 2733	42 § 14132
§ 7(a)(1)	114 Stat 2734	18 § 3563
§ 7(a)(2)	114 Stat 2734	18 § 3563
§ 7(a)(3)	114 Stat 2734	18 § 3563
§ 7(b)	114 Stat 2734	18 § 4209
§ 7(c)	114 Stat 2734	42 § 14135c
§ 7(d)	114 Stat 2734	42 § 14135c
§ 8(a)	114 Stat 2734	42 § 3733
§ 8(b)	114 Stat 2735	42 § 3796kk-2
§ 8(c)	114 Stat 2735	42 § 14133
§ 9	114 Stat 2735	42 § 14135d
§ 10	114 Stat 2735	42 § 14135e
§ 11	114 Stat 2735	42 § 14135 nt
106-547...§ 1	114 Stat 2738	18 § 700 nt
§ 2(a)	114 Stat 2738	18 § 1036
§ 2(b)	114 Stat 2738	18prec. 1001
§ 3(a)	114 Stat 2739	18 §716
§ 3(b)	114 Stat 2740	18prec. 700
106-548...—	114 Stat 2741	– § —............Uncl.
106-549...—	114 Stat 2743	– § —............Uncl.
106-550...§ 1	114 Stat 2745	36prec. 101 nt
§ 2	114 Stat 2745	36prec. 101 nt
§ 3	114 Stat 2746	36prec. 101 nt
§ 4	114 Stat 2746	36prec. 101 nt
§ 5	114 Stat 2747	36prec. 101 nt
§ 6	114 Stat 2748	36prec. 101 nt
§ 7	114 Stat 2749	36prec. 101 nt
§ 8	114 Stat 2749	36prec. 101 nt
§ 9	114 Stat 2750	36prec. 101 nt
§ 10	114 Stat 2750	36prec. 101 nt
§ 11	114 Stat 2751	36prec. 101 nt
§ 12	114 Stat 2751	36prec. 101 nt
Dec. 20, 2000..... 106-331... § 1	114 Stat 2752	42 § 201 nt
§ 2	114 Stat 2752	42 § 287a-3a
§ 3	114 Stat 2759	42 § 287-3a nt

Public law number

Statutes at Large citation

USCA Citation

Exhibit 4—8
USCA Excerpt from Conversion Table.
West, a Thomson Reuters business, *United States code Annotated*, Conversion Table (2000), p. 1542. Used with permission of Thomson Reuters/West.

3. United States Code Service

LexisNexis publishes the *United States Code Service* (USCS), which consists of approximately 150 volumes and contains the wording of the federal statutes published in the *United States Statutes at Large*. The *United States Code Service* and *United States Code Annotated* are competitive sets, produced by different publishers to accomplish the same basic task—to publish the federal laws and provide the information necessary for researchers to interpret and answer questions concerning federal law. An example of pages from the USCS is presented in Exhibit 4–9.

The sets are similar in most respects; therefore, most researchers do not use both sets. Which set you use is often based on what's available or on personal preferences. The similarities and dissimilarities of the sets are presented here.

---

18 USCS § 1201, N 64 CRIMES & CRIMINAL PROCEDURE

64. Appellate review

In prosecution under predecessor to 18 USCS § 1201, objection that letter which codefendant had taken from kidnapped victim and which was later found by police in defendant's apartment was obtained by illegal search could not be raised for first time on appeal from conviction. Eaker v United States (1935, CA.10 Colo) 76 F2d 267.

Defendant who had been convicted of interstate transportation of person who had been unlawfully kidnapped could not by writ of habeas corpus applied for in United States District Court for Western District of Oklahoma affect his sentence for such unlawful interstate transportation rendered in United States District Court for Northern District of Texas, nor cause his trial for kidnapping offense in Western District of Oklahoma, wherein no charge for such offense was pending

against him. Trafford v Yellow Cab Co. (1961, CA3 Pa) 293 F2d 43.

65. Habeas corpus proceedings

Whether defendant was member of conspiracy and did conspire in violation of law raised issue of fact, and where that issue was resolved against him in trial court, it could not be relitigated in habeas corpus proceeding. Hudspeth v McDonald (1941, CA10 Kan) 120 F2d 962, cert den (1941) 314 US 617, 86 L Ed 496, 62 S Ct 110, reh den (1945) 325 US 892, 89 L Ed 2004, 65 S Ct 1181.

Motion to vacate sentence for kidnapping conviction of 30 years will be denied when petitioner was adequately made aware of charge against him and where his plea of guilty was voluntarily entered into without fear of death penalty. Wilson v United States (1969, WD Va) 303 F Supp 1139.

§ 1202. Ransom money

Whoever receive, possesses, or disposes of any money or other property, or any portion thereof, which has at any time been delivered as ransom or reward in connection with a violation of section 1201 of this title, knowing the same to be money or property which has been at any time delivered as such ransom or reward, shall be fined not more than $10,000 or imprisoned not more than ten years, or both. (June 25, 1948, ch 645, § 1, 62 Stat. 760.)

HISTORY; ANCILLARY LAWS AND DIRECTIVES

Prior law and revision:
This section is based on Act June 22, 1932, ch 271, § 4, as added Jan. 24, 1936, ch 29, 49 Stat. 1099 (former 18 U.S.C. § 408c-1).
The words "in the penitentiary" after "imprisoned" were omitted in view of 18 USCS § 4082 committing prisoners to the custody of the Attorney General.
Minor charges in phraseology were made.

Exhibit 4–9
Title 18 USCS 1202.
LexisNexis®, *United States Code Service*, Title 18 Crimes & Criminal Procedure § 1202 (1994), p. 200. LexisNexis® Screen Captures reprinted with the permission of LexisNexis. LexisNexis and *Shepard's* are registered trademarks and Focus and KWIC are trademarks of Reed Elsevier Properties, Inc., used with the permission of LexisNexis.

CROSS REFERENCES

Sentencing guidelines, Statutory Index, Sentencing Guidelines for U.S. Courts, 18 USCS Appendix.

RESEARCH GUIDE

Annotations:
What constitutes violation of 18 USCS 1202, Prohibiting receipt, possession, or disposition of ransom money. 31 ALR Fed 916.

INTERPRETIVE NOTES AND DECISIONS

1. Generally
2. Relationship with other laws
3. Delivery of ransom

4. Conspiracy
5. Jurisdiction
6. Indictment

CRIMES   **18 USCS § 1203**

1. Generally

18 USCS § 1202 was intended to extend federal jurisdiction to persons having only indirect connection with actual kidnapping and to discourage any co-operation with those primarily responsible. United States v Ortega (1975, CA3 NJ) 517 F2d 1006, 31 ALR Fed 909.

2. Relationship with other laws

18 USCS § 1202 Is not separate, detached violation with regard to primary federal kidnapping statute (18 USCS § 1201) and § 1202 is directed to only portion of larger offense which includes number of components. United States v Ortega (1975, CA3 NJ) 517 F2d 1006, 31 ALR Fed 909.

Establishing violation of 18 USCS § 1202 requires proof of money or property which was delivered as ransom or reward, elements that are clearly not identical to any of elements of USCS § 1201 kidnapping offense, and therefore trial court was correct in refusing to instruct that § 1201. Durns v United States (1977, CA8 Mo) 562 F2d 542, 2 Fed Rules Evid Serv 462, cert den (1977) 434 US 959, 54 L Ed 2d 319, 98 S Ct 490.

3. Delivery of ransom

For ransom to have been "delivered" within meaning of § 1202 does not require transfer of possession to kidnappers; all that is needed is for transferor to have placed ransom at place specified by kidnappers, and fact that transferor may have mistakenly placed ransom at wrong location

does not vitiate "delivery" for purposes of § 1202; thus, violation thereof occurred where defendant found and appropriated ransom mistakenly delivered and concealed fact after learning that it was ransom United States v Ortega (1975, CA3 NJ) 517 F2d 1006, 31 ALR Fed 909.

4. Conspiracy

Conspiracy to violate predecessor to 18 USCS § 1202 began with plan to abduct and ended when ransom money was changed into unmarked money. Laska v United States (1936, CA10 Okla) 82 F2d 672, cert den (1936) 298 US 689, 80 L Ed 1407, 56 S Ct 957.

5. Jurisdiction

18 USCS § 1202 being prohibition of integral part of kidnapping scheme which concededly is within federal jurisdiction, violation of prohibition is within federal jurisdiction even if interstate commerce is not directly involved. United States v Ortega (1975, CA3 NJ) 517 F2d 1006, 31 ALR Fed 909.

6. Indictment

Indictment charging defendant with three separate offenses of transmitting communications in interstate commerce demanding ransom money under 18 USCS § 875(a) and with receiving, possessing and disposing of ransom money in violation of 18 USCS § 1202, is not duplicitious as each count charges separate offense. Amsler v United States (1967, CA9 Cal) 381 F2d 37.

Exhibit 4–9
Continued

Similarities:

✦ *Organization*—Both are organized in the same way. The organization is based on the 50 titles of the *United States Code*. For example, Title 42 Section 1983, will be found at 42 USCA § 1983 and 42 USCS § 1983.

✦ *Contents*—Both have general indexes, popular name tables, and conversion tables.

✦ *Annotation*—In both sets, the annotations provide information on the history of the statute, direct you to other research sources, and briefly summarize cases that have construed the statute.

✦ *Updates*—Both sets are updated annually with pocket parts for each volume and supplemental pamphlets.

Differences:

✦ The USCA includes more court decisions in the Notes of Decisions section of the annotations. The USCS tends to be more selective and reference the more significant cases.

✦ The Research Guide section of USCS annotations is more comprehensive than the Library Reference section of the USCA in that it includes more references to research sources.

✦ The supplements to the USCS, called the *Cumulative Later Case and Statutory Service*, are cumulative. Therefore, only the latest supplement needs to be checked. The USCS also publishes a monthly pamphlet called *USCS Advance*, which includes new public laws, presidential proclamations, and executive orders.

✦ In the USCA, the topics covered in the Notes to the Decisions are arranged alphabetically; in the USCS, the Interpretive Notes and Decisions are arranged according to topic (see Exhibits 4–2 and 4–9).

B. State Statutory Law and Codes

The enactment and publication of state legislation varies in detail from state to state, but they are similar in many respects to the federal system. Most states initially publish their laws in pamphlets similar to the federal slip laws. When the legislative session is over, the laws are published in books often referred to as session laws. These are similar to the *United States Statutes at Large* in that the laws are presented in the order in which they were passed.

State laws are then organized according to topic (codified) and published with annotations similar to the USCA and USCS. Most state codes are similar to the USCA and USCS in the following ways:

✦ Each set has a general index, and some sets have a separate index following each title.

✦ Some statutes have popular name tables and conversion tables that allow you to locate statutes that have been renumbered or repealed.

✦ The statutes are organized by subject with each subject title being subdivided into chapters and so on. (See Exhibit 4–1 and "Numbers" in Section IIA earlier in this chapter.)

✦ The state constitution with annotations is included in the code.

✦ State codes are usually updated annually by some form of supplement. These may be pocket parts inserted in the statutory volume or separate pamphlets.

✦ State statutes are annotated. The annotations include the history of the section, cross-references to other statutes, research guides, and notes to court decisions (see Exhibit 4–1).

C. The Research Process—Techniques and Strategies

1. Step 1: Locate the Statute

Inasmuch as federal and state codifications share similar features, the process for locating and researching federal and state constitutional and statutory law is essentially the same and will be discussed together here. The beginning step of all research, including statutory research, is to identify what you are looking for as precisely and narrowly as possible. Define your research question in as concise terms as possible. Time spent narrowing the focus of your search will save a great deal of research time later. A tightly focused identification of the research question saves time because the researcher is immediately directed to the specific area of the law in question and does not waste time searching multiple statutes.

> **FOR EXAMPLE** The question involves the issue of whether a shareholder of a corporation must attend a meeting in person to vote on an issue. If a researcher thinks, "Oh, this is a corporation question" and immediately looks at corporations in the index to the statutes, the researcher will waste time looking through the entire corporation section. If the research is conducted electronically, and the search term is simply "corporations," all the corporation statutes will come up. If, however, the research is focused to "corporations, shareholders, meetings" or "corporations, shareholders, voting," the search is narrowed at the outset and the statute is located more quickly, whether the research is manual or electronic.

After you have defined your search as concisely as possible, there are three main ways to approach locating a statute.

a. The General Index

The most common approach to locating statutes is to use the general index. When using this approach, identify as specifically as possible the words that describe the problem. If the term you use is not the term used in the index, the index often will refer you to the correct term. For example, if you are looking for statutes concerning trailers, the index under *trailers* may read, *See Manufactured Homes.* (See Exhibit 4–4 for an example of an index page.)

After you have found the correct index entry, the index will list the appropriate title and section. With this information, you can locate statutes in the appropriate statutory volume. Most statutes are arranged by title, and the titles covered in each volume are indicated on the spine. For example, the spine may read *Titles 5-7,* thus indicating that Titles 5 through 7 of the code are included in that volume. Be sure to check the index pocket part if you cannot find a term in the main index volume. The term may have been recently added to the index.

b. Title Table of Contents

Most statutory codifications include a table of contents at the beginning of each title that lists the name and number of the chapters within the title. At the beginning of each chapter, a table of contents typically lists the statutory section number and name of each section. If you know the number of the title you are looking for, you can go directly to the volume and scan the table to quickly locate a statute. It is not necessary to consult the general index.

> **FOR EXAMPLE** You want to locate the statutory definition of a term in the Indiana Commercial Code, and you know from experience that the commercial code is Title 26. You can directly go to Title 26, scan the table of contents to Chapter 1, and immediately locate the appropriate section, 26-1-1-201 General definitions. (See the first page of Exhibit 4–1.)

Beginning researchers should be aware that some subjects are covered by more than one set of laws. Therefore, referring to a specific title requires the researcher to be sufficiently familiar with the law to know that what he or she is looking for is covered only by that title.

> **FOR EXAMPLE** The question being researched involves identifying the statutes that govern a loan. Several statutes may cover loans: the commercial paper chapter of the commercial law title of the code, the state's small loan act, and the federal truth in lending statutes.

Always consult the general index and identify all the possible titles that cover the research topic.

c. Popular Name

Many laws are commonly known by their popular name, such as the Good Samaritan Act or the Truth in Lending Act. Many state statutes and the USCA and the USCS have popular name tables listing in alphabetical order the popular names and citation. The tables are usually located with the table of contents volume(s) or as a separate volume. *Shepard's Acts and Cases by Popular Name: Federal and State* also lists the popular names and citations of federal and state laws. If you know the popular name of the act you are looking for, consult the popular name table, and you will be directed to the appropriate section of the statutes.

2. Step 2: Update Your Research

After you locate a statute, you must check the pocket parts and *supplementary pamphlets* to ensure that the statute published in the main volume has not been amended or repealed. Also, check the annotations to locate new case law that may affect the interpretation of the statute. *Shepard's Citations* provides updates to state and federal statutes and is published more frequently than state and federal pocket parts and supplementary pamphlets. The process of updating research through the use of *Shepard's Citations* is called Shepardizing. *Shepard's* is discussed in Chapter 7.

D. Computer-Aided Research

You may research state and federal statutes by using Westlaw and LexisNexis. In addition, you can access federal and most state laws without a fee through various sites on the Internet. You may locate many laws through state and federal government Web sites, and many may be located through college and university Web sites and Findlaw.com. Some of these sites are located in the Internet Resources section of this chapter. Also, many annotated statutes are available on CD-ROM through the publisher. Statutory research using Westlaw, LexisNexis, and FindLaw is discussed in Chapter 10.

E. Ethics—Competence and Diligence

There are ethical considerations to keep in mind when conducting any type of research, whether it is enacted law, case law, or secondary authority. Rule 1.1 of the American Bar Association's *Model Rules of Professional Conduct* requires that a client be provided competent representation. Rule 1.3 provides that a client be represented with diligence and promptness. These rules mean that a researcher must possess sufficient knowledge of the law and legal research to research completely the issues raised by the facts of the client's case. In addition, all avenues of research must be pursued promptly and explored thoroughly.

IV. ADMINISTRATIVE LAW

As discussed in Chapter 1, federal and state legislatures delegate the task of administering laws to administrative agencies. The legislatures pass enabling legislation that authorizes administrative agencies to carry out the intent of the legislature. This enabling legislation usually includes a grant of authority to create rules and regulations necessary to carry out the law. These rules and regulations have the authority of law; they are primary authority. The body of law that results from the rules and regulations and the court opinions interpreting them is called administrative law. The terms *rules* and *regulations* are often used interchangeably when discussing administrative law. To avoid repetition, the term *regulation*, when used in this section, includes both administrative rules and regulations.

On occasion, you may be called upon to research issues involving the interpretation or application of an administrative agency regulation.

> **FOR EXAMPLE** The client's business is fined by the Occupational Safety and Health Administration (OSHA) for failure to have fire extinguishers located in the proper places in the business. The client challenges OSHA's interpretation of the agency's regulation governing fire extinguishers. Research would be necessary to locate the regulation and the court opinions that have addressed the regulation.

This section discusses research involving the location and interpretation of administrative regulations.

A. Federal Administrative Law

1. Publication

Administrative regulations are published in two sources:

+ *Federal Register*—The *Federal Register* is a daily publication of the federal government that publishes:

  + Presidential documents such as executive orders

  + Rules and regulations

  + Proposed rules and regulations including summaries of proposed rules and notices of hearings, persons to contact, and so on (see Exhibit 4–10)

  + A table of contents in the front of each issue arranged by agency. At the end of each issue is a section called Reader Aids that includes valuable information such as a list of telephone numbers and a table of CFR Parts Affected that lists parts and sections of the *Code of Federal Regulations* affected. The pagination of the *Federal Register* is continuous beginning with the first issue of a year and ending with the last. Therefore, the first page of the first issue of the year will be page 1 and the last issue of the year will end with a page number

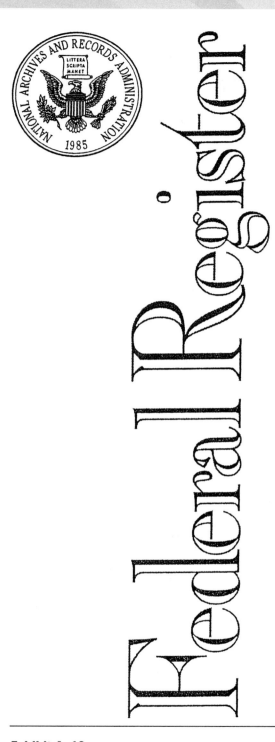

6–28–01

Vol. 66   No. 125

Pages 34353–34522

Thursday

June 28, 2001

Exhibit 4–10

Federal Register Cover Page.

Federal Register, Vol. 66 No. 125, June 28, 2001, Office of the Federal Register, National Archives and Records Administration, Washington, DC.

somewhere around 90,000. The issues are not cumulative; therefore, using the *Federal Register* as a research source is difficult.

In addition, a cumulative *Federal Register Index* is published at the end of each month. This index is arranged by agency and references all the information published in the previous months of the year.

◆ *Code of Federal Regulations* (CFR)—It is much easier to conduct regulatory research using the *Code of Federal Regulations*. The regulations of administrative agencies are codified in this multivolume, softbound set of books. The regulations are published in 50 titles, each of which represents a different subject area. The title numbers often, but not always, correspond to the titles assigned in the *United States Code*. The titles are subdivided into chapters, and each chapter usually covers the regulations of an individual agency. The chapters are divided into parts that consist of regulations governing a specific topic. The parts are divided into sections that are the specific regulations (see Exhibit 4–11). The code is reprinted annually on a quarterly basis, that is, one fourth of the code is reprinted each quarter.

There is a table of contents for each title, chapter, and part. At the end of each title is an index. In addition, there is an index volume (*CFR Index and Finding Aids*) through which regulations may be located by subject matter or agency (see Exhibit 4–12). The index includes a parallel table that allows you to locate the CFR title if you know the citation of the *United States Code* statute that established the agency. The index also includes a list of the agencies and 50 titles, chapters, and parts.

2. Researching Federal Administrative Law

Due to its organization, it is easier to locate federal rules and regulations through the *Code of Federal Regulations* rather than the *Federal Register*; therefore, the following guides focus on researching the CFR.

a. Indexes and Table of Contents

You may locate regulations in the CFR by subject matter or agency by consulting the *CFR Index and Finding Aids* volume. If you know the USC statute number, you can locate the code title in the parallel table in the index volume.

If you already know the code title or section, you can directly go to the code volume and scan the table of contents for the title to locate the appropriate section. You could also consult the index following the title.

You may also locate regulations through the *Index to the Code of Federal Regulations*. This is a commercial publication by the Congressional Information Service that indexes the CFR by subject and geographic information. It is usually available at law libraries.

b. Other Sources for Locating Rules and Regulations

You may be directed to specific CFR sections by other publications. If you know the statute that established the administrative agency, the annotations following the statute in the USCA or the USCS may include cross references to specific CFR sections. Other secondary sources such as law review articles and ALR annotations may reference specific CFR sections.

c. Federal Register

Inasmuch as the CFR is updated annually, it may be necessary to refer to the *Federal Register* to locate recently published rules and regulations. Consult the latest *Federal Register Index* to locate the rules and regulations.

d. Computer-Aided Research

The CFR and the *Federal Register* are available on Westlaw and LexisNexis. Federal administrative rules and regulations also may be researched through the Government Printing Office's Access site (listed in this chapter's Internet Resources). Also, you may obtain information from individual agency Web sites.

Subchapter ———————— # SUBCHAPTER A—GENERAL

Part ————————

PART 1000—COMMISSION ORGANIZATION AND FUNCTIONS

Section

AUTHORITY: 5 U.S.C. 552(a).

SOURCE: 56 FR 30496, July 3, 1991, unless otherwise noted.

§1000.1 The Commission.

(a) The Consumer Product Safety Commission is an independent regulatory agency which was formed on May 14, 1973, under the provisions of the Consumer Product Safety Act (Pub. L. 92-573, 86 Stat. 1207, as amended (1.5 U.S.C. 2051, et seq.)). The purposes of the Commission under the CPSA are:

(1) To protect the public against unreasonable risks of injury associated with consumer product;

(2) To assist consumers in evaluating the comparative safety of consumer products;

(3) To develop uniform safety standard for consumer products and to minimize conflicting State and local regulations; and

(4) To promote research and investigation into the causes and prevention of product-related deaths, illnesses, and injuries.

(b) The Commission is composed of five members appointed by the President, by and with the advice and consent of the Senate, for terms of seven years.

§ 1000.2 Laws administered.

The Commission administers five acts:

(a) The Consumer Product Safety Act (Pub. L. 92-573, 86 Stat. 1207, as amended (15 U.S.C. 2051, et seq.)).

(b) The Flammable Fabrics Act (Pub. L. 90-189, 67 Stat. 111, as amended (15 U.S.C. 1191, et seq.)).

(c) The Federal Hazardous Substances Act (15 U.S.C. 1261, et seq.).

(d) The Poison Prevention Packaging Act of 1970 (Pub. L. 91-601, 84 Stat. 1670, as amended (15 U.S.C. 1471, et seq.)).

(e) The Refrigerator Safety Act of 1956 (Pub. L. 84-930, 70 Stat. 953, (15 U.S.C. 1211, et seq.)).

§ 1000.3 Hotline.

(a) The Commission operates a toll-free telephone Hotline by which the public can communicate with the Commission. The number for use in all 50 states is 1-800-638-CPSC (1-800-638-2772).

(b) The Commission also operates a toll-free Hotline by which hearing or speech-impaired persons can communicate by teletypewriter with the Commission. The teletypewriter number for use in all states is 1-800-638-8270.

(c) The Commission also makes information available to the public product recall information, its public calendar, and other information through its

---

Exhibit 4–11

Page from the Code of Federal Regulations (CFR).

Code of Federal Regulations, Title 16 Part 100 to End, Commercial Practices (2001), p. 7, National Archives and Records Administration, Washington, DC.

Teachers, Christa McAuliffe Fellowship Program, 34 CFR, 237

Upward bound program, 34 CFR 645

Vocational and applied technology education

Demonstration projects for integration of vocational and academic learning program, 34 CFR 425

State-administered tech-prep education program, 34 CFR 406

State programs, 34 CFR 403

Subject

Emergency medical services

Cargo air carriers, special authorization for emergency transportation, 14 CFR 206

Medicare, conditions for payment, 42 CFR 424

Private land mobile radio services, 47 CFR 90

Public safety officers' death and disability benefits, rescue squad or ambulance crew members, 28 CFR 32

Special nuclear material, domestic licensing, 10 CFR 70

Surface coal mines and surface work areas of underground coal mines, safety standards, 30 CFR 77

Underground coal mines, mandatory safety standards, 30 CFR 75

Emergency mobilization
See Civil defense

Emergency Oil and Gas Guaranteed Loan Board
Emergency oil and Gas Guaranteed Loan Program, 13 CFR 500

Emergency powers
Employment of military resources in event of civil disturbance, 32 CFR 215

Passport requirement and exceptions, 22 CFR 53

Procedures for use and coordination of radio spectrum during wartime emergency, 47 CFR 214

Telecommunications emergency preparedness
Emergency restoration priority procedures for telecommunications services, 47 CFR 211

Executive policy, 47 CFR 201

Government and public correspondence telecommunications precedence system, 47 CFR 213

Planning and execution, 47 CFR 202

Procedures for obtaining international telecommunication service for use during wartime emergency, 47 CFR 212

Emergency Steel Guarantee Loan Board
Emergency Steel Guarantee Loan Program, 13 CFR 400

Employee benefit plans
See also pensions

Age Discrimination in Employment Act, 29 CFR 1625

Bona fide profit-sharing plans or trusts, requirements under Fair Labor Standards Act, 29 CFR 549

Bona fide thrift or savings plans, requirements under Fair Labor Standards Act, 29 CFR 547

Consolidated Rail Corporation, certain standards relating to Corporation's employee stock ownership plan, attainment determination, 49 CFR 49

Convicted persons, applications for certificates of exemption from certain laws. 28 CFR 4

Employee Retirement Income Security Act of 1974
Administration and enforcement, 29 CFR 2560

Administrative definitions, 29 CFR 2510

Civil penalties adjustment under Title I, 29 CFR 2575

Fiduciary responsibilities, 29 CFR 2550

Group health plans, health insurance portability and renewability. 29 CFR 2590

Interpretive bulletins, 29 CFR 2509

Procedural regulations, 29 CFR 2570

Reporting and disclosure, 29 CFR 2520

Temporary bonding rules, 29 CFR 2580

Family and Medical Leave Act of 1993, 29 CFR 825

Form and content of and requirements for financial statements, Securities Act of 1933, Securities Exchange Act of 1934, Public Utility Holding Company Act of 1935, Investment Company Act of 1940, Investment Advisers Act of 1940, and Energy Policy and Conservation Act of 1975, 17 CFR 210

Income taxes

Exhibit 4–12
CFR Index and Finding Aids Page.
Code of Federal Regulations, Index and Findings Aids (2001), p. 186, National Archives and Records Administration, Washington, DC.

e. Court and Administrative Decisions

Your research may require you to consult administrative agency or court decisions for an interpretation of a rule or regulation. Agency decisions may be available through the Government Printing Office and through commercial publishers such as Commerce Clearing House (CCH) and Bureau of National Affairs (BNA) (discussed in Chapter 8). Administrative and court decisions can also be accessed through Westlaw and LexisNexis.

Shepard's United States Administrative Citations and Shepard's Code of Federal Regulations Citations include citations to administrative agency and court decisions. West's Federal Practice Digest will direct you to federal cases and secondary sources that have interpreted federal regulations.

f. Updating Administrative Law Research

The Code of Federal Regulations is updated by consulting the List of CFR Sections Affected (LSA). This is a softbound, monthly publication that lists changes to any CFR regulation. It is cumulative; therefore, you must check only the most recent issue. The cover indicates the time period covered in the pamphlet (see Exhibit 4–13). The LSA is organized

Code of Federal Regulations

LSA

List of CFR Sections Affected

May 2001

Title 1–16
Changes January 2, 2001
through May 31, 2001

Title 17–27
Changes April 2, 2001
through May 31, 2001

Title 28–41
Changes July 3, 2000
through May 31, 2001

Title 42–50
Changes October 2, 2000
through May 31, 2001

Exhibit 4–13
CFR LSA Cover Page.
Code of Federal Regulations, LSA (2000). National Archives and Records Administration, Washington, DC.

by title and part, indicates the nature of the change such as "revised" or "removed," and includes a reference to the page number in the *Federal Register* where the revised section is published.

To locate changes that have occurred since the last LSA publication, you must check the Reader Aids at the end of the most recent *Federal Register*. As discussed in subsection A of Section IV, the Reader Aids includes a table of CFR Parts Affected that lists parts and sections of the *Code of Federal Regulations* affected. The CFR can be updated to the current date through reference to the LSA and Reader Aids.

The CFR can also be updated through Westlaw and LexisNexis. If you are updating through the Government Printing Office Access Web site, you must consult both the LSA and the Reader Aids.

Administrative agency and court decisions can be updated through *Shepard's United States Administrative Citations* and *Shepard's Code of Federal Regulations Citations*.

B. State Administrative Law

The publication of state rules and regulations varies from state to state, and it would require a separate text to cover each state. However, the publication and research of state administrative law often follows in varying degrees that of federal administrative law. Therefore, an understanding of the federal administrative law discussed in the previous two subsections will help you when researching state administrative law. Some states publish agency rules and regulations in a single code similar to the CFR. In some states, the regulations are published by each agency. Probably the quickest way to locate where an agency's regulations and administrative decisions are published is to contact the individual agency. Often individual agencies have Web sites, and the information may be available through the agency or state government Web site.

V. COURT RULES

Court rules regulate the conduct of matters brought before the court. They range in the subjects they cover from the technical, such as the format of pleadings, to the substantive, such as grounds for dismissal or when an appeal must be filed. Usually the rules are divided into two categories: rules of civil procedure and rules of criminal procedure. Each jurisdiction has the authority to promulgate its own set of rules, although many states follow in substantial part the Federal Rules of Civil and Criminal Procedure.

On occasion, you may need to research matters involving the rules to determine what a rule requires or how a rule has been interpreted.

> **FOR EXAMPLE** Rule 60 B of the Federal Rules of Civil Procedure provides that a judgment may be set aside on the grounds of "excusable neglect." It may be necessary to research the case law to determine how the courts have defined "excusable neglect."

The Federal Rules of Civil and Criminal Procedure are included in the *United States Code*. By consulting the USCA or the USCS, you will find annotations that direct you to summaries of cases and secondary sources such as legal encyclopedia sections and ALR annotations that have interpreted the rules. Like the federal rules, state court rules are usually published with the state statutes. Locating the rules in the annotated statutes is usually the starting point when researching rules.

The state and federal rules are available on Westlaw and LexisNexis through <http://www.findlaw.com> and the state or individual court Web site. In addition, multivolume treatises provide exhaustive analysis of the federal rules such as West's *Federal Practice and Procedure.*

In addition to the rules governing civil and criminal procedure, federal courts and many state courts have what are referred to as **local rules**. Consult these rules before filing any pleading or other document with the court. These rules are specific to the court and generally govern administrative matters such as the size of papers accepted, the number of copies of pleadings that must be filed with the original, and how to file by facsimile transmission. If the court has a Web site, the local rules may be available on the site. If not, local rules are available through the clerk of the court.

VI. STATUTORY ANALYSIS—THE PROCESS

The analysis of enacted law and court rules is the process of determining if a law applies, how it applies, and the effect of that application to a specific fact situation. When analyzing a legal problem or addressing an issue that is governed by constitutional, statutory, administrative law provision, or a court rule, it is helpful to have an approach, that is, an analysis process. This process should allow you to approach the matter in a way that efficiently solves the problem in the least amount of time with the least confusion and greatest accuracy. For the sake of clarity, throughout this section the discussion and examples focus upon laws passed by legislative bodies, statutory law. Note, however, that the principles presented here apply to the analysis of constitutions, statutes, administrative law, and court rules.

The three-step approach presented in Exhibit 4–14 is recommended when addressing a legal problem or issue governed by statutory law. These steps may be summarized as follows:

✦ Step 1: Determine if the statute applies in any way to the legal problem or issue.

✦ Step 2: Carefully read the statute and identify the required elements.

✦ Step 3: Compare or match the required elements to the facts of the problem and determine how the statute applies.

These steps are a helpful approach to statutory analysis, although in some instances a step may be unnecessary—for example, step 1 is unnecessary if you already know that the statute applies—and in other instances, a different approach may be required. Each step in this recommended approach is discussed separately in the following sections.

A. Step 1: Determine if the Statute Applies

The first step in the process is to determine which law if any covers the legal issue raised by the client's fact situation. Statutes govern certain people and situations. The first task then is to determine which statute or statutes govern the question.

Step 1	Determine if the statute applies. ✦ Part 1. Locate all possible applicable statutes. ✦ Part 2. Determine which statutes apply.
Step 2	Analyze the statute. ✦ Part 1. Read the statute. ✦ Part 2. Identify the statutory elements—what does the statute specifically declare, require, or prohibit.
Step 3	Apply the statute to the legal problem or issue. ✦ Chart format ✦ Narrative format

Exhibit 4–14
Statutory Analysis Three-Step Approach.

This step involves two parts:

+ Part 1. Locate all possible applicable statutes.
+ Part 2. Determine which statutes apply.

Part 1. Locate All Possible Applicable Statutes

Before you can determine if a particular statute applies, you first must locate all statutes that possibly apply. Locating one applicable statute does not mean you should stop your search. Make sure your research is thorough and complete. Continue researching until you are confident that all areas of law that may govern the problem have been explored and all potential applicable statutes have been located. Some matters are covered by more than one statute.

Part 2. Determine Which Statutes Apply

Determine whether each statute applies by asking yourself, "Does the general area of law covered by this statute apply to the issue or question raised by the facts of my client's case?" You can usually answer this question by referring to the scope of the statute, the definitions section, or case law.

Reference to the scope section of the statute will often answer the question of whether the statute applies.

> **For Example** The problem involves the validity of a contract for the sale of a security interest in a car. The scope section of the Commercial Code–Sales statute provides, "This chapter applies to the sale of goods, it does not apply to any transaction which . . . is a sale of a security interest or intended to operate only as a security transaction. . . ." This section clearly indicates that this statute does not cover such transactions. If the facts involved the sale of the car, rather than the sale of a security interest in the car, the statute might apply.

Often reference to the definitions section of a statute will help you determine whether a statute applies.

> **For Example** The legal problem involves the sale of a farm. The question of whether this sale is governed by the provisions of the Commercial Code–Sales statute is answered by reference to the definitions section of the statute. In that section goods are defined as "all things that are movable at the time of the contract for sale. . . ." The statute clearly does not apply to the sale of a farm.

In some instances, reference to case law may be necessary to determine if a statute governs a situation.

> **For Example** The client's case involves the lease of goods, and neither the scope nor definitions sections of the Commercial Code–Sales statute indicates whether the term *sale* includes a lease of goods. Reference to case law may be necessary. Court decisions often define terms not defined in a statute.

Note that you may often locate the relevant case law by looking to the reference information following the section of the statute.

It may be that two laws apply and govern a legal question. In this event, two causes of action may be available.

> **FOR EXAMPLE** A small loan may violate provisions of both the federal Truth in Lending Act and the state Usury Law. In this case, there may be a cause of action under the federal law and a cause of action under the state law.

If this occurs, follow steps 2 and 3 in regard to each statute.

When determining if a statute applies, always check the effective date of the statute to be sure that the statute is in effect. This information is usually found in the statute itself or in the historical notes or comments in the reference sections following the statute. Also, *always* check the statute's supplements to ensure that the statute you are researching is the latest version. Supplementary material published after the publication of the main text is often located immediately following the statute or in a separate section or pamphlet. The supplements include any changes in the statute or reference material that have occurred since the publication of the book containing the statute.

B. Step 2: Analyze the Statute

After you determine that a statute applies, you must carefully read and analyze it to determine how it applies. Some statutes are lengthy and difficult to understand. You may need to check the library references to locate other library sources that explain and interpret the statute. It may be necessary to make a chart to assist you in understanding the specific provisions and operation of a statute.

Step 2 involves two parts, which are addressed in the text that follows:

✦ Part 1. General concerns when reading statutory law.

✦ Part 2. Identify the statutory elements—what does the statute specifically declare, require, or prohibit?

Part 1. General Concerns When Reading Statutory Law

Several points should be kept in mind when reading statutory law:

1. Read the statute carefully several times.

2. Does the statute set a standard or merely provide factors that must be considered?

3. Does the statute provide more than one rule or test? Are other rules or tests available? Are there exceptions to the rule or test?

4. All the words and punctuation have meaning. Always check the definitions section for the meaning of terms. If there is no definition section, consult case law, a legal dictionary, or *Words and Phrases*. Don't assume you know what a term means. Your assumption may be wrong. A legal term may have several meanings, some of which may be unknown to you. All punctuation counts. If you cannot understand how to read a statute, consult a secondary source, such as a treatise or legal encyclopedia.

5. Review the entire statute (all sections) to determine if other sections in some way affect or relate to the section you are researching.

> **FOR EXAMPLE** Section 611-9 of the statute provides:
>
> a. A will that does not comply with Section 611-8 is valid as a holographic will if the signature and the material provisions are in the handwriting of the testator.
>
> b. If a holographic will does not contain a statement as to the date of its execution, and it is established that the testator lacked testamentary capacity at any time during which

the will might have been executed, the will is invalid unless it is established that it was executed at a time when the testator had testamentary capacity.

c. Any statement of testamentary intent contained in a holographic will may be set forth either in the testator's own handwriting or as part of a commercially printed form will.

Note that a holographic will is a will written entirely by the testator in his own handwriting and not witnessed. Subsection (a) sets the standard for when a holographic will is valid. Subsection (b), however, addresses a situation that affects the validity of a holographic will even if the requirements of subsection (a) are met. Subsection (c) establishes how testamentary intent may be set forth.

The preceding example illustrates a point that cannot be overemphasized: *read and consider all parts of a statute.* Suppose the legal question is, "What is required for a holographic will to be valid?" If you stopped reading the statute at subsection (a) because it appeared to answer your question, you would miss the other provisions that also affect the answer to the question. Always read the entire statute. Also, if the statute refers to another section, read that section to determine how the section affects the statute.

6. Certain common terminology must be understood. Be aware of the meaning of commonly used terms, such as *shall, may, and,* and *or.*

Shall makes the duty imposed mandatory; it must be done. *May* leaves the duty optional. If *and* is used, all the conditions or listed items are required. If the term *or* is used, only one of the conditions or listed items is required.

FOR EXAMPLE Section 24-6-7-9 provides "A person is concerned in the commission of a crime if he:

a. directly commits the crime;

b. intentionally causes some other person to commit the crime; or

c. intentionally aids or abets in the commission of the crime."

The use of *or* means that a person is covered by the statute if he/she does *any* one of the listed acts.

7. Keep in mind the canons of construction when reading statutes. These are presented in the General Considerations section of this chapter.

Part 2. Identify the Statutory Elements

What does the statute specifically declare, require, or prohibit? After carefully reading the statute, the next part of step 2 is to analyze the section of the statute in question. How does the statute apply? Ask yourself, "What specific requirements must be met for the statute to apply? What are the elements?" For a statute to apply, certain conditions established by the statute must be met. These conditions or components of the statute are called **statutory elements**. After the elements are identified, you can determine how the statute applies.

After you have a sufficient understanding of the statute, begin this part of step 2 by breaking the statute down into its elements. Identify and list the elements that must be met for the statute to apply. This is necessary because you must know what the elements are before you can proceed to step 3 and apply them to the legal problem or issue raised by the client's facts.

Identify the elements or requirements of the statute by reading the entire statute, analyzing each sentence word by word, and listing everything that is required to comply with the statute. This includes listing all the various conditions and exceptions contained in the subsections of the statute in question and the conditions and exceptions included in other statutes that may affect the statute in question.

> **FOR EXAMPLE** Consider section 2-2-315 of the Commercial Code–Sales Act of State X: Where the seller at the time of contracting has reason to know any particular purpose for which the goods are required and that the buyer is relying on the seller's skill or judgment to select or furnish suitable goods, there is an implied warranty that the goods shall be fit for such purpose.

Read the statute in the preceding example and determine the elements. For the implied warranty of § 2-2-315 to apply, the following requirements must be met:

1. *The person must be a seller of goods.* How do you know "of goods" is required? Section 2-2-315 quoted previously does not read "seller of goods"; it only states "the seller." You know "of goods" is required because in step 1 to determine if the statute applied to the issue in the client's case, you reviewed the scope section of the act. It provides that the act applies only to the sale of goods.

   How is the term *goods* defined? Assume the term is defined in the definitions section of the Commercial Code–Sales Act as "All things movable at the time of sale." The statute also requires the individual to be a "seller." How is *seller* defined in the definitions section of the act? Assume the term is defined as anyone who sells goods.

2. *The seller has reason to know the purpose for which the goods are required.* The seller must have reason to know of the purpose for which the buyer wants the goods. The statute does not require actual knowledge on the part of the seller. It provides, "has reason to know." You may need to refer to case law to determine what "reason to know" means or requires.

3. *The seller has reason to know the buyer is relying on the seller's skill or judgment.* This is usually established by the words or actions of the buyer that indicate to the seller the buyer's reliance on the seller's skill or judgment.

4. *The buyer must actually rely on the seller's skill or judgment in furnishing suitable goods.* This is required because the statute provides "the seller . . . has reason to know . . . that the buyer is relying."

5. *The seller must have known of the purpose for which the goods were required and the buyer's reliance on the seller's skill or judgment in furnishing the goods at the time the sale was taking place, not later.* This is required because the statute provides, "the seller at the time of contracting. . . ."

Be sure to complete both parts of step 2 before proceeding to step 3.

C. Step 3: Apply the Statute to the Legal Problem or Issue

After you have identified the elements, which are the conditions necessary for the statute to apply, apply the elements to the legal problem or issue raised by the client's fact situation. This entails applying or matching the facts of the client's case to the elements of the statute.

This may be accomplished in several ways. One way is to prepare a chart that lists the elements of the statute. Next to this, list the facts from the client's case that match or establish each of the elements or requirements of the statute. Another way is to prepare a narrative summary of the elements and how the facts of the case apply to match or establish the elements. The following examples illustrate the performance of step 3 in both chart and narrative summary format.

1. Chart Format

In the following example, a chart format is used.

> **FOR EXAMPLE** Tom goes to the local hardware store and informs the salesperson that he needs to grind metal with a power metal grinder. He tells the salesperson that he needs goggles to protect his eyes. The salesperson, after looking through his stock, hands Tom a pair of goggles and tells him, "These are what you need." Tom purchases the goggles, and when he uses them, a piece of metal pierces the lens of the goggle and damages Tom's eye.

Can Tom state a claim under the provisions of the implied warranty statute, § 2-2-315, presented in the previous example? How does the statute apply?

STATUTORY ELEMENTS	FACTS OF CLIENT'S CASE
1. Seller of goods	The seller was a salesperson at the local hardware store a seller within the meaning of the statute. The item sold, goggles, meets the definition of goods (the goggles are "things movable at the time of sale").
2. Has reason to know the buyer's	Tom explicitly told the seller the purpose for buying the goggles. purpose in purchasing the goods.
3. Has reason to know of buyer's	This is implied from Tom's conduct of allowing the seller to select the reliance on seller's judgment goods without any input from Tom.
4. Reliance by buyer on seller's	Tom relied on the salesperson's judgment. He indicated the purpose skill or judgment and accepted, without independent judgment or act, what the seller selected.
5. At the time of contracting	The seller knew at the time of the sale, not later, of Tom's purpose and reliance.

After you identify the elements of the statute and compare and match the facts of the client's case with the required elements of the statute, you can determine how the statute applies. In this example, you can conclude that the statute covers the conduct of the salesperson and that an implied warranty was created. All the required elements of the statute are established by the facts in Tom's case:

1. The salesperson was a seller within the meaning of the statute, and the item sold meets the definition of goods.

2. At the time of the sale, the buyer informed the seller of the specific purpose for which the goods were being purchased.

3. The seller knew of the buyer's reliance on his skill and judgment.

4. The buyer relied on the expertise and judgment of the seller.

5. The seller knew at the time of sale, not later.

2. Narrative Summary

In the following example, a narrative summary is used rather than a chart format.

> **FOR EXAMPLE** Section 56-6-1 of the Open Meetings Act provides that "all meetings of two or more members of any board . . . at which any public business is discussed or at which any action may be taken or is taken are declared to be public meetings open to the public." The section further provides:
>
> "a. Such meetings shall be held only after full and timely public notice.
>
> b. This section does not apply to chance meetings or social gatherings at which discussion of public business is not the central purpose."
>
> Ida and Dan are members of a three-person state board. They run into each other at a Christmas party and discuss board business.

Is this meeting an open meeting governed by § 56-6-1? The application of step 2 reveals the statute requires an open meeting when the following elements are present:

1. Two or more board members

2. Meet at other than a chance or social gathering where discussion of public business is not the central purpose

3. Public business is discussed or action may be or is taken

A narrative summary of the elements and the application of the statute to the facts illustrates step 3:

1. Two or more board members. This element is met. Both Dan and Ida are board members.

2. Meet at other than a chance or social gathering where discussion of public business is not the central purpose. It appears that this element is not met by the facts. This was a social gathering and also possibly a chance meeting. The gathering was a Christmas party. It does not appear that the discussion of public business was the central purpose. If it is discovered that the sole reason they went to the party was to discuss public business, the exclusion in subsection b of the statute probably does not apply and the meeting may be covered by the act.

3. Public business is discussed or action may be or is taken. This element is met. Public business was discussed.

After performing step 3, it appears that this was not a public meeting within the meaning of the act. Although the requirements of the first and third element are met (two or more board members met and discussed public business), the requirements of the second element are not.

When performing step 3, remember to match the client's facts with the required elements of a statute. When this is accomplished, you can determine how the statute applies. In the example concerning the purchase of goggles, all the required statutory elements were met by the facts of the client's case and an implied warranty was created. In the public meetings example, the facts did not meet the requirements of the second element of the statute, and therefore the meeting was not a public meeting within the meaning of the statute.

D. Summary of the Statutory Analysis Process

The three steps presented in this section are a useful approach to statutory analysis. These steps may be summarized as follows:

+ Step 1: Determine if the statute applies in any way to the legal problem or issue.
+ Step 2: Carefully read the statute and identify the required elements.
+ Step 3: Compare or match the required elements to the facts of the problem and determine how the statute applies.

In addition to this three-step approach, keep in mind other general considerations when analyzing statutory law. These considerations are presented in the following section.

VII. GENERAL CONSIDERATIONS

In addition to this three-step approach, always keep in mind two major considerations and guides when you are engaged in statutory analysis:

+ Legislative history
+ Canons of construction

These considerations come into play, and are of the greatest importance, when the meaning of the statute is unclear and the meaning has not been determined by a court.

When required to interpret a statute, a court will first look to the plain meaning of the language of the statute. This is called the **Plain Meaning Rule**, which mandates that a statute will be interpreted according to its plain meaning. Words will be interpreted according to their common meaning. The court will render an interpretation that reflects the plain meaning of the language and is consistent with the meaning of all other sections of the act. If the meaning is clear on its face, no additional inquiries concerning the meaning of a statute are allowed. If there is ambiguity in the meaning of a statutory section, the court will look to the legislative history of the statute and apply canons of construction.

When engaging in statutory analysis, you should be aware of and keep in mind the considerations that the court applies when interpreting the meaning of a statute. The reason for this is obvious. You want your interpretation of the meaning of a statute and how it will be applied to coincide with that of the court. Each of these considerations is addressed in this section.

A. Legislative History

To determine the meaning of a statute, a court may look to the legislative history of the statute to discover what the legislature intended it to mean. **Legislative history** is the record of the legislation during the enactment process before it became law. It is composed of committee reports, transcripts of hearings, statements of legislators concerning the legislation, and any other material published for legislative use in regard to the legislation.

Legislative history may be of assistance in several ways when interpreting a statute. The history may identify why an ambiguous term was used and what meaning the legislature intended, what the legislature intended the statute to accomplish, the general purpose of the legislation, and so on. Researching legislative history is discussed in Chapter 8.

B. Canons of Construction

Canons of construction are rules and guidelines the courts use when interpreting statutes. A fundamental rule of construction that determines when canons of construction are applied by a court is the Plain Meaning Rule. If the meaning is clear on its face, there is no room for interpretation, and a court will not apply the canons of construction.

The canons of construction are too numerous to be individually addressed in this text. Some of the more well known canons are presented here.

1. Expressio Unius

The entire Latin phrase is *expressio unius est exclusio alterius*, which translates as "the expression of one excludes all others." If the statute contains a list of what is covered, everything else is excluded.

> **FOR EXAMPLE** If a statute governing artists lists potters, glass blowers, painters, poets, writers, and sculptors, but does not include weavers, weavers are not covered by the statute. Only the occupations listed are covered; all other occupations are not covered.

Note, however, that a statute often is written to state that a list is not exclusive. When so written, this canon of construction does not apply, and the statute is not limited to the items listed.

> **FOR EXAMPLE** "A 'Building' as used in this statute means a structure on private or commercial property and includes *but is not limited to* a dwelling, an office of fixed location, ..."

2. Ejusdem Generis

This term means of the same genus or class. As a canon of construction, it means that whenever a statute contains a specific list followed by a general term, the general term is interpreted to be limited to other things of the same class or kind as those in the list.

> **FOR EXAMPLE** A statute regulating self-propelled vehicles lists "bicycles, tricycles, unicycles, and other devices." "Other devices" is limited to mean devices of the same class or kind as bicycles, tricycles, and unicycles. Motorized vehicles are not "other devices" within the meaning of the statute.

3. Pari Materia

The Latin translates as "on the same subject matter." This canon means that statutes dealing with the same subject should be interpreted consistently.

> **FOR EXAMPLE** A state's Fair Housing Act prohibits discrimination against an individual on the basis of "gender preference." The state's Fair Employment Act also uses the term *gender preference*. The term should be interpreted consistently in both statutes unless each statute has a definitions section that gives a clearly different meaning.

4. Last Antecedent Rule

Qualifying words and phrases apply to the words or phrase immediately preceding and do not extend to other more remote words or phrases.

> **FOR EXAMPLE** A DWI statute provides, "driver means every person who drives or is in actual physical control of a motor vehicle upon a highway. . . ." The phrase *upon a highway* modifies the term *motor vehicle*. It does not modify the term *drives*.

5. Intended Remedy

Statutes are to be interpreted in a manner that furthers the intended legislative remedy.

6. Entire Context

The words, phrases, and subsections of a statute are to be interpreted in the context of the entire statute.

7. Constitutionality

Statutes are assumed to be constitutional and should be construed in a manner that preserves their constitutionality, if possible.

8. Criminal Statutes

Criminal statutes are to be narrowly interpreted.

It is important to remember that, as with all matters involving case law, when a court interprets a statute, the principle of stare decisis applies. A court will follow the interpretation previously adopted unless the previous interpretation is overruled and a new interpretation is adopted.

VIII. KEY POINTS CHECKLIST: *Working with Statutes*

The following key points should be kept in mind when working with statutes:

+ When conducting research, identify the question or research terms as narrowly and concisely as possible.

+ *Always* update your research—check the pocket parts and supplements to make sure that the statute has not been changed or repealed.

+ When researching federal regulatory law, it is easier to use the *Code of Federal Regulations* rather than the *Federal Register*.

+ When reviewing a statute, do not limit your focus to a specific section. Remember, a section is one part of an entire act that usually contains several statutory sections. Read a section in the context of the entire act. Be sure you are familiar with all the sections of the act; there may be another section, such as a definitions section, that affects the interpretation of the statute you are reading.

+ When you find a statute that appears to apply, do not stop your research. In many instances, more than one statute or legislative act applies to a specific question or fact situation.

+ Read statutes carefully and slowly. Several readings may be necessary. You may have to make a chart or diagram of the various sections and subsections of a statute to gain an understanding of the operation of the statute.

+ All the words of a statute have meaning. If a word does not seem necessary or appears repetitive, you may have misread the statute. Read it again. Consult a secondary source that contains a discussion or interpretation of the statute.

+ Do not assume a word means what you think it does. Many statutory words are terms of art, loaded with meaning. Check the definitions section of the statute, case law, or a legal dictionary to ensure you give the correct meaning to a term.

✦ The plain meaning of a statute governs its statutory interpretation. If the meaning is clear, it is not subject to interpretation.

✦ If the statute is unclear or ambiguous, look to other sources for guidance, such as legislative history or applicable canons of construction. Are there court opinions that interpret the statute? Are there secondary sources, such as law review articles and encyclopedia sections, which discuss the statute?

IX. APPLICATION

The application of the principles of statutory research and analysis is illustrated in the following examples.

A. Chapter Hypothetical

In the hypothetical situation presented at the beginning of the chapter, Alan's assignment is to determine if Mrs. Jackson has a cause of action against Beauty Care Beauty Salon for breach of warranty under the sales provisions of the state's commercial code. The scope of his research has been narrowed greatly by the assignment. He needs to locate the sales provisions of the commercial code and then identify the statutes that address warranties. Alan can look to various terms in the index of the statutes such as *sales, commercial code, warranties,* and *contracts.* He may look to the popular name table for commercial code, or sales of goods. If he is conducting research electronically, he may begin with the terms "contracts, sales, warranties." His research turns up five sections of the state's Commercial Code Sales Act that may apply:

✦ Section 29-2-102 provides that the act applies to the sale of goods only; services are specifically excluded in the act.

✦ Section 29-2-105 defines goods as "all things which are movable at the time of the contract for sale."

✦ Section 29-2-313 provides that "an express warranty is created by a seller's affirmation of fact or promise that relates to the quality of the goods."

✦ Section 29-2-314 states that "a warranty that the goods shall be merchantable is implied in a contract for their sale if the seller is a merchant with respect to goods of that kind."

✦ Section 29-2-315 provides "Where the seller at the time of contracting has reason to know any particular purpose for which the goods are required and that the buyer is relying on the seller's skill or judgment to select or furnish suitable goods there is a warranty that the goods shall be fit for such purpose."

After conducting research on how to analyze statutory law, Alan applies the steps recommended in this chapter.

Step 1: Determine if the statute applies

When reviewing the statutes, Alan notes that § 29-2-102 provides that the Commercial Code Sales Act applies only to the sale of goods. If this transaction is not a sale of goods, the statute does not apply and the warranty provisions of the act do not apply.

Section 29-2-105 defines goods as "all things which are movable. . . ." This definition is of no help. Is a permanent hair treatment movable within the meaning of the act? In this case, both goods and services are involved. The service portion, the beautician applying the permanent, does not appear to be goods within the meaning of the statute but is clearly a service. The invoice, however, shows that Mrs. Jackson paid $20 for a perm kit. The perm kit is clearly goods under the act. The transaction is a mixed transaction involving both services and goods. Alan's review of the statute indicates that there is no section that addresses mixed transactions.

Because the statute does not give guidance concerning mixed transactions, Alan must refer to case law. In the case of *Elie v. American Saloon*, the court provides guidance for determining when a mixed transaction is a sale of goods covered by the Commercial Code Sales Act.

The court adopted what it called the predominant factor test. Under this test, the nature of the contract will be determined by what predominates. If the transaction involves primarily a service, it is a service contract and not covered by the act. If the transaction involves primarily the sale of goods, it is a sale of goods and is covered by the act. In its discussion of the application of the test, the court stated that the bill or receipt should be examined. If the largest portion of the bill applies to the cost of the goods sold, the transaction is predominately a sale of goods and the act applies. If the majority of the bill applies to the services provided, the transaction is a service transaction, not covered by the act.

Applying this test to Mrs. Jackson's facts, the bill clearly indicates that the largest portion of the transaction applied to the service of giving the permanent. Mrs. Jackson was charged $20 for the perm kit (goods) and $80 for the permanent (services). Alan concludes that under the predominant factor test, the service predominates the transaction, and it appears to be a service contract not covered by the act. After performing step 1, Alan concludes that there is no warranty relief available against Beauty Care Beauty Salon because the Commercial Code Sales Act does not apply to the transaction.

Alan's conclusion is based on his interpretation of the law. Because he is new at statutory analysis, he knows his analysis could be wrong. To be on the safe side, he continues his analysis to provide his supervisory attorney a complete review of the law. He proceeds to steps 2 and 3.

Step 2: Analyze the statute

If the act does apply, that is, if it is concluded that the transaction is a sale of goods rather than a service, which of the warranty remedies, if any, would be available to Mrs. Jackson? Alan carefully reads the statute and determines that the three warranties included in sections 29-2-313, 29-2-314, and 29-2-315 are the only possible warranties available in the act. Which of these would apply?

Clearly sections 29-2-313 and 29-2-315 would not apply. Section 29-2-313 requires some affirmation or promise by the seller relating to the quality of the goods. In Mrs. Jackson's case, there was no statement by the beautician, either oral or written, concerning the quality of the permanent. Section 29-2-315 also would not apply, as Mrs. Jackson did not communicate any particular purpose for which the goods were required. Also, there are no facts to indicate that she in any way relied on the beautician's expertise in selecting the permanent, although it could be argued that this is implicit in getting a permanent. To be on the safe side, Alan reviews the courts' interpretation of the term *particular purpose*. The case law indicates that the term refers to a unique and specific purpose for which the goods are required that is clearly and specifically communicated by the buyer to the seller. The facts in Mrs. Jackson's case show there was no specific communication.

Alan's last hope is section 29-2-314. He reads the statute and identifies the following as the elements of an implied warranty of merchantability:

1. The transaction must be a contract for the sale of goods.
2. The seller must be a merchant of those goods.

On the face of it, it appears that this statute would apply. Alan proceeds to step 3.

Step 3: Apply the statute to the legal problem or issue

Alan applies the statute to the problem through the use of a chart format.

STATUTORY ELEMENTS

1. Contract for sale of goods.

2. Seller is a *merchant* of those goods.

FACTS OF CLIENT'S CASE

Assuming that the predominant factor test did lead to the conclusion that this transaction is a sale of goods, not services, then this is a sale of goods transaction.

The act defines *merchant* as a person who deals in goods of the kind sold. If the beauty salon and the beautician routinely sell perm kits, then the seller is a "merchant." Here, the salon routinely sells perm kits when it charges for them as a part of a permanent. Therefore, the seller is a "merchant."

After performing this step, Alan can reach a conclusion on whether the statute applies and whether Mrs. Jackson has a cause of action for breach of warranty under section 29-2-314. Assuming that the transaction is a sale of goods which is doubtful in light of the conclusion reached in step 1, it appears that the statute would apply: there was a contract for the sale of goods by a merchant of those goods.

Under section 29-2-314, the seller warrants that the goods are merchantable, which is defined in case law as meaning, "fit for the ordinary purposes for which such goods are used." In Mrs. Jackson's case, the goods obviously were not fit for their ordinary purpose. Her hair broke off and changed color. If section 29-2-314 applies, Mrs. Jackson clearly has a claim for breach of warranty. Remember, however, the conclusion in step 1 was that section 29-2-314 does not apply because the transaction is probably a sale of a service, not goods.

Note: Alan went through steps 2 and 3 because he is new at statutory analysis and wanted to make sure his analysis was correct. An experienced researcher would stop at step 1.

B. Chapter 1 Hypothetical *Reins v. Stewart*

Research—Locate the Statute

Vanessa focuses on civil battery as a cause of action under state law. Her first step is to research the state statutes to determine if the state legislature has passed a law defining civil battery. She starts here because statutory law is the primary authority the court will first look to when deciding the question. Also, if there is statutory law, the annotations to the statute may include a reference to a court opinion that addresses the liability of bystanders who encourage the perpetrator of a battery.

Based upon her training and paralegal education, Vanessa knows that the applicable area of civil law is tort and that battery is often categorized under "assault and battery." Vanessa would start her search by identifying all the possible terms that the statute may be listed under such as *torts, assault, battery, civil action,* and *bystanders.* After she identifies the terms, she would consult the index of the state statutes to determine if there is any legislative act governing the question. If she conducted an electronic search using an electronic database such as Westlaw, she would locate the state statute database and search, using key terms such as "assault and battery."

As discussed in the hypothetical in Chapter 1, there is no statute in Vanessa's state addressing civil assault or battery and the matter is governed by the case law. One of the more difficult problems is to determine when to quit looking for a statute. As discussed in Chapter 1, not all matters are governed by statutory law; some matters are governed by case law. How does Vanessa know when to quit looking for the statutory law? After she has conducted her research using all the possible terms the statute may be categorized under, it's time to look to another source, such as case law. Therefore, to avoid missing the statute because you failed to look under the proper term, it is critical that all the possible terms be identified at the outset.

At this point Vanessa looks to case law, the next major source of primary authority. When she finds a case that applies, if there is statutory law that governs the issue (and Vanessa missed it), the court will likely refer to the applicable statute in the opinion. Vanessa can then go back and refer to the statute. How Vanessa locates the applicable case law is discussed in the Application section of Chapter 5.

C. Chapter 2 Hypothetical *United States v. Canter*

Research—Locate the Statute

In this case, the location of the applicable statute is fairly simple because the cause of action and area of law are identified in the assignment and included in the issue. The area of law is the federal criminal law and the cause of action is bank robbery with a dangerous weapon. Therefore, the research task is to locate the federal criminal law governing bank robbery.

As discussed earlier in the chapter, federal laws are published in the *United States Code*. A researcher should use the *United States Code Annotated* or the *United States Code Service* when looking for federal law because both of these publications are annotated— they include with each statute references to other sources that may be helpful in understanding how the statute applies and notes to court cases that have interpreted the statute.

The researcher, Dustin in the hypothetical, could locate the statute by referring to the general index under the terms *Robbery* or *Bank Robbery* or look under the general category of Criminal Law and the subcategory Bank Robbery. Using any of these terms, he will be led to the bank robbery statute, 18 USC § 2113.

Another way to locate the law is to refer to the table of contents. Because in the hypothetical Dustin knows that the area of law is criminal law, he could go directly to the criminal law volume of the *United States Code Annotated* or the *United States Code Service* and scan down the list of statutory sections until he locates the robbery sections. He would then go directly to the bank robbery statute.

If Dustin conducts the search using an electronic database such as Westlaw, he could locate the bank robbery statute by using the search terms "bank robbery."

Analyze the Statute

An analysis of the statute is performed in the Application section of Chapter 2. The result of that analysis after applying the statutory elements to the facts of Mr. Canter's case is clearly that a bank robbery took place. The question that is not answered is whether the robbery took place with a "dangerous weapon." Is the wooden replica of a handgun Mr. Canter used a dangerous weapon within the meaning of the statute? This question cannot be answered by simply applying the facts of Mr. Canter's case to the statute. Further research must be conducted to determine how the courts have defined dangerous weapon. Case law must be consulted. The Application section of Chapter 5 discusses how to locate the case law that answers this question.

SUMMARY

This chapter focused on how to research and analyze enacted law and court rules. The principles presented in the chapter apply to the research and analysis of constitutions, statutory law, administrative law, and court rules.

An increasingly expanding source of law in the United States is statutory law. This body of law is assuming a greater role because many matters once covered by the case law are now addressed by state and federal legislative bodies. As a result of this growth, researchers more frequently engage in analyzing legal problems and issues governed by statutory law.

Statutory research is the process of finding the statutory law that applies to a problem. Most federal and state laws are organized according to topic (codified) and published with annotations. The beginning step of all research, including statutory research, is to identify what you are looking for as precisely and narrowly as possible. Most statutes are located through the use of the general index, although they also may be found through the use of the table of contents or the popular name table.

Administrative law is the body of law that results from the rules and regulations of administrative agencies and the court opinions interpreting them. The main research source for locating federal administrative law is the *Code of Federal Regulations*. Court rules regulate the conduct of matters brought before the court.

The analysis of enacted law and court rules is the process of determining if a law applies, how it applies, and the effect of that application. For the sake of clarity, the chapter discussion and examples focus upon the analysis of laws passed by legislative bodies, statutory law. A prerequisite to analyzing a law is a familiarity with the parts or components of the law.

The most efficient way to address a problem involving a statute is to have a process for or an approach to statutory analysis. This chapter presents a three-step approach.

The first step is to determine whether the statute governs the situation in any way. This step involves locating all the possible statutes that may apply and then deciding which ones apply to the facts raised by the legal problem.

The second step is to carefully read the statute and identify what is required for the statute to apply. These requirements are usually referred to as the elements of the statute. A careful analysis may require several readings of the statute and reference to interpretative sources, such as court opinions, or secondary sources, such as treatises and law review articles.

The third step is to apply the elements to the facts of the legal problem. This involves matching the elements of the statute to the facts of the case and determining how the statute applies.

When engaging in statutory analysis, there are considerations and guidelines that should be kept in mind. Most of these come into play when the meaning of a statute is unclear or ambiguous. In addition to court opinions, which give guidance to the interpretation of a statute, legislative history and canons of construction may be consulted. Legislative history is composed of all the legislative material and records concerning a statute before it became law. Canons of construction are guidelines developed by courts for use in interpreting ambiguous statutes. These sources should not be used if the meaning of the statute is clear on its face.

The ease with which you are able to locate and analyze statutes increases with practice. The more you read and analyze statutes, the easier it becomes. The exercises at the end of this chapter may prove helpful in this regard.

CHAPTER REFERENCES

INTERNET RESOURCES

<http://www.law.cornell.edu>

> Through this site maintained by Cornell Law School, you may obtain the *Code of Federal Regulations*, the Federal Rules of Civil Procedure, and other court rules.

<http://www.law.cornell.edu/uscode/>

> The *United States Code* is also available at this site.

<http://www.findlaw.com/>

> FindLaw is an excellent source to locate state statutes. Just click on the Search Cases & Codes tab, then click on the state you are searching for. Court rules and some state administrative regulations may be found at this site.

<http://www.lawsonline.com>

> Links to state and federal law sources.

<http://www.access.gpo.gov>

> This Government Printing Office site provides access to the *United States Code*, the *Code of Federal Regulations*, the *Federal Register* and other documents.

<http://www.house.gov/>

> United States House of Representatives home page.

<http://www.senate.gov/>

> United States Senate home page.

<http://www.loc.gov/>

> Site for the Library of Congress.

 For additional materials, please go to the CD accompanying this book

 For additional resources, visit our Web site at www.paralegal.delmar.cengage.com

STATUTORY CITATION

The *Bluebook* and *ALWD Citation Manual* rules governing statutory citation are discussed in Chapter 11. If the document you are working on may be filed in a court, such as a state supreme court, check the court rules for any citation rule that may differ from the *Bluebook* or the *ALWD*. Following are some examples of federal and state citations:

A. Constitutions

U.S. Const. art. IV, § 3
N.M. Const. art. IV § 1

B. Federal Citation

18 U.S.C. § 1112 (1994)	*United States Code*
18 U.S.C.A. § 1112 (West 1996)	*United States Code Annotated*
18 U.S.C.S. § 1112 (Lawyers Co-op. 1994)	*United States Code Service*

C. State Statutes

Ind. Code Ann. § 26-1-2-315 (Michie 1992)
Cal. Com. Code § 2314 (West 1964)
Colo. Rev. Stat. Ann. § 19-2-919 (West 1999)

D. Administrative Law

7 C.F.R. pt. 215 (2001)
66 Fed. Reg. 34636 (2001)

E. Court Rules

The rules are cited according to *Bluebook* format. See Chapter 11, Rules of Evidence and Procedure, for additional information on citing rules.
Fed. R. Civ. P. 4
Fed. R. Crim. P. 18

EXERCISES

Additional exercises are located on the Student CD-ROM accompanying the text and Online Companion.

ASSIGNMENT 1

Mary and Tom have lived together for eight years in the state, but they have never married. They are buying a home together and share a checking and savings account. Do the laws of your state recognize common law marriage? If so, do Tom and Mary have a common law marriage?

ASSIGNMENT 2

Irene has good credit and a good job. She believes that a landlord refused to rent her an apartment because she is a single woman. Refer to either the USCA or the USCS and identify the federal law that governs this.

ASSIGNMENT 3

Refer to the USCA. What is the definition of a digital audio recording device under the copyright law?

ASSIGNMENT 4

Refer to the USCS. Cite the title and section of the code that addresses equal opportunity in contract solicitation, housing, and community development by the Federal Home Loan Mortgage Corporation.

ASSIGNMENT 5

What is the authorized term of imprisonment for a Class A felony under title 18 of the *United States Code?* Cite the title and section.

ASSIGNMENT 6

Refer to the Fifth Amendment to the U.S. Constitution in the USCA. Cite a 1967 U.S. Supreme Court decision addressing the applicability of the privilege against self incrimination in the case of juveniles.

ASSIGNMENT 7

Look up a statute in your state and identify the component parts. You may find it on the Web through

<http://www.findlaw.com/> or look up the statute at a local law or public library (most public libraries have the state statutes).

ASSIGNMENT 8

In the following exercises, a statute is presented followed by questions concerning the statute.

Statute: Criminal code section 20-4-102, Arson. A person who knowingly sets fire to, burns, causes to be burned, or by use of any explosive, damages or destroys, or causes to be damaged or destroyed, any property of another without his consent commits arson.

Questions

A. What are the required elements of arson?

B. Tom breaks into a neighbor's barn, sets off 20 sticks of dynamite, and blows up the barn. The barn does not catch fire, but it is blown to small bits and completely destroyed. Has Tom committed arson? Why?

C. Lois breaks into a house intending to steal cash and jewelry. She lights a match to locate a safe. She drops the match; it falls in a trash can and the house catches fire. Has Lois committed arson? Why?

D. Dai's Diner is losing money and about to go out of business. Dai and Steve own the building where the diner is located. One evening Dai sets the building on fire to collect the insurance on the building. Has Dai committed arson? Why?

ASSIGNMENT 9

Answer the questions in Assignment 8 using your state law governing arson.

ASSIGNMENT 10

What, if any, federal regulation applies to environmental impact statements for activities in Antarctica?

ASSIGNMENT 11

Refer to the *Federal Register* for 2001. On what page of the *Federal Register* is the Drug Enforcement Administration's proposed rule for schedules of controlled substances involving electronic commerce?

ASSIGNMENT 12

Statute: Section 30-1-6 Nuncupative wills.

A. A nuncupative will may be made only by a person in imminent peril of death and shall be valid only if the testator died as a result of the impending peril, and must be:

1. Declared to be his last will by the testator before two disinterested witnesses;

2. Reduced to writing by or under the direction of one of the witnesses within 30 days after such declaration; and

3. Submitted for probate within 6 months after the death of the testator.

B. The nuncupative will may dispose of personal property only and to an aggregate value not exceeding $1000.

C. A nuncupative will does not revoke an existing written will. Such written will is changed only to the extent necessary to give effect to the nuncupative will.

Note: A nuncupative is an oral will, a will that is not written.

Questions

A. What type of wills does this statute apply to?

B. What requirements must be met for a nuncupative will to be valid? That is, what are the elements?

C. Mr. Lang, on his death bed, writes his will on a piece of note paper, signs it, and delivers it to his sister for safekeeping. Does the statute govern the validity of this will?

D. Larry, on his death bed, declares that it is his will and that all his property should go to his girlfriend Beth. There are three witnesses present: Beth, Larry's sister Mary, and the next-door neighbor, Tom. Tom is in an adjoining room. The door to the adjoining room is open. Tom hears what Larry is saying. Assume for this example that the will is reduced to writing within 30 days and submitted for probate within 6 months.

1. Is this a valid will under this statute? What additional information may be necessary?

2. Assume this is a valid will, and Tom had a previous valid written will. What impact does the nuncupative will have on the written will? What is disposed of by the nuncupative will?

ASSIGNMENT 13

Statute: The following statute is a section of the Commercial Code Sales Act adopted by the state legislature.

Section 2-201. Statute of Frauds.

A contract for the sale of goods for the price of $500 or more is not enforceable by way of action or defense unless there is some writing sufficient to indicate that a contract for sale has been made between the parties and signed by the party against whom enforcement is sought or by the party's authorized agent or broker. A writing is not insufficient because it omits or incorrectly states a term agreed upon, but the contract is not enforceable under this paragraph beyond the quantity of goods shown in such writing.

Assume that the act applies to the sale of goods. Goods are defined in § 2-100 as "those things movable" and do not include real property.

Questions

A. Does the statute apply to the lease of goods?

B. What are the required elements of the statute? In other words, for a contract for the sale of goods of $500 or more to be enforceable, what is required?

C. Mary orally contracts to buy 10 car tires at $70 each. The seller prepares a contract and gives it to Mary. Neither party signs the contract.

1. Who can enforce the contract under the provisions of the statute?

2. The contract is signed by Mary only. Who can enforce the contract?

3. Both parties sign the contract, and the written contract incorrectly provides for nine tires at $70 each. Is the contract enforceable under the statute? If so, to what extent?

4. Both parties sign the contract and it reads 15 tires at $70 each. Is the contract enforceable under the statute? If so, to what extent?

5. There is no written contract. The seller hands Mary a slip of paper upon which he has written "This is to confirm our oral agreement." He and Mary both sign the paper. Is there an enforceable contract under the provisions of the statute? If so, to what extent?

ASSIGNMENT 14

Statute: Section 35-1-4 Privileged Communications— Husband and Wife

In all actions, husband and wife may testify for or against each other, provided that neither may testify as to any communication or admission made by either of them to the other during the marriage, except in actions:

a. between such husband and wife, and,

b. where the custody, support, health or welfare of their children or children in either spouse's custody or control is directly in issue.

Questions

A. Prepare an outline of the statutory elements.

B. When can a husband or wife testify against each other? When are they prohibited from testifying against each other?

C. Husband, while driving under the influence of alcohol, ran a stop sign and his vehicle collided with a vehicle driven by Mr. Smith. The Husband's spouse (Wife) and two children were passengers in the car. The day after the wreck Husband told Wife that he knew that he ran the stop sign because he was drunk. Mr. Smith sues Husband for negligence. When answering the following questions identify any additional information that may be necessary to answer the question.

1. Can Wife be compelled to testify concerning her conversation with Husband? Why or why not?

2. Can Wife voluntarily testify concerning the conversation? Why or why not?

3. If Husband and Wife are legally separated, can Wife voluntarily testify concerning the conversation? Why or why not?

4. Is the conversation admissible if they are divorced at the time of the lawsuit? Why or why not?

5. Husband and Wife have lived together as husband and wife for the past 20 years. They have never been formally married. Can Wife testify against Husband concerning the conversation? Why or why not?

6. Is the conversation admissible in a divorce action between Husband and Wife? Why or why not?

CHAPTER 5

Case Law—Research and Briefing

Outline

Learning Objectives

After completing this chapter, you should understand:

✦ The role and importance of court opinions

✦ The elements of a court opinion

✦ How to find a court opinion

✦ The role and importance of a case brief

✦ The elements of a case brief

✦ How to brief a case

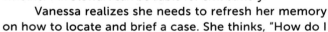

Refer to the *Reins v. Stewart* hypothetical presented in Chapter 1. Now that Vanessa has identified the key facts and issue in the case (see the Application sections of Chapters 2 and 3), her next task is to locate and brief a case that answers the question of whether Mr. Stewart can be liable for civil battery.

Vanessa realizes she needs to refresh her memory on how to locate and brief a case. She thinks, "How do I

find a case that supports our position? How do I brief the case?" (The case Vanessa located is presented in the Court Opinion—Elements section of this chapter, Exhibit 5–1. How she located and briefed it is presented in the Application section of this chapter.)

I. INTRODUCTION

The focus of this chapter is on court opinions and addresses the same questions Vanessa faced when undertaking her assignment—that is, what are the elements of court opinions, where are they published, how do you find them, and how do you brief them. Throughout this chapter, a court opinion will be referred to as a *court case* and a brief of a court opinion will be referred to as a *case brief*. Chapter 6 discusses case law analysis. Case law analysis is the process you engage in to determine if a court opinion governs or applies to a client's case, that is, if a case is "on point."

II. COURT OPINIONS—IN GENERAL

As discussed in Chapter 1, the two major sources of law are enacted law (constitutions; laws enacted by legislative bodies, including ordinances; and so on) and the common law. **Case law** is the body of law on a particular subject created by the court opinions and is sometimes referred to as common law or judge-made law. The case law is found in the written opinions of the courts.

Common law consists of the law made by courts when they interpret existing law or create new law. It is composed of the legal rules, doctrines, and principles adopted by the courts. Courts often announce rules of law when interpreting statutory or constitutional provisions or create new law when there is no statutory or constitutional law governing a legal dispute.

> **FOR EXAMPLE** ***Statutory Interpretation:*** A statute uses the term *publication* but fails to define it. The court, addressing the issue of what constitutes publication, announces a rule of law that the term *publication* as used in the statute means "communication to a third party."
>
> ***Creating Law:*** A state has not enacted legislation recognizing strict liability as a cause of action in tort. The highest court in the state, in a case before it, announces a rule of law adopting strict liability as a cause of action in the state.

A **court opinion** is the court's written statement explaining its decision in a case. It is the court's resolution of the legal dispute before the court and the reasons in support of its resolution. The court opinion usually includes a statement of facts, points of law, and rationale.

Often the terms *court opinion*, *case*, and *decision* are used interchangeably to refer to a court's resolution of an issue or a decision in a dispute. In this chapter, the terms *court opinion* and *case* are used to refer to the written opinion of a court.

III. COURT OPINIONS—IMPORTANCE

Of the two major sources of law, enacted law and case law, case law constitutes the largest body of law, far larger in volume than constitutional or statutory law. It is essential to acquire a general familiarity with this body of law because it represents such a large portion of the law. Also, you must study case law because so many areas of law are governed by case law.

Reading and analyzing court opinions and studying case law are important for numerous reasons. Overall, the major reasons are the following:

✦ *To learn the case law*—Much of the law is court-made. To determine the elements of a cause of action for a court-made law, you must refer to case law. Case law may govern your client's fact situation, and to determine what law applies and the probable outcome, you must analyze case law.

> **FOR EXAMPLE** In most states, the cause of action for civil battery is a creation of case law, not statutory law. To identify the elements necessary to state a battery claim, the case law must be researched.

✦ *To interpret constitutional or statutory law*—Court opinions often announce rules of law that govern how a statutory or constitutional term or provision is interpreted or applied. Therefore, you must consult case law to understand how to interpret and apply statutes and constitutional provisions.

> **FOR EXAMPLE** The U.S. Supreme Court has issued many opinions on the types of speech protected by the First Amendment. To determine if an individual who burns a state flag in front of the state capital is protected by the First Amendment's freedom of speech provisions, Supreme Court opinions interpreting freedom of speech must be consulted.

✦ *To understand the litigation process*—Court opinions often address legal questions that arise in the context of the litigation process—either before, during, or after trial. Court opinions give insight into the process by explaining what conduct is appropriate, which arguments are successful, where errors are made, how procedural rules apply, how trials and motion hearings should proceed, and so on.

✦ *To gain insight into legal analysis*—In a court opinion, the court often analyzes the law. The court discusses what law applies, how it applies, the reasons for its application, and how the reasons operate to govern the application of the law to the facts of the case. By studying court opinions, you learn how to assemble a legal argument, how to determine if a law applies, and how to support a legal argument.

✦ *To develop legal writing skills*—Judges are usually experienced in legal writing, and most opinions are well written. You may read opinions with an eye to how sentences and paragraphs are structured, how case law and statutory law are referred to and incorporated into legal writing, and how transitions are accomplished. If you have a problem putting some aspect of your research into writing, look at an opinion to see how a court handled a similar matter.

> **FOR EXAMPLE** You are preparing a research memorandum. You are unsure about how to introduce the persuasive precedent in your memorandum. By reading a court opinion where the court relied on persuasive precedent, you can study the language the court used to introduce the persuasive precedent and use the court's language as a guide after which to model your introduction. For example, in *Smith v. Jones,* the court stated, "There is no case law in this jurisdiction interpreting the term 'publication' as used in § 55-5-67A. The state of Texas, however, has an identical statute, and the Supreme Court of Texas, in the case of *Frank v. Inex,* interpreted 'publication' to mean communication to a third party." You can use this language as a guide in your introduction of persuasive precedent.

For the preceding reasons and many others, the study of case law is important. The skill of being able to correctly locate, analyze, and apply case law is essential to legal research and analysis.

IV. COURT OPINIONS—ELEMENTS

A. In General

The first requirement in properly analyzing a court opinion is to be familiar with the elements of an opinion. A court opinion usually includes some or all of the following components:

- The facts that gave rise to the legal dispute before the court.
- The procedural history and posture of the case—that is, what happened in the lower court or courts, who appealed the decision, and why.
- The issue or issues addressed and resolved by the court.
- The rule of law that governs the dispute.
- The application of the rule of law to the facts—in other words, the holding.
- The reason or reasons supporting the court's application of the rule of law to the facts, that is, why the court decided as it did.
- The relief granted or denied. For example, "The judgment of the trial court is upheld."

B. Elements of a Reported Case

West, the publisher of the regional reporters and most of the federal reporters, follows a uniform format when publishing court opinions. A similar format is followed by LexisNexis in its publication *Supreme Court Reports: Lawyers' Edition*. Because the majority of court opinions are published by West, an example of an opinion published by West, is presented in Exhibit 5–1. The case, *Rael v. Cadena*, is published in the *New Mexico Reports* and the *Pacific Reporter*. Note that the components of the case are identified in the left margin next to each section of the opinion. These components are summarized in the following text.

1. Citation

The citation refers to the volume number, the page number, and the name of the reporter where the case may be found. The citation for *Rael v. Cadena* is 93 N.M. 684, 604 P.2d 822. That means the printed opinion of this case is published and may be found in two reporters: volume 93 of the *New Mexico Reports* on page 684, and volume 604 of the *Pacific Reporter*, Second Series, on page 822. (See CITATION in Exhibit 5–1.) When an opinion may be found in more than one set of books, the citations are referred to as **parallel citations**.

Court decisions are increasingly available through court Web sites or other publications such as public domain citations (also referred to as neutral citations or vendor neutral citations). Therefore, an additional citation number may be present.

FOR EXAMPLE *State v. Foster*, 1998-NMCA-163, 126 N.M. 177, 976 P.2d 852. 1998-NMCA-163 is the public domain citation. The publication year is 1998. NMCA is the court—the New Mexico Court of Appeals. The last number, 163, is the case number. In this example there are three parallel citations.

The format for neutral citations is discussed in greater detail in Chapter 11, subsection II A 9, Neutral/Public Domain Citations.

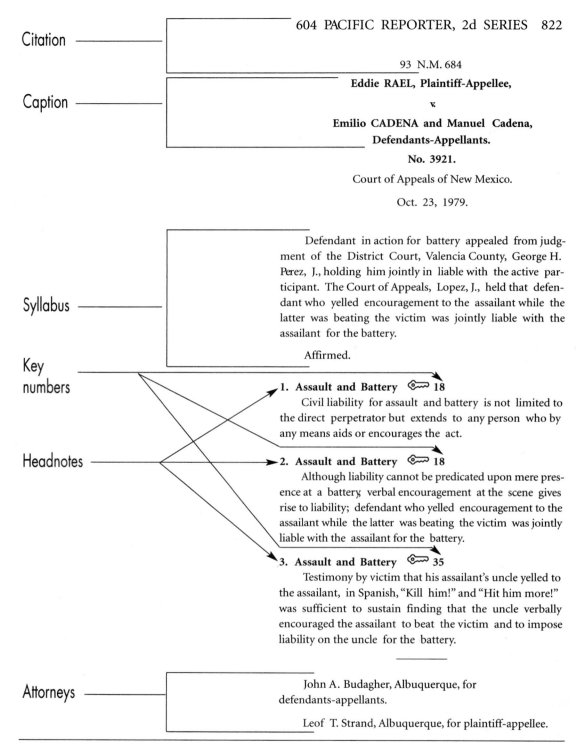

Exhibit 5–1
Court Opinion—*Rael v. Cadena.*
West Publishing, 604 Pacific Reporter 2d 822, (1979). Used with permission of Thomson Reuters/West.

Judge ————————

Body of
the
opinion

OPINION

LOPEZ, Judge.

Defendant Emilio Cadena, a non-active participant in the battery of plaintiff Eddie Rael, appeals the judgment of the trial court finding him, along with the active participant, jointly and severally liable for the battery. We affirm.

The issue on appeal is whether a person present at a battery who verbally encourages the assailant, but does not physically assist him, is civilly liable for the battery.

On a visit in Emilio Cadena's home, Eddie Rael was severely beaten on the head and torso by Emilio's nephew, Manuel Cadena. As a result of the beating, he suffered a fractured rib and was hospitalized. Eddie Rael testified that once the attack had started, Emilio yelled to Manuel in Spanish, "Kill him!" and "Hit him more!" The trial court sitting without a jury found that Emilio encouraged Manuel while Manuel was beating Eddie. Based on this finding, the court held the Cadenas jointly and severally liable for the battery.

Emilio urges that in order for the trial court to have held him jointly liable for the battery, it had to find either that he and Manuel acted in concert, or that Manuel beat and injured Eddie as a result of Emilio's encouragement. This is a misstatement of the law.

[1] This is an issue of first impression in New Mexico. It is clear, however, that in the United States, civil liability for assault and battery is not limited to the direct perpetrator, but extends to any person who by any means aids or encourages the act. *Hargis v. Herrine,* 230 Ark. 502, 323 S.W.2d 917 (1959); *Ayer v. Robinson,* 163 Cal. App.2d 424, 329 P.2d 546 (1958); *Guilbeau v. Guilbeau,* 326 So.2d 654 (La.App.1976); *Duke v. Feldman,* 245 Md. 454, 226 A.2d 345 (1967); *Brink v. Purnell,* 162 Mich. 147, 127 N.W. 322 (1910); 6 Am.Jur.2d *Assault and Battery* § 128 (1963); 6A C.J.S. *Assault and Battery* § 11 (1975); Annot., 72 A.L.R.2d 1229 (1960). According to the Restatement:

[f]or harm resulting to a third person from the tortious conduct of another, one is subject to liability if he

* * * * * *

(b) knows that the other's conduct constitutes a breach of duty and gives substantial assistance or encouragement to the other so to conduct himself. * * *

Restatement (Second) of Torts § 876 (1979).

[2] Although liability cannot be predicated upon mere presence at a battery, *Duke, supra;* 6 Am.Jur., *supra,* verbal encouragement at the scene gives rise to liability. *Hargis, supra; Ayer, supra; Brink, supra.*

[A] person may be held liable for the tort of assault and battery if he *encouraged* or incited *by words* the act of the direct perpetrator. * * * (Emphasis added.)

6 Am.Jur., *supra* at 108. Because he yelled encouragement to his nephew while the latter was beating Eddie Rael, Emilio Cadena is jointly liable with his nephew for the battery.

[3] Contradictory evidence was offered as to whether Emilio Cadena did yell anything during the beating. Eddie Rael claimed that Emilio urged Manuel to beat him; Emilio denied that he said anything; and Manuel testified that he never heard Emilio. However, the trial court found that Emilio did verbally encourage Manuel to beat Eddie. Although the evidence was in conflict, the court could conclude from the testimony of Eddie Rael that Emilio Cadena verbally encouraged his nephew to attack. This testimony, if believed, is substantial evidence to support the trial court's finding. It is not the function of the appellate court to weigh the evidence or its credibility, or to substitute its judgment for that of the trial court. So long as the findings are supported by substantial evidence, they will stand. *Getz v. Equitable Life Assur. Soc. of U.S.,* 90 N.M. 195, 561 P.2d 468, *cert. denied,* 434 U.S. 834, 98 S.Ct. 121, 54 L.Ed.2d 95 (1977).

The judgment of the trial court is affirmed.

IT IS SO ORDERED.

SUTIN and ANDREWS, JJ., concur.

Exhibit 5–1
Continued

2. Caption

The caption includes the names of the **parties** to the lawsuit and their court status. Eddie Rael was the plaintiff at the trial court level, and he is the appellee on appeal. (The appellee is the person against whom the appeal is filed, the person who won at the trial court level.) Emilio Cadena was the defendant at the trial court level and is the appellant on appeal. (The appellant is the person who lost at the trial court level and who filed the appeal.) Manuel Cadena is listed as a defendant-appellant, but he is not involved in the appeal. The caption of the case used on appeal is usually the same as the caption used in the trial court. The caption of the case in the trial court includes both Cadenas as defendants, and therefore, the caption on appeal is the same. Note that the plaintiff and defendant's last names are printed in all capitals. (See CAPTION in Exhibit 5–1.) When referring to or citing the case, only the names in all capitals are used.

> **FOR EXAMPLE** When citing this case, the citation should read: *Rael v. Cadena,* 93 N.M. 684, 604 P. 2d 822 (Ct. App. 1979).

Note that below the caption is "No. 3921." This is the docket number of the case assigned by the court of appeals. Below the docket number is the name of the court that decided the case and the date of the decision. This is indicated in the citation as (Ct. App. 1979). If the decision had been rendered by the highest court in the jurisdiction, such as the supreme court of New Mexico, only the year of the decision would appear in the parentheses: (1979). If the citation does not include a state reporter citation, a reference to the state is included in the parentheses.

> **FOR EXAMPLE** *Smith v. Jones,* 292 S.W.2d 425 (Tex. 1980).

3. Syllabus

The syllabus is a brief summary of the opinion. It is written by West, not the court, and cannot be relied upon as the holding of the court. It is presented as a useful aid in providing the reader with a brief overview of the opinion. (See SYLLABUS in Exhibit 5–1.)

4. Headnotes

The headnotes are summaries of the points of law discussed in the case. Headnotes follow in sequential order the relevant paragraphs of the opinion. The number to the left of the headnote corresponds to the bracketed number in the body of the opinion. (See HEADNOTES in Exhibit 5–1.)

> **FOR EXAMPLE** In *Rael v. Cadena,* headnote 1 contains a summary of the point of law discussed in the body of the opinion between [1] and [2]. Headnote 2 is a summary of the point of law discussed in the opinion between [2] and [3]. Headnote 3 is a summary of the law discussed in the opinion between [3] and the end of the opinion.

Note: Headnotes are prepared by West. They are included for the convenience of individuals researching the case and are useful in providing a quick overview of the law and legal principles addressed in the opinion. They are not the opinion of the court and have no authority of law. Any reference to or quote from an opinion must be taken from the opinion itself, not from the headnotes.

5. Key Numbers

A few words in bold print next to the headnote number indicate the area of law addressed in the headnote. Next to this bold print description of the area of law is a small key symbol and a number. (See KEY NUMBERS in Exhibit 5–1.) West has divided all areas of U.S. law into various topics and subtopics. Each area is identified by a topic name (the bold print), and each specific topic or subtopic is assigned a key number. West publishes separate volumes called digests that contain summaries of court opinions organized by topic and subtopic.

FOR EXAMPLE Next to headnote 1 in *Rael v. Cadena* is "Assault and Battery," followed by a key symbol and the number 18. The key symbol and the number 18 refer to a specific subtopic of assault and battery. The subject of this subtopic can be determined by consulting the index to "Assault and Battery" in the digest (the use of a digest is discussed in Chapter 7). A reference to the digest reveals that key number 18 is the specific subtopic of assault and battery concerning the liability of persons who aid or encourage an assault or battery. In the body of the opinion between [1] and [2], and between [2] and [3], this is the area of assault and battery law discussed. If you want to read other court opinions in which liability for battery was based upon the conduct of aiding or encouraging a batterer at the scene of a battery, refer to the volume of the digest containing the topic "Assault and Battery." Look to the subtopic key number 18. Under that key number is a summary of all court opinions that have addressed this subtopic and the citations of those opinions.

Through this system you have easy access to all court opinions dealing with the question you are considering. The key number system is an invaluable research tool.

6. Attorneys

This section provides the names and cities of the attorneys in the case and the parties they represent. (See ATTORNEYS in Exhibit 5–1.)

7. Judge

At the beginning of the opinion is the name of the judge who wrote it. (See JUDGE in Exhibit 5–1.)

8. Body of the Opinion

The body of the opinion usually includes the facts of the case, the prior proceedings, the issue or issues addressed by the court, the rule of law governing the dispute, the holding, the reasoning in support of the holding, and the relief granted. (See BODY OF THE OPINION in Exhibit 5–1.) There are no hard-and-fast rules dictating what must be contained in a court opinion, and often one or more of the elements listed here may be missing. Each of the elements of the body are discussed separately here:

a. Facts

Opinions usually include the facts that gave rise to the legal dispute. Often the opinion includes few facts or more facts than appear relevant to the matter decided.

b. Prior Proceedings

In this part of the opinion, the court presents a summary of what happened in the lower court and who appealed. This may be a brief summary, as in *Rael v. Cadena*, or it may be extensive and detailed.

c. Issue or Issues

The issue is the legal question addressed by the court in the opinion. The court may present the issue narrowly in the context of the facts.

FOR EXAMPLE Under New Mexico tort law, does a battery occur when an individual, present at a battery, verbally encourages the assailant by yelling "Kill him!" and "Hit him more!", but does not in any other way participate in the battery?

Or the court may state the issue broadly, merely phrasing the issue in the context of the area of law.

> **FOR EXAMPLE** Did the defendant commit a civil battery?

In many instances, a case addresses more than one legal issue. Also, the court may not present a statement of the issue or issues at all, and it may be difficult to determine what they are.

Identifying and understanding the issue is the most important task of reading an opinion. If the issue is not understood, the rule of law applied by the court may not be understood, and the opinion consequently may be misanalyzed and misapplied.

d. Rule of Law

The rule of law governs the issue. It may be a statutory or constitutional provision or a case law doctrine, rule, principle, and so on. In *Rael v. Cadena*, case law governs the law of civil assault and battery.

e. Holding

The holding is the court's application of the rule of law to the facts of the case. It is the court's answer to the issue(s) in the case. The holding is usually presented immediately after the rule of law in the opinion or after the reasoning at the end of the opinion.

f. Reasoning

The reasoning is the court's explanation of how or why the rule of law applies to the dispute. On occasion, the reasoning is difficult to follow. Often it is helpful to read the holding first and determine how the court ruled, and then read the reasoning. By first understanding the decision, you may be better able to understand the reasoning in support of the decision.

g. Disposition/Relief Granted

The relief granted is usually a one-sentence statement by the court that includes the order of the court as a result of the holding.

> **FOR EXAMPLE** In *Rael v. Cadena*, next to the last sentence where the court states, "The judgment of the trial court is affirmed," the court presents the relief granted.

A court has several options when granting relief:

- ✦ It may agree with the trial court and *affirm* the trial court's decision.
- ✦ It may disagree with the trial court and *reverse* the trial court's decision. If it reverses the decision, it will *remand*, that is, send the case back to the trial court. When a case is remanded, the appellate court may order the trial court to:
  1. Enter a judgment or order in accordance with the appellate court decision
  2. Retry the case (conduct a new trial)
  3. Conduct further proceedings in accordance with the appellate court decision
- ✦ If there are several issues, it may affirm the trial court on some of the issues and reverse the trial court on other issues.

h. Concurring Opinion

In some instances, a judge may agree with the majority holding but for different or additional reasons than those presented by the majority. The judge may then set out his or her reasons in support of the majority in what is called a concurring opinion. There may be more than one concurring opinion if other judges also agree with the majority conclusion but for different or additional reasons.

i. Dissenting Opinion

If a judge disagrees with the majority decision, the judge may present his or her reasons in what is called a dissenting opinion. Because a dissenting opinion does not agree with the majority view, it does not have the force of law. It is valuable, however, because it may help a reader understand the majority opinion.

FOR EXAMPLE The dissent may summarize what the court stated in the majority opinion. Note, however, that because the dissent disagrees with the majority view, it may mischaracterize the majority opinion.

The dissenting opinion is also important because it may become the majority view in the future when the composition of the court changes or there is a shift in the court's position. The dissent may provide the basis for future arguments in support of overruling outdated precedent. Remember, at one time the U.S. Supreme Court ruled that segregation on the basis of race was legal, *Plessey v. Ferguson*, 163 U.S. 537, 16 S. Ct. 1138, 41 L. Ed. 256 (1896). Now, segregation on the basis of race is illegal, *Brown v. Board of Education of Topeka*, 347 U.S. 483, 74 S. Ct. 686, 98 L. Ed. 873 (1954).

V. COURT OPINIONS—RESEARCHING

Researching case law is the process of finding a court opinion that answers a question being researched. Usually the search is for case law that governs or guides the resolution of an issue in a client's case. Such a court opinion is often referred to as being "on point." This section focuses on how to find court opinions. The first part of this section discusses case law research sources, that is, where federal and state court opinions are published. The second part presents research strategies or techniques—how to conduct case law research.

A. Publication of Court Opinions

1. In General

Not all court opinions are published in the national or state reporters discussed in subsection 3 (National Reporter System). Most federal and state trial court decisions are not published. Due to the large number of cases, many but not all federal and state appellate court decisions are published. Sometimes an appellate court will not choose to publish a decision because the decision does not have value as precedent. The opinion may address a question already well settled in the law, or it may merely reflect the court's correction of a trial court error. Publication is limited primarily to cases establishing a new rule of law or changing existing law, criticizing existing law, involving matters of public interest, or resolving conflicts of authority.

Just as there are official and unofficial publications of statutory law, there are official and unofficial publications of case law. The official publications of case law are those published at the direction of the government. Court opinions that are not published at the direction of the government are unofficial publications. Both official and unofficial publications include at a minimum the full text of court opinions.

2. Forms of Publication

Most court opinions are published three times in three formats: slip opinions, advance sheets, and bound volumes called *reports* or *reporters*.

a. Slip Opinion

Most court decisions are first published by the court in the form of a slip opinion. Where there is a court Web site, the opinions may also be published on the site. The slip opinion is usually in the form of a pamphlet that contains the full text of the court's opinion in a single case. It includes any concurring or dissenting opinion in the case. It is individually paginated and includes the case name, the date of the decision, and the name of the attorneys.

Slip opinions do not usually include a syllabus (synopsis or summary of the facts, issues, and holding of a case), nor do they include headnotes. They are not organized by legal topic and are distributed to the parties involved in the lawsuit. In some jurisdictions, they are also available by subscription.

b. Advance Sheets

The permanent hardbound volumes of court decisions are published when there are a large number of court decisions sufficient to fill an entire volume. Therefore, many opinions may not appear in a bound volume until up to a year after the decision is rendered. Advance sheets are temporary pamphlets (often softcovered books) that contain the full text of a number of recent court decisions. They are designed to provide quick access to the recent court decisions. The publishers of the permanent volumes publish advance sheets frequently, often weekly. They are placed next to the last hardbound volume and are discarded when a permanent volume is published that contains the opinions printed in the advance sheet cases.

The decisions are presented chronologically and are sequentially paginated; that is, the volume and page number in the advance sheet will be the same as the page and volume number of the bound volume when the bound volume is published.

FOR EXAMPLE An opinion that appears in volume 525, page 756 of the advance sheet will appear in volume 525, page 756 of the permanent bound volume.

The advance sheets usually contain a case synopsis and headnotes for each case, and the index and tables that appear in the permanent volume. They include a Key Number Digest section that arranges the cases by digest topic and subtopic.

c. Reporter

Court opinions are permanently published in hardbound volumes usually referred to as "reporters" or "reports." A reporter volume is published when there are a sufficient number of advance sheets to fill a bound volume. The cases are presented chronologically and, as mentioned previously, paginated with the same page numbers as the advance sheets. Each bound volume usually includes a subject index and an alphabetical list of the opinions reported in the volume. The volumes are numbered consecutively so that the highest numbered volume contains the most recent cases. Often when a large number of volumes are in a series, a second or third series is started. The new series begins at volume 1.

FOR EXAMPLE West's *Pacific Reporter* publishes the state court opinions for the western states. When the number of volumes of the *Pacific Reporter* (cited as P.) reached 300, a second series, *Pacific Reporter,* Second Series (cited as P.2d), beginning at volume 1 was started. When the second series reached 999 volumes, the *Pacific Reporter,* Third Series (cited as P.3d.), beginning at volume 1 was started. The series number is indicated in the citation. The P.2d in the citation 662 P.2d 646 indicates that the decision is found in *Pacific Reporter,* Second Series. The volume number is 662 and the page number is 646.

3. National Reporter System

Most court decisions, both federal and state, are published by West in multivolume sets called reporters. These sets are available from the publisher in hardbound volumes or on CD-ROM. The decisions of the U.S. Supreme Court are published in the *Supreme Court Reporter,* the decisions of the U.S. Courts of Appeals are published in the *Federal Reporters,* and the decisions of the various state appellate courts are published in regional or state-specific reporters.

The following sections discuss the various reporters. Features common to all these reporters are presented here rather than repeated in the discussion of each reporter. Most reporter volumes include the following:

✦ A table of cases that lists in alphabetical order the opinions presented in the volume. Most sets have an additional table of cases, which arranges the cases by state or by circuit.

FOR EXAMPLE Each volume of the *Federal Reporter* has a table of cases listing all the cases alphabetically and a table that arranges the cases alphabetically by circuit. All the cases from the First Circuit, Second Circuit, and so on are arranged alphabetically by circuit. The *South Western Reporter* includes a table of cases that lists the cases alphabetically and a table that arranges the cases alphabetically by state so that all the cases from each state are listed separately.

✦ A table of statutes that lists the various statutes, constitutional provisions, rules interpreted or reviewed, and relevant court opinions.

FOR EXAMPLE If you are researching cases that have interpreted the First Amendment to the U.S. Constitution, the table will direct you to all the cases in the volume that have interpreted the amendment.

✦ A table of words and phrases that lists alphabetically words and phrases judicially defined and indicates the page number in the volume where they are defined.

✦ A key number digest at the back of each volume that provides a summary of each case in the volume arranged by topic and key number.

✦ A case syllabus (a synopsis case summary), headnotes, and key numbers at the beginning of each case presented in the volume. This allows a researcher quick access to all related cases through West's digest system. (See the first page of Exhibit 5–1.)

4. Publication of Federal Court Decisions

a. U.S. Supreme Court

Three different sets publish the decisions of the U.S. Supreme Court: *United States Reports, Supreme Court Reporter,* and *United States Supreme Court Reports, Lawyers' Edition.* This information may also be available in other forms, both printed and electronic.

(1) United States Reports. The *United States Reports* (cited as U.S.) is the official reporter for the Supreme Court of the United States. It is published by the U.S. Government Printing Office and contains the full text of all the decisions of the Supreme Court. The decisions are initially published as slip opinions, advance sheets follow, and then finally come hardbound volumes. The reports are indexed but do not include headnotes or key numbers.

(2) Supreme Court Reporter. The *Supreme Court Reporter* (cited as S.Ct.) is an unofficial publication of the decisions of the U.S. Supreme Court, published by West and

part of West's National Reporter System. It includes the decisions of the Supreme Court since 1882. It is published more quickly than the *United States Reports*. Advance sheets are published at least twice a month.

The headnotes with links to the key numbers make the *Supreme Court Reporter* a valuable research tool. The key numbers, through their link to West's digest system, allow a researcher to research a point of law discussed in a Supreme Court opinion in all reported decisions—both federal and state (see Exhibit 5–2).

(3) United States Supreme Court Reports, Lawyers' Edition. The *United States Supreme Court Reports, Lawyers' Edition* (cited as L.Ed. or L.Ed.2d for volumes since

---

525 U.S. 154   **IN RE KENNEDY**   635
Cite as 119 S.Ct. 635 (1999)

525 U.S. 153, 142 L.Ed.2d 573
⌊153In re Michael KENNEDY
No. 98-6945.
Decided Jan. 11, 1999

Pro se petitioner sought extraordinary writ in noncriminal matter. On petitioner's motion to proceed in forma pauperis, the Supreme Court held that, because petition was petitioner's twelfth frivolous filing with Supreme Court in a noncriminal matter, he would not be allowed to proceed in forma pauperis, and would be barred prospectively from bringing further petitions for certiorari or for extraordinary writs in noncriminal matters without paying fee and complying with rule governing document preparation.

So ordered.

Justice Stevens dissented with statement.

Federal Courts ⊙⇒ 453

Because pro se petitioner's petition for extraordinary writ was his twelfth frivolous filling with Supreme Court in a noncriminal matter, he would not be allowed to proceed in forma pauperis, and would be barred prospectively from bringing further petitions for certiorari or petitions for extraordinary writs in noncriminal matters without paying docketing fee and complying with rule governing document preparation. U.S.Sup.Ct.Rules 33.1, 38, 39, 39.8, 28 U.S.C.A.

PER CURIAM.

Pro se petitioner Kennedy seeks leave to proceed *in forma pauperis* under Rule 39 of this court. We deny this request pursuant to Rule 39.8, Kennedy is allowed until February 1, 1999, within which to pay the docketing fee required by Rule 38 and to submit his petition in compliance with this Court's Rule 33.1. We also direct the Clerk of the Court not to accept any further petitions for certiorari nor petitions for extraordinary writs from Kennedy in

noncrimainal matters unless he pays the docketing fee required by Rule 38 and submits his petition in compliance with Rule 33.1.

Kennedy has abused this Court's certiorari and extraordinary writ processes. In October 1998, we invoked Rule 39.8 to deny Kennedy *in forma pauperis* status. See *In re Kennedy*, 525 U.S. 807, 119 S.Ct. 38, 142 L.Ed.2d 30 (1998). At this time, Kennedy had filed four petitions for extraordinary writs and six petitions for certiorari, all of which were both patently frivolous and had been denied without recorded dissent. The instant petition for an extraordinary writ thus constitutes Kennedy's 12th frivolous filing with this Court.

We enter the order barring prospective filings for the reasons discussed in *Martin v. District of Columbia Court* ⌊154*of Appeals*, 506 U.S. 1, 113 S.Ct. 397, 121 L.Ed.2d 305 (1992) (*per curiam*). Kennedy's abuse of the writ of certiorari and of the extraordinary writ has been in noncriminal cases, and so we limit our sanction accordingly. The order therefore will not prevent Kennedy from petitioning to challenge criminal sanctions which might be imposed on him. The order, however, will allow this Court to devote its limited resources to the claims of petitioners who have not abused our process.

It is so ordered.

Justice STEVENS, dissenting.

For reasons previously stated, see *Martin v. District of Columbia Court of Appeals*, 506 U.S. 1, 4, 113 S.Ct. 397, 121 L.Ed.2d 305 (1992) (STEVENS, J., dissenting), and cases Cited, I respectfully dissent.

Exhibit 5–2

Opinion from *Supreme Court Reporter.*

In Re Kennedy, 525 U.S. 153, 119 S.Ct. 635, 142 L.Ed.2d 573 (1999). Used with permission of Thomson Reuters/West.

GEISSAL V MOORE MEDICAL CORP.
(1998) 524 US 74,141 L Ed 2d 64,118 S Ct 1869

Defendants (1) had violated COBRA by renouncing an obligation to provide continuing coverage, and (2) were estopped to deny him COBRA continuation coverage. The parties agreed to have a magistrate judge conduct all proceedings. The individual (1) moved for partial summary judgment on the first two counts, and (2) included an argument that the defendants' reliance upon § 1162(2)(D)(i) to deny him continuation coverage was misplaced, as he had first been covered under his wife's plan before he had elected continuation coverage. While the motion was pending, the individual died and his wife, who was also the personal representative of his estate, replaced him as plaintiff. The magistrate judge granted partial summary judgment in favor of the defendants on the two counts, as the magistrate judge expressed the view that under § 1162(2)(D)(I), an employee with coverage under another group health plan as of the date on which the employee elected COBRA continuation coverage was ineligible for such coverage (927 F Supp 352, 1996 US Dist LEXIS 7145). On appeal, the United States Court of Appeals for the Eight Circuit, in affirming, expressed the view that (1) under § 1162(2)(D)(i), it was within the defendants' rights to cancel the individual's COBRA benefits unless there was a "significant gap" between the coverage afforded under the corporation's plan and that afforded under his wife's plan; and (2) the wife had failed to carry her burden of showing that such a significant gap existed (114 F3d 1458, 1997 US App LEXIS 13589).

On certiorari, the United States Supreme Court vacated the Court of Appeals' judgment and remanded the case for further proceedings. In an opinion by SOUTER, J., expressing the unanimous view of the court, it was held that § 1162(2)(D)(i) did not allow an employer to deny COBRA continuation coverage to a qualified beneficiary who was covered under another group health plan at the time that the beneficiary made a COBRA election, as (1) under the plain meaning of § 1162(2)(D)(i) as it read at the time pertinent to the case at hand, the medical corporation could not cut off the individual's COBRA continuation coverage, where the individual (a) was covered under his wife's plan before he made his COBRA election, and (b) so did not first become covered under his wife's plan after the date of election; and (2) there was no justification for disparaging the clarity of § 1162(2)(D)(i).

HEADNOTE

Classified to United States Supreme Court Digest, Lawyers' Edition

Pensions and Retirement Funds § 1—Employee Retirement Income Security Act—group health plan—continuation coverage

For purposes of some provisions (29 USCS §§ 1161 et seq.) of the Employee Retirement Income Security Act of 1974 as amended by the Consolidated Omnibus Budget Reconciliation Act of 1985 (COBRA)-which provisions authorize a qualified beneficiary of an employer's group health plan to obtain continued coverage under the plan when the beneficiary might otherwise lose that benefit for certain reasons, such as the termination of employment-29 USCS § 1162(2)(D)(i) (later amended) does not allow an employer to deny COBRA continuation coverage to qualified beneficiary who is covered.

Exhibit 5–3

Page Showing Headnote from Opinion Published in *United States Supreme Court Reports, Lawyers' Edition*.

Geissal v. Moore Medical Corp., 524 U.S. 74, 118 S.Ct. 1869, 141 L.Ed.2d 64 (1998), page 65. LexisNexis® Screen Captures reprinted with the permission of LexisNexis. LexisNexis and Shepard's are registered trademarks and Focus and KWIC are trademarks of Reed Elsevier Properties, Inc., used with the permission of LexisNexis.

1956) is an unofficial publication of the decisions of the U.S. Supreme Court, published by LexisNexis. It includes all the decisions of the Supreme Court since 1789. Advance sheets are published at least twice a month.

Like the *Supreme Court Reporter,* a summary of the case and headnotes precede each opinion. Each headnote is assigned a topic and section number (see Exhibit 5–3). The topics are printed in the *United States Supreme Court Digest, Lawyers' Edition.* This allows researchers to locate other cases addressing the same topic. In addition, there are summaries of the briefs of counsel, and for some cases, annotations that analyze important points of law covered in the case.

Note: The publisher prepares the case summaries and headnotes in both *Supreme Court Reporter* and *United States Supreme Court Reports, Lawyers' Edition;* case summaries and headnotes are not part of the actual court opinion. They are valuable research tools, but they are not the law. Any reference or quotation in research should be to the court opinion itself and not to the material prepared by the publisher.

(4) Loose-Leaf Services and Newspapers.   There are various sources to obtain quick access to the decisions of the Supreme Court of the United States. The *United States Law Week,* published by the Bureau of National Affairs, is a loose-leaf service that publishes weekly the decisions of the Supreme Court. The service includes additional information such as summaries of cases pending before the court and reports on oral arguments. Often law firms and law libraries subscribe to legal newspapers that print the decisions of the U.S. Supreme Court and other federal courts.

(5) Computer and Internet Resources.   Access to most federal court opinions is available through Westlaw and LexisNexis. In addition, court opinions are often available through the official court Web site and other Internet resources. See Internet Resources at the end of this chapter for more specific information. Many federal reporters are also available from the publisher on CD-ROM. Chapters 9 and 10 discuss computer-aided research in detail.

b. U.S. Courts of Appeal

West publishes the decisions of the U.S. Circuit Courts of Appeals in the *Federal Reporter* (cited F), the *Federal Reporter,* Second Series (cited F.2d), and the *Federal Reporter,* Third Series (cited F.3d). Like the *Supreme Court Reporter,* it is part of West's National Reporter System. The cases are initially published in advance sheets, which are later compiled in hardbound volumes. The *Federal Reporter* is an unofficial reporter, but it is the only reporter that publishes the decisions of the U.S. Circuit Courts of Appeal. Therefore, there are no parallel citations for these decisions.

Over the years, the *Federal Reporter* has included decisions of courts other than the U.S. Circuit Courts of Appeals such as decisions of the U.S. District Courts up to 1932 and the U.S. Court of Claims from 1960 to 1982. As mentioned at the beginning of this section, due to the large number of cases, not all the decisions are published.

c. U.S. District Courts

West publishes selected decisions of the U.S. District Court since 1932 in the *Federal Supplement* (cited F. Supp.). This reporter set includes the decisions of the U.S. International Trade Commission since 1956 and the Judicial Panel on Multidistrict Litigation since 1932. Like the *Federal Reporter,* this set is unofficial, but it is the only reporter that publishes the decisions of the U.S. District Courts. Therefore, there are no parallel citations for these decisions. This reporter is part of the National Reporter System. Like the other reporters, the cases are initially published in advance sheets, which are later compiled in hardbound volumes.

d. Other West Federal Reporters

West publishes the following specialized federal reporter sets:

(1) Federal Rules Decisions (cited F.R.D.).   This set includes selected opinions of the U.S. District Courts concerning the Federal Rules of Civil Procedure and Criminal Procedure. Some cases involving court rules will appear in the *Federal Supplement.* If a decision is published in one set such as the *Federal Rules Decisions,* however, it generally will not be published in the other set.

(2) West's Bankruptcy Reporter.   This reporter publishes selected decisions of the U.S. Bankruptcy Courts and District Courts involving bankruptcy. It includes bankruptcy opinions from the U.S. Supreme Court and the Courts of Appeals.

(3) United States Claims Court Reporter.   This set publishes selected trial court decisions of the Claims Court and relevant opinions from the Supreme Court and the Courts of Appeals.

(4) West's Military Justice Reporter.   This set includes the decisions from the U.S. Court of Military Appeals and Courts of Military Review.

(5) West's Veterans Appeals Reporter.   This reporter publishes decisions of the U.S. Court of Veterans Appeals.

5. Publication of State Court Decisions

a. Regional Reporters

In addition to the reporters that publish the federal court decisions (discussed in the previous subsection), West's National Reporter System includes sets of reports and reporters that publish selected decisions of the state appellate courts. Each reporter volume includes the features discussed earlier in subsection VA 3—National Reporter System of this chapter—a table of cases reported, words and phrases defined, and so on. The National Reporter System publishes state court decisions by geographic region in reporters called regional reporters. The reporters are the following: *Pacific Reporter, North Western Reporter, South Western Reporter, North Eastern Reporter, Atlantic Reporter, South Eastern Reporter,* and *Southern Reporter.* West created the geographic grouping of regions, and there is no particular significance to the organization of the regions. The map in Exhibit 5–4 shows the reporter regions and the states in each region.

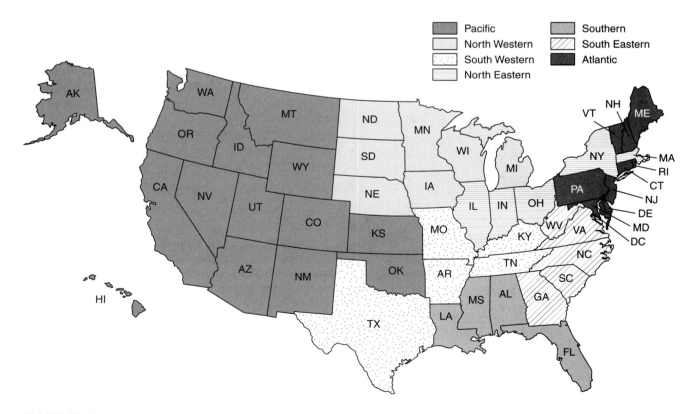

Exhibit 5–4
West's National Reporter System Map.
West, a Thomson Reuters business, Copyright 2002. Used with permission of Thomson Reuters/West.

Due to the large number of cases from California, New York, and Illinois, West created separate reporters for these states. The *California Reporter* publishes the decisions of the California Supreme Court and appellate courts. The Supreme Court decisions are published in both the *Pacific Reporter* and the *California Reporter;* the appellate court decisions are published in the *California Reporter* only. The *New York Supplement* publishes the decisions of the New York Court of Appeals, intermediate appellate decisions, and a few trial court decisions. The New York Court of Appeals decisions are also printed in the *North Eastern Reporter;* the intermediate appellate decisions are not printed in the *North Eastern Reporter.* The *Illinois Decisions* publishes decisions from the Illinois Supreme Court and appellate courts.

West also publishes individual reporters for many states. These reporters are limited to the states' supreme and appellate court decisions. These reporters are designed for attorneys who are mostly interested in the decisions of the state in which they practice. These decisions are also published in the regional reporters.

> **FOR EXAMPLE** A practitioner in New Mexico may need ready access to New Mexico case law for 90 percent of his or her work and only occasionally need access to case law from other states. It may be worthwhile to purchase a set of the *New Mexico Reports,* which consists of less than 180 volumes, whereas it may be cost prohibitive to purchase the *Pacific Reporter* that consists of several hundred volumes.

Advance sheets are published for each regional reporter, and the advance sheets include the features discussed in the earlier subsection VA 2—Forms of Publication in this chapter.

Many states have discontinued the official publication of state appellate court decisions. In those states, the court decisions are published only in the regional reporter, and the only citation is to the regional reporter.

> **FOR EXAMPLE** Colorado discontinued its official publication of cases in 1980. The only citation to Colorado decisions is to the *Pacific Reporter* cite, for example, *People v. J.D.,* 989 P.2d 762 (Col. 1999).

Some states have an official publication as well as a public domain citation (also referred to as medium neutral citations or vender neutral citations). When this is the case, three citation numbers are required.

> **FOR EXAMPLE** *State v. Foster,* 1998-NMCA-163, 126 N.M. 177, 976 P.2d 852. The public domain citation is 1998-NMCA-163. The official publication citation is 126 N.M.177 (volume 126 of the *New Mexico Reports*). The unofficial *Pacific Reporter* citation is 976 P.2d 852. In this instance, there are three parallel citations, and the opinion may be found in three publications.

b. Computer and Internet Resources

Access to most state court opinions is available through Westlaw and LexisNexis. In addition, court opinions are often available through the official court Web site and other Internet sites. See the Internet Resources section at the end of this chapter. Many state and regional reporters are also available from the publisher on CD-ROM.

6. Attorney General Opinions

The chief attorney for the federal or state government is usually referred to as the **Attorney General**. Upon the request of legislators or other government officials, an

Research Sources and Techniques for Locating Cases	
Statutory Annotations	If your research involves a situation that requires the interpretation of a statute, read the statute and look to the case annotations following the statute.
Digest	If the question being researched does not involve a statute or the annotations do not direct you to a relevant case, look to a digest.
Other Case Law Research Sources	If you need to locate additional court opinions, use other research sources such as legal encyclopedias, treatises, ALR's, and law review articles.
***Shepard's Citations* and Updating Research**	If you know the citation of a case and you are looking for other cases that have referred to the case or if you want to know if the case has been reversed or modified, refer to the appropriate *Shepard's* citator.
Computer-Aided Research	Research sources and court opinions may be located through Westlaw and LexisNexis.

Exhibit 5–5
Researching Court Opinions.

attorney general may issue a written opinion interpreting how the law applies. This usually occurs when there is no court opinion interpreting how a specific law applies or when there are conflicting court opinions. These opinions are **secondary authority**; they are not enacted law or the opinion of a court. They are not primary authority and do not have to be followed by a court. Since they are written by the attorney general, they are often relied on in the absence of a law or court opinion addressing a specific question.

Attorney general opinions are available through Westlaw and LexisNexis. In addition, they are often available through federal or state government Web sites and other internet resources. The opinions are also individually available through the attorney general's office in slip form. Bound volumes of all the opinions are usually available at law libraries.

B. Researching Court Opinions—Locating Case Law

After you know where the various court opinions are published, the next step is to become familiar with the many research sources and techniques for locating cases (see Exhibit 5–5). Whenever you are conducting case law research, remember to check the advance sheets, pocket parts, or whatever is used to update the source you are researching to ensure that you locate the most recent court decision that answers your question. Where and how you conduct research depends on the amount and type of information you have at the outset. The main ways to locate case law are discussed next.

1. Statutory Annotations

If your research involves a situation that requires the interpretation of a statute, the first step is to read the statute and look to the case annotations following the statute. Often the annotations to the key court decisions following the statute will include a case that is on point. This saves time spent in using another research source such as a digest.

FOR EXAMPLE The client robbed a bank with a toy handgun that looked exactly like a real handgun. The client is charged with bank robbery with a dangerous weapon under 18 U.S.C. § 2113(a) & (d). The question is whether a toy handgun is a dangerous weapon under the statute. Referring to the annotations to the statute in the *United States Code Annotated* or the *United States Code Service,* you will find cases that address the question of whether a toy gun is considered a dangerous weapon. Other than check-ing to determine if the case has been reversed or modified, or that there are no recent cases also on point, no further search may be necessary; a digest does not need to be consulted.

If the case you locate is not exactly the case you are looking for, that is, it is not quite on point, the opinion may reference other cases that are on point or provide you with a key number that will lead you to the proper case. Always read the statute first be-cause the answer may be in the statute itself or in the annotations.

2. Digests

If the question being researched does not involve a statute or the annotations do not direct you to a relevant case, the next step is to look to a digest. West publishes sets of vol-umes called digests for the various reporters. There is a digest for each regional and state reporter, such as the *Pacific Digest* for the *Pacific Reporter,* and a *Federal Practice Digest.* As discussed earlier in section IV B 5—Key Numbers, West has divided the areas of law into various topics and subtopics. Each area is identified by a topic name such as "ASSAULT AND BATTERY" and each topic is divided into subtopics and assigned a key number. The digests contain summaries of all the court opinions under each key number subtopic.

If you know a case name, you can quickly locate it in a digest's table of cases. If you don't have a particular case in mind but you are looking for a case that addresses the question you are researching, scan the topic area, locate the relevant key, and scan the case summaries to locate the case on point.

If there are no cases under a particular key number, the digest will refer you to other research sources such as a legal encyclopedia cite.

3. Computer-Aided Research

Court opinions may be located through Westlaw and LexisNexis. Also, court opinions may often be found through other Internet sources (see Chapters 9 and 10).

4. Other Case Law Research Sources

You may also locate court opinions through other research sources such as legal ency-clopedias, treatises, ALRs, and law review articles. Usually, however, there are quicker ways of locating cases than through these sources.

> **FOR EXAMPLE** The question you are researching is similar to the question raised in *Rael v. Cadena* (presented in Exhibit 5–1): When may a person who is present at a battery be liable for a battery if the person does not physically participate in the battery? You can look under Assault and Battery in an encyclopedia and eventually find a section that addresses this question and be directed to specific cases. But you may spend a lot of time reading before you locate the specific topic you are looking for and spend even more time checking the numerous cases listed before you find the case on point. By using a di-gest, Westlaw, or LexisNexis, your search is more focused and you will usually find cases quicker.

If there is an ALR annotation on the question you are researching, it will provide an in-depth analysis of a specific question and references to key cases addressing the question. First, however, follow the steps mentioned in Subsections 1 and 2 above be-cause if you find a case on point, you may not need the in-depth analysis, or the case you find may mention a relevant ALR annotation and save you the time of locating it.

5. *Shepard's Citations* and Updating Research

If you know the citation of a case and you are looking for other cases that have referred to the case or if you want to know if the case has been reversed or modified, refer to the appropriate *Shepard's* citator. The use of *Shepard's* is discussed in Chapter 7.

You must always check to determine if the case you have located is good law, that is, whether the court opinion or part of the opinion you are relying on has been reversed or modified by a subsequent court decision. This may be accomplished through the use of the appropriate *Shepard's* or electronically through Westlaw or LexisNexis.

VI. COURT OPINIONS—BRIEFING (CASE BRIEF)

A. Introduction

As a researcher, you may be assigned the task of reading and briefing court opinions. A court opinion is usually called a case, and a brief of a court opinion is usually called a case brief or a case abstract. A **case brief** is a written summary identifying the essential components of a court opinion.

B. Importance of Briefing

Briefing a case serves several useful purposes and functions:

1. *Analysis/Learning.* Writing a summary of the essential elements of an opinion in an organized format leads to better understanding of the case and the reasoning of the court. Opinions are often complex, and the reasoning is hard to identify, difficult to follow, or spread throughout the opinion. The preparation of a case brief requires studying the opinion, identifying the essential, and eliminating the nonessential. This process of studying a case and analyzing it helps the reader gain a better understanding of it. The analytical process of focusing on the structure of the case helps you gain an understanding of the reasoning, thereby assisting your analysis of the law.

2. *Research/Reference.* A case brief is a time-saving research tool. It provides a summary of the essentials of a case that can be quickly referred to when reviewing the case. This saves the time that would be spent rereading and reanalyzing the entire case to remember what the court decided and why. When working on a complex legal problem involving several court opinions or when time has passed since a case was read, the availability of case briefs can result in a considerable saving of time because it is often difficult to remember which opinion said what.

   A case brief is a valuable tool for the attorney assigned to the case. The attorney may not need to read all the cases related to an issue. The attorney can read the case briefs prepared by the researcher and save time by quickly weeding out those cases that are not key and identify and focus on the cases that should be read.

3. *Writing.* The process of briefing a case serves as a valuable writing tool. It provides you with an exercise in which you learn to sift through a court opinion, identify the essential elements, and assemble your analysis into a concise written summary.

C. How to Read a Case

Before you can brief a case, you must first read it carefully. Sometimes it is necessary to read the entire opinion or parts of it several times to gain an understanding of the decision and the court's reasoning. You cannot expect to skim or quickly read an opinion and hope to understand it. It cannot be read like a newspaper or novel for several reasons:

- ✦ Judges write opinions with the assumption that the reader has an understanding of the law, legal terminology, and the legal system. If you are a beginner, you are slowed by having to look up the meaning of legal terms and become familiar with the style of legal writing.

    Do not get discouraged if at first it takes a long time to read and understand case law. It is normal to "crawl through" court opinions when you are a novice at reading them. As you become familiar with the terminology and style of legal opinions, you will read them faster and with greater understanding. The process, however, is gradual and usually takes months rather than days to learn. No matter how skilled you are, cases always must be read carefully to be fully understood.

- ✦ Some opinions are difficult to read and take time because they involve complex, abstract, or unfamiliar subjects involving multiple issues. In such instances, you may have to read the entire case or portions of it several times. You may have to prepare outlines or charts as you read to help you follow and understand the court's reasoning. You may have to refer to a treatise, encyclopedia, or other research tool to understand the area of law involved in the case.

- ✦ Some opinions are difficult to read because they are poorly written. Not all judges are great writers. The reasoning may be scattered throughout the case or not completely presented.

- ✦ Some opinions are difficult to read and understand because the court may have incorrectly interpreted or applied the law. You may be surprised when you read the holding that the court reached a conclusion that is the opposite of the outcome you expected. Remember that some decisions are overruled because a higher or subsequent court determined that the earlier opinion was incorrect. Therefore, it is important to read each case with a critical eye.

    In regard to the last two reasons presented in this list, the difficulty in reading and understanding an opinion may have nothing to do with your ability to read the case.

The purpose of reading a court opinion is to obtain an understanding of the law or principle addressed by the court. To gain this understanding, cases must be read and analyzed with *close scrutiny*.

D. Case Brief—Elements

There is no standard form for a brief of a court opinion, nor are there any hard-and-fast rules governing format. Some texts recommend that case briefs contain as few as five parts, some as many as 16. The style of a case brief may vary from individual to individual and office to office. Be prepared to adapt to different styles.

The goal of a good case brief is a concise summary of the essentials of the court opinion that may be used as a quick reference in the future. Therefore, the brief should be concise. It certainly should not be as long as or longer than the case. Do not fill the brief with excessive quotes from the case or long summaries. Spend more time thinking than writing. Reduce the opinion to its essence.

A recommended outline for a case brief format is presented in Exhibit 5–6. This format should be viewed as a basic outline of the essential parts of a case brief. It can be adapted as necessary to meet your needs. A discussion of each section of the outline follows.

CASE BRIEF FORMAT	
CITATION:	Name of case and where it can be found.
PARTIES:	Names and legal status of the parties.
FACTS:	A summary of those facts that describe the history of events that caused the parties to be in court (background facts), and those facts to which the law applies and are essential to the decision reached by the court (key facts).
PRIOR PROCEEDINGS:	What happened in the lower court or courts.
ISSUE:	The specific question(s) addressed and answered by the court. State the issue as narrowly and concretely as possible in the context of the case facts. It should include the rule of law and the key facts.
HOLDING:	The court's answer to the issue.
REASONING:	Why the court ruled as it did. This is the court's application of the case or statutory law to the facts of the case. It should include a. The rule of law that applies b. How the court applied the rule of law to the facts
DISPOSITION:	What order was entered as a result of the holding, e.g., "The judgment of the trial court is reversed."
COMMENTS:	Observations concerning the opinion.

Exhibit 5–6
Case Brief Format.

1. Citation

The citation includes the name of the parties, where the case can be found, the court that issued the opinion, and the year of the opinion.

> **FOR EXAMPLE** In *Rael v. Cadena,* the citation is *Rael v. Cadena,* 93 N.M. 684, 604 P.2d 822 (Ct. App. 1979).
>
> ✦ *Rael v. Cadena*—Name of the case.
>
> ✦ *93 N.M. 684, 604 P.2d 822*—The volume and page numbers of the books where the case can be found. This case can be found in volume 93 of the *New Mexico Reports* on page 684, and in volume 604 of the *Pacific Reporter,* Second Series, on page 822.
>
> ✦ *(Ct. App. 1979)*—The court that rendered the opinion and the year of the opinion. The New Mexico Court of Appeals rendered the opinion in 1979. If the date alone appears in parentheses—(1979)—the highest court of the state wrote the opinion. If there is no reference to a state reporter, a reference to the state would also be included with the date: (N.M. Ct. App. 1979).

2. Parties

The caption at the beginning of the opinion gives the full name and legal status of each party.

> **FOR EXAMPLE** ✦ Eddie Rael, Plaintiff-Appellee
>
> ✦ Emilio Cadena, Defendant-Appellant
>
> ✦ Manuel Cadena, Defendant-Appellant

The legal status refers to the litigation status of the parties. This includes the status at the trial and appellate court level. The status is usually indicated in the caption. The plaintiff is the person who brought the lawsuit, and the defendant is the party against whom the suit is brought. Often terminology other than *plaintiff* and *defendant* is used.

> **FOR EXAMPLE** *Petitioner* and *respondent* are often used in divorce cases. The petitioner is the party who filed the divorce petition, and the respondent is the person against whom the divorce petition is filed.

The appeal status of the parties immediately follows the trial court status in the caption.

> **FOR EXAMPLE** In *Rael v. Cadena*, Eddie Rael was the plaintiff at trial (he filed the lawsuit), and he is the party against whom the appeal was filed (Appellee—he won at the trial level).

3. Facts

The fact section of a case brief includes a summary of those facts that describe the history of the events giving rise to the litigation. The fact section should include key and background facts.

a. Key Facts

The key facts are those facts in the opinion to which the law applies and that are essential to the decision reached by the court. The outcome of the case is determined upon these facts. If the key facts were different, the outcome of the case would probably be different.

b. Background Facts

Background facts are those facts that put the key facts in context. They are facts necessary to make sense of the story and thereby provide the reader with an overall context within which the key facts occur, an overall picture of the events of the case.

In some texts, the case brief format presents the Prior Proceedings before the Facts. It is recommended that the Facts section precede the Prior Proceedings section of the brief. Because the facts of the case are the events that led to the litigation and, therefore, occurred prior to the litigation, it is logical that in the case brief format, they should precede the court events (the prior proceedings). Also, it is easier from a briefing standpoint to identify what happened before the matter went to the trial court and then identify what happened in court.

4. Prior Proceedings/Procedural History

Prior proceedings are those events that occurred in each court before the case reached the court whose opinion you are briefing. Most opinions are not written by trial courts; they are written by courts of appeals reviewing the decision(s) of a trial court, either:

+ An intermediary court of appeals, such as the U.S. Court of Appeals
+ The highest court of the jurisdiction, such as the U.S. Supreme Court

Therefore, there are usually prior proceedings. If you are briefing an opinion of a trial court, there may be no prior proceedings because the trial court was the first court to hear the case.

The prior proceedings should include the following:

1. The party initiating the proceeding and the cause of action

2. The court before which the proceeding was brought

3. The result of the proceeding

4. The party appealing and what is being appealed

> **FOR EXAMPLE** "The plaintiff sued the defendant, claiming medical malpractice. The trial court granted the defendant's motion to dismiss, ruling that the statute of limitations had run. The plaintiff appealed the trial court's ruling that the statute had run."

5. Issue or Issues

The issue is the legal question addressed and answered by the court. It is the precise legal question raised by the specific facts of the case. The issue should be stated as narrowly and concisely as possible in the context of the facts of the case. A court opinion may address several issues. Identify each issue separately in the case brief unless you are instructed to brief only one of the issues.

> **FOR EXAMPLE** In an opinion involving an automobile collision case, the court addresses several issues, some involving insurance, some involving evidence, some involving negligence, and some involving battery. The attorney working on a client's case is interested only in the court's resolution of an evidentiary question raised by the facts in the court case. The client's case involves an evidentiary question and fact situation similar to that addressed in the court opinion. Therefore, a researcher may be instructed to provide a case brief of only the portion of the opinion that addresses the evidentiary question. Although the opinion involves several issues, the case brief will address only one issue.

Refer to Chapter 3 for a discussion of how to identify and state an issue in a court opinion.

6. Holding

The holding is the court's resolution of the issue. It is the decision of the court, the answer to the issue. There should be a separate holding for each issue identified in the Issue section of the case brief. In some brief formats, the holding is a simple, one-word, "yes" or "no" response to the issue. The holding should be presented as a complete response to the issue, which means that the presentation of the holding should include all the elements of the issue and should be in the form of a statement.

> **FOR EXAMPLE** The issue in the case is "Under Indiana's probate code, Ind. Code § 29-1-5-2, is a will valid if the witnesses are brothers of the testator?" If the court ruled that the will was valid, the holding should be presented as follows: "Under Indiana's probate code, Ind.Code § 29-1-5-2, a will is valid if the witnesses are brothers of the testator as long as there is no evidence of undue influence."

7. Reasoning

Usually the largest part of an opinion is the court's presentation of the reasons in support of the holding. Just as for each issue there is a holding, for each holding there should be reasons explaining why the holding was reached.

The reasoning portion of an opinion usually consists of two parts:

+ The rule of law that governs the facts of the dispute. It may be constitutional, legislative, or case law, and it may consist of any legal principle, doctrine, or rule of law that applies to the issue in the case.

+ The court's application of the rule to the facts of the case.

> **FOR EXAMPLE** The issue in the case is, "Under state tort law, does a battery occur when law enforcement officers, while making a lawful arrest, encounter resistance, use force to overcome that resistance, and continue to use force after the resistance ceases?"

The reasoning presented in the opinion is as follows:

+ *Rule of law*—"In *Smith v. Jones*, the supreme court ruled that a civil battery occurs whenever unauthorized harmful contact occurs."

+ *Application of this rule to the facts of the case*—"The defendants argue that inasmuch as they were making a lawful arrest, they were authorized to use force; therefore, their conduct was not unauthorized within the meaning of *Smith v. Jones*. In this case, however, although the officers were making a lawful arrest, their conduct ceased to be lawful when they continued to use force against plaintiff after plaintiff ceased resisting. Law enforcement officers are authorized to use the amount of force necessary to overcome resistance. After resistance ceases, any continued use of force is unauthorized within the meaning of *Smith v. Jones* and constitutes a civil battery."

In some instances, it is difficult to identify the reasoning in a court opinion because it is scattered throughout the opinion. A helpful approach is to work backward from the holding. Look to the holding first, and keep it in mind while reading the case. It may be easier to see how the court assembled the reasons in support of the holding if you know the holding or outcome while reading the case.

Also, the rule of law or legal principle governing the issue is usually clearly stated by the court and is easy to identify. The reasons for the application of the rule or principle to the facts of the case usually follow the presentation of the governing law. Therefore, identification of the governing law may also help you locate the reasoning.

Lengthy quotations from the case should be avoided. The reasoning should be summarized.

> **FOR EXAMPLE** In the excessive force example presented in the previous example, the Reasoning section of the case brief is as follows: "A civil battery occurs whenever unauthorized harmful contact occurs. *Smith v. Jones*. Law enforcement officers are authorized to overcome resistance. After resistance ceases, any continued use of force is unauthorized and constitutes a civil battery."

Also included in the Reasoning section is a summary of the reasoning of any concurring opinion.

8. Disposition

In this section, include the relief granted by the court, which is the order entered by the court. This is usually located at the very end of the opinion.

> **FOR EXAMPLE** The judgment of the trial court was affirmed.

9. Comments

Include in this section of the case brief any observations you may have concerning the court opinion. This could include any of the following:

+ Why you agree or disagree with the decision.

+ A summary of any dissenting opinions. Does the dissenting opinion contain information that is useful in understanding the majority opinion? Does the dissenting opinion contain valuable legal arguments that may be useful in arguing against the use of the case as precedent? This is especially helpful if the holding of the court goes against your client's position.

Note: Some case brief formats have a separate section for dissenting opinions.

✦ Why the case may or may not be on point.

> **FOR EXAMPLE** Referring to the excessive force example, assume that in the client's case there is evidence that the client never ceased resisting. You might include the following comment in the comment section of the brief: "It is questionable whether this case can be relied on as precedent due to the differences between the facts of the case and our client's facts. In the court case, force continued after resistance ceased, and the court held that the continued use of force constituted a battery. Inasmuch as in our case there is evidence that resistance never ceased, the court opinion may not be applicable."

✦ References to the opinion in subsequent cases or secondary sources, such as a law review article.

✦ Any information updating the case, that is, concerning whether the case is still good law. This is discussed in the next section.

E. Case Brief—Updating

Whenever an assignment requires you to brief a case, you should determine if the case is still good law, which means you must check to determine if the opinion has been reversed, modified, or in any way affected by a later court decision. The primary method of accomplishing this is through the use of the appropriate *Shepard's* citator. *Shepard's* citators are published by LexisNexis. A researcher must be familiar with *Shepard's Citations* to update a court opinion. Instructions on how to use a *Shepard's* citator are included in the beginning of each volume.

In addition, computerized services provide on-line citators that are usually more up-to-date than the *Shepard's* printed citators. Some of these on-line services are the following:

✦ *LexCite*—Includes a list of the recent cases citing a case (available through LexisNexis)

✦ *Insta-Cite*—Provides a summary of the prior and subsequent history of a case and includes references to the case in *Corpus Juris Secundum* (available through Westlaw)

✦ *Key Cite*—Includes a list of all cases citing a case (available through Westlaw)

✦ *Shepard's Citator Services*—Presents information not yet included in the *Shepard's* printed volumes

VII. KEY POINTS CHECKLIST: *Locating, Reading, and Briefing Court Opinions*

◼ If the research question involves a statute, look to the statute and the statutory annotations first to locate case law. If the statutory annotations do not provide help, next look to a digest.

◼ Read opinions carefully and slowly. You cannot speed-read case law. Often you may have to take notes as you read a case.

- If you have a problem identifying the key facts, refer to Chapter 2.

- Watch for the court's statement of the issue. The court may state the issue in a broad or procedural context. If you have a problem identifying or stating the issue, refer to Chapter 3.

- If you have trouble understanding the majority opinion, often the concurring or dissenting opinion summarizes and clarifies the arguments and reasoning adopted by the majority. Be aware that the dissenting opinion may mischaracterize the majority opinion in support of its own position.

- If you have trouble understanding the opinion, shepardize the case to determine if there are any other cases, law review articles, ALR citations, or other secondary sources of information concerning the case. Consult a treatise that discusses the area of law involved in the opinion. Refer to the digest for other cases addressing the same area of law.

- Do not be discouraged if you have trouble reading and understanding opinions. It takes time and experience. The more you read opinions, the easier it becomes. Your skill improves only through doing; therefore, read as many cases as possible.

- Read opinions with a critical eye. Court opinions are just that—opinions. On occasion, courts are wrong. Do not read with unquestioning blind faith. Read critically. Question! Ask yourself, "Does the reasoning support the conclusion?"

VIII. APPLICATION

A. Chapter 1 Hypothetical *Reins v. Stewart*

Vanessa's assignment is to locate and brief a case that answers the question of whether Mr. Stewart can be liable for civil battery. The brief of the case she found, *Rael v. Cadena*, follows a discussion of how the research is conducted for this and the Chapter 2 hypothetical. The text and brief of *Sterling Computer Systems of Texas, Inc. v. Texas Pipe Bending Company* follows the brief of *Rael v. Cadena*. The brief of the *Sterling* case is included to provide another example of a case brief.

Locating *Rael v. Cadena*

Vanessa begins her search for an appropriate case by looking for a statute that establishes a civil cause of action for battery. She looks under "battery" based on her preliminary research and identification of the issue. Civil battery is tort law and in most states the majority of tort law is case law, not statutory law. If there is a statute, Vanessa looks to the statutory annotations to see if there is a case on point. That is, a case where the court addressed the question of whether an individual present at the scene of a battery, who did nothing more than strongly encourage the perpetrator, could be liable for civil battery.

If there is no statute or a case on point in the annotations, Vanessa next looks to the regional or state reporter digest under "battery." Assume that Vanessa resides in New Mexico. She refers to the index of either the *New Mexico Reports* or *Pacific Digest* to locate the volume number for battery. Battery is indexed under Assault and Battery. By scanning the topic key numbers, she locates Key 18—Persons Liable. She looks under "Persons Liable" because that key is closest to the facts identified in the issue—is Mr. Stewart liable when he encouraged his son to hit Mr. Reins? Looking at the case summaries under Key 18 she finds *Rael v. Cadena*, 93 N.M. 684, 604 P.2d 822 (Ct. App. 1979), a case that is on point (see Exhibit 5–1). She continues her search to locate any other cases that may be on point. She also checks to determine if the case has been overruled or otherwise modified by subsequent court decisions.

If there is no case under Key 18, the digest refers to a legal encyclopedia cite that addresses the topic and provides reference to cases. At this point, Vanessa could also look under other key topics that might apply such as Key 5, "Overt act in general." In addition, she could look for an ALR annotation that discusses the question. She could also perform this search electronically using Westlaw or LexisNexis.

B. Chapter 2 Hypothetical *United States v. Canter*

Dustin begins his search by looking to the annotations following 18 U.S.C. § 2113 (a) and (d), to see if there is a case on point. That is, a case where the court addresses the question of whether a fake weapon, such as the carved replica of a handgun, could be considered a dangerous weapon.

Dustin scans the Notes of Decisions to locate the section that appears closest to the facts of the issue. Under the Notes of Decisions, Part II Offenses, is subdivision 75, "Putting Life in Jeopardy by Dangerous Weapons-Toy Guns." In this subdivision, *United States v. Martinez-Jimenez*, 864 F.2d 664 (9th Cir. 1989) is a case on point (see Appendix C). He continues his search to locate any other cases that may be on point. He also checks to determine if the case has been overruled or otherwise modified by subsequent court decisions.

If there is no case on point in the annotations, Dustin next looks to the *West's Federal Practice Digest 4th* index. He looks in this digest because Mr. Canter is charged with a federal crime. Based on the information included in the statement of the issue, he looks under all related terms—*bank robbery, robbery, weapons, dangerous weapons*, and so on. Under Robbery, he finds Key 11, "Degrees, Armed Robbery." He researches "Degrees, Armed Robbery" because that key is closest to the facts identified in the issue. Looking at the case summaries under Key 11, he finds *United States v. Martinez-Jimenez*.

If he cannot find a case in the digest, he looks for a legal encyclopedia cite that addresses the topic and provides reference to cases. He could also look for an ALR annotation that discusses the question. For how Dustin conducts this search electronically using Westlaw or LexisNexis, see Chapter 10.

C. Brief of *Rael v. Cadena*

The sample brief is presented first, followed by comments on the brief.

Citation:	*Rael v. Cadena*, 93 N.M. 684, 604 P.2d 822 (Ct. App. 1979)
Parties:	Eddie Rael, Plaintiff-Appellee Emilio Cadena and Manuel Cadena, Defendants-Appellants
Facts:	While visiting Emilio Cadena's home, Eddie Rael was beaten by Emilio's nephew, Manuel Cadena. After the attack began, Emilio yelled to Manuel "Kill him!" and "Hit him more!" Emilio never actually struck Rael nor physically participated in the battery. Rael was hospitalized as a result of the beating.
Prior Proceeding:	Eddie Rael sued Emilio and Manuel Cadena for battery. The trial court, sitting without a jury, found Emilio jointly liable with

	Manuel for the battery. Emilio appealed the judgment of the trial court.
Issue:	Under New Mexico tort law, does a battery occur when an individual, present at a battery, encourages the perpetrator of the battery by yelling "Kill him!' and "Hit him more!", but does not in any other way participate in the battery?
Holding:	Yes. An individual may be liable for battery by encouraging or inciting the perpetrator by words or acts.
Reasoning:	The rule of law in the United States is that civil liability for assault and battery is not limited to the direct perpetrator, but extends to any person who by any means aids or encourages the act. The act of verbal encouragement at the scene may give rise to liability. The trial court found that Emilio Cadena yelled encouragement to his nephew while the nephew was beating Rael and, therefore, under the rule of law, is jointly liable for the battery.
Disposition:	The judgment of the trial court was affirmed.
Comments:	If, in the client's case, less aggressive language were used, it may be valuable to review other cases to determine the type of encouragement necessary to constitute a battery. Here, Emilio's comments were very aggressive. Would he have been liable for battery had he merely said, "Go ahead, Manuel"?

Comments on the Case Brief

Note that the brief includes the essential information of the case:

1. The name of the case and where it can be found
2. The names of the parties and their status before the court
3. The facts that gave rise to the dispute
4. The actions of the trial court
5. The issue or legal question
6. The holding
7. The law governing the issue and the application of that law to the facts of the dispute
8. The disposition
9. Relevant comments

You may include in the Comments section a notation that the issue in the case was a matter of first impression in New Mexico—that is, the issue addressed in the case had never been decided by New Mexico courts. That is why the reasoning refers to non–New Mexico law and secondary authority rather than to New Mexico law. See the Reasoning section of the brief.

D. Brief of *Sterling Computer Systems of Texas, Inc. v. Texas Pipe Bending Company*

A second example of the application of the principles presented in this chapter is illustrated with the brief of the Sterling Computer Systems case. The case is presented in the following text. Comments concerning the case brief follow the brief.

CASE

STERLING COMPUTER SYSTEMS OF TEXAS, INC.,
Appellant,

v.

TEXAS PIPE BENDING COMPANY, Appellee.
No. 965. Court of Civil Appeals of Texas.
Houston (14th Dist.).
March 20, 1974.
Rehearing Denied April 10, 1974.
507 S.W.2d 282 (Tex. Ct. App. 1974)

Action for breach of contract for data-processing service. The District Court, Harris County, Paul Pressler, J., granted summary judgment for defendant, and plaintiff appealed. The Court of Civil Appeals, Tunks, C. J., held that contract, which contained an express provision that plaintiff would not be liable for an outright refusal to perform dataprocessing services for defendant, and which contained no requirements that plaintiff make a reasonable effort to perform, failed for want of mutuality and was unenforceable.

AFFIRMED.

Contracts 10(2)
Contract, which contained an express provision that plaintiff would not be liable for an outright refusal to perform dataprocessing services for defendant, and which contained no requirement that plaintiff make a reasonable effort to perform, failed for want of mutuality and was unenforceable.

Alvin L. Zimmerman, Houston, for appellant.
Robert H. Singleton, Percy D. Williams, Houston, for appellee.

TUNKS, Chief Justice.

The issue in this case is the propriety of a summary judgment for the defendant in a breach of contract suit, which was granted on the theory that the contract lacked mutuality.

The appellant, Sterling Computer Systems of Texas, Inc., brought suit for breach of contract against the appellee, Texas Pipe Bending Company. In essence, the contract in question provided that Texas Pipe Bending was to provide Sterling with digitized cards and computer programs each month, with which Sterling was to perform data processing services for Texas Pipe Bending. Certain prices were quoted in the agreement, which were "based on a minimum of 20,000 digitized cards per month." The term of the agreement was to have been for one year, but after providing cards and paying in full for eight months, Texas Pipe Bending refused to further provide Sterling with digitized cards. The trial court granted Texas Pipe Bending's motion for summary judgment. Although the judgment does not so recite, it was apparently based on the argument proposed by Texas Pipe Bending that the contract was unenforceable because of the lack of mutuality. Sterling has appealed.

The relevant portion of the contract is found in a clause denominated as "LIMITATION OF LIABILITY." This clause provides in part as follows:

> SCS [Sterling] shall not be liable for its failure to provide [sic] the services herein and shall not be liable for any losses resulting to the client [Texas Pipe Bending] or anyone else by reason of such failure.

The general rule as stated in *Texas Farm Bureau Cotton Ass'n v. Stovall*, 113 Tex. 273, 253 S.W. 1101, 1105 (1923), is:

> [A] contract must be based upon a valid consideration, and . . . a contract in which there is no consideration moving from one party, or no obligation upon him, lacks mutuality, is unilateral, and unenforceable.

Under the express terms of the contract in question Sterling would not be liable for an outright refusal to perform the dataprocessing services. This fact renders its obligation a nullity.

Sterling cites various cases which purportedly support its position that the trial court erred in granting summary judgment for Texas Pipe Bending. The gist of these cases is that although a contract may not expressly obligate a party to perform, such an obligation may be implied by its terms. In *Texas Gas Utilities Company v. Barrett*, 460 S.W.2d 409 (Tex.Sup.1970), the Texas Supreme Court held, under a similar contention, that there was a mutuality of obligation. In that case, the contract provided that the Gas Company would not be liable for failure to deliver when such failure was "caused by conditions beyond its reasonable control," and then enumerated certain situations which exemplified the above phrase (over none of which would the Gas Company have control). The Court noted, "It [Gas Company] was bound, however, to supply available natural gas to respondents. . . ." *Texas Gas Utilities Company v. Barrett*, supra 460 S.W.2d at 413. In the present case, there existed no requirement that Sterling make a reasonable effort to perform. The exculpatory clause allowed Sterling to refuse to perform with impunity.

Clement v. Producers' Refining Co., 277 S.W. 634 (Tex. Comm'n App. 1925, jdgmt adopted), was another case in which mutuality was found. That case involved a contract for an agent's commission. By the terms of the agreement, the principal was to pay the agent a commission on goods which "may be supplied" by the principal. Notwithstanding this provision, the Commission of Appeals held that the contract impliedly obligated the principal to supply goods to the agent. However, the Court stated:

> [A]s there is no language used which would clearly indicate that the company was not obligated to furnish goods and products, the courts are not warranted in holding that no such obligation was imposed . . . by its terms.

Clement v. Producers' Refining Co., supra at 635.

The case at bar is distinguishable because the contract contained an express provision that Sterling would not be liable if it did not perform. Various other cases cited by appellant are similarly distinguishable because in those cases, contracts were involved which did not expressly provide that one of the contracting parties could fail to perform without incurring liability.

As a matter of law, the contract in question fails for want of mutuality. The trial court correctly granted summary judgment for the defendant, Texas Pipe Bending Company.

AFFIRMED.

***

Citation:	*Sterling Computer Systems of Texas, Inc. v. Texas Pipe Bending Company,* 507 S.W.2d 282 (Tex. Ct. App. 1974).
Parties:	Sterling Computer Systems of Texas, Inc., Plaintiff-Appellant Texas Pipe Bending Company, Defendant-Appellee
Facts:	Sterling Computer Systems (Sterling) entered into a contract with Texas Pipe Bending (Texas Pipe) under which Texas Pipe was to provide Sterling with digitized cards and computer programs each month with which Sterling was to perform data-processing services for Texas Pipe. After complying for eight months, Texas Pipe refused to provide Sterling with the cards. The contract contained the following provision, "SCS [Sterling] shall not be liable for its failure to profide [sic] the services herein and shall not be liable for any losses resulting to the client [Texas Pipe] or anyone else by reason of such failure."
Prior Proceedings:	Sterling sued Texas Pipe for breach of contract. Texas Pipe moved for summary judgment, arguing that the contract was unenforceable because it lacked mutuality. The trial court granted the motion. Sterling appealed.
Issue:	Under Texas contract law, does a contract lack consideration and is, therefore, unenforceable if it contains a limitation of liability clause that provides that a party "shall not be liable for its failure to provide the services herein and shall not be liable for any losses resulting . . . by reason of such failure?"
Holding:	Yes. Under Texas contract law, a contract lacks consideration and is unenforceable if it contains a limitation of liability clause that provides that a party "shall not be liable for its failure to provide the services herein and shall not be liable for any losses resulting . . . by reason of such failure."
Reasoning:	The rule of law presented in *Texas Farm Bureau Cotton Association v. Stovall,* 113 Tex. 273, 253 S.W. 1101 (1923), is that where there is no obligation upon a party to a contract, the contract lacks mutuality, is unilateral, and is unenforceable. Under the limitation clause, Sterling is not liable for its refusal to perform. Therefore, as a matter of law, the contract fails for want of mutuality.
Disposition:	The trial court's granting of the motion for summary judgment was affirmed.

Comments: The court did not address any potential avenues of relief that may be available to Sterling in equity, such as equitable restitution or reliance. Such avenues may be available in our case and should be explored. Also, does Sterling have a claim against the drafters of the contract for legal malpractice?

Comments on the Case Brief—*Procedural vs. Substantive Issues*

Note that the court identifies the issue as: "The issue in this case is the propriety of a summary judgment for the defendant in a breach of contract suit, . . ." The actual issue in the case, however, is whether a contract is enforceable when it contains a clause that allows a party to escape liability when it fails to perform. Often a court will state the issue in the procedural context of how the matter came before the court.

> **FOR EXAMPLE** "The issue in this case is whether the motion for summary judgment was properly granted by the trial court." This is how the matter came before the court procedurally: an appeal was taken from the trial court's ruling on the motion for summary judgment. The real issue involves a question of whether, in light of the facts and the applicable law, there was a sufficient basis for the court to rule as it did.

In answering the procedural question, the court actually addresses the substantive question raised by the facts of the case. *The substantive question is what the case is actually about.* In this case, summary judgment was granted because, as a matter of law, the contract failed for want of mutuality (lack of consideration) due to the limitation of liability clause. Therefore, Sterling could not enforce the contract because it was not valid. The substantive issue addressed by the court was whether the clause rendered the contract unenforceable due to the lack of consideration. Always look for the substantive issue when the court states the issue in a procedural context.

SUMMARY

A court opinion, often referred to as a case, is the court's resolution of a legal dispute and the reasons in support of its resolution. When resolving disputes, courts often interpret constitutional or statutory provisions or create law when there is no governing law. The body of law that emerges from court opinions is called case law. It constitutes the largest body of law in the United States, far larger than constitutional, legislative, or other sources of law.

Because you must read court opinions to learn case law, it is necessary to become familiar with and proficient at reading and analyzing case law. There are several additional reasons, however, for reading opinions. A court opinion:

✦ Helps you understand and interpret constitutional provisions and statutory law

✦ Helps you understand the litigation process

✦ Provides insight into the structure of legal analysis and legal argument

✦ Provides a guide to proper legal writing

Most court opinions are composed of the facts of the case, the procedural history of the case (what happened in the lower court), the legal questions (issues) that are addressed by the court, the decision or holding of the court, the reasons for the decision reached, and the disposition (the relief granted).

Federal and state court opinions are published in books called reports and reporters, which are available through Westlaw and LexisNexis. In addition, court opinions are often available through official court Web sites and other Internet resources. If the question involves a statute, the search for case law should begin with a review of the annotations following the statute. If the question does not involve a statutory law, the search usually begins with a digest.

A case brief is a written summary of a court opinion that presents, in an organized format, all the essential information of the opinion. A researcher may be assigned the task of briefing a case. A case brief is valuable because it:

+ Saves an attorney the time of reading the case
+ Serves as a valuable learning tool
+ Is a reference tool
+ Is a writing tool

The first and possibly most important step in briefing a case is to read it carefully and slowly. Reading case law is often a difficult process, especially for the beginner. It becomes easier as more opinions are read.

Chapters 2 and 3 provide guidelines that are helpful in identifying many of the elements of a case brief.

The importance of case law cannot be overemphasized. The difficulties you encounter in reading and briefing court opinions can be lessened through the use of the guidelines presented in this chapter.

CHAPTER REFERENCES

INTERNET RESOURCES

<http://supct.law.cornell.edu/supct>
    The U.S. Supreme Court opinions are located at this site.

<http://oyez.org>
    You can hear the oral arguments or read the court briefs of U.S. Supreme Court cases at this site. The oral arguments are available for cases from 1960 to the present.

<http://www.supremecourtus.gov>
    This official page of the U.S. Supreme Court features court opinions, orders, rules, calendars and schedules, news releases, and general information.

<http://www.law.emory.edu>
    This site provides access to U.S. Federal Court cases.

<http://www.uscourts.gov>
    The site for the home page for the federal courts.

<http://www.findlaw.com/>
> Through this FindLaw site you can locate court cases in general.

<http://www.courts.net>
> This site provides access to Web sites maintained by courts nationwide.

<http://www.usdoj.gov>
> U.S. Attorney General opinions are available at this U.S. Department of Justice Web site.

<http://www.naag.org>
> Many state attorney general opinions are available at this National Association of Attorneys General Web site.

For additional materials, please go to the CD accompanying this book

For additional resources, visit our Web site at www.paralegal.delmar.cengage.com

CASE LAW CITATION

The *Bluebook* and *ALWD Citation Manual* rules governing case law citation are discussed in Chapter 11. Some brief notes and examples are presented here. If the document you are working on may be filed in a court, such as a state supreme court, check the court rules for any citation rule that may differ from the *Bluebook*.

A. Federal Courts

1. **U.S. Supreme Court.** The *Bluebook* provides that cases from the U.S. Supreme Court require citation to the official reporter, the *United States Reports.*

   Stone v. Powell, 428 U.S. 465 (1976) Citations may be to all three reporters:

   In Re Kennedy, 525 U.S. 807, 119 S.Ct. 38, 142 L.Ed2d 30 (1998)

2. **U.S. Court of Appeals.** Cite to the *Federal Reporter.*

   Essex Ins. Co. v. Davidson, 248 F.3d 716 (8th Cir. 2001)

3. **U.S. District Court.** Cite to the *Federal Supplement* or the *Federal Rules Decisions.*

   McCollum v. McDaniel, 136 F. Supp.2d 472 (D. Md. 2001)

B. State Courts

According to the *Bluebook,* in documents submitted to a state court, all citations to opinions decided by that state's courts must include citation to the official state reporter and any other parallel citation.

> *Ford v. Revlon, Inc.,* 153 Ariz. 38, 734 P.2d 580 (1987)

If the state has a public domain citation, citation should be to that citation and citation to the regional reporter may be added.

> In all other documents, the citation is to the regional reporter.

> *Ford v. Revlon, Inc.,* 734 P.2d 580 (Ariz. 1987)

EXERCISES

Additional exercises are located on the Student CD-ROM accompanying the text and Online Companion.

ASSIGNMENT 1

List and describe the elements of a case brief.

ASSIGNMENT 2

Why are court opinions important?

ASSIGNMENT 3

Consult West's *General Digest* Tenth Series.

A. Give the name and citation of a 2001 Minnesota case that lists the elements of battery.

B. Referring to the Minnesota case, does battery require the intent to injure?

C. Cite a Kentucky case that provides that fourth degree assault can be proved only if the result of the assault is physical injury, not death.

D. You are researching a question concerning the admissibility of evidence in an arson case. What key number would you refer to?

E. You are looking for the case *Adams v. Noble.* What is the Federal Supplement citation? What U.S. District Court rendered the decision? What key numbers can the case be found under?

ASSIGNMENT 4

Refer to the regional digest for your state (refer to Exhibit 5–4) or to your state court digest. Give the name and citation of a decision from your state that discusses the elements of assault or battery. Refer to the case. What are the elements of assault and battery? If there is no decision from your state, what legal encyclopedia reference is listed?

ASSIGNMENT 5

The client has been charged with bank robbery with a dangerous weapon in federal court. Refer to the *United States Code Annotated* and answer the following questions:

A. Give the ALR cite that addresses the question of how the use of an unloaded gun affects criminal responsibility.

B. Give the name and citation of the 1986 U.S. Supreme Court case that addresses the question of when an unloaded handgun is a "dangerous weapon."

C. Give the name and citation of a 1993 Eleventh Circuit case that answers the question of whether a toy gun is a "dangerous weapon."

ASSIGNMENT 6

Look to your state statute concerning aggravated or armed robbery and the annotations that follow the statute.

A. Give the legal encyclopedia reference(s) that refer to aggravated or armed robbery.

B. Give the ALR cite (if any) that addresses the question of how the use of an unloaded gun affects criminal responsibility.

C. Give the name and citation of any case that answers the question of whether a toy or fake gun is a "dangerous weapon."

ASSIGNMENT 7

Describe the importance of briefing a case.

ASSIGNMENT 8

Refer to *Morgan v. Greenwaldt* in Appendix C. Identify the citation, holding, and disposition.

ASSIGNMENT 9

Refer to *People v. Sanders* and *United States v. Martinez-Jimeniz* in Appendix C. For each of these cases, identify the parties, citation, holding, and disposition.

ASSIGNMENT 10

Following the format presented in this chapter, read and brief the following court opinions:

A. *United States v. Leon* (see Appendix C).

B. *Acacia Mutual v. American General* (see Chapter 3).

C. *Commonwealth v. Shea* (see Appendix C). Brief only the issue of whether the ocean can be considered a deadly weapon.

D. *Atlantic Beach Casino, Inc. v. Morenzoni* (see Appendix C). Brief only the issue concerning the constitutionality of the municipal ordinances.

E. *Cardwell v. Gwaltney* (see Appendix C).

F. *State v. Benner* (see Appendix C). Brief only the issue of the sufficiency of the evidence to support the conviction.

G. *McClain v. Adams* (see Appendix C).

H. *Cooper v. Austin* (see Appendix C). Brief only the issue of the validity of the codicil.

CHAPTER 6

Case Law Analysis—Is a Case on Point?

Learning Objectives

After completing this chapter, you should understand:

✦ What "on point" means when discussing case law

✦ The role and importance of a case being on point in legal analysis

✦ How to determine whether a case is on point

"That bum has cheated us for the last time," David Simms said as he walked out the office door. David Simms and his brother, Don, had just finished their initial interview with Ms. Booth, the attorney who would handle their case. Their tale was one of financial abuse by their older brother, Steve.

Their father, Dilbert Simms, died in December 1997 and left his plumbing business, Simms Plumbing, Inc., to his three sons—Steve, Don, and David. Steve, who had been running the business since 1995, was left 52 percent of the stock. David and Don, who never worked at Simms Plumbing and were employed in other occupations, were each left 24 percent.

As the majority shareholder, Steve completely controls the business. To date, he refuses to issue stock dividends even though the corporation has an accumulated cash surplus of $500,000. He has given himself three large salary increases and several cash bonuses since his father's death. When questioned by David and Don about stock dividends, he tells them, "You don't work in the business. You don't deserve any money out of it. If you want any money, you're going to have to work at the store, every day, just like I do."

After this conversation, David and Don consulted the supervising attorney, Ms. Booth. They seek redress for the wrong they feel their brother has committed in refusing to issue dividends.

The paralegal's task, assigned by Ms. Booth, is to find the applicable statute and the leading case on point in the jurisdiction. The statute, section 96-25-16 of the Business Corporation Act, provides that a court may order the liquidation of a corporation when a majority shareholder has engaged in oppressive conduct. The statute, however, does not define what constitutes oppressive conduct.

The hard part of the assignment is locating a case on point, in the jurisdiction, that defines or provides the elements of oppressive conduct. After an extensive search, the paralegal locates only one case dealing with oppressive conduct, *Karl v. Herald.* In this case, a husband and wife owned a small corporation in which the husband owned 75 percent of the stock and the wife owned 25 percent. When they divorced, he fired her from her salaried position of bookkeeper, took away her company car, and refused to issue stock dividends. The company was very profitable, had a large cash surplus, and was clearly in a financial position to issue dividends. After the divorce, the husband gave himself a hefty salary increase. The court held that he had engaged in oppressive conduct in freezing his wife out of the corporation. It defined oppressive conduct as "any unfair or fraudulent act by a majority shareholder that inures to the benefit of the majority and to the detriment of the minority."

Upon finding this case, several questions run through the paralegal's mind. Is this case on point? How do you determine if a case is on point? Why does it matter?

I. INTRODUCTION

Legal research, analysis, and writing are all related and are often part of a single process. Research locates the law, analysis determines how the law applies, and legal writing assembles and integrates the results into a useable form.

The focus of this chapter is on the application of case law to a legal question. It covers **case law analysis**—the analytical process you engage in to determine if and how the decision in a court opinion either governs or affects the outcome of a client's case. A case that governs or affects the outcome of a client's case is commonly referred to as being on point. The purpose of case law research is to locate cases that are on point, that is, cases that illustrate how law applies to the client's facts. Therefore, it is critical for a researcher to be able to determine whether a case is on point.

Throughout the chapter, reference is made to single issues and single rules of law or legal principles when discussing court opinions and clients' cases. The focus is on how to determine if a single issue, addressed in a court opinion, is on point and how, therefore, it may affect or govern an issue in a client's case. Always be aware that multiple issues and legal rules/principles are often involved in court opinions, some of which may be on point, and therefore govern the outcome of an issue in the client's case, and some of which may not be on point. When determining if an opinion is on point, follow the steps discussed in this chapter separately for each issue in a client's case.

The chapter opens with a definition of the term *on point,* followed by a discussion of the importance of locating a case on point and the process of determining if a case is on point.

II. DEFINITION—*ON POINT*

Throughout this chapter, the term *on point* is used to describe a court opinion that applies to the client's case. What do "on point" and "applies to the client's case" mean? A case is **on point** if the similarity between the key facts and the rule of law or legal principle of the court opinion and those of the client's case is sufficient for the court opinion to govern or provide guidance to a later court in deciding the outcome of the client's case. In other words, does the court opinion govern or guide the resolution of an issue in the client's case? Is the court opinion precedent? If a case is on point, it is precedent. The terms *on point* and *precedent* are often used interchangeably.

III. ON POINT—IMPORTANCE

Before discussing the process involved in determining if a case is on point, it is helpful to understand why you must engage in the process of finding past court decisions that affect the client's case. Why is it important?

As discussed in Chapter 1, case law is a major source of law in the legal system. Through case law, courts create law and interpret the language of constitutions, legislative acts, and regulations. The determination of whether a case is on point is important because of two doctrines covered in Chapter 1—precedent and stare decisis. The doctrines of precedent and stare decisis govern and guide the application of case law and thereby provide uniformity and consistency in the case law system. They help make the law more predictable. A brief review of these doctrines is helpful in obtaining an understanding of the process involved in determining whether a case is on point.

A. Precedent

Precedent is an earlier court decision on an issue that governs or guides a subsequent court in its determination of an identical or similar issue based on identical or similar key facts. This chapter identifies the steps involved in determining when a case may be either mandatory or persuasive precedent. A case is precedent (on point) if there is a sufficient similarity between the key facts and rule of law or legal principle of the court opinion and the matter before the subsequent court.

FOR EXAMPLE The state collections statute provides that efforts to collect payment for a debt must be made in a reasonable manner. The statute does not define "reasonable." In the case of *Mark v. Collections, Inc.,* the supreme court of the state held that it is not reasonable, within the meaning of the collection statute, for a bill collector to make more than one telephone call a day to a debtor's residence, nor is it reasonable to make calls before sunrise or after sunset.

The facts of the case were that the collector was making seven calls a day, some of which were after sunset.

The facts of the client's case are that a bill collector is calling the client six times a day between the hours of 9 A.M. and 5 P.M. The ruling in *Mark v. Collections, Inc.,* applies as precedent to the issue of whether the frequency of the calls by the collector is unreasonable and, therefore, in violation of the act. The *Mark* case is sufficiently similar to the current case to apply as precedent. Both cases involve the following:

✦ *The same law*—The collections statute

✦ *The same question*—A determination of when the frequency of the telephone calls constitutes unreasonable conduct within the meaning of the act

✦ *Similar key facts*—Six telephone calls per day and seven calls per day

The application of *Mark* as precedent guides the court in its resolution of the question presented in the client's case of whether six calls a day violate the act. The court in *Mark* held that more than one call a day is unreasonable. Therefore, the six calls a day in the client's case are unreasonable in light of the holding in the *Mark* case. This example is referred to as the collections example in this chapter.

B. Mandatory Precedent

Mandatory precedent is precedent from a higher court in a jurisdiction. If a court opinion is on point, that is, if it is precedent, the doctrine of stare decisis mandates that the lower courts in the jurisdiction follow it. In the preceding example, if the decision in *Mark v. Collections, Inc.,* is the ruling of the highest court in the jurisdiction, the lower courts in the jurisdiction must follow it.

C. Persuasive Precedent

Persuasive precedent is precedent that a court may look to for guidance when reaching a decision, but that it is not bound to follow. In the collections example, courts in other jurisdictions are not bound to follow the *Mark* decision. Also, if the decision was by a lower court in the jurisdiction, such as a trial court, then a higher court, such as a court of appeals, is not bound to follow the decision. A higher court, however, may choose to refer to and use a lower court decision as guidance when deciding a similar case before it.

D. Stare Decisis

The doctrine of **stare decisis** is a basic principle of the case law system that requires a court to follow a previous decision of that court or a higher court in the jurisdiction when the current decision involves issues and key facts similar to those involved in the previous decision. In other words, the doctrine of stare decisis requires that similar cases be decided in the same way—that cases that are precedent should be followed. The doctrine applies unless there is good reason not to follow it.

> **FOR EXAMPLE**   In regard to the *Mark* case discussed previously, stare decisis is the doctrine that holds that after it is determined that the case is precedent, the lower courts in the jurisdiction must follow it unless good cause is shown. It is mandatory precedent.

Without the doctrines of stare decisis and precedent, there would most likely be chaos in the court decision-making process. Judges and attorneys would not have guidance about how matters should be decided. Similar cases could be decided differently based upon the whims and diverse beliefs of judges and juries. These doctrines provide stability, predictability, and guidance for courts and attorneys. An individual can rely on a future court to reach the same decision on an issue as an earlier court did when the cases are sufficiently similar.

With the preceding in mind, it becomes clear why determining whether a case is on point is important and why a researcher needs to find a case that is on point:

+ The determination must be made before the case may apply as precedent and be used and relied upon by a court in its determination of how an issue will be decided. Note that if the court is unaware of the case, it may be necessary to bring it to the court's attention.

+ Inasmuch as the court will consider precedent in reaching its decision, a researcher needs to find cases that are on point to provide guidance to the attorney as to how the issue in the client's case may be decided. Cases that are on point must be located and analyzed to determine what impact they may have on the decision in the client's case. Also, they must be analyzed to help the attorney determine what course of action to take. If a case that is on point indicates that the decision will most likely be against the client, it may be appropriate to pursue settlement or other options.

IV. DETERMINING WHETHER A CASE IS ON POINT

The process of deciding if a court opinion is on point involves determining how similar the opinion is to the client's case. The more similar the court opinion is to the client's case, the more likely it will be considered precedent—that is, the more likely the rule/principle applied in the opinion will govern or apply to the client's case.

In the Definition—*On Point* section of this chapter, a case is defined as being on point if there is a sufficient similarity between the key facts and rule of law or legal principle of the court opinion and those of the client's case. Therefore, for a case to be on point and apply as precedent, there are two requirements:

+ The significant or key facts of the court opinion must be sufficiently similar to the key facts of the client's case; or if the facts are not similar, the rule of law or legal principle applied in the court opinion must be so broad that it applies to many diverse fact situations.

+ The rule of law or legal principle applied in the court opinion must be the same or sufficiently similar to the rule of law or legal principle that applies in the client's case. *Rule of law* and *legal principle*, as used here, include any constitutional, legislative, or case law provision, act, doctrine, principle, or test relied on by the court in reaching its decision.

For a court opinion to be on point and apply as precedent, the requirements of the following steps must be met.	
Step 1	**Are the key facts sufficiently similar for the case to apply as precedent?** The key facts of the court opinion must be sufficiently similar to the key facts of the client's case. If the facts are not similar, the opinion will serve as precedent only if the rule of law or legal principle is broad enough to apply to other fact situations, including the client's.
Step 2	**Are the rules/principles of law sufficiently similar for the case to apply as precedent?** The rule of law or legal principle applied in the court opinion must be the same or sufficiently similar to the rule of law or legal principle that applies in the client's case.

Exhibit 6–1
Steps in Determining whether a Case Is on Point.

If these two criteria are not met, the court opinion is not on point and may not be used as precedent for the client's case. The two-step process presented in Exhibit 6–1 is recommended for determining if the two requirements are met.

A. Step 1: Are the Key Facts Sufficiently Similar?

The first step in the analysis process is to determine if the significant or key facts in the court opinion are sufficiently similar to the key facts in the client's case so that the court opinion may apply as precedent. This is accomplished by comparing the key facts of the court opinion with those of the client's case. A key fact is a fact that, if it were changed, would affect the outcome of the case. You must identify key facts before you can determine if a case is on point. If there is not a sufficient similarity between the key facts of the client's case and the court opinion, the opinion *usually* cannot be used as precedent—that is, it is not on point.

You may encounter two situations when comparing the key facts of a client's case and a court opinion:

✦ The key facts are directly on point, that is, they are identical or nearly identical.
✦ The key facts are different.

1. Identical or Nearly Identical Key Facts

When the key facts in the court opinion are identical or nearly identical with those of the client's case, the opinion is on point factually and can be a precedent that applies to the client's case if the requirements of step 2 are met. The phrase **on all fours** is often used to describe such opinions: opinions where the facts of the opinion and those of the client's case and the rule of law that applies are identical or so similar that the court opinion is clearly on point. When such an opinion is the opinion of a higher court in a jurisdiction, it is mandatory precedent that the lower courts in the jurisdiction must follow.

FOR EXAMPLE In the case of *Davis v. Davis,* Ms. Davis had sole custody of her two daughters, ages 8 and 10. Ms. Davis had a boyfriend who occasionally stayed overnight at her home. The children were aware of the overnight visits. Mr. Davis, her former husband, filed a motion with the court asking for a change of custody. He based his claim solely upon his ex-wife's alleged "immoral conduct." No evidence was presented indicating how the overnight visits impacted the children. The trial court granted a change of custody.

The court of appeals overturned the trial court, ruling that "mere allegations of immoral conduct are not sufficient grounds to award a change of custody." The court required the presentation of evidence showing that the alleged immoral conduct harmed the children.

The client was divorced one year ago and was granted sole custody of his two minor daughters, ages 8 and 12. On occasion, his girlfriend stays overnight, and the children are aware of the overnight visits. The client's former spouse has filed a motion for change of custody alleging that his immoral conduct is grounds for a change of custody. She does not have evidence that the children have been harmed or negatively impacted.

Clearly, the requirements of step 1 are met. *Davis v. Davis* is factually on point and, therefore, is precedent that applies to the client's case. Note that the requirements of step 2 are also met. The same legal principle is being applied in the court opinion and the client's case: mere allegations of immorality are not sufficient grounds for granting a change of custody. Step 2 addresses the requirement that the legal principles must be sufficiently similar.

Although some of the facts are different—in the client's case, it is the father who has custody and his girlfriend stays overnight, while in *Davis v. Davis* it is the mother who has custody and her boyfriend who stays overnight—these facts are not key facts. The gender of the custodial parent and the gender of the person staying overnight are not key facts. The key facts are identical: occasional overnight visits, the children are aware of the visits, the children are preteen (the age of the children is always an important consideration), and there is no evidence presented that the children are harmed. This example is referred to as the custody example throughout the remainder of this chapter.

It is rare to find instances where the key facts are identical. Usually there is some difference in the key facts. When you find a case with identical facts that you determine is mandatory precedent, be thankful if the holding supports your client's position. It is difficult for a lower court not to follow the higher court's decision when it is so clearly on point.

2. Different Key Facts

When the key facts of the court opinion and the key facts of the client's case are not identical, the opinion *may* be on point and *may* apply as precedent. It depends on the degree of the difference. If some of the key facts are different, you must determine whether the differences are of such a nature or degree that they render the court opinion unusable as precedent. Use the following three-part process when making this determination:

* *Part 1*—Identify the similarities between the key facts.
* *Part 2*—Identify the differences between the key facts.
* *Part 3*—Determine if the differences are of such a significant degree that the opinion cannot apply as precedent. (See Exhibit 6–2.)

Throughout this discussion of different key facts, assume that the requirements of step 2 are met—that is, the rule of law applied in the court opinion is the same or sufficiently similar to the rule of law that applies in the client's case.

FOR EXAMPLE The client's case is the same as the custody example except that instead of occasional overnight visits by the girlfriend, the girlfriend has moved in with the client. Is the case of *Davis v. Davis* on point?

Three-part process for determining if a case is on point when the key facts of the court opinion are different from the key facts of the client's case.	
Part 1	Identify the similarities between the key facts.
Part 2	Identify the differences between the key facts.
Part 3	Determine if the differences are of such a significant degree that the opinion cannot apply as precedent.

Exhibit 6–2
Three-Part Process for Addressing Different Key Facts.

To answer this question, use the following process:

a. Part 1—Identify the Similarities Between the Key Facts

In both the client's case and the *Davis case*:

✦ The minor children are under the age of 12.

✦ Someone of the opposite sex is staying overnight with the custodial parent.

✦ There is no showing that the children have been harmed by the conduct.

b. Part 2—Identify the Differences Between the Key Facts

The difference in the key facts is that in *Davis v. Davis*, the overnight visits are occasional. In the client's case, there is cohabitation rather than occasional overnight visits.

c. Part 3—Determine If the Differences Are of Such a Significant Degree That the Opinion Cannot Apply as Precedent

To determine the significance of the differences, substitute the client's key facts for those of the court opinion. If the substitution of the key facts would result in changing the outcome of the case, the court opinion cannot be used as precedent.

In this example, would the court in *Davis v. Davis* have reached the same conclusion if Ms. Davis' boyfriend had moved in with her? Probably. The same legal principle applies—that is, allegations of immoral conduct alone are not sufficient grounds to award a change of custody; there must be a showing that the conduct harmed the children.

As indicated in *Davis v. Davis*, an essential element necessary before a change of custody is granted is a showing of harm to the children. A key fact in the *Davis* decision was the lack of showing of harm to the children. In both the court opinion and the client's case, there is a lack of showing of harm to the children, and therefore, the principle applied in *Davis* should apply to the client's case even though the *Davis* opinion involved overnight visits and the client's case involves cohabitation.

You must be careful, however. There may be another statute or case law doctrine providing that cohabitation is per se harmful to children—that is, in cohabitation cases such as the client's case, the law presumes that cohabitation is harmful to the children. If this is the situation, the plaintiff would not need to establish harm in cohabitation cases such as the client's and the *Davis* opinion would not be on point and could not be used as precedent. The difference in the key facts would be so significant that the substitution of the client's cohabitation fact with the *Davis* opinion's occasional overnight visits fact would change the decision reached by the court because a different statute would apply.

Four variations may be encountered when dealing with different key facts. These variations are presented in Exhibit 6–3.

(1) Minor Differences in Key Facts—Case on Point. Some key facts are so insignificantly different that they clearly do not affect the use of a court decision as precedent.

Exhibit 6-3
Different Key Fact Variations.

Variations that may be encountered when dealing with different key facts.
1. Minor Differences in Key Fact—case on point
2. Major Difference in Key Facts—case not on point
3. Major Difference in Key Facts—case on point
4. Major Difference in Key Facts—case on point, broad legal principle

> **FOR EXAMPLE** In the custody example, if the client's children were 9 and 11 years old as opposed to 8 and 10, *Davis v. Davis* would clearly apply as precedent. Although the age of the children is a key fact, a minor difference of one year in the ages of the children is not a significant difference in the key facts. If the client's children were several years older than the children in *Davis v. Davis,* such as ages 17 and 18, the age difference could be a major difference in the key facts because a different standard might apply if the children were in their late teens.

(2) Major Difference in Key Facts—Case Not on Point. The following example presents a situation where the key facts of the court opinion and the key facts of the client's case are different, the opinion is not on point, and it does not apply as precedent. This example is referred to in this chapter as the arrest example.

> **FOR EXAMPLE** In the court case of *State v. Thomas,* Mr. Thomas was handcuffed and taken to the police station after officers broke up a fistfight. Thomas was not read his rights at the scene of the fight. He was read his rights and formally arrested at the police station 30 minutes later. The court, ruling that he was under arrest when handcuffed at the scene, stated that "an arrest takes place when a reasonable person does not believe he is free to leave."

In the client's case, the client explains that the police handcuffed him and told him to stay in the hallway of the house while they executed a search warrant. He was not allowed to leave. It appears that the key facts regarding whether an arrest has taken place are nearly the same. In both the court opinion and the client's case, the individual was handcuffed and not free to leave. The critical difference in the facts is the context of the seizure of the individual. In *Thomas,* the seizure took place at the scene of a fight. There were no warrants involved. In the client's case, the seizure took place during the execution of a search warrant.

In regard to the question of whether the client was under arrest when handcuffed and detained in the hallway, is *State v. Thomas* on point? The answer is no. Although the facts of the detention are similar, the difference in the context of the seizure is a critical key fact difference. Other case law holds that a seizure during the execution of a search warrant is an exception to the rule stated in *Thomas,* and such seizures do not constitute an arrest.

The other case law provides that a search warrant implicitly carries with it the authority to detain an individual for the purposes of the officer's safety and to determine if there is cause to make an arrest. Therefore, such detentions do not constitute an arrest within the meaning of the law. Because of this authority, the difference between the key facts of *Thomas* and the client's case is critical, and the case is not on point. This example is referred to as the arrest example throughout the remainder of this chapter.

(3) Major Difference in Key Facts—Case on Point.   A major difference in the key facts does not necessarily result in a determination that the case is not on point. The opinion may still be on point, but the outcome may be different. The legal principle applied by the court may still apply. Its application may just lead to a different result.

> **FOR EXAMPLE**   In the custody example, if there is an additional key fact in the client's case that the spouse seeking custody has evidence showing that the children were being harmed by exposure to the cohabitation, *Davis v. Davis* could still be on point. This could occur even though there was no evidence of harm to the children presented in the *Davis* case. Although there is now a major difference between the key facts of the court opinion and the client's case, the court opinion may still apply as precedent and govern the outcome of the change of custody question.
>
> The court in the *Davis* case concluded that sufficient grounds did not exist to award a change of custody because there was *no evidence* presented showing harm to the children. The same principle governing *Davis* governs the facts here—that is, allegations of immorality, *standing alone,* are not sufficient for an award of a change of custody; there must be a showing of harm to the children.
>
> A corollary of the rule, however, is that if there is a *showing of harm* to the children, there may be sufficient grounds for a change of custody. It can be argued that when the key fact of evidence of harm is present, the corollary of the rule applies. Even though the facts of the court opinion and the client's case are different, the corollary applies to support a change of custody award—a result different from the result reached in the court opinion.

(4) Major Difference in Key Facts—Case on Point, Broad Legal Principle.   Generally, if key facts are significantly different, it is highly probable that a different rule or principle applies and a court case will not apply as precedent. There are, however, instances where the key facts are different, but the court opinion is on point because the rule of law or legal principle is so broad that it applies to many different fact situations. This situation is addressed in greater detail in step 2 in the next section.

> **FOR EXAMPLE**   The client was detained with a group of exotic dancers in a bar. The officers who detained the client were not executing a search or arrest warrant. Before informing the dancers that they were under arrest, or in any way informing them what was taking place, the officers moved them to a separate room where they were detained for more than an hour. They were clearly not free to leave. They were formally arrested two hours later and then taken to jail.
>
> In regard to the question of whether the client was under arrest when detained in the room prior to arrest, *State v. Thomas* (presented in the preceding arrest example) is probably on point. The definition of arrest presented in *Thomas* applies to the client's case even though the factual context of the seizures is different. Applying that definition to the client's case results in the conclusion that an arrest occurred when the client was moved to a separate room and detained for over an hour. A reasonable person in the client's situation would not believe he was free to leave. The definition of arrest presented in *Thomas* is so broad that it applies to a wide range of detention situations.

Note: Be careful. It is always preferable to locate an opinion that is as factually similar to the client's case as possible. The more dissimilar the key facts, the easier it is for the other side to argue that the differences are critical, the opinion is not on point, and it does not apply as precedent to the case at hand.

A difference in key facts should alert you to be careful and cause you to explore all potential legal avenues that may arise due to the fact differences. Focus on the differences. Ask yourself, "Are they important?" Conduct further research and Shepardize the case to determine if there are other cases more on point.

In summary, if the key facts are the same and the same rule of law applies (step 2), the court opinion is usually on point and can be considered as a precedent that applies to your client's case. If the key facts are different, either in part or totally, you must perform careful analysis to ensure that the factual differences are not so significant that they are fatal to the use of the court opinion as precedent.

B. Step 2: Are the Rules/Principles of Law Sufficiently Similar?

By applying the principles presented in step 1, you determined whether the key facts of the court opinion are sufficiently similar to the key facts of the client's case for the opinion to apply as precedent factually. After this is accomplished, half of the task is completed. Note that this is a *two-step* process—you *must* complete both steps before you can determine whether a case is on point and whether it can apply as precedent.

The second step is to determine whether the rule of law or legal principle applied in the court opinion is the same rule of law or legal principle that applies in the client's case. If it is not the same rule of law, is it sufficiently similar to the rule that applies in the client's case for the opinion to still apply as precedent? As mentioned at the beginning of the Determining Whether a Case Is on Point section, the rule of law or legal principle includes any constitutional, legislative, or case law provision, act, doctrine, principle, or test relied on by the court in reaching its decision. You may encounter one of two situations when performing step 2:

1. The rule or principle applied in the court opinion is the same rule or principle that applies in the client's case.

2. The rule or principle applied in the court opinion is different from the rule or principle that applies in the client's case.

1. Same Rule or Principle

If you determine that the key facts are sufficiently similar so that the court opinion can apply as precedent and the same rule of law is involved in both the opinion and the client's case, the requirements of step 2 are met, and the case is on point. The rule of law comparison is simple. The rule of law applies in the client's case in the same way as it was applied in the court's opinion.

> **FOR EXAMPLE** In the custody example, if the client's case involves the situation of the client having occasional overnight visits by his girlfriend, the same rule of law governs the court opinion and the client's facts—that is, allegations of immorality without evidence of harm to the children are not sufficient grounds to support a change of custody. The rule applies in the same way in the client's case as in the court opinion— a change of custody will not be granted where there is no showing of harm to the children.

Note: The same rule of law may apply, but its application in the client's case may result in an outcome different from the outcome in the court case. See the example presented in the earlier Major Difference in Key Facts—Case on Point subsection. In that example, the same legal principle was applied in both the client's case and the court opinion, but the result was different.

2. Different Rule or Principle

What if the rule of law applied in the opinion is different from the rule of law that applies in the client's case? In other words, what if there is no court decision in your jurisdiction applying or interpreting the rule or legal principle that applies to your client's case? What if the rule or principle applied in the closest court opinion you can find is different from the rule or principle that applies in the client's case? Can the court opinion apply as precedent? The general rule is *no.* Usually this is obvious. For example, a child custody opinion rarely can be precedent for a murder case.

Again, there are exceptions. The court's interpretation of a provision of a legislative act or case law rule or principle may be so broad in scope that it applies to the different law or rule that governs the client's case. Keep in mind, however, that because the law or rule applied in the court opinion is different from that which applies to the client's case, the court opinion is *persuasive* precedent. The court hearing the client's case does not have to follow it—it is not *mandatory* precedent. The court has discretion and must be persuaded.

There are two areas to explore when considering these exceptions: legislative acts and case law rules or principles. In regard to these two areas, it is important to remember that the discussion involves *only* those situations where there is *no court opinion* in the jurisdiction that directly interprets the same legislative act or case law rule that applies to the client's case.

a. Legislative Acts

A court opinion interpreting one legislative act may be used as precedent for a client's case that involves the application of a different legislative act when the following is true:

+ There is a similarity in language between the legislative acts.
+ There is a similarity in function between the legislative acts. (See Exhibit 6–4.)

Requirements that must be met for a case to be on point when the legislative act applied in the court opinion differs from the legislative act that applies in the client's case.
1. There is a similarity in language between the legislative acts.
2. There is a similarity in function between the legislative acts.

Exhibit 6–4
Requirements When Different Legislative Acts Apply.

FOR EXAMPLE There are three statutes adopted in the jurisdiction:

+ Section 56 provides that an individual must be a resident of the county to be eligible to run for the position of county animal control officer.

+ Section 3105 provides that an individual must be a resident of the county to run for a seat on the county school board.

+ Section 4175 provides that an individual must be a resident of the state to be eligible to run for the office of governor.

The term *resident* is not defined in any of the statutes, and none of the statutes establishes a length of residency requirement. The only case in the jurisdiction that defines the term is *Frank v. Teague,* a case involving section 3105. In this case, the court ruled that to be eligible to run for a seat on the school board, the candidate must be a resident of the county of the school board district for a minimum of three months immediately prior to the election. This example is referred to in this chapter as the residence example.

1. The client, a resident of the county for three and one-half months, wants to run for the office of governor. Does the *Frank* opinion apply as precedent and support the client's claim of eligibility to run for the office of governor? Probably not.

Although there is a similarity in the language of the statutes in that both use the term *resident*, there is not a similarity in function. The considerations involved in determining the length of residence required as a prerequisite for eligibility to run for each office are quite different. The court's decision in *Frank*, imposing a three-month residency requirement for the school board position, may be based upon the court's determination that this is the amount of time an individual needs to become sufficiently familiar with the county to perform the duties of a school board member. The position of governor, however, involves different considerations. The office is statewide, and the court could conclude that a longer residency period is necessary for an individual to become sufficiently familiar with the state to adequately perform the duties of governor.

2. The client wants to run for the position of animal control officer. He has been a resident of the county for four months. In this situation, it is more likely that *Frank* will apply as precedent, that it is on point, and that it supports the position that the client is eligible to run for animal control officer.

Again, both statutes use the same language, *resident*. They are more closely related in function than the school board and governor statutes. Both involve countywide positions wherein the duties are focused on county concerns. It can be argued that no more time is required to become familiar with the county to perform the duties of animal control officer than is required to perform the duties of a school board member.

The court, following this line of reasoning, could conclude that the residency requirement for the position of animal control officer should not exceed the minimum residency set for a seat on the school board. It could, therefore, adopt the three-month standard established in the *Frank* case as the standard for the animal control officer statute.

Because the statutes are different, you are always open to a counterargument pointing out some critical difference in function between the statutes.

In this example, it could be argued that the duties of animal control officer are much different than those of a school board member. The duties of the animal control officer require a great degree of familiarity with the geography of the county, and a longer period of residency should therefore be required to ensure that a candidate has sufficient time to become familiar with the county.

In every situation where the statutes are different in function, even if they have some similarities, an argument can be made that the difference, no matter how slight, dictates that a court's interpretation of one statute in one case cannot apply to another statute in a different case.

The preceding examples involve statutes from the same state. All the statutes were passed by the same state legislature, and the court opinion came from a court in that state. What if, in the residence example, there is no case law in the state interpreting the term *resident*, and the *Frank v. Teague* opinion is a decision from another state interpreting a statute of that state that is identical or very similar to section 3105? Can *Frank* apply as precedent?

The answer is the same as the answer discussed in the preceding examples. If there is sufficient similarity in language and function of the statutes, the opinion can apply as precedent. If there is not sufficient similarity, it cannot apply as precedent. As long as the court is convinced that the similarity is sufficient, it can apply.

Bear in mind that a decision from another jurisdiction is only persuasive precedent, and a court is more likely to adopt persuasive precedent from a court within the jurisdiction than from a court without. It is best to locate authority within your jurisdiction. Look out of state only if there is no opinion that could apply as persuasive precedent within the jurisdiction.

Realistically, it is always risky to argue that a court's interpretation of a provision of one statute applies as precedent for the interpretation of a provision of a different statute. You are always open to, and will probably have to fend off, counterarguments that the statutes are functionally different and that reliance on a particular court opinion is misplaced. Your position is never solid. Always try to find another opinion or pursue another avenue of research.

b. Case Law Rule or Principle

The same principles mentioned in the preceding section apply when you attempt use as precedent a court opinion interpreting a case law rule or principle. Can a court opinion interpreting a case law rule or principle apply as precedent for a client's case that requires the application of a different case law rule or principle? Are the case law rules or principles similar in language and function? A court opinion interpreting one case law rule or principle may be used as precedent for a client's case that involves the application of a different case law rule or principle when the following is true:

1. There is a similarity in language between the case law rules or principles.

2. There is a similarity in function between the case law rules or principles. (See Exhibit 6–5.)

Requirements that must be met for a case to be on point when the common law rule or principle applied in the court opinion differs from the common law rule or principle that applies in the client's case.
1. There is a similarity in language between the common law rules or principles.
2. There is a similarity in function between the common law rules or principles.

Exhibit 6–5
Requirements When Different Common Law Rules/Principles Apply.

FOR EXAMPLE The jurisdiction recognizes the torts of intrusion and public disclosure of a private fact. Intrusion protects against the act of prying or probing into the private affairs of an individual. Public disclosure of a private fact protects against the act of publishing information concerning the private affairs of an individual. Both of these torts have been established by the highest court in the jurisdiction. There is no statutory law defining or governing the torts. One of the elements of the tort of *intrusion* is an act of intrusion into the *private affairs* of the plaintiff. One of the elements of the tort of *public disclosure of a private fact* is the public disclosure of a fact concerning the *private affairs* of the plaintiff.

In the client's case, the client was having an affair with the wife of a city council member. A campaign rival of the client disclosed the existence of the relationship at a campaign rally. The campaign rival acquired the information from a campaign aide who obtained the information by peeking through the client's bedroom window. The client wants to sue for public disclosure of a private fact. The question is whether the affair is a private fact.

The only relevant case in the jurisdiction is *Claron v. Clark,* an intrusion case where a private investigator, through the means of a wiretap, discovered that the plaintiff was engaged in an affair. The court ruled that the term *private affairs* includes any sexual activity that takes place within the confines of an individual's residence.

Is the *Clark* opinion, an intrusion case, on point? Can it be precedent in the client's case, which involves a different tort—public disclosure of a private fact? May it be used as precedent in the client's case to guide the court in its interpretation of the meaning of the term *private affairs?* There is a similarity in the elements of the torts; both use the term *private affairs.* Both torts are similar in function. They are designed to protect the private affairs and lives of individuals.

If the court is convinced that the similarities are sufficient, the case can apply as precedent. It can always be argued, however, that because the torts are different, there is a difference in function, no matter how slight, which dictates that a court's interpretation of one tort cannot apply to a different tort. In this case, it can be argued that prying is different from publication, and therefore, the difference in the interest being protected in the two torts is sufficient to prevent an interpretation of a term in intrusion from being used to interpret the same term in public disclosure of a private fact.

Again, be careful. The same pitfalls exist here as when different legislative acts apply. A court opinion within the jurisdiction interpreting a different rule of law is only persuasive precedent. It is not mandatory precedent that must be followed. It is easy to present a counterargument that the functions of the two doctrines are clearly different, so the court opinion cannot apply as precedent. Also, keep in mind that when the decision is from another jurisdiction, it is still only persuasive precedent, and a court is more likely to adopt persuasive precedent from a court within the jurisdiction than from a court without.

Note: Be careful. It is always preferable to locate an opinion that applies a rule or legal principle that is the same as the rule or principle that applies in the client's case. If different rules or principles are involved, it is easier for the other side to argue that the opinion is not on point and, therefore, does not apply as precedent for the case at hand.

Where different rules or principles are involved, you should conduct further research and *Shepardize* the case to determine if there are other cases more on point.

V. KEY POINTS CHECKLIST: *Is a Case on Point?*

- Focus on the key facts and the rule of law/legal principle of both the court opinion and the client's case.
- Where there are differences between the key facts of the court opinion and the client's case, carefully determine whether the differences are significant. Beware! Different key facts may lead to the application of an entirely different law or principle despite other key fact similarities. The rule of law or legal principle, however, may be so broad that it applies to many different fact situations.
- Clearly identify the rule of law/legal principle that applies in the court opinion and in the client's case.
- Where the rule of law applied in the court opinion is different from the rule that applies in the client's case, consider using the court opinion as precedent *only when there is no authority* interpreting or applying the rule/principle that applies in the client's case.
- Consider authority from another jurisdiction *only* when there is no authority in the jurisdiction.

- If in doubt about whether a fact is a key fact, continue your analysis until you are certain. Refer to the steps presented in Chapter 2.

- Follow your instincts. If an opinion does not appear to be on point but your intuition tells you it is on point, continue your analysis until you are certain. If you never reach the point of feeling certain, search elsewhere.

VI. APPLICATION

This section presents four examples illustrating the application of the principles presented in this chapter for determining when a case is on point.

A. Chapter Hypothetical

This example is based on the fact pattern presented at the beginning of this chapter. Returning to that problem, is the case of *Karl v. Herald* on point so that it applies as precedent for the client's case?

STEP 1: Are the key facts sufficiently similar? The first step is to determine whether the key facts of *Karl v. Herald* are sufficiently similar to the client's case for *Herald* to apply as precedent—to be on point. Although the facts in *Herald* are somewhat different, they are sufficiently similar. In both cases, the corporation was in a position to pay dividends. In both cases, while refusing to pay dividends, the majority shareholder allegedly enriched himself through excessive raises and/or bonuses. In both cases, the minority shareholders were effectively frozen out from benefiting in the corporation.

A difference in *Herald* is that the plaintiff worked in the business. In the client's case, the brothers did not work in the business. This difference in the cases is not a key fact difference. The fact that the plaintiff in *Herald* worked in the business relates to her status as an employee, but it is not related to her status as a shareholder. In *Herald,* the court defined oppressive conduct as conduct against shareholders, not employees. The plaintiff's status as an employee may give rise to employee rights, but it is not related to rights as a shareholder and, therefore, is not a key fact.

STEP 2: Are the rules/principles sufficiently similar? Is there a sufficient similarity between the law that applies in *Karl v. Herald* and that which applies in the client's case for the case to be considered on point and apply as precedent? The same statute, section 96-25-16 of the Business Corporation Act, applies to both the court opinion and the client's case. Both cases involve allegations of oppressive conduct by a minority shareholder against a majority shareholder and are governed by the same section of the statute.

In the *Herald* opinion, oppressive conduct was defined as "any unfair or fraudulent act by a majority shareholder that inures to the benefit of the majority and to the detriment of the minority." The client's case also involves questions of oppressive conduct by the majority shareholder and is governed by the same definition. Just as in *Herald,* there is alleged unfair conduct by the majority shareholder that inures to the benefit of the majority and to the detriment of the minority. There are no major differences between *Herald* and the client's case that restrict the application of *Herald* as precedent.

Note: What if you concluded that *Herald* was not on point, but it was the only case in the jurisdiction that discusses oppressive conduct? You would need to be sure to analyze the case in the memorandum to your supervisor and point out why the case is not on point.

B. Chapter 1 Hypothetical *Reins v. Stewart*

The following example involves the application of the principles to the hypothetical presented at the beginning of Chapter 1. Vanessa located *Rael v. Cadena*, 93 N.M. 684, 604 P.2d 822 (Ct. App.1979), a case she believes is on point. She performs the following steps to determine if the case is on point.

STEP 1: Are the key facts sufficiently similar? The first step is to determine whether the key facts of *Rael v. Cadena* are sufficiently similar to the client's case for *Rael* to apply as precedent—to be on point. The facts Vanessa identified as the key facts in the client's case are listed here followed by the key facts in *Rael v. Cadena:*

✦ Mr. Stewart was present at the fight and encouraged his son by yelling, "Hit him again, beat him." He did not otherwise participate. The son attacked Mr. Reins.

In *Rael*, Emilio Cadina was present at the fight and encouraged his nephew by yelling, "Kill him" and "Hit him more!" Emilio did not otherwise participate. The nephew, Manuel Cadena, attacked Mr. Rael. The facts are almost identical. The only difference is in the words of encouragement. This difference is insignificant. In both cases the words strongly encouraged the perpetrator and were yelled by the nonactive participant.

✦ Mr. Reins suffered a broken jaw as a result of the beating.

In *Rael*, Mr. Rael suffered a fractured rib and was hospitalized. Again, the facts are almost identical. In both cases, the victim suffered severe injuries.

✦ Mr. Stewart said the words after the son started to attack Mr. Reins.

In *Rael*, Mr. Cadena said the words after his nephew began the attack. In both cases, the facts match.

STEP 2: Are the rules/principles sufficiently similar? There is sufficient similarity between the law that applies in *Rael v. Cadena* and that which applies in the client's case for the case to be considered on point and apply as precedent. Both cases involve the same law: battery. In both cases, the question is whether an individual present at the scene of a battery, who did nothing more than strongly encourage the perpetrator, is liable for civil battery.

There are no major differences between the law and key facts of *Rael v. Cadena* and the client's case that restrict the application of *Rael* as precedent.

C. Chapter 2 Hypothetical *United States v. Canter*

The following example involves the application of the principles to the hypothetical presented at the beginning of Chapter 2. The case Dustin believes to be on point is *United States v. Martinez-Jimenez*, 864 F.2d 664 (9th Cir. 1989). He performs the following steps to determine if the case is on point.

STEP 1: Are the key facts sufficiently similar? The first step is to determine if the key facts of *United States v. Martinez-Jimenez* are sufficiently similar to the client's case for *Martinez-Jimenez* to be on point. The facts Dustin identified as the key facts in the client's case are listed here followed by the key facts in *United States v. Martinez-Jimenez*.

✦ Mr. Canter approached the teller, displayed a crudely carved replica of a gun, and demanded money.

In *Martinez-Jimenez*, Mr. Martinez-Jimenez remained in the lobby and ordered the people in the bank to lie down. He displayed a toy gun. He and his partner took money from the bank. The facts in both cases are substantially the same except for one difference. In *Martinez-Jimenez*, the fake gun was a toy gun that looked exactly like a real weapon. In the client's case, the fake was a crudely carved replica of a gun. This distinction is probably not significant because in both cases, the person being robbed believed it was a real weapon. The court noted that the statute focuses on the harm created, not the manner in which it is created. In both cases, the belief that the gun was real created a dangerous situation and fear and apprehension in the victims.

✦ Mr. Canter took the money and fled the bank.

In *Martinez-Jimenez*, Mr. Martinez-Jimenez and his partner took cash and fled the bank. In both cases, the facts match.

✦ In the client's case, the money belonged to the bank.

In *Martinez-Jimenez*, the money belonged to the bank.

✦ The teller that Mr. Canter approached believed Mr. Canter had a real handgun. The only other witness was fairly certain the gun was not real.

In *Martinez-Jimenez*, Mr. Martinez-Jimenez displayed a toy gun that all the eyewitnesses thought was a handgun (two bank employees and a customer). There is a difference in these facts. In the client's case, one witness did not believe it was a real gun. The court in *Martinez-Jimenez* did not address the question of whether all the witnesses must believe the instrumentality is a real weapon for it to be considered a dangerous weapon. It should not, however, make a difference if some of the witnesses do not believe the instrumentality is real. In *Martinez-Jimenez*, the court focused upon the increased risk to the physical security of those present at the scene created by the appearance of dangerousness. As long as some of the witnesses (in this case the teller being robbed) believe the instrumentality is real, that risk is created. The goal of the court's holding was to eliminate or reduce that risk, and, therefore, the holding should apply whenever the risk is created, even if all the witnesses do not believe the risk is present.

Note: To be on the safe side, other cases involving bank robberies with fake weapons should be checked to determine if the fact that some witnesses do not believe the weapon is real makes a difference.

STEP 2: Are the rules/principles sufficiently similar? There is sufficient similarity between the law that applies in *Martinez-Jimenez* and that which applies in the client's case for the case to be considered on point. Both cases involve the same law: bank robbery with a dangerous weapon. In both cases, the question is whether sufficient evidence exists to support charges of bank robbery with a dangerous weapon when the weapon is fake and the victims believe it is real.

There are no major differences between the law and key facts of *United States v. Martinez-Jimenez* and the client's case that restrict the application of *Martinez-Jimenez* as precedent.

D. Libel Case

The following fact situation and court opinion illustrate another example of the use of the steps discussed in this chapter.

FOR EXAMPLE Jerry lives in an apartment building. He often sees couples, and sometimes individuals, entering and leaving Eve's apartment in the late evening and early morning. Convinced that Eve is engaged in immoral behavior, he prepares a petition requesting that Eve be kicked out of the building. He intends to present copies of the petition to the other tenants of the building and submit the signed petitions to the landlord. In the petition, he refers to Eve as an immoral person.

Early one evening he decides to confront Eve. In the ensuing conversation, he discovers that Eve is a marriage counselor employed by a local business. The couples he has seen visiting her apartment are workers at the business who, due to their schedules, can come to counseling only during the late evening. She has an agreement with her employer that allows her to counsel couples and individuals in her apartment.

Jerry, realizing he is mistaken about Eve, decides to destroy the petition. On the way to the incinerator, he unknowingly drops a copy of the petition. It is found by another tenant and ultimately is circulated among the tenants of the building. Eve hears about the petition and decides to sue Jerry for libel.

The state has a libel statute in which libel is defined as "the intentional publication, in writing, of false statements about a person." A leading libel case in the jurisdiction is *Cox v. Redd*. In this case, Redd wrote a letter he intended to mail to Cox wherein he called Cox a crook and a thief.

The statements were not true. Redd intended for Cox, and no one else, to read the letter. The day before he planned to mail the letter, he invited several friends over to spend the evening. He forgot to put the letter away. He left it opened on the dining room table, and some of the guests read it. Redd was not aware that his guests had read the letter. Cox heard about it and sued Redd for libel.

The court, interpreting the libel statute, ruled that "intentional publication" means either the actual intent to publish or, where there is no intent to publish, reckless or grossly negligent conduct that results in publication. The court held that Redd's conduct of leaving the letter opened where he knew his guests could see it was grossly negligent conduct, and therefore, he had intentionally published the letter and had committed libel. The court commented that Redd knew company was coming to his house, and his failure to exercise care in securing the letter in light of that knowledge was gross negligence.

In this example, is *Cox v. Redd* on point so that it applies as precedent in Jerry's case?

STEP 1: Are the rules/principles sufficiently similar? Both cases involve false written statements that were published. In both cases, there is the question of whether the publication was intentional. In the *Cox* case, even though he may not have intended to publish the letter, Redd's carelessness in leaving it out resulted in its publication.

Are the facts concerning intentional publication in Eve's case sufficiently similar? It is questionable. In the *Cox* case, Redd was careless and took no steps to secure the letter. In Eve's case, Jerry was taking steps to avoid publication and accidentally dropped a copy of the petition. It could be argued that some key facts are clearly different, that his conduct was simple negligence and not gross negligence, and therefore, the case is not on point. It could also be argued that due to the extreme sensitivity of the contents of the petition, Jerry should have taken great care to ensure that all the copies of the petition were burned, and the failure to exercise that care constitutes gross negligence. Under this argument, the case can apply as precedent.

It is important to note that there is a difference in the key facts that makes it questionable whether the case is on point. To remove doubt, additional research must be conducted to determine what constitutes gross negligence and whether Jerry's conduct rises to the level of gross negligence.

STEP 2: Are the rules/principles sufficiently similar? If it is decided that there is a sufficient similarity in the facts, is there a sufficient similarity between the law that applies in the *Cox* opinion and that which applies in the client's case for the opinion to be considered on point and apply as precedent? Both cases are libel cases that apply the same libel statute. Both cases involve the element of intent to publish. Both cases are concerned with an aspect of that element—whether there is "intentional publication" when the conduct that results in publication is unintentional.

Therefore, there is little question that *Cox* is on point in regard to step 2. If it is determined that Jerry's conduct is gross negligence, under the rule of law applied in *Cox*, Jerry's conduct is intentional publication.

SUMMARY

Court opinions are important because under the doctrines of precedent and stare decisis, judges reach decisions according to principles laid down in similar cases. Therefore, a researcher should find a case that is precedent (on point) because it guides the attorney as to how the issue in the client's case may be decided. An opinion is on point, and may be considered as precedent, if a sufficient similarity exists between the key facts and the rule of law/legal principle that governs both the court opinion and the client's case.

When considering the key facts, the heart of the process is identifying the similarities and differences between them. The more pronounced the differences between the facts of the court opinion and those of the client's case, the greater the likelihood that the opinion is not on point. Be critical in your analysis when there are differences. Always check other avenues of research when the key facts are different.

Where the key facts are sufficiently similar for the opinion to be considered on point, look to the rule of law that governs the court opinion and the client's case. Where the same rule applies in the same way, the opinion is usually on point. Where a different rule applies, a court opinion usually cannot apply as precedent. Where the language and function of the applicable rules/principles are sufficiently similar, however, it can be argued that an opinion is on point and can be used as precedent.

Reliance on a court opinion that applies a different rule/principle than that which applies in the client's case is risky and should occur only when there is no case that interprets the rule or principle governing the client's case.

CHAPTER REFERENCES

INTERNET RESOURCES

Various Web sites discuss the subject of cases on point. Most sites discuss specific cases and topics. These sites may be accessed by searching for "case law on all fours" or "cases on all fours." Most sites provide information without charge. Information you obtain free may not be closely monitored and may not be as accurate or have the same quality as that obtained from fee-based services. Therefore, exercise care when using freely obtained material.

For additional materials, please go to the CD accompanying this book

 For additional resources, visit our Web site at www.paralegal.delmar.cengage.com

EXERCISES

Additional exercises are located on the Student CD-ROM accompanying the text and Online Companion.

ASSIGNMENT 1

What does it mean when a case is on point? When is a case on point?

ASSIGNMENT 2

Describe the two-step process for determining when a case is on point.

ASSIGNMENT 3

Describe the three-part process for determining if a case is on point when there are different key facts.

ASSIGNMENT 4

Describe the two steps to follow when the doctrine/rule applied by the court is different from the doctrine that applies in the client's case.

ASSIGNMENT 5

Why is it important for a researcher to find a case on point?

ASSIGNMENT 6

In the following examples, use the statutory and case law presented in the hypothetical at the beginning of the chapter, that is, section 96-25-16 and *Karl v. Herald*. The client seeks redress for the refusal of the other party to issue dividends. In each example, determine if *Karl v. Herald* is on point.

Example 1

Client and his sister, Janice, are shareholders in a corporation. Janice is the majority shareholder, the sole member of the board of directors, and the manager of the corporation. For the past five years, she has paid herself a lucrative salary twice that paid to managers of similar corporations. The corporation has a $400,000 cash surplus that Janice claims is necessary for emergencies. No emergency has occurred in the last five years that would require more than $50,000.

Example 2

Client and Claire own a fabric store. The business is a corporation and Claire holds 80 percent of the stock and makes all the business decisions. Client, an employee of the business, owns 20 percent of the stock. The business has a large cash surplus, but Claire has never issued dividends. Claire's salary is three times Client's. When Client asks that dividends be issued, Claire responds, "Your dividend from this corporation is your job."

Example 3

Client and Don are partners in a business. Don owns 70 percent of the partnership and Client owns 30 percent. Client does not work for the business. Don runs the business and pays himself a large salary that always seems to equal the profits. Client thinks this is fishy and that Don should have a set salary and the profit above Don's salary should be shared 70/30. There is no partnership case law in the jurisdiction that addresses this question.

ASSIGNMENT 7

In each of the following examples, a brief summary of the court opinion is presented, followed by a client's fact situation. For each client fact situation, Parts A–G, determine the following:

1. What are the fact similarities and differences between the court opinion and the client's situation?
2. Is the court opinion on point? Why or why not?
3. If the opinion is on point, what will the probable decision be in regard to the question raised by the client's facts?

Example 1

Court Opinion: *State v. Jones.* Mr. Jones, a first-time applicant for general relief funds, was denied relief without a hearing. The denial was based on information in Mr. Jones' application indicating that his income was above the threshold maximum set out in the agency regulations. The regulation provides that when an applicant's income, or the financial support provided to an applicant plus income, exceeds $12,000 a year, the individual may be denied general relief funds. The regulation is silent about the right to a hearing.

Mr. Jones' application reflected that the gross income from his two part-time jobs exceeded by $2,000 the maximum allowable income for eligibility. He believed there were special circumstances that would allow him to be eligible for general relief. His demand for an appeal hearing to explain his special circumstances was denied.

The court held that the due process clause of the state constitution entitles a first-time applicant for general relief funds to a hearing when special circumstances are alleged. The question in the following three fact situations is whether the client is entitled to a hearing.

Part A

Client's Facts: Tom lives at home with his parents. He has a part-time job. He does not pay rent and utilities. He uses the money from his job to attend school. He has very little left over. His application for general relief was denied. The written denial stated that the combination of the support provided by his parents and his part-time income exceeded the maximum allowable income. His application for an appeal hearing was denied.

Part B

Client's Facts: In the last session of the state legislature, the legislature passed legislation that provided that when applicants for general relief were denied relief based on information provided in the application, they were not entitled to an appeal hearing. The purpose of the legislation was to cut costs.

Mr. Taylor, a first-time applicant for general relief funds, was denied benefits based solely on his application. He believes that he has special circumstances that entitle him to benefits. His request for an appeal hearing was denied.

Part C

Client's Facts: Client has been receiving general relief funds for the past year. Last week he received notice that his relief is being terminated due to information received from his employer indicating that he had received a raise, and his income is now over the statutory maximum. His request for an appeal hearing on the termination of relief was denied.

Example 2

Court Opinion: *Rex v. Ireland.* Mr. Rex, the landlord, filed an eviction suit against his tenant, Mr. Ireland. Mr. Rex served notice of default upon Mr. Ireland by rolling up the notice of default and placing it in Mr. Ireland's mailbox. The mailbox was situated next to the street. Mr. Ireland retrieved the notice the next day. Mr. Ireland, in his defense to the eviction suit, stated that he was not given proper notice of default under the provisions of section 55-67-9 of the Landlord/Tenant Act; therefore, the case should be dismissed. The statute provides that notice of default may be accomplished by:

1. Delivery by certified mail
2. Hand delivery to the individual to be evicted
3. Posting at the most public part of the residence

The statute further provides that the court may enter an order of eviction if the notice of default is not responded to within 30 days.

The court, denying the request for dismissal, ruled that the intent of the statute was to ensure that tenants receive notice of default. The court noted that although the method of delivery by Mr. Rex did not comply with the statute, the intent of the act was accomplished inasmuch as Mr. Ireland had actual notice of default and was not prejudiced by the improper notice. The question in the following four fact situations is whether the notice of default is effective.

Part D

Client's Facts: The client is a tenant. The landlord told the client's daughter to inform the tenant that he was in default and, under the terms of the lease, would be evicted if he did not pay or otherwise respond within 30 days. The daughter informed the tenant the next day. Would it make any difference if the daughter informed the tenant after 30 days but before the eviction suit was filed?

Part E

Client's Facts: Client, the tenant, was on vacation when the landlord posted the notice of default on the front door. Client did not return from vacation and learn of the default until after the 30-day default period had passed.

Part F

Client's Facts: Landlord sent the notice of default by regular mail, and the tenant received it.

Part G

Client's Facts: The landlord sent the notice by certified mail, but the client refused to accept it.

CHAPTER 7

Secondary Authority and Other Research Sources—Encyclopedias, Treatises, *American Law Reports*, Digests, *Shepard's*

Outline

Learning Objectives

After completing this chapter, you should understand:

✦ The role of secondary authority in general

✦ The role of encyclopedias, treatises, *American Law Reports*, Digests, and *Shepard's* in research

✦ How to locate and conduct research using encyclopedias, treatises, *American Law Reports*, Digests, and *Shepard's*

In early May, Melissa was accepted to law school for the term beginning the following fall. In June, after attending a party where there was a lot of drinking, she left with Damon, a young man she had known since high school. Both of them had been drinking, and rather than take her home as she expected, Damon took her to Lookout Point to "talk." He had something other than talk on his mind, and when Melissa resisted his advances, he slapped her, cutting her lip and loosening two of her teeth. As she exited the car, he grabbed for her and tore her blouse. Fortunately, there were other cars parked at Lookout Point, and Damon drove off rather than pursue her.

Melissa was furious; she had never been treated like that. She talked to the police and they informed her that she could file assault and battery charges and she should consult an attorney about obtaining civil relief by filing a battery tort claim. She didn't even know what the officer meant by "battery tort claim." She assumed the only thing she could do was to file criminal charges. She decided that since she was going to law school, she might as well find out for herself what the officer was talking about. The research sources Melissa would consult to learn about the tort law of battery are discussed in the Application section of this chapter.

I. INTRODUCTION

Chapters 4 and 5 covered primary authority, the law itself—constitutions, enacted law (statutes), and case law. Courts refer to and rely on primary authority first when resolving legal problems. In many instances, a court may be bound to follow the primary authority.

Therefore, locating the primary authority that may apply to a problem is *usually* the first step of legal research. However, it may be necessary to consult secondary authority, such as a legal encyclopedia, as a preliminary step if you do not have a basic familiarity with the area of law involved.

This and the next chapter address **secondary authority** and other research sources. Secondary authority consists of legal research, sources a court may rely on that are not the law, that is, not primary authority. These sources summarize, compile, explain, comment on, interpret, or in some other way address the law. As mentioned in Chapter 1, secondary authority is used for several purposes:

+ *To obtain a background or overall understanding of a specific area of the law.* If you are unfamiliar with an area of law, legal encyclopedias, treatises, and periodicals are useful.

> **FOR EXAMPLE** If the researcher is unfamiliar with a specific area of law, such as defamation, a treatise on tort law or a legal encyclopedia will provide an overview of the area. If the researcher seeks an organized summary of the case law on the topic, the Restatement (Second) of Torts should be consulted.

These sources are valuable because they explain and often analyze the law.

+ *To locate primary authority (the law) on a question being researched.* Secondary authority usually guides the researcher by providing references to statutory and case law. *American Law Reports* (ALR) and digests are particularly useful for this purpose. This chapter discusses these sources and *Shepard's Citations*. Cases may also be located through reference to legal encyclopedias, treatises, periodicals, Restatements of the Law, and uniform laws.

+ *To be relied upon by the court when reaching a decision.* This usually occurs only when there is no primary authority governing a legal question, or it is unclear how the primary authority applies. Treatises, law reviews, and Restatements of the Law are some secondary sources relied upon by courts.

There are literally hundreds of secondary sources. This chapter covers the more frequently used secondary sources. It addresses sources that provide the researcher with either an overview or a detailed treatment of specific areas of law: legal encyclopedias and treatises. The chapter also discusses other research sources that are of great assistance in locating case law: ALRs digests, and *Shepard's* citators. A table showing the primary use of the secondary sources and other research sources discussed in this chapter is presented in Exhibit 7–1.

Note: Secondary authority is not the law. It is persuasive authority, not binding on the courts. But courts may rely on and follow it. Therefore, secondary authority is usually consulted after primary authority. Most legal research focuses on primary authority with little reference to secondary authority. If there is primary authority that answers a question being researched, such as statutory or case law, then secondary authority is not necessary. If secondary authority describes and refers to primary authority on a subject, locate and refer to primary authority when analyzing the law.

Exhibit 7–1
Secondary Authority—
Primary Use as a
Research Tool.

AUTHORITY	PRIMARY USE AS A RESEARCH TOOL
Legal Encyclopedias	Use to obtain an overview of a specific area of the law and to locate case law in that area.
Treatises	Use when you are seeking more than the general summary of the law available in a legal encyclopedia. Treatises provide in-depth discussions of legal topics and explain, analyze, and criticize the law.
American Law Reports	Use to obtain a comprehensive analysis of individual legal issues. ALRs provide a greater in-depth discussion of specific legal issues than is available in a treatise. Legal issues are analyzed through synthesis and discussion of cases from every jurisdiction.
Digests	Use to locate case law that addresses specific point(s) of law. Digests are helpful in two situations: ✦ You know the name of a case that addresses the point of law being researched and are looking for other cases that address the same point. ✦ You do not know of any cases that address the point of law being researched.
***Shepard's* Citators**	Use to determine whether a case or other authority is "good law." *Shepard's* indicates whether a case has been reversed, modified, or overruled. It also refers to any case law or secondary sources that have discussed the primary authority being researched.

II. LEGAL ENCYCLOPEDIAS

Legal encyclopedias are designed to provide an overview of all the areas of law. They do not provide the in-depth coverage that is available in a treatise or periodical article. They are similar to other encyclopedias in that the subject matter is arranged alphabetically; there is a table of contents for each topic, and there is a detailed general index.

> **FOR EXAMPLE**   In the hypothetical presented at the beginning of the chapter, reference to assault and battery in an encyclopedia would be a good starting point for Melissa to begin her research because it would provide her with an overview of the law.

Legal encyclopedias are designed to provide an overview of all areas of the law. They do not provide the in-depth coverage that is available in a treatise or periodical article. They provide a summary of the law; they do not criticize or analyze it. Legal encyclopedias summarize the law primarily through a summary of case holdings. For that reason, they are valuable for locating cases on a subject. However, due to the large number of cases on any subject, one-half or less of a page of the encyclopedia may be text, with the remainder of the page listing citations in support of the narrative. The problem becomes one of too many cases. Also, in legal encyclopedias, there is less emphasis on statutes and statutory law than case law. Because of their general treatment of topics, legal encyclopedias are not frequently cited in court opinions or documents filed in court. Keep in mind that legal encyclopedias are secondary authority.

Legal encyclopedias are similar to other encyclopedias in that the subject matter is arranged alphabetically; there is a table of contents for each topic, and there is a detailed general index.

The two types of legal encyclopedias are national and local or state.

A. National Encyclopedias

There are two national encyclopedias: *American Jurisprudence 2d*, commonly known as Am. Jur. 2d and *Corpus Juris Secundum,* referred to as CJS. Both of these encyclopedias are national in scope, that is, they present a general overview of federal and state law. Both *American Jurisprudence 2d* and *Corpus Juris Secundum* are preceded by earlier sets: *American Jurisprudence* and *Corpus Juris.* Many law libraries maintain the earlier sets, but they are rarely used because their coverage ends in the 1930s.

Each encyclopedia covers more than 400 legal topics. Originally they were published by different publishers and were competitive sets. Today West, a Thomson business, publishes them. Inasmuch as they are similar in most respects and share many features, a researcher will use one set or the other, not both.

1. Features

The similar and dissimilar features of *American Jurisprudence 2d* and *Corpus Juris Secundum* are discussed here.

a. Similarities

Both sets share the following similarities:

◆ *Topic presentation*—Topics are arranged alphabetically with each topic beginning with a table of contents (see Exhibit 7–2). The presentation of topics is in the form of a narrative summary, with the narrative and citations presented on each page (see Exhibits 7–3 and 7–4).

◆ *General index*—Accompanying each set is a comprehensive general index that covers the entire set, and each individual volume has indexes for the topics covered in the volume (see Exhibit 7–5 for a page from a general index).

◆ *Topic summary*—At the beginning of each topic is a summary of what is covered, what topics are treated elsewhere, and West's key number references. This allows the use of the West's Digests to locate other cases on the same topic (see Exhibit 7–4). Both sets will refer you to other research sources.

◆ *Updates*—Pocket parts are used to update each volume, and replacement volumes are provided as necessary (see Exhibit 7–6).

◆ *Tables*—Each set has a table of statutes, rules, and regulations that list the title and section where specific statutes, rules, and regulations are cited (see Exhibit 7–7). Neither set has a table of cases.

b. Dissimilarities

The sets are different in the following ways:

◆ *Size*—CJS is larger than Am. Jur. 2d.; it has more than 100 volumes compared to more than 80 for Am. Jur. 2d. This does not mean that CJS provides a more comprehensive coverage of topics. CJS attempts to include every case reported in its discussion of topics. This results in many pages having one or two sentences of narrative, with the rest of the page consisting of footnotes to cases, which largely accounts for the additional number of volumes.

Am. Jur. 2d. is more selective in its inclusion of cases, presenting a cross section of leading cases, and includes citations in its footnotes and other research references (see Exhibit 7–4).

◆ *Emphasis*—Am. Jur. 2d emphasizes statutory law somewhat more than CJS. Neither set, however, focuses on statutory analysis.

◆ *New Topic Service*—Am. Jur. 2d. includes a New Topic Service binder that introduces new topics. New topics are presented here until they are incorporated in revised volumes in the main set.

6A C. J. S.

ASSAULT AND BATTERY

Analysis

Sub-Analysis

See also descriptive word index in the back of this Volume

Exhibit 7–2
CJS Table of Contents for Assault and Battery.
West, a Thomson Reuters business, *Corpus Juris Secundum*, Vol. 6A (1975) p. 309. Used with permission of Thomson Reuters/West.

§§ 1–2 ASSAULT & BATTERY

I. IN GENERAL

Main Text

§ 1. Scope of Title

This title discusses and includes acts of violence towards the person of another, either with or without any actual touching or striking, which do not constitute an element in or an attempt to commit any other specific injury or offense. Defenses, justification, and excuse for such acts are covered, as well as circumstances of aggravation. Liabilities and remedies therefor, both civil or criminal, are likewise treated.

Subjects which are covered in other titles and not treated in this title include civil liability for assault resulting in death,[1] assaults in connection with unlawful arrest,[2] assaults by operation of motor vehicles,[3] and assaults committed in obstructing process or resisting an officer.[4]

The commission of an assault with intent to, or in an attempt to, perpetrate other offenses, is discussed in connection with the particular offense, in C.J.S. titles Homicide, Rape, and Robbery. Convictions of assault in prose-cutions for other offenses are treated in C.J.S. Indictments and Informations.

§ 2. Definitions
   a. Assault
   b. Battery or assault and battery

a. Assault

An assault is any unlawful offer or attempt to injure another with apparent present ability to effectuate the attempt under circumstances creating a fear of imminent peril.

Quoted in: Fla.—Motley v. State, 20 So.2d 798, 800, 155 Fla. 545.

Library References
   Assault and Battery ⬤━1, 2, 48.

References to West's Key Numbers

An assault may be defined as any intentional, unlawful offer of corporal injury to another by force, or force unlawfully directed toward the person of another, under such circumstances as create a well founded fear of imminent peril, coupled with the apparent present ability to effectuate the attempt if not prevented.[5] Also, the

Citations to Case Law

1. C.J.S. Death.
2. C.J.S. False Imprisonment.
3. See C.J.S. Motor Vehicles.
4. See C.J.S. Obstructing Justice.
5. Ala.—Western Union Telegraph Co. v. Hill, 150 So. 709, 25 Ala.App. 540, certiorari denied 150 So. 711, 227 Ala. 469.
   Fla.—Motley v. State, 20 So.2d 798, 155 Fla. 545.
   McDonald v. Ford, App., 223 So.2d 553—Albright v. State, App., 214 So.2d 887.
   Ill.—People v. Allen, 254 N.E.2d 103, 117 Ill.App.2d 20.
   Kan.—Corpus Juris Secundum cited in State v. Hazen, 165 P.2d 234, 239, 160 Kan. 733.
   Ky.—Jenkins v. Kentucky Hotel, 87 S.W. 2d 951, 261 Ky. 419—Smith v. Gowdy, 244 S.W. 678, 196 Ky. 281, 29 A.L.R. 1353.
   La.—Osborne v. People's Benev. Industrial Life Ins. Co. of Louisiana, 139 So. 733, 735, 19 La.App. 667.
   Mich.—Corpus Juris Secundum quoted in Tinkler v. Richter, 295 N.W. 201, 203, 295 Mich. 396.
   Mo.—Corpus Juris Secundum cited in Adler v. Ewing, App., 347 S.W.2d 396, 402—State v. Higgins, App., 252 S.W.2d 641.
   N.C.—State v. Roberts, 155 S.E.2d 303, 270 N.C. 655—State v. Johnson, 142 S.E.2d 151, 264 N.C. 598.
   Okl.—Dunbar v. State, 131 P.2d 116, 75 Okl.Cr. 275.

Or.—State v. Carroll, 62 P.2d 830, 155 Or. 85.
S.C.—Kirven v. Kirven, 160 S.E. 432, 435, 162 S.C. 162.
Tenn.—Thomasson v. Western Union Tel. Co., 5 Tenn.Civ.App. 640.
Wash.—Corpus Juris Secundum cited in Peasley v. Puget Sound Tug & Barge Co., 125 P.2d 681, 691, 13 Wash.2d 485—Howell v. Winters, 108 P. 1077, 58 Wash. 436.
5 C.J. p 615 note 5.
Other definitions
   (1) In general.
U.S.—Anderson v. Crawford, C.C.A.Kan., 265 F. 504.
   Ransom v. Matson Navigation Co., D.C.Wash., 1 F.Supp. 244.
   U. S. v. Hand, Pa., 26 F.Cas.No. 15,-297, 2 Wash.C.C. 435.
Ala.—Republic Iron & Steel Co. v. Self, 68 So. 328, 192 Ala. 403, L.R.A.1915F 516.
   Taylor v. State, 175 So. 698, 27 Ala. App. 538.
Cal.—People v. Yslas, 27 Cal. 630.
Del.—Marker v. Hanratty, 97 A. 904, 6 Boyce 217.
Ga.—Copeland v. Dunehoo, 138 S.E. 267, 36 Ga.App. 817.
Iowa.—Holdorf v. Holdorf, 169 N.W. 737, 185 Iowa 838.
Ky.—Commonwealth v. Remley, 77 S.W. 2d 784, 257 Ky. 209.
Mich.—Warmelink v. Tissue, 241 N.W. 203, 257 Mich. 228—People v. Doud, 193 N.W. 884, 223 Mich. 120—Drew v.

Comstock, 23 L.W. 721, 57 Mich. 176.
Minn.—State v. Intihar, 152 N.W.2d 315, 277 Minn. 223.
Miss.—Cittadino v. State, 24 So.2d 93, 199 Miss. 235.
N.J.—State v. Staw, 116 A. 425, 97 N.J. Law 349.
N.Y.—People v. Wood, 199 N.Y.S.2d 342, 10 A.D.2d 231.
Ohio.—State v. Hetzel, 112 N.E.2d 369, 159 Ohio St. 350.
   State v. Theisen, 115 N.E.2d 863, 94 Ohio App. 461.
Or.—Cook v. Kinzua Pine Mills Co., 293 P.2d 717.
Va.—The Hardy Case, 17 Gratt. 592. 5 C.J. p 712 note 82a.
   (2) Assault is threat of injury.
U.S.—Daly v. Pedersen, D.C.Minn., 278 F.Supp. 88.
   (3) An offer or attempt to inflict bodily harm on another person.
R.I.—Liu v. Sugarman, 254 A.2d 753, 105 R.I. 727.
   (4) Act which is legal cause of contact with another person and which is offensive to reasonable sense of personal dignity if act is done with intention of inflicting harmful or offensive contact upon the other.
Pa.—Esmond v. Liscio, 224 A.2d 793, 209 Pa.Super. 200.
   (5) An intentional attempt by violence to injure the person of another.
Fla.—Bailey v. State, 79 So. 639, 76 Fla. 230.

Exhibit 7–3
CJS Main Volume Entry for Assault and Battery.

West, a Thomson Reuters business, *Corpus Juris Secundum*, Vol. 6A (1975) p. 316. Used with permission of Thomson Reuters/West.

§ 1 ASSAULT AND BATTERY 6 Am Jur 2d

I. INTRODUCTION [§§ 1-9]

Research References
18 USCA § 113
ALR Digest: Assault and Battery §§ 1, 3, 25
ALR Index: Assault and Battery
2 Am Jur Proof of Facts 81, Assault and Battery; 1 Am Jur POF 3d 613, Assault and Battery
36 Am Jur Trials 241, Defending Assault and Battery Cases
West Digest, Assault and Battery ⚷ 1-7, 47-53
Topic Summary —————————

§ 1. Generally; assault

Generally speaking, an assault is a demonstration of an unlawful intent by one person to inflict immediate injury or offensive contact on the person of another then present.[1] Although physical contact is not an essential element, violence or offensive contact—threatened or offered—is.[2] The threat must be to cause immediate injury, not injury in the future.[3]

- *Definition:* Assault is frequently defined as an intentional attempt by a person, by force or violence, to do an injury to the person of another, or as any attempt to commit a battery, or any threatening gesture showing in itself or by words accompanying it an immediate intention, coupled with a present ability, to commit a battery.[4]

1. Yale v. Town of Allenstown, 969 F. Supp. 798, 12 I.E.R. Cas. (BNA) 1209, 72 Empl. Prac. Dec. (CCH) ¶; 45184 (D.N.H. 1997) (applying New Hampshire law); Mount Vernon Fire Ins. Co. v. DLRH Associates, 967 F. Supp. 105 (S.D.N.Y. 1997), judgment aff'd, 152 F.3d 919 (2d Cir. 1998) (applying New York law); Billado v. Parry, 937 F. Supp. 337 (D. Vt. 1996) (applying Vermont law); Rivera ex rel. Rivera v. City of Nappanee, 704 N.E.2d 131 (Ind. Ct. App. 1998); Bacon on Behalf of Bacon v. Bacon, 567 N.W.2d 414 (Iowa 1997); City of Greenville v. Haywood, 130 N.C. App. 271, 502 S.E.2d 430 (1998), review denied, 349 N.C. 354, 1998 WL 1014898 (1998); Epps v. Com., 28 Va. App. 58, 502 S.E.2d 140 (1998), reh'g en banc granted, 28 Va. App. 270, 503 S.E.2d 813 (1998) and opinion withdrawn and vacated on reh'g en banc, 29 Va. App. 169, 510 S.E.2d 279 (1999).

As to the liability of accessories or participants in an assault and battery, see 21 Am Jur 2d, Criminal Law §§ 186 et seq.

As to the need for intent, see § 8.

Practice References: 1 Am Jur POF 3d 631, Assault and Battery.

2. Yanez v. City of New York, 29 F. Supp. 2d 100 (E.D.N.Y. 1998) (applying New York law); U.S. v. LeCompte, 108 F.3d 948, 46 Fed. R. Evid. Serv. (LCP) 833 (8th Cir. 1997) (applying 18 USCA § 113(a)(3)); Wilson v. Meeks, 98 F.3d 1247 (10th

Cir. 1996) (called into doubt on other grounds by, Ensminger v. Terminix Intern. Co., 102 F.3d 1571 (10th Cir. 1996)) (applying Kansas law); Jense v. Runyon, 990 F. Supp. 1320 (D. Utah 1998); People v. Aguilar, 16 Cal. 4th 1023, 68 Cal. Rptr. 2d 655, 945 P.2d 1204 (1997); Dickens v. Puryear, 302 N.C. 437, 276 S.E.2d 325 (1981) (distinguished on other grounds by, Bryant v. Thalhimer Bros., Inc., 113 N.C. App. 1, 437 S.E.2d 519 (1993)); Epps v. Com., 28 Va. App. 58, 502 S.E.2d 140 (1998), reh'g en banc granted, 28 Va. App. 270, 503 S.E.2d 813 (1998) and opinion withdrawn and vacated on reh'g en banc, 29 Va. App. 169, 510 S.E.2d 279 (1999).

3. City of Seattle v. Allen, 80 Wash. App. 824, 911 P.2d 1354 (Div. 1 1996) (distinguished by, State v. Aguilar, 1999 WL 261752 (Wash. Ct. App. Div. 1 1999)).

4. Abraham v. Raso, 15 F. Supp. 2d 433 (D.N.J. 1998) (applying New Jersey law); McVay v. Delchamps, Inc., 707 So. 2d 90 (La. Ct. App. 5th Cir. 1998); Thompson v. Williamson County, Tenn., 965 F. Supp. 1026, 23 A.D.D. 381 (M.D. Tenn. 1997) (applying Tennessee law); Waag v. Thomas Pontiac, Buick, GMC, Inc., 930 F. Supp. 393, 74 Fair Empl. Prac. Cas. (BNA) 12, 69 Empl. Prac. Dec. (CCH) ¶; 44507 (D. Minn. 1996) (disagreed with on other grounds by, Torres v. National Precision Blanking, a Div. of Nat. Material L.P., 943 F. Supp. 952, 73 Fair Empl. Prac. Cas. (BNA) 1843, 70

Exhibit 7–4

Am. Jur. 2d Main Volume Entry for Assault and Battery.

West, a Thomson Reuters business, *American Jurisprudence, 2nd Ed.*, Vol. 6 (1999) p. 10. Used with permission of Thomson Reuters/West.

Entry for Assault and Battery

ASHES OR CINDERS—Cont'd
Municipal regulations as to, Mun Corp § 455, 456, 465
Nuisances, Nuis § 182, 190, 202
Railroads (this index)
Workers' compensation, Work C § 138

ASHPANS
Railroads, RR § 150

AS INTEREST MAY APPEAR
Insurance, Ins § 2002

AS IS SALE
Generally, Sales § 336, 835
Conspicuousness of disclaimer or exclusion of warranty, Sales § 844
Disclaimers, Sales § 844
Fraud and deceit, Fraud § 388, 453
Merchantability, use of word, Sales § 833

Reference to Multiple Sections

Parol evidence, Sales § 325, 327
Real property, sale or transfer of, V & P § 327
Sleep or Sleeping (this index)

AS PER CONTRACT
Generally, Contracts § 378

ASPHALT AND ASPHALT PRODUCTS
Exemptions from claims of creditors, asphalt roller, Exemp § 100
Municipal, county, school, and state tort liability, asphalt heating machine, Mun Tort Liab § 239
Nuisances, Nuis § 185, 186
Premises liability, Prem Liab § 545
Special or local assessments, Spec A § 49
Taxation (this index)

ASPHYXIATION
Suffocation (this index)

ASPIRIN
Anacin (this index)
Insurance, Ins § 622
Malpractice by medical profession, Phys & S § 259
Proximate cause, Negl § 544

ASPORTATION
Larceny (this index)
Receiving and transporting stolen property, necessity of asportation by thief, Rec St P § 4
Robbery, Rob § 13, 14, 38, 132

ASS
Mules (this index)

ASSASSINATION
Argument of counsel abusing defendant, Trial § 681
Extradition, Extrad § 116
Rewards, Reward § 11
Sedition, subversive activities and treason, seditious conspiracy, Sedit § 5
United States President, assassination of, Reward § 11

ASSAULT AND BATTERY
Generally, Asslt & B § 1-177
Abatement, survival, and revival, Abat & R § 102
Abusive language, defense of provocation by, Asslt & B § 49
Actions and remedies, generally, Asslt & B § 94-177
Admiralty jurisdiction over, Admir § 93
Affray, assault as included offense, Breach P § 23
Agency, Asslt & B § 106
Aggravated assault
  generally, Asslt & B § 34-42
  arms, Asslt & B § 41
  deadly or dangerous weapon requirement, Asslt & B § 39-42
  degree of assault, Asslt & B § 35
  feet, Asslt & B § 41
  hands, Asslt & B § 41
  included offenses, Asslt & B § 44
  indictments and informations, Asslt & B § 72
  intent, Asslt & B § 36, 37
  lesser included offenses, Asslt & B § 45
  objects, Asslt & B § 42
  type of weapon used, Asslt & B § 38
  types of aggravated assault, Asslt & B § 38-42
  unloaded firearms, Asslt & B § 40
Aggravation of damages
  generally, Asslt & B § 150
  punitive damages, Asslt & B § 157
Aliens and citizens, Aliens § 3367
Ambassadors and other diplomats, protection from assault, Ambass § 9
Answers, Asslt & B § 161, 162
Apprehension. Threats and fear, below
Arrests, Asslt & B § 63
Associations and clubs
  fraternal order or benefit society member refusing to submit to ceremony involving assault, Frat § 67
  religious societies, liability of priest or minister for assault, Relig Soc § 24
Assumption of risk, Asslt & B § 122
Attempts, Asslt & B § 11
Attorney fees and costs, Asslt & B § 148
Attorneys, disciplinary proceedings, Attys § 89
Automobile insurance, Auto Ins § 159, 174, 175
Automobiles and Highway Traffic (this index)
Aviation, Avi § 220
Bank Robbery Act (this index)
Battered person syndrome, Asslt & B § 82
Benefit society or fraternal order member refusing to submit to ceremony involving, Frat § 67
Bodily injury requirement, Asslt & B § 4
Burden of proof. Presumptions and burden of proof, below
Business premises, defense of, Asslt & B § 66

ASSAULT AND BATTERY—Cont'd
Carriers (this index)
Cause of contact, Asslt & B § 5
Character or reputation
  generally, Asslt & B § 176, 177
  criminal prosecutions, Asslt & B § 85
Children and minors
  generally, Asslt & B § 104; Par & C § 14, 22, 35, 44
  criminal prosecutions, Asslt & B § 32, 33
  defense of privilege, Asslt & B § 119
Citizen's arrest, Asslt & B § 63
Clubs or clubbing
  expert and opinion evidence, Expert § 214
  firearm used as club, Rob § 7; Weap § 3
  robbery, Rob § 6, 7
Comparative negligence, Asslt & B § 135; Negl § 1463, 1519, 1690
Complaints, Asslt & B § 159, 160
Compromise and settlement, validity of, Contract § 203
Consent, defense of
  generally, Asslt & B § 124-128
  ability to give consent, Asslt & B § 126
  criminal prosecutions, below
  duress, Asslt & B § 126
  fraud. Asslt & B § 126
  medical care, Asslt & B § 127
  mutual combat, Asslt & B § 128
  nature of consent, Asslt & B § 125
  scope of consent, Asslt & B § 125
Conspiracy
  generally, Asslt & B § 107; Consp § 58
  criminal prosecutions, Asslt & B § 13
Constitutional law
  generally, Asslt & B § 10
  sentence and punishment, Asslt & B § 91, 92
Contempt, Contempt § 22, 32, 68
Contributory negligence, Asslt & B § 122; Negl § 912, 915
Conviction or acquittal, record of, Asslt & B § 170, 171
Corporal Punishment (this index)
Counterclaim, recoupment, and setoff, Countcl § 42
Credit card issuer's liability for wrongful billing, cancellation, dishonor or disclosure, Cred Cards § 44
Criminal conviction or acquittal, record of, Asslt & B § 170, 171
Criminal prosecutions
  generally, Asslt & B § 10-93
  abusive language, defense of provocation by, Asslt & B § 49
  aggravated assault, above
  arrests, Asslt & B § 63
  attempts, Asslt & B § 11
  battered person syndrome, Asslt & B § 82
  burden of proof, Asslt & B § 73

For assistance using this Index, call 1-800-328-4880

Exhibit 7–5
Am. Jur. 2d Index Page.
West, a Thomson Reuters business, *American Jurisprudence, 2nd Ed.*, General Index (2001) p. 342. Used with permission of Thomson Reuters/West.

ASSAULT AND BATTERY

> **KeyCite®**: Cases and other legal materials listed in KeyCite Scope can be researched through West Group's KeyCite service on Westlaw®. Use KeyCite to check citations for form, parallel references, prior and later history, and comprehensive citator information, including citations to other decisions and secondary materials.

I. INTRODUCTION [§§ 1–9]

§ 3 Battery

§ 4 — Need for bodily injury

Research References

Apprehending the weapon within: The case for criminalizing the intentional transmission of HIV, 36 Am Crim LR 2:313 (1999).

§ 9 Relationship between assault and battery

Cases

Defendant was guilty of assault in the third degree, where defendant choked victim, his wife, by placing his hands around her throat, causing her to lose consciousness for brief period of time. C.G.S.A. § 53a-61(a)(2). State v. Atkinson, 46 Conn. Supp. 130, 741 A.2d 991 (Super. Ct. 1999).

II. CRIMINAL LIABILITY [§§ 10–93]

A. IN GENERAL [§§ 10–15]

§ 10 Generally; constitutionality of statutes

Cases

Stalking statute, as narrowly construed to supply requirements of genuine threat and intent to carry out the threat, is not facially overbroad under First Amendment, though statute does not contain express exemption for all forms of constitutionally protected speech. U.S.C.A. Amend. 1; ORS 163.732. State v. Rangel, 328 Or. 294, 977 P.2d 379 (1999).

D. EFFECT OF FAMILY RELATIONSHIP OR POSITION OF AUTHORITY [§§ 29–33]

§ 29 Generally; husband and wife; domestic partners

Research References

The domestic violence dilemma: How our ineffective and varied responses reflect our conflicted views of the problem, 71 S Cal LR 3:641 (1999).

Cases

Statute making a parent guilty of permitting sexual abuse of a child, if parent knowingly allowed act of criminal sexual abuse or criminal sexual assault upon his or her child and failed to take "reasonable steps" to prevent commission or future occurrences of such

an act, was unconstitutionally vague under Due Process Clause; it was unclear what reasonable steps were required in order to comply with statute, and statute provided no guidelines for authorities in determining what constituted reasonable steps. U.S.C.A. Amend. 14; S.H.A. Const. Art. 1, § 2; S.H.A. 720 ILCS 150/5 .1. People v. Maness, 191 Ill. 2d 478, 247 Ill. Dec. 490, 732 N.E.2d 545 (2000).

§ 30 Peace officer

Cases

Off-duty, uniformed police officer who was engaged in secondary employment as store security guard for private employer was acting in his "official capacity" as police officer when he investigated confrontation between store employee and defendant, and thus, defendant's ensuing assault on officer warranted convictions for assault on police officer and obstructing police officer; even though officer received compensation from store, duties officer performed as security guard were supplemental to his primary duties as law enforcement officer. Code, 61-2-10b(d, e), 61-5-17(a). State v. Phillips, 205 W. Va. 673, 520 S.E.2d 670 (1999).

§ 32 Parents and persons vested with quasi-parental authority

Research References

Spanking and other corporal punishment of children by parents: Overvaluing pain, undervaluing children, 35 Houston LR 1:147 (1999).

§ 33 —Domestic violence statutes

Research References

Domestic violence and mediation: A tragic combination for victims in California Family Court, 35 Cal West LR 2:355 (1999).

The Lautenberg Amendment: Congress hit the mark by banning firearms from domestic violence offenders, 30 St Mary's LJ 3:801 (1999).

Cases

Standard form for Domestic Violence Protective Order (DVPO), Form AOC-CV-306, is disapproved; form combines several possible find . . .

© West Group, 5/2001   3

Notes in margin:
No New Information on Sections 5 Through 8
New Cases
New Research References

Exhibit 7–6
Am. Jur. 2d Pocket Part Page.
West, a Thomson Reuters business, *American Jurisprudence, 2nd Ed.*, Vol. 6 (2001) p. 3. Used with permission of Thomson Reuters/West.

TABLE OF STATUTES AND RULES CITED

UNITED STATES CODE ANNOTATED

Title and Section	Am Jur 2d title and section	Title and Section	Am Jur 2d title and section
5 USCA		**28 USCA**	
8130	Assign § 95	1450	Attach § 29
11 USCA		2405	Attach § 66
365(a)	Assist § 23	2710 et seq.	Attach § 261
12 USCA		2710-2717	Attach § 67
91	Attach § 70, 87	2710	Attach § 187
15 USCA		2710(b)	Attach § 314
61	Asso § 2	2711	Attach § 273
714b(c)	Attach § 84	2713	Attach § 444, 614
1671-1677	Attach § 178	2717	Attach § 540
1671(b)	Attach § 178	3001-3308	Attach § 239
1672(c)	Attach § 2, 178	3101	Attach § 265
1673(a)	Attach § 178	3101(b)	Attach § 223
1673(b)(1)	Attach § 178	3101(c)(1)	Attach § 267
1673(b)(2)	Attach § 178	**29 USCA**	
1673(c)	Attach § 178	206(a)(1)	Attach § 178
1674(a)	Attach § 11	**31 USCA**	
16 USCA		192	Assign for Crs § 115
3	Assign § 95	3713	Assign for Crs § 115
18 USCA		3713(a)(1)(A)(I)	Assign for Crs § 115
111	Asslt & B § 2, 15, 18, 63	3713(b)	Assign for Crs § 115
112	Asslt & B § 14	3727(a)	Assign § 95
113	Asslt & B § 9, 14	3727(b)	Assign § 95
113(a)(3)	Asslt & B § 1	3727(c)	Assign § 95
113(a)(4)	Asslt & B § 14	**40 USCA**	
113(f)	Asslt & B § 17	308	Attach § 184
115	Asslt & B § 14	309	Attach § 184
116	Asslt & B § 14	**41 USCA**	
1114	Asslt & B § 15	15	Assign § 95
1501	Asslt & B § 14	15(a)	Assign § 95
2114	Asslt & B § 14	15(b)	Assign § 95
26 USCA		**42 USCA**	
501(i)	Asso § 4	1983	Asso § 5

Exhibit 7–7
Am. Jur. 2d Table of Statutes and Rules Cited.
West, a Thomson Reuters business, *American Jurisprudence, 2nd Ed.*, Vol. 6 (2001) p. xiii. Used with permission of Thomson Reuters/West.

◆ *Desk Book*—Am. Jur. 2d includes the *Am. Jur. 2d. Desk Book* that includes general information such as statistical charts, tables, data, and diagrams. It includes, for example, a diagram of various federal agencies, the text of the U.S. Constitution, and the addresses and telephone numbers of the federal courts.

2. Research Techniques—National Encyclopedias

You use legal encyclopedias to obtain an overview of a specific area of the law and to locate case law in that area. The following are techniques for locating legal topics.

a. General Index

Usually research begins by consulting the general index that accompanies each set.

> **FOR EXAMPLE** If you are interested in researching aggravated assault with a dangerous weapon, you would look in the index under assault and battery to be directed to the appropriate topic and section (see Exhibit 7–5).

b. Table of Contents

If you know the area of law that covers the subject you are researching, you can refer to the volume that covers the topic and scan the table of contents for the specific topic.

> **FOR EXAMPLE** If you are interested in who is entitled to sue for an assault, you could retrieve the volume that covers the topic and scan the table of contents to locate the appropriate section (see Exhibit 7–2).

Note that the spine of each volume identifies the range of subjects covered, for example, "Private Franchise Contracts to Process."

c. Statute, Rules, and Regulations

If you are looking for a specific statute, rule, or regulation, the Table of Statutes and Rules Cited will direct you to the sections where it is discussed (see Exhibit 7–7).

Always consult the pocket part to update your research to ensure that the narrative summary in the main text has not changed and to locate the most recent cases.

3. Computer-Aided Research

American Jurisprudence 2d and *Corpus Juris Secundum* are available on Westlaw. Am. Jur. 2d is also available on LexisNexis and CD-ROM. Neither set is available on nonfee-based Web sites. Note that copyrighted secondary sources are generally not available free on the Internet. Computer-aided research is discussed in detail in Chapters 9 and 10.

B. State Encyclopedias

Some legal encyclopedias are published for individual states. These encyclopedias are organized like the national encyclopedias and include many of the same features, such as a table of contents for each section, a general index, and pocket part supplements. Some sets have tables of cases, statutes, and regulations. They provide a narrative summary of the laws of the state with citations to state and federal case law that have interpreted state law. Research is conducted in the same manner as a national encyclopedia. State encyclopedias are most valuable when conducting research on questions involving state law. Note that most states do not have state encyclopedias. Consult your local law library to determine if one is published for your state.

III. TREATISES

Treatises are texts that provide a comprehensive analysis of a single area of law such as torts or criminal law. Where a legal encyclopedia presents a broad overview of an area of law, a treatise does much more. It provides a much more in-depth discussion of the law and explains, analyzes, and criticizes the law. Some treatises include guidance for the legal practitioner such as practice tips, checklists, and legal forms. Legal experts in the field write treatises and, therefore, courts rely on and cite treatises more often than legal encyclopedias. Treatises, however, are secondary authority; they are not the law, and courts do not have to follow a position or adopt an interpretation advocated by the author.

A. Types and Features of Treatises

There are several types of treatises, ranging from single-volume texts to multivolume sets. Single-volume treatises exist on hundreds of legal topics, and the topics covered can be very specific, such as the *First Amendment Law Handbook* by James L. Swanson, or they can cover an entire area of law, such as *The Law of Torts* by Dan B. Dobbs. The broader the topic covered by the single-volume text, the less detailed the coverage.

Multivolume treatises exist for most major areas of law. A multivolume treatise is like an expanded version of a single-text treatise. Due to its greater size, it provides a more in-depth treatment of a legal topic than a single-text treatise.

FOR EXAMPLE *Fletcher Cyclopedia Corporations* consists of 33 hardbound and loose-leaf volumes. It analyzes corporate law and addresses in detail the legal issues corporations may face. Obviously, this publication covers the area of corporate law in much greater detail than a single-volume treatise.

The multivolume sets are more likely to include aids for the practitioner such as forms, checklists, and practice guides.

Most treatises have the following features:

✦ *Narrative presentation*—The subject matter is presented in a narrative format similar to a legal encyclopedia. Documentation supporting the narrative text, including case citations and references to other sources, is presented in footnotes (see Exhibit 7–8).

✦ *Index*—An index is included at the end of the single-volume treatise or as a separate volume(s) in multivolume sets.

✦ *Table of cases*—Most treatises include a table of cases arranged alphabetically and a table of contents for each subject area.

✦ *Updates*—Most multivolume treatises are updated annually or semiannually through the use of pocket parts for each volume or separate supplements. Most single-volume treatises are updated through the publication of a new edition. Some single-volume treatises, such as the softbound *Corporate Communications Handbook* by Walton and Seghetti, are published annually rather than updated. Always check the pocket part or supplement to ensure your research is up to date.

B. Research Using Treatises

Most law libraries have a treatise section where both the single- and multivolume treatises are arranged alphabetically by legal topic, for example, treatises on criminal law follow treatises on contracts, and so on. Some public libraries may have single-volume treatises located in the legal section. Check the catalog or with the librarian to determine which treatises are available.

1. Use as a Research Tool

Use a treatise when you are seeking more than the general summary of the law provided by a legal encyclopedia. The issue you are researching may not be covered in sufficient detail in an encyclopedia. Also, the analysis or criticism of the law provided in a treatise

TOPIC D. ASSAULT

§ 33. Simple Assault

Nature of the tort. Newspapers and even judges and lawyers sometimes use the term assault to mean a battery. More technically, assault is a quite different tort, although it often precedes a battery. An assault is an act that is intended to and does place the plaintiff in apprehension of an immediate unconsented-to touching that would amount to a battery.[1] The plaintiff's subjective recognition or apprehension that she is about to be touched in an impermissible way is at the core of the assault claim.

Intent and transferred intent. As in other cases, intent may be based either on the defendant's purpose or on his substantial certainty that a

5. Because employers are generally protected from negligence claims under workers' compensation laws, but sometimes not for intentional tort claims. See generally, Jean Love, Actions for Nonphysical Harm: The Relationship Between the Tort System and No-Fault Compensation (With an Emphasis on Workers' Compensation), 73 CAL. L. REV. 857 (1985).

6. *Employers liable for negligence:* E.g., Ford v. Revlon, Inc., 153 Ariz. 38, 734 P. 2.d 580 (1987). *Hospital liable for negligence:* Sumblin v. Craven

County Hospital Corp., 86 N.C. App. 358, 357 S.E. 2d 376 (1987) (viewing claim against hospital for failure to protect psychiatric patient from molestation as a negligence case).

7. E.g., West v. LTV Steel Co., 839 F. Supp. 559 (N.D.Ind. 1993).

8. See Chapter 22 on vicarious liability generally.

§ 33

1. Restatement §§ 21 & 32.

Exhibit 7–8
Sample Treatise Page.
West, a Thomson Reuters business, Dan B. Dobbs, *The Law of Torts*, (2000) p. 63. Used with permission of Thomson Reuters/West.

may be necessary when seeking information on how to counter an opponent's interpretation of, or reliance on, a law.

> **FOR EXAMPLE** The research question involves the actions of a majority shareholder in a family corporation that harm the minority shareholders. The majority shareholder controls the board of directors and refuses to issue dividends or allow the minority shareholders to benefit from the corporation in any way. The minority shareholders want to know what remedies are available to them. A legal encyclopedia may not address the subject in sufficient detail to be of assistance. *Fletcher Cyclopedia Corporations* certainly covers the topic in greater detail and will likely provide the answer. The two-volume treatise *O'Neal's Oppression of Minority Shareholders*, will provide an even greater in-depth discussion of the subject along with citations to cases that discuss various types of oppressive conduct.

Treatises are also extremely valuable in locating cases. In the preceding example, *Fletcher Cyclopedia Corporations* and *O'Neal's Oppression of Minority Shareholders* will provide numerous case citations to instances of oppressive conduct, one of which may match the fact situation being researched. A legal encyclopedia usually does not address as many specific fact situations as a treatise.

2. Research Techniques—Treatises

The following are the techniques for locating specific topics in treatises.

a. General Index

Usually research begins by consulting the index at the end of the text or the set.

> **FOR EXAMPLE** If you are interested in oppressive conduct by majority shareholders, look in the index under "shareholders," "majority shareholders," or "oppressive conduct."

b. Table of Contents/Table of Cases

If you know where the topic you are researching is covered in the treatise, go to the section or volume that covers the subject and scan the table of contents for the specific subtopic. If you are looking for the treatment of a specific case in a treatise, consult the table of cases.

c. Reference from Other Sources

Often another source such as a citation in a case or legal encyclopedia may direct you to a specific treatise section.

> **FOR EXAMPLE** A court opinion may read, "For an exhaustive treatment of derivative actions, see 4 Alan R. Bromberg & Larry E. Ribstein, *Partnership* § 15.059."

As with a legal encyclopedia, *always* consult the pocket part or supplement to update your research to locate the most recent cases and ensure that the narrative summary in the main text has not changed. If the treatise is a single volume that is not updated, check the case citations through *Shepard's* or some other source to make sure the cases are still good law. *Shepard's Citations* is discussed in *Shepard's Citations*, section VI of this chapter.

3. Computer-Aided Research

Many treatises are available on Westlaw and LexisNexis. Many treatises are available on CD-ROM. Treatises, like other copyrighted secondary sources, usually are not available on nonfee-based Web sites.

IV. *AMERICAN LAW REPORTS*

One approach to reporting and analyzing the case law is that taken by the *American Law Reports* (ALR). The ALR publishes the text of leading state and federal court opinions addressing specific issues. Following the opinion is an analysis (referred to as annotations) of the legal issues raised in the opinion and a summary of the cases from every jurisdiction that have addressed the same or similar issues. The case summaries are arranged by jurisdiction and provide the researcher with a view of the treatment of the legal issue or issues raised in the case.

> **FOR EXAMPLE** The ALR annotation analyzes this question: "When is a worker entitled to compensation for injuries suffered after termination of employment when there is some connection between the injury and the employment?" The annotation organizes and presents the cases according to how the courts have answered the question. The cases that have allowed compensation are presented together by state. The cases that have not allowed compensation are also presented together.

In addition to the case summaries, the annotations provide references to various other research sources. Lawyers with expertise in the area of law select the cases and prepare the annotations.

The annotations following the text of the court opinion are thoroughly researched and may range in length from a few pages to more than 100 pages. A single ALR volume may be more than 1,000 pages and provide annotations to less than 15 cases. The annotations cover only selected legal issues. If the issue you are researching is addressed by an annotation, the annotation is a research shortcut. It often provides, in one place, all your research: a comprehensive analysis of the issue, references to and summaries of the case law on point, and references to other research sources.

ALR began publication in 1919 and for years was published by Lawyers' Co-op. Today, West publishes ALR. It is composed of the following six multivolume series:

ALR (First Series)	Federal and state cases from 1919 to 1948—175 volumes
ALR 2d (Second Series)	Federal and state cases from 1948 to 1965—100 volumes
ALR 3d (Third Series)	Federal cases from 1965 to 1969 and state cases from 1965 to 1980—100 volumes
ALR 4th (Fourth Series)	State cases from 1980 to 1991—100 volumes
ALR 5th (Fifth Series)	State cases from 1991 to June 2005—125 volumes
ALR 6th	State cases from June 2005 to present
ALR Federal	Federal cases from 1969 to present

A. ALR Components

There were changes in organization and updating when the second series was published and again with the publication of the third series. The annotations in the third, fourth, fifth, sixth, and federal series are generally similar in format and updating, and they share the following components:

✦ *Prefatory Statement*—An annotation begins with a statement that briefly describes the topic of the annotation and cites the case used to illustrate the legal issue discussed in the annotation. At the end of the statement is a reference to the page where the case is printed in the ALR volume (see Exhibit 7–9).

---

10 ALR5th 337

WHAT PROJECTS INVOLVE WORK SUBJECT TO STATE STATUTES REQUIRING PAYMENT OF PREVAILING WAGES ON PUBLIC WORKS PROJECTS

Prefatory
Statement

In some cases involving state statutes requiring the payment of prevailing wages to employees on public works projects, issues arise as to whether the activity in question should be considered a project subject to the statute. Focusing on the type of work that the project calls for, some courts have examined the statutory description of covered work and the type of work called for by the contract. In C & C Teletronics, Inc. v U. S. West Information Systems, Inc. (1987, Minn App). 414 NW2d 758, 10 ALR 5th 980, for example, the court held that a general contract for the installation of a new telephone system in the state's university buildings was not subject to prevailing wage requirements, where it did not constitute a "project," "construction," or "repair," for purposes of M.S.A. §§ 177.42 subd. 2 and 177.43 subd. 1, the prevailing wage law. This annotation collects and analyzes such cases, dealing with various types of work.

C & C Teletronics, Inc. v U. S. West Information Systems, Inc. is fully reported at page 980, infra.

Exhibit 7–9
ALR Annotation.
Lawyers Cooperative Publishing, *American Law Reports, 5th Ser.,* Vol. 10 (1993) p. 337. Used with permission of Thomson Reuters/West.

Table of Contents

Research References

Index

Jurisdictional Table of Cited Statutes and Cases

ARTICLE OUTLINE

I. PRELIMINARY MATTERS

§ 1. Introduction
   [a] Scope
   [b] Related annotations
§ 2. Summary

II. COVERAGE OF WORK UNDER PARTICULAR STATUTORY TERMS

A. TERMS OF INCLUSION

§ 3. "Public work" or "public works"
   [a] Term applicable
   [b] Term inapplicable
§ 4. "Project" or "state project"
   [a] Term applicable
   [b] Term inapplicable
§ 5. "Alteration"
   [a] Term applicable
   [b] Term inapplicable
§ 6. "Construction"
   [a] Term applicable
   [b] Term inapplicable
§ 7. "Demolition"
§ 8. "Fixed work"
§ 9. "Repair"

B. TERMS OF EXCLUSION

§10. Maintenance
   [a] Statutory exclusion applicable
   [b] Statutory exclusion inapplicable

Exhibit 7–10
ALR Annotation—Table of Contents.
Lawyers Cooperative Publishing, *American Law Reports, 5th Ser.*, Vol. 10 (1993) p. 338. Used with permission of Thomson Reuters/West.

◆ *Table of Contents*—Following the prefatory statement is a detailed table of contents for the annotation (see Exhibit 7–10).

◆ *Research References and Sources*—A research section follows the table of contents that lists references related to the annotation. This section includes references to related ALR annotations, encyclopedia sections, texts, key numbers, law review articles and other publications, practice aids, and computer-assisted research sources (see Exhibit 7–11).

◆ *Article Index*—Next is an index that lists the subjects and where each subject is covered in the annotation.

10 ALR 5th   PREVAILING WAGES LAWS—PROJECTS
                                                    10 ALR 5th 337

Research References

TOTAL CLIENT-SERVICE LIBRARY® REFERENCES

The following references may be of related or collateral interest to a user of this annotation:

Annotations

See the related annotations listed in § 1[b].

Encyclopedias and Texts

65 Am Jur 2d, Public Works and Contracts §§ 204-215
15A Federal Procedure, L Ed, Government Contracts §§ 39:939-39:997
RIA Employment Coordinator, Public Contracts C-13,051 through C-13,326

Practice Aids

10 Federal Procedural Forms, L Ed, Government Contracts §§ 34:61-34:94
20A Am Jur Pl & Pr Forms (Rev), Public Works and Contracts, Forms 101-104
15 Am Jur Legal Forms 2d, Public Works and Contracts §§ 216:201-216:204
14 Am Jur Trials 437, Representing the Government Contractor

Federal Statutes

40 USCS §§ 276a through 276a-5

Digests and Indexes

L Ed Digest, Contracts § 171; Counties § 8; Municipal Corporations § 42; States, Territories, and Possessions
§ 51; Towns § 3; United States § 165
ALR Digests, Contracts § 556; Counties § 46; Municipal Corporations §§ 125, 129(1); States § 13; Towns
§ 11; United States § 5
ALR Index, Building and Construction Contracts and Work; Counties; Davis-Bacon Act; Labor and Employment; Municipal Corporations; Public Works and Contracts; States; Towns

Auto-Cite®

Cases and annotations referred to herein can be further researched through the Auto-Cite® computer-assisted research service. Use Auto-Cite to check citations for form, parallel references, prior and later history, and annotation references.

RESEARCH SOURCES

The following are the research sources that were found to be helpful in compiling this annotation:

Encyclopedias

65 Am Jur 2d, Public Works and Contracts §§ 204-215
56 CJS Master and Servant § 153

Exhibit 7–11
ALR Annotation—Research References.
Lawyers Cooperative Publishing, *American Law Reports, 5th Ser.*, Vol. 10 (1993) p. 339. Used with permission of Thomson Reuters/West.

◆ *Jurisdictional Tables*—Following the index is a table that lists all the cases cited in the annotation by jurisdiction and the statutes relevant to the annotation (see Exhibit 7–12).

◆ *Scope*—The body of the annotation begins with a scope section that identifies what is and what is not covered in the annotation (see Exhibit 7–13).

◆ *Related Annotations*—Next is a reference to related ALR annotations (see Exhibit 7–13).

10 ALR 5th   PREVAILING WAGES LAWS—PROJECTS
                                   10 ALR 5th 337

Scope of annotation, § 1[a]   Telecommunications system, §§ 3[a], 4[b], 5[b],
Sewers, §§ 3, 9   6[b]
Shrubbery removal, §§ 3[a], 10[a]   Train service, § 3[b]
Sidewalk removal, § 7   Transmission lines, § 10[a]
Streets, § 3   Tree removal or maintenance, §§ 3[a], 10[a]
Summary, § 2   University campus, §§ 3[a], 4[b], 5[b], 6[b]
Sweeping of streets, § 3[a]   Warranty work, § 3[a]

Jurisdictional Table of Cited Statutes and Cases*

CALIFORNIA

Cal Lab Code § 1720 (Deering). See §§ 3[a, b], 5[a], 7
Cal Lab Code §§ 1771, 1773 (Deering). See § 10[a]

Franklin v Riverside (1962) 58 Cal 2d 114, 23 Cal Rptr 401, 373 P2d 465, 45 CCH LC ¶ 50591—§ 10[a]
International Brotherhood of Electrical Workers v Harbor Comrs., Board of (1977, 2nd Dist) 68 Cal App
    3d 556, 137 Cal Rptr 372, 82 CCH LC ¶ 55083, 57 OGR 329—§ 3[b]
Priest v Housing Authority of Oxnard (1969, 2nd Dist) 275 Cal App 2d 751, 80 Cal Rptr 145—§§ 3[a], 5[a], 7

ILLINOIS

Ill Ann Stat ch 48 para 39s-1 et seq., 39s-2, 39s-3 (Smith-Hurd). See § 10[a]
Ill Rev Stat ch 48 para 39s-1 et seq. (1987). See § 3[a]
Ill Rev Stat ch 48 para 39s-2 (1975). See § 10[a]
Ill Rev Stat ch 48 para 39s-2 (1989). See § 8

Beaver Glass & Mirror Co. v Education, Board of (1978, 2d Dist) 59 Ill App 3d 880, 17 Ill Dec 378, 376
    NE2d 377, 84 CCH LC ¶ 55143—§ 10[a]
Frye v Iroquois, County of (1986, 3d Dist) 140 Ill App 3d 749, 95 Ill Dec 185, 489 NE2d 406, 27 BNA
    WH Cas 979—§ 10[a]

---

* Statutes, rules, regulations, and constitutional provisions bearing on the subject of the annotation are included in this table only to the extent, and in the form, that they are reflected in the court opinions discussed in this annotation. The reader should consult the appropriate statutory or regulatory compilations to ascertain the current status of relevant statutes, rules, regulations, and constitutional provisions.

For federal cases involving state law, see state headings.

Exhibit 7–12
ALR Annotation—Jurisdictional Tables.
Lawyers Cooperative Publishing, *American Law Reports, 5th Ser.,* Vol. 10 (1993) p. 341. Used with permission of Thomson Reuters/West.

- ✦ *Summary and Comment*—This section presents a summary of the topic that includes background and other information helpful in understanding the topic.
- ✦ *Practice Pointers*—The next section of the body presents case preparation and other guidelines for practitioners.
- ✦ *Substantive Provisions*—The bulk of the body of an annotation is composed of the substantive sections that organize, summarize, analyze, and evaluate the case law on the topic of the annotation. For each case discussed in the annotation, there is a presentation of the facts and issue(s) before the court related

§ 1 [a]   PREVAILING WAGES LAWS—PROJECTS   10 ALR 5th
                                              10 ALR 5th 337

I. Preliminary Matters

Scope

§ 1. Introduction

[a] Scope

This annotation[1] collects and analyzes the cases discussing whether a project involves work of a nature rendering the project subject to a state statute requiring nongovernmental employers to pay prevailing wages to workers on public works projects.[2]

A number of jurisdictions have rules, regulations, constitutional provisions, or legislative enactments directly bearing on this subject. These provisions, including prevailing wage statutes, are discussed herein only to the extent and in the form that they are reflected in the court opinions that fall within the scope of the annotation. The reader is consequently advised to consult the appropriate statutory or regulatory compilations to ascertain the current status of all statutes discussed herein, including those listed in the Jurisdictional Table of Cited Statutes and Cases.

Related Annotations

[b] Related annotations

Employees' private right of action to enforce state statute requiring payment of prevailing wages on public works projects. 10 ALR 5th 360.

What employers are subject to prevailing wage requirement of state statutes requiring payment of prevailing wages on public works projects. 7 ALR 5th 444.

What are "prevailing wages," or the like, for purposes of state statute requiring payment of prevailing wages on public works projects. 7 ALR 5th 400.

Who is "employee," "workman," or the like, of contractor subject to state statute requiring payment of prevailing wages on public works projects. 5 ALR 5th 513.

What entities or projects are "public" for purposes of state statutes requiring payment of prevailing wages on public works projects. 5 ALR 5th 470.

Validity, construction, and effect of state and local laws requiring governmental units to give "purchase preference" to goods manufactured or services performed in state. 84 ALR 4th 419.

What constitutes "public work" within statute relating to contractor's bond. 48 ALR 4th 1170.

Validity of state statute or local ordinance requiring, or giving

---

1. This annotation, together with 5 ALR 5th 470, 5 ALR 5th 513, 7 ALR 5th 400, 7 ALR 5th 444, and 10 ALR 5th 360, supersedes the annotation at 93 ALR 1249.

2. As to the question whether a project is of a "public" nature so as to render the project subject

to a state prevailing wage statute, see 5 ALR 5th 470. As to the question whether a particular employer involved in a public works project is covered by a state prevailing wage statute, see 7 ALR 5th 444.

Exhibit 7–13

ALR Annotation—Body of Annotation.

Lawyers Cooperative Publishing, *American Law Reports, 5th Ser.,* Vol. 10 (1993) p. 344. Used with permission of Thomson Reuters/West.

---

to the topic of the annotation, the court's conclusions on the issue(s), and the court's reasons for its conclusions.

In addition to the components of each annotation, the ALR series have the following general features:

✦ *ALR Index*—There is an ALR general index that lists terms and phrases alphabetically with references to all related annotations. The index is comprehensive with extensive cross-references (see Exhibit 7–14).

FOR EXAMPLE   If you are looking for annotations on asphyxiation, the index will direct you to suffocation.

The index is a multivolume set that provides references to annotations in ALR 2d, ALR 3d, ALR 4th, ALR 5th, ALR 6th, and ALR Federal.

ALR INDEX

Reference

ASPHALT AND ASPHALT PRODUCTS—Cont'd
frauds exception in UCC § 2-201(3)(a), **45 ALR4th 1126, § 10**

ASPHYXIATION
Suffocation (this index)

ASPIRIN
Drugstores and druggists, liability of pharmacist who accurately fills prescription for harm resulting to user, **44 ALR5th 393, § 15, 20[a], 42[b]**
Malpractice, negligence in diagnosing or treating aspirin poisoning, liability for, **36 ALR3d 1358**

ASPORTATION
Interstate or foreign shipments, what constitutes offense under provisions of 18 U.S.C.A. § 659 penalizing theft from interstate or foreign shipments, **8 ALR Fed 938**
Motor vehicle, asportation of motor vehicle as necessary element to support charge of larceny, 70 ALR3d 1202
Pawning, taking, and pledging or pawning, another's property as larceny, **82 ALR2d 863**
Privacy, false light invasion of, accusation or innuendo as to criminal acts, **58 ALR4th 902, § 11**
Separate offense
seizure or detention for purpose of committing rape, robbery, or other offense as constituting separate crime of kidnapping, **39 ALR5th 283**
shoplifting, validity, construction, and effect of statutes establishing shop-lifting or its equivalent as a separate criminal offense, **64 ALR4th 1088**

ASSASSINATION
Alien's entitlement, due to threat to life or freedom, to withholding of deportation under § 243(h) of Immigration and Nationality Act of 1952 (8 U.S.C.A. § 1253(h)), **83 ALR Fed 16, § 8[a, c], 10[c], 11[i], 13[b]**
Contact with attorney, denial or interference with accused's right to or request

ASSASSINATION—Cont'd
for initial contact with attorney, **18 ALR4th 669, § 3[a]; 18 ALR4th 743, § 3** — **Topic**

ASSAULT AND BATTERY
For related topics, see Abuse of Persons; — **Related Topic**
Fighting
Admiralty, what constitutes assault resulting in serious bodily injury within the special maritime or territorial jurisdiction of the United States for purposes of 18 U.S.C.A. § 113(f), providing punishment for such act, **55 ALR Fed 895**
Agents and agency
employer's liability to employee or agent for injury or death resulting from assault or criminal attack by third person, **40 ALR5th 1**
franchisor's tort liability for injuries allegedly caused by assault or other criminal activity on or near franchise premises, 2 **ALR5th 369**
Aggravated assault
kicking as aggravated assault, or assault with dangerous or deadly weapon, **19 ALR5th 823**
stationary object or attached fixture as deadly or dangerous weapon for purposes of statute aggravating offenses such as assault, robbery, or homicide, **8 ALR5th 775** — **Annotation**
sufficiency of bodily injury to support charge of aggravated assault, **5 ALR5th 243**
Aggravation of damages, see group Mitigation or aggravation of damages in this topic
AIDS, transmission or risk of transmission of human immunodeficiency virus (HIV) or acquired immunodeficiency syndrome (AIDS) as basis for prosecuting or sentencing defendant for criminal offense, **13 ALR5th 628**
Amusements and exhibitions
employee, liability of amusement operator for a personal assault by employee upon customer, patron, or other invitee, **34 ALR2d 422**
patron, liability of owner or operator of theater or other amusement to patron

Stationary Object

Consult POCKET PART for Later Annotations

Exhibit 7–14
ALR Index.
West, a Thomson Reuters business, *American Law Reports*, Index A—B (1999) p. 324. Used with permission of Thomson Reuters/West.

ANNOTATION HISTORY TABLE

This table lists annotations in ALR (First Series), ALR 2d, ALR 3d, ALR 4th, ALR 5th through Volume 69, ALR Fed through Volume 155, which have been superseded or supplemented by later annotations. Consult the pocket part in this volume for later history.

ALR (First Series)

1 ALR 148
Superseded 74 ALR 2d 828

1 ALR 222
Subdiv VIII Superseded 71
ALR 2d 1140

1 ALR 329
Superseded 36 ALR 2d 861

1 ALR 343
Superseded 51 ALR 2d 1404

1 ALR 383
Superseded 13 ALR 4th 1153

1 ALR 449
Superseded 28 ALR 2d 662

1 ALR 528
Superseded 87 ALR 4th 11

1 ALR 546
Superseded 50 ALR 2d 1324

1 ALR 834
Superseded 91 ALR 2d 1344

1 ALR 861
Superseded 41 ALR 2d 1213

1 ALR 884
Superseded, as to private
easements 25 ALR 2d 1265

1 ALR 1163
Superseded 28 ALR 4th 482

1 ALR 1267
Superseded 87 ALR 2d 271

1 ALR 1368
Superseded 46 ALR 2d 1140

1 ALR 1528
Superseded 13 ALR 3d 42

1 ALR 1632
Superseded 53 ALR 2d 572

1 ALR 1688
Superseded 99 ALR 2d 7

2 ALR 6
Supplemented 49 ALR 2d 982

2 ALR 61
Superseded 14 ALR 3d 783

2 ALR 225
Supplemented 41 ALR 2d 1263

2 ALR 287
Superseded 11 ALR 4th 345

2 ALR 345
Superseded 44 ALR 2d 1242

2 ALR 545
Superseded 54 ALR 3d 9

2 ALR 579
Superseded 50 ALR 2d 1161

2 ALR 592
Superseded 12 ALR 3d 933

2 ALR 867
Superseded 25 ALR 3d 941

2 ALR 1008
Superseded 90 ALR 2d 1210

2 ALR 1068
Superseded 6 ALR 3d 1457

2 ALR 1368
Superseded 56 ALR 3d 1182

2 ALR 1376
Superseded 45 ALR 2d 1296

2 ALR 1389
Superseded 28 ALR 3d 1344

2 ALR 1428
Superseded 61 ALR 5th 739

2 ALR 1522
Superseded 157 ALR 1359

2 ALR 1576
Superseded 77 ALR 2d 1182

3 ALR 242
Superseded 72 ALR 2d 342

3 ALR 312
Superseded 24 ALR 2d 194

3 ALR 610
Superseded 12 ALR 2d 611

3 ALR 664
Superseded 48 ALR 2d 894
74 ALR 4th 90

3 ALR 824
Superseded 13 ALR 3d 848

3 ALR 833
Superseded 22 ALR 3d 1346

3 ALR 902
Superseded 57 ALR 3d 1083

3 ALR 1003
Superseded 98 ALR 3d 605

3 ALR 1096
Superseded 89 ALR 3d 551

3 ALR 1104
Superseded 8 ALR 4th 886

3 ALR 1109
Superseded 92 ALR 2d 1009

3 ALR 1130
Supplemented 41 ALR 2d 739

3 ALR 1279
Subdiv II Superseded 100
ALR 2d 227

3 ALR 1304
Superseded 82 ALR 2d 611

Consult POCKET PART for Later Entries

Exhibit 7–15
ALR Annotation History Table.
West, a Thomson Reuters business, *American Law Reports*, General Index (1999) p. 1325. Used with permission of Thomson Reuters/West.

◆ *Table of Laws, Rules, and Regulations*—The index includes a table that indicates where statutes, rules, and regulations are cited in annotations.

◆ *Annotation History Table*—The last volume of the general index includes a history table that indicates if an annotation has been supplemented in or superseded by a later annotation (see Exhibit 7–15).

✦ *ALR Digests*—There are multivolume ALR digests similar to the *West Digests* (discussed in the next section). In the digests, the law is divided into more than 400 topics and arranged alphabetically. Each topic is divided into numerical subsections. The sections include a summary of the annotations, and references to other sources, such as encyclopedia references and practice references. There are separate digests for ALR and ALR 2d, and a combined digest for ALR 3d, ALR 4th, ALR 5th, ALR 6th, and ALR Federal.

✦ *Updates*—ALR and ALR 2d are updated differently than the other ALR series.

ALR. ALR is updated by checking the *ALR Blue Book of Supplemental Decisions.* This is a noncumulative multivolume set; that is, each volume covers supplemental cases for a set period of years. For example, Volume 3 covers supplemental decisions from 1952 to 1958. There is an annual paperback pamphlet for decisions subsequent to the last hardbound volume. This means that each volume and supplement must be checked to locate all the supplemental cases. Fortunately, because ALR covers cases only through 1948, it is not frequently used. The *Blue Book* lists the ALR citation (e.g., 121 ALR 616-627) followed by a list of cases decided after the citation was published. The *Blue Book* also indicates if an annotation has been supplemented or superceded by another annotation.

ALR 2d. ALR 2d is updated by reference to the multivolume *ALR 2d Later Case Service.* Each volume is updated with a pocket part, so you must check the pocket part as well as the main volume. The *Later Case Service* lists the ALR 2d citation followed by a summary of the new cases, and it lists supplemental or superseding annotations.

ALR 3d, ALR 4th, ALR 5th, ALR 6th, and ALR Federal. These are updated through the use of annual cumulative pocket part supplements inserted in the back of each volume. The pocket part lists the ALR citation followed by a list of new sections and subsections, a list of new research references, and a summary of the new cases. It also indicates if an annotation has been supplemented or superceded by another annotation.

Latest Case Service Hotline. In the front of each pocket part supplement of ALR 3d, ALR 4th, ALR 5th, ALR 6th, and ALR Federal is a toll-free number for obtaining cites to cases decided since the publication of the pocket part.

Auto-Cite and Insta-Cite. Cases may be updated through Auto-Cite on LexisNexis, and Insta-Cite on Westlaw. These databases are discussed in Chapter 10.

B. Research Using ALR

1. Use as a Research Tool

Legal research is usually focused on a very specific issue raised by the facts of a client's case. The value of ALR as a research tool lies in its comprehensive analysis of specific legal issues. If there is an annotation that addresses the legal issue you are researching, most of your research is done. The issue is analyzed through the discussion and synthesis of cases from every jurisdiction. Secondary sources such as treatises, *West Digest* key numbers, and practice aids are identified.

FOR EXAMPLE The question being researched involves the admissibility of polygraph evidence by the defendant in a malicious prosecution case. This is a specific question that could require a great deal of research. There is an ALR cite that directly addresses this topic: Steven J. Gaynor, Annotation, *Admissibility of Evidence of Polygraph Test Results or Offer or Refusal To Take Test, in Action for Malicious Prosecution*, 10 ALR 5th 663 (1993). Reference to this ALR annotation saves the researcher an immense amount of time because all the research to the year of the publication is consolidated in one source.

2. Research Techniques

The following research techniques will help you locate specific ALR annotations.

a. Index to Annotations

Probably the most frequently used approach to locating annotations is to consult the multivolume index. If you know the general area of law, the index will direct you to the appropriate annotation.

> **FOR EXAMPLE** The question is whether a stationary object can be a deadly weapon under a criminal statute enhancing the penalty for assault with a deadly weapon. By looking in the index under Assault and Battery, the researcher will be quickly directed to the appropriate annotation (see Exhibit 7–14).

b. ALR Digest

Like the index, annotations can be located by looking up the topic in the general area of law in the digest. In addition to references to annotations, the digest will summarize relevant cases printed in ALR.

c. Table of Laws, Rules, and Regulations

If you know the statute that governs the issue being researched, you can refer to the table and be directed to the annotations that discuss the statute.

d. Reference from Other Sources

Often you may be directed to a specific ALR annotation from another source such as a citation in a case, article, or *Shepard's Citations*. In such cases, you could go directly to the volume and section cited.

Always consult the pocket part and supplement to update your research and to locate the most recent cases. In addition, *always* consult the Appendix volume to ensure that you have located all the case summaries. Note that the Appendix volumes are not cumulative; each must be checked.

3. Computer-Aided Research

The ALR are available on CD-ROM, Westlaw, and LexisNexis.

V. DIGESTS

As discussed in Chapter 5, court opinions are printed in reporters in chronological order; they are not organized by topic. If you are attempting to locate a case that addresses a specific issue, that is, a case on point, it would take you forever to find it by randomly looking through case after case in the reporters. A digest is not secondary authority, that is, it is not a source a court will rely on to interpret the law. Rather, it is a source designed to allow researchers to locate cases easily.

A digest is a set of books that organizes the law by topic, such as corporations or torts, and each topic is divided into subtopics. The digest provides the citation to and a brief summary or "digest" of all the court opinions that have addressed the subtopics. The ability to review the case summaries allows the researcher to select the case most similar to the client's case, which is the case most on point. Thus, a digest serves as a tool for locating cases on specific questions being researched.

A. West Key-Number Digest System

The most comprehensive and frequently used digests are the *West Digests* published by West. Appellate court decisions in the United States are published in the various West's reporters. West developed its digest system to facilitate access to those decisions. An understanding of how the system is organized is helpful when learning how to use it.

West organizes the law into the following main categories: Persons, Property, Contracts, Torts, Crimes, Remedies, and Government. These broad categories are divided into subcategories, and the subcategories are subdivided into more than 400 topics (see Exhibit 7–16). Each topic is listed in alphabetical order in the digest. Each topic is subdivided into subtopics, and each subtopic is assigned a number called a **key number** (see Exhibit 7–17). Each subtopic is referred to by both its topic and key number.

FOR EXAMPLE Assault and Battery 7 refers to key number 7 of the topic of Assault and Battery, and Constitutional Law 7 refers to key number 7 of the topic of Constitutional Law.

To determine the subtopic title of a key number, look at the table of contents of the topic in the digest (see Exhibit 7–17).

FOR EXAMPLE If you want to know what the title of the subtopic Assault and Battery 7 is, you would look up Assault and Battery in the digest and then look to key number 7 to find that it refers to "Excessive force in doing lawful act" (see Exhibit 7–17).

Following the topic table of contents is the body of the digest, which lists the key number followed by a summary (digest) of all the court opinions that have in some way discussed the topic (see Exhibit 7–18).

FOR EXAMPLE The client wants to sue the police for beating him up when he was arrested for a DUI. To find cases that addressed that topic, you would look to the digest under Assault and Battery. In the body of the digest under key number 7, "Excessive force in doing a lawful act," is a summary of all the cases that have addressed the topic.

Every court opinion published in the West's reporters is linked to the digests through the use of headnotes. As you will recall from Chapter 5, headnotes are summaries of all the points of law discussed in the opinion. The headnotes follow the relevant paragraphs of the opinion in sequential order. Each headnote is assigned a topic and subtopic key number from the West classification system according to the area of law discussed in the case.

FOR EXAMPLE Refer to Exhibit 5–1 in Chapter 5. In *Rael v. Cadena*, headnote 1 contains a summary of the point of law discussed in the body of the opinion between [1] and [2]. The topic is Assault and Battery and the subtopic is Key 18 (Persons Liable). Headnote 2 is a summary of the point of law discussed in the opinion between [2] and [3], also Assault and Battery Key 18. Headnote 3 is a summary of the law discussed in the opinion between [3] and the end of the opinion, Assault and Battery Key 35 (Weight and Sufficiency of Evidence).

The beauty of the classification system is that the same numbering system is used for all the decisions published by West, essentially all the published federal and state

OUTLINE OF THE LAW

Digest Topics are arranged for your convenience by Seven Main Divisions of Law. Complete alphabetical list of Digest Topics with topic numbers follows this section.

1. PERSONS
2. PROPERTY
3. CONTRACTS
4. TORTS
5. CRIMES
6. REMEDIES
7. GOVERNMENT

1. PERSONS

RELATING TO NATURAL PERSONS IN GENERAL

Civil Rights
Dead Bodies
Death
Domicile
Drugs and Narcotics
Food
Health and Environment
Holidays
Intoxicating Liquors
Names
Seals
Signatures
Sunday
Time
Weapons

PARTICULAR CLASSES OF NATURAL PERSONS

Absentees
Aliens
Chemical Dependents
Children Out-of Wedlock
Citizens
Convicts
Indians
Infants
Mental Health
Slaves
Spendthrifts

PERSONAL RELATIONS

Adoption
Attorney and Client
Child Custody
Child Support
Employers' Liability
Executors and Administrators
Guardian and Ward
Husband and Wife
Labor Relations
Marriage
Master and Servant
Parent and Child
Principal and Agent
Workers' Compensation

ASSOCIATED AND ARTIFICIAL PERSONS

Associations
Beneficial Associations
Building and Loan Associations
Clubs
Colleges and Universities
Corporations
Exchanges
Joint-Stock Companies and Business Trusts
Partnership
Religious Societies

PARTICULAR OCCUPATIONS

Accountants
Agriculture
Auctions and Auctioneers
Aviation
Banks and Banking

Exhibit 7–16
West's Outline of the Law.
West, a Thomson Reuters business, *Eleventh Decennial Digest*, Vol. 5 (2001) p. IX. Used with permission of Thomson Reuters/West.

Topic

ASSAULT AND BATTERY

Subjects Included ———————————————— **SUBJECTS INCLUDED**

Acts of violence toward the person of another, with or without actual touching or striking, not
  constituting an element in, or attempt to commit, any other specific injury or offense
Justification or excuse for such acts, and circumstances of aggravation
Liabilities and remedies therefor, civil or criminal

SUBJECTS EXCLUDED AND COVERED BY OTHER TOPICS

Death, assault resulting in civil liability, see DEATH
Motor vehicles, assaults by operation of, see AUTOMOBILES
Subjects   Obstructing process or resisting officer, assaults committed in, see OBSTRUCTING JUSTICE
Covered   Other offenses—
Elsewhere   Commission of assault with intent to, or in attempt to, perpetrate, see HOMICIDE, RAPE,
                ROBBERY
            Convictions of assault in prosecutions for, see INDICTMENT AND INFORMATION
Unlawful arrest, assaults in connection with, see FALSE IMPRISONMENT

For detailed references to other topics, see Descriptive-Word Index

Analysis

I. CIVIL LIABILITY, ☞1–46.
  (A) ACTS CONSTITUTING ASSAULT OR BATTERY AND LIABILITY THEREFOR, ☞ 1-18.
  (B) ACTIONS, ☞ 19-46.

II. CRIMINAL RESPONSIBILITY, ☞ 47–100.
  (A) OFFENSES, ☞ 47-71.
  (B) PROSECUTION, ☞ 72-99.
  (C) SENTENCE AND PUNISHMENT, ☞ 100.

I. CIVIL LIABILITY.

(A) ACTS CONSTITUTING ASSAULT
       OR BATTERY AND LIABILITY
              THEREFOR.

Key
Numbers

☞ 1. Nature and elements of assault and battery.
   2. —— In general.
   3. —— Intent and malice.
   4. —— Ability to execute intent.
   5. —— Overt act in general.
   6. —— Unlawful act.
   7. —— Excessive force in doing lawful act.
   8. Defenses.
   9. —— In general.
  10. —— Exercise of authority or duty.
  11. —— Consent.
  12. —— Provocation.
  13. —— Self-defense.
  14. —— Defense of another.
  15. —— Defense of property.

16. —— Accident.
17. Persons entitled to sue.
18. Persons liable.

       (B) ACTIONS.

☞ 19. Grounds and conditions precedent.
20. Jurisdiction and venue.
21. Time to sue and limitations.
22. Parties.
23. Process.
24. Pleading.
     (.5). In general.
     (1). Declaration, petition, or complaint.
     (2). Plea or answer and replication.
     (3). Issues, proof, and variance.
25. Evidence.
25.1. —— In general.

Exhibit 7–17
Assault and Battery Key Number Outline.
West, a Thomson Reuters business, *Eleventh Decennial Digest*, Vol. 5 (2001). Used with permission of Thomson Reuters/West.

⚷ 1   ASSAULT & BATTERY

For later cases see same Topic and Key Number in Pocket Part

I. CIVIL LIABILITY.

(A) ACTS CONSTITUTING ASSAULT
OR BATTERY AND LIABILITY
THEREFOR.

⚷ **1. Nature and elements of assault and battery.**

Library references

C.J.S. Assault and Battery § 2.

⚷ 2. —— In general.

C.A.D.C. 1988. Under District of Columbia law, surgeon who performs operation on minor patient without consent of minor's parents commits assault for which he is liable in damages, absent exceptional circumstances, such as when there is bona fide medical emergency, patient is "mature minor," parents are not readily accessible, or parents have given their implied consent.

Kozup v. Georgetown University, 851 F.2d 437, 271 U.S.App.D.C. 182, on remand 1989 WL 39006, appeal after remand 906 F.2d 783, 285 U.S.App.D.C. 89.

C.A.9 (Ariz.) 1987. Person commits tort of "assault" if he acts with intent to cause another harmful or offensive contact or apprehension thereof, and other person apprehends imminent contact.

Garcia v. U.S., 826 F.2d 806.

Person commits tort of "battery" if he acts with intent to cause harmful or offensive contact, or apprehension thereof, and contact occurs.

Garcia v. U.S., 826 F.2d 806.

C.A.9 (Cal.) 1991. Employee union steward's state law battery claim against management employee arose from right created by independent state common law and not by collective bargaining agreements and, thus, state law claim was not preempted by Labor Management Relations Act; whatever parties' rights and duties under collective bargaining agreement, they could not possibly have negotiated infringement of employee union steward's state law right to be free from battery. Labor Management Relations Act, 1947, § 301, 29 U.S.C.A. § 185.

Hayden v. Reickerd, 957 F.2d 1506.

Employee's state law right to be free from battery, continuing infliction of stress, and verbal abuse he alleged was retaliation for his union activities did not turn on interpretation of any term of collective bargaining agreement and were not preempted by Labor Management Relations Act. Labor Management Relations Act, 1947, § 301, 29 U.S.C.A. § 185.

Hayden v. Reickerd, 957 F.2d 1506.

C.A.9 (Cal.) 1991. An employee's state law assault and battery claim against his supervisor was not preempted by the Labor Management Relations Act, as the acts alleged would violate state law irrespective of the identity of the wrongdoer or his victim and did not require interpretation of collective bargaining agreement provisions. Labor Management Relations Act, 1947, § 301, 29 U.S.C.A. § 185; West's Ann.Cal.Penal Code §§ 240, 242.

Galvez v. Kuhn, 933 F.2d 773.

Allegation that supervisor's conduct was motivated by desire to find reason to fire employee was too tenuous a connection to collective bargaining agreement discharge provisions to preempt employee's state law claims of assault and battery against supervisor. Labor Management Relations Act, 1947, § 301, 29 U.S.C.A. § 185.

Galvez v. Kuhn, 933 F.2d 773.

C.A.10 (Colo.) 1979. Hackbart v. Cincinnati Bengals, Inc., 601 F.2d 516, certiorari denied 100 S.Ct. 275, 444 U.S. 931, 62 L.Ed.2d 188.

C.A.11 (Ga.) 1990. In absence of consent, surgery constitutes battery.

Bendiburg v. Dempsey, 909 F.2d 463, certiorari denied 111 S.Ct. 2053, 500 U.S. 932, 114 L.Ed.2d 459, appeal after remand 19 F.3d 557.

C.A.6 (Mich.) 1986. Prison guard's waving of knife in front of paraplegic prisoner constituted common-law assault, from which general damages were presumed to flow, and thus, prisoner was entitled to general damages for that conduct.

Parrish v. Johnson, 800 F.2d 600.

C.A.5 (Miss.) 1983. Under Mississippi law, mere words, without threat of physical violence, are insufficient to support finding of civil assault.

Hart v. Walker, 720 F.2d 1436.

Where county supervisor displayed firearm in purporting to arrest plaintiff, finding that supervisor committed civil assault upon plaintiff under Mississippi law was not clearly erroneous.

Hart v. Walker, 720 F.2d 1436.

C.A.2 (N.Y.) 1993. "Assault" is intentional placing of another person in fear of imminent harmful or offensive contact.

United Nat. Ins. Co. v. Waterfront New York Realty Corp., 994 F.2d 105.

"Battery" is an intentional wrongful physical contact with another person without consent.

United Nat. Ins. Co. v. Waterfront New York Realty Corp., 994 F.2d 105.

For cited U.S.C.A. sections and legislative history, see United States Code Annotated

---

Exhibit 7–18

Body of Digest for Assault and Battery—Case Summaries.

West, a Thomson Reuters business, *Federal Practice Digest 4th*, Vol. 3A (1994), p. 766. Used with permission of Thomson Reuters/West.

appellate court decisions in the United States. All reported decisions are summarized (provided headnotes) using the same key number classification system, and all cases are linked through the same system to digests that identify all other cases that address the same topic.

> **FOR EXAMPLE** If you are interested in any reported case anywhere in the United States, state or federal, that discusses when persons may be liable for an assault or battery, you can refer to any *West Digest* under Assault and Battery Key 18 and find the other cases. Assault and Battery Key 18 is the same in all the headnotes and all the digests.

B. Components of the *West Digests*

West prepares numerous digests, which are discussed in the next section. These digests follow the same format and share the following components.

Each topic presented in a digest begins with the name of the topic such as "ASSAULT AND BATTERY." After each topic title is the following:

✦ *Subjects Included and Excluded*—This section lists the areas covered in the topic and the areas not covered. For the subjects excluded, there are references to the topics where the subjects are covered (see Exhibit 7–17).

✦ *Table of Contents*—Next is a table of contents listing the title and key number of all the subtopics (see Exhibit 7–17).

✦ *Case Summaries*—Following the table of contents is the body of the digest that presents a summary by key number of every case reported that has addressed a specific subtopic. The digest presents a summary of only that portion of the case that addressed the specific key number.

> **FOR EXAMPLE** In the body of the digest under Assault and Battery Key 18, "Persons liable" will be a summary of only that portion of each case that discussed the topic of when a person is liable for an assault or battery.

This saves you from having to read a summary of the entire case and allows you to focus on the specific question being researched. If there are no cases that address a key number subtopic, the digest will list an encyclopedia reference where the topic is covered (see Exhibit 7–18).

In addition to the components of each annotation, each digest set includes the following:

✦ *Outline of The Law and List of Topics*—At the beginning of each digest volume is West's outline of the law and a list of digest topics (see Exhibit 7–16).

✦ *Topics Covered*—Indicated on the spine are the topics covered in the volume, such as "Gas to Habeas Corpus." This allows you to locate the volume you are looking for without having to look in the book. In addition, inside each volume is a list of topics covered in the volume and the page number where the topic begins, such as "Gas . . . 1, Gifts . . . 249."

✦ *Descriptive-Word Index*—A comprehensive descriptive-word index accompanies each set. The index is a multivolume set that lists words or phrases in alphabetical order. Following the word or phrase is a reference to the topic and key number where it is discussed (see Exhibit 7–19).

DESCRIPTIVE-WORD INDEX

Volume 1 General Digest, Tenth Series

References are to Digest Topics and Key Numbers

ABANDONMENT
AUTOMOBILES. Autos 12
BANKRUPTCY, abandonment of
    property, see this index Bankruptcy
DEFENSE to criminal charge. Crim Law
    31.10

ABORIGINAL PEOPLES
See generally, this index Indians

ABORTION
FAMILY planning—
    Government grants and grantees.
        Social S 4.6

ABSENCE AND ABSENTEES
BALLOTS, see this index Absent Voters
LIMITATION of actions—
    Guarantors, effect as to. Lim of
        Act 94
    Jointly or severally liable parties,
        effect as to. Lim of Act 94
    Sureties, effect as to. Lim of Act 94

ABUSE OF PROCESS
BANKRUPTCY. Bankr 2253, 3502

ABUSED CHILDREN
EVIDENCE—
    Expert testimony. Crim Law
        474.4(4)

ACCESS
CABLE television systems—
    Access rules. Tel 449(10)

ACCOMPLICES AND ACCESSORIES
RACKETEERING. RICO 21

ACCOUNTANTS
BANKRUPTCY—
    Compensation. Bankr 3161
RACKETEERING—
    Enterprise, accounting firm as.
        RICO 42
SECURITIES regulation—
    Federal regulation, see this index
        Securities Regulation
    State regulation, see this index Blue
        Sky Law

ACTIONS AND OTHER PROCEEDINGS
COMMENCEMENT of actions—
    Bankruptcy case. Bankr 2202
INJUNCTIONS—
    Preliminary injunction—
        Grounds and objections. Inj
            138.27
        Proceedings. Inj 139–159.5

ADDITUR
LEGAL or equitable, see this index Legal
    or Equitable Nature of Proceedings

ADEQUATE PROTECTION
BANKRUPTCY, see this index
    Bankruptcy

ADMINISTRATIVE LAW
    AND PROCEDURE
APPEAL and error—
    Ripeness. Admin Law 704
COMMODITY futures trading
    regulation—
    Administrative agencies, sanctions
        and proceedings. Com Fut 51–61
DISCOVERY. Admin Law 466
DOUBLE jeopardy, proceedings affected.
    Double J 24
REVIEW, see Appeal and error, ante

ADMIRALTY
INTEREST—
    Prejudgment. Interest 39(2.25)

ADOPTION
HABEAS CORPUS—
    Grounds for relief. Hab Corp 534

ADOPTION OF CHILDREN
HOMOSEXUALS, ability to adopt. Adop 4

ADVERTISEMENT
ATTORNEYS, see this index Attorney
    and Client
CONTRACTS—
    United States, advertisement for
        proposals or bids. U S 64.25
EMPLOYMENT, discrimination. Civil
    R 156
FREEDOM of speech and press. Const
    Law 90.3

ADVICE OF COUNSEL
DEFENSE—
    Criminal charge. Crim Law 37.20

ADVISORS
COMMODITY futures trading
    regulation, see this index
    Commodity Futures Trading
    regulation, passim

AFFIRMATIVE ACTION
EMPLOYMENT discrimination. Civil R
    154
    Relief in equal employment
        opportunities actions. Civil R 392
EMPLOYMENT discrimination suit,
    relief in, see this index Civil Rights

AFFIRMATIVE DEFENSES
BANKRUPTCY, relief from stay,
    proceedings. Bankr 2436

AGE
DISCRIMINATION. Civil R 106
    Employment—
        Generally. Civil R 168–172
    Presumptions and burden of proof.
        Civil R 380
    Relief in age discrimination in
        employment actions. Civil R
        406, 407
    Remedies and proceedings. Civil
        R 331–431
    Weight and sufficiency of evidence.
        Civil R 388

AGGRAVATION OF DAMAGES
RELIEF in equal employment
    opportunities actions. Civil R 402

AGRICULTURAL COMPOSITIONS AND
    EXTENSIONS
FAMILY farmers, see this index Family
    Farmer Debt Adjustment

AIDERS AND ABETTORS JURORS—
    Representation of community. Jury
        33(1.4)
    Waiver—
        Challenge based on age of
            prospective juror. Jury 110(4)

AIR
POLLUTION, see this index Air Pollution

AIR POLLUTION
Generally. Health & E 25.6
ENVIRONMENTAL impact statement.
    Health & E 25.10
Judicial review or intervention—
    Scope of inquiry or review.
        Health & E 25.15(10)
JUDICIAL review of regulations or
    intervention. Health & E 25.15
    Scope of inquiry or review. Health &
        E 25.15(9)
MUNICIPAL regulation. Mun Corp 606
NUISANCES—
    Health & E 28
    Nuis 3(3)

AIRPORTS AND LANDING FIELDS
SEARCHES and seizures. Searches 72
    Drug searches. Drugs & N 183.5

Exhibit 7–19
Descriptive-Word Index.
West, a Thomson Reuters business, *West General Digest*, Vol. 6 (2001) p. 929. Used with permission of Thomson Reuters/West.

✦ *Table of Cases*—Each digest has a table of cases listing cases alphabetically by the names of the plaintiffs (see Exhibit 7–20). Some digests also have a table of cases listing cases alphabetically by the name of the defendant, followed by the plaintiff's name.

✦ *Words and Phrases*—Most federal and state digests include a Table of Words and Phrases that lists alphabetically words and phrases that have been interpreted or defined in court opinions and the citation to the opinions.

✦ *Updates*—Digests are updated through the use of the following:

Pocket Parts. Each digest volume is updated through the use of an annual pocket part placed at the back of the volume. The pocket part presents by key number the summaries of new cases that address the key number topic (see Exhibit 7–21).

Supplementary Pamphlets. Supplementary pamphlets with further updates are published between annual pocket parts.

Later Cases. Both the pocket parts and supplementary pamphlets include a "Closing" table that lists the names of all the reporters covered in the digest. If there is a reporter volume subsequent to the one listed, it must be checked to determine if there are cases published after the ones in the supplement. A key number digest is in the back of each reporter volume for the cases presented in the volume.

FOR EXAMPLE If the closing table reads, "Closing with cases reported in 243 F.3d 713," then you must check the key number digest at the back of any *Federal Reporter 3d Series* volume subsequent to volume 243, page 713 for later cases.

C. Types of Digests

West publishes several digests, each of which serves to fulfill a specific need. Each of these digests includes the components discussed in the previous section. A brief description of the digests and their functions is presented here.

1. American Digest System

The most comprehensive and inclusive digest is the *American Digest System*. This digest presents summaries of all the reported state and federal court decisions. Due to the large number of cases covered, the digest consists of several multivolume sets with each set covering a specific time period. The sets are not cumulative; therefore, if you want to find all cases for a specific key number, you need to check each set for all the cases.

FOR EXAMPLE If you want to locate the cases addressing Assault and Battery Key 18, you have to consult the *General Digest* for cases from 1996 to present, the *Tenth Decennial Digest* for cases from 1986 to 1996, the *Ninth Decennial Digest* for 1976–1986, the *Eighth Decennial Digest* for 1966–1976, and so on.

The weakness of the digest is its strength; that is, it covers all the cases. You may be interested only in federal cases, cases from your region of the United States, or cases from your state. With the *American Digest*, you may have to wade through a lot of case summaries to find the case you want. Fortunately, West publishes other more focused digests.

A.A.

For Later Case History Information, see INSTA-CITE on WESTLAW

AA Ambulance Co., Inc. v. Multnomah County, OrApp, 794 P2d 813, 102 Or-App 398.—Records 54, 57, 63, 68.

AA Ambulance Co., Inc. v. Multnomah County, OrApp. 777 P2d 997, 97 OrApp 618. See Care Ambulance Co., Inc. v. Multnomah County.

AA, Charles, Matter of, NYAD 3 Dept, 550 NYS2d 180. See Charles AA, Matter of.

AA. Faith, Matter of, NYAD 3 Dept, 530 NYS2d 318, 139 AD2d 22. See Faith AA, Matter of.

AA. on behalf of A.A. v. Cooperman, NJSuperAD, 526 A2d 1103, 218 NJSuper 32.—Const Law 278.5(7); Schools 159½(4).

A.A. Poultry Farms, Inc. v. Rose Acre Farms. Inc., CA7 (Ind), 881 F2d 1396, cert den 110 SCt 1326, 494 US 1019, 108 LEd2d 501.—Fed Civ Proc 630; Monop 17(1.8); Trade Reg 918.

A.A. Poultry Farms, Inc. v. Rose Acre Farms, Inc., SDInd. 683 FSupp 680, aff 881 F2d 1396, cert den 110 SCt 1326, 494 US 1019, 108 LEd2d 501.—Fed Civ Proc 2333, 2339, 2608; Fed Cts 660, 660.20; Monop 12(1), 12(1.2), 12(16.5); Trade Reg 911, 913, 914, 920, 929, 931.

A.A. Profiles, Inc. v. City of Ft. Lauderdale, CA11 (Fla), 850 F2d 1483, reh den 861 F2d 727, cert den 109 SCt 1743, 490 US 1020, 104 LEd2d 180.—Civil R 209; Em Dom 2(1.2), 277; Zoning 167, 196.

A.A. Quality Const. v. Thomas, Mont, 728 P2d 416, 224 Mont 108.—Damag 189; Mech Liens 154(2).

AA, Ricky, Matter of, NYAD 3 Dept, 541 NYS2d 264, 146 AD2d 433. See Ricky AA, Matter of.

AAA Bail Bonding Co. v. State, Ga. 383 SE2d 125, 259 Ga 411.—Bail 80.

AAA Bonding Co. v. State, GaApp, 386 SE2d 50, 192 GaApp 684.—Bail 77(1).

AAA Crane Service, Inc. v. Omnibank University Hills, N.A., ColoApp, 723 P2d 156.—Costs 2; Courts 85(1); Mech Liens 272, 281(1); Pretrial Proc 746.

AAA Distributors and Associates, In re, CA4 (NC), 922 F2d 1146. See Raynor, In re.

AAA Elec. Service v. Farmers Home Mut. Ins. Co., Utah App. 763 P2d 814. See American Bonding Co. v. Nelson.

AAA Guaranteed Mortg., Inc. v. State, Dept. of Banking and Finance, Div. of Finance, FlaApp 2 Dist, 517 So2d 761.—Brok 3.

AAA Sod, Inc. v. Weitzer Corp., FlaApp 4 Dist, 513 So2d 750.—Mech Liens 281(1), 304(1), 310(3).

AAA Van Services, Inc. v. Willis, GaApp, 354 SE2d 631, 182 GaApp 46.—App & E 358; Costs 260(5).

AAA Van Services, Inc. v. Willis, GaApp, 348 SE2d 475, 180 GaApp 18.—App & E 215(1); Bailm 33.

AAAA Enterprises, Inc. v. River Place Community Urban Redevelopment Corp., Ohio, 553 NE2d 597, 50 Ohio St3d 157, appeal after remand 598 NE2d 711, 74 Ohio App3d 170, jurisdictional motion overr 579 NE2d 214, 62 Ohio St3d 1441.—Em Dom 18.5; Judgm 181(15), 185(2), 185(6).

AAAA Enterprises, Inc. v. U.S., ClCt, 10 ClCt 191.—Fed Cts 1104, 1105, 1109, 1111, 1139.

AAAction Plumbing Co. v. Stewart, Tex-App-Hous | 1 Dist |, 792 SW2d 501, error den.—Time 10(9).

Aaberg By and Through Aaberg v. Aaberg, Ala, 512 So2d 1375.—Marriage 13, 50(1).

Aagaard-Juergensen, Inc. v. Lettelier, FlaApp 5 Dist, 579 So2d 404.—Damag 227.

Aagaard-Juergensen, Inc. v. Lettelier, FlaApp 5 Dist, 540 So2d 224.—App & E 79(2); Corp 363; Judgm 185(2), 185(5).

AAI Corp. v. U.S., ClCt, 22 ClCt 541.—Fed Cts 1078; U S 73(9).

Aaker v. Aaker, MinnApp, 447 NW2d 607, review den.—Divorce 224, 240(1), 240(2), 245(2), 247, 286(1), 308, 310, 312.6(1); Parent & C 3.3(6).

Aakjer v. Spagnoli, SCApp, 352 SE2d 503, 291 SC 165.—App & E 1048(7), 1058(1), 1067; Autos 242(1), 246(39), 246(55); Jury 149; New Tr 30; Trial 18, 30, 115(5), 260(8); Witn 208(1), 275(6), 379(1), 405(1).

A.A.L., In Interest of, WisApp, 448 NW2d 239, 152 Wis2d 159.—App & E 945; Const Law 82(10), 274(5); Counties 138; Courts 1; Infants 212, 243, 252; States 111.

A.A.L., Matter of Adoption of, WisApp, 448 NW2d 239, 152 Wis2d 159. See A.A.L., In Interest of.

Aalbers v. Iowa Dept. of Job Service, Iowa, 431 NW2d 330.—Social S 437, 589.

Aalco-Barney Co. v. Harry Sander Realty Co., Inc., MoApp, 771 SW2d 922. See Shockley v. Harry Sander Realty Co., Inc.

Aalgaard v. Merchants Nat. Bank, Inc., CalApp 3 Dist, 274 CalRptr 81, 224 CA3d 674, review den, cert den 112 SCt 278, 116 LEd2d 230.—Banks 251; Civil R 449; Consp 11; Mast & S 9.5, 34; States 18.23, 18.45.

Aalund v. Williams County, ND, 442 NW2d 900.—Em Dom 187, 238(4).

A.A.M., State in Interest of, NJSuperCh. 548 A2d 524, 228 NJSuper 9.—Drugs & N 107; Infants 68.7(2), 68.7(3).

Aamco Transmissions v. General Cas. Co. of Wisconsin, WisApp. 422 NW2d 154, 143 Wis2d 661. See Silverton Enterprises, Inc. v. General Cas. Co. of Wisconsin.

AAMCO Transmissions, Inc. v. Harris, EDPa, 759 FSupp 1141.—Contracts 168; Fed Civ Proc 2492; Fraud 7; Lim of Act 2(1); Trade Reg 871.3.

Aamco Transmissions, Inc. v. Smith, EDPa, 756 FSupp 225.—Fed Cts 31, 214, 217.

Aamodt v. U.S., ClCt, 22 ClCt 716, aff 976 F2d 691.—Labor 416.1.

A & A Acoustics, Inc. v. Valinsky, IllApp 1 Dist, 147 IllDec 840, 559 NE2d 1180, 202 IllApp3d 516, appeal den 151 IllDec 379, 564 NE2d 834, 135 Ill2d 553.—App & E 984(5); Atty & C 24, 32(11); Costs 2; Mech Liens 249.

A & A Cake Decorating Supplies Inc. v. Ramos, LaApp 3 Cir, 502 So2d 1171.—App & E 1106(1).

A & A Grocery v. State Liquor Authority, NYAD 1 Dist, 556 NYS2d 330. See Mohsin v. State Liquor Authority.

A & A Intern., Inc. v. U.S., CIT, 676 FSupp 263. —Cust Dut 17, 18, 19, 26(1), 26(3), 84(7).

A & A Invalid Van Service v. Medevac Midamerica of Kansas, Inc., DKan, 719 FSupp 1014. See Freeman v. Medevac Midamerica of Kansas, Inc.

A & B Cattle Co. of Nevada, Inc. v. City of Escondido, CalApp 4 Dist, 238 CalRptr 580, 192 CA3d 1032.—Mun Corp 65, 592(1).

A & B Heating & Air Conditioning, Matter of, CA11 (Fla), 861 F2d 1538.—Bankr 3781.

A & B Heating & Air Conditioning, Matter of, CA11 (Fla), 823 F2d 462, cert gr and vac US v. A & B Heating and Air Conditioning, Inc, 108 SCt 1724, 486 US 1002, 100 LEd2d 189, on remand 861 F2d 1538.—Int Rev 4832.

A & B Homes, Ltd., In re, Bkrtcy EDVa, 98 BR 243.—Bankr 2678, 3064; Sec Tran 10, 89.

A & B Horse Farms v. U.S., ClCt, 18 ClCt 302. See Haberman v. U.S.

A & B Pipe and Supply Co. v. Turnberry Towers Corp., FlaApp 3 Dist, 500 So2d 261.—Judgm 188.

A & B Restaurant Equipment, Inc. v. Homeseekers Sav. and Loan, LaApp 4 Cir, 506 So2d 137, writ den 512 So2d 852, reconsideration den 513 So2d 1195.—Brok 106; Refer 100(6); Ven & Pur 34, 113, 143, 334(1), 341(3).

A & C Bldg. and Indus. Maintenance Corp. v. U.S., ClCt, 11 ClCt 385.—Fed Cts 1077.

A & D Care, Inc., In re, BkrtcyMDPa, 86 BR 43.—Bankr 2084.5, 2085, 2102.

A & D Care, Inc., In re, BkrtcyWDPa, 90 BR 138.—Bankr 2045; Fed Cts 47.

A & D Supermarkets, Inc., No. 2 v. United Food and Commercial Workers. Local Union 880, NDOhio. 732 FSupp 770.—Monop 12(9), 17(1.7), 28(1.7), 28(5), 28(6.2); States 18.33.

A & E Pacific Const. Co. v. Saipan Stevedore Co., Inc., CA9 (NMariana Islands), 888 F2d 68.—Civil R 181; Fed Cts 776; Monop 16(1), 24(7), 28(1.6); Ship 103; Territories 18; Treaties 8.

A & E Supply Co., Inc. v. Nationwide Mut. Fire Ins. Co., CA4 (Va), 798 F2d 669, cert den 107 SCt 1302, 479 US 1091, 94 LEd2d 158.—Damag 184; Fraud 58(4); Insurance 11, 602.1; Trover 40(4).

A & H, Inc., In re, BkrtcyWDWis, 122 BR 84.—Bankr 2828, 3544.

A & H Vending Service, Inc. v. Village of Schaumburg, IllApp 1 Dist, 118 IllDec 733, 522 NE2d 188, 168 IllApp3d 61, appeal den 125 IllDec 210, 530 NE2d 238, 122 Ill2d 569.—Licens 7(1), 7(9).

A & J Auto Body, In re, BkrtcyDMass, 63 BR 335. See Russo, In re.

A & J Gifts Shop v. Chu, NYAD 3 Dept, 536 NYS2d 209, 145 AD2d 377, appeal den 542 NYS2d 518, 74 NY2d 603, 540 NE2d 713.—Tax 1311, 1316.

A & J Tie Beam Service v. Kendle. FlaApp 1 Dist, 511 So2d 653.—Work Comp 853, 1861.

A & K Produce, In re, BkrtcySDNY, 106 BR 42. See New York Produce American & Korean Auction Corp., In re.

For Later Case History Information, see INSTA-CITE on WESTLAW

Name and Citation of Case

Topic and Key Number Reference

Exhibit 7–20

Table of Cases.

West, a Thomson Reuters business, *Tenth Decennial Digest*, Vol. 40 (1993), p. 10th D. Pt 1–4. Used with permission of Thomson Reuters/West.

No Cases Under Key Number

Library Reference

ASSAULT & BATTERY 🔑 2

I. CIVIL LIABILITY.

(A) ACTS CONSTITUTING ASSAULT OR BATTERY AND LIABILITY THEREFOR.

🔑 1. Nature and elements of assault and battery.

Library references

C.J.S. Assault and Battery § 2.

🔑 2. — In general.

C.A.11 (Ala.) 1998. Under Alabama law, assault consists of intentional, unlawful offer to touch the person of another in rude or angry manner under such circumstances as to create in mind of party alleging assault a well-founded fear of imminent battery, coupled with apparent present ability to effectuate the attempt, if not prevented.—Peterson v. BMI Refractories, 132 F.3d 1405.

Court of Appeals was not required to interpret collective bargaining agreement (CBA) to determine whether employer was liable under Alabama law for alleged assault and battery that occurred when supervisor allegedly threatened employee with pistol, and employee's assault and battery claims thus were not preempted by LMRA. Labor Management Relations Act, 1947, § 301(a), 29 U.S.C.A. § 185(a).—Id.

C.A.10 (Kan.) 1996. Under Kansas law, "assault" is defined as intentional threat or attempt, coupled with apparent ability, to do bodily harm to another, resulting in immediate apprehension of bodily harm; no bodily contact is necessary.—Wilson v. Meeks, 98 F.3d 1247.

Under Kansas law, elements of battery include touching or striking another person with intent of bringing about either contact, or apprehension of contact that is harmful and offensive.—Id.

C.A.10 (N.M.) 1999. One of the key distinctions between claims sounding in negligence and those sounding in intentional tort like assault and battery is that the latter requires an unconsented touching. Restatement (Second) of Torts § 13 comment.—Benavidez v. U.S., 177 F.3d 927.

C.A.3 (Pa.) 1998. Under Pennsylvania law, tort of intentional exposure to hazardous substances is predicated on theory of battery; plaintiff must prove as constituent element he or she did not consent to the tortious conduct.—Barnes v. American Tobacco Co., 161 F.3d 127, certiorari denied 119 S.Ct. 1760, 526 U.S. 1114, 143 L.Ed.2d 791.

C.A.5 (Tex.) 2000. Dangerous nature of cigarettes was common knowledge, and thus smokers' assault action against tobacco manufacturer was barred by Texas Product Liability Act provision relieving manufacturers and sellers of inherently unsafe products from products liability suits, even if addictive nature of tobacco was not itself common knowledge. V.T.C.A., Civil Practice & Remedies Code § 82.004(a).—Harris v. Philip Morris Inc., 232 F.3d 456.

Tobacco manufacturer's concealment of addictive nature of cigarettes did not preclude application of Texas Product Liability Act provision relieving manufacturers and sellers of inherently unsafe products from products liability suits to bar smokers' civil assault action against manufacturer. V.T.C.A., Civil Practice & Remedies Code §§ 82.001(2), 82.004(a).—Id.

Under Texas law, smokers' claims against tobacco manufacturer for civil assault arising from its manufacture and sale of products that induced nicotine addition were based on "products liability," and thus were barred by Texas Product Liability Act provision relieving manufacturers and sellers of inherently unsafe products from products liability suits. V.T.C.A., Civil Practice & Remedies Code § 82.004(a).—Id.

C.A.5 (Tex.) 2000. Under Texas law, action against cigarette manufacturer brought by survivors and estate of deceased smoker, alleging civil assault as result of manufacturer's failure to warn smoker of dangers of nicotine addiction, was barred by Texas Products Liability Act; addictive properties of nicotine were common knowledge, application of Act was not against public policy, action was predicated on existence of product defect, and claims arose out of smoker's personal injuries allegedly caused by smoking addictive cigarettes. V.T.C.A., Civil Practice & Remedies Code § 82.004.—Davis ex rel. Davis v. R.J. Reynolds Tobacco, Inc., 231 F.3d 928, rehearing denied.

M.D.Ala. 2000. To establish a claim for "battery" under Alabama law, plaintiff must show that he or she was subjected to the touching of the person of another in rudeness or anger.—Taylor v. Alabama, 95 F.Supp.2d 1297.

M.D.Ala. 1999. Under Alabama law, "assault" is defined as an intentional, unlawful offer to touch the person of another in a rude or angry manner under such circumstances as to create in the mind of the party alleging the assault a well-founded fear of an imminent battery, coupled with the apparent present ability to effectuate the attempt, if not prevented.—Martin v. Anderson, 107 F.Supp.2d 1342.

Under Alabama law, a "battery" is a successful assault, and consists of touching another in a hostile manner.—Id.

M.D.Ala. 1999. Under Alabama law, "battery" consists of touching of another in hostile manner.—Hardy v. Town of Hayneville, 50 F.Supp.2d 1176.

M.D.Ala. 1998. To recover for assault and battery under Alabama law, plaintiff must provide evidence of touching by one person of person of another in rudeness or anger.—Portera v. Winn Dixie of Montgomery, Inc., 996 F.Supp. 1418.

There is no requirement under Alabama law that there be injury or threat of injury to constitute assault and battery; wrong consists, not in touching, so much as in manner or spirit in which it is done, and question of bodily pain is important only as affecting damages.—Id.

M.D.Ala. 1997. "Assault and battery" under Alabama law is touching by one person of person or clothes of another in rudeness, in anger, or in hostile manner; intent to injure is not required.—Mills v. Wex-Tex Industries, Inc., 991 F.Supp. 1370.

M.D.Ala. 1997. Under Alabama law, "assault" consists of an intentional, unlawful offer to touch a person coupled with the present ability to do so, such that the words or action create a reasonable fear of imminent contact.—Morrow v. Auburn University at Montgomery, 973 F.Supp. 1392.

Although words, standing alone, do not constitute assault under Alabama law, when considered in combination with an offender's show of force or other action, a cause of action for assault may lie.—Id.

University department head did not assault instructor under Alabama law by allegedly "playing footsie," rubbing instructor's neck and shoulder, or standing too close behind her, though instructor described conduct as unwelcomed and humiliating, where no menacing or offensive comments were claimed and instructor did not contend that at any time she felt threatened.—Id.

M.D.Ala. 1996. Assault, under Alabama law, is unlawful offer to touch person coupled with present ability to do so, such that words or action create reasonable fear of imminent contact.—Brassfield v. Jack McLendon Furniture, Inc., 953 F.Supp. 1438.

Although words alone cannot constitute assault, under Alabama law, words accompanied by show of force or other action may be sufficient.—Id.

Female employee's allegations that male manager clenched his fist while telling her he was going to knock her teeth down her throat were sufficient to support employee's assault claim against manager under Alabama law.—Id.

Female employee's allegation that she told corporate employer's president about manager's violent threat and that employer failed to take adequate steps to prevent future incidents were sufficient to sustain employee's assault claim against employer under Alabama law.—Id.

Successful assault becomes battery under Alabama law.—Id.

M.D.Ala. 1996. Under Alabama law, assault and battery consists of touching by one person of person of another in rudeness or anger.—Patterson v. Augat Wiring Systems, Inc., 944 F. Supp. 1509.

Reasonable jury could find that supervisor's entering employee's vehicle against employee's wishes and placing his hand on employee in rude and angry manner constituted assault and battery under Alabama law by supervisor.—Id.

N.D.Cal. 1998. In order to state a cause of action for assault plaintiff must establish that: (1) defendant intended to cause harmful or offensive contact, or the imminent apprehension of such contact, and (2) plaintiff was put in imminent apprehension of such contact. Restatement (Second) of Torts § 21.—Brooks v. U.S., 29 F.Supp.2d 613, affirmed 162 F.3d 1167.

Merely reckless behavior cannot give rise to an assault cause of action.—Id.

S.D.Cal. 1998. Under California law, sheriff's deputies were not liable for assault or battery to family and estate of arrestee based on deputies' failure to administer cardiopulmonary resuscitation (CPR) on arrestee, as CPR involved neither touching nor apprehension thereof. Restatement (Second) of Torts §§ 18, 21.—Price v. County of San Diego, 990 F.Supp. 1230.

Assault involves apprehension of a touching. Restatement (Second) of Torts § 21.—Id.

D.Colo. 2000. Under Colorado law, elements of assault are: (1) defendant intended to make physical contact with plaintiff or intended to place plaintiff in apprehension of physical contact; (2) defendant placed plaintiff in apprehension of immediate physical contact; and (3) that contact was harmful or offensive.—O'Hayre v. Board of Educ. for Jefferson County School Dist. R-1, 109 F.Supp.2d 1284.

Under Colorado law, elements of battery are: (1) defendant's act resulted in physical

For references to other topics, see Descriptive-Word Index

Exhibit 7–21

Pocket Part for Assault and Battery.

West, a Thomson Reuters business, *Eleventh Decennial Digest*, Pocket Part Assault and Battery, Vol. 5 (2001), p. 10th D Pt 1–17. Used with permission of Thomson Reuters/West.

2. Digests of Federal Court Opinions

West publishes separate digests for decisions of the federal courts.

✦ *United States Supreme Court Digest*—The *United States Supreme Court Digest* provides a summary of all the decisions of the Supreme Court of the United States. Thus, if your research is focused on Supreme Court decisions that have addressed a specific topic, then you could consult this digest to find the cases.

✦ *Federal Court System*—West publishes several digests that cover the decisions of the U.S. Supreme Court, the U.S. Courts of Appeals, and the U.S. district courts. Each digest covers a specific time period.

Federal Digest	1754–1938
Modern Federal Practice Digest	1939–1961
West's Federal Practice Digest 2d	1961–1975
West's Federal Practice Digest 3d	1975–1983
West's Federal Practice Digest 4th	1983–

The digest summaries of the Supreme Court cases are listed first, the Court of Appeals cases are listed next, followed by the U.S. district courts and other federal courts. In addition, specialized federal digests cover the decisions of other specific federal courts, for example, *West's Bankruptcy Digest*.

3. Regional Digests

West publishes digests for four of the regional reporters:

✦ *Atlantic Digest* for cases reported in the *Atlantic Reporter*

✦ *North Western Digest* for cases reported in the *North Western Reporter*

✦ *Pacific Digest* for cases reported in the *Pacific Reporter*

✦ *South Eastern Digest* for cases reported in the *South Eastern Reporter*

Each regional digest includes summaries of the cases presented in the reporter, organized by state.

> **FOR EXAMPLE** If you want to locate the cases addressing Assault and Battery Key 18 in the *Pacific Digest*, you will find the digest summaries of the cases from Arizona presented together, the digest summaries of the cases from California presented together, and so on.

To locate cases for the states covered in the *North Eastern Reporter*, the *South Western Reporter*, and the *Southern Reporter*, you must consult the *American Digest* or the state reporter digest.

4. State Digests

West publishes 46 state digests and a digest for the District of Columbia. No state digests are published for Delaware, Nevada, or Utah. The Delaware decisions are included in the *Atlantic Digest*, and the Nevada and Utah decisions are in the *Pacific Digest*. The decisions of Delaware, Nevada, and Utah along with all the other states are included in the *American Digest System*. The *Dakota Digest* includes both North and South Dakota. The *Virginia and West Virginia Digest* includes both Virginia and West Virginia.

The state digests usually include the reported state court decisions as well as federal court decisions arising in the state.

D. Research Using Digests

1. Use as a Research Tool

Digests are used to locate case law that addresses specific point(s) of law. You use digests in two situations:

> ✦ You know the name of a case that addresses the point of law being researched and are looking for other cases that address the same point.

FOR EXAMPLE The question being researched is the same as that raised in *Rael v. Cadena*, that is, "When may a bystander be liable for a battery?" (See Exhibit 5–1 in Chapter 5.) This question is identified in the case headnotes as being covered under the topic Assault and Battery, Key Number 18. You are familiar with the *Rael* case, but the client's facts are somewhat different from those in *Rael*. Checking Assault and Battery Key 18 in a digest will lead you to all the other cases that address the question. A scan of the case summaries may lead to a case that is factually closer to the client's facts, a case that is on point.

> ✦ You do not know of any cases that address the point of law being researched. In most instances, a researcher has identified the question being researched but needs to locate court opinions that address the topic.

FOR EXAMPLE The client was severely beaten by police when he was arrested for a traffic violation. He wants to sue the police for using excessive force. The question is: "What constitutes excessive force when an arrest is being made?" Consulting the topic Assault and Battery in a digest will lead you to Key 7, "Excessive force in doing lawful act," and a summary of all the cases that have addressed the question. One of those cases may be directly on point.

2. Research Techniques

The starting point for conducting digest research is to locate the correct digest set. Refer to the types of digests discussed in the earlier subsection C—Types of Digests and select the appropriate digest. If you are looking for federal cases, consult a federal digest; if you are looking for a state case, use the state court digest for that state; for state cases from a particular region such as the western part of the United States, check the regional digest (e.g., the *Pacific Digest*). If no state or regional digest is available, refer to the *American Digest*.

After a digest is selected, you can use several techniques to locate specific cases.

a. Case Headnotes

If you already know of a case that is related to the issue being researched, refer to the topic and key number of the relevant headnote from the case and consult that topic and key number in the digest. By going directly to the key number, you avoid other research steps such as having to refer to the index.

FOR EXAMPLE You are researching the issue of who may be liable in a battery. You are familiar with *Rael v. Cadena*, but the client's facts are quite different. Even though *Rael* is not on point, the case headnote, Assault and Battery Key 18, will lead you directly to the cases that have addressed the topic.

This is by far the quickest way to locate other cases. Therefore, it is helpful if you know of a related case when you begin. This is why it is important when conducting statutory research to consult the case summaries in the annotations to the statute. Although there may not be a case directly on point, there may be a related case summarized in the annotations that will provide the digest key number for the point of law being researched.

b. Descriptive-Word Index

If you are unaware of a specific case, think of all the areas of law or words and phrases that may be related to the topic being researched and consult the index. The index will refer you to the digest topic and key number.

> **FOR EXAMPLE** The question involves the firing of a person because of age. You may look under several index topics such as age, discrimination, civil rights, or employment (see Exhibit 7–19).

c. Topic Outline

If you know the topic that covers the issue, go directly to the topic in the digest and review the topic outline of all the key numbers under the topic. By scanning the outline, you can identify the relevant key numbers and review the relevant cases in the digest.

d. Table of Cases

If you know the name of a case but do not know the citation, consult the table of cases. The table lists the cases alphabetically, provides the citations, and includes the topic and key numbers for the digest entries (see Exhibit 7–20).

e. Reference from Other Sources

Often you may be directed to a specific digest topic and key number from another source such as an ALR citation, encyclopedia cite, or an article. In such cases, you could go directly to the volume and section cited.

f. Update

Always consult the pocket part and supplement to update your research and to locate the most recent cases.

3. Computer-Aided Research

The digests are not available on nonfee-based Internet sites. However, Westlaw provides a Key Number Service database that provides access to all the key number case summaries.

VI. *SHEPARD'S CITATIONS*

When you locate primary authority that provides an answer to a question being researched, it is necessary to determine if the authority has been reversed or modified by a subsequent law or court decision. That is, you must determine if the authority is still valid; is it still "good law." Throughout this text, a great deal of emphasis is placed on updating research through consulting pocket parts and supplements. The next step to ensure an authority is good law is to consult *Shepard's Citations*, which is published by LexisNexis Publishing. The process of consulting a *Shepard's* to determine the current validity of an authority is called **Shepardizing**. You Shepardize a case or statute when you check it in *Shepard's Citations*. Whenever you refer to a case, statute, or constitutional provision in any legal writing, you must Shepardize it. Obviously you don't want to rely on a legal authority that is no longer valid. Like a digest, *Shepard's* is not secondary authority; that is, it is not a source a court will rely on to interpret the law.

Shepard's Citations is a set of books that consists of citations to legal authorities such as a court opinion followed by a list of citations to cases and other authorities that discuss, analyze, or in some way affect the legal authority. A *Shepard's* will not only tell you whether a case or other authority has been reversed, modified, or overruled, it will also refer you to any other case or authority that has discussed the case. Although there are differences between the types of *Shepard's Citations*, the process of Shepardizing is essentially the same. *Included in the front of each volume are instructions on how to use Shepard's.* Because a researcher frequently uses a *Shepard's* for case citations, the process of using a *Shepard's* in that context will be discussed in detail followed by a summary of the other *Shepard's*.

A. Format and Components of *Shepard's Citations*

A *Shepard's* citator page is covered with numbers and may look incomprehensible at first glance. But after you understand the format and components, a citator is easy to use. Case and statutory law citators share the same basic format, and their components are discussed next. The various types of *Shepard's* case and statutory law citators are discussed in subsection B—Types of *Shepard's Citations*.

1. *Shepard's* Case Law Citators

Case law citators share the following features:

✦ *Abbreviations—Analysis and introductory material*—At the front of the citator is a table of abbreviations page that identifies all of the abbreviations used in the citator (see Exhibit 7–22). Following this page are instructions on how to use the citator. These instructions usually include an illustration interpreting a sample citation. If you need guidance on how to use the citator, these pages are invaluable.

✦ *Case location*—The reporter volume number is printed in the upper-right or upper-left corner of each page of the citator (see Exhibit 7–23). The case page number is printed in bold on the page, for example,—**1055**—. The name of the case and year follows the page number (see Exhibit 7–23).

> **FOR EXAMPLE** You are looking for the citations to *Young v. Wyoming*, 695 P.2d 1055 (Wyo. 1985). You would look to the *Shepard's Pacific Reporter Citations*, locate the page with Vol. 695 at the top of the page, and then look for —**1055**— (see Exhibit 7–23).

✦ *Parallel citations*—Following the case name and year are the parallel citations (if any) in parentheses (see Exhibit 7–23). When a case is printed in more than one reporter, the citation to each reporter is called a parallel citation, for example, *Commonwealth v. DeMichael*, 442 Pa. 553, 277A.2d 159 (1971). The parallel citations are included in the first *Shepard's* volume published after the parallel citation is available. They are not included in the supplements. If the state court opinions are published only in the regional reporter, no parallel citation is listed.

✦ *History of the case*—Following the parallel citation are citations to cases that involve the same case. This is the most important section of the case citations because any subsequent decision dismissing, modifying, or reversing the

HISTORY AND TREATMENT ABBREVIATIONS

Abbreviations have been assigned, where applicable, to each citing case to indicate the effect the citing case had on the case you are Shepardizing. The resulting "history" (affirmed, reversed, modified, etc.) or "treatment" (followed, criticized, explained, etc.) of the case you are Shepardizing is indicated by abbreviations preceding the citing case reference. For example, the reference "f434F2d872" means that there is language on page 872 of volume 434 of the *Federal Reporter,* Second Series, that indicates the court is "following" the case you are Shepardizing. Instances in which the citing reference occurs in a dissenting opinion are indicated in the same manner. The abbreviations used to reflect both history and treatment are as follows.

History of Case

a	(affirmed)	The decision in the case you are Shepardizing was affirmed or adhered to on appeal.
cc	(connected case)	Identifies a different case from the case you are Shepardizing, but one rising out of the same subject matter or in some manner intimately connected therewith.
D	(dismissed)	An appeal from the case you are Shepardizing was dismissed.
m	(modified)	The decision in the case you are Shepardizing was changed in some way.
p	(parallel)	The citing case is substantially alike or on all fours, either in law or facts, with the case you are Shepardizing.
r	(reversed)	The decision in the case you are Shepardizing was reversed on appeal.
s	(same case)	The case you are Shepardizing involves the same litigation as the citing case, although at a different stage in the proceedings.
S	(superseded)	The citing case decision has been substituted for the decision in the case you are Shepardizing.
US	cert den	Certiorari was denied by the U.S. Supreme Court.
US	cert dis	Certiorari was dimissed by the U.S. Supreme Court.
US	cert gran	Certiorari was granted by the U.S. Supreme Court.
US	reh den	Rehearing was denied by the U.S. Supreme Court.
US	reh dis	Rehearing was dismissed by the U.S. Supreme Court.
v	(vacated)	The decision in the case you are Shepardizing has been vacated.

Treatment of Case

c	(criticized)	The citing case disagrees with the reasoning/decision of the case you are Shepardizing.
d	(distinguished)	The citing case is different either in law or fact, for reasons given, from the case you are Shepardizing.
e	(explained)	The case you are Shepardizing is interpreted in some significant way. Not merely a restatement of facts.
Ex	(Examiner's decision)	The case you are Shepardizing was cited in an Administrative Agency Examiner's Decision.
f	(followed)	The citing case refers to the case you are Shepardizing as controlling authority.
h	(harmonized)	An apparent inconsistency between the citing case and the case you are Shepardizing is explained and shown not to exist.
j	(dissenting opinion)	The case is cited in a dissenting opinion.
L	(limited)	The citing case refuses to extend the holding of the case you are Shepardizing beyond the precise issues involved.
o	(overruled)	The ruling in the case you are Shepardizing is expressly overruled.
q	(questioned)	The citing case questions the continuing validity or precedential value of the case you are Shepardizing.

Exhibit 7–22

Abbreviations for Case History and Treatment.

LexisNexis®, *Shepard's Federal Citations,* 8th Ed., Vol. 15, (1995), inside cover of text. LexisNexis® Screen Captures reprinted with the permission of LexisNexis. LexisNexis and *Shepard's* are registered trademarks and Focus and KWIC are trademarks of Reed Elsevier Properties, Inc., used with the permission of LexisNexis.

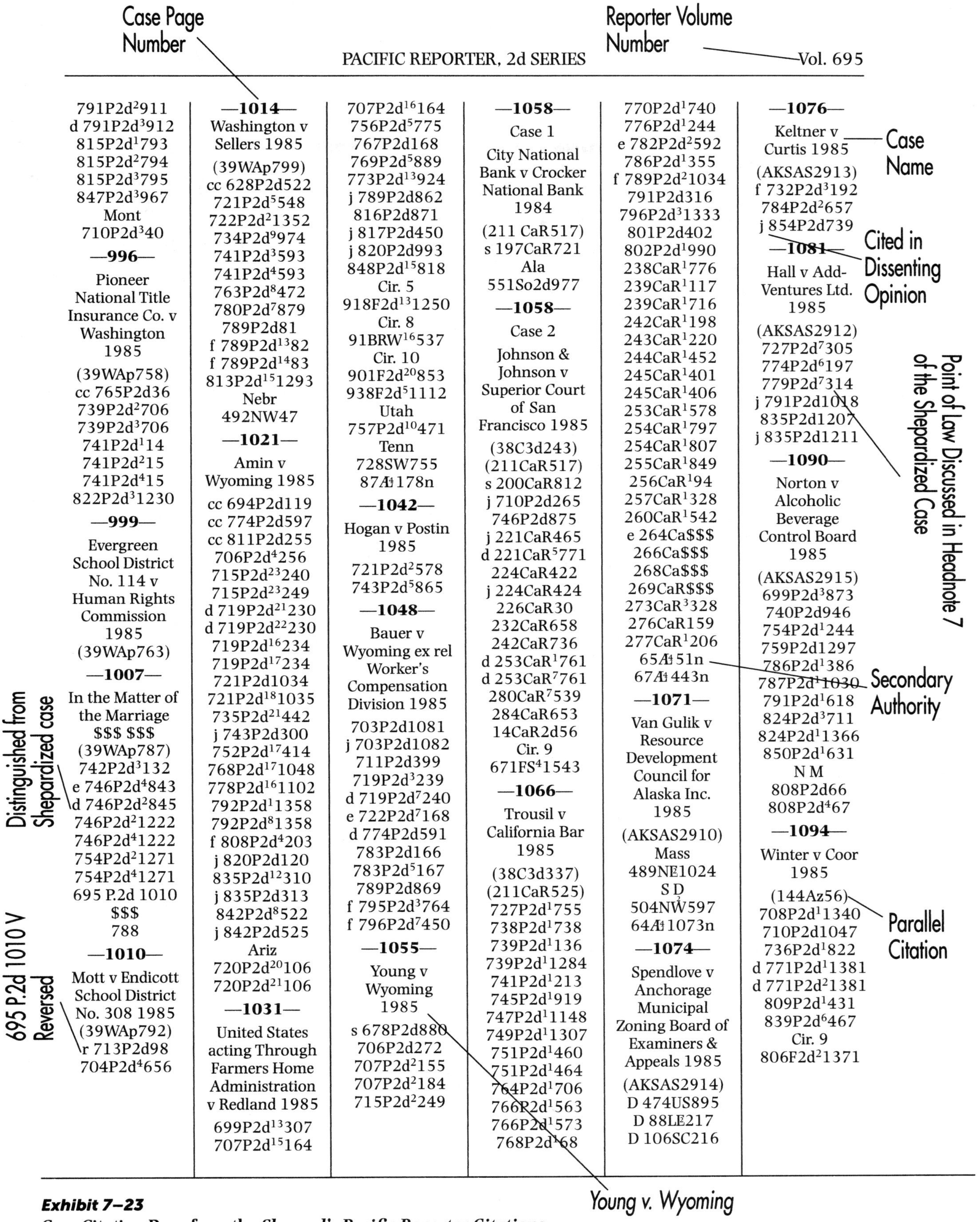
Case Page Number
Reporter Volume Number
Case Name
Cited in Dissenting Opinion
Point of Law Discussed in Headnote 7 of the Shepardized Case
Secondary Authority
Parallel Citation
Young v. Wyoming
Distinguished from Shepardized case
695 P.2d 1010 V Reversed

PACIFIC REPORTER, 2d SERIES — Vol. 695

791P2d[2]911
d 791P2d[3]912
815P2d[1]793
815P2d[2]794
815P2d[3]795
847P2d[3]967
Mont
710P2d[3]40

—996—

Pioneer National Title Insurance Co. v Washington 1985

(39WAp758)
cc 765P2d36
739P2d[2]706
739P2d[3]706
741P2d[1]14
741P2d[2]15
741P2d[4]15
822P2d[3]1230

—999—

Evergreen School District No. 114 v Human Rights Commission 1985

(39WAp763)

—1007—

In the Matter of the Marriage $$$ $$$

(39WAp787)
742P2d[3]132
e 746P2d[4]843
d 746P2d[2]845
746P2d[2]1222
746P2d[4]1222
754P2d[2]1271
754P2d[4]1271
695 P.2d 1010
$$$
788

—1010—

Mott v Endicott School District No. 308 1985

(39WAp792)
r 713P2d98
704P2d[4]656

—1014—

Washington v Sellers 1985

(39WAp799)
cc 628P2d522
721P2d[5]548
722P2d[2]1352
734P2d[9]974
741P2d[3]593
741P2d[4]593
763P2d[8]472
780P2d[7]879
789P2d81
f 789P2d[13]82
f 789P2d[14]83
813P2d[15]1293
Nebr
492NW47

—1021—

Amin v Wyoming 1985

cc 694P2d119
cc 774P2d597
cc 811P2d255
706P2d[4]256
715P2d[23]240
715P2d[23]249
d 719P2d[21]230
d 719P2d[22]230
719P2d[16]234
719P2d[17]234
721P2d1034
721P2d[18]1035
735P2d[21]442
j 743P2d300
752P2d[17]414
768P2d[17]1048
778P2d[16]1102
792P2d[1]1358
792P2d[8]1358
f 808P2d[4]203
j 820P2d120
835P2d[12]310
j 835P2d313
842P2d[8]522
j 842P2d525
Ariz
720P2d[20]106
720P2d[21]106

—1031—

United States acting Through Farmers Home Administration v Redland 1985

699P2d[13]307
707P2d[15]164
707P2d[16]164
756P2d[5]775
767P2d168
769P2d[5]889
773P2d[13]924
j 789P2d862
816P2d871
j 817P2d450
j 820P2d993
848P2d[15]818
Cir. 5
918F2d[13]1250
Cir. 8
91BRW[16]537
Cir. 10
901F2d[20]853
938F2d[5]1112
Utah
757P2d[10]471
Tenn
728SW755
87A4178n

—1042—

Hogan v Postin 1985

721P2d[2]578
743P2d[5]865

—1048—

Bauer v Wyoming ex rel Worker's Compensation Division 1985

703P2d1081
j 703P2d1082
711P2d399
719P2d[3]239
d 719P2d[7]240
e 722P2d[7]168
d 774P2d591
783P2d166
783P2d[5]167
789P2d869
f 795P2d[3]764
f 796P2d[7]450

—1055—

Young v Wyoming 1985

s 678P2d880
706P2d272
707P2d[2]155
707P2d[2]184
715P2d[2]249

—1058—

Case 1

City National Bank v Crocker National Bank 1984

(211 CaR517)
s 197CaR721
Ala
551So2d977

—1058—

Case 2

Johnson & Johnson v Superior Court of San Francisco 1985

(38C3d243)
(211CaR517)
s 200CaR812
j 710P2d265
746P2d875
j 221CaR465
d 221CaR[5]771
224CaR422
j 224CaR424
226CaR30
232CaR658
242CaR736
d 253CaR[1]761
d 253CaR[7]761
280CaR[7]539
284CaR653
14CaR2d56
Cir. 9
671FS[4]1543

—1066—

Trousil v California Bar 1985

(38C3d337)
(211CaR525)
727P2d[1]755
738P2d[1]738
739P2d[1]136
739P2d[1]1284
741P2d[1]213
745P2d[1]919
747P2d[1]1148
749P2d[1]1307
751P2d[1]460
751P2d[1]464
764P2d[1]706
766P2d[1]563
766P2d[1]573
768P2d[1]68
770P2d[1]740
776P2d[1]244
e 782P2d[2]592
786P2d[1]355
f 789P2d[2]1034
791P2d316
796P2d[3]1333
801P2d402
802P2d[1]990
238CaR[1]776
239CaR[1]117
239CaR[1]716
242CaR[1]198
243CaR[1]220
244CaR[1]452
245CaR[1]401
245CaR[1]406
253CaR[1]578
254CaR[1]797
254CaR[1]807
255CaR[1]849
256CaR[1]94
257CaR[1]328
260CaR[1]542
e 264Ca$$$
266Ca$$$
268Ca$$$
269CaR$$$
273CaR[3]328
276CaR159
277CaR[1]206
65A451n
67A4443n

—1071—

Van Gulik v Resource Development Council for Alaska Inc. 1985

(AKSAS2910)
Mass
489NE1024
S D
504NW597
64A41073n

—1074—

Spendlove v Anchorage Municipal Zoning Board of Examiners & Appeals 1985

(AKSAS2914)
D 474US895
D 88LE217
D 106SC216

—1076—

Keltner v Curtis 1985

(AKSAS2913)
f 732P2d[3]192
784P2d[2]657
j 854P2d739

—1081—

Hall v Add-Ventures Ltd. 1985

(AKSAS2912)
727P2d[7]305
774P2d[6]197
779P2d[7]314
j 791P2d1018
835P2d1207
j 835P2d1211

—1090—

Norton v Alcoholic Beverage Control Board 1985

(AKSAS2915)
699P2d[3]873
740P2d946
754P2d[1]244
759P2d1297
786P2d[1]386
787P2d[1]1030
791P2d[1]618
824P2d[3]711
824P2d[1]1366
850P2d[1]631
N M
808P2d66
808P2d[4]67

—1094—

Winter v Coor 1985

(144Az56)
708P2d[1]1340
710P2d1047
736P2d[1]822
d 771P2d[1]1381
d 771P2d[2]1381
809P2d[1]431
839P2d[6]467
Cir. 9
806F2d[2]1371

Exhibit 7–23

Case Citation Page from the *Shepard's Pacific Reporter Citations*.

Shepardized case will be indicated here. A letter before the citation will indicate the action taken.

> **FOR EXAMPLE** Refer to the citations following 695 P.2d 1010 in Exhibit 7–23. The citation reference "r 713 P.2d 98" means that the case at 695 P.2d 1010 was reversed by the decision found at 713 P.2d 98.

The list of what the *r* and other abbreviations stand for is presented on the Abbreviations page at the front of the citator.

✦ *Later case treatment*—Following the history of the case are citations to every other case that has mentioned the cited case and references to secondary authorities. The cases are arranged in chronological order with the earlier cases mentioned first. The case citation is to the page in the case where the Shepardized case is discussed. Thus, if a case citation is to "746 P.2d. 875," 875 is the page in the case where the Shepardized case is discussed rather than the beginning page of the case.

The case citations include treatment codes that indicate how the Shepardized case was treated in the cited case.

> **FOR EXAMPLE** There are several citations following 695 P.2d.1048 (see Exhibit 7–23) that show different ways the case was treated by subsequent courts: in "j 703 P.2d 1082," the treatment code *j* means the Shepardized case (695 P.2d 1048) was cited in the dissenting opinion in 703 P.2d at page 1082; in "d 774 P.2d 591" the *d* means that the court distinguished the case from the Shepardized case in 774 P.2d at page 591.

The treatment codes are included in the table of abbreviations at the beginning of each *Shepard's* citator.

In addition to the treatment codes, the citations include references to specific points of law discussed in the Shepardized case that are also addressed in the cited case. This is accomplished through the use of small raised numeral references following the reporter abbreviation in the citation. These numbers correspond to the headnote number of the Shepardized case.

> **FOR EXAMPLE** The case being Shepardized appears at 695 P.2d 1081. One of the case citations is 779 P.2d[7] 314. The raised "7" means that the point of law discussed in headnote 7 of the Shepardized case (695 P.2d 1081) is discussed in 779 P.2d at page 314 (see Exhibit 7–23).

These reference numbers are invaluable to a researcher because they allow you to compare the treatment of a specific point of law in both cases. If there is no raised number given in a citation, then the case discusses the Shepardized case in general or does not summarize a point of law from the case.

✦ *Secondary sources*—Following the case citations are references to secondary sources such as ALR annotations that in some way reference the Shepardized case (see Exhibit 7–23).

2. *Shepard's* Statutory Law Citators

In addition to case law citators, *Shepard's Citations* publishes citators that allow you to determine the history of a statute, constitutional provision, or regulation; whether it is still valid; and how the courts have interpreted it. For the purpose of clarity, *statute* will be used in the following discussion. The guidelines discussed here also apply to constitutional provisions and regulations. *Shepard's* citators to enacted law are similar to the case law citators in many respects:

✦ *Abbreviations—Analysis and introductory material*—At the front of the citator is a table of abbreviations page that identifies all the abbreviations used in the citator (see Exhibit 7–24). Following this page are instructions on how to use the citator.

✦ *Statute location*—Printed in the upper corner of each page of the citatory is the statute title, volume, or chapter number. As discussed in Chapter 4, statutory or code numbering systems vary from state to state. When more than one title is covered on a page, the title number is usually included in a box. The separate section numbers are printed in bold (see Exhibit 7–25).

✦ *History*—The first entries under a section indicate any legislative action taken that affects the statute.

> **FOR EXAMPLE** If it has been amended, an *A* followed by the citation to the amendment is presented (see Exhibit 7–25).

✦ *Case treatment*—After the history of the statute are citations to cases that have mentioned the statute. Preceding the case citations are treatment codes that indicate how the statute was treated in the cited case (see Exhibit 7–25).

> **FOR EXAMPLE** A *C* preceding a case citation indicates the statute was held constitutional.

If no letter precedes the citation, then the case merely discusses the statute generally.

✦ *Secondary sources*—Following the case citations are references to secondary sources such as ALR annotations that in some way reference the statute (see Exhibit 7–25).

3. Updating *Shepard's Citations*

Most sets of *Shepard's Citations* consist of one or more hardbound volumes accompanied by one or more supplement pamphlets. In most cases, advance sheets are published between the publication of the pamphlets. The pamphlets and advance sheets update the hardbound volumes. On the cover of each pamphlet is a "WHAT YOUR LIBRARY SHOULD CONTAIN:" section listing all the hardbound volumes and supplements for the set (see Exhibit 7–26). Check this list to ensure that your research is complete. If one of the *Shepard's* is missing, check with the librarian.

COMPUTERIZED UPDATING. *Shepard's* is available on LexisNexis. LexisNexis also offers citation updates through *Auto-Cite*. Westlaw offers a citation update service called *KeyCite*. These services are more current than the advance sheets, often providing information that is current within 24 hours.

B. Types of *Shepard's Citations*

A brief description of the various *Shepard's Citations* and their functions is presented here.

1. Case Law

Shepard's publishes a set of citators for each case reporter. In law libraries, usually the citators are located next to the case reporters. Some of the citators and the courts they cover are as follows:

✦ *United States Supreme Court Cases—Shepard's United States Citations.*

✦ *Lower Federal Courts—Cases from the Federal Reporter, Federal Supplement, Federal Rules Decisions, Court of Claims Reports and United States Claims Court Reporter— Shepard's Federal Citations.*

ABBREVIATIONS—ANALYSIS

Form of Statute

Amend.	Amendment	J.R.	Joint Resolution
Appx.	Appendix	No.	Number
Art.	Article	p	Page
C or Ch.	Chapter	¶	Paragraph
CA	Code Amendments	P.L.	Public Law
Cl.	Clause	Res.	Resolution
C. R.	Concurrent Resolution	§	Section
Ex. Ord.	Executive Order	St.	Statutes at Large
Ex. or		Stand.	Standard
Ex. Sess.	Extra Session	Subd.	Subdivision
GRP	Governor's Reorganization Plan	Sub ¶	Subparagraph
		Subs. or	
		Subsec.	Subsection

Operation of Statute

Legislative

A	(amended)	Statute amended.
Ad	(added)	New section added.
E	(extended)	Provisions of an existing statute extended in their application to a later statute, or allowance of additional time for performance of duties required by a statute within a limited time.
GP	(granted and citable)	Review granted and ordered published.
L	(limited)	Provisions of an existing statute declared not to be extended in their application to a later statute.
R	(repealed)	Abrogation of an existing statute.
Re-en	(re-enacted)	Statute re-enacted.
Rn	(renumbered)	Renumbering of existing sections.
Rp	(repealed in part)	Abrogation of part of an existing statute.
Rs	(repealed and superseded)	Abrogation of an existing statute and substitution of new legislation therefor.
Rv	(revised)	Statute revised.
S	(superseded)	Substitution of new legislation for an existing statute not expressly abrogated.
Sd	(suspended)	Statute suspended.
Sdp	(suspended in part)	Statute suspended in part.
Sg	(supplementing)	New matter added to an existing statute.
Sp	(superseded in part)	Substitution of new legislation for part of an existing statute not expressly abrogated.

Judicial

C	Constitutional.		V	Void or invalid.
U	Unconstitutional.		Va	Valid.
Up	Unconstitutional in part.		Vp	Void or invalid in part.

Exhibit 7–24

Shepard's Statutory Citator **Abbreviations.**

Section —

Amended —

Secondary Source —

Held Constitutional —

§ 908 (j)
Ad 98St1646
Cir. 1
11F3d254
Cir. 5
957F2d1205
20F3d661
23F3d109
Cir. 9
953F2d557
§ 908 (j) (3)
Cir. 5
17F3d786
§ 909 et seq.
Cir. 7
702FS722
§ 909
A 86St1251
A 98St1647
285US38
287US537
317US391
386US736
398US407
440US31
461US633
76LE605
77LE480
87LE353
18LE492
26LE360
59LE123
76LE202
52SC287
53SC232
63SC289
87SC1423
90SC1791
99SC906
103SC2050
Cir. DC
77F2d543
101F2d255
107F2d264
131F2d233
147F2d563
190F2d30
512F2d941
545F2d210
607F2d1381
607F2d1386
670F2d210
749F2d68
834F2d1030
929F2d737
173FS381

Cir. 1
91F2d130
599F2d468
646F2d712
688F2d863
851F2d4
885F2d984
885F2d986
Cir. 2
93F2d663
209F2d914
241F2d766
272F2d15
C 548F2d1113
607F2d1039
702F2d412
19FS907
96FS95
192FS564
202FS859
411FS1181
822FS949
Cir. 3
98F2d1016
183F2d936
209F2d200
545F2d338
C 577F2d852
24FS245
C 117FS605
225FS461
336FS800
Cir. 4
43F2d983
154F2d560
184F2d79
C 539F2d378
591F2d985
594F2d407
9FS315
9FS745
47FS568
186FS805
245FS234
475FS10
Cir. 5
35F2d346
49F2d807
54F2d212
57F2d257
57F2d263
68F2d56
133F2d305
204F2d173
519F2d536
601F2d1307
C 634F2d844
681F2d288

785F2d1318
790F2d420
797F2d213
818F2d398
820F2d1411
958F2d1300
65F3d461
29FS377
344FS325
391FS1360
662FS99
Cir. 6
600F2d1221
850F2d285
Cir. 7
554F2d310
647F2d719
46FRD34
Cir. 8
583F2d877
58F3d1236
Cir. 9
31F2d153
328F2d877
496F2d1249
567F2d1385
C 596F2d900
708F2d415
717F2d1284
882F2d1437
938F2d983
14FS159
98FS1021
313FS314
Cir. 11
766F2d1517
CtCl
305F2d378
16ARF689n
§ 909 (a to g)
Cir. DC
749F2d75
§ 909 (a)
A 86St1251
A 98St1647
Cir. DC
670F2d211
Cir. 1
885F2d993
Cir. 3
183F2d937
24FS245
Cir. 5
601F2d1308
Cir. 6
850F2d294

§ 909 (b)
A 86St1251
440US33
461US626
59LE122
76LE197
99SC904
103SC2047
Cir. DC
57F2d440
131F2d234
135F2d258
218F2d860
545F2d211
548F2d1049
352FS195
Cir. 1
585F2d1169
885F2d985
Cir. 2
963F2d542
160FS784
Cir. 3
183F2d937
267F2d60
545F2d338
16FS677
24FS245
56FS62
166FS909
354FS330
Cir. 5
110F2d269
150F2d79
168F2d873
601F2d1308
322FS1232
Cir. 7
46FRD34
Cir. 9
169F2d988
188F2d457
567F2d1385
60FS806
Cir. 11
672F2d848
766F2d1514
§ 909 (c)
A 86St1251
Cir. DC
545F2d211
548F2d1049
Cir. 1
885F2d985
Cir. 3
183F2d937

Cir. 4
37FS717
Cir. 5
601F2d1319
Cir. 9
567F2d1387
§ 909 (d)
A 86St1251
436US601
56LE568
98SC2001
Cir. DC
160F2d253
545F2d211
Cir. 2
135F2d152
304FS321
Cir. 4
53F2d300
198F2d237
475FS10
Cir. 5
62F2d122
150F2d79
319FS1376
Cir. 9
175F2d911
567F2d1387
§ 909 (e)
A 86St1251
A 98St1647
440US29
461US626
59LE122
76LE197
99SC904
103SC2047
Cir. DC
545F2d211
Cir. 1
885F2d984
Cir. 3
183F2d937
545F2d338
Cir. 4
56F2d216
Cir. 5
322FS1232
Cir. 6
850F2d285
Cir. 9
41F2d154
46F2d541
567F2d1385

Cir. 11
672F2d848
§ 909 (f)
Cir. DC
75F2d236
160F2d254
Cir. 1
91F2d133
136F2d657
Cir. 2
56F2d1052
60F2d896
Cir. 4
154F2d560
47FS566
Cir. 5
150F2d79
818F2d399
Cir. 6
138FS834
Cir. 9
175F2d912
188F2d455
§ 909 (g)
Cir. 2
192FS569
§ 910
285US38
317US390
76LE605
87LE353
52SC287
63SC289
Cir. DC
85F2d411
183F2d819
233F2d701
290F2d358
628F2d89
793F2d321
173FS381
Cir. 1
489F2d1041
646F2d711
851F2d4
885F2d991
942F2d819
11F3d250
Cir. 2
769F2d67
884F2d57
969F2d1408
244FS112
329FS697

Exhibit 7–25
Citation Page from the *Shepard's Federal Statute Citations*.
Shepard's® Federal Statute Citations, 1996 Bound Volume, Vol. 1, p. 65. LexisNexis® Screen Captures reprinted with the permission of LexisNexis. LexisNexis and *Shepard's* are registered trademarks and Focus and KWIC are trademarks of Reed Elsevier Properties, Inc., used with the permission of LexisNexis.

VOL. 91   APRIL 1, 2001   NO. 7

Shepard's
Federal Citations
Part 1B

ANNUAL CUMULATIVE SUPPLEMENT

FEDERAL REPORTER (3rd Series)

(USPS 656490)

Announcing:
New Updating System
- fewer steps for researchers
- easier to maintain your library

Questions?
1-800-899-6000, option 5

WHAT YOUR LIBRARY SHOULD CONTAIN:

1995 Bound Edition, Volumes 1 to 15*
1995-1999 Bound Supplement Volumes 1 to 7*
1999-2000 Bound Supplement Volumes 1 to 3*

*Supplemented with:

—*April 1, 2001 Gold Annual Cumulative Supplement, Vol. 91, No. 7, Parts 1A & 1B*

For information on "What Your Library Should Contain" for Federal Supplement, Federal Rules decisions and Federal Claims Court Reporters cases, please refer to Part 2, page vi of the most recent softcover supplement.

LEXIS Publishing™

LEXIS*NEXIS* • MARTINDALE-HUBBELL*
MATTHEW BENDER* • MICHIE* • SHEPARD'S*

Exhibit 7–26

Cumulative Supplement Cover Page.

LexisNexis® *Shepard's®* *Federal Citations*, Annual Cumulative Supplement, Vol. 91, No. 7 (Apr. 2001), cover page. LexisNexis® Screen Captures reprinted with the permission of LexisNexis. LexisNexis and *Shepard's* are registered trademarks and Focus and KWIC are trademarks of Reed Elsevier Properties, Inc., used with the permission of LexisNexis.

✦ *State Court Decisions*—A separate set of *Shepard's* covers the decisions of each state and Puerto Rico. In addition, a set of *Shepard's* exists for each of the regional reporters.

> **FOR EXAMPLE** The cases published in the New Mexico Reporter are covered in Shepard's New Mexico Citations. The cases published in the Pacific Reporter are covered in Shepard's Pacific Reporter Citations.

An advantage of a state citator is that it will direct you to more research sources such as law review articles and attorney general opinions. A disadvantage of a state citator is that while it includes citations to state and federal cases, it does not include citations from other states.

✦ *Specialized citators*—Topical citators provide citations to cases in specific areas of law such as Shepard's Bankruptcy Citations and Shepard's Federal Labor Law Citations.

2. Statutory, Constitutional, and Other Enacted Law

Just as you must Shepardize case law to determine if it is good law, you must also Shepardize statutory provisions. *Shepard's* publishes various citators that allow you to Shepardize a law to determine its history, current status, and how the courts have interpreted it. Some of these citators are listed here:

✦ *Statutory, constitutional, and court rules*—The *Shepard's* citator for a state's statutes is either included with the *Shepard's* state case citator or published as a separate volume. Citations to state constitutions and state court rules are included with the *Shepard's citations* to the state statutes. *Shepard's Federal Statute Citations* covers the federal statutes and includes the citations to the U.S. Constitution and *Federal Court Rules*.

✦ *Federal and state regulations*—You may Shepardize the regulations of the federal agencies published in the *Code of Federal Regulations* by using *Shepard's Code of Federal Regulations Citations*. Some state administrative agency regulation citations are included in the *Shepard's* state citations.

C. Research Using *Shepard's Citations*

1. Use as a Research Tool

Shepard's Citations are used for two purposes:

a. To determine if the authority you have located is still good law. This is the most important use of a *Shepard's* citator. It is critical to know if subsequent court or legislative action has affected a case or statute you have located. If a higher court has reversed a court decision or if a statute has been repealed by subsequent legislation, it no longer is authoritative and cannot be relied on. One of the worst things that can happen is to support a legal argument with a court case and have the other side note to the court that the case has been reversed. A failure to Shepardize *all* the primary authority you rely on indicates either sloppy or incompetent work.

b. To locate case law or secondary sources that have discussed primary authority being researched. Even though a court opinion has not been reversed, it is important to determine how other courts have analyzed it. If the later courts have uniformly criticized the holding and reasoning of a court opinion or it has been limited in some way, you may not want to rely on it. Also, you may wish to locate additional authority to support and add weight to the case relied on. It is also possible that the reasoning in the case being researched is not clear and other cases or secondary authority is necessary to help clarify it.

2. Research Steps

The following steps are guidelines for using *Shepard's Citations*.

a. Select the Appropriate Shepard's Citator

The starting point for conducting research with a *Shepard's* citator is to locate the correct citations set. If you are Shepardizing federal cases, consult the *Shepard's Federal Citations*. If you are looking just for U.S. Supreme Court citations, select *Shepard's United States Citations*. If you are checking state court citations, refer to the regional or state reporter *Shepard's*. If you are Shepardizing statutory, constitutional, or regulatory law, consult the appropriate *Shepard's* citator. The various types of *Shepard's* citators are presented in the previously shown subsection B—Types of *Shepard's Citations*.

After you have located the appropriate set, select the correct volume, supplement, and advance sheet(s). Be sure to check the "WHAT YOUR LIBRARY SHOULD CONTAIN:" box on the most recent supplement to ensure you have all the supplements and advance sheets (see Exhibit 7–26). Also note that the spine of the hardbound volume indicates which reporter volumes are covered in the citator.

> **FOR EXAMPLE** If you are Shepardizing *Young v. Wyoming*, 695 P.2d 1055 (Wyo. 1995) and want to locate cases in the state and region that address the case, you would refer to *Shepard's Pacific Reporter Citations*. You would select the hardbound volume (the spine reads 695 P.2d—855 P.2d), supplement pamphlet, and advance sheets that cover 695 P.2d 1055.

b. Locate and Review the Entry for the Authority Being Shepardized

Refer to the upper corner of the pages to find the page of the citation being Shepardized (see Exhibits 7–23 and 7–25). The case volume number or statutory title number is printed on the upper corner of the page. Scan the page and locate the case page number or statutory section printed in bold.

Thoroughly review the citations and references to secondary authorities. When reviewing the entries keep the following in mind:

1. Carefully review the history for subsequent cases or legislative action that have reversed, overturned, repealed, amended, modified, or in any way affected the authority being Shepardized. Any such action may mean that the authority may no longer be relied upon—it is no longer good law.

2. Carefully review the treatment of the authority in subsequent court opinions. Even though the authority being Shepardized may not have been reversed or repealed, reliance on it may be questionable if it has received a negative treatment by the courts.

> **FOR EXAMPLE** If many of the citations to the Shepardized case are preceded by negative letters such as *c* (criticized) or *q* (questioned), it may indicate that the case, although not overruled or reversed, is not being relied upon by subsequent courts as good authority.

You must read the cases that treat the Shepardized case negatively. It is possible that the case is being criticized for the treatment of an issue that is different from the one you are researching. You may be researching a negligence issue raised in the case being Shepardized, and the negative treatment in the subsequent cases involves a different issue such as one involving an improper jury instruction.

3. If you are concerned with one issue in the Shepardized case, then it may be necessary to only review those cited cases that addressed that issue.

> **FOR EXAMPLE** You are researching headnote 1 of the case being Shepardized. Your research would focus on those cited cases that addressed headnote 1; that is, cases with the raised 1 following the reporter name such as 779 P.2d^1 314.

4. If a case does not appear in a *Shepard's* volume, such as a supplement, it may mean that no court opinion discussed the case during the time period covered by the supplement.

   Always check the citation to be sure it is correct.

c. Update Your Research

Check the supplementary pamphlets and advance sheets and perform the research steps mentioned previously. Any authority relied upon should also be checked electronically through LexisNexis or Westlaw in addition to *Shepard's*.

3. Computer-Aided Research

Shepard's is available on LexisNexis. It is not available on Westlaw, although both Westlaw and LexisNexis offer citation update services. See Computerized Updating in subsection A—Computer-Aided Reasearch previously. As of the date of this publication, there were no Internet nonfee-based update services.

VII. KEY POINTS CHECKLIST: *Secondary Authority*

- The first step of legal research is to locate primary authority (the law) because courts look to primary authority first when resolving legal problems. Secondary authority is used when there is no primary authority on a topic in a jurisdiction, in support of the existing primary authority, to help you understand the primary authority, or to locate court opinions and other research sources interpreting the primary authority.

- None of the research sources discussed in this chapter are primary authority (the law). A court may refer to and rely upon the secondary authorities mentioned in the chapter, but it is not bound to follow them.

- Legal encyclopedias and treatises are primarily used to obtain a familiarity with or understanding of a specific area of the law.

- Use an ALR if you are looking for a comprehensive analysis and synthesis of cases from every jurisdiction on very specific legal issues.

- Refer to a digest when you need to locate cases that have addressed a specific legal question or when you have a case and want to locate other cases that address the same legal questions.

- Always Shepardize the primary authority you rely on to ensure that the authority has not been overturned, reversed, repealed, or amended.

- Like all research sources, you must check the pocket parts, supplements, or whatever is used to update the source to ensure that your research is current.

VIII. APPLICATION

This section presents three examples illustrating the application of the information presented in this chapter.

A. Chapter Hypothetical

This example is based on the fact pattern presented at the beginning of the chapter. This section explores the avenues of research Melissa may pursue to learn about the tort law of battery. Melissa could begin her search by consulting a legal encyclopedia such as *American Jurisprudence 2d* or *Corpus Juris Secundum* at the local law library. By consulting the general index, she would be directed to the volume that addresses assault and battery. If she knows that the topic she is looking for is assault and battery, she can go to the volumes on the shelf. The spine of each book will indicate the range of coverage of the volume such as "Assault and Battery to Attachment and Garnishment." She would pull the appropriate volume and read about assault and battery. The encyclopedia will give her a general overview of the topic. She can also access *American Jurisprudence 2d* through both Westlaw and LexisNexis.

If Melissa wants a more in-depth summary or analysis of the law of civil assault and battery, she could consult a treatise such as Prosser and Keeton on the *Law of Torts* or *The Law of Torts* by Dobbs. She would locate these books by going to the local law library and asking for the treatise section. The treatises are usually arranged alphabetically by topic. Therefore, the tort treatises are shelved together. Melissa is interested in assault and battery in situations such as hers where the attack takes place in a date situation. The treatise will provide a discussion of the topic in greater analytical detail than an encyclopedia. If she has access to Westlaw or LexisNexis, she could check to see if a tort treatise is available.

For a more detailed analysis of the subject in specific date situations, she could look for an *ALR* annotation. If she were to locate an annotation that addresses the question in a situation similar to hers, it will provide, in one place, a comprehensive analysis of the issue, references to and summaries of the case law on point, and references to other research sources.

If Melissa is unable to locate an annotation, she could refer to a *West Digest* and look under the topic of assault and battery. There she would locate summaries of specific court opinions that discuss assaults and batteries that take place during a date. She would then select the case or cases that are most similar factually to her situation and read how the law applies.

Through these sources, Melissa could explore the subject in detail and determine what the officer meant when he said she could file a battery tort claim. She could also determine what remedies are available to her.

B. Chapter 1 Hypothetical *Reins v. Stewart*

The following example discusses the application of the information presented in the chapter to the hypothetical presented at the beginning of Chapter 1. Vanessa located *Rael v. Cadena*, 93 N.M. 684, 604 P.2d 822 (Ct. App. 1979), a case she believes is on point. Therefore, it may not be necessary to consult secondary authority. However, if she wants to obtain an overview of the topic of bystander liability, she could consult a legal encyclopedia such as *American Jurisprudence 2d*. Referring to the general index under assault and battery, she would be directed to 6 Am. Jur. 2d *Assault and Battery*. Section 108 addresses the topic of bystander liability.

If she needs a very detailed analysis of the topic and additional cases, she could look for an *ALR* annotation. Looking in the ALR index under assault and battery and bystander liability or persons liable, *she would find Civil Liability of One Instigating or Inciting an Assault or Assault and Battery Notwithstanding Primary or Active Participant therein has been absolved of Liability*, 72 A.L.R. 2nd 1229, an annotation on the topic by H. C. Hind.

C. Chapter 2 Hypothetical *United States v. Canter*

The following example refers to the hypothetical presented at the beginning of Chapter 2. The case Dustin believes to be on point is *United States v. Martinez-Jimenez*, 864 F.2d 664 (9th Cir. 1989). Therefore, just as in the previous hypothetical, it may not be necessary to consult secondary authority.

To obtain additional information on the topic of whether a fake gun may be considered a dangerous weapon, Dustin could consult a legal encyclopedia. By referring to the general index of *American Jurisprudence 2d* under *bank robbery, robbery, robbery degrees, weapons, dangerous weapons*, and so on, he would be directed to 67 Am. Jur. 2d *Robbery*. Section 7 addresses the topic of robbery with toy or simulated weapons. For a more detailed overview he should consult a legal treatise on criminal law. He would look in ALR for an in-depth analysis of the topic. By consulting the general index and using the search terms mentioned previously, he would be directed to an annotation by Lynn Considine Cobb, *Robbery by Means of Toy or Simulated Gun*, 81 ALR 3d 1006.

SUMMARY

The focus of this chapter is secondary authority, that is, sources of law a court may rely on that are not the law (not primary authority). Secondary authority consists of legal research sources that summarize, compile, explain, comment on, interpret, or in some other way address the law. Secondary authority is used for several purposes including the following:

✦ *To obtain a background or overall understanding of a specific area of the law.* Legal encyclopedias, treatises, and periodicals are useful for these purposes.

✦ *To locate primary authority (the law) on a question being researched.* ALR and digests are particularly useful for this purpose.

✦ *To be relied upon by the court when reaching a decision.* This usually occurs only when there is no primary authority governing a legal question, or it is unclear how the primary authority applies to the question.

There are literally hundreds of secondary sources. This chapter covered those secondary sources that provide the researcher with treatment of the law that ranges from the general to the specific. These sources are legal encyclopedias and treatises.

Legal encyclopedias provide an overview of all the areas of law. They do not provide in-depth coverage, and they are similar to other encyclopedias in their general treatment of topics.

Treatises are single or multivolume texts that provide a comprehensive analysis of a single area of law such as torts or criminal law. Where a legal encyclopedia presents a broad overview of an area of law, a treatise provides a much greater in-depth discussion and explains, analyzes, and criticizes the law.

This chapter also focuses on sources that help a researcher locate and analyze case law: ALR and digests. ALR provides a researcher with an exhaustive coverage of specific legal issues. A digest organizes the law by topic and provides a summary or "digest" of all the court opinions that have addressed the topic. It is an excellent case finder when a researcher needs to locate court opinions on specific topics.

Before any primary authority can be relied upon, it must be checked to determine if it is still "good law"; that is, it has not been reversed, modified, or affected by some subsequent opinion or statute. This chapter concludes with a discussion of *Shepard's Citations*, which allow a researcher to determine if primary authority is still good law and locate other cases and secondary authority that discuss a specific court opinion.

CHAPTER REFERENCES

INTERNET RESOURCES

Most of the secondary authority and other research sources discussed in this chapter are available on Westlaw or LexisNexis (see Chapter 10). Most of the sources are not available on nonfee-based Web sites.

For additional materials, please go to the CD accompanying this book

For additional resources, visit our Web site at www.paralegal.delmar.cengage.com

CITATION

The Bluebook and *ALWD Citation Manual* rules governing citation to the various secondary authority sources are discussed in Chapter 11. Some examples of citations to the secondary authority sources discussed in this chapter are presented here.

A. Legal Encyclopedias

6 Am. Jur. 2d *Assault and Battery* § 2 (1999)
6A C.J.S. *Assault and Battery* § 11 (1975)

B. Treatises

Dan B. Dobbs, *The Law of Torts* § 23 (West, a Thomson business 2000)

C. ALR Annotations

Jeffrey F. Ghent, *Annotation, Modern Status of Sudden Emergency Doctrine*, 10 ALR 5th 680 (1993)

D. Digests, *Shepard's*

The cases you locate through digests and *Shepard's* are cited according to *The Bluebook*. The digests themselves are not cited.

EXERCISES

Additional exercises are located on the Student CD-ROM accompanying the text and Online Companion.

ASSIGNMENT 1
What are the uses of secondary authority?

ASSIGNMENT 2
The client seeks advice concerning the actions of the majority stockholder in a small corporation. The majority stockholder owns 58 percent of the stock, and the client and another shareholder own 42 percent. The majority stockholder controls the board of directors and is president of the corporation. He refuses to allow the corporation to issue any stock dividends. Until recently, the client and the other minority stockholder worked for the corporation. Last month, the majority stockholder fired the client and the minority stockholder.

What sections of Am. Jur. 2d discuss this topic?

ASSIGNMENT 3
Which Am. Jur. 2d title and sections address 18 U.S.C.S. §204?

ASSIGNMENT 4
The client's brother was killed in an automobile collision. Family members disagree about whether viewing of the deceased should be allowed due to the degree of damage to the body. What section of Am. Jur. 2d discusses this topic?

ASSIGNMENT 5
Refer to Corpus Juris Secundum. What section defines the term *name*, and what is the definition?

ASSIGNMENT 6
The client, a shareholder in a corporation, believes that the corporation exceeded its authority when it expanded the corporation's business from the repair of automobiles to the sale of automobile parts. What section of *Fletcher Cyclopedia of the Law of Private Corporations* addresses this topic? What is the term for the action of a corporation that exceeds its power?

ASSIGNMENT 7
The client's son belongs to a religious cult. The client believes the cult used improper means to indoctrinate his son and keep him in the cult. The son has given all his goods to the cult and refuses to see or talk to his parents. Is there an ALR annotation that addresses the liability of a cult for improper activities?

ASSIGNMENT 8
Has 2 ALR 347 been replaced or superseded? By what annotation?

ASSIGNMENT 9
Your assignment is to obtain some general information on the criminal aspects of causing or procuring the termination of a human pregnancy. Consult the ALR 3d, ALR 4th, ALR 5th, and ALR Federal Digest. Under the Practice References, what is the reference to the Defense of Paternity Charges in Am. Jur. Proof of Facts 2d? What is the citation of a 1999 Nebraska case involving the state's partial-birth abortion statute?

ASSIGNMENT 10
What ALR annotation discusses 42 U.S.C.A. § 740?

ASSIGNMENT 11
The client's husband attacked her so severely that she was hospitalized. They are now separated, and the client wants to sue her husband. The husband still lives on the military base where they lived at the time of the incident. Refer to the *Federal Practice Digest* and locate the digest topic and key number that address this topic.

ASSIGNMENT 12
Give the name and citation of a 1994 Nevada case that held that the use of a toy gun to carry out a kidnapping is not a defense to a kidnapping charge. Refer to the Tenth Decennial Digest.

ASSIGNMENT 13
Your supervising attorney asks you to locate the digest topic and key numbers that *Glover v. Lockheed Corp.* is listed under. He remembers it is a Federal Supplement case, but he can't remember the citation.

ASSIGNMENT 14
The assignment requires reference to a *Shepard's* citator. In regard to 18 U.S.C. § 1201(a), what is the citation of the United States Reports decision that held the provision unconstitutional in part? What Sixth Circuit case found the provision constitutional? What Second Circuit case, in 2001, discussed section 1201(a)(1)?

ASSIGNMENT 15
The assignment requires reference to a *Shepard's* citator. What is the name of the case that appears at 904th volume of the Federal Reporter Second on page 1482? What Tenth Circuit opinion distinguished the case?

ASSIGNMENT 16
The assignment requires reference to a *Shepard's* citator. On what dates in the 1980s was Rule 11 of the Federal Rules of Civil Procedure amended?

Secondary Authority—Periodicals, Restatements, Uniform Laws, Dictionaries, Legislative History, and Other Secondary Authorities

Outline

Learning Objectives

After completing this chapter, you should understand:

✦ The role of periodicals, Restatements, uniform laws, dictionaries, and miscellaneous secondary sources in legal research

✦ How to conduct research using periodicals, Restatements, uniform laws, dictionaries, and other secondary sources

"Luis, the city council is considering drafting a zoning ordinance restricting the location of adult entertainment businesses. I need some preliminary research on First Amendment and other constitutional limitations on such ordinances. How would you like to take a crack at this?" Assistant City Attorney Genevieve Gray said to her intern Luis Sisneros. Luis had just started his internship with the city attorney's office. The city provided three internships for paralegal students. "Yes, I'll start right away," Luis responded, thinking to himself, "This is great. I expected some go-fer type assignments like locating and copying statutes and cases."

The steps Luis follows when performing this assignment and the results of his search are discussed in the Application section of this chapter.

I. INTRODUCTION

Chapter 7 addressed the more frequently used sources that help a researcher summarize, explain, interpret, locate, and update the law. This chapter presents other frequently used secondary authority sources. The chapter discusses legal periodicals that can be used when you are seeking an analysis and critique of a specific legal topic that is more in-depth or narrower in focus than that provided by a legal encyclopedia or a treatise. It also covers those secondary sources that present definitions or uniform statements of the law such as dictionaries, Restatements of the Law, and uniform laws. In addition, the chapter covers legislative history and practice aids such as form books. Exhibit 8–1 presents a table showing the primary use of the secondary sources discussed in this chapter.

II. LEGAL PERIODICALS

Legal periodicals publish articles on legal topics, and through the various publications, articles are available on literally every legal topic. The articles are usually authored by individuals who have expertise in the area, such as law professors and expert practitioners in the field, or by law students who have conducted extensive research on a topic. The articles are valuable for their depth of research; citation to numerous primary and secondary sources; and in-depth analysis of current legal issues, recently emerging areas of the law, or very specific topics.

| FOR EXAMPLE | S. K. Hom, *Lexicon Dreams and Chinese Rock and Roll: Thoughts on Culture, Language, and Translation Strategies of Resistance and Reconstruction*, 53 U. Miami L. Rev. 1003 (1999), is an example of a law review article addressing a very specific topic. |

Publications in legal periodicals are secondary authority. They are not primary authority, but courts on occasion cite them when there is no primary authority on a topic or when interpreting primary authority such as a statute.

AUTHORITY	PRIMARY USE AS A RESEARCH TOOL
Periodicals	Use when you are seeking an analysis and critique of a specific legal topic that is more in-depth or narrower in focus than that provided by a legal encyclopedia or treatise. You may also refer to a periodical when seeking information on a recently emerging legal issue that is not yet addressed in treatises or other sources.
Restatements of the Law	Use a Restatement to locate a standardized definition or statement of the law, reasons in support of the definition or statement of the law, and citations to related cases, treatises, and other secondary authority.
Uniform Laws and Model Acts	Use to locate a model text from which a law may be crafted, arguments in support of the law, and citations to cases, treatises, and articles interpreting the law.
Dictionaries	Use to obtain the spelling, pronunciation, and legal meaning of terms used in the law.
Legislative History	Use to determine the meaning or application of a law. Legislative history may be helpful when the meaning of a law that governs a fact situation is unclear or when the law is written so broadly that its application to a specific fact situation is unclear.

Exhibit 8–1
Secondary Authority—Primary Use as a Research Tool.

> **FOR EXAMPLE** "The courts of this state have not addressed the question of the liability of a majority shareholder in a situation such as the one presented in this case. Guidance, however, is provided in (name of law review article) where the question has been thoroughly analyzed."

A. Types of Legal Periodicals

Legal periodicals can be classified into four distinct categories.

1. Law Reviews

Law reviews are scholarly periodicals published by law schools. They contain articles written by law professors, judges, practitioners, and law students and are usually published four times a year. Most accredited law schools in the United States publish at least one law review. Law students edit law reviews under the guidance of the law school faculty and administration. Rigorous standards are employed to ensure high quality. Due to their scholarly nature, they are often cited by courts.

Law reviews are valuable for their detailed analysis of current legal issues, recently emerging areas of the law, and specific topics (see Exhibit 8–2). Law reviews usually include the following:

- ✦ *Articles*—Articles are written by scholars, judges, or practitioners and usually present a comprehensive analysis of specific topics such as the *Lexicon Dreams* article mentioned previously. The articles are thoroughly researched with footnotes citing numerous cases, studies, and other sources. They often criticize the law and recommend changes or alternative legal solutions.
- ✦ *Notes and Comments*—These are shorter pieces written by students. They are like the articles in that they are narrow in focus, thoroughly researched, and extensively footnoted. Inasmuch as students and not experts in the field write them, they have less authority and are less frequently cited.
- ✦ *Recent Development/Cases*—This section discusses recent cases and developments in the law such as new statutes. Students author this section.
- ✦ *Book Reviews*—Most law reviews include book reviews of recent legal publications.

2. Bar Association and Other Association Publications

Every state has a bar association whose members are attorneys licensed to practice law in the state. There are national bar associations open to practitioners nationally, the largest and most well known being the American Bar Association. Most of these associations publish journals that are similar in many respects to law reviews. The journals include articles on specific legal subjects, recent developments in the case and statutory law, and tips and guides for practitioners. They also include book reviews, news about the association, and technology updates. Similar to law reviews, the articles are thoroughly researched with footnotes citing cases and other sources.

State bar association journals tend to publish articles that are local in nature and of interest primarily to practitioners of that jurisdiction. The American Bar Association publishes the *American Bar Association Journal*, which includes articles concerning national legal developments. In addition to bar associations, there are associations for paralegals and legal assistants. Some of these associations publish newsletters that include articles of interest to paralegals and legal assistants.

3. Commercial Publications

Numerous commercial journals and periodical publications focus on specific areas of law, for example, the *Journal of Taxation*. Individuals interested in a specific area of law

PROTECTING THE GENDER NONCONFORMIST FROM THE GENDER POLICE—WHY THE HARASSMENT OF GAYS AND OTHER GENDER NONCONFORMISTS IS A FORM OF SEX DISCRIMINATION IN LIGHT OF THE SUPREME COURT'S DECISION IN *ONCALE V. SUNDOWNER*

TONI LESTER[*]

INTRODUCTION—THE SILENCE SURROUNDING HARASSMENT BASED ON HOMOPHOBIA

Traditionally, people who are harassed at work because they are gay[1] have found that they have not been granted the same kind of legal protections that their heterosexual counterparts have received.[2] This is true despite the fact that the sexual harassment of gays is motivated by homophobia, which in turn is motivated in large part by misogyny. Since misogyny in all its many manifestations is one of the things that Title VII's prohibition against sex discrimination is supposed to attack,[3] the failure of the courts to recognize that harassment against gays is a kind of sex discrimination is at best misguided and at worst very dangerous.

---

[*] Affiliated Research Scholar Wellesley Centers for Women; former Visiting Law Scholar, Institute for Research on Women and Gender, Stanford University; Associate Professor of Law, and Johnson Research Chair, Babson College; B.S., J.D., Georgetown University.

[1] I use the term "gay" here broadly to mean those who identify themselves as homosexual men, lesbians, bisexuals, and transsexuals. I recognize that the term is the subject of great debate today, however. I will talk about the debate and explain my use of the term in greater detail in Part I.

[2] *See* Ulane v. Eastern Airlines, Inc., 742 F.2d 1081, 1084–86 (7th Cir. 1984) (stating that Title VII does not protect transsexuals, homosexuals or transvestites); Desantis v. Pacific Tel. & Tel. Co., 608 F.2d 327, 329–30 (9th Cir. 1979) (stating that "Title VII's prohibition of "sex" discrimination . . . should not be judicially extended to include sexual preference"); *see also* Regina L. Stone-Harris, *Same-Sex Harassment—The Next Step in the Evolution of Sexual Harassment Law Under Title VII,* 28 ST. MARY'S L.J. 269, 289 (1996) (stating that in dealing with "hostile or abusive work environment claims" brought by a male victim against a male offender "who believed the victim was homosexual," courts have "rule[d] against the plaintiff," with the author finding it "notable . . . how closely the offensive conduct [in these cases] parallels other conduct which courts have found to be discriminatory").

[3] *See, e.g.,* Price Waterhouse v. Hopkins, 490 U.S. 228, 251 (1989) ("An employer who objects to aggressiveness in women but whose positions require this trait places women in an intolerable and impermissible catch 22: out of a job if they behave aggressively and out of a job if they do not. Title VII lifts women out of this bind."); Meritor v. Vinson, 477 U.S. 57, 67 (1986) ("Sexual harassment which creates a hostile or offensive environment for members of one sex is every bit the arbitrary barrier to sexual equality at the workplace that racial harassment is to racial equality." (citing Henson v. Dundee, 682 F.2d 897, 902 (11th Cir. 1982))); Ellison v. Brady, 924 F.2d 872, 881 (9th Cir. 1991) ("Congress designed Title VII to prevent the perpetuation of stereotypes and a sense of degradation which serve to close or discourage employment opportunities for women." (citing Andrews v. Philadelphia, 895 F.2d 1469, 1483 (3d Cir. 1990))); Barnes v. Costle, 561 F.2d 983, 987 (D.C. Cir. 1977) (noting that "[n]umerous studies have shown that women are placed in the less challenging, the less responsible and the less remunerative positions on the basis of their sex alone," and finding "such blatantly disparate treatment . . . particularly objectionable in view of the fact that Title VII has specifically prohibited sex discrimination since its enactment in 1964."); Torres v. Nat'l Precision Blanking, 943 F. Supp. 952, 954 (N.D. Ill. 1996) (stating that "the principal purpose of including the term 'sex' in the Act was to 'do some good for the minority sex.'" (citing 110 CONG. REC. 2577 (1964))).

Some have argued that Title VII's prohibition against sex discrimination was the result of a fluke, in which Congressman Howard Smith of Virginia hoped to stymie the bill's passage by adding the word, "sex" to the bill, never expecting it to be approved. *See* CHARLES & BARBARA WHALEN, THE LONGEST DEBATE—A LEGISLATIVE HISTORY OF THE CIVIL RIGHTS ACT 115-118 (1985).

Exhibit 8–2

Sample Law Review Page.

University of New Mexico School of Law, Toni Lester, *Protecting the Gender Nonconformist from the Gender Police—Why the Harassment of Gays and Other Gender Nonconformists Is a Form of Sex Discrimination in Light of the Supreme Court's Decision in Oncale v. Sundowner.* 29 New Mexico L. Rev. (1999) p. 89. Reprinted with permission from the New Mexico Law Review.

can subscribe to such a publication. The articles are similar to bar journal articles in that they are well researched. They often include book reviews, practitioner guides and tips, and technology updates.

4. Legal Newspapers and Newsletters

A number of legal newspapers are available by subscription such as the *National Law Journal* and the *Legal Times*. The *National Law Journal* and the *Legal Times* are published weekly and include articles and features on trends in litigation, developments in the law, information on attorneys and the legal profession, and book reviews. There are also many subject-specific newspapers such as the *Corporate Legal Times*. In many cities, local newspapers publish legal notices, court docket information, and articles of local interest.

In addition to newspapers, thousands of newsletters are published by commercial as well as public interest groups. These newsletters are usually issued weekly or monthly and focus on current information in specific areas of the law.

Many legal newspapers and newsletters can be accessed on-line. This is discussed in the Internet Resources section of this chapter.

B. Research Using Legal Periodicals

1. Use as a Research Tool

Refer to a legal periodical when you are seeking an analysis and critique of a specific legal topic that is more in-depth or narrower in focus than that provided by a legal encyclopedia or a treatise. In many instances an article in a legal periodical will go into much greater depth than a treatise and will provide more case citations, statistical information, and references to other sources. You may also refer to a periodical when seeking information on a recently emerging legal issue that is not yet addressed in treatises.

2. Research Techniques—Legal Periodicals

As is apparent from the previous section, the hundreds of periodical publications make it impractical to research each publication for articles on a specific topic. There are research tools designed to help you locate specific articles:

a. Index to Legal Periodicals (ILP)

The ILP provides an index to the contents of most legal periodicals in the United States, the United Kingdom, and most Commonwealth countries. Exhibit 8–3 presents an index page. Hardbound volumes are published annually with monthly updates. The volumes and updates are not cumulative. Therefore, if you are looking for an article published in the current year, you must check the hardbound volume and each update.

> **FOR EXAMPLE** If you are interested in an article published sometime in the past five years, you would have to check the hardbound volume for each year and each update.

The index includes the following features:

(1) Subject/Author Index. Articles are indexed alphabetically by both subject and author in the Subject/Author index. If you know the name of the author or you know the subject, such as "assault and battery," you can use this index to locate articles. The index includes the title of the article, the name of the author, and the name and date of the publication (see Exhibit 8–3).

INDEX TO LEGAL PERIODICALS & BOOKS

Ashton, Bruce L.—cont.
New safe harbors for employers in the Service's qualified plan correction examples; by C. F. Reish, B. L. Ashton, N. J. White. 91 no6 *J. Tax'n* 349-57 D 1999

Ashton, Roger D.
Consolidation in the financial services sector: tax implications to stakeholders. 49 *Rep. Proc. Ann. Tax Conf. Convened by Can. Tax Found.* 21.1-.58 1997

Ashworth, Andrew
Article 6 and the fairness of trials. 1999 *Crim. L. Rev.* 261-72 Ap 1999
Restorative justice and victims' rights. 2000 *N.Z. L.J.* 84-8 Mr 2000

Asia-Pacific Economic Cooperation (Organization)
The role of APEC in the achievement of regional cooperation in Southeast Asia. L. C. Cardenas, A. Buranakanits. 5 no1 *Ann. Surv. Int'l & Comp. L.* 49-80 Spr 1999

Asia-Pacific legal development; edited by Douglas M. Johnston and Gerry Ferguson. University of B.C. Press 1998 611p ISBN 0-7748-0673-7 LC 99-183418

Asiain, Jorge Hugo
Financing of real estate projects in Argentina. 4 no1 *NAFTA Rev.* 96-104 Wint 1998

Asian Americans
All the themes but one. E. L. Muller. 66 no4 *U. Chi. L. Rev.* 1395-33 Fall 1999
Are Asians black?: The Asian-American civil rights agenda and the contemporary significance of the black/white paradigm. J. Y. Kim, student author. 108 no8 *Yale L.J.* 2385-412 Je 1999
Asian Americans, the law, and illegal immigration in post-civil rights America: a review of three books. H. Gee. 77 no1 *U. Det. Mercy L. Rev.* 71-81 Fall 1999
Beyond black and white: selected writings by Asian Americans within the critical race theory movement. H. Gee. 30 no3 *St. Mary's L.J.* 759-99 1999
Emerging from the margins of historical consciousness: Chinese immigrants and the history of American law. R. P. Cole, G. J. Chin. 17 no2 *Law & Hist. Rev.* 325-64 Summ 1999
Justice held hostage: U.S. disregard for international law in the World War II internment of Japanese Peruvians—a case study. N. T. Saito. 40 no1 *B.C. L. Rev.* 275-348 D 1998
Lexicon dreams and Chinese rock and roll: thoughts on culture, language, and translation as strategies of resistance and reconstruction. S. K. Hom. 53 no4 *U. Miami L. Rev.* 1003-17 H 1999
Lochner [Lochner v. New York, 25 S. Ct. 539 (1905)], parity, and the Chinese laundry cases [Yick Wo v. Hopkins, 6 S. Ct. 1064 (1886)] D. E. Bernstein. 41 no1 *Wm. & Mary L. Rev.* 211-94 D 1999
McCarthyism, the internment and the contradictions of power. M. J. Matsuda. 40 no1 *B.C. L. Rev.* 9-36 D 1998
No right to own?: The early twentieth-century "Alien Land Laws" as a prelude to internment. K. Aoki. 40 no1 *B.C. L. Rev.* 37-72 D 1998
Out of the shadow: marking intersections in and between Asian Pacific American critical legal scholarship and Latina/o critical legal theory. E. M. Iglesias. 40 no1 *B.C. L. Rev.* 349-83 D 1998
Praising with faint damnation—the troubling rehabilitation of Korematsu [Korematsu v. United States, 63 S. Ct. 1124 (1944)] A. C. Yen. 40 no1 *B.C. L. Rev.* 1-7 D 1998
Race, rights, and the Asian American experience: a review essay. H. Gee. 13 no4 *Geo. Immigr. L.J.* 635-51 Summ 1999
Racial reparations: Japanese American redress and African American claims. E. K. Yamamoto. 40 no1 *B.C. L. Rev.* 477-523 D 1998
Reparations and the "model minority" ideology of acquiescence: the necessity to refuse the return to original humiliation. C. K. Iijima. 40 no1 *B.C. L. Rev.* 385-427 D 1998
The stranger who resides with you: ironies of Asian-American and American Indian legal history. J. W. Singer. 40 no1 *B.C. L. Rev.* 171-7 D 1998
Symposium: the long shadow of Korematsu [Korematsu v. United States, 63 S. Ct. 1124 (1944)] 40 no1 *B.C. L. Rev.* 1-535 D 1998
A tale of new precedents: Japanese American internment as foreign affairs law. G. Gott. 40 no1 *B.C. L. Rev.* 179-274 D 1998
Using DSM-IV to diagnose mental illness in Asian Americans. T. B. Tran, student author. 10 *J. Contemp. Legal Issues* 335-57 1999

See/See also the following book(s):
Chang, R. S. Disoriented; Asian Americans, law, and the nation-state. New York University Press 1999 x, 180p

California
The Chinese American challenge to court-mandated quotas in San Francisco's public schools: notes from a (partisan) participant-observer. D. I. Levine. 16 *Harv. BlackLetter L.J.* 39-145 Spr 2000
Redeeming whiteness in the shadow of internment: Earl Warren, Brown, [Brown v. Board of Education, 74 S. Ct. 686 (1954)] and a theory of racial redemption. S. Cho. 40 no1 *B.C. L. Rev.* 73-170 D 1998

Asian Pacific Economic Cooperation (Organization) *See* Asia-Pacific Economic Cooperation (Organization)

Asimow, Michael
Bad lawyers in the movies. 24 no2 *Nova L. Rev.* 533-91 Wint 2000
Interim-final rules: making haste slowly. 51 no3 *Admin. L. Rev.* 703-55 Summ 1999
"Justice with an attitude": Judge Judy and the daytime television bunch. 38 no4 *Judges' J.* 24-8+ Fall 1999

Askin, Frank, 1932
A law school where students don't just learn the law; they help make the law. 51 no4 *Rutgers L. Rev.* 855-74 1999

Askin, Kelly Dawn
Crimes within the jurisdiction of the International Criminal Court. 10 no1 *Crim. L.F.* 33-59 1999
Issues surrounding the creation of a regional human rights system for the Asia-Pacific. 4 no2 *ILSA J. Int'l & Comp. L.* 599-601 Spr 1998
Sexual violence in decisions and indictments of the Yugoslav and Rwandan tribunals: current status. 93 no1 *Am. J. Int'l L.* 92-123 Ja 1999

Åslund, Anders, 1952- ———————————— Entry by Author
Law in Russia. 8 no4 *E. Eur. Const. Rev.* 96-101 Fall 1999

Asmus, Daniel G.
Service provider liability: Australian High Court gives the world a first—should the United States follow suit? 17 no1 *Dick. J. Int'l L.* 189-228 Fall 1998

Asouzu, Amazu A.
The adoption of the UNCITRAL model law in Nigeria: implications on the recognition and enforcement of arbitral awards. 1999 *J. Bus. L.* 185-204 Mr 1999

Aspen, Marvin E., 1934-
about
It's how you play the game. L. Leshne. 34 no7 *Trial* 28-32 Jl 1998

Aspin, Larry
Trends in judicial retention elections, 1964-1998. 83 no2 *Judicature* 79-81 S/O 1999

Asplen, Christopher H.
Integrating DNA technology into the criminal justice system. 83 no3 *Judicature* 144-9 N/D 1999

Assafa Endeshaw *See* Endeshaw, Assafa, 1950-
Assault and battery ——————— Entry by Topic Assault and Battery
See also
Battered women
Child abuse
A jurisprudence in disarray: on battery, wrongful living, and the right to bodily integrity. M. P. Strasser. 36 no4 *San Diego L. Rev.* 997-1041 Fall 1999
Score and pierce: crimes of fashion? Body alteration and consent to assault. A. J. Watkins, student author. 28 no2 *Vict. U. Wellington L. Rev.* 371-98 My 1998

Canada
Fraud, HIV and unprotected sex: R. v. Cuerrier [[1998] 2 S.C.R. 371] R. K. Yamada, student author. 6 no1 *Sw. J.L. & Trade Am.* 157-76 Spr 1999
Secrets and lives—the public safety exception to solicitor-client privilege: Smith v. Jones [[1999] 169 D.L.R.4th 385] W. N. Renke. 37 no4 *Alta. L. Rev.* 1045-70 D 1999

Great Britain
Assault, battery and indirect violence. M. Hirst. 1999 *Crim. L. Rev.* 557-60 Jl 1999
Consent, threats and deception in criminal law. J. Horder. 10 no1 *King's C. L.J.* 104-8 1999
Corporal punishment of children: a caning for the United Kingdom. A. Bainham. 58 pt2 *Cambridge L.J.* 291-3 Jl 1999
Theorising the limits of the 'sadomasochistic homosexual' identity in R v Brown [[1994] 1 A.C. 212] S. Chandra-Shekeran, student author. 21 no2 *Melb. U. L. Rev.* 584-600 D 1997

Exhibit 8–3

Page from the *Index to Legal Periodicals and Books.*
From *Index to Legal Periodicals and Books.* Copyright © 2000. Reprinted with permission from The H.W. Wilson Company.

(2) Table of Cases.   Cases that have been noted or discussed in articles are indexed alphabetically by the names of both plaintiff and defendant. Following the case name are citations to the articles.

(3) Table of Statutes.   If you know the name of a statute, this index will direct you to articles that have discussed the statute.

(4) Book Reviews.   The Book Review Index lists by book title the periodicals that have reviewed the title.

b. Current Law Index (CLI)

The CLI is a periodical index similar to ILP. It provides an index of articles of several hundred periodicals. Exhibit 8–4 presents an index page. Hardbound volumes are published annually with monthly updates. Like the ILP, the volumes and updates are not cumulative. The CLI includes articles beginning in 1980; it does not reference articles published prior to 1980. The index includes the following features:

(1) Subject Index.   The CLI has a separate subject index where articles are indexed alphabetically by subject. If you know the name of the subject, such as "assault and battery," you can use this index to locate articles. The index includes the title of the article, the name of the author, and the name and date of the publication (see Exhibit 8–4).

(2) Author/Title Index.   There is a separate index where articles are indexed alphabetically by author and title. This index also includes book reviews indexed by author and title.

(3) Table of Cases.   Cases that have been noted or discussed in articles are indexed alphabetically by the names of both plaintiff and defendant. Following the name are citations to the articles.

(4) Table of Statutes.   If you know the name of a statute, this index will direct you to articles that have discussed the statute.

c. Legal Resource Index (LRI)

The LRI is published by the same company that publishes the CLI, the Information Access Company. The LRI includes the same information as the CLI as well as references to several legal newspapers. It is available in microfilm, and each month a new microfilm is issued. Each issuance is cumulative; therefore, you have to check only the most recent issuance to obtain all the relevant articles on a topic. Like CLI, it does not reference articles published prior to 1980. It is available at most law libraries and can be purchased from the publisher. The CD-ROM version is called *LegalTrac*.

d. Other Periodical Indexes

In addition to the major indexes discussed previously, there are several other indexes. Check with a law library for specific indexes.

> **FOR EXAMPLE**   The *Index to Foreign Legal Periodicals* focuses on journals published outside of the United States and the British Commonwealth. The *Current Index to Legal Periodicals* is published weekly and provides access to articles not yet indexed in the ILP or the CLI.

e. Reference from Other Sources

Another source, such as a citation in a court opinion, legal encyclopedia, or treatise, may direct you to a legal periodical article. Often references to law review articles that have

The role of philanthropy in the intersection between culture and commerce. by Cora Mirikitani
29 Journal of Arts Management, Law and Society 128 Summer, 1999

-Cases

The death of a subsidy and the birth of the entitlement in funding of the arts. (Case Note) Brooklyn Institute of Arts & Sciences v. City of New York by Danielle E. Caminiti
10 Fordham Intellectual Property, Media & Entertainment Law Journal 875-904 Spring, 2000

ARTS, Useful *see*
perspective (electronic commerce) (Interview) by Richard Stavros
238 Public Utilities Fortnightly (1994) 28 April 15, 2000

ASARIOTIS, Regina
Proposed amendments to the U.S. Carriage of Goods by Sea Act: a response to English criticisms (response to article by Regina Asariotis and Michael N. Tsimplis in previous issue of this journal, 1999) by Michael F. Sturley
Hoyds Maritime and Commercial Law Quarterly 519-529 Nov, 1999

United we stand (solicitor Ken Beruldsen diagnosed with mesothelioma from working in a pipe factor and solicitors Jim Taylor handled his case) (Victoria) by Kevin Childs
74 Law Institute Journal 10(2) August, 2000
see also
Asbestos industry
Asbestos removal

-Cases

The Louisiana long-arm statute stretches beyond its reach. (Case Note) Ruckstuhl v. Owens Corning Fiberglas Corp. by Kelly Elizabeth Grieshaber
45 Loyola Law Review 765-781 Winter, 1999
ASBESTOS abatement *see*
Asbestos removal

ASBESTOS abatement industry *see*
Asbestos industry

Reference to Author ─── ~~ASBESTOS industry~~
Asbestos legislation: Could it be the end? by Kristin Loiacono *36 Trial 11 June, 2000*
In the Beltway; Federal Claims Court may quench asbestos fires; DOJ still in hot seat. by Terry Carter
86 ABA Journal 32(1) April, 2000
ASBESTOS mines and mining *see*
Mining industry
ASBESTOS removal
Asbestos fines give warning to construction clients. (United Kingdom) by Lucinda Ponting
Health and Safety Bulletin 8(1) Dec, 1999
see also
Asbestos industry
ASBESTOS removal industry *see*
Asbestos industry
ASBESTOS servicing industry *see*
Reference to Subject Asbestos industry
~~ASEAN *see*~~
Association of South East Asian Nations
ASH disposal
Trash, ash, and the phoenix: a fifth anniversary review of the Supreme Court's City of Chicago waste-to-energy combustion ash decision. City of Chicago v. Environmental Defense Fund, Inc. by Markus G. Puder
26 Boston College Environmental Affairs Law Review 473-518 Spring, 1999

ASHES, Removal of *see*
Ash disposal
ASHURST Morris Crisp
Merger waves. (law firms) by Sean Farrell
22 American Lawyer 24 August, 2000
ASIA, Southwest *see*
Middle East
ASIA, Western *see*
Middle East
ASIAN Americans
Comparative racialization: racial profiling and the case of Wen Ho Lee. (Race and the Law at the Turn of the Century) by Neil Gotanda
47 UCLA Law Review 1689-1703 August, 2000
The interrelationship between anti-Asian violence and Asian America. (Hate Crimes 2000: A Symposium and Community Forum on Hate in America) by Victor M. Hwang
21 Chicano Latino Law Review 17-37 Spring, 2000
Long struggle for justice; Asian Pacific Americans have played a key role in this country's civil rights struggles. Their fight is not yet over. by Rockwell Chin, William G. Paul, Robert S. Chang, Kristin Choo, Frank H. Wu, Laura Kingsley Hong and Peter M. Suzuki
85 ABA Journal 66(8) Nov, 1999
Finding the me in LatCrit theory: thoughts on language acquisition and loss. (Substantive Self-Determination: Democracy, Communicative Power and Inter/national Labor Rights) (LatCrit III Symposium) by John Hayakawa Torok
53 University of Miami Law Review 1019-1036 July, 1999
Using DSM-IV to diagnose mental illness in Asian Americans. (Diagnostic and Statistical Manual of Mental Disorders) (Rethinking Mental Disability Law: Resolving Old issues in a New Millennium.) by Tam B. Tran
10 The Journal of Contemporary Legal Issues 335-357 Spring, 1999
ASIAN refugees *see*
Refugees, Asian
ASKA, Gail
Is workfare working? (government programs requiring welfare recipients to work) (New York) (Panel Discussion)
8 Journal of Law and Policy 107-177 Fall, 1999
ASPHALT cement
Paving contractor was not required to use accrual method. by Nicholas J. Fiore
31 The Tax Adviser 748 Oct, 2000
ASPHALTIC cement *see*
Asphalt cement
ASPHYXIA
Fatal suffocation by rubber balloons in children: mechanism and prevention. by H.A. Abdel-Rahman *108 Forensic Science International 97-105 Feb 14, 2000*
see also
Drowning
Strangling
ASSAULT and battery
Costs - defendant's costs order - Prosecution of Offences Act 1985, s. 16 - proceedings discontinued - whether costs order appropriate. (United Kingdom) R. v. South West Surrey Magistrates' Court (ex parte James) by D.C. Ormerod and Tom Rees
Criminal Law Review 690-692 August, 2000

Liability of partnership for a partner's assault. (United Kingdom) Flynn v. Thompson & Partners by J.A. Coutts
64 Journal of Criminal Law 368-370 August, 2000
Recalcitrant HIV-positive persons: the problem of people who are unwilling or unable to prevent the transmission of communicable diseases. (Canada) R. v. Cuerrier by Timothy Christie
20 Health Law in Canada 53-57 May, 2000
Offences against the Person Act 1861, s. 20 - inflicting grievous bodily harm - whether reasonable man foreseeing injury must be taken to have the same age and sex as defendant. (United Kingdom) R. v. Marjoram by Clare Barsby and J.C. Smith
Criminal Law Review 372-374 May, 2000
Racially aggravated assault occasioning actual bodily harm - approach to sentence. (United Kingdom) R. v. Saunders by D.A. Thomas
Criminal Law Review 314-315 April, 2000
Racist assaults - sentencing guildelines. (United Kingdom) R. v. Saunders by Philip Plowden
64 Journal of Criminal Law 158-160 April, 2000
Enforcement of the assault and battery exclusion in Louisiana: Hickey v. Centenary Oyster House. Hickey v. Centenary Oyster House by David A. Szwak
60 Louisiana Law Review 793-807 Spring, 2000
Treating spousal violence 'differently'. (Special Issue on Domestic Violence) by Kathy Laster and Roger Douglas
7 International Review of Victimology 115-139 Spring-Fall, 2000
Paved with good intentions: mandatory arrest and decreasing the threshold for assault. (Women, Children and Domestic Violence: Current Tensions and Emerging Issues) (Panel Discussion)
27 Fordham Urban Law Journal 629-671 Feb, 2000
Crown Court's power to make a restriction order. (United Kingdom) R. v. Avbunudje
64 Journal of Criminal Law 30-32 Feb, 2000
Joint enterprise - withdrawal. (United Kingdom) R. v. Mitchell
63 Journal of Criminal Law 538-539 Dec, 1999
Finding clarity in a Gray option: a critique of Pennsylvania's informed consent doctrine. Gray v. Grunnagle by Nathan A. Kottkamp
61 University of Pittsburgh Law Review 241-285 Fall, 1999
A jurisprudence in disarray: on battery, wrongful living, and the right to bodily integrity. by Mark Strasser
36 San Diego Law Review 997-1041 Fall, 1999
see also
Affray
Indecent assault
Poisoning
ASSAULT, Criminal *see*
Rape
ASSAULT, Sexual *see*
Rape
ASSAULT weapons

Exhibit 8—4

Sample Subject Page from the *Current Law Index*.

analyzed a statute are included in the annotations to the statute. In such instances, you would go directly to the periodical and an index is not necessary.

3. Computer-Aided Research

The *Index to Legal Periodicals, Current Law Index,* and *LegalTrac* are available in CD-ROM. The ILP and CLI are available on Westlaw and LexisNexis. *LegalTrac* is available on the Internet by subscription. Many law reviews, periodicals, and legal newspapers are available on both Westlaw and LexisNexis. Some law reviews are available through law school Web sites, and some periodical articles are available through the publisher's Web site. See Chapters 9 and 10 for further discussion of computers and legal research.

III. RESTATEMENTS OF THE LAW

The American Law Institute was founded in 1923 to address two major defects in American law: uncertainty and complexity. Uncertainty existed because of a lack of agreement among members of the profession on fundamental principles of the common law. Also, there was a lack of precision in the use of legal terms and often poorly drafted statutes. Complexity was due to numerous differences in the law in the various jurisdictions in the United States.

The primary goal of the Institute is to promote clarification and simplification of the law. The founders decided that this goal could be accomplished through a restatement of the law defining the law for basic legal subjects. To accomplish this task, the Institute recruited nationally known scholars to draft the Restatements. From 1923 to 1944, Restatements of the Law were published for Agency, Conflict of Laws, Contracts, Judgments, Property Restitution, Security, Torts, and Trusts. In 1952, the original Restatements were republished with updates, expanded comment, and analysis. New Restatements were published in such areas as Landlord Tenant and Foreign Relations Law. This second set of publications is called *Restatement Second.* In 1987 *Restatement Third* was begun. It includes revisions and updates of the Restatements and new subjects such as Suretyship and Guarantee and Unfair Competition.

Restatements are the product of the work of highly competent scholars in each area of the law and are a highly respected and valuable research tool. Due to the authoritativeness of the Restatements, they are frequently cited by the courts and often accorded recognition greater than that accorded to treatises.

> **FOR EXAMPLE** Most of the law of torts is not statutory law; that is, it is established in court opinions. A state court has not defined a term such as *superseding cause* in negligence law. An appellate court of the state when faced with a case that requires the term to be defined may refer to the Restatement of the Law of Torts § 440 and adopt the Restatement's definition of the term.

Note: The Restatements of the Law are secondary authority and are used to support primary authority or when there is no primary authority.

There are currently Restatements for the following areas of the law:

Agency	Restitution and Unjust Enrichment
Conflicts of Law	Security
Contracts	Suretyship and Guaranty
Foreign Relations Law of the United States	Torts
Judgments	Trusts
Law Governing Lawyers	Unfair Competition
Property	

A. Restatement Features

The Restatements of the Law have the following features:

✦ *Organization*—Each *Restatement of the Law* is divided into chapters that cover major areas. The chapters are then divided into broader *Topics*, and the topics into individual sections that present a general principal of law.

> **FOR EXAMPLE** One of the chapters of the Restatement of the Law of Torts, Products Liability is "Liability of Commercial Product Sellers Based on Product Defects at Time of Sale." This chapter is divided into topics. Topic 1 is "Liability Rules Applicable to Products Generally." This topic is divided into four sections. Section 1 presents the general principle of law governing the "Liability of Commercial Seller or Distributor for Harm Caused by Defective Products." (See Exhibit 8–5.)

At the beginning of each volume and each chapter is a table of contents listing the topic and sections covered in the chapter (see Exhibits 8–5 and 8–6).

✦ *Restatement of the Law*—Each Restatement section begins with a statement of the principle of law or a rule of law, summarizing and defining U.S. law on the topic (see Exhibits 8–6 and 8–7).

✦ *Comments*—Following the rule of law is a comment section that includes an analytical discussion of the rule and may present hypothetical illustrations of the application of the rule (see Exhibits 8–6 and 8–7). The authority who drafted the Restatement prepares the comments and reporters' notes (see Reporters' Notes next). As the work product of a well-known authority, they add value to the Restatement.

✦ *Reporters' Notes*—Following the comments are reporters' notes that include general information concerning the Restatement and citations to cases, treatises, articles, and other secondary sources in support and opposition to the Restatement (see Exhibit 8–8).

✦ *Cross References*—Cross references to the West's Digests' key numbers and ALR annotations accompany each Restatement.

✦ *Appendix Volumes*—Beginning with the *Restatement Second*, there are *noncumulative* Appendix volumes that categorize and summarize decisions of courts from different jurisdictions that have cited Restatements (see Exhibit 8–9).

✦ *Updates*—The Restatements are updated with pocket parts for each hardbound volume and supplements that are placed beside the appropriate hardbound volume. The title page of the pocket part or supplement provides the dates of the cases reported and instructions for locating earlier citations (see Exhibit 8–10). Semiannually, Interim Case Citations pamphlets are published that are used in conjunction with the pocket parts and supplements.

✦ *Index*—A comprehensive index accompanies each Restatement, referencing sections, comments, and reporters' notes (see Exhibit 8–11).

B. Research Using Restatements of the Law

1. Use as a Research Tool

Restatements have several uses as a research tool. You may refer to a Restatement when a specific legal term, principle, or rule has not been defined in your jurisdiction. In such situations, a court may refer to and adopt the Restatement as the law in the jurisdiction. The Restatement provides guidance as to how the law should be defined or stated, reasons in support of the definition or statement of the law, and citations to cases, treatises, and other secondary authority.

TABLE OF CONTENTS

CHAPTER 1

**LIABILITY OF COMMERCIAL PRODUCT SELLERS
BASED ON PRODUCT DEFECTS AT TIME OF SALE**

TOPIC 1. LIABILITY RULES APPLICABLE TO
PRODUCTS GENERALLY

Exhibit 8–5
Restatement (Third) of Torts, Products Liability Table of Contents Page.
American Law Institute, *Restatement (Third) of Torts*, 3d Ed., Vol. 1, (1998) p. xxi. Copyright 1998 by the American Law Institute. All rights reserved. Reprinted with permission.

When a Restatement has been adopted, the comments and reporters' notes are invaluable aids in locating cases from other jurisdictions and other secondary sources interpreting the Restatement. A Restatement may be also used to locate authority to challenge an existing law.

FOR EXAMPLE   The client's case requires the challenge of a rule or statement of the law adopted by a state that differs from the one recommended by the Restatement. The Restatement may provide reasons and persuasive authority that can be used to challenge the existing rule or statement of the law.

CHAPTER 1

LIABILITY OF COMMERCIAL PRODUCT SELLERS BASED ON PRODUCT DEFECTS AT TIME OF SALE

TOPIC 1. LIABILITY RULES APPLICABLE TO PRODUCTS GENERALLY

TOPIC 1. LIABILITY RULES APPLICABLE TO PRODUCTS GENERALLY

§ 1. Liability of Commercial Seller or Distributor for Harm Caused by Defective Products

Rule ———

One engaged in the business of selling or otherwise distributing products who sells or distributes a defective product is subject to liability for harm to persons or property caused by the defect.

Comment ——— **Comment:**

a. History. This Section states a general rule of tort liability applicable to commercial sellers and other distributors of products generally. Rules of liability applicable to special products

Exhibit 8–6

Restatement (Third) of Torts, **Products Liability § 1.**

American Law Institute, *Restatement (Third) of Torts*, 3d Ed., Vol. 1, (1998) p. 5. Copyright 1998 by the American Law Institute. All rights reserved. Reprinted with permission.

§ 2. Categories of Product Defect

Rule ————
A product is defective when, at the time of sale or distribution, it contains a manufacturing defect, is defective in design, or is defective because of inadequate instructions or warnings. A product:

(a) contains a manufacturing defect when the product departs from its intended design even though all possible care was exercised in the preparation and marketing of the product;

(b) is defective in design when the foreseeable risks of harm posed by the product could have been reduced or avoided by the adoption of a reasonable alternative design by the seller or other distributor, or a predecessor in the commercial chain of distribution, and the omission of the alternative design renders the product not reasonably safe;

(c) is defective because of inadequate instructions or warnings when the foreseeable risks of harm posed by the product could have been reduced or avoided by the provision of reasonable instructions or warnings by the seller or other distributor, or a predecessor in the commercial chain of distribution, and the omission of the instructions or warnings renders the product not reasonably safe.

Comment:

Comment ————
a. Rationale. The rules set forth in this Section establish separate standards of liability for manufacturing defects, design defects, and defects based on inadequate instructions or warnings. They are generally applicable to most products. Standards of liability applicable to special product categories such as prescription drugs and used products are set forth in separate sections in Topic 2 of this Chapter.

The rule for manufacturing defects stated in Subsection (a) imposes liability whether or not the manufacturer's quality control efforts satisfy standards of reasonableness. Strict liability without fault in this context is generally believed to foster several objectives. On the premise that tort law serves the instrumental function of creating safety incentives, imposing strict liability on manufacturers for harm caused by manufacturing defects encourages greater investment in product safety than does a regime of fault-based liability under which, as a practical matter, sellers may escape their appropriate share of responsibility. Some courts and commentators also have said that strict liability discourages the consumption of defective products by

Exhibit 8–7
Restatement (Third) of Torts, **Products Liability § 2.**
American Law Institute, *Restatement (Third) of Torts,* 3d Ed., Vol. 1, (1998) p. 14. Copyright 1998 by the American Law Institute. All rights reserved. Reprinted with permission.

Ch. 1   LIABILITY BASED ON TIME-OF-SALE DEFECTS   § 1

nonmanufacturing sellers or distributors do not themselves render the products defective and regardless of whether they are in a position to prevent defects from occurring. See § 2, Comment *o*. Legislation has been enacted in many jurisdictions that, to some extent, immunizes nonmanufacturing sellers or distributors from strict liability. The legislation is premised on the belief that bringing nonmanufacturing sellers or distributors into products liability litigation generates wasteful legal costs. Although liability in most cases is ultimately passed on to the manufacturer who is responsible for creating the product defect, nonmanufacturing sellers or distributors must devote resources to protect their interests. In most situations, therefore, immunizing nonmanufacturers from strict liability saves those resources without jeopardizing the plaintiffs interests. To assure plaintiffs access to a responsible and solvent product seller or distributor, the statutes generally provide that the nonmanufacturing seller or distributor is immunized from strict liability only if: (1) the manufacturer is subject to the jurisdiction of the court of plaintiff's domicile; and (2) the manufacturer is not, nor is likely to become, insolvent.

In connection with these statutes, two problems may need to be resolved to assure fairness to plaintiffs. First, as currently structured, the statutes typically impose upon the plaintiff the risk of insolvency of the manufacturer between the time an action is brought and the time a judgment can be enforced. If a nonmanufacturing seller or distributor is dismissed from an action at the outset when it appears that the manufacturer will be able to pay a judgment, and the manufacturer subsequently becomes insolvent and is unable to pay the judgment, the plaintiff may be left to suffer the loss uncompensated. One possible solution could be to toll the statute of limitations against nonmanufacturers so that they may be brought in if necessary. Second, a nonmanufacturing seller or distributor occasionally will be responsible for the introduction of a defect in a product even though it exercised reasonable care in handling or supervising the product in its control. In such instances, liability for a § 2(a) defect should be imposed on the nonmanufacturing seller or distributor. See § 2, Illustration 2.

REPORTERS' NOTE

Comment a. History.

1. Abundant authority recognizes the division of product defects into manufacturing defects, design defects, and defects based on inadequate instructions or warnings. See, e.g., Caterpillar Tractor Co. v. Beck, 593 P.2d 871, 881–82 (Alaska 1979) (Accord, Shanks v. Upjohn Co., 835 P.2d 1189, 1194 (Alaska 1992)); Dart v. Wiebe Mfg., Inc., 709 P.2d 876, 878–79 (Ariz. 1985) (en banc); Barker v. Lull Eng'g Co., 573 P.2d 443, 454 (Cal. 1978) (recognizing that different

---

Exhibit 8–8

Restatement (Third) of Torts, **Products Liability Notes.**

American Law Institute, *Restatement (Third) of Torts,* 3d Ed., Vol. 1, (1998) p. 9. Copyright 1998 by the American Law Institute. All rights reserved. Reprinted with permission.

RESTATEMENT OF THE LAW

OF

TORTS

Second

APPENDIX

COURT CITATIONS TO FIRST RESTATEMENT

DIVISION TWO

NEGLIGENCE

CHAPTER 14

**LIABILITY OF PERSONS SUPPLYING CHATTELS
FOR THE USE OF OTHERS**

TOPIC 6. INDEPENDENT CONTRACTORS

§ 403. Chattel Known to be Dangerous

Kan. 1964. Com. (a) cit. in sup. An excavator had cleaned a drainage ditch after constructing it. He knew of a pipeline under the ditch, but ruptured it while he was cleaning it. The court held that since the pipeline was not inherently dangerous, the excavator was not liable to the landowner for the damage the ruptured pipe caused. Phillips Pipe Line Co. v. Kansas Cold Storage, Inc., 192 Kan. 480, 389 P.2d 766, 770.

§ 404. Negligence in Making, Rebuild-ing, or Repairing Chattel

C.A.4, 1965. Cit. in sup. The Department of the Navy contracted to have an old bridge crossing a certain channel removed. The defendant removed the bridge but failed to remove a steel piling which was vertical in the water but did not protrude above the surface. The contract called for removal of all such pilings. The plaintiff's boat was sunk as a result of striking the piling. The court held that even though the plaintiff was not a party to the contract,

---

Cit.-cited; fol.-followed; quot.-quoted; sup.-support.
A complete list of abbreviations faces page 1.

Exhibit 8–9

Restatement (Second) of Torts, **Appendix Page.**

American Law Institute, *Restatement (Second) of Torts,* 2nd Ed., Appendix through December 1975, §§ 403 (1986) p. 1. Copyright 1986 by the American Law Institute. All rights reserved. Reprinted with permission.

Insert this Pocket Part in the back of the Restatement
of the Law Third, Torts: Products Liability (1998)

CASE CITATIONS TO THE RESTATEMENT OF THE LAW

Cumulative Annual Pocket Part
For Use In 2000

Dates of the Cases Reported ——————————— Reporting Cases From July 1984
Through June 1999 That Cite

Restatement of the Law Second,
Torts 2d, §§ 402A and 402B
and
Restatement of the Law Third,
Torts: Products Liability §§ 1 to End

Instructions for Locating
Earlier and Subsequent ——
Citations

This Pocket Part contains all citations to the Restatement of the Law Third,
Torts: Products Liability, as well as citations, for the period from July 1984
through June 1999, to §§ 402A–402B of the Restatement Second of Torts. For
earlier citations to §§ 402A–402B, see the Volume titled "Torts 2d Appendix
§§ 402A to 402B Reporting All Cases through June 1984." For subsequent
citations see also the *Interim Case Citations to the Restatements of the Law*
pamphlets designated for use with the 2000 Pocket Parts and Supplements.

Editor: Marianne McGettigan Walker
The American Law Institute
4025 Chestnut Street
Philadelphia, PA 19104

ST. PAUL, MN
AMERICAN LAW INSTITUTE PUBLISHERS
2000

Exhibit 8–10
Restatement (Third) of Torts, Pocket Part Cover Page.

INDEX

References are to Sections, Comments, and Reporters' Notes

A

ABOVE GROUND POOLS
Reference to Comments
Design defect considerations, **§ 2 Com. *d*** ————————— Reference to Comments

ACQUISITIONS
See Mergers and Acquisitions

ADMINISTRATIVE REGULATIONS
See Statutes, Rules, and Regulations

ADULTERATION
Food products, harm caused by defective, **§ 7 Com. *6;* § 7 RN to Com. *b***

ADVERTISING FIRMS
Commercial distribution, other means of, **§ 20 Com. *g***

ADVERTISING
Direct advertising to patients, **§ 6 RN to Com. *e*** ————————— Reference to Reporters Notes
Sellers' or distributors' liability for defective used products, **§ 8 Com. *a***
Used product sellers' or distributors' liability for defective used products,
       buyer's expectations of risk of defect, **§ 8 Com. *h***

AFFIRMATIVE DEFENSES
Generally, **§§ 17–18**

AGE AND CONDITION
Lessor as one who otherwise distributes a product, **§ 20 Com. *c***
Proof incident that harmed plaintiff not solely result of causes other than
       defect at time of sale, **§ 3 Com. *d***
Used product sellers' or distributors' liability for defective used products,
       risk of defect, **§ 8 Com. *h***

AGREEMENTS
See Contracts and Agreements

ALCOHOLIC BEVERAGES
Design defect considerations, **§ 2 Com. *d***

ALLERGIC REACTIONS
Adverse reactions, Warnings of, § 2 Com. *k;* **§ 2 RN to Com. *k***
Food products, harm caused by defective, **§ 7 Com, *a***

ALTERATION
See Misuse, Modification, and Alteration

ALTERNATIVE DESIGN
Design defect factors in determining omission as, **§ 2 RN 1, 3-4 to Com. *f***
Foreseeable risks of harm reduced or avoided by, **§ 2(b); § 2 Com. *f;***

Exhibit 8–11

Restatement (Third) of Torts, **Products Liability Index Page.**

2. Research Techniques—Restatements

The following research techniques will help you locate specific Restatement topics.

a. Index

You may locate Restatement topics by consulting the alphabetical index usually located at the end of each Restatement (see Exhibit 8–11).

> **FOR EXAMPLE** If you are interested in the definition of *superceding cause* in a negligence case, you should refer to the index in the *Restatement of the Law of Torts, Second*.

b. Table of Contents

If you are familiar with the area and topic, you can scan the Table of Contents of the Restatement volume for the specific section.

> **FOR EXAMPLE** You are researching strict liability in a torts case involving manufacturing defects. You could look in the table of contents or the *Restatement of the Law of Torts, Products Liability* volume (see Exhibit 8–5).

c. Appendix Volumes

Refer to the noncumulative Appendix volumes for summaries of court opinions addressing the Restatement section you are researching.

d. Reference from Other Sources

Often you may be directed to a specific Restatement section from another source such as a citation in a case, article, and *Shepard's Restatement of the Law Citations*. You could go directly to the volume and section cited rather than consult the index.

Always check the pocket part and supplement to update your research and to locate the most recent cases. In addition, *always* consult the Appendix volume to ensure that you have located all the case summaries. Note that the Appendix volumes are not cumulative, so each must be checked.

3. Computer-Aided Research

The Restatements are available on CD-ROM, and on Westlaw and LexisNexis.

IV. UNIFORM LAWS AND MODEL ACTS

The National Conference of Commissioners on Uniform State Laws was formed to draft and promote uniform laws. The members of the conference are judges, attorneys, law professors, and legal scholars. The goal of the conference is to make available for adoption by states uniform laws and model acts in areas of the law where uniformity would be beneficial to the states.

> **FOR EXAMPLE** For commerce to take place smoothly and efficiently between states, it is beneficial if the laws governing commerce, such as the sale of goods, are uniform among the states. To this end, the National Conference of Commissioners on Uniform State Laws and the ALI drafted the Uniform Commercial Code. Every state has adopted the code in whole or in part.

"Model acts" are drafted for those situations where a state does not intend to adopt an entire law, but rather intends to modify a uniform law to meet the state's requirements.

The ALI has drafted several model codes. Some of these are the Model Penal Code, the Model Code of Evidence, The Model Land Development Code, and the Model Business Corporations Act.

The uniform laws and model acts are secondary authority. They become primary authority only when they are adopted by a state's legislature. When adopted, they are assigned statutory numbers that fit within the state's statutory numbering scheme.

> **FOR EXAMPLE** The first two sections of Article 2 Sales of the Uniform Commercial Code are numbered and titled Section 2-101, Short Title, and Section 2-102, Scope. When the State of Colorado adopted these sections, the numbers were amended to fit within the state's statutory numbering system—Section 2-101 is Section 4-2-101, Short Title; Section 2-102 is Section 4-2-102, Scope.

A. Features of Uniform Laws and Model Acts

The uniform laws annotated have the following features:

- ✦ *Organization*—Each law or act is divided into topics and subtopics by articles and sections (see Exhibit 8–12).
- ✦ *Uniform Law*—Each section presents a statement of the uniform law (see Exhibit 8–13).
- ✦ *Commissioners' Notes*—The law may be followed by the commissioners' comments on the law that include, among other things, the purpose of the law, a discussion of the variations adopted by the states, references to law review articles, and a list of the states that have adopted the law.
- ✦ *Library References*—Following the law are library references or guides to other research sources such as digest key numbers and encyclopedia cites (see Exhibit 8–13).
- ✦ *Notes to Decisions*—Each law includes a summary of court decisions interpreting the law from all adopting states (see Exhibit 8–14).
- ✦ *Tables*—Each volume has tables that list states that have adopted the law.
- ✦ *Index*—Each uniform law has an index at the back of the volume.
- ✦ *Updates*—Pocket parts update each volume (see Exhibit 8–14).

B. Research Using Uniform Laws and Model Acts

1. Use as a Research Tool

If a researcher is proposing or drafting legislation, uniform laws and model acts are invaluable guides. Not only do they provide a model text from which a law may be crafted, but they also provide access to arguments in support of the law and citations to cases, treatises, and articles interpreting the law.

When a jurisdiction has adopted a uniform law, the commissioners' comments and notes to decisions are invaluable aids in locating cases from other jurisdictions and other secondary sources interpreting the law. This is especially helpful when the state courts have not interpreted the law.

The commissioners' comments and notes to decisions may be helpful in locating persuasive authority to challenge an existing law.

> **FOR EXAMPLE** The client's case requires challenging the applicable state statute, which differs from the uniform law. The annotations to the uniform law may provide reasons and persuasive authority that can be used to challenge the existing statute.

PART II

DEFINITION OF SPECIFIC CRIMES

OFFENSES INVOLVING DANGER TO THE PERSON

Article 210

CRIMINAL HOMICIDE

Sec.

210.0   Definitions.
210.1   Criminal Homicide.
210.2   Murder.
210.3   Manslaughter.
210.4   Negligent Homicide.
210.5   Causing or Aiding Suicide.
[210.6   Sentence of Death for Murder; Further Proceedings to Determine
            Sentence.]

Article 211

ASSAULT; RECKLESS ENDANGERING; THREATS

211.0   Definitions.
211.2   Recklessly Endangering Another Person.
211.3   Terroristic Threats.

Article 212

KIDNAPPING AND RELATED OFFENSES; COERCION

212.0   Definitions.
212.1   Kidnapping.
212.2   Felonious Restraint.
212.3   False Imprisonment.
212.4   Interference with Custody.
212.5   Criminal Coercion.

Article 213

SEXUAL OFFENSES

213.0   Definitions.
213.1   Rape and Related Offenses.
213.2   Deviate Sexual Intercourse by Force or Imposition.
213.3   Corruption of Minors and Seduction.
213.4   Sexual Assault.

Exhibit 8–12
ULA Page Showing Topic, Articles, and Sections.
West, a Thomson Reuters business, *Uniform Laws Annotated*, Model Penal Code, Vol 10 (1975), p. 527. Used with permission of Thomson Reuters/West.

§ 211.0   MODEL PENAL CODE

ARTICLE 211

ASSAULT; RECKLESS ENDANGERING; THREATS

§ 211.0. Definitions
  In this Article, the definitions given in Section 210.0 apply unless a different meaning plainly is required.

§ 211.1. Assault

Text ———————————— (1) Simple Assault. A person is guilty of assault if he:
    (a) attempts to cause or purposely, knowingly or recklessly causes bodily injury to another; or
    (b) negligently causes bodily injury to another with a deadly weapon; or
    (c) attempts by physical menace to put another in fear of imminent serious bodily injury.

  Simple assault is a misdemeanor unless committed in a fight or scuffle entered into by mutual consent, in which case it is a petty misdemeanor.

  (2) Aggravated Assault. A person is guilty of aggravated assault if he:
    (a) attempts to cause serious bodily injury to another, or causes such injury purposely, knowingly or recklessly under circumstances manifesting extreme indifference to the value of human life; or
    (b) attempts to cause or purposely or knowingly causes bodily injury to another with a deadly weapon.

  Aggravated assault under paragraph (a) is a felony of the second degree; aggravated assault under paragraph (b) is a felony of the third degree.

Library References

Library References ———————————
Assault and Battery ⚷48 to 58.   C.J.S. Assault and Battery §§ 51, 57 et seq., 69, 73 et seq.

§ 211.2. Recklessly Endangering Another Person
  A person commits a misdemeanor if he recklessly engages in conduct which places or may place another person in danger of death or serious bodily injury. Recklessness and danger shall be presumed where a person knowingly points

Exhibit 8–13
Sample ULA Assault Page.

PENAL CODE   § 211.1

Caldwell, Pa.1987, 532 A.2d 813, 516 Pa. 441, reargument denied 550 A.2d 785, 520 Pa. 69.

In all cases charged under the Code's murder provisions, in order for the death penalty to be imposed, State must prove beyond a reasonable doubt that aggravating factors outweighed the mitigating factors. State v. Biegenwald, N.J.1987, 524 A.2d 130, 106 N.J. 13.

To support aggravating factor under N.J.S.A. 2C:11–3, subd. e(4)(f), for murder committed for purpose of escaping detection, apprehension, trial, punishment or confinement for another offense committed by defendant or another, there must be evidence from which jury could infer that at least one reason for killing was to prevent victim from informing police and testifying against defendants. State v. Moore, N.J.Super.L.1985, 504 A.2d 804, 207 N.J.Super. 561.

14. Indictment
Defendant may not be subject to possible imposition of death penalty unless indictment contains allegation that homicidal act was committed by defendant's own conduct or that defendant procured commission of offense by payment or promise of payment of anything of pecuniary value. State v. Moore, N.J.Super.L.1985, 504 A.2d 804, 207 N.J.Super. 561.

15. Prosecution witness
Defendant's admission that he killed victims because of his concern that they could later identify defendant or his accomplices was not sufficient to establish, as aggravating circumstance, for purposes of determining whether death sentence could be imposed, that one victim was prosecution witness killed to prevent his testimony against defendant. Com. v. Caldwell, Pa.1987, 532 A.2d 813, 516 Pa. 441, reargument denied 550 A.2d 785, 520 Pa. 69.

16. Nature and extent of punishment
Sentence of death imposed on defendant for murder of his mother was neither excessive nor disproportionate to penalty imposed in similar cases. Com. v. Jermyn, Pa.1987, 533 A.2d 74, 516 Pa. 460, denial of post-conviction relief affirmed 620 A.2d 1128, 533 Pa. 194, reargument denied, certiorari denied 114 S.Ct. 703, 510 U.S. 1049, 126 L.Ed.2d 669, denial of post-conviction relief affirmed 652 A.2d 821, 539 Pa. 371, certiorari denied 115 S.Ct. 2285, 132 L.Ed.2d 287.

Case Summaries Interpreting Law

17. Vacated sentence
Death sentence was properly vacated and sentence of life imprisonment imposed upon defendant convicted of murder, based on improper submission to jury, as aggravating circumstance, of aggravated assault conviction subsequently overturned by virtue of grant of defendant's motion to withdraw his guilty plea to aggravated assault charge, which was pending at time of sentencing, notwithstanding defendant's subsequent conviction for aggravated assault, where although jury was properly presented with other aggravating circumstance, that defendant was serving life sentence for murder at time of commission of second

murder, there was no way of determining whether jury would have found one proper aggravating circumstance outweighed any mitigating circumstances, without additional aggravated assault conviction. Com. v. Karabin, Pa.Super.1987, 524 A.2d 516, 362 Pa.Super. 300, appeal granted 531 A.2d 1119, 516 Pa. 617, affirmed 559 A.2d 19, 521 Pa. 543.

Sentence of death could not be allowed to stand where half of jury heard that defendant was wanted on other murder charges prior to verdict on defendant's penalty. Com. v. Williams, Pa.1987, 522 A.2d 1058, 514 Pa. 62.

17a. Resentencing
Admission of murder conviction that was entered after capital murder conviction, but before resentencing phase, and that was to be considered as aggravating factor at resentencing phase did not violate double jeopardy clauses of State and Federal Constitutions. State v. Biegenwald, N.J.1988, 542 A.2d 442, 110 N.J. 521.

18. Intent
Mere fact that murder is preceded by warning to victim would not fulfill requirement that murderer intends to, or has explicit purpose to, inflict severe psychological or physical pain prior to death for purpose of provision in death penalty statute listing as aggravating circumstance fact that murder was outrageously or wantonly vile, horrible, or inhuman and that it involved depravity of mind. State v. Ramseur, N.J.1987, 524 A.2d 188, 106 N.J. 123, denial of habeas corpus affirmed 983 F.2d 1215, certiorari denied 113 S.Ct. 2433, 508 U.S. 947, 124 L.Ed.2d 653.

19. Depravity of mind
Facts that murderer committed murder because he liked it or it made him feel better, that he killed bystanders without reason, that he killed children or others whose helplessness would indicate that there was no reason to murder, or that murderer intentionally mutilated body he believed was no longer a live human being, evidence "depravity of mind" for purposes of provision in death penalty statute listing as aggravating circumstance fact that murder was outrageously or wantonly vile, horrible, or inhuman in that it involved depravity of mind. State v. Ramseur, N.J.1987, 524 A.2d 188, 106 N.J. 123, denial of habeas corpus affirmed 983 F.2d 1215, certiorari denied 113 S.Ct. 2433, 508 U.S. 947, 124 L.Ed.2d 653.

20. State of mind
In determining whether murder was outrageously or wantonly vile, horrible, or inhuman in that it involved torture or aggravated battery to victim for purposes of aggravating circumstance in death penalty statute, court must look at defendant's state of mind, and not mere fact that victim actually suffered as result of attack, and extreme physical or mental suffering must be precisely what defendant wanted to occur in addition to death. State v. Ramseur, N.J.1987, 524 A.2d 188, 106 N.J. 123, denial of habeas corpus affirmed 983 F.2d 1215, certiorari denied 113 S.Ct. 2433, 508 U.S. 947, 124 L.Ed.2d 653.

ARTICLE 211
ASSAULT; RECKLESS ENDANGERING; THREATS

§ 211.1. Assault.

Notes of Decisions

Note to Decisions Topics

Generally 1
Adequacy of counsel 9a
Admissibility of evidence
    Generally 16

Excited utterances 18a
Motive and intent 18b
Photographs 18

Exhibit 8–14

ULA Cumulative Annual Pocket Part Page.

2. Research Techniques—Uniform Laws

The following research techniques will help you locate specific uniform laws and model acts.

a. Uniform Laws Annotated, Master Edition

The *Uniform Laws Annotated, Master Edition* (ULA) published by West, a Thomson business, includes the uniform laws and annotations to all uniform laws that have been adopted by one or more states. Exhibits 8–12 through 8–14 are from the ULA. The annotations include the features listed in the preceding subsection A and are invaluable research tools. The set includes uniform laws and model acts. A pamphlet entitled the *Directory of Uniform Acts and Codes: Tables and Codes* is published with the set. The Directory lists the uniform laws and model laws by name, subject, and adopting jurisdiction.

b. Reference from Other Sources

Often you may be directed to a specific uniform law section from another source such as a citation in a case, article, or ALR's Index to Annotations.

3. Computer-Aided Research

Uniform laws and model acts are available on Westlaw and LexisNexis.

V. DICTIONARIES AND *WORDS AND PHRASES*

A. Legal Dictionaries

Words often have a more complex or different meaning when used in a legal context than in everyday use.

> **FOR EXAMPLE** Most people think the word *publication* means to make something known to the public in general, such as through publication in a newspaper. When used in conjunction with the law of defamation, the term means communicating information to one or more persons. In this context, telling defamatory information about an individual to one other person is publication.

Legal dictionaries provide the spelling, pronunciation, and legal meaning assigned to terms used in the law. Law dictionaries are similar to other dictionaries in that the terms are arranged alphabetically. They differ from other dictionaries in that they cite the source of the definition, such as a treatise or court opinion.

> **FOR EXAMPLE** Following the definition of a term such as *salesman* will be a citation to the court opinion or a secondary authority source where the term is defined.

Legal dictionaries, therefore, are valuable not only for their definitions, but also for the citations that serve as a research source for both primary and secondary authority (see Exhibit 8–15).

The two most well known law dictionaries are *Black's Law Dictionary* published by West and *Oran's Dictionary of the Law* published by Delmar Cengage Learning. The dictionaries are similar. Both dictionaries arrange the terms alphabetically, provide citations to the definitions, and consist of a single volume.

Black's is available on Westlaw.

109   assault

"as is" means that the property is sold in its existing condition, and use of the phrase *as is* relieves the seller from liability for defects in that condition. — Also termed *with all faults.*

as-is warranty. See warranty (2).

asked price. See price.

asking price. See price.

as of. On; at. • This is often used to signify the effective legal date of a document, as when the document is backdated or the parties sign at different times <the lease commences as of June 1>.

as of right. By virtue of a legal entitlement <the case is not one triable to a jury as of right>.

as per. In accordance with; per (3). • This phrase has traditionally been considered a barbarism, *per* being the preferred form in commercialese <per your request>. But even *per* can be improved on <as you requested>.

asportation (as-pǝr-**tay**-shǝn), *n.* The act of carrying away or removing (property or a person). • Asportation is a necessary element of larceny. — Also termed *carrying away.* — **asport,** *vb.* See LARCENY.

> "There is no larceny unless the personal goods of another which have been taken by trespass are 'carried away,' but this technical requirement may be satisfied by a very slight movement. There must be 'asportation,' to use the word commonly found in the early cases, but the slightest start of the carrying-away movement constitutes asportation." Rollin M. Perkins & Ronald N. Boyce, *Criminal Law* 323 (3d ed. 1982).

> "To constitute larceny, there must be a taking or caption and carrying away or asportation of the property of another. There is a caption when the defendant takes possession. He takes possession when he exercises dominion and control over the property. There is an asportation when he carries away the property; any carrying away movement, however slight, is sufficient. An asportation presupposes a prior caption; therefore, there can be no asportation unless there has first been a caption." 3 Charles E. Torcia, *Wharton's Criminal Law* § 357, at 412-13 (15th ed. 1995).

asportavit (as-por-**tay**-vit). [Law Latin] He carried away.

ASR. *abbr.* ACCOUNTING SERIES RELEASE.

assart. *Hist.* **1.** The action of pulling up trees and bushes in a forest to make the land arable. • This was a crime if done without a license. **2.** A piece of land made arable by clearing a forest.

assassination, *n.* The act of deliberately killing someone, esp. a public figure, usu. for hire or for political reasons. — **assassinate,** *vb.* — **assassin,** *n.*

assault, *n.* **1.** *Criminal & law.* The threat or use of force on another that causes that person to have a reasonable apprehension of imminent harmful or offensive contact; the act of putting another person in reasonable fear or apprehension of an immediate battery by means of an act amounting to an attempt or threat to commit a battery. **2.** *Criminal law.* An attempt to commit battery, requiring the specific intent to cause physical injury. — Also termed (in senses 1 and 2) *simple assault.* **3.** Loosely, a battery. **4.** Popularly, any attack. — **assault,** *vb.* — **assaultive,** *adj.* Cf. BATTERY.

> "Ordinary usage creates a certain difficulty in pinning down the meaning of 'assault.' Etymologically, the word is compounded of the Latin *ad* + *saltare*, to jump at. In popular language, it has always connoted a physical attack. When we say that D assaults V, we have a mental picture of D attacking V, by striking or pushing or stabbing him. In the middle ages, however, the terms 'assault' and 'battery' were given technical meanings which they have retained ever since. It became settled that though an assault could be committed by physical contact, it did not require this, since a show of force raising an apprehension in the mind of the victim was sufficient. Also, a 'battery' did not require an actual beating; the use of any degree of force against the body would suffice. The acts of spitting on a person and kissing without consent are both batteries." Glanville Williams, *Textbook of Criminal Law* 135–36 (1978).

> "In addition to the classic definitions of assault, some jurisdictions have used assault as a generic term to describe either assault or battery. Thus, a defendant who intentionally injures somebody may be convicted of assault rather than battery." Arnold H. Loewy, *Criminal Law in a Nutshell* 57 (2d ed. 1987).

aggravated assault. Criminal assault accompanied by circumstances that make it more severe, such as the use of a deadly weapon, the intent to commit another crime, or the intent to cause serious bodily harm.

> "The common law did not include any offense known as 'aggravated assault.' However, it did make provision for certain situations in this field, under other names. If, for example, the intended application of force to the person would have resulted in murder, mayhem, rape or robbery, if successful, and the scheme proceeded far enough to constitute an attempt the prosecution was for an attempt to commit the intended felony." Rollin M. Perkins & Ronald N. Boyce, *Criminal Law* 180 (3d ed. 1982).

assault purpensé (ǝ-**sawlt** poor-**pawn**-say). *Hist.* Premeditated assault. — Also termed

---

Exhibit 8–15
Page from *Black's Law Dictionary*.
West, a Thomson Reuters business, *Black's Law Dictionary*, Seventh Edition, (1999) p. 109. Used with permission of Thomson Reuters/West.

B. *Words and Phrases*

Words and Phrases is a multivolume set published by West, which provides the judicial definition of words and phrases. It includes only terms that have been defined in federal and state court opinions. If a term has not been defined in an opinion, it will not appear in *Words and Phrases*. It provides every court definition of a term and a brief summary of the opinion. A term will usually have multiple definitions, sometimes covering several pages. The set is kept up to date with annual pocket parts for each volume. It is *not* available on either Westlaw or LexisNexis as a separate database. However, court definitions of specific terms are available on both databases.

Words and Phrases is a valuable case finder, especially in those situations where you are looking for a term's unique definition.

> **FOR EXAMPLE** You are looking for the definition of *Indian trader* for the purpose of determining whether a traveling salesman's one-time sale of goods on an Indian reservation makes the salesman an "Indian trader" within the meaning of the Indian Trader Act. Black's does not define the term, but *Words and Phrases* includes a definition.

VI. LEGISLATIVE HISTORY

Legislative history is the record of the legislation during the enactment process before it became law. It is composed of committee reports, transcripts of hearings, statements of legislators concerning the legislation, and any other material published for legislative use in regard to the legislation. It is a secondary authority source sometimes relied upon by the courts when interpreting laws.

There are several different sources of legislative history for federal statutes. The research sources for locating the legislative history for state statutes may be similar to some or all of the federal legislative history sources. Therefore, the research sources for locating federal legislative history are discussed here. The state sources vary from state to state and may be limited or nonexistent, depending upon the state. Consult the appropriate state legislative records or service office for the availability of legislative history.

It is important to note that legislative history is considered only if the plain meaning of a statute is not clear or sections of a statute are internally inconsistent. If the meaning is clear, that meaning will be applied by the court even if the legislative history indicates the legislature intended a different meaning.

A. Federal Legislative History Sources

The following are the main sources of legislative history. Usually information from more than one of these sources is necessary to determine legislative intent.

1. Congressional Bills

Each bill goes through several versions before it is passed. An examination of the terms or provisions deleted or added in the various versions of the bill may reveal the legislative intent.

> **FOR EXAMPLE** An early version of the Housing Discrimination Act may have used the term *citizen* rather than *person*. The substitution of the more expansive term *person* in a later version may support an argument that the legislature intended that the act have an expansive application rather than a limited one.

Information gained through this source concerning legislative intent is based upon the *researcher's interpretation* of what the legislature intended when it adopted different versions of a bill. Therefore, other legislative history sources are necessary to obtain additional support for a particular interpretation of legislative intent.

2. Committee Hearings

Congressional committees hold hearings to receive public input and expert testimony concerning proposed legislation. The records of hearings are composed of transcripts of the legislators' questions and witness testimony along with exhibits and documents submitted. Some of the information may help explain how the legislation applies or the reason certain terms or phrases were used. But the hearing records include all arguments and information submitted by individuals and groups both in support and opposition to some or all of the legislation. It is difficult to determine which testimony and information the committee relied upon. Therefore, the information from this source is usually used in support of other legislative history sources.

3. Committee Reports

A committee report on a bill usually includes the text of the bill, the majority's reasons for recommending the bill, an analysis of the contents of the bill, and the minority's reasons for opposing the bill. Because the report clearly states the legislators' intent and is prepared by those who worked with the bill, the courts usually consider the report the most authoritative source of legislative history.

4. Congressional Debates

Congress may hold debates on a bill, and the records of the debates are published in the *Congressional Record*. During the debates, members of Congress present arguments for and against a bill and amendments to a bill. The debates often include explanations of provisions of the bill, its purpose, or how it applies. Often many different and contradictory reasons may be presented in support of a bill. For this reason, it may be difficult to determine legislative intent from the debates.

B. Researching Federal Legislative History

1. Use of Legislative History

On some occasions, a law that governs a client's fact situation may be written in such a manner that its meaning is unclear. The lack of clarity may be due to the use of an ambiguous term or phrase. Or, the law may be written so broadly that it is unclear how it is supposed to apply in a specific fact situation. The courts may resolve the matter by looking to the legislative history of the law to determine the legislature's intended meaning of a term or phrase or when or how the law applies. Legislative history may be of assistance in several ways. The history may identify why an ambiguous term was used and what meaning the legislature intended, what the legislature intended the statute to accomplish, what the general purpose of the legislation is, and so on.

FOR EXAMPLE Section A (9) of the state Housing Discrimination Act provides that no person shall deny an individual housing on the basis of gender preference. The court is called upon to interpret the term *person*. Does it include corporations and businesses such as partnerships? In the case before the court, a closely held corporation that owned an apartment complex refused to rent an apartment to a couple because of their gender preference. The corporation argued that a corporation is not a person within the meaning of the statute.

Included in the legislative history of the statute is a committee report recommending the passage of the legislation. The report contains the following language, "the intent of the legislation is to eliminate any and all forms of gender discrimination in housing. The term 'person' is intended to include all individuals and business entities, including corporations." The legislative history in this example provides the court guidance in interpreting the statute.

2. Sources for Locating and Compiling Federal Legislative History

There are several avenues to pursue when you compile the legislative history of a federal statute. The starting point of your research is to locate the statute in the USC, USCA, or the USCS and review the history of the statute in the annotations. This will provide you with several pieces of information necessary to locate the legislative history: the public law number, the date the law was enacted, the statutes at large number, and where it is published in the *United States Code Congressional and Administrative News Service* (USCCAN, discussed later). The legislative history may include the Senate report number, the House conference report number, and the popular name.

> **FOR EXAMPLE** Following the text of 42 U.S.C.A. § 2000aa is the following information: Pub. L. 96-440, Title I § 101, Oct 13, 1980, 94 Stat. 1879, Senate Report No. 96-874, House Conference Report No. 96-1411, 1980 *United States Code Congressional and Administrative News Service*, page 3950.

The public law number is most important because most of the sources index laws by the public law number. If you do not know the public law number, some of the sources listed here include subject indexes. The following are the main sources for locating and compiling legislative history.

a. Compiled Legislative Histories

A starting point for researching legislative history is to determine if the legislative history has already been compiled. For many laws, the government agency charged with regulating the legislation, a commercial publisher, or other groups have already compiled the legislative history. If there is a compiled legislative history, your research may be done, and there is no need to look further. Several publications list compiled legislative histories; check the catalog listings at a law library. Some of the sources for locating compiled legislative histories are listed here:

✦ *Public Laws Legislative Histories on Microfiche*, published by Commerce Clearing House (CCH)

✦ *Sources of Compiled Legislative Histories*, sponsored by the American Association of Law Libraries and published by Fred B. Rothman Publications (see Exhibit 8–16)

✦ Check with the federal agency responsible for administering the legislation

b. Congressional Information Service (CIS)

The CIS is a commercial publication considered one of the most comprehensive publications of legislative history documents. Pamphlets are published monthly that are assembled into annual bound volumes. The CIS includes summaries of the law; committee reports, documents, and hearing testimony; and references to debates published in the *Congressional Record*. The CIS makes the summarized documents available on microfiche. The CIS includes a comprehensive index volume that allows you to locate documents in several ways such as by bill number, subject, and popular name (see Exhibit 8–17).

c. United States Code Congressional and Administrative News Service (USCCAN)

United States Code Congressional and Administrative News Service publishes the texts of federal statutes and committee reports. It is published by West and is available at most law libraries. West publishes an edition for each session of Congress in monthly pamphlets that are subsequently assembled in bound volumes. In each pamphlet and bound volume is a legislative history table that lists information relating to the law,

PUBLIC LAW BILL NUMBER	STATUTE	ACT ENTRY	CONTENTS					
			ACTUAL DOCS.			CITES TO DOCS.		
			REPORTS	HEARINGS	DEBATES	INDEX	DISCUSSION	LISTS CITES
96-487 H.R. 39	94 Stat. 2371	ALASKA NATIONAL INTEREST LANDS CONSERVATION ACT						
		IHS Legislative Histories Microfiche Program.						
		Quarles, Steven P. "The Alaska Lands Act's Innovations in the Law of Access Across Federal Lands: You Can Get There from Here." 4 Alaska Law Review 1 (1987).					X	X
96-502 H.R. 8117	94 Stat. 2737	SAFE DRINKING WATER ACT AMENDMENTS OF 1980						
		U.S. Congress. Senate. Committee on Environment and Public Works. A Legislative History of the Safe Drinking Water Act. Wash., D.C.: GPO, 1982. SuDoc: Y4.P96/10:97-9 Microfiche: CIS, 82-S322-5	X		X	X		
96-510 H.R. 7020	94 Stat. 2767	COMPREHENSIVE ENVIRONMENTAL RESPONSE, COMPENSATION, AND LIABILITY ACT OF 1980						
		Grad, Frank P. "A Legislative History of the Comprehensive Environmental Response, Compensation and Liability ("Superfund") Act of 1980." 8 Columbia Journal of Environmental Law 1 (1982).					X	X
		IHS Legislative Histories Microfiche Program.						
		Needham, Helen and Cohn, Menefee, ed. Superfund: A Legislative History. Wash., D.C: Environmental Law Institute, 1984.	X		X	X		
96-517 H.R. 6933	94 Stat. 3015	PATENT AND TRADEMARK LAW AMENDMENT OF 1980						
		Chisum, Donald S. Patents: A Treatise on the Law of Patentability, Validity, and Infringement. New York: Matthew Bender, 1978-, vol.6, app.28. LC.: KF3114.C47	X					
96-561 S. 2163	94 Stat. 3296	AMERICAN FISHERIES PROMOTION ACT OF 1980						
		Stanley, Stephen. "Mare Clausum: The American Fisheries Promotion Act of 1980." 9 Syracuse Journal of International Law and Commerce 403 (1982).					X	X

Rev 2-88

Exhibit 8–16

Page from *Sources of Compiled Legislative Histories.*

Sources of Compiled Legislative Histories: A Bibliography of Government Documents, Periodical Articles, and Books, by Nancy P. Johnson, AALL Publ Series No. 14, Fred B. Rothman Publications, a division of Willam S. Hein & Co., Inc., Buffalo, New York, 2000, p. B 124. Reprinted with permission from William S. Hein & Co, Inc.

INDEX OF BILL NUMBERS

This index lists all the Public Bills that were the subjects of publications abstracted in the 1979 through 1982 CIS/Annuals.

The bills are referenced to CIS accession numbers, as well as to Public Law numbers where appropriate. In each case the referenced number begins with a bold face year number indicating the particular CIS/Annual in which that abstract will be found.

This index contains bills from the 91st through the 95th Congresses. All bills are preceded by (91), (92), (93), (94), (95), (96), or (97) identifying the Congress in which they were considered.

Separate lists are provided for each Congress. Within Congresses, House and Senate bills are listed separately arranged by bill type.

91st CONGRESS
House Bills

(91) H. Res. 108.......................... **82** H523–35
(91) H.R. 10351 .... **81** H343–5
(91) H.R. 17070 .... **79** H623–4
(91) H.R. 17968 .... **82** H523–35

91st CONGRESS
Senate Bills

(91) S.J. Res. 1............................ **79** S523–5
(91) S. 2007 .... **81** H343–5
(91) S. 3842 .... **79** H623–4

92nd CONGRESS
House Bills

(92) H. Con. Res. 243................. **82** H703–14
(92) H. Con. Res. 296................. **82** H703–14

(92) H.R. 850 .... **81** PL97–34
(92) H.R. 9265 .... **79** PL96–22
(92) H.R. 12350 .... **81** H343–5
(92) H.R. 13076 .... **80** PL96–283
(92) H.R. 13416 .... **79** H563–2
(92) H.R. 13416 .... **80** PL96–487
(92) H.R. 13904 .... **80** PL96–283
(92) H.R. 14100 .... **81** PL97–34
(92) H.R. 14121 .... **81** PL97–34
(92) H.R. 14193 .... **81** PL97–34
(92) H.R. 14918 .... **80** PL96–283
(92) H.R. 16188 .... **82** S523–15
(92) H.R. 16932 .... **80** H343–7

92nd CONGRESS
Senate Bills

(92) S. 215 .... **81** S521–4
(92) S. 343 .... **79** PL95–521
(92) S. 344 .... **79** PL95–521
(92) S. 643 .... **80** PL96–517
(92) S. 643 .... **81** PL96–517
(92) S. 1255 .... **80** PL96–517
(92) S. 1255 .... **81** PL96–517
(92) S. 1876 .... **80** PL96–486
(92) S. 2087 .... **80** H343–7
(92) S. 2108 .... **79** S763–2
(92) S. 2108 .... **79** PL96–22
(92) S. 2657 .... **82** S521–65.4
(92) S. 2801 .... **79** S313–21
(92) S. 2801 .... **80** PL96–283
(92) S. 3010 .... **81** H343–5
(92) S. 3040 .... **80** PL96–308

(92) S. 3040 .... **81** PL96–308
(92) S. 3116 .... **80** PL96–308
(92) S. 3116 .... **81** PL96–308
(92) S. 3133 .... **80** S523–8
(92) S. 3133 .... **80** PL96–308
(92) S. 3133 .... **81** PL96–308
(92) S. 3145 .... **80** PL96–308
(92) S. 3145 .... **81** PL96–308
(92) S. 3587 .... **80** PL96–308
(92) S. 3587 .... **81** PL96–308

93rd CONGRESS
House Bills

(93) H. Con. Res. 40................... **82** H703–14
(93) H. Con. Res. 152................. **82** H703–14
(93) H. Con. Res. 292................. **82** H703–14
(93) H. Con. Res. 340................. **82** H703–14
(93) H. Con. Res. 404................. **82** H703–14
(93) H.J. Res. 784 .... **79** PL95–521
(93) H.R. 9 .... **80** PL96–283
(93) H.R. 12 .... **80** H343–7
(93) H.R. 122 .... **80** PL96–308
(93) H.R. 122 .... **81** PL96–308
(93) H.R. 982 .... **82** S523–15
(93) H.R. 1858 .... **81** PL97–34
(93) H.R. 2295 .... **79** H563–2
(93) H.R. 2295 .... **80** PL96–487
(93) H.R. 6265 .... **80** H343–6
(93) H.R. 7732 .... **80** PL96–283
(93) H.R. 9298 .... **80** H343–6
(93) H.R. 10014 .... **80** PL96–308
(93) H.R. 10014 .... **81** PL96–308
(93) H.R. 10792 .... **79** PL95–598
(93) H.R. 11067 .... **79** PL95–521
(93) H.R. 11081 .... **79** PL95–521
(93) H.R. 11135 .... **79** PL95–521
(93) H.R. 11145 .... **79** PL95–521
(93) H.R. 11321 .... **80** H343–7
(93) H.R. 11401 .... **79** PL95–521
(93) H.R. 11555 .... **79** PL95–521
(93) H.R. 11754 .... **82** PL97–446
(93) H.R. 11838 .... **79** PL95–511
(93) H.R. 12233 .... **80** PL96–283
(93) H.R. 12993 .... **80** S263–47
(93) H.R. 14027 .... **79** PL95–572
(93) H.R. 14212 .... **79** PL96–122
(93) H.R. 14212 .... **80** PL96–122
(93) H.R. 14449 .... **81** H343–5
(93) H.R. 15002 .... **80** S961–11.3
(93) H.R. 15139 .... **79** H303–6
(93) H.R. 15139 .... **79** PL96–122
(93) H.R. 15139 .... **80** PL96–122
(93) H.R. 15276 .... **80** H343–6
(93) H.R. 15856 .... **79** H563–2

(93) H.R. 15856 .... **80** PL96–487
(93) H.R. 16643 .... **79** PL95–598

93rd CONGRESS
Senate Bills

(93) S.J. Res. 1........................... **79** S523–5
(93) S. Res. 71 .... **79** S381–5
(93) S. 1 .... **80** H523–42
(93) S. 1 .... **80** S521–14
(93) S. 1 .... **82** S523–1
(93) S. 15 .... **80** H343–7
(93) S. 284 .... **79** S763–2
(93) S. 284 .... **79** PL96–22
(93) S. 500 .... **79** PL95–572
(93) S. 590 .... **80** S381–28
(93) S. 798 .... **79** S523–31
(93) S. 978 .... **80** S523–8
(93) S. 978 .... **80** PL96–308
(93) S. 978 .... **81** PL96–308
(93) S. 1040 .... **80** S313–19
(93) S. 1134 .... **79** S313–21
(93) S. 1134 .... **80** PL96–283
(93) S. 1270 .... **79** PL95–625
(93) S. 1321 .... **80** PL96–517
(93) S. 1321 .... **81** PL96–517
(93) S. 1400 .... **82** S523–1
(93) S. 1401 .... **80** S523–2
(93) S. 1401 .... **81** S523–8
(93) S. 1724 .... **80** H523–6
(93) S. 2504 .... **82** PL97–247
(93) S. 2575 .... **79** PL95–483
(93) S. 2576 .... **79** PL95–483
(93) S. 2600 .... **79** PL95–521
(93) S. 2603 .... **79** PL95–521
(93) S. 2611 .... **79** PL95–521
(93) S. 2615 .... **79** PL95–521
(93) S. 2616 .... **79** PL95–521
(93) S. 2631 .... **79** PL95–521
(93) S. 2642 .... **79** PL95–521
(93) S. 2733 .... **79** PL95–521
(93) S. 2878 .... **80** PL96–283
(93) S. 2879 .... **82** S313–35
(93) S. 2994 .... **81** S543–4
(93) S. 3265 .... **79** PL95–572
(93) S. 3368 .... **80** S961–11.3
(93) S. 3440 .... **79** PL95–511
(93) S. 3776 .... **79** PL95–572
(93) S. 4026 .... **79** PL95–598
(93) S. 4051 .... **80** PL96–479
(93) S. 4062 .... **79** PL95–511
(93) S. 4153 .... **80** PL96–458
(93) S. 4178 .... **81** H343–5
(93) S. 4227 .... **79** PL95–521
(93) S. 4259 .... **80** S523–5

Exhibit 8–17

CIS Index of Bill Numbers.

LexisNexis® Academic & Library Solutions, *CIS® Four-Year Cumulative Index 1979–1982*, Index of Subjects and Names R-Z Supplementary Indexes (1982) p. 3481. LexisNexis® Screen Captures reprinted with the permission of LexisNexis. LexisNexis and *Shepard's* are registered trademarks and Focus and KWIC are trademarks of Reed Elsevier Properties, Inc., used with the permission of LexisNexis.

such as the public law number, date of approval, bill number, the House and Senate report number, and dates the House and Senate considered the bill. With the text of each act is a legislative history section that provides references to all reports related to the act. Although USCCAN does not publish all committee reports, it is a good source for committee and conference report references and an overview of the legislative history of the law. Through this source, you can identify the reports and other sources from which you can assemble the legislative history.

d. Congressional Record

The *Congressional Record* is a record of the debates on the floor of the Senate and House. It is useful if you are interested in reviewing the floor debates on a bill. It includes an index that references such things as debates, committee reports, and passage information. Information is indexed by subject matter and history. For information in the history section, you must know the House and Senate bill numbers of the legislation.

e. Congressional Index

The *Congressional Index* is a loose-leaf service published by CCH. It includes various information on bills such as indexes of bills by subject and sponsor, a summary of each bill, tables of actions taken on a bill, companion bills, and voting records on a bill. It does not include the text of the bill, debates, committee reports, and so on, but it is a valuable aid in locating documents.

f. Congressional and Other Sources

Copies of legislative history documents such as bills and committee reports usually are available through your congressional representatives. You can also Shepardize a statute and locate law review articles and ALR annotations that have analyzed the statute. Often the analysis will include a summary of the legislative history.

g. Computer-Aided Research

There are several on-line services that may be used to locate and compile legislative history. It is helpful and often necessary to have the public law number of the law or the Senate or House bill numbers.

✦ *Westlaw and LexisNexis*—Both of these services have databases that allow you to access the full text of bills, selected legislative history documents such as committee reports, and the *Congressional Record*. Both have bill tracking services. CIS is available on LexisNexis.

✦ *LEGI-SLATE*—LEGI-SLATE is an on-line bill-tracking service. Legislation can be located by several means such as bill number, subject, and sponsor. It is a subscription service available at many law libraries.

✦ *Access and Thomas*—Access and Thomas are sites maintained by the federal government that provide access to legislative history documents. Access is a legislative history site maintained by the Government Printing Office. Thomas is a legislative history site maintained by the Library of Congress. The Web site addresses are listed in the Internet Resources section of this chapter.

C. State Legislative History

Just as courts may look to federal legislative history to resolve an ambiguity in a federal law, state courts may look to state legislative history as a guide to interpret state law. The research sources and processes for locating the legislative history for state statutes are similar to that for federal law. State legislative history and its location vary from state to state and may be limited. Consult the appropriate state legislative records or service office for the availability of legislative history. Information on state legislation may be available from the state legislative Web site, and Westlaw and LexisNexis offer state databases. In addition, the local law librarian should be able to guide you to the sources for state legislative history.

VII. JURY INSTRUCTIONS AND OTHER RESEARCH SOURCES

In addition to the research authorities discussed in Chapter 7 and this chapter, other sources should be mentioned. These sources are briefly discussed next.

A. Jury Instructions

Following the presentation of the evidence in a trial, the jury is instructed on the law that applies to the case, such as how terms are defined and what must be proved for a party to prevail (see Exhibit 8–18). Most states adopt uniform or model jury instructions for the courts to follow when instructing the jury. These jury instructions are often published with the annotated statutes. If not, check at the local law library or with the court. If there is no approved set of jury instructions, several texts exist that include model jury instructions such as *Am. Jur. Pleading and Practice Forms.*

It is important to know how to locate jury instructions because you may be called on to prepare the instructions for a case. In addition, they provide the definitions of terms, the elements of a cause of action that must be proved, and so on, which the state has adopted. Also, the instructions often provide annotations that reference court opinions that discuss the instruction.

FOR EXAMPLE If you want to determine what your state requires to establish a negligence claim, you can consult the state's approved jury instructions. The annotations to the instructions will reference court opinions that have discussed the topic.

B. Practice and Form Books

Many types of single- and multivolume texts are designed to assist practitioners. They range from form books to texts that provide detailed litigation guides and strategy.

FOR EXAMPLE If you are called upon to prepare a legal document, such as a contract for the sale of a business, you should check a form book to make sure you do not leave anything out.

In some states, there are texts with forms specific to that state. Check the treatise section of your library or with the librarian. Some of the better known texts are listed here:

- ✦ *West's Federal Forms*—Model forms for all procedural aspects of trials
- ✦ *West's Legal Forms, 2d*—Model practice forms such as contracts and real estate forms
- ✦ *Fletcher Corporation Forms Annotated*—Corporation law forms
- ✦ *Am. Jur. Pleading and Practice Forms*—Model litigation documents such as complaints and interrogatories
- ✦ *Am. Jur. Legal Forms 2d*—Model practice forms such as contracts and wills
- ✦ *Am. Jur. Proof of Facts*—Information ranging from interviews and discovery to what must be proved in a case
- ✦ *Am. Jur. Trials*—Information on conducting a trial such as opening arguments and trial strategy

2.09   CIVIL INSTRUCTIONS

2.09 IMPEACHMENT OF WITNESS, PRIOR CONVICTION

Jury Instruction

You have heard evidence that witness[1] _____ has been convicted of [a crime] [crimes]. You may use that evidence only to help you decide whether to believe the witness and how much weight to give his [her] testimony.

Committee Comments

The admissibility of prior convictions to impeach a witness' credibility is governed by Fed. R. Evid. 609. In civil cases tried before December 1, 1990, the trial judge had no discretion to balance the probative value against the prejudicial effect. The conviction had to be admitted if it came within the rule. *Green v. Bock Laundry Machine Co.,* 490 U.S. 504 (1989); *Jones v. Board of Police Comm'rs,* 844 F.2d 500, 504–05 (8th Cir.1988). Effective December 1, 1990, Rule 609 reinstates the balancing feature. If the conviction involves dishonesty or false statements, it may be admitted even if not a felony. Fed. R. Evid. 609. There is substantial dispute about how much information may be injected concerning the prior conviction. Some judges do not even allow evidence of what crime, or what punishment was involved. The judge may allow evidence of the specific crime committed and the sentence. *Ross v. Jones,* 888 F.2d 548, 551 (8th Cir.1989). Fed. R. Evid. 105 gives a party the right to require a limiting instruction explaining that the use of this evidence is limited to credibility.

See Manual of Model Criminal Jury Instructions for the Eighth Circuit, 2.18; 3 Edward J. Devitt, et al., FEDERAL JURY PRACTICE AND INSTRUCTIONS: Civil § 73.05 (4th ed. 1987); F.J.C.C. Instruction 30; *Fifth Circuit Pattern Jury Instructions—Civil,* Instruction 2.17 (West 1998); *Ninth Circuit Manual of Model Jury Instructions—Criminal,* Instruction 4.8 (West 1997). *See generally* Fed. R. Evid. 609, 105; West Key #"Witnesses" 344(1–5), 345 (1–4).

Notes on Use

1. If the party in a civil case has a conviction which is introduced in evidence, it would be appropriate to modify Eighth Cir. Crim. Inst. 2.16 and give the following instruction, unless the evidence is admitted under Fed. R. Evid. 404(b) to prove motive, intent, plan, etc. Crim, Inst. 2.16, modified for civil cases is as follows:

Exhibit 8–18
Sample Jury Instruction.
West, a Thomson Reuters business, *Manual of Model Civil Jury Instructions for the District Courts of the Eighth Circuit,* by Committee on Model Civil Jury Instructions within the Eighth Circuit, 1999, p. 28. Used with permission of Thomson Reuters/West.

Many of the form and practice books are also available on Westlaw and LexisNexis. Links to form sources are provided in the Internet Legal Resource Guide at <http://www.ilrg.com> and at FindLaw at <http://www.findlaw.com>.

C. Loose-Leaf Services

Loose-leaf services are publications that focus on a specific area of law and include primary authority such as statutes, regulations, and summaries of court and administrative decisions. Also, they usually include an analysis of the law and references to secondary sources. Each publication includes indexes and finding aids that differ according to the subject matter and the publisher. They are not updated by pocket parts; rather the pages are individually placed in binders and are updated by replacement pages. Several different publishers publish loose-leaf services that cover many subjects such as labor law, environmental law, family law, and tax law. Some of the major publishers are Commerce Clearing House (CCH), Bureau of National Affairs (BNA), and Matthew Bender (MB).

D. Presidential Materials

The two main types of directives issued by the president are proclamations and executive orders. Proclamations are announcements that have no legal effect such as declaring a week as National Bicyclers Week. Executive orders cover a wide range of topics and are usually directives to agencies. These directives have the force of law. Presidential proclamations and executive orders are published in the *Federal Register*, CFR, USCCAN, and the *Weekly Compilation of Presidential Documents* (published by the Office of the Federal Register). They are also available on Westlaw, LexisNexis, and the GPO Web site.

E. Martindale-Hubbell Law Directory

The *Martindale-Hubbell Law Directory*, published by LexisNexis, is a comprehensive directory of attorneys. The multivolume set, arranged alphabetically by state, provides the names of attorneys and biographical information such as date of admission to the bar, law school attended, and publications. There is a multivolume *International Law Directory* listing attorneys from foreign countries. *Martindale-Hubbell* is available on CD-ROM, LexisNexis, and the directory Web site (listed at the end of this chapter).

Included with the law directory set is a *Martindale-Hubbell Law Digest*. The *Law Digest* contains brief summaries of some (but not all) of the laws of the states and many foreign countries. The set also includes some uniform laws, model acts, and the American Bar Association's *Model Rules of Professional Conduct*.

VIII. KEY POINTS CHECKLIST: *Periodicals, Restatements, Uniform Laws, Dictionaries, Legislative History, and Other Secondary Authorities*

- Use periodicals primarily to obtain an analysis and critique of a specific legal topic that is more in-depth or narrower in focus than that provided by a legal encyclopedia or a treatise, or an analysis of recently emerging areas of the law.

- Restatements of the Law, uniform laws, and model acts provide a model text from which a law may be crafted. They provide access to reasons in support of a recommended statement of the law and citations to cases, treatises, and articles interpreting the law.

- Consult the legislative history of a law when its meaning or application is unclear. If the meaning or application of a law is clear, a court will not refer to legislative history.

- Do not try to draft legal documents or pleadings from scratch. Refer to the forms or samples available in the law office or consult a form book, such as *Am. Jur. Legal Forms 2d* or *Am. Jur. Pleading and Practice Forms*.

- Like all research sources, you must check the pocket parts, supplements, or whatever is used to update the source to ensure that your research is current.

IX. APPLICATION

This section applies the information presented in the chapter to the hypotheticals presented at the beginning of this chapter and Chapters 1 and 2.

A. Chapter Hypothetical

This example is based on the fact pattern presented at the beginning of the chapter.

Luis thinks to himself, "The issue here in the broadest sense is, 'What are the constitutional limitations on the city restrictively zoning adult entertainment businesses?' I remember from my constitutional law class that the First Amendment's freedom of speech guarantees are involved. So I could start by looking at the annotations to the First Amendment in the *United States Code Annotated* and locate the section dealing with adult entertainment. This would lead me to case law on the subject. The problem with this is it would take me a while to find the section, and then I would have to wade through all the cases. I could look through a treatise on the First Amendment, but again I may have to wade through a lot of material before I find what I need. I need a source focused on my specific topic that has addressed the question, such as a law review article."

Luis has performed the important first step in his quest. He has identified the question he needs to research and weighed the research avenues available. He could look for a law review article on the topic by consulting the *Index to Legal Periodicals* or the *Current Law Index*, where he will find several articles that address the topic. Both the *Index to Legal Periodicals* and *Current Law Index* are available on Westlaw and LexisNexis and may be available in the local law library on CD-ROM. A law review article will thoroughly analyze the topic through a discussion of the constitutional issues and synthesis of cases that have addressed such ordinances. It will include references to other research sources.

Luis could consult the *Uniform Laws Annotated, Master Edition* to determine if there is a uniform law or model zoning ordinance restricting the location of adult entertainment businesses. If there is, Luis will be presented not only with the uniform law, but also with references to law review articles that have adopted the act, discussion of variations adopted by the states, references to law review articles, research references such as digest key numbers and encyclopedia cites, and summaries of court decisions that have interpreted the law.

B. Chapter 1 Hypothetical *Reins v. Stewart*

As discussed in Chapter 5, Vanessa located a case on point, *Rael v. Cadena*, 93 N.M. 684, 604 P.2d 822 (Ct. App. 1979). In reading the case, she notes that the court referred to Restatement (Second) of Torts § 876, which addresses bystander liability. She could refer to this section for information on how bystander liability is defined, reasons in support of the definition, and citations to cases, treatises, and other secondary authority on the topic. Note that the court opinion directs Vanessa to secondary authority sources. This is one of the reasons to look for primary authority first.

If Vanessa wants to locate additional information, she could look for a law review article on the topic of assault and battery and bystander liability by consulting the *Index to Legal Periodicals* or the *Current Law Index*.

C. Chapter 2 Hypothetical *United States v. Canter*

The case Dustin believes to be on point is *United States v. Martinez-Jimenez*, 864 F.2d 664 (9th Cir. 1989). To obtain an in-depth analysis of the question of whether a fake gun may be considered a deadly weapon, Dustin could look for a law review article on the topic. By consulting the *Index to Legal Periodicals* or the *Current Law Index* under the topics of robbery, deadly weapon, and toy or fake gun, he would be directed to an article that discusses *United States v. Martinez-Jimenez*: Gary Garrigues, *United States v. Martinez-Jimenez [864 F. 2d 664]; use a toy gun, go to prison*, 20 Golden Gate ULRev. 167. This article will provide Dustin with an exhaustive analysis of the topic.

The ALI does not publish a Restatement of the Law on the topic of criminal law. Therefore it is not a reference source for information on what constitutes a dangerous weapon.

SUMMARY

This chapter discussed frequently used research sources designed to locate, interpret, and analyze statutory and case law: legal periodicals, Restatements of the Law, uniform and model laws, legislative history, and other sources.

Legal periodicals publish articles on legal topics in every area of the law. Periodical articles are valuable for their detailed analysis of current legal issues, recently emerging areas of the law, or very specific topics; depth of research; and citation to primary and secondary sources.

Restatements of the Law present a uniform statement of the law for areas of the case law such as torts and contracts. A Restatement provides guidance as to how the law should be defined or stated, reasons in support of the definition or statement of the law, and citations to cases, treatises, and other secondary sources.

Uniform laws and model acts provide uniform statements of the law that are available for adoption by states. They are invaluable guides when drafting or interpreting legislation.

The chapter also covered other topics such as legislative history and other research sources such as form books. The legislative history is the record of the legislation during the enactment process. It often includes guidance as to the meaning or application of the statute.

The chapter briefly covered other research sources that may be valuable to a researcher:

✦ *Jury instructions*—Provide the definition of terms, elements of a cause of action, and so on that a jurisdiction has adopted

✦ *Practice and Form Books*—Provide guidance when drafting legal documents or pleadings

✦ *Loose-leaf Services*—Publications that focus on specific areas of law and compile primary authority such as statutes and summaries of court and administrative decisions

✦ *Presidential Materials*—Proclamations and executive orders by the president

✦ *Martindale-Hubbell Law Directory*—A comprehensive directory of attorneys

CHAPTER REFERENCES

INTERNET RESOURCES

The *Index to Legal Periodicals*, *Current Law Index*, Restatements, Uniform Laws, and Model Acts are available on Westlaw and LexisNexis. LegalTrac is available on the Internet by subscription. Both Westlaw and LexisNexis have databases that allow you to access the full text of bills, selected legislative history documents such as committee reports, and the *Congressional Record*. *Black's* is available on Westlaw. CIS is available on LexisNexis.

Some law reviews and periodicals are available on the publishers' Web sites. You can check a particular law school's Web site to determine if a law review is published on its Web site.

Using "legal newspaper" or "legal newsletters" as a topic, you can find thousands of Web sites that provide access to legal newspapers, law journals, and newsletters. One site from Washburn University School of Law provides links to legal newspapers, newsletters, and magazines: <http://www.washlaw.edu>.

<http://thomas.loc.gov>
> Legislative history is available at this site maintained by the Library of Congress.

<http://www.access.gpo.gov>
> Legislative history is also available at this site maintained by the Government Printing Office. You can access legislative history, presidential documents, the *United States Code*, the *Code of Regulations*, *Federal Register*, and numerous other documents.

<http://www.whitehouse.gov/library>
> The White House virtual library Web site provides access to presidential material.

<http://www.house.gov/>
> U.S. House of Representatives home page.

<http://www.senate.gov/>
> U.S. Senate home page.

<http://www.martindale.com>
> Martindale-Hubbell locator site.

Loose-Leaf Services. Some major publishers of loose-leaf services are CCH at <http://www.cch.com> and BNA at <http:///www.bna.com>.

<http://www.ilrg.com>
> Links to form sources are provided at this Internet Legal Resource Guide site.

For additional materials, please go to the CD accompanying this book

For additional resources, visit our Web site at www.paralegal.delmar.cengage.com

CITATION

The *Bluebook* and *ALWD Citation Manual* rules governing citation to the various secondary authority sources are discussed in Chapter 11. Some examples of citations to the primary and secondary authority sources discussed in this chapter are presented here.

A. Legal Periodicals

Michael Asimow, *Bad Lawyers in the Movies*, 24 Nova L. Rev. 533 (2000)

B. Restatements

Restatement (Second) of Torts § 21 (1965)

C. Uniform Laws

U.C.C. § 2-315, 1 U.L.A. 111 (1997)

Model Penal Code § 210 (1974)

D. Dictionaries

Black's Law Dictionary 361 (7th ed. 1999)

E. Legislative History

1. Bill—S. 201, 107th Cong. § 2 (2001).

   H.R. 60, 106th Cong. § 8 (1999).

2. Committee Hearing—The Freedom to E-File Act: Hearings on H.R. 852.

   Before the Subcomm. On Department Operations, Oversight, Nutrition, and Forrestry, 106th Cong. 56-77 (2000).

3. Committee Report—H. R. Rep. No. 106-986, at 17 (2000).

4. Committee Report—H. R. Rep. No. 101-665, at 279, *reprinted in* 1990 U.S.C.C.A.N. at 3004 (1990).

F. Presidential Proclamations and Executive Orders

Rule 14.7 of *The Bluebook* provides that the citation should be to the CFR cite with a parallel citation to USC. If the material is not in the CFR, then the material is cited in the *Federal Register*.

- Proclamation: Proclamation No. 6642, 58 Fed. Reg. 67625 (1993)
- Executive Order: Exec. Order No. 13202, 66 Fed. Reg. 11225 (2001)

G. Loose-Leaf Services

- *Brito v. County of Palm Beach, Florida*, [1999 Transfer Binder] Prod. Liab. Rep. (CCH) ¶ 15403 (Fla. Dist. Ct. App. Nov. 9, 1998)

EXERCISES

Additional exercises are located on the Student CD-ROM accompanying the text and Online Companion.

ASSIGNMENT 1

Refer to the *Index to Legal Periodicals*. What 1998 article distinguishes between euthanasia and the withdrawal of life-sustaining treatment?

ASSIGNMENT 2

The supervising attorney is interested in on-line patent searching. Refer to the *Current Law Index*. What 1997 law review addresses this topic?

ASSIGNMENT 3

Refer to the *Current Law Index*. What *Illinois Bar Journal* law review article addresses *Ward v. KMART Corp.*, 554 N.E.2d 233 (Ill. 1990)?

ASSIGNMENT 4

Refer to *Restatement (Second) of Torts*. What section provides the elements of false imprisonment? What are the elements of false imprisonment? Is a person liable if the person unintentionally causes the confinement of another? What section addresses confinement caused indirectly by the institution of criminal proceedings?

ASSIGNMENT 5

Refer to *Restatement (Third) of Unfair Competition*. What section defines a trade secret? What is the definition? What is the reason for providing protection to trade secrets? What Rhode Island law addresses trade secrets? What 1998 case from the U.S. District Court for the Southern District of Indiana discussed trade secrets?

ASSIGNMENT 6

The client owns a clothing store. She has questions concerning what constitutes an offer and an acceptance. Refer to the *Uniform Laws Annotated, Master Edition*. What uniform law governs this question? What section of that law addresses offer and acceptance? What CJS reference is included in the Library References? What 1998 case held that a fax stating that an electric utility was willing to accept shipments of coal from a coal company on a probationary basis if specific conditions were accepted by the coal company constituted an offer?

ASSIGNMENT 7

The supervising attorney's son was able to log on to a Web site that showed children how to torture cats. She seems to remember that some legislation was introduced in the 106th Congress that dealt with on-line protection of children. Consult the *United States Code Congressional and Administrative News Service* and locate what, if any, legislation was introduced.

ASSIGNMENT 8

The client was struck while crossing an intersection by a vehicle driven by a minor. The minor's parents owned the vehicle, and the minor was driving with their knowledge and consent. The minor has been cited twice for speeding in the past three years. Refer to *Am. Jur. Pleading and Practice Forms* and locate the proper negligence complaint form for suit against the parents.

CHAPTER 9

Computer and Internet Research

Outline

I. Introduction
II. Nonfee-Based Law-Related Web Sites
III. CD-ROM
IV. Key Points Checklist: *Computers and Legal Research*
V. Application

Learning Objectives

After completing this chapter, you should understand:

✦ The role of computers in legal research
✦ The role and types of nonfee-based law-related Web sites
✦ The role of CD-ROMs in legal research

Dmitri Rostov works as a paralegal for a small, three-attorney law firm. The firm has a small law library consisting of the state statutes, the state court case reports, and some civil form books and treatises. It does not have a commercial research service such as Westlaw or LexisNexis. Any extensive research must be performed through nonfee-based sources on the Internet or at the nearest law school, a half hour's drive from the office.

A new client of the law firm runs a restaurant and is preparing to jar and sell her favorite sauce recipe.

One of the additives that will be in the sauce is malic acid. Dmitri's assignment is to check the federal regulations to determine if malic acid is considered a safe food additive. Dmitri hopes he can find the answer through the Internet; he would prefer to avoid having to drive to the law school to check the federal regulations. The answer to this question and the research steps Dmitri follows are discussed in the Application section of this chapter.

I. INTRODUCTION

The earlier chapters of the text focus on the techniques for conducting research using print resources such as treatises and bound volume sets. As technology develops and research is increasingly conducted using electronic resources, it is still important to know how to research using print resources for at least four reasons:

✦ The organization and elements of the electronic databases are based on the structure of the print material. Therefore, a familiarity with the print source makes it much easier to understand the structure of the electronic database and conduct electronic research.

✦ The material you are looking for may not be in an electronic database. This is especially true in the case of treatises. Experienced researchers recognize that a research project may require knowledge of and reference to print resources. They do not rely exclusively on computer-assisted legal research.

✦ An occasion may occur where access to electronic research is unavailable such as when the local server is down. In such situations you are helpless if you don't know how to conduct research using print material.

✦ In addition, cost concerns may limit the amount of time you can spend using commercial electronic services. Some firms use electronic services only to double-check what they have located in print sources or to update their research. This limits the time spent on electronic resources and cuts costs.

This chapter presents an overview of the various nonfee-based Internet and other computer-based legal research sources. Commercial (fee-based) research sources such as Westlaw and LexisNexis are addressed in Chapter 10.

A. Ethics

There are literally thousands of nonfee-based Web sites on the Internet. Note that a nonfee-based service is not in a contractual relationship with the consumer of its information. No laws or regulations govern the accuracy of the content of nonfee-based Web sites. Such sites do not have a legal duty to provide information that is accurate or up to date. As noted in Chapter 2, it is an ethical obligation to provide the client with competent representation. *Therefore, you must verify the accuracy of information you obtain from such sites and determine if it is up to date.*

When selecting a nonfee-based site, there are no hard and fast rules for determining what makes a "good" site. Sites maintained by law schools are usually accurate and well maintained. Always consider the author/publisher and content of the information, and check the site to determine how frequently the information is updated. Beware that advocacy groups publish some sites, and information may be limited or slanted in favor of the position advocated by the group. Links to documents that help you evaluate Web sites can be found at the sites "Evaluation of Information Sources" at http://www.vuw.ac.nz/staff/alastair_smith/evaln/evaln.htm, "Evaluating Internet Resources: A Selective Bibliography" at http://www.lib.auburn.edu/madd/docs/eir.html>, and "The Virtual Chase" at <http://www.virtualchase.com>.

B. Limitations

In addition to the disadvantages of nonfee-based Internet research mentioned so far, there are additional limitations. On many Web sites, when you are searching for statutory law, only the statute is available, not the annotations. Therefore, none of the valuable research information, such as ALR annotations, law review articles, and case references are included.

> **FOR EXAMPLE** If you are searching the *United States Code* for the bank robbery statute using <http://www.law.cornell.edu/uscode/>, the statute will be retrieved, but not the annotations.

When looking for case law, many sites require that you know the name or citation of the case. If you are trying to find any case that answers the question raised by the issue, you may not be able to conduct the search based on search terms (see Boolean searching in the upcoming section IIA, Search Terms). For many sites that allow Boolean searching, the search capability is not as sophisticated as that of fee-based services such as Westlaw or LexisNexis. Most nonfee-based sites do not provide you with the ability to update research.

> **FOR EXAMPLE** If you locate a case that is on point, most sites do not allow you to check the history or treatment of the case to determine if it has been overturned or affected by a subsequent case. They have no mechanism like *Shepard's* to identify cases, articles, and other secondary sources that have cited the case.

II. NONFEE-BASED LAW-RELATED WEB SITES

The following is a discussion of various nonfee-based law-related Web sites. The addresses of Web sites are referred to as **Uniform Resource Locators** or **URLs**. The addresses are current as of the date of publication of this text. If a Web site is not at the address listed, it does not mean that the site no longer exists. The site could be down temporarily due to technical problems, or the address may have changed. To determine if the address has changed, use a search engine to search for a key term in the address.

> **FOR EXAMPLE** If you are looking for Legal-Pad and the site does not come up at the address listed in the upcoming subsection B, Legal Search Engines, perform a search using "Legal Pad" as the search term. If you are looking for a school's law library, search under the name of the school and "law library."

Also, you may have a specific Web page address such as <http://www.willamette.edu/law/wlo/us-supreme>. This is the address of a specific page from the Willamette College of Law's Web site. Summaries of recent U.S. Supreme Court opinions are available at this page. Often specific page addresses change. If you are not able to receive a specific page, go to the home page. In this example, the home page is <http://www.willamette.edu/>. The directory of information on the home page will lead you to the information. In this case, the home page directory includes links to the Supreme Court opinions.

A. Search Terms

This section presents a brief discussion of how to conduct Internet legal research, followed by discussion of nonfee-based Internet legal research sites. The initial steps for conducting a search discussed in Chapter 13 apply to the process for conducting a computer-assisted search: analyzing the assignment, performing preliminary preparation, identifying key facts, and identifying the issue. Computer searches are usually conducted using key words or terms from the issue (often referred to as *Boolean* Searches or *terms and connectors* searches). The basic steps for determining the search terms are as follows:

1. *State the issue you are researching as specifically as possible in the context of the facts.*

2. *Formulate the search query.* Review the issue and select the significant terms. Ask yourself "What terms in the issue are likely to be included in the constitutional provision, statute, or case being researched?"

> **FOR EXAMPLE** The issue is: "Under federal statutory law does bank robbery with a dangerous weapon occur when the weapon is a toy gun?" The assignment is to locate the federal law that governs bank robbery with a dangerous weapon. You are looking for a statute that includes the terms *bank, robbery, dangerous*, and *weapon*.

After you have identified the terms, type them in the search query box and execute the search by clicking on the appropriate command such as "search" or "submit." See the "Quick Search" and "Submit" boxes in Exhibit 9–1. Also, most Web sites that allow searches by search terms include instructions about how to conduct a search (see Exhibit 9–2).

If you are conducting a broad search for general information on a topic, think of all the terms the topic may be categorized under and conduct the search using any combination or all of the terms.

> **FOR EXAMPLE** The question involves child custody, and the researcher wants to gain familiarity with this area of law. The first step is to list all the terms child custody may be indexed under such as *divorce, marriage, custody, parent and child, child custody, children*, and *domestic relations*. The topic will be found under at least one of those search terms.

B. Legal Search Engines

Several sites provide **general access** and links to legal research sites. The links are to Web sites that have access to statutory law, case law, and other research sources. Some of the most comprehensive sites are the following:

 ✦ <http://www.findlaw.com>. FindLaw is considered one of the best and most comprehensive sites providing links to sources for federal and state statutory law, case law, government directories, law firms, legal organizations, law schools, legal practice materials, and numerous other sources.

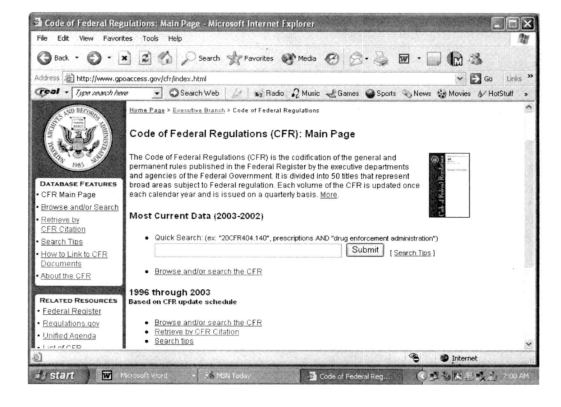

Exhibit 9–1
United States Government Printing Office Search by Terms Query Screen.

Exhibit 9–2
Government Printing Office Search Instructions Screen.

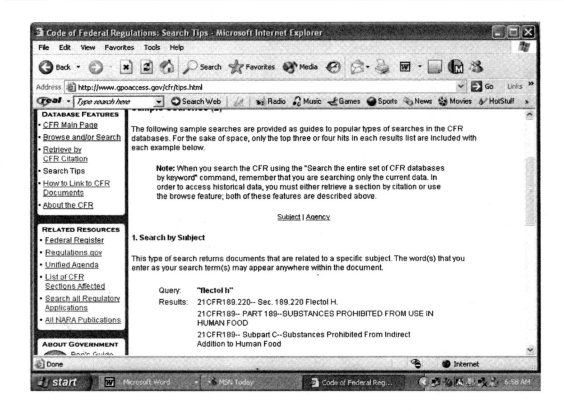

♦ <http://lawcrawler.findlaw.com>. LawCrawler uses simple search terms or phrases to search the Internet for legal information sites. FindLaw is the parent site of LawCrawler.

♦ <http://law.gsu.edu/>. This Georgia State University College of Law site provides access to U.S. federal resources. It allows you to conduct searches of major topics such as judicial opinions, federal regulations, and federal legislation (House and Senate Bills and the Congressional Record). On the home page, click on "Law Library."

♦ <http://www.abanet.org/>. This American Bar Association site includes links to legal research sources, law school libraries, branches of government, courts, and numerous other sources.

♦ <http://www.legal-pad.com>. This site includes legal clip art and a large number of links to law-related sites.

♦ <http://www.jflax.com/law.htm>. Jeff Flax's Law Related Resources includes a comprehensive list of links to law-related Web sites.

♦ <http://lcweb.loc.gov/>. Through this Library of Congress Web site you can locate any book that has been published and has an ISBN.

♦ <http://www.legaldocs.com/>. This site provides templates for legal documents in many areas such as wills, trusts, sales, and real estate. Many documents are free. The law of the state where the document is to be used must be checked to ensure the document complies with state law.

♦ <http://www.llr.com>. This site provides links to various legal research databases. On the home page, type "legal research" in the search box.

♦ <http://www.lawguru.com>. Law Guru includes links to hundreds of legal resource Web sites.

♦ <http://www.ilrg.com>. Internet Legal Resource Guide provides links to forms and other research sources.

♦ <http://www.lectlaw.com>. Links to numerous research sources may be found at the 'Lectric Law Library.

♦ <http://www.megalaw.com>. Like FindLaw this comprehensive site provides links to sources for federal and state statutory law, case law, government directories, law firms, legal organizations, law schools, legal practice materials, and numerous other sources.

Law Schools

Most law schools have Web sites, and most sites provide links to the school's law library. The list of all the law school Web sites is too extensive to include here. To locate the site of a school you are interested in, use a search engine and insert the name of the law school, such as Harvard Law School.

Research may be conducted through many law school library Web sites. The following is a list of law school sites that provide comprehensive legal research links, resources, and information:

♦ <http://www.law.indiana.edu/v-lib/>. This Indiana Virtual Law Library includes links to sites of specialty areas of law, government resources, search engines, and law journals.

♦ <http://www.law.cornell.edu/index.html>. This Cornell University Law School site provides extensive resource guides and access to many different legal topics.

♦ <http://www.washlaw.edu>. In addition to links to numerous law- and legal research–related Web sites, this Washburn University School of Law site provides links to state and federal court and government sites.

♦ <http://www.law.utexas.edu/>. This University of Texas School of Law site includes a legal resource guide on many different legal topics.

♦ <http://www.kentlaw.edu/>. Information on how to find legal materials on the Internet is available at this Chicago-Kent College of Law site. Included are lists governing various areas such as the federal government, computer law, and health law.

♦ <http://www.law.emory.edu/>. This Emory University Law School site provides access to links to many federal circuit court decisions and other research material.

♦ <http://www.law.villanova.edu/>. At this site, you can use "locators" to find official Web sites for federal and state courts and federal government information resources.

C. Federal Government Sources

1. General Access Sources

The following sites are helpful in locating federal government on-line resources.

a. <http://www.firstgov.gov>. FirstGov is the U.S. government's official Web portal. This site provides information and access links to various federal government on-line resources.

b. <http://www.fedworld.gov/>. FedWorld allows you to search for government reports, locate U.S. government Web sites, locate government documents and studies, and so on.

Exhibit 9–3
Home Page for the
Federal Courts.

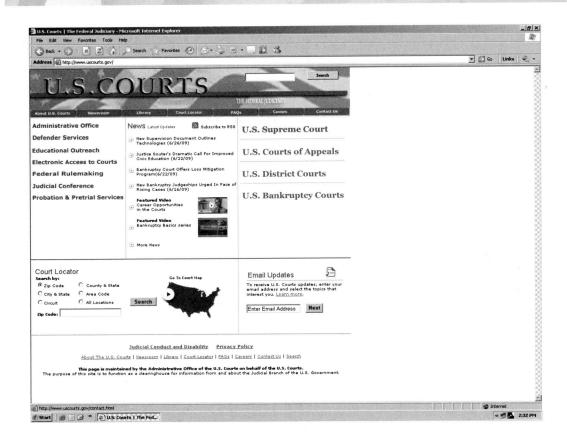

c. <http://www.uscourts.gov/>. This site is the home page for the Federal Courts (see Exhibit 9–3).

d. <http://www.gpoaccess.gov/index.html>. This is the address for the Government Printing Office (see Exhibit 9–4). The site provides information on the executive branch, including the *Code of Federal Regulations*, the *Federal Register*, the *Congressional Record*, and government reports.

2. Federal Courts Opinions

The following sites provide access to the U.S. Supreme Court, the U.S. Circuit Courts of Appeal, and the Federal District Court resources.

U.S. Supreme Court

a. <http://www.supremecourtus.gov>. This official page of the United States Supreme Court features court opinions, orders, rules, calendars and schedules, news releases, and general information.

b. <http://www.findlaw.com/casecode/supreme.html>. This FindLaw site includes Supreme Court cases and the *United States Code*.

c. <http://www.law.cornell.edu/>. At the Cornell Law School home page, click on "Court Opinions" and in the drop-down box, click on "US Supreme Court." You may access transcripts, court orders, and decisions.

d. <http://www.fedworld.gov/>. This FedWorld site allows you to locate opinions from 1937 to 1975 if you know the names of the parties but do not know the citation.

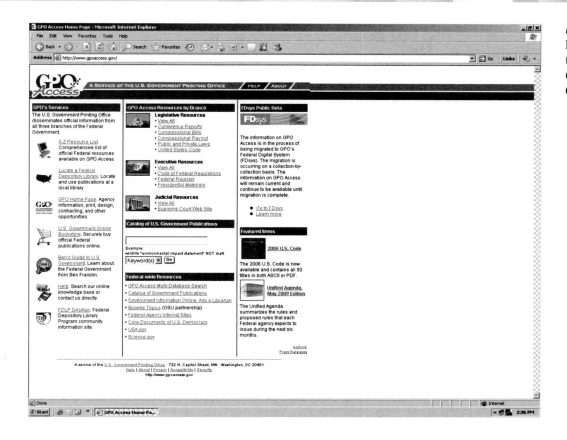

e. <http://www.oyez.org>. You may hear the oral arguments or read the court briefs of U.S. Supreme Court cases at this site. The oral arguments are available for cases from 1960 to present.

f. <http://www.willamette.edu/law/wlo/us-supreme>. Summaries of recent U.S. Supreme Court opinions and the text of the opinions are available at this Willamette College of Law site. Cases from 2002 to present are available.

United States Circuit Courts of Appeal

Access to federal circuit court cases is available through several sources. A few are listed here.

a. <http://findlaw.com/casecode/courts>. Through this FindLaw site, you can locate court cases in general.

b. <http://www.law.vill.edu/library/researchguides/fedcourtlocator.asp>. This Villanova University School of Law site includes Circuit Court opinions and rules.

c. <http://www.law.emory.edu/fedcircuit>. Circuit Court opinions may be accessed through this Emory Law School site.

U.S. District Courts

As discussed in Chapter 1, the U.S. district courts are the primary trial courts in the federal system. Most federal district courts list their opinions on the court Web page. The home page for the federal courts, <http://www.uscourts.gov/>, provides information about the courts and links to the district court Web sites.

Attorney General Opinions. www.usdoj.gov. U.S. Attorney General Opinions are available at this U.S. Department of Justice Web site.

3. Federal Statutes, Court Rules, and Regulations

The *United States Code*, federal court rules, and the *Code of Federal Regulations* are available at the following sites.

United States Code

The Cornell Law School site, at http://www.law.cornell.edu/uscode/, provides access to the *United States Code*. You may search by title and chapter, popular name, title of individual sections, and table of contents. The *United States Code* is also available at the Government Printing Office Web site at <http://www.gpoaccess.gov/>.

Federal Court Rules

The federal court rules are included in the *United States Code* discussed in the previous section. Local court rules are usually available through the federal court's Web site, which may be accessed at <http://www.uscourts.gov/>. The federal court rules are also available at many law school Web sites such as <http://www.law.cornell.edu/>. Cornell Law School's Web site allows you to search the *Federal Rules of Civil Procedure and Evidence* by key word search.

Code of Federal Regulations (CFR)

    a. <http://www.law.cornell.edu/cfr>. This Cornell Law School site allows searches by title and section, index of section headings, the Government Printing Office search engine, or the CFR table of contents.

    b. <http://www.gpoaccess.gov/cfr/index.html>. This Government Printing Office site includes the CFR and a search engine for finding code sections.

Federal Register

The *Federal Register* is available at the Government Printing Office Web site: <http://www.gpoaccess.gov/fr/index.html>.

4. Legislation

Information on federal legislation is available at <http://thomas.loc.gov>. Legislative history is available at this site, which is maintained by the Library of Congress. It includes information on legislation, the full text of the *Congressional Record*, and committee information.

    Legislative history is also available at this site maintained by the Government Printing Office: <http://www.access.gpo.gov>. Access to legislative history and presidential documents is available.

5. Congress and Federal Agencies

The following is a partial list of addresses for Congress and various federal agencies. The addresses for Web sites of agencies not listed here may be accessed through the Library of Congress Web site: <http://www.lcweb.loc.gov/>.

<http://www.census.gov/>	Census Bureau
<http://www.cia.gov/>	Central Intelligence Agency
<http://uscis.gov/>	Citizenship and Immigration Service
<http://www.cpsc.gov/>	Consumer Product Safety Commission
<http://www.usda.gov/>	Department of Agriculture
<http://www.uspto.gov/>	Department of Commerce/Patent and Trademark Office

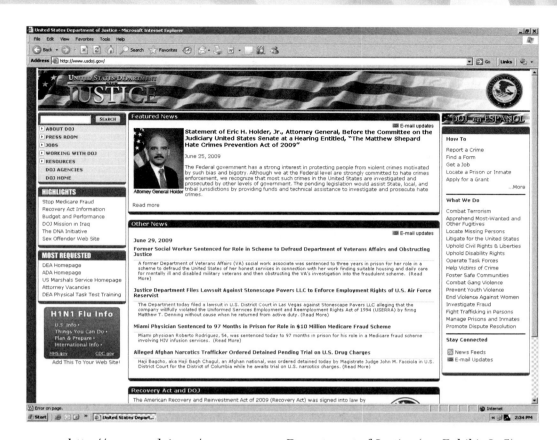

Exhibit 9–5
United States Department of Justice Home Page.

<http://www.usdoj.gov/>	Department of Justice (see Exhibit 9–5)
<http://www.dol.gov/>	Department of Labor
<http://www.dot.gov/>	Department of Transportation
<http://www.epa.gov/>	Environmental Protection Agency
<http://www.faa.gov/>	Federal Aviation Administration
<http://www.fbi.gov/>	Federal Bureau of Investigation
<http://www.ftc.gov/>	Federal Trade Commission
<http://www.fda.gov/>	Food and Drug Administration
<http://www.irs.ustreas.gov/>	Internal Revenue Service
<http://www.nhtsa.dot.gov/>	National Highway Traffic Safety Administration (NHTSA)
<http://www.sec.gov/>	Securities and Exchange Commission (SEC)
<http://www.ssa.gov/>	Social Security Administration
<http://www.state.gov/index.html>	State Department
<http://www.house.gov/>	U.S. House of Representatives
<http://www.senate.gov/>	U.S. Senate
<http://www.whitehouse.gov/>	White House

D. State Sources

The amount of legal research material available via the Internet varies from state to state.

> **FOR EXAMPLE** Some states may provide on-line access to state agency regulations, some may not.

Law-related material is usually available through state court, state government, local law school, or state bar association Web sites. Consider accessing these sites when conducting a search within your state. The legal materials most commonly available are state statutes, court opinions, law reviews, and agency regulations. Rather than list all the Web sites for all the states, a list of the Web addresses for those sites that provide links to state sources follows.

a. <http://www.findlaw.com/>. Through FindLaw, you can access state statutes, case law, administrative law, law schools, professional legal organizations, and some law reviews.

b. <http://www.lawsonline.com/>. Lawsonline provides links to state sources including state codes.

c. <http://www.llr.com>. You can access the recent opinions of the highest state courts through this site.

d. <http://www.law.vill.edu/>. This Villanova University Law school site provides links to state courts and court opinions.

e. <http://www.law.indiana.edu/v-lib>. At the Indiana Virtual Law library, you can find information on many state sources and links to many different specialty areas of law such as family law.

f. <http://www.kentlaw.edu/>. Access to instructions on finding legal materials on the Internet are available at this Chicago-Kent College of Law site. Lists are provided of state government and specialty areas sites such as health law.

g. <http://www.nass.org/acr/internet.html>. This site provides links to official administrative codes and registers for all 50 states and the District of Columbia.

h. <http://www.ncsconline.org/>. The National Center for States Courts (NCSC) Web site includes a list of state courts. Also, law-related Internet sites can be found at this site.

i. <http://www.hg.org/usstates-govt.html>. The site provides access to state and local government information on uniform laws, on-line journals, and other topics.

j. <http://www.courts.net>. This site provides access to Web sites maintained by courts nationwide.

k. <http://www.washlaw.edu>. State Statutes—Links to state laws available at the Washburn University Web site.

l. <http://www.statelocalgov.net>. Links to state government sources are available at this Piper Resources site.

m. <www.naag.org>. Many state attorney general opinions are available at this National Association of Attorneys General Web site.

E. Secondary Authority and Specialty Areas

Many **secondary authority** and other sources such as ALR, *West's Digests*, and treatises are available only at fee-based Web sites such as Westlaw or LexisNexis. Many secondary sources such as Shepard's are available on fee-based Web sites and CD-ROM (see section III, CD-ROM later). However, many secondary and other materials in specialty areas are available at no charge on the Internet. These specialty area and secondary source materials are discussed here. A good source for information and links to numerous sources for the specialty areas listed here can be found at the Amicus Attorney Web site, <http://amicus.ca/resources/index.html>. Another site for accessing information and research sources in numerous specialty areas is the LawyerExpress site located at <http://www.lawyerexpress.com>.

1. Specialty Area Sources

The following is a list of legal topics and Web sites that provide access to information concerning these topics.

a. Arbitration and Mediation, at <http://www.firstgov.gov/>. At the FirstGov Web site, you can locate numerous sources of information on arbitration and mediation. Type in either "arbitration" or "mediation" in the search query box on the home page.

b. Administrative Law, at <http://www.findlaw.com>. FindLaw provides access to federal administrative codes, regulations, orders, and agency rulings. State and local administrative laws are available through the Municipal Code Corporation site, <http://www.municode.com>. Administrative law research may be conducted through the American Bar Association's Administrative Procedure Database at <http://www.law.fsu.edu/library/admin>. The Government Printing Office (GPO) site, <http://www.access.gpo.gov>, provides access to the *United States Code*, the *Code of Regulations*, the *Federal Register*, and numerous other documents. Also, the *LSA: List of CFR Sections Affected* (LSA) (a monthly pamphlet accompanying the *CFR*) is available at this site.

c. Bankruptcy, at <http://www.findlaw.com/>. FindLaw provides access information on the various types of bankruptcy, bankruptcy law, and links to bankruptcy courts. The Internet Bankruptcy Library can be found at <http://bankrupt.com/>. It provides access to publications and resource materials, and links to bankruptcy resources.

d. Civil Litigation, at <http://amicus.ca/resources/index.html>. This Amicus Attorney site includes links to numerous civil litigation support materials such as deposition techniques and tort law sources. A directory of expert witnesses is available at <http://www.claims.com/claims.php>. A site that provides links to experts is <http://www.expertpages.com>. A site that includes information on damages is <http://www.lawcatalog.com>. In the search box, type "damages" for a list of sources of information concerning damages.

e. Civil Rights, at <http://www.findlaw.com/>. The civil rights provisions of the *United States Code* may be found through FindLaw. The American Civil Liberties Union (ACLU) Web site, <http://www.aclu.org/>, provides extensive information on issues concerning civil rights.

f. Consumer Law, at <http://www.consumerlaw.org>. This National Consumer Law Center site includes comprehensive information on consumer law.

g. Corporate Law. General information about corporate law is available through the LawyerExpress Web site, <http://www.lawyerexpress.com>, and the Amicus AttorneyWeb site, <http://amicus.ca/resources/index.html>. State Business and Professional Codes are available through the Cornell University Web site at <http://www.law.cornell.edu>. The Office of the Secretary of State has information on incorporating in a state. Usually forms and documents are available. Secretary of state offices can be contacted through the state government Web site or through <http://www.nass.org/sos/sos.html>.

h. Criminal Law, at <http://www.criminology.fsu.edu>. This Florida State University School of Criminology site provides extensive information on criminal law.

Links to criminal justice sites can be found at the Institute for Law and Justice site, at <http://www.ilj.org/>.

i. Elder Law. Information concerning Medicare, Medicaid, and rights of the elderly can be found at <http://www.seniorlaw.com>.

j. Environmental Law. The Environmental Protection Agency Web site is <http://www.epa.gov>. Links to environmental law resources are at the WWW Virtual Library site at <http://vlib.org>.

k. Estate Planning. State probate statutes should be consulted when the question involves estate planning. They are available through FindLaw. Estate planning material may also be located at the Amicus Attorney site, <http://amicus.ca/resources/index.html>.

l. Family Law, at <http://www.divorcenet.com>. This DivorceNet site provides information on state divorce laws. Information on numerous family law matters such as property issues, custody, and tax planning is available at <http://www.nolo.com/>.

m. Immigration. The Citizenship and Immigration Service Web site is <http://uscis.gov>. Links to all types of material on immigration are available at <http://www.immigrationusa.com/is.html>. Immigration procedures, forms books, and other related materials are available at <http://www.us-immigration.com>.

n. International Law. International legal resources are available at the Cornell Law School Legal Information Institute site at <http://www.law.cornell.edu/topics/> and the United Nations System of Organizations site at <http://www.unsystem.org/>. See also the American Society of International Law's *ASIL Guide to Electronic Resources for International Law* at <http://www.asil.org/resource/home.htm>.

o. Intellectual Property and Copyright. The U.S. Copyright Office Web site is <http://www.lcweb.loc.gov/copyright>. The U.S. Patent and Trademark Office can be accessed via <http://www.uspto.gov>. Information about copyrights is available at the Copyright Clearance Center, <http://www.copyright.com>.

p. Legal Documents and Forms. Legal documents and forms can be found at several sites. Two popular sites are <http://www.lectlaw.com/form.html> (the 'Lectric Law Library) and <http://www.legaldocs.com/> (LegalDocs). Links to form sources are provided in the Internet Legal Resource Guide at <http://www.ilrg.com/forms.html> and FindLaw at <http://www.findlaw.com>.

q. Personal Injury. Links to numerous sites that provide information on personal injury law are available at the Amicus Attorney site at <http://amicus.ca/resources/index.html>. The National Highway Traffic Safety Administration (NHTSA) provides information on traffic safety, consumer complaints, and so on at <http://www.nhtsa.dot.gov>. Data on consumer products is available at the Consumer Product Safety Commission's site at <http://www.cpsc.gov>. The Americans with Disabilities Act Document Center is located at <http://www.jan.wvu.edu/links/adalinks.htm>. Medical information is available at the Virtual Medical Law Center at <http://www.martindalecenter.com>.

r. Real Property and Landlord Tenant Law. Along with many other specialty sites, the Amicus Attorney site at <http://amicus.ca/resources/index.html> includes links to numerous sites that provide information on real property law. The National Association of Realtors site is <http://www.realtor.com>. The site provides links to a wide variety of sources on real estate matters. Nolo Press maintains a landlord/tenant site at <http://www.nolo.com/index.cfm>.

s. Tax Law. The Web site for the Internal Revenue Service is <http://www.irs. ustreas.gov/>. Links to numerous tax law resources are available through the Tax Prophet Web site at <http://www.taxprophet.com>.

t. Uniform Commercial Code. Comprehensive information on the Uniform Commercial Code is available at the Cornell University Law School Legal Information site at <http://www.law.cornell.edu/>. In addition to the Uniform Commercial Code, the site provides links to state commercial code statutes and information about the code. The Amicus Attorney site, <http://amicus.ca/resources/index. html>, also provides numerous links to resources on the commercial code.

2. Secondary Authority and Other Sources

In this section is a list of some secondary authority and other source material sites that are available at nonfee-based Web sites.

a. Law Firms. Information on law firms and locating attorneys is available through FindLaw at <http://www.findlaw.com> and Martindale-Hubbell at <http://www.martindale.com>.

b. Law Reviews, Journals, and Periodicals. Many law reviews, journals, and periodicals are available on-line. Many law schools publish their law reviews and journals. Some examples are the Harvard Law Review at <http://www. harvardlawreview.org> and the Cornell Law Review at <http://www.lawschool. cornell.edu/clr>.

   Directories that provides links to law reviews and law journals include FindLaw at <http://stu.findlaw.com/journals> and the University of Chicago D'Angelo Law Library at <http://www.lib.uchicago.edu/e/law/lawreviews. html>. The University Law Review Project provides information on the availability of law reviews on the Internet at <http://www.lawreview.org/>. See also Anderson's Directory of Law Reviews and Scholarly Legal Publications at <http://www.andersonpublishing.com/law school/directory/>.

   Hiros Gamos Journals, at <http://www.hg.org/journals.html>, includes a listing of law review articles available on the Internet.

c. Legal Dictionaries. Legal dictionaries are available at the following sites: <http:// www.duhaime.org/diction.htm> and <http://www.lectlaw.com/def.htm>.

d. Legal Newspapers and Newsletters. Many legal newspapers and newsletters may be accessed on-line by using the name as a search term. Many may also be accessed through FindLaw. The Washburn University School of Law Web site, <http://www.washlaw.edu>, and the Law News Network at <http://www.law. com> provide links to legal newspapers, newsletters, and magazines.

e. Statistical Information. Statistical information on the federal courts may be found on-line at <http://www.uscourts.gov/publications.html>. The Federal Bureau of Investigations *Uniform Crime Reports* is available at <http://www.fbi.gov>. The Bureau of Justice Statistics provides information at <http://www.usdoj.gov/bjs/>.

f. Treaties. An extensive collection of treaties is available through the *Treaties & International Agreements Researchers' Archive*. It is available through subscription at <http://www.oceanalaw.com>.

g. Uniform State Laws and Model Acts. Uniform state laws and model acts are available at the National Conference of Commissioners on Uniform State Laws (NCCUSL) Web site at <http://www.nccusl.org/>. Access to information on uniform laws is also available through the University of Pennsylvania Law School Web site at <http://www.law.upenn.edu/bll/ulc/ulc_frame.htm>.

F. Listservs

A listserv is an e-mail discussion group. A listserv links people with common interests to share information on a topic or area of expertise. To participate, you must subscribe to or join the group. Once you have joined a listserv discussion group, you may send (post) messages and receive messages from group members. When a message is posted, it is available to all members who subscribe to the group. In essence, the information is public; it is not like private e-mail.

There are hundreds of discussion groups on various legal topics. Listservs are valuable because they allow you to receive the input of colleagues who are interested in and are often experts on a certain legal topic. If you have difficulty finding an answer to a legal question, you can post the question on the listserv and obtain an answer or guidance from other members of the group. However, you must always verify the information you receive.

There are two types of listservs:

+ *Unmoderated*—All messages by group members are sent to the group
+ *Moderated*—Messages are sent to a moderator, who reviews each message and decides whether to return it to the sender, edit it and send it in on to the group, or send it on to the group as is.

The rules established by the group usually govern the activities of the moderator.

Two Web sites that provide information on legal listservs are the Washburn University School of Law site at <http://www.washlaw.edu/listservs> and the Westchester Library System site at <http://www.wls.lib.ny.us/resources/legallistservs.html>.

G. Organizations

The following is a list of law-related organizations and associations:

<http://www.aallnet.org/>	American Association of Law Libraries (AALL)
<http://www.abanet.org/>	American Bar Association (ABA)
<http://www.aclu.org/>	American Civil Liberties Union (ACLU)
<http://www.alanet.org/>	Association of Legal Administrators (ALA)
<http://www.aafpe.org/>	American Association for Paralegal Education (AAFPE)
<http://www.nala.org/>	National Association of Legal Assistants (NALA)
<http://www.nals.org/>	National Association of Legal Secretaries (NALS)
<http://www.nass.org/sos/sos.html>	National Association of Secretaries of State (NASS)
<http://www.paralegals.org>	National Federation of Paralegal Associations (NFPA)

State Bar Organizations. State Bar organizations may be accessed by using a search engine and typing in the name of the state bar such as "New York State Bar."

International Organizations

<http://www.europa.eu.int>	European Union
<http://www.icj-cij.org>	International Court of Justice (World Court)
<http://www.oas.org>	Organization of American States
<http://www.un.org/>	United Nations
<http://www.wto.org>	World Trade Organization

III. CD-ROM

Many legal research sources are available on CD-ROM. These include *American Jurisprudence 2d*, *American Law Reports*, the *United States Code Annotated*, *Shepard's*, state statutory and case law, treatises such as Wright and Miller's *Federal Practice and Procedure*, and practice aids such as *American Jurisprudence Legal Forms* to name a few. For obvious space-saving reasons, many law firms now purchase legal materials in CD-ROM form rather than paper texts.

CD-ROMs have the advantage of allowing the researcher to conduct research through the use of a laptop computer at home, at court, or while traveling. Publishers usually update their CD-ROMs with replacement disks at regular intervals, such as monthly or quarterly. A disadvantage is the material is only as current as the update. Many law libraries have research sources on CD-ROM, and as long as you are familiar with computerized research, it may be easier to perform your search using a CD-ROM rather than a text.

CD-ROMs, just as texts, vary in their organization and search features. However, performing a search on most CD-ROMs is similar to performing a search on Westlaw or LexisNexis. That is, a search may be conducted by citation, natural language, and terms and connectors. If the material is updated only monthly or quarterly, it may be necessary to update your research using Westlaw or LexisNexis for more timely information. For a list of law-related CD-ROM products, see the *Directory of Law Related CD-ROMs* by Information Publishing at <http://www.infosourcespub.com>. This is a subscription service. A reference book that includes a law-related CD-ROM product list is *Directory of Law Related CD-ROMs* by Arlene L. Eis (Infosources Publishing).

IV. KEY POINTS CHECKLIST: *Computers and Legal Research*

- It is important to know how to research using print resources because electronic resources may not be available or may be too expensive. Electronic research systems are based on print resources, and a familiarity with print resources makes it easier to understand electronic research.

- The most critical step in the research process is framing the issue in the context of the specific facts of the case. A well-framed issue, stated in the context of the facts, provides a researcher with the information necessary to conduct research using natural language or terms and connectors.

- Nonfee-based on-line research sources do not have a contractual duty to provide information that is accurate or up to date. You should verify the accuracy of any information that you obtain from such sites and check to determine if the information is current.

- When using a CD-ROM, always check to see how current the disk is. It may be necessary to use another source to update the material.

V. APPLICATION

This section presents three examples illustrating the application of the information presented in this chapter.

A. Chapter Hypothetical

Dmitri knows that a good place to check the Code of Regulations is through the Government Printing Office Web site at <http://www.gpoaccess.gov/cfr/index.html>. This site includes the code and a search engine for finding code sections. He formulates his search query based on the question of whether malic acid is considered safe as a food substance. After accessing the Web site, he types in "food substances considered as safe malic acid" in the "Quick Search" query box. One of the search results is 21 C.F.R. § 184, Direct Food Substances Affirmed as Generally Recognized as Safe. Malic acid is included in the list of substances recognized as safe.

B. Chapter 1 Hypothetical *Reins v. Stewart*

Vanessa's assignment is to locate a case that addresses the question of whether Mr. Stewart may be liable for battery. She reviews the issue to formulate her search query. The issue as determined in the Application section of Chapter 3 is "Under (name of state) tort law, does a battery occur when an individual, present at a battery, encourages the perpetrator of the battery by yelling, 'Hit him again, beat him,' but does not in any other way participate in the battery?" Based on the issue, she formulates the following search query: Battery and bystander and verbally encourages and perpetrator.

She accesses the FindLaw Web site at <http://www.findlaw.com>. On the home page, she clicks on "States" under the "For Legal Professionals" box, then "New Mexico" under the list of states, and then "Supreme Court and Court of Appeals Opinions." At this point, she discovers that the only search options are by title or document number (as of the date of this publication). A search using search terms is not an option. In fact, none of the nonfee-based state sources listed in this chapter provide for a case law search by search terms, such searches are available through commercial sites such as Westlaw or LexisNexis. Vanessa could also consult either the *Pacific* or *New Mexico Digest*. These are available through commercial sites such as Westlaw. They are also available at local libraries. This example highlights one of the weaknesses of nonfee-based Internet research.

C. Chapter 2 Hypothetical *United States v. Canter*

Dustin's assignment is to locate a federal case where the court addresses the question of whether a fake weapon such as the carved replica of a handgun could be considered a dangerous weapon. Based on the issue, he formulates the following query: bank robbery and dangerous weapon and toy gun or fake gun.

Dustin discovers FindLaw queries by search terms only allow you to search back until 1996 (as of the date of this publication). The case on point, identified in the Application section of Chapter 5, *United States v. Martinez-Jimenez*, is a 1989 case and therefore cannot be located using a FindLaw word search. Dustin could locate the case through a commercial site. He could also consult *West's Federal Practice Digest 4th*, available through commercial sites such as Westlaw. It is also available at the local library. This example, like the previous one, highlights one of the weaknesses of nonfee-based Internet research: cases can be found if you have a name or citation but are not usually accessible through a word search.

SUMMARY

The earlier chapters of the text focused on the techniques for conducting research using print resources such as texts and bound volumes. It is important to know how to research using print resources for at least four reasons:

- ✦ A familiarity with the print source makes it much easier to understand the structure of the electronic database and conduct electronic research.
- ✦ The material you are looking for may not be in an electronic database.
- ✦ An occasion may occur where access to electronic research is unavailable such as when the local server is down.
- ✦ Cost concerns may limit the amount of time you can spend using commercial electronic services.

Experienced researchers do not rely exclusively on computer-assisted legal research.

This chapter presents an overview of the various nonfee-based Internet and other computer-based legal research sources such as CD-ROMs.

Thousands of nonfee-based Web sites provide access to various types of legal information on the Internet. There are no laws or regulations governing the accuracy of the content of nonfee-based Web sites; therefore, they do not have a legal duty to provide information that is accurate or up to date. You must verify the accuracy and determine if any information you obtain from such sites is up to date. When selecting a nonfee-based site, always consider the author/publisher and content of the information, and check the site to determine how frequently the information is updated.

A limitation of most nonfee-based Internet sources is that they do not have as extensive databases as the commercial sources mentioned in Chapter 10. Many sites that provide statutory law do not include the annotations. Many sites that provide access to case law, do not allow searches based on search words or terms (Boolean searches).

This chapter discusses and provides the Web addresses for many of the nonfee-based Web sites that provide access to various types of legal information. Included are federal and state government Web sites, secondary authority and specialty area sources, and e-mail discussion groups (listservs).

This chapter closes with a discussion of legal research information available on CD-ROMs.

CHAPTER REFERENCES

INTERNET RESOURCES

See the earlier Section II, NONFEE-BASED LAW-RELATED WEB SITES.

 For additional materials, please go to the CD accompanying this book

 For additional resources, visit our Web site at www.paralegal.delmar.cengage.com

CITATION

The 18th edition of the *Bluebook* and the *ALWD Citation Manual: A Professional System of Citation* state that if the authority is readily available in print, cite to the print source. It is not necessary to reference the electronic source. This rule applies unless the documents are not available in a printed source or are difficult to obtain, such as unpublished cases. Citation to electronic sources is discussed in detail in the ELECTRONIC RESOURCES subsection of Chapter 11.

EXERCISES

Additional exercises are located on the Student CD-ROM accompanying the text and Online Companion.

ASSIGNMENT 1

The client is a shareholder of a corporation in Tennessee. What is required for an action be taken by shareholders without a meeting?

ASSIGNMENT 2

Perform Assignment 1 using your state law.

ASSIGNMENT 3

Using the Cornell Law School Web site, locate a 1998 U.S. Supreme Court Case from the state of Minnesota that involved a warrantless search.

ASSIGNMENT 4

The Hobbs Bridge Act is included in which section of the *United States Code?*

ASSIGNMENT 5

What is the fee charged by the U.S. district courts for a search of the court records?

ASSIGNMENT 6

Under the *Federal Rules of Civil Procedure*, must leave of the court be obtained to take the deposition of a person detained in prison? Include the rule citation.

ASSIGNMENT 7

How is "claim" defined in National Park Services regulations dealing with minerals management? Include the CFR citation.

ASSIGNMENT 8

What was the topic of the Federal Reserve notice issued on January 2, 2004 (published in the *Federal Register*)?

ASSIGNMENT 9

The supervising attorney is working on an employee disability benefits claim involving the Employment Retirement Security Act (ERISA). He remembers that there was a 2003 U.S. Supreme Court Case on the subject. He remembers that one of the parties was Black and Decker. Locate the case.

ASSIGNMENT 10

The client's son is forming a Bible club at the local high school. The club wants to meet during the school's activity period. The school principal refuses to allow them to meet. Using <http://www.findlaw. com/casecode/>, what is the name, case number, and date of a Third Circuit case, involving the Punxsutawney schools, decided after 2000 that addresses this question?

ASSIGNMENT 11

Your supervisory attorney is working on a consumer law case involving a savings and loan company's refusal to grant our client a loan. Our client is female.

The supervisory attorney wants to know the cost of the National Consumer Law Center's Credit Discrimination with CD-ROM Manual.

ASSIGNMENT 12

The client resides in Pennsylvania and has a question concerning child support. Locate information on Pennsylvania child support. Hint: This is a family law matter.

ASSIGNMENT 13

You are working on a simple will. Describe how you can locate a simple will form on the Internet.

ASSIGNMENT 14

Describe how you would obtain, free of charge, a law review article from the Buffalo Criminal Law Review.

ASSIGNMENT 15

What legal research links are provided by the American Bar Association?

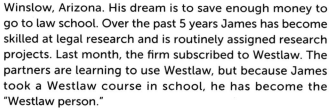

CHAPTER 10

Commercial Internet Research

Outline

Learning Objectives

After completing this chapter, you should understand:

✦ The role of computers in legal research

✦ An overview of legal research using the most frequently used commercial services: Westlaw and LexisNexis

✦ The role and types of nonfee-based on-line legal research sources

James Redhorse was born and raised in Window Rock, Arizona, on the Navajo Reservation. His parents insisted that all their children graduate from high school and encouraged them to go to college. After graduating from paralegal school 5 years ago, James got a job at a law firm in Winslow, Arizona. His dream is to save enough money to go to law school. Over the past 5 years James has become skilled at legal research and is routinely assigned research projects. Last month, the firm subscribed to Westlaw. The partners are learning to use Westlaw, but because James took a Westlaw course in school, he has become the "Westlaw person."

The senior partner called James into his office and said, "I just had an interview with Mrs. Burgess. She is 80 years old, and since her husband died 5 years ago, her closest companion is her cat, Alice. Her next-door neighbor hates cats and repeatedly warned Mrs. Burgess that if Alice continued to use his rose garden as a bathroom he would 'get rid of her.' Last week he set a cat trap for Alice. She was caught in the trap and died. The next day, when Mrs. Burgess asked the neighbor if he had seen Alice, he replied, 'I told you I would take care of her and I did.' He then showed her the trap with Alice still in it. She became so upset over the incident that she went to her doctor. Mrs. Burgess is extremely distraught over the actions of the neighbor and the loss of her cat. She feels that she is now all alone and has lost her best friend. She wants to sue. I want you to get on Westlaw and do some research into what type of damages may be recovered for loss of a pet. I'm especially interested if she can recover for the distress this has caused her."

The answer to this question and the research steps James follows are discussed in the Application section of this chapter.

I. INTRODUCTION

While Chapters 4 through 8 mention if and where the print resources are available on electronic databases such as Westlaw or LexisNexis, they do not discuss how to conduct electronic research. This chapter presents an overview of legal research using the two most frequently used commercial (fee-based) services: Westlaw and LexisNexis. It also includes a brief discussion of Loislaw and VersusLaw, smaller and somewhat less frequently used services. Although other electronic research services are available a familiarity with the major sources will provide you with sufficient information to use other services.

Although the focus of the chapter is on Westlaw and LexisNexis the discussion is limited to an overview of the information available and how to conduct basic research. There are two reasons for this:

 ✦ Inasmuch as there are entire texts devoted to how to use Westlaw and LexisNexis, a detailed discussion is beyond the scope of this text. See Judy A. Long, *Legal Research Using Westlaw* (West Legal Studies, a division of Thomson Delmar Learning, 2002).

 ✦ Westlaw LexisNexis, and most commercial services update and modify their services frequently, rendering a detailed discussion outdated by the time of publication of this text. Because of the frequent modifications, the screen exhibits in this chapter may differ somewhat from current screens.

Westlaw and LexisNexis each have thousands of databases that include primary and secondary authority research sources and numerous other sources. There are databases for all areas of federal and state law, including statutory and case law. Materials are available on specific practice areas, forms, access to public records of all types, news sources, business materials, periodicals, legal treatises, litigation materials, legal and other statistical information sources, directories of all types, law reviews, and international materials. The databases are not limited to law-related information and are too extensive to list here. For example, the *LexisNexis 2005 Directory of Online Services* is more than 950 pages.

II. WESTLAW

Westlaw, by West, a Thomson business, provides access to thousands of primary and secondary research sources. It is available directly on the Internet at <http://www.westlaw.com>. This section first discusses signing on to Westlaw, followed by finding primary and secondary authority, viewing search results, updating research, and printing search results.

A. Signing On

The first step in the research process is to access Westlaw on-line. This is accomplished by performing the following steps:

1. Access the Internet with your Web browser (e.g., Microsoft Explorer).
2. Type the Westlaw address: <http://www.westlaw.com>.
3. Type in your Westlaw password and Client Identifier.
4. Click GO.

After you have signed on, the Welcome page appears. It is from this page that your search will begin (see Exhibit 10–1).

Find by Citation   Directory

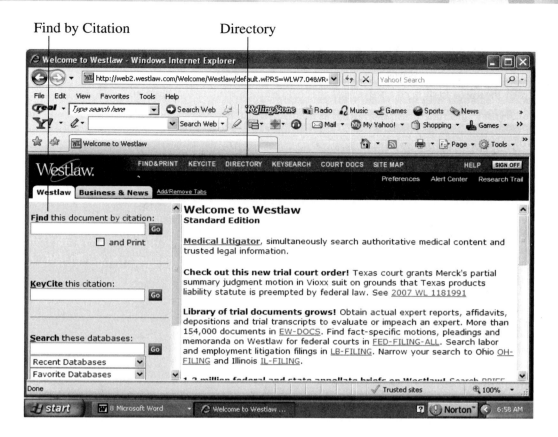

Exhibit 10–1
Westlaw Welcome Screen.
Used with permission of Thomson Reuters/West.

B. Finding Primary Authority

As mentioned in Chapter 1, primary authority is the law itself—constitutional law, enacted law (statutes), and case law. This section focuses on locating statutory and constitutional law (note that constitutions are usually located with the statutes) and case law.

1. Finding Statutory Laws and Constitutional Provisions

There are several ways to locate a statute or constitutional provision depending on the amount of information you have.

a. Search by Citation

When you know the citation of a statute or constitutional provision, you can locate it by performing the following steps:

1. On the Westlaw Welcome page, type the citation in the "Find this document by citation" box and click "Go." The document will come up (see Exhibit 10–1).

> **FOR EXAMPLE** If you wanted to find 18 U.S.C.S. Sec. 2113, you would type 18 usca s 2113.

2. If you are not at the Welcome page, click on "Find" at the top of the page. "Find a Document" will appear (see Exhibit 10–2). Type the citation in the "Enter a citation" box and click "Go."

b. Search by Issue—Natural Language

In most instances, you will not know the citation of the statute that governs the issue being researched. Therefore, you must locate the statute by using the information from the issue. *The most critical step in the research process is framing the issue in the context of the specific facts of the case.* A well-framed issue, stated in the context of the facts, provides a researcher with the information necessary to frame the research query by using the two most common research methods: natural language and terms and connectors (see the next subsection). For help in identifying and stating issues, see Chapter 3.

Natural Language *is a search method that allows you to research by stating the search query (the issue) using plain English.* To conduct a natural language search perform the following steps:

1. *State the issue you are researching as specifically as possible in the context of the facts.*

> **FOR EXAMPLE** The facts of the case are that an individual robs a bank using a toy gun. The question is whether under the federal law a "dangerous weapon" is used in the robbery. The assignment is to locate the federal statute that governs this question. The issue may be stated as follows: Under federal statutory law, does bank robbery with a dangerous weapon occur when the weapon is a toy gun?

2. *Locate the appropriate database.* As with any search, first narrow your search to the sources that contain the material for which you are searching for, such as the U.S.C.A. for federal law and the state statutes for state law. Just as you would look in different sets of books for different laws, Westlaw has different databases for different research areas (see Exhibit 10–2).

Exhibit 10–2
Westlaw Databases Page.
Used with permission of Thomson Reuters/West.

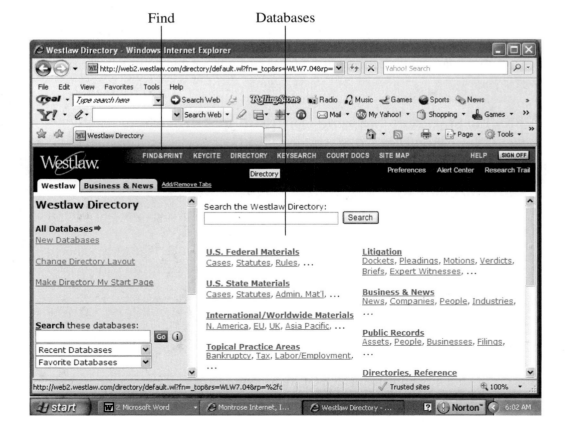

> **FOR EXAMPLE** When you are looking for federal statutory law, click on "View Westlaw Directory" or "Directory" on the Welcome page. On the "Westlaw Directory" page, click on "U. S. Federal Materials," then click on "Statutes," then "United States Code."

3. *Enter the natural language description.* After the database page comes up, on the left side of the page, click on "Natural Language" and type the natural language description of the issue in the "Natural Language description" box. Then click on "Search." (see Exhibit 10–3). The search results will then appear.

c. Search by Issue—Terms and Connectors

Another way to find the statute that governs the issue is through the use of "Terms and Connectors." *A terms and connectors search (often referred to as a Boolean searching) allows you to conduct a search using key words of the issue and symbols (connectors).* The connectors specify the relationships between the key terms, and the search retrieves documents based upon the relationship between the terms.

> **FOR EXAMPLE** In the search query -deadly /p weapon /p bank /p robbery-, the connector "/p" locates all of the documents in which the words deadly, weapon, bank, and robbery appear in the same paragraph of the document.

To perform a terms and connectors search, you must be familiar with the following information:

✦ *Plurals and possessives.* Westlaw automatically retrieves plurals and possessives of terms. If you type *robber*, Westlaw will search for *robber, robbers, robbers',* and *robber's.* It will not retrieve the singular forms if you type the plural.

Terms and Connectors   Natural Language   Fields

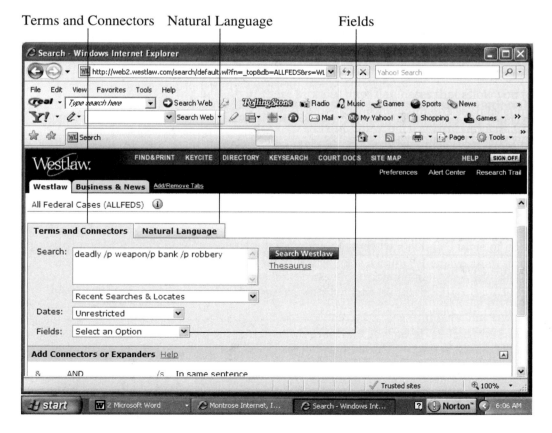

Exhibit 10–3
Natural Language/ Terms and Connectors Search Page.
Used with permission of Thomson Reuters/West.

✦ *Root expander (!).* To search for all forms of a word, place the root expander *"!"* at the end of the root of the word.

| FOR EXAMPLE | The query *-work!-* will retrieve the various forms of the word: *worker, working, works,* and so on. |

✦ *Universal Character (*).* To search for all variations of a word, place an asterisk (*), the universal character, in place of the variable character.

| FOR EXAMPLE | The query *-r*ng-* will retrieve all the documents with *ring, rang,* and *rung.* |

✦ *Connectors.* Connectors specify the relationship between the search terms. They govern the scope of the search. Always use a space to separate the connector from the search term with a space. The list of connectors can be accessed by clicking on "Connectors/Expanders" at the bottom of the page. Following is a list of the connectors and an explanation of how they are used.

CONNECTOR	RULES GOVERNING USE OF CONNECTOR
& (and)	The use of an ampersand "(&)" between the terms retrieves all documents that contain both terms. Thus, the search query—*bank & robber*—retrieves all documents with both terms: *bank* and *robber.*
space (or)	A space between words retrieves all documents that contain either search term. Thus, the search query—*bank robber*—retrieves all documents that contain either the word *bank* or *robber.*
/s	The use of */s* between the terms retrieves all documents that contain both terms in the same sentence. Thus, the search query—*bank /s robber*—retrieves all documents in which *bank* and *robber* appear in the same sentence.
/p	The use of */p* between the terms retrieves all documents that contain both terms in the same paragraph. Thus, the search query—*bank /p robber*—retrieves all documents in which *bank* and *robber* appear in the same paragraph.
/n	The use of */n* between the terms retrieves all documents in which the terms appear within a certain number of words of each other. The *n* is the specified number of words. Thus, the search query—*bank /5 robber*—retrieves all documents in which *bank* and *robber* appear within five words of each other.
" "	Place terms in quotation marks when you want to locate documents in which the terms appear in the same order as they appear in the quotation marks. Thus, the search query—*"bank robbery"*—locates all documents in which the terms *bank* and *robbery* appear together and *bank* precedes *robbery.*
%	To exclude a term from a search query, place the % symbol before the term. Thus, the search query—*bank & robber % weapon*—retrieves all documents that contain the words *bank* and *robber* and which do not contain the word *weapon.*

Following are some examples of search queries using the connectors. The queries are shown in bold.

✦ **bank robbery dangerous weapon** The search retrieves all documents that contain any one of the terms.

✦ **bank & robbery & dangerous & weapon** The search retrieves only documents that contain all of the terms.

✦ **bank /p robbery /p dangerous /p weapon** The search retrieves only documents that contain all of the terms in the same paragraph.

✦ **bank /8 weapon** The search retrieves only documents that contain the word *bank* within eight words of the word *weapon*.

✦ **"dangerous weapon" & bank & robbery** The search retrieves only those documents that include the terms *bank, robbery, dangerous,* and *weapon* where the terms *dangerous* and *weapon* appear together.

✦ **bank & robbery % dangerous & weapon** The search retrieves only those documents that include *bank* and *robbery* and do not include the words *dangerous* and *weapon.*

To conduct a terms and connectors search, perform the following steps:

1. *State the issue you are researching as specifically as possible in the context of the facts.* This step is the same for both natural language and terms and connectors searches.

2. *Formulate the terms and connectors search query.* Review the issue and select the key terms that are significant to the issue being researched. Ask yourself, "What terms in the issue are likely to be included in the constitutional provision or statute being researched?"

FOR EXAMPLE The issue is as follows: "Under federal statutory law, does bank robbery with a dangerous weapon occur when the weapon is a toy gun?" The assignment is to locate the federal law that governs a bank robbery with a dangerous weapon. You are looking for a statute that includes the terms *bank, robbery, dangerous,* and *weapon.*

After you have identified the terms, formulate the query using the appropriate connectors.

FOR EXAMPLE Referring to the previous example, the search is for a statute that includes the terms *bank, robbery, dangerous,* and *weapon.* The terms *dangerous* and *weapon* probably appear in the same order, so they are placed in quotation marks in the query. The query is—*"dangerous weapon" & bank & robbery.* Using the *United States Code Annotated* as a database, your search will retrieve all statutes that include the terms *bank, robbery,* and *dangerous weapon.* The search will retrieve only those statutes in which the terms *dangerous* and *weapon* appear together. To then narrow the search, the query could read—*"dangerous weapon" /p bank /p robbery.* The search will retrieve only those statutes in which the terms appear in the same paragraph.

3. *Locate the appropriate database.* This step is the same as the second step used for a natural language search.

4. *Enter the terms and connectors.* After the database search page comes up, on the left side of the page, click on "Terms and Connectors." In the Terms and

Connectors box, type the terms and connectors for the issue you are searching. Then click on "Search" (see Exhibit 10–3). The search results will then appear.

Natural Language vs. Terms and Connectors Searches. When comparing natural language and terms and connectors searches, you will see certain advantages and disadvantages for both. A terms and connectors search has the disadvantage of requiring a familiarity with the use of the connectors. It has the advantage of allowing the researcher to tailor the search.

> **FOR EXAMPLE** A terms and connectors search using the /p connector retrieves only those documents in which the terms appear in the same paragraph. A natural language search retrieves all the documents that contain the search terms.

Although it takes some practice to become familiar with terms and connectors searches, most researchers prefer them because of the ability to limit the search.

d. Search by Table of Contents (TOC)

In some instances, you may be able to locate a statute or constitutional provision by reviewing the tables of contents of the laws you are searching.

> **FOR EXAMPLE** You are looking for the federal law that governs bank robbery. Rather than construct a natural language or terms and connectors search, you may be able to locate the statute simply by looking at the criminal law section of the table of contents of the *United States Code* or the *United States Code Annotated*.

To conduct a TOC search, perform the following steps:

1. Select the appropriate database.
2. Select "Tables of Contents." Click on the table of contents you want to view.
3. To retrieve a specific title, check its box and click "Go."

2. Finding Case Law

On Westlaw, there are several ways to locate court opinions. Most of the search methods and steps for locating case law are similar to those used to search for statutory and constitutional law.

a. Search by Citation

If you know the citation of a case, you can locate the case by using either of the following steps:

1. On the Westlaw Welcome page, type the citation in the "Find this document by citation" box and click on "Go" (see Exhibit 10–1). The document will come up.

> **FOR EXAMPLE** If the citation is to 713 F Supp 1296, type 713 fs 1296 and click on "Go."

2. If you are not at the Welcome page, click on "Find" at the top of the page. "Find a Document" will appear. Type the citation in the "Enter a citation" box and click on "Go."

b. Search by Issue—Natural Language

In most instances, when you are trying to find the case law that governs the issue being researched, you do not know its name or citation (as is often the case when you are searching for statutes). Therefore, you must locate the case law using the information from the issue. The steps for performing a natural language search for statutory and case law are the same. See "Search by Issue—Natural Language" in Subsection B1b previously. In constitutional, statutory, and case law searches, the most critical step in the research process is framing the issue in the context of the specific facts of the case.

To conduct a natural language search for case law, perform the following steps:

1. *State the issue you are researching as specifically as possible in the context of the facts.*

2. *Locate the appropriate database.* Locate the appropriate case law database.

> **FOR EXAMPLE** If you are looking for federal case law, click on the U.S. Federal Materials, Cases database.

3. *Enter the natural language description.* After the database page comes up, type the natural language description of the issue in the "Natural Language description" box. Then click on "search." The search results will then appear (see Exhibit 10–3).

c. Search by Issue—Terms and Connectors

The steps for performing a terms and connectors search for statutory and case law are the same. The same terms and connectors are used for all searches. See "Search by Issue—Terms and Connectors" in Subsection B1c previously.

Following is a summary of the steps for conducting a terms and connectors search for case law.

1. *State the issue you are researching as specifically as possible in the context of the facts.* This first step is the same for both natural language and terms and connectors searches.

> **FOR EXAMPLE** Under federal statutory law, does bank robbery with a dangerous weapon occur when the weapon is a toy gun?

2. *Formulate the terms and connectors search query.* Review the issue and select the key terms that are significant to the issue being researched. Ask yourself, "What terms in the issue are likely to be included in a court opinion?"

> **FOR EXAMPLE** The issue is as follows: "Under federal statutory law, does bank robbery with a dangerous weapon occur when the weapon is a toy gun?" The assignment is to locate court opinions that address the question of whether a toy gun used in a bank robbery is a dangerous weapon. You are looking for case law that includes the terms *bank, robbery, dangerous weapon,* and *toy gun.*

After you have identified the terms, formulate the query using the appropriate connectors.

> **FOR EXAMPLE** Referring to the previous example, the search is for court opinions that include the terms *bank, robbery, dangerous weapon,* and *toy gun*. The terms dangerous and weapon and toy gun probably appear in the same order, so they will be placed in quotation marks in the query. The query would be—*"dangerous weapon" & bank & robbery & "toy gun"*. If you wanted to narrow the search, then the query could read —*"dangerous weapon" /p bank /p robbery /p "toy gun"*. The search would retrieve only those cases in which the terms appear in the same paragraph.

3. *Locate the appropriate database.* This step is the same as the second step one for a natural language search. See step two in the "Search By Issue—Natural Language" in Subsection B1b(2) previously.

4. *Enter the terms and connectors.* After the database page comes up, type the terms and connectors for the issue being searched in the "Terms and Connectors" box. Then click on "search" (see Exhibit 10–3). The search results will then appear.

d. Search by Title/Name

If you know the name of one or more of the parties in a case, you can locate the case by performing the following steps:

1. *Find.* Click on "Find." On the left side of the "Find a Document" screen, click on "Find by Title."

2. *Find Document by Title.* On the "Find Document by Title" screen, type the name of at least one of the parties, select a jurisdiction, and click "Go."

e. Search by Digest—Topic and Key Numbers

If you are searching for case law that addresses an issue, you can perform a digest search on Westlaw. As discussed in Chapter 5, the West's digests organize the law by topic and subtopics and each subtopic is assigned a key number. The Westlaw "Custom Digest" allows you to access the digests on-line using its Custom Digest. To use the digest, perform the following steps:

1. *Access the Custom Digest page.* On the welcome page, click "Site Map" and then click "Key Numbers & Digest."

2. *Select topic and key number.* On the West Key Number Digest page, review the topics and select the key number for the subject you are researching. To see all of the key numbers under a topic, click the plus sign (+) next to the topic number. Check the box next to the key number you want to search; or if you already know the key number, type it in the box at the top of the page and click "Go." The Key Number Search page with your key number selection will appear.

3. *Select the jurisdiction.* Select the federal or state jurisdiction you want to search, and add additional search terms in the terms and connectors box (optional). When you click the search box at the bottom of the page, the case summaries will appear on the right side of the page.

   You also can access key numbers through the use of **KeySearch**™. To access KeySearch, click "KeySearch" on the tool bar. A page with a list of legal topics will appear, and you can select a legal topic from that list. From there, you are directed to select a specific jurisdiction and to direct your search by search terms. KeySearch retrieves documents that contain key numbers and other documents, such as law reviews.

3. Field Restrictions

When you are researching case law, through the use of Field Restrictions, Westlaw allows you to limit your search to specific portions of documents or documents published on certain dates. You can access the list of field restrictions by clicking on the "Fields" box on the Search page (See Exhibit 10–3). Type the field restriction initials before the terms and connectors, which are placed in parentheses.

> **FOR EXAMPLE** To locate the federal law governing bank robbery, your query might be—*bank & robbery*. To narrow your search to only those documents in which the terms *bank* and *robbery* appear in the caption of the statute, your query would be—*TI (bank & robbery)*. The search then would retrieve only those statutes in which the terms *bank* and *robbery* appeared in the title. It would not retrieve all of the other statutes in which the terms appear in other places, such as in the text or annotations. This would significantly narrow the search.

4. Search Results

The search results are displayed on a split screen. The text of the document retrieved is on the right frame, and the left frame contains information links concerning the search.

a. Document Text

In the document text, the search terms are highlighted in yellow. In a natural language search, the portion of the document most closely related to the query is in red.

KeyCite flags, which are discussed in the next section, appear at the beginning of the document. Clicking on hyperlinks allows you to immediately view a case or statute cited in the document by clicking on the hyperlink.

b. Information

The left frame of the screen provides access to information relevant to the document. This includes KeyCite results, headnotes for cases, tables of authorities, annotations for statutes, constitutional provisions, and so on. The left frame also lists the number of documents retrieved. The "Results List" allows you to view the list of documents selected; click the link to retrieve documents from the list (see Exhibit 10–4). When there are KeyCite flags, they appear in the citations list.

5. Updating Research—KeyCite

It is essential to determine whether the statute or case you have found is still "good law." *Shepard's Citations* was created to allow a researcher to make that determination. *KeyCite is a Westlaw feature, that, like* Shepard's Citations, *allows you to update primary authority and some secondary authority research.* Cases are included in KeyCite the day they appear in Westlaw.

The following is a summary of the main features of the KeyCite system:

+ *Coverage.* KeyCite covers all reported cases, over 1 million unpublished decisions, selected administrative decisions, the *United States Code Annotated* (U.S.C.A.), statutes from all 50 states, the *Code of Federal Regulations* (CFR), and *American Law Reports* (ALR).

+ *Status Flags. A status flag in a document header or next to a citation in the citation list lets you know the current status of a case.* A red flag means that at least one of the points of law in the case is no longer good law. The case has been overruled, reversed, or vacated. A red flag next to a statute means that the statute has been

Exhibit 10–4
**Westlaw Search Result
Screen—Single Case.**
Used with permission of
Thomson Reuters/West.

KeyCite Flag   KeyCite   Print Options

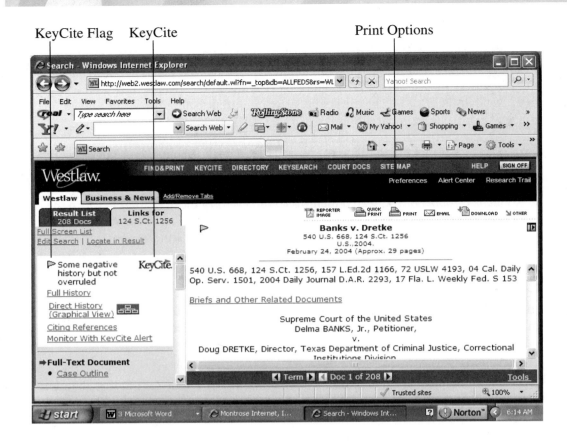

amended or repealed. A yellow flag means that the case has been criticized but
not reversed or overruled or that there is pending legislation that may affect the
statute. Flags indicate that a case has a negative history. A blue H means that
the case has some history. A green C indicates that the case has no direct or negative indirect history.

✦ *Depth of Treatment Stars. Green stars are placed next to a list of cases and secondary
authorities that discuss the case being researched. The stars indicate the depth of the
treatment of the cited case.* Four stars mean an extended discussion of the cited case,
usually more than a page. Three stars indicate a substantial discussion, usually
more than one paragraph but not an entire page. Two stars refer to a discussion
of less than a paragraph. One star means a brief reference, often just a citation.

✦ *Key Number System.* KeyCite is integrated with the Key Number System®. It
allows you to track specific legal issues discussed in a case.

✦ *Information Tabs.* The left frame of the screen provides access to information
relevant to the document (as discussed in the previous subsection), including
the history of a case and citations to secondary sources such as ALR annotations and law review articles.

The guidelines for using KeyCite for constitutional, statutory, and case law are
essentially the same.

C. Finding Secondary Authority

Westlaw provides access to thousands of secondary sources. There are databases for Am.
Jur. 2d, ALR, and legal periodicals including law reviews, treatises, legislative history,
and legal forms, just to name a few. To view the available databases, click on "Directory"
on the Welcome page. On the "Westlaw Directory" page, the databases will appear in

the right frame. Select the appropriate secondary authority database category, such as "Treatises, CLEs, Practice Guides." Then click on the appropriate secondary authority database.

The steps for performing a secondary authority search are generally the same as those used for a primary authority search. That is, you may search by citation, terms and connectors, natural language, and so on. Review "Finding Primary Authority" in Subsection B previously.

D. Printing and Saving

Westlaw provides several printing and saving options. You can download documents to a disk, have them sent to an e-mail address or to a fax number, or print them. If you want documents to be printed as they appear in print, select one of the print options: Composed Single or Dual Column. Documents also can be printed as they appear on the computer screen. Documents can be printed immediately or printed upon exiting Westlaw. On the top of the document being researched are print options (see Exhibit 10–4).

III. LEXISNEXIS®

LexisNexis, like Westlaw, is a commercial legal research service that provides access to thousands of primary and secondary research sources. The LexisNexis research service is operated by LexisNexis, a division of Reed Elsevier Inc. It is available directly on the Internet at <http://www.LexisNexis.com>. There are differences between LexisNexis and Westlaw, but the basic organization and research principles are the same. If you understand how to conduct research on one, with a little practice, you can use the other.

Rather than repeating the information that applies to both searches on LexisNexis and Westlaw, reference is made to the appropriate subsections of the previous section II Westlaw. This section first discusses signing on to LexisNexis, followed by finding primary and secondary authority, viewing search results, updating your research, and printing search results.

A. Signing On

The first step in the research process is to access LexisNexis on-line by following these steps:

1. Access the Internet with your Web browser.
2. Type the LexisNexis address: <http://www.LexisNexis.com>.
3. Type in your LexisNexis ID and password.
4. Click the "Sign On" button.

After you have signed on, the Legal tab appears (unless customized differently). It is from this page that your search will begin (see Exhibit 10–5).

B. Finding Primary Authority

This section focuses on locating statutory law, constitutional law, and case law.

1. Finding Statutory and Constitutional Law

There are several ways to locate a statute or constitutional provision depending upon the amount of information you have.

Exhibit 10–5
LexisNexis Search Screen.
LexisNexis® Screen Captures reprinted with the permission of LexisNexis. LexisNexis and *Shepard's* are registered trademarks and Focus and KWIC are trademarks of Reed Elsevier Properties, Inc., used with the permission of LexisNexis.

Jurisdiction   Source Categories   Terms and Connectors   Natural Language

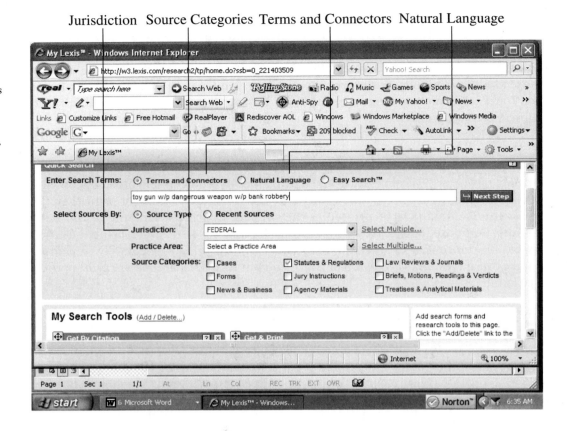

a. Search by Citation

If you know the citation of a statute or constitutional provision, you can locate it by performing the following steps:

> 1. On the Legal tab, at the bottom of the page click on "Get a Document." Then click on "Citation," type the citation in the "Get by Citation" box, and click "Get" (see Exhibit 10–6). The document will come up.

> **FOR EXAMPLE**   If you wanted to find 18 U.S.C.S. Sec. 2113, type 18 uscs 2113 in the "Get by Citation" box and click "Get."

> 2. If you are not on the Legal tab, you can retrieve a document by following step 1 on any page that has the "Get a Document" tab at the top of the page.

b. Search by Issue—Natural Language

As with Westlaw, you can conduct searches by using natural language. The most critical step in the research process is framing the issue in the context of the specific facts of the case. See "Search by Issue—Natural Language," in Subsection B1b earlier in this chapter.

To conduct a natural language search, perform the following steps:

> 1. *State the issue you are researching as specifically as possible in the context of the facts.*

> 2. *Locate the appropriate database.* Like Westlaw, LexisNexis has hundreds of different databases for different research areas (see Exhibit 10–7). Click on the database name to access the database.

Get by Citation   Get by Party Name   Get by Document Number

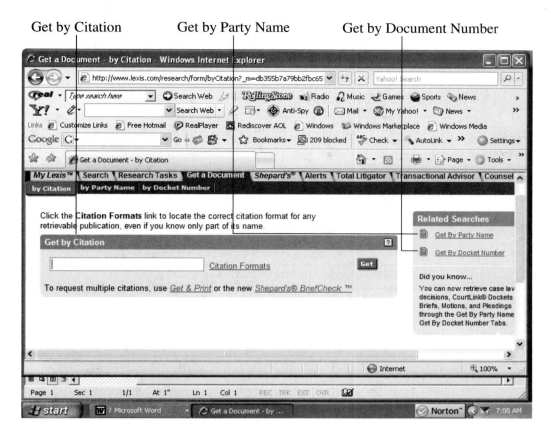

Exhibit 10–6
LexisNexis Get a Document Page.
LexisNexis® Screen Captures reprinted with the permission of LexisNexis. LexisNexis and *Shepard's* are registered trademarks and Focus and KWIC are trademarks of Reed Elsevier Properties, Inc., used with the permission of LexisNexis.

> **FOR EXAMPLE** When looking for federal statutory law, look under "Jurisdiction," select "Federal," and under source categories select "Statutes and Regulations."
> Click on "Natural Language" and type the natural language search terms in the box. Then click on "Search" (see Exhibit 10–5). The search results will appear.

c. Search by Issue—Terms and Connectors

Another way to find a constitutional provision or statute that governs the issue is through the use of terms and connectors. A terms and connectors search on LexisNexis is the same as it is on Westlaw. However, there are some differences in terminology and connectors.

To perform a terms and connectors search on LexisNexis, note the following information:

+ *Plurals and possessives.* Like Westlaw, LexisNexis automatically retrieves plurals and possessives of terms. If you type *robber,* it will search for *robber, robbers, robbers',* and *robber's.* LexisNexis will also search for the singular word when you type a plural. These rules apply to words that form the plural by adding an *s* or *es* or by changing a *y* to an *ies.*

+ *Root expander (!).* To search for extensions of a word, place the root expander *!* at the end of the root of the word. This is the same in both LexisNexis and Westlaw.

> **FOR EXAMPLE** The search -*work!*- retrieves the various forms of the word: *worker, working, works,* and so on.

+ *Universal character* (*). Use the asterisk as a placeholder for one character anywhere but at the beginning of a word. This is the same in both LexisNexis and Westlaw.

> **FOR EXAMPLE** The search -r*ng- retrieves all the documents with *ring, rang,* and *rung*.

+ *Space between words.* Unlike Westlaw, where a space between words is the same as *or,* a space between words in LexisNexis means that the words will be searched for together. The search will locate documents in which the terms appear in the same order. Thus, the search—*bank robbery*—locates all documents in which the terms *bank* and *robbery* appear together and *bank* precedes *robbery*.

+ *Connectors.* In both LexisNexis and Westlaw, connectors specify the relationship between the search terms. Always use a space to separate the connector from the search term with a space.

The connectors are somewhat different in LexisNexis. Following is a list of the LexisNexis connectors and an explanation of how they are used.

CONNECTOR	RULES GOVERNING USE OF CONNECTOR
and	The use of *and* between the terms retrieves all documents that contain both terms. Thus, the search—*bank and robber*—retrieves all documents with both terms: *bank* and *robber*.
or	Place *or* between words to retrieve all documents that contain either search term. Thus, the search—*bank or robber*—retrieves all documents that contain either the term *bank* or the term *robber*.
/s	The use of */s* between the terms retrieves all documents that contain both terms in the same sentence. Thus, the search—*bank /s robber*—retrieves all documents in which *bank* and *robber* appear in the same sentence.
/p	The use of */p* between the terms retrieves all documents that contain both terms in the same paragraph. Thus, the search—*bank /p robber*—retrieves all documents in which *bank* and *robber* appear in the same paragraph.
/n	The use of */n* between the terms retrieves all documents in which the terms appear within a certain number of words of each other. The *n* is the specified number of words. Thus, the search—*bank /5 robber*—retrieves all documents in which *bank* and *robber* appear within five words of each other.
PRE/n	*PRE/n* placed between words locates documents in which the first word precedes the second word by *n* words. Thus, the search—*bank PRE/2 robbery or holdup*—locates all documents that contain the word *bank* within two preceding words of either *robbery* or *holdup*.
and not	To exclude a term from a search, place *and not* before the term. Thus, the search—*bank and robber and not weapon*—retrieves all cases that contain the words *bank* and *robber* and do not contain the word *weapon*. All words after *and not* are excluded from the search.

Following are some examples of search queries using the connectors. The queries are shown in bold.

+ **bank or robbery or dangerous or weapon** The search retrieves all documents that contain any one of the terms.

+ **bank and robbery and dangerous and weapon** The search retrieves only documents that contain all of the terms.

- ✦ **bank /p robbery /p dangerous /p weapon** The search retrieves only documents that contain all of the terms in the same paragraph.

- ✦ **bank /8 weapon** The search retrieves only documents that contain the word *bank* within eight words of the word *weapon.*

- ✦ **dangerous pre/2 weapon and bank and robbery** The search retrieves only those documents that contain the word *dangerous* within two preceding words of *weapon* and that also contain the words *bank* and *robbery.*

- ✦ **bank pre/3 robbery or holdup.** The search retrieves only those documents that contain the word *bank* within three preceding words of either *robbery* or *holdup.*

- ✦ **bank and robbery and not dangerous and weapon** The search retrieves those documents that include *bank* and *robbery*, but excludes documents with both *dangerous* and *weapon.*

To conduct a terms and connectors search, perform the following steps:

1. *State the issue you are researching as specifically as possible in the context of the facts.* This first step is the same for both natural language and terms and connectors searches.

2. *Formulate the terms and connectors search.* This step is the same step for both LexisNexis and Westlaw searches. See the discussion of "Search by Issue—Terms and Connectors" in the Westlaw Subsection B1c earlier in this chapter.

> **FOR EXAMPLE** The issue may be stated as follows: "Under federal statutory law, does bank robbery with a dangerous weapon occur when the weapon is a toy gun?" A LexisNexis terms and connectors search could be—*dangerous weapon and bank and robbery.* With the *United States Code* as a database, the search would retrieve all statutes that include the terms *bank, robbery,* and *dangerous weapon.* The search would retrieve only those statutes in which the terms *dangerous* and *weapon* appear together in that order.

3. *Locate the appropriate database.* This step is the same as the second step for a natural language search. See step 2 in the "By Issue—Natural Language" in Subsection B1b earlier in this chapter.

4. *Enter the terms and connectors.* After the search page comes up, click on "Terms and Connectors." In the search box, type the terms and connectors for the issue being searched then click on "search" (see Exhibit 10–9). The search results will then appear.

d. Search by Table of Contents (TOC)

In some instances, you may be able to locate a statute or constitutional provision by reviewing the TOC of the laws you are searching.

To conduct a TOC search, perform the following steps:

1. On the home page, select the source you are searching, such as United States Code Service—Titles 1 through 50. See Exhibit 10–7.

2. When you click on "United States Code Service," a Table of contents option appears. The various titles of the statutes (the TOC) will appear.

3. To retrieve a specific title, check its box.

Exhibit 10–7
LexisNexis Databases.
LexisNexis® Screen Captures
reprinted with the permission of LexisNexis. LexisNexis
and *Shepard's* are registered
trademarks and Focus and
KWIC are trademarks of
Reed Elsevier Properties, Inc.,
used with the permission of
LexisNexis.

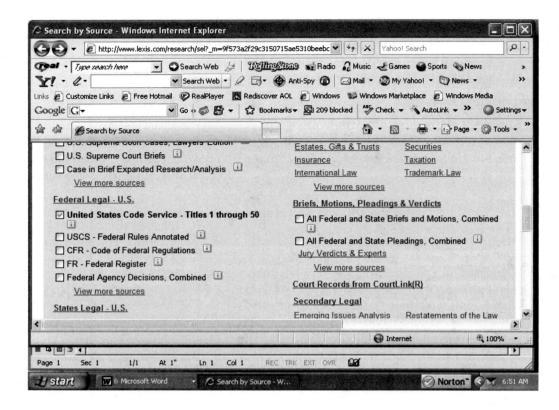

> **FOR EXAMPLE** You are looking for the federal law that governs bank robbery. Rather
> than performing a natural language or terms and connectors search, you
> may be able to locate the statute simply by looking at the criminal law section of the table
> of contents of the *United States Code Service.* Under "Federal Legal—US," click on "United
> States Code Service—Titles 1 through 50" on the LexisNexis Legal tab screen. Then click
> on "CRIMES AND CRIMINAL PROCEDURE," then "Crimes," then "ROBBERY & BURGLARY,"
> then "Bank Robbery." The bank robbery statute then will come up.

2. Finding Case Law

There are several ways to locate court opinions on LexisNexis. Most of the search methods
and steps are similar to those used to search for statutory and constitutional law.

a. Search by Citation, Name, or Docket Number

If you know the name of a party, the citation, or the docket number of a case, you can
locate the case by performing the following steps:

1. On the Legal tab, click on "Get a Document." Then click on "Party Name,"
   "Citation," or "Docket Number" and type the information in the "Get by Party
   Name," "Get by Citation," or "Get by Docket Number" box. Select a jurisdiction
   when using "Get by Party Name" or "Get by Docket Number." Click "Get" or
   "Search" (see Exhibit 10–6). The document will be retrieved.

2. If you are not on the home page, you can retrieve a document by following
   step a on any page that has the "Get a Document" tab at the top of the page.

b. Search by Issue—Natural Language

In most instances, when you are trying to find the case law that governs the issue, you do
not know its name or citation. Therefore, you must locate the case using the information
from the issue. The steps for performing a natural language search for statutory and case

Search by Topic or Headnote

Exhibit 10–8
Search by Topic or Headnote.
LexisNexis® Screen Captures reprinted with the permission of LexisNexis. LexisNexis and *Shepard's* are registered trademarks and Focus and KWIC are trademarks of Reed Elsevier Properties, Inc., used with the permission of LexisNexis.

law are the same. See "Search by Issue—Natural Language" in Subsection B1b earlier in this chapter.

c. Search by Issue—Terms and Connectors

The steps for performing a terms and connectors search for statutory and case law are the same. The same terms and connectors are used for all searches. (See Subsection B1c previously and Exhibit 10–5.)

3. Search by Topic or Headnote

Search by Topic or Headnote is a finding tool designed to help you find research materials within a specific area of law (see Exhibit 10–8).

> **FOR EXAMPLE**   If you are unfamiliar with an area of law or are unsure what terms to include in a search, Search by Topic or Headnote runs searches on specific legal topics for you.

4. Restrict Search

The "Restrict by Document Segment or Restrict by Date" option in LexisNexis performs the same function as "Field Restrictions" in Westlaw (see Exhibit 10–9). *That is, it allows you to limit your search for terms to specific portions of documents, such as the headnotes of a case or the title of a statute.*

To conduct a search using "Restrict Search," perform the following steps:

a. On the search page, select the "Restriction by Document Segment" option and type the term to be searched or date range.

b. The search will be limited to the terms within the sections of the document selected.

Restrict Search by Document Segment or Date

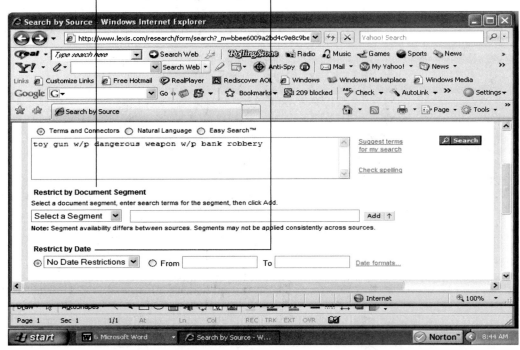

5. Search Results

The search results will list all the documents that match your search (see Exhibit 10–10 for a specific search result). You have several options for viewing any document listed.

a. Cite

To view the citations or bibliographic references of a document, click on "Cite" in the upper left corner of the screen.

b. KWIC™

If you want to view only the portions of the document that include the search terms surrounded, click on "KWIC" in the upper left corner of the screen. KWIC (key words in context) displays a window of 15–25 words on each side of your search words.

c. Full

To view the complete text of a document the search has retrieved, click on "Full" in the upper left corner of the screen.

d. Custom

To view only a portion of a document, such as the dissent in a court opinion or an annotation of a statute, click on "Custom." Select the segment of the field that you want to view.

e. FOCUS™

The "FOCUS" feature allows you to further narrow your search within your retrieved documents. Click on "FOCUS" above the retrieved document, type in the additional search terms, and click on "FOCUS."

Cite KWIC Full Custom   Focus   *Shepard's*   Print

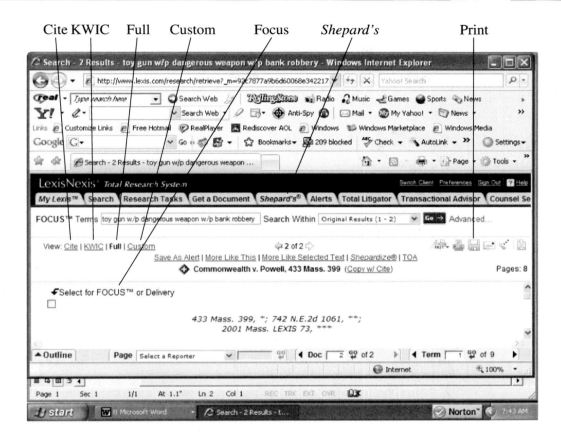

Exhibit 10–10
LexisNexis Case Law Search Result Screen— Single Case.
LexisNexis® Screen Captures reprinted with the permission of LexisNexis. LexisNexis and *Shepard's* are registered trademarks and Focus and KWIC are trademarks of Reed Elsevier Properties, Inc., used with the permission of LexisNexis.

f. Term

To move to any of your search terms while viewing a document in KWIC, click on the arrow next to the number in the bottom right lower navigation bar at the bottom right.

g. Outline

After you have retrieved a full document and you want to go immediately to a specific portion, such as the dissent, click on "Explore" on the bottom left of the page and select the part of the document that you want to view.

6. Updating Research—*Shepard's*® *Citations*

This service provides the history and treatment of a document necessary to verify its current status (see Exhibit 10–10). It also allows a researcher to locate additional cases, articles, and other secondary sources that have cited the document being researched. Cases are included in the service within 24 to 48 hours of their receipt.

Following is a summary of the main features of the *Shepard's*® *Citations Service*:

✦ *Coverage.* The service covers federal and state case law, federal and state statutory law, the *Code of Federal Regulations*, federal rules, U. S. patents, law reviews, and periodicals.

✦ *Shepard's Signal™.* LexisNexis uses a *Shepard's Signal* as an indicator of the current status of a document. The signals are similar to the status flags used by Westlaw. A red stop sign means that the document has received negative treatment, such as a case being reversed or overruled or a statute being repealed. A yellow triangle means that there is possible negative treatment, such as the case has been criticized or distinguished but not reversed or overruled. A diamond with a plus in it means that the document has received positive treatment, such as a case being followed or affirmed.

✦ *Information.* *Shepard's Citations Service* includes the history of a case, including the appellate history and citations to secondary sources such as ALR annotations and law review articles.

C. Finding Secondary Authority

LexisNexis, like Westlaw, provides access to thousands of secondary sources. There are databases for Am. Jur. 2d, ALR, and legal periodicals including law reviews, treatises, legislative history, and legal forms, just to name a few. Most of these databases are listed on under "Secondary Legal." You can also use "Search by Topic or Headnote" to find research materials within a specific area of law. Secondary sources for legal topics are available on the Analytical Materials tab.

The steps for performing a secondary authority search are generally the same as those used to conduct a primary authority search. That is, you can search by citation, terms and connectors, natural language, and so on.

Following are the basic steps for conducting a secondary authority search when you do not know the citation:

1. *State the issue or research question as specifically as possible in the context of the facts.*

2. *Formulate the terms and connectors or natural language search.*

3. *Locate the appropriate database.* Locate and click on the appropriate database on the Legal tab.

4. *Perform the search.* After the database page comes up, perform the search using terms and connectors, natural language, and so on.

D. Printing and Saving

LexisNexis provides several printing and saving options (see Exhibit 10–10). You can download documents to a document or disk, have them sent to an e-mail address or a fax number, or print them. Documents can be printed in single or dual column, with the search terms in bold or italics, among other options. In the upper right corner of the document, click on "Fast Print," "Print," "Download," "Fax," or "Email."

IV. LOISLAW

Loislaw is another commonly used commercial legal research service. Like Westlaw and LexisNexis, Loislaw provides access to thousands of databases. The databases include federal and state cases; statutory, constitutional, and administrative law; and other authority. The secondary authority databases include treatises, practical tools and forms from Wolters Kluwer companies—Aspen Publishers and CCH—State Bar Partners, and other sources, all of which cover a wide variety of practice areas. The secondary authority databases are not quite as extensive as those of Westlaw and LexisNexis. A list of Loislaw services and prices is available on its Web site at <http://www.loislaw.com>. Searches are conducted in a terms and connectors format similar to the one used in both Westlaw and LexisNexis.

V. VERSUSLAW

VersusLaw provides access to the *United States Code*; state statutes; full-text appellate decisions from 50 states, the U.S. Supreme Court from 1900, 13 federal circuits from 1930, and federal district courts; and specialty practice collections. Searches are conducted in a terms and connectors format. A list of VersusLaw services and prices is available on its Web site at <http://versuslaw.com>.

VI. KEY POINTS CHECKLIST: *Fee-Based Internet Research*

- The most frequently used commercial services are Westlaw, LexisNexis, and Loislaw. A familiarity with any of these sources will provide you with sufficient information to use other services.

- The most critical step in the research process is framing the issue in the context of the specific facts of the case (see Chapter 3). A well-framed issue, stated in the context of the facts, provides a researcher with the information necessary to conduct research using natural language or terms and connectors.

- A terms and connectors search has the disadvantage of requiring a familiarity with the use of the connectors. It has the advantage of allowing the researcher to tailor the search.

- As with any research, it is essential to determine if the results of electronic research are still good law. Westlaw, LexisNexis, and Loislaw include services that allow you to update your research.

VII. APPLICATION

A. Chapter Hypothetical

As James Redhorse learned in his legal research course, the first step of any research project is to identify the issue as concretely as possible in the context of the facts. He knows a concise statement of the issue will allow him to focus his search and identify the search terms. After considering the facts of the case and several drafts, his preliminary formulation of the issue is "Under Arizona law, may damages for emotional distress be recovered when an individual traps and kills a neighbor's pet and shows the dead pet to the owner causing the owner severe distress?" James knows the issue may become more refined as research is conducted.

The next step is to determine where to look. Will he look for statutory law, case law, or secondary authority? Although research normally begins with a search for a governing statute, James knows that recovery for emotional distress is usually governed by tort law and most torts are not statutory. He decides to check Arizona case law for a court opinion that has addressed this question.

Reviewing the issue, he concludes that a terms and connectors search should include *emotional distress, damages*, and *pet*. He chooses the Westlaw Arizona courts database and formulates his search as: "emotional distress" and damages and pet. The search results reveal no cases on point. This doesn't surprise James because Arizona doesn't have a large body of case law. This means he will have to look to the law from other jurisdictions.

Rather than search state by state, James decides to look for an ALR article that addresses the subject. If there is one, it will provide an analysis of the question and include relevant state statutory law, case law, and secondary authority. He selects the ALR database and enters the search: "emotional distress" and damages and pet. The results show more than 180 documents.

James doesn't want to wade through that many annotations, so he decides to edit his search by restricting the search to the titles of those ALR annotations that include his search terms. He clicks on "Edit Search" and using field restrictions, limits the search to titles that include the search terms.

The search reads: TI ("emotional distress" and damages and pet). The search results in one annotation: "Recovery of Damages for Emotional Distress Due to Treatment of Pets and Animals" by Jay M. Zitter, 91 ALR 5th 545.

This annotation answers the question. It summarizes all the case and statutory law that has addressed this question. It reveals that some states allow damages for emotional distress for the loss of a pet and some do not. With this information, James can review the cases that are factually close to Mrs. Burgess' case and prepare a memorandum to the senior partner summarizing the law.

B. Chapter 1 Hypothetical *Reins v. Stewart*

Vanessa's assignment is to locate a case that addresses the question of whether Mr. Stewart may be liable for battery. She reviews the issue to formulate her search query. The issue as determined in the Application section of Chapter 3 is "Under (name of state) tort law, does a battery occur when an individual, present at a battery, encourages the perpetrator of the battery by yelling, 'Hit him again, beat him,' but does not in any other way participate in the battery?" Assume Vanessa is using LexisNexis. Because the jurisdiction is New Mexico, she selects "States Legal-U.S.," then "New Mexico" and "NM Cases, Combined." Based upon the statement of the issue, she formulates a natural language search query as follows: "Does a battery occur when an individual present at a battery verbally encourages the perpetrator, but does not in any other way participate?" When she clicks on "Search," the case of *Rael v. Cadena* is located.

C. Chapter 2 Hypothetical *United States v. Canter*

Dustin's assignment is to locate a case where the court addresses the question of whether a fake weapon, such as a carved replica of a handgun, could be considered a dangerous weapon. Assume Dustin is using Westlaw and decides to perform a terms and connectors search. Because Mr. Cantor is charged under a federal statute, Dustin selects "U.S. Federal Materials," "Cases," and then "All Federal Cases after 1944." Based upon the statement of the issue, he formulates the following query: "dangerous weapon" /s "toy gun" or "fake gun" /s bank /s robbery. After typing this search query in the "Terms and Connectors box," 17 cases come up. One case directly on point is *United States v. Martinez-Jimenez*.

SUMMARY

The earlier chapters of the text focus on the techniques for conducting research using print resources such as texts and bound volumes. Chapter 9 discusses computer and Internet research in general. This chapter focuses on research using fee-based Internet resources. Although fee-based Internet resources are reliable, it is important to know how to research using print resources. Experienced researchers do not rely exclusively on fee-based Internet legal research.

This chapter presents an overview of legal research using the most frequently used commercial services: Westlaw, LexisNexis, and Loislaw. Although many other electronic research services are available, a familiarity with either Westlaw or LexisNexis provides sufficient information to use the other services.

There are differences between Westlaw, LexisNexis, and Loislaw, but the basic organization and research principles are the same. The services share the following features:

✦ Documents can be located by name, title, or citation.

✦ In Westlaw and LexisNexis, documents can be located by natural language, a search method that allows you to state the search query using plain English.

✦ Documents can be located by using terms and connectors.

✦ Searches can be conducted through reference to the tables of contents of research sources.

✦ In Westlaw and LexisNexis, documents can be located by focusing research on specific areas of law through Westlaw's Key Number and KeySearch services and LexisNexis's Search Advisor.

✦ Research may be updated through the use of Westlaw's KeyCite, LexisNexis's *Shepard's*, or Loislaw's GlobalCite services.

In addition to Westlaw, LexisNexis, and Loislaw, there are other commercial Web-based legal research services such as VersusLaw.

CHAPTER REFERENCES

INTERNET RESOURCES

In addition to Westlaw, LexisNexis, and Loislaw, there are other commercial Web-based legal research services such as VersusLaw and Commerce Clearing House (CCH). The Web site addresses for Westlaw, LexisNexis, Loislaw, VersusLaw, and CCH are as follows:

<http://www.westlaw.com>
<http://www.lexisnexis.com>
<http://loislaw.com>
<http://www.versuslaw.com>
<http://www.cch.com>

For additional materials, please go to the CD accompanying this book

For additional resources, visit our Web site at www.paralegal.delmar.cengage.com

CITATION

The 18th edition of the *Bluebook* and the *ALWD Citation Manual: A Professional System of Citation* provide that if the authority is readily available in print, cite to the print source. It is not necessary to reference the electronic source, such as Westlaw or LexisNexis. This rule applies unless the documents are not available in a printed source or are difficult to obtain, such as unpublished cases. Citation to electronic sources is discussed in detail in subsection IV. M. Electronic Resources of Chapter 11.

EXERCISES

Additional exercises are located on the Student CD-ROM accompanying the text and Online Companion.

For Assignments 1–7, use Westlaw.

ASSIGNMENT 1

The client is the chairman of the board of directors of an Ohio corporation. The board of directors has decided to merge the corporation with another Ohio corporation. The client wants to know if shareholder approval is required for the merger. Identify the Ohio statute that governs this question and what it provides concerning shareholder approval.

ASSIGNMENT 2

Perform Assignment 1 using your state law.

ASSIGNMENT 3

Your supervising attorney recalls that there was a 1989 Arkansas case where a county court judge was convicted in federal court of vote buying. After the U.S. Court of Appeals denied the appeal, the state circuit court declared the judge ineligible to hold public office. The judge claimed that he had received insufficient notice of the state court hearing because he had less than 24 hours notice to appear at the hearing. What is the name and citation of the case? Under the holding of the case, when is a person "convicted" for purposes of removal of a public official from office?

ASSIGNMENT 4

What is the citation of a 1993 ALR annotation that discusses the admissibility of polygraph test results in an action for malicious prosecution? What Am. Jur. 2, Evidence research references are listed? What Malicious Prosecution key numbers are referred to? What 1987 U.S. 6th Circuit Court of Appeals case held that generally the use of polygraph results to prove a party's innocence is prohibited?

ASSIGNMENT 5

Locate a 1998 Alabama criminal case where the defendant, Colbert, appealed his criminal conviction claiming that there was not sufficient evidence to support the conviction and his probation was revoked improperly.

A. What is the citation to the case?

B. What was the defendant convicted of?

C. Why was the case remanded?

ASSIGNMENT 6

Access "Key Numbers" from the top of the "Welcome" page.

A. What is the topic and key number that applies to the arrest and detention of juveniles charged with a crime?

B. Give the citation of a 1970 Oregon case that held that a reasonable search for weapons may be made when an officer takes temporary custody of a juvenile.

ASSIGNMENT 7

Select "KeyCite" on the "Welcome" page. For the case of *United States v. Martinez-Jimenez*, 864 F.2d 664 (9th Cir. 1989), what are the citations of the 1995 and 1993 cases listed under "Positive History" that have a yellow flag?

For Assignments 8–14, use LexisNexis.

ASSIGNMENT 8

While walking her dog in a city park, Client's dog was attacked by another dog. Before the dogs could be separated, Client's dog was severely injured and died later that day. Client's dog was on a leash and the other dog was not leashed. Client was very close to her pet and she wants to sue the owner of the other dog for the emotional distress she suffered as a result of witnessing the attack and death of her pet. Your supervisory attorney remembers that there was an Arizona case where, under similar facts, recovery was denied. Find the case.

ASSIGNMENT 9

There is a question in the Client's negligence case of whether there is an intervening force that may cut off Client's right to recover. What *Restatement 2d* sections define intervening force and superseding cause? How are the terms defined?

ASSIGNMENT 10

The Client and her husband are residents of the state of Georgia. She wants to sue for divorce claiming adultery. She does not want to file a no-fault divorce. Is adultery a ground for divorce in Georgia? If so, what is the statute and what does it provide? What law review article presents a survey of Georgia cases dealing with domestic relations?

ASSIGNMENT 11

Answer Assignment 10 using your state law.

ASSIGNMENT 12

Client's son was hitchhiking along a highway where hitchhiking was prohibited. Find an ALR annotation that addresses the construction and effect of antihitchhiking laws in an action for injury to a hitchhiker. What case mentioned in the annotation addresses an action by a hitchhiker to recover for injuries sustained when a driver went past him on an interstate, stopped, backed up along the shoulder to give him a ride, and hit him?

ASSIGNMENT 13

Select "Check a Citation." For the case of *Harris v. Cincinnati*, 79 Ohio App. 3d 163, 607 N.E. 2d 15 (1992),

how many citing decisions are listed? Are there any cases showing a negative history? How many law review and periodical references are listed?

ASSIGNMENT 14

Under federal law, what law governs murder? What is the penalty for murder in the first degree? What 1968 case addressed the constitutionality of this statute?

CHAPTER 11

Legal Citation

Outline

Learning Objectives

After completing this chapter, you should understand:

✦ The general citation rules that apply when citing most types of legal sources

✦ The specific citation rules that apply when citing primary authority, that is, case, constitutional, and enacted (statutory) law

✦ The specific citation rules that apply when citing secondary authority

Mike Myers is a second semester paralegal student enrolled in an introductory research and writing class. After a six-week introduction to basic research, the class is given an assignment that requires drafting a simple, one-issue legal research memorandum. The assignment involves the question of when a mother can lose her parental rights due to drug use and other misconduct. Students are instructed to include parallel citations in the case citations used in the memo. The instructor divided the class into groups, and Mike's group's assignment was to answer the question using Georgia law. Based on two Georgia cases and one statute, Mike prepared the rough draft of the memo. For the final draft, he had to make sure his citations are correctly presented. The authorities Mike found and the steps he took to ensure the citation formats were correct are discussed in the Application section of this chapter.

I. INTRODUCTION

A. In General

Chapters 4 through 8 addressed how to find primary and secondary authority. This chapter discusses how to present authority after you find it. Whenever a reference is made in legal writing to the law (primary authority) or a nonlaw source that a court may rely on (secondary authority), you must identify the source of the reference. The writer cannot simply say, "This is what the law provides" without a reference to the legal authority that supports the statement. Thus, when an argument is made that a certain legal principle governs a particular set of facts or legal question, a reference must be made to the source of the principle. This reference is called a **citation**.

A citation provides the information necessary for the reader to locate the reference, that is, the specific statute, court opinion, law review, or encyclopedia, thus allowing the reader to check the reference's content. Citations are usually required in court opinions, office legal memoranda, court briefs, and scholarly writings such as law review articles. They also may be included in general legal correspondence or other documents when there is reference to legal authority.

The information included in a citation must be correct. The writer serves no purpose by referring a reader to a source of information and incorrectly identifying the location of the source. The reader will not be pleased if he or she takes the time to look up the authority and the authority is not located at the page or volume indicated in the citation. It is important that citations be correct for several additional reasons:

✦ A citation that is incorrect in form or content sends the message that the drafter is either not careful or lacks education. If there are errors in citation, the reader may wonder if there are also errors in the substance of the research.

✦ Errors in documents submitted to a court may cause the judge to question the competence of the attorney and the quality and content of the research and analysis. Court rules require proper form, and improper citation exhibits a disregard for those rules and disrespect for the court.

✦ Opposing counsel may question the ability of the attorney to mount an effective opposition and be less inclined to settle a case.

✦ The writer's research and analysis skills may become suspect if research sources are not properly presented. Professional reputation is often determined by the quality of the work product.

B. *The Bluebook* and the *ALWD Citation Manual*

Unfortunately, no single standard set of rules governing citation form has been adopted by the jurisdictions in the United States. The main guide and source of authority on legal citations for the past 75 years has been *The Bluebook: A Uniform System of Citation* (*Bluebook*) published by the Harvard Law Review Association. It presents the rules and proper format for citing constitutions, statutes, regulations, rules, cases, and other legal sources such as legal encyclopedias and law reviews. Some states have adopted the *Bluebook* in whole or in part as the official citation reference for pleadings and papers filed in the state courts. Many states have adopted at least some citation rules that differ from the *Bluebook*, especially in the area of citation to state court opinions and statutes. Therefore, it is necessary to check the state rules whenever preparing a document to be submitted to a court.

The *Bluebook* is not designed as a teaching tool and many students, instructors, and practitioners find it difficult to use. As an alternative to the *Bluebook*, the Association of Legal Writing Directors created the *ALWD Citation Manual: A Professional System of Citation* (*ALWD*). The Association's members are professors from nearly all American law schools. An authority on American legal citation, Professor and Associate Dean Darby Dickerson of the Stetson University College of Law, drafted the *ALWD*. Aspen Publishers published the first edition in 2000. It is designed to be easy to understand and use by providing a single set of rules for all forms of legal writing. Within three months of its publication, the manual was adopted by 80 law schools and more than 35 paralegal schools. The second edition was published in 2003.

At the time of this publication, the *Bluebook* and the *ALWD* are the primary sources for rules on citation used by law and paralegal schools. Inasmuch as the *Bluebook* is composed of 415 pages and the *ALWD*, third edition, 572 pages, a detailed discussion of the citation rules of either text is beyond the scope of this chapter. The following discussion presents a brief review of the main rules of citation with references to rules from both the *ALWD* and the *Bluebook*. The goal of the chapter is to provide you with quick access to the main rules of *citation* in either authority. The discussion and examples are based upon *The Bluebook: A Uniform System of Citation* (18th ed. 2005) and the *ALWD Citation Manual: A Professional System of Citation* (3rd ed. 2006). The format of both texts begins with an introduction followed by the general/basic rules of citation, and then citation to primary sources (cases, constitutions, and statutes) and secondary sources. Because researchers most frequently refer to the citation rules for primary and secondary authority, the chapter presents those rules first, followed by the general rules of citation.

The *Bluebook* notes some differences between the citation format used when citing authorities in court documents and legal memoranda and the citation format used in scholarly pieces such as law review articles. Most of the differences involve the use of different typefaces. In the *ALWD*, the same format is used for all types of documents. The type of formal legal writing usually engaged in by practitioners, law students, and paralegals involves court documents and legal memoranda, rather than law review articles. Therefore, this chapter focuses on the citation format used in court documents and legal memoranda, and the examples are to citation forms used in those types of legal writing.

Most of the examples provided in the white pages of the *Bluebook* are for citation when writing a law review. The light blue pages of the *Bluebook*, called Bluepages, provide guidance on how to adapt the examples found throughout the body of the *Bluebook* to the drafting of legal memoranda and court documents. There are cross-references to the Bluepages in the margins of the *Bluebook* rules and tables. Also, at the end of the *Bluebook* is a Quick Reference section that provides examples of citation forms commonly used in court documents and legal memoranda.

II. PRIMARY AUTHORITY

This section presents an overview of rules of citation to be used when citing primary authority, that is, case, constitutional, and enacted (statutory) law. The citation format for rules such as procedural and evidentiary rules are also included in this section. The examples are to citation forms used in court documents and legal memoranda rather than law review articles. See Exhibit 11–1 for a chart listing the primary authority sources and the citation rule references.

The rules discussed in this section and in the following sections are referenced as follows: References to *The Bluebook: A Uniform System of Citation* are *Bluebook* R ___ (rule number) or *Bluebook* B___ (Bluepages number); references to the *ALWD Citation Manual: A Professional System of Citation* are *ALWD*-___ (rule number).

Primary Authority Citation Rules		
Authority	***Bluebook* Rules and Bluepages Notes (B)**	***ALWD* Rules**
Case Law	Rule 10 and B5	Rule 12
Constitutions	Rule 11 and B7	Rule 13
Statutory Law	Rule 12 and B5	Rule 14
Rules of Evidence and Procedure	Rule 12.8.3	Rule 17
Administrative Law	Rule 14	Rule 19
Secondary Authority Citation Rules		
American Law Reports (ALR)	Rule 16.6.5	Rule 24
Dictionaries	Rule 15.7	Rule 25
Legal Encyclopedias	Rule 15.7	Rule 26
Periodicals (Law Reviews, etc.)	Rule 16	Rule 23
Restatements	Rule 12.8.5	Rule 27
Treatises/Books	Rule 15	Rule 22

Exhibit 11–1
Primary and Secondary
Authority Citation Rule
References.

FOR EXAMPLE *Bluebook* R-2 refers to rule 2 of the *Bluebook*. *Bluebook* B1 refers to number 1 of the *Bluebook's* Bluepages. *ALWD* 1 refers to rule 1 of the *ALWD Citation Manual: A Professional System of Citation.*

The general rules governing each type of primary authority are listed following the subsection title. A detailed discussion of each rule is beyond the scope of this text.

Note: Although most of the citation conventions are the same in both manuals, there are differences between the *Bluebook* and the *ALWD Citation Manual*. Do not assume that you can substitute one for the other; always check the rules when preparing these citations.

If the citation rules of the jurisdiction where you are filing a brief or other court document require the use of the *Bluebook*, then you must cite according to the *Bluebook* rules. Do not substitute *ALWD* format if it differs from the *Bluebook*.

A. Case Law—*Bluebook* R-10 & B2 & B5; *ALWD*-12

The following is a list of the components of case citations with examples and a summary of the applicable rules. Citations to federal and state cases are similar in form.

1. Citation Components—*Bluebook* R-10.1; *ALWD*-12.1

The components of a case citation are the following:

1. The case name
2. The reporter in which the case is published (the volume number, abbreviation of the reporter, and page number where the case begins)

3. Pinpoint page if the citation is to a specific page

4. The parallel (unofficial) publication, if any (the volume number, abbreviation of the publication, and page number where the case begins)

5. The abbreviation for the court issuing the opinion, unless the issuing court is included in the reporter abbreviation

6. The year of the decision in parentheses

7. Subsequent history of the case, if any

Some examples are presented first with a ^ symbol indicating where spaces are placed, followed by the example without the space symbol.

FOR EXAMPLE | *Federal Court Decisions*
United States Supreme Court

United ^ States ^ v.^ Matlock, ^ 415 ^ U.S.^ 164 ^ (1974)
United States v. Matlock, 415 U.S. 164 (1974)

1. **United States v. Matlock**—Case name.

2. **415 U.S. 164**—The reporter in which the case is published: 415 is the volume number, 164 is the page number, and U.S. is the abbreviation of the case reporter.

3. No parallel publication is included in this citation.

4. The court issuing the opinion is not identified because it is apparent from the citation. *U.S. Reports* contains the opinions of the U.S. Supreme Court. Notice that in the next two examples the identity of the court issuing the opinion is included—9th Cir. and N.D. Ill.

5. **1974**—The year of the decision.

U.S. Court of Appeals

United ^ States ^ v. ^ Martinez-Jimenez, ^ 864 ^ F.2d ^ 664 ^ (9th Cir.^1989)
United States v. Martinez-Jimenez, 864 F.2d 664 (9th Cir. 1989)

U.S. District Court

United ^ States ^ v.^ Central ^ R.R.,^ 436^ F.^ Supp.^ 739 ^ (N.D.^ Ill.^1990)
United States v. Central R.R., 436 F. Supp. 739 (N.D. Ill. 1990)

State Court Decisions

Britton ^ v.^ Britton, ^ 100 ^ N.M.^ 424,^ 671^ P.2d ^1135 ^ (1983)
Britton v. Britton, 100 N.M. 424, 671 P.2d 1135 (1983)
Burnon^ v.^ State,^ 55 ^S.W.3d ^752^ (Tex.^ Crim.^ App.^ 2001)
Burnon v. State, 55 S.W.3d 752 (Tex. Crim. App. 2001)

1. **Britton v. Britton** and *Burnon v. State*—Case names.

2. **100 N.M. 424**—The state reporter in which the case is published: 100 is the volume number, 424 is the page number, and N.M. is the abbreviation of the case reporter; **55 S.W.3d 752**—The regional reporter where the Texas cases are published. Texas does not have a state reporter, therefore, there is no parallel citation.

3. **671 P.2d 1135**—The parallel (unofficial) publication: 671 is the volume number, 1135 is the page number, and P.2d is the abbreviation of the parallel publication.

4. The New Mexico court issuing the opinion is not identified because it is apparent from the citation. The decision was rendered by the New Mexico Supreme Court.

> If a court other than the New Mexico Supreme Court issued the decision, the initials of the court would be included with the year of the opinion, i.e., (Ct. App. 1983); **Tex. Crim. App.**—the Texas court that rendered the decision.
>
> 5. **1983 and 2001**—the year of the decisions.

2. Case Names—*Bluebook* R-10.2; *ALWD*-12.2

The *Bluebook*'s rules for abbreviating case names have many more exceptions than the *ALWD*; however, both books have numerous detailed rules governing case names. Always check the rules when preparing case citations. The following is a summary of the rules on case names. The case names may be italicized or underlined. The names are italicized in most of the examples in this chapter. (The *ALWD* provides that case names are printed the same in both court documents and other documents.)

a. Individual Names

Cite the last names of the individuals, not the first name.

FOR EXAMPLE	Correct: *Clothier v. Guillez*
	<u>Clothier v. Guillez</u>
	Incorrect: *Daniel J. Clothier v. Mary Guillez*

b. Organization and Business Names

Include an organization's full name. When a business has more than one legal designation (e.g., Co., Ltd., Corp., Inc.), use the first designation and omit the others.

FOR EXAMPLE	Correct: *Clothier v. David Johnson Packing Co.*
	Incorrect: *Clothier v. Johnson*
	Correct: *Davis v. Sally Smits Co.*
	Incorrect: *Davis v. Sally Smits Co., Inc.*

When an organization or business is commonly known by its initials, you may substitute the initials for the name. Do not use periods with the initials.

FOR EXAMPLE	Correct: *ACLU v. Houseman*
	Incorrect: *A.C.L.U. v. Houseman*

c. Abbreviations

The abbreviations to be used in party names are presented in Table T.6 of the *Bluebook* and Appendix 3 of the *ALWD*. Do not abbreviate names that are not listed.

FOR EXAMPLE	Corporation—Corp.; Market—Mkt.

d. Multiple Parties

If the case has multiple plaintiffs or defendants, include only the first party on each side of the case. Do not use *et al.* or *et ux.*, to indicate additional parties.

FOR EXAMPLE	Correct: *Pugh v. Holmes*
	Incorrect: *Pugh, Smith, Reasoner v. Holmes, Taylor, Johnson*
	Incorrect: *Pugh, et al. v. Holmes, et al.*

e. Consolidated Cases

If the case consists of more than one case consolidated together, list only the first case.

> **FOR EXAMPLE**   Correct: *Davis v. Outland*
> Incorrect: *Davis v. Outland, McCray v. Whensal*

f. United States

When the United States is a party, both the *Bluebook* and the *ALWD* provide that "America" should be omitted. The *Bluebook* requires that United States be spelled out. The *ALWD* provides that it be abbreviated.

> **FOR EXAMPLE**   *Bluebook: United States v. Leon*
> *ALWD: U.S. v. Leon*

g. State or Commonwealth

When citing a decision of a court of your state where the state or commonwealth is a party, refer only to the state, commonwealth, or people. Do not refer to the state such as "State of Colorado" or "Commonwealth of Massachusetts."

> **FOR EXAMPLE**   Correct: *State v. Benner*
> Incorrect: *State of Maine v. Benner*
> Correct: *Commonwealth v. Shae*
> Incorrect: *Commonwealth of Massachusetts v. Shae*

If you are referring to the decision of another state where the state or commonwealth is a party, refer to the party by state name and do not include "State of" or "Commonwealth of."

> **FOR EXAMPLE**   Correct: *Maine v. Benner*
> Incorrect: *State v. Benner*
> Correct: *Massachusetts v . Shae*
> Incorrect: *Commonwealth of Massachusetts v. Shae*

h. Geographical Terms

Include in the citation only the first geographical location in a party's name.

> **FOR EXAMPLE**   Correct: *Smith v. City of Boston*
> Incorrect: *Smith v. City of Boston, Massachusetts*
> Correct: *Smith v. County Commission*
> Incorrect: *Smith v. County Commission of Johnson County*

i. Procedural Phrases—In re, Ex parte, and Ex rel.

In re refers to an action that does not involve adversarial parties, but something such as an estate. *Ex parte* refers to an action on behalf of one party without contest by the other side such as a divorce where one party does not participate. *Ex rel.* refers to an action by one person on behalf of another such as a parent on behalf of a child. When using *ex rel.*, include the names of both parties. These phrases are included when they appear in case names.

> **FOR EXAMPLE** *In re Estate of Jones; Ex Parte Turner; New York ex rel. Smith v. Hardworth; Johnson ex rel. Casey v. Carrington*

j. "The"

Do not include "The" in a citation when it is the first word of a party name.

> **FOR EXAMPLE** Correct: *Los Angeles Times v. Jones*
> Incorrect: *The Los Angeles Times v. Jones*

k. Property

When property is a party, such as when the government is seizing property, include only the first listed piece of property.

> **FOR EXAMPLE** Correct: *Maine v. One 1998 Cadillac Seville*
> Incorrect: *Maine v. One 1998 Cadillac Seville, Serial No. 134998 and One 2001 Toyota Corolla, Serial No. 77564432*

l. Punctuation

The case name is followed by a comma (then the reporter information); the comma is not italicized or underlined.

> **FOR EXAMPLE** Correct: *Smith v. Jones,* or <u>Smith v. Jones</u>,
> Incorrect: *Smith v. Jones,* or <u>Smith v. Jones,</u>

m. Citations as Part of a Sentence

See subsection IV D2f Authorities Included in the Text of a Sentence later in this chapter.

3. Volume, Reporter, and Page—*Bluebook* R-10.3; *ALWD*-12.3 to 12.5

Following the case name in a citation is the reference to the reporter where the case is printed. This reference includes the volume number of the reporter and the page where the case begins. The volume number precedes the abbreviation for the reporter followed by the page of the case. The following is a summary of the rules governing citation to reporters. Note that local court rules may require differences in citation; therefore, always check the rules.

a. Abbreviations

Do not assume you know the abbreviations for the various reporters. Always consult either *Bluebook* Table T.1 or the *ALWD* Chart 12.1 and Appendix 2. Also, refer to the general rules governing abbreviations presented in section IV D Abbreviations later in this chapter.

b. Spacing

Refer to the general rules governing spacing presented in subsection IV D2 Spacing later in this chapter.

c. U.S. Supreme Court

Unless required by local rule, citation to decisions of the U.S. Supreme Court should be to the official reporter only, the *United States Reports*. A parallel citation to another reporter such as the *Supreme Court Reporter* or *United States Supreme Court Reports, Lawyers' Edition*, should not be included.

> **FOR EXAMPLE** Correct: *United States v. Matlock*, 415 U.S. 164 (1974).
>
> Incorrect: *United States v. Matlock*, 415 U.S. 164, 94 S. Ct. 988, 39 L. Ed. 2d 242 (1974). Note that this would be correct if the court rule required or allowed parallel citations.

If the *United States Reports* citation is not available, then you may cite to another reporter such as the *Supreme Court Reporter* (S. Ct.). The order of preference is to cite to the *Supreme Court Reporter* and if it is not available, then cite to *United States Supreme Court Reports, Lawyers' Edition*.

> **FOR EXAMPLE** If the opinion in the previous example was not yet available in the *United States Reports*, a proper citation would be: *United States v. Matlock*, __U.S.__, 94 S. Ct. 988, (1974).

d. U.S. Court of Appeals

Decisions of the U.S. Court of Appeals are cited to the *Federal Reporter*. Note that the circuit that rendered the decision is included in the citation in parentheses.

> **FOR EXAMPLE** *United States v. Martinez-Jimenez*, 864 F.2d 664 (9th Cir. 1989)

e. U.S. District Courts

Decisions of the U.S. District Courts are cited to the *Federal Supplement*. Note that the district that rendered the decision is included in the citation in parentheses.

> **FOR EXAMPLE** *United States v. Central R.R.*, 436 F. Supp. 739 (N.D. Ill. 1990)

f. State Court and Parallel Citations

The format and abbreviations for citing state court decisions are presented in Table T.1 of the *Bluebook* and the *ALWD* Appendix 1. Again, be sure to check local rules. The general rule for state court decisions is to cite to the relevant regional reporter.

> **FOR EXAMPLE** *Guilbear v. Guilbear*, 326 So.2d 654 (La. App. 1976)

Many state court decisions are published in a regional reporter and a state reporter. When a citation includes a reference to more than one reporter, it is called a parallel citation. Generally a parallel citation is used only when it involves a citation to a state court case in a document submitted to a court in that state. Check the state court citation rules to determine when parallel citations are required.

When a parallel citation is required, cite the official reporter before the unofficial reporter, and separate each citation with a comma and one space.

> **FOR EXAMPLE** *Race Fork Coal v. Turner*, 5 Va. App. 350, 363 S.E.2d 423 (1985).

g. Page Numbers

The page number on which the case begins follows the reporter abbreviation. If the reference is to a specific page within the case, the reference to the specific page (pinpoint citations) follows the initial page reference. See Subsection IV G, Page Numbers (Pinpoint Citations) later in this chapter.

FOR EXAMPLE	*Guilbear v. Guilbear*, 326 So.2d 654, 658 (La. App. 1976)
	Race Fork Coal v. Turner, 5 Va. App. 350, 352, 363 S.E.2d 423, 425 (1985)

Note that in the second example the pinpoint citation is included with both the state and the parallel regional reporter citations.

Some of the West reporters, such as the *Supreme Court Reports*, include throughout the text of reported cases cross-references to the pages in the official reporter. This cross-reference system is called **star paging**. It saves you the time of looking up a case in more than one reporter when citing page numbers in parallel citations. The cross-reference appears as an upside down *T* with the page number ($\perp$234) and is inserted in the text to indicate the beginning of a page in an official reporter.

FOR EXAMPLE	"Thus, the tolling provision does$\perp$234 not apply, and count two is subject to the two-year statute of limitations and was properly dismissed." Page 234 of the official reporter begins with "not apply."

h. Cases Not Yet Reported—Slip Opinions

A case may be unreported or not yet published in a reporter and may be available only as a separate slip opinion or in loose-leaf form. When this is the situation, the citation should include the case name, docket number, court abbreviation, and date of disposition.

FOR EXAMPLE	*Jason v. Kelly*, No. 22-231 (Colo. App. Aug. 15, 2002)

4. Date and Court Abbreviation—*Bluebook* R-10.4 & 10.5; *ALWD*-12.5 & 12.6

In parentheses following the reporter and page citation are the court abbreviation (if necessary) and the date on which the case was decided. If the decision is by the U.S. Supreme Court or highest court of a state, you do not have to insert the court abbreviation. The date appears alone in parentheses. The fact that the date alone appears in the parentheses tells the reader it is the highest court. The information in the parentheses is separated from the reporter page by a space. There is no comma.

FOR EXAMPLE	*United States v. Matlock*, 415 U.S. 164 (1974);
	Kline v. Angle, 216 Kan. 328, 532 P.2d 1093 (1975)

For any other court decision, include the court abbreviation. The abbreviations are in the *Bluebook* Tables T.1, T.7, and T.10 and the *ALWD* Appendices 1 and 4.

FOR EXAMPLE	*United States v. Central R.R.*, 436 F. Supp. 739 (N.D. Ill. 1990);
	Burnon v. State, 55 S.W.3d 752 (Tex. Crim. App. 2001)

The court abbreviation is not required if the court that decided the case is apparent from the name of the reporter.

> **FOR EXAMPLE**   *Race Fork Coal v. Turner*, 5 Va. App. 350, 353, 363 S.E.2d 423, 425 (1985).
> It is apparent from the citation (Va. App.) that the court is the Virginia
> Court of Appeals.

5. Subsequent History—*Bluebook* R-10.7; *ALWD*-12.8

The *Bluebook* and the *ALWD* provide that the subsequent history should be included in the citation unless it refers to the history on remand, a denial of rehearing, or a denial of certiorari or similar discretionary appeals (where the cited case is more than two years old). The *ALWD* Rule 12.8(a) includes an exhaustive list of subsequent history actions that should be included. The subsequent history is placed after the full citation. Place a comma after the court and date parenthetical, followed by the italicized history designation, a comma, and the citation.

> **FOR EXAMPLE**   *Jackson v. State*, 225 Ga. 790, 167 S.E.2d 628 (1969), *rev'd, Furman v.*
> *Georgia*, 408 U.S. 238 (1972)

6. Prior History—*Bluebook* R-10.7; *ALWD*-12.9

The prior history of a case is not required and should be included in a citation only when it is significant to a point presented in your writing. Place the prior history after the full citation.

> **FOR EXAMPLE**   *Furman v. Georgia*, 408 U.S. 238 (1972), *rev'g, Jackson v. State*, 225 Ga.
> 790, 167 S.E.2d 628 (1969)

7. Parenthetical Information—Concurring, Dissenting, and Plurality Opinion—*Bluebook* R-10.6; *ALWD*-12.11

If the reference in your writing is to a part of an opinion other than the majority opinion, you must so indicate in a parenthetical following the full citation. You may also include parenthetically information about the weight of the case such as the size of the majority. Insert one space, without a comma, between the court and date parenthetical of the full citation and the parenthetical containing the additional information. If the information in the parenthetical is not a full sentence, do not include final punctuation, such as a period, in the parenthetical.

> **FOR EXAMPLE**   *United States v. Leon*, 468 U.S. 897 (1984) (Powell, J., dissenting);
> *United States v. Leon*, 468 U.S. 897 (1984) (5-4 decision)

8. Short Citation Format— *Bluebook* B5.2; *ALWD*-12.21

After a case has been cited in full, several short citation formats may be used depending on the situation. Do not include subsequent or prior history with a short citation. If the use of *id.* is appropriate (see subsection IV I1 *Id.* as a Short Citation later in this chapter), it is the preferred short citation format.

> **FOR EXAMPLE**   *Id.* at 755

If *id.* cannot be used and the case name or part of the case name *is not* included in the sentence, then use one party's name, the volume number, reporter, and page reference. Use the first party's name unless it would be confusing.

> FOR EXAMPLE | Full Citation: *Burnon v. State*, 55 S.W.3d 752 (Tex. Crim. App. 2001)
> Short Citation: *Burnon*, 55 S.W.3d at 755

When making a reference to the case in general rather than to a specific page, do not use "at."

> FOR EXAMPLE | Full Citation: *Burnon v. State*, 55 S.W.3d 752 (Tex. Crim. App. 2001)
> Short Citation: *Burnon*, 55 S.W.3d 752

If the case name or part of the case name is included in the sentence, then use only the volume number, reporter, and page reference.

> FOR EXAMPLE | In *Burnon* the court held that the defendant had the required intent.
> 55 S.W.3d at 755 (or 55 S.W.3d 752 if the reference is to the case in general).

If the case has a parallel citation, the short citation includes the parallel citations.

> FOR EXAMPLE | Full Citation: *Race Fork Coal v. Turner*, 5 Va. App. 350, 363 S.E.2d 423 (1985)
> Short Citation: *Race Fork Coal*, 5 Va. App. at 355, 363 S.E.2d at 427. The
> *ALWD* also allows reference to the regional reporter only—Race Fork Coal, 363 S.E.2d at 427.

The Bluepages note 5.2 allows the use of *id.* as a short form with parallel citations. The *ALWD* Rule 12.21(f) states that the use of *id.* "is not appropriate with parallel citations."

> FOR EXAMPLE | Full Citation: *Race Fork Coal v. Turner*, 5 Va. App. 350, 363 S.E.2d 423 (1985)
> Short Citation: *Bluebook: Id.* at 355, 363 S.E.2d at 427

9. Neutral/Public Domain Citations—*Bluebook* R-10.3.3; *ALWD*-12.16

Court decisions are increasingly available through court Web sites or other sources as public domain citations (also referred to as neutral or vendor neutral citations). These citations do not refer to a particular vendor source such as a West, a Thomson business reporter. When such citations are available in a jurisdiction, you must check the local rule to determine the citation format and whether the neutral citation is required. See *Bluebook* Table T.1 and *ALWD* Appendix 2. The standard neutral citation includes the case name, year of the decision, court abbreviation, case number, and citation to a reporter or online source.

> FOR EXAMPLE | *State v. Foster*, 1998-NMCA-163, 976 P.2d 852. The year published is
> 1998. NMCA is the court—the New Mexico Court of Appeals. The last
> number, 163, is the case number. The reporter citation is 976 P.2d 852.

10. Cases—Electronic Sources

See subsection IV M Electronic Sources later for citations to electronic sources.

B. Constitutions—*Bluebook* R-11; *ALWD*-13

Constitutions are usually composed of articles and amendments. According to the *Bluebook*, the citation form for a constitution consists of the abbreviated name of the constitution, the article or amendment number, and the section number. The *ALWD* requires the abbreviated name of the constitution and a pinpoint reference (the pinpoint reference is the article or amendment number and the section number). Regardless of these descriptive differences, the citation format is the same in both the *Bluebook* and the *ALWD*. The *Bluebook* provides that constitutional subdivisions should be abbreviated according to Table T. 16; the *ALWD* provides that the jurisdictional and subdivision abbreviations in Appendix 3 should be used. Each example is presented first with a ^ symbol indicating where spaces are placed, followed by the example without the space symbol.

> **FOR EXAMPLE**   U.S.^ Const.^ art. ^ IV, ^ § ^ 3
> U.S. Const. art. IV, § 3
> Conn.^ Const. ^ art. ^ XII,^ § ^ 1
> Conn. Const. art. XII, § 1

In the examples, the elements of the citation are as follows:

- ✦ **U.S. Const.; Conn. Const.**—The abbreviated name
- ✦ **art. IV; art. XII**—The article number
- ✦ **§ 3; § 1**—The section number (pinpoint reference)

Include in parentheses information about an article or amendment if the provision has been repealed or superseded.

> **FOR EXAMPLE**   U.S. Const. amend XVIII (repealed 1933 by U.S. Const. amend. XXI).

The only short-form citation appropriate for use with constitutional citations is *id*. If the use of *id*. is not appropriate (see subsection IV I1 Id. as a Short Citation later), then the full citation must be given.

C. Statutory Law—*Bluebook* R-12 & B6; *ALWD*-14

Statutes may be cited to the official or unofficial code, session law, or secondary sources. The preference is to cite to the official code, then the unofficial code if the citation is not available in the official code; if the citation is not available in the official or unofficial codes, then to the session law. The abbreviations and formats for codes and session laws are presented in *Bluebook* Table T.1 and *ALWD* Appendix 1.

1. General Rules when Citing Statutes

The following rules apply when citing both federal and state statutes.

a. Main Text and Supplements

If the cited material is taken from the main text, the year of the volume of the text is placed in parentheses at the end of the citation (the year the volume was published; it usually appears on the spine of the volume). If the cited material appears only in the supplement, you must so indicate in the parentheses with the date. If the cited material is taken from the main text and the supplement, it must be indicated with the date.

> **FOR EXAMPLE**   Citation from main text: 15 U.S.C. § 7 (1988)
> Citation from supplement only: 15 U.S.C. § 7 (Supp. 2002)
> Citation from main text and supplement: 15 U.S.C. § 7 (1988 & Supp. 2002)
> Citation from main text and supplement, unofficial commercial publisher: 15 U.S.C.A. § 7 (West 1984 & Supp. 2002)

b. Section Symbol (§) and Multiple Sections

The section symbol (§) is used to indicate a section of a statute. Note, however, that you may not use the symbol to start a sentence. In such cases the word *section* is used.

> **FOR EXAMPLE**   Correct: "Section 2253 of the Act provides . . . ."
>
> Incorrect: "§ 2253 of the Act provides . . . ."

Refer to subsection IV L Sections and Paragraphs later for the rules on citing multiple sections.

c. Name of Act

Although it is not required, the name of the act may be included in the citation. In the examples in the *Bluebook*, the name of the act is in regular print. In the *ALWD*, Rule 14.2(g) provides that the name should be in italics.

> **FOR EXAMPLE**   Robinson-Patman Act, 15 U.S.C. § 7 (1988)—*Bluebook*
>
> *Robinson-Patman Act*, 15 U.S.C. § 7 (1988)—*ALWD*

2. Federal Statutes—*Bluebook* R-12; *ALWD*-14.2

The federal statutes of general public interest are printed in three separate publications:

- ✦ *United States Code* (U.S.C.)—the official code
- ✦ *United States Code Annotated* (U.S.C.A.)—West, a Thomson business
- ✦ *United States Code Service* (U.S.C.S.)—LexisNexis

The citation format for federal statutes is composed of the following elements:

1. Title number
2. Code abbreviation
3. Section symbol (§)
4. Section number
5. Publisher if it is a commercial publication—in parentheses
6. The year of the publication or supplement (the year the volume was published; usually appears on the spine of the volume)—in parentheses

> **FOR EXAMPLE**   Official code: 15 ^ U.S.C.^ § ^ 7 ^ (1988)
>   15 U.S.C. § 7 (1988)
>
> Unofficial codes: 15 U.S.C.A. § 7 (West 1984)
>   15 U.S.C.S. § 7 (LexisNexis 1984)
>
> 1. **15**—Title number
> 2. **U.S.C., U.S.C.A, and U.S.C.S.**—Abbreviated name of the codes
> 3. **§ 7**—Section symbol and number
> 4. **(1988) (West 1984) (LexisNexis 1984)**—The year of the publication and publisher for unofficial codes

When citing to the Internal Revenue Code, substitute I.R.C. for U.S.C. and omit the title number.

> **FOR EXAMPLE**   Correct: I.R.C. § 100 (1994)
>
> Incorrect: 26 U.S.C. § 100 (1994)

a. Short Citation Format State and Federal Statutes—Bluebook R-12.9; ALWD-14.5

If the use of *Id.* is appropriate (see subsection IV I1 *Id.* as a Short Citation later), it is the preferred short citation format. Otherwise, the short citation is the full citation format minus the parenthetical information.

> **FOR EXAMPLE** Full Citation: 15 U.S.C. § 7 (1988 & Supp. 2002); Minn. Stat. § 519 (1990)
>
> Short Citations: 15 U.S.C. § 7; *Id.* § 7; Minn. Stat. § 519; *Id.* § 519

3. State Statutes—*Bluebook* R-12; *ALWD*-14.4

The citation form for state statutes varies from state to state. The abbreviations and formats for state statutes are presented in *Bluebook* Table T.1 and *ALWD* Appendix 1. Also note that some states have local citation rules that require a citation format different from that presented in the *Bluebook* and the *ALWD*. The local court rules should be consulted for the proper citation format. The local rules are included in Appendix 2 of the *ALWD*.

The citation format for state statutes usually includes the following elements:

1. Name of the code
2. Section symbol (§)
3. Chapter/title/section number
4. Publisher if it is a commercial publication—in parentheses
5. The year of the publication or supplement (the year the volume was published; usually appears on the spine of the volume)—in parentheses

> **FOR EXAMPLE** Official Code: Minn.^ Stat.^ § ^519^ (1990)
>   Minn. Stat. § 519 (1990)
>
> Unofficial Code: Minn. Stat. Ann. § 519 (West 1991)
>
> 1. **Minn. Stat**.—Name of the code
> 2. **§**—Section symbol
> 3. **519**—Section number
> 4. **West**—The publisher of the unofficial code in the second example
> 5. **1990 & 1991**—The year of the publications in both examples

Some states such as California identify portions of their codes by subject matter rather than by title. For those states, the subject matter code is included in the citation.

> **FOR EXAMPLE** Cal. Corp. Code § 200 (West 1986); Tex. Fam. Code Ann. § 2.101 (Vernon 1993)

4. Session Laws—*Bluebook* R-12.4; *ALWD*-14.6 to 14.8

If a citation is not available in the official or unofficial codes, then it is appropriate to cite to the session law. This may occur when a recently passed law has not yet been published in the official or unofficial codes. As with state statutes, the citation form for session laws varies from state to state. The abbreviations and formats for state session laws are presented in *Bluebook* Table T.1 and *ALWD* Appendix 1.

The basic elements of a federal session law citation are the following:

1. Name or title of the act may be included; it is optional. In the *ALWD* example, the name/title is italicized. In the *Bluebook* Quick Reference examples, the name/title is not italicized or underlined.

2. Law abbreviation and number.

3. Pinpoint reference when citing a specific section.

4. Volume, statute, and initial page number.

5. Pinpoint page reference when referring to a specific page.

6. Date—year (in parentheses) of the cited volume of the Statutes at Large.

> **FOR EXAMPLE** Uniformed Services Former Spouses Protection Act, Pub. L. No. 101-510, § 554, 104 Stat. 1569, 1572 (1993)
>
> 1. **Uniformed Services Former Spouses Protection Act**—Name or title of the act italicized or underlined
> 2. **Pub. L. No. 101-510**—Law abbreviation and number
> 3. **§ 554**—Pinpoint reference to a specific section
> 4. **104 Stat. 1569**—Volume, statute, and initial page number
> 5. **1572**—Pinpoint page reference to a specific page
> 6. **1993**—Date

D. Rules of Evidence and Procedure—*Bluebook* R-12.8.3; *ALWD*-17

The *Bluebook* rule governing citations to evidentiary and **procedural rules** differs from the *ALWD* rule. The *Bluebook* provides that the citation should include the abbreviated name of the rule and the number of the rule.

> **FOR EXAMPLE**
>
> | | |
> |---|---|
> | Fed. R. Civ. P. 4 | Rule 4 of the Federal Rules of Civil Procedure |
> | Fed. R. Evid. 407 | Rule 407 of the Federal Rules of Evidence |
> | Fed. R. Crim. P. 18 | Rule 18 of the Federal Rules of Criminal Procedure |

The *ALWD* rule states that the citation should include, in addition to the abbreviated name and rule number, the name of the publisher if the source is other than an official code and the year of the publication, both in parentheses.

> **FOR EXAMPLE**
>
> | | |
> |---|---|
> | Fed. R. Civ. P. 4 (2001) | Rule 4 of the Federal Rules of Civil Procedure |
> | Fed. R. Evid. 407 (West 2002) | Rule 407 of the Federal Rules of Evidence, published by West, a Thomson business |
> | Fed. R. Crim. P. 18 (2001) | Rule 18 of the Federal Rules of Criminal Procedure |

E. Administrative Law—*Bluebook* R-14; *ALWD*-19

The components of citations to administrative rules or regulations are the following:

1. The title (topic or agency) number in the code publication
2. The abbreviated name of the publication (e.g., *Code of Federal Regulations*—C.F.R.; *Federal Register*—Fed. Reg.)
3. The section number or page number of the rule or regulation
4. The year of the publication

FOR EXAMPLE	27 C.F.R. § 20.235 (1988)
	48 Fed. Reg. 37,315 (1983)

1. **27 & 48**—The title (topic or agency) number
2. **C.F.R. & Fed. Reg.**—The abbreviated name of the publication
3. **§ 20.235 & 37,315**—The section number or page number
4. **1988 & 1983**—The year of the publication

III. SECONDARY AUTHORITY

This section presents an overview of rules of citation to be used when citing secondary authority, that is, sources a court may rely on that are not the law (not primary authority). The examples are to citation forms used in court documents and legal memoranda rather than law review articles. See Exhibit 11–1 for a chart listing the secondary authority sources and the citation rule references.

A detailed discussion of the citation rules for each type of secondary authority is beyond the scope of this text. Therefore, this section presents the citation format for the most commonly used secondary authorities. As with the previous sections, there are differences between the *Bluebook* and the *ALWD* Citation Manual. Do not assume that you can substitute one for the other.

A. American Law Reports—*Bluebook* R-16.6.5; *ALWD*-24

1. Full Citation Format

The components of an *American Law Report* (ALR) citation are the following:

1. The full name of the author
2. The word *Annotation*

Note: The *ALWD* omits the use of *Annotation* following the author name.

3. The title (italicized or underlined)
4. The volume number
5. The abbreviated name of the publication
6. The page number where the annotation begins (followed by the pinpoint page if a specific page is referred to, i.e., 852, 860)
7. The year of the publication

FOR EXAMPLE	Michael J. Weber, Annotation, *Application of Statute of Limitations to Actions for Breach of Duty in Performing Services of Public Accountant,*

7 A.L.R.5th 852 (1992).

1. **Michael J. Weber**—Full name of the author
2. **"Annotation"**—Included if using the *Bluebook*; not included if using the *ALWD*
3. ***Application of Statute of Limitations to Actions for Breach of Duty in Performing Services of Public Accountant***—The title (italicized or underlined)
4. **7**—The volume number
5. **A.L.R.5th**—The abbreviated name of the publication—no spaces
6. **852**—The page number where the annotation begins
7. **1992**—The year of the publication

2. Short Citation Format

Use *id.* if appropriate (see subsection IV I1 *Id.* as a Short Citation later). If *id.* is not appropriate, include the author's last name, volume number, ALR series, "at," and the pinpoint reference.

FOR EXAMPLE	*Id.* at 861; Weber, 7 A.L.R.5th at 861

B. Legal Dictionary—*Bluebook* R-15.7; *ALWD-25*

1. Full Citation Format

A legal dictionary citation should include the following:

1. Author (if any)
2. The full name of the dictionary (underlined or italicized)
3. Page of the definition—no comma after name of the dictionary and the page
4. Editor—only required in the *ALWD* format—beginning of parentheses
5. Edition
6. Publisher—only required in the *ALWD* format
7. The year of the publication—end of parentheses

FOR EXAMPLE	*Bluebook* format:
	Black's Law Dictionary 451 (7th ed. 1992)

1. ***Black's Law Dictionary***—The full name of dictionary (italicized or underlined)
2. **451**—Page of the definition
3. **7th ed. 1992**—Edition and the year of the publication

FOR EXAMPLE	*ALWD* format:
	Black's Law Dictionary 451 (Bryan A. Garner ed., 7th ed., West 1992)

1. ***Black's Law Dictionary***—The full name of dictionary (italicized or underlined)
2. **451**—Page of the definition
3. **Bryan A. Garner ed.**—Name of editor
4. **7th ed.**—Edition
5. **West**—Publisher
6. **1992**—The year of the publication

2. Short Citation Format

Use *id.* if appropriate (see subsection IV I1 *Id.* as a Short Citation later). If *id.* is not appropriate, repeat the name and the page number.

FOR EXAMPLE	*Id.* at 451; *Black's Law Dictionary* at 451

C. Legal Encyclopedia—*Bluebook* R-15.7; *ALWD-26*

1. Full Citation Format

A full citation to a legal encyclopedia should contain the following:

1. The volume number of the encyclopedia
2. The abbreviated name of the encyclopedia, usually either Am. Jur. 2d or C.J.S. (no underlining or italics)
3. The title or topic name (italicized or underlined)
4. The section symbol (§) and section number within the article
5. The year of the publication in parentheses

> **FOR EXAMPLE** 88 C.J.S. *Trial* § 105 (1980)
> 59A Am. Jur. 2d *Partnership* § 925 (Supp. 1995)
>
> 1. **88 and 59A**—The volume number of the encyclopedia
> 2. **C.J.S. and Am. Jur. 2d**—The abbreviated name of the encyclopedia
> 3. ***Trial* and *Partnership***—The topic name (italicized)
> 4. **§ 105 and § 925**—The section symbol and section number within the article
> 5. **1980 and Supp. 1995**—The year of the publication

2. Short Citation Format

Use *id.* if appropriate (see subsection IV I1 *Id.* as a Short Citation later). If *id.* is not appropriate, repeat the full citation minus the date.

> **FOR EXAMPLE** *Id.* § 925; *Id.* § 105; 59A Am. Jur. 2d *Partnership* § 925; 88 C.J.S. *Trial* § 105

D. Periodicals—Law Review/Journal Citations—*Bluebook* R-16; *ALWD-23*

1. Full Citation Format

The following are the components of a law review, journal, or other periodical citation:

1. The full name of the author
2. The title of the article (italicized or underlined)
3. The volume number
4. The abbreviated title of the periodical
5. The page number where the article begins (followed by the pinpoint page if a specific page is referred to, i.e., 159, 165)
6. The year of the publication in parentheses

> **FOR EXAMPLE** Patricia W. Bennett, After White v. Illinois: Fundamental Guarantees to a Hollow Right to Confront Witnesses, 40 Wayne L. Rev. 159 (1993).
>
> 1. **Patricia W. Bennett**—The full name of the author
> 2. ***After White v. Illinois: Fundamental Guarantees to a Hollow Right to Confront Witnesses***—The title of the article
> 3. **40**—The volume number
> 4. **Wayne L. Rev.**—The abbreviated title of the periodical

5. **159**—The page number where the article begins

6. **1993**—The year of the publication

2. Short Citation Format

Use *id.* if appropriate (see subsection IV I1 *Id.* as a Short Citation later). If *id.* is not appropriate, include the author's last name, volume number, periodical abbreviation, "at," and the pinpoint reference.

> **FOR EXAMPLE** *Id.* at 165; Bennett, 40 Wayne L. Rev. at 165

E. Restatements—*Bluebook* R-12.85; *ALWD-27*

1. Full Citation Format

A citation to a *Restatement* should include the following components:

1. The full name and edition of the *Restatement*. In the *ALWD*, the full name and edition is italicized or underlined, including a subtitle if the reference is to a subtitle.

2. The section symbol (§) and number of the *Restatement*.

3. The year of the publication in parentheses.

> **FOR EXAMPLE** *Bluebook*—Restatement (Second) of Judgments § 28 (1982)
>
> *ALWD*—*Restatement (Second) of Judgments* § 28 (1982)
>
> *Bluebook*—Restatement (Second) of Torts: Products Liability § 52 (1989)
>
> *ALWD*—*Restatement (Second) of Torts: Products Liability* § 52 (1989)

1. **Restatement (Second) of Judgments**—The full name of the Restatement and the edition; Restatement (Second) of Torts: Products Liability—The full name of the *Restatement*, edition, and subtitle

2. **§ 28 and § 52**—The section numbers

3. **1982 and 1989**—The year of the publications

2. Short Citation Format

Use *id.* if appropriate (see subsection IV I1 *Id.* as a Short Citation later); otherwise, repeat the full citation minus the date.

> **FOR EXAMPLE** *Id.* § 28; *Restatement (Second) of Judgments* § 28

F. Treatises/Books—*Bluebook* R-15; *ALWD-22*

1. Full Citation Format

Treatise and book citations should include the following:

1. The volume number if there is more than one volume

2. The full name of the author or editor if a name is given

3. The full title of the publication as it appears on the title page, in italics or underlined

4. Number of the section, paragraph, or page if you are referring to a specific number, paragraph, or page

5. The editor if there is an editor, the edition or series number of the book if not the first edition, and the publisher (the *Bluebook* does not require the inclusion of the publisher)—beginning of parentheses

6. The year of the publication—end of parentheses

> **FOR EXAMPLE** 6A Richard R. Powell, *Powell on Real Property* ¶ 899 (Patrick J. Rohan ed. Matthew Bender 1994)

1. **6A**—The volume number
2. **Richard R. Powell**—The full name of the author
3. ***Powell on Real Property***—The full title of the publication as it appears on the title page
4. **¶ 899**—The number of the paragraph
5. **(Patrick J. Rohan ed., Matthew Bender 1994)**—The editor, publisher, and year of the publication. This is the first edition, therefore, there is no edition number such as 3d ed

2. Short Citation Format

Use *id.* if appropriate (see subsection IV I1 *Id.* as a Short Citation later). If *id.* is not appropriate, include the author's last name, title, "at," and the pinpoint reference.

> **FOR EXAMPLE** *id.* ¶ 899; Powell, *Powell on Real Property* ¶ 899

IV. GENERAL RULES OF CITATION

This section presents an overview of basic rules of citation to be used when citing most legal sources. The general rule or rules governing each area are listed following the subsection title. See Exhibit 11–2 for a chart listing the general rules of citation and the citation rule references. A detailed discussion of each rule is beyond the scope of this text.

General Rules of Citation		
Topic	***Bluebook* Rules and Bluepages Notes (B)**	***ALWD* Rules**
Abbreviations	Rule 6 Tables T.5 to T.16 & BT1	Rule 2 Appendices 3 to 5
Capitalization	Rule 8 & B10.6	Rule 3
Electronic Sources	Rule 18	Rules 38 to 42
Internal Cross References (*supra* and *infra*)	Rule 3.6	Rule 10
Italics and Underscoring	B.2	Rule 1.3
Page Numbers (Pinpoint Citations)	Rules 3.3 to 3.5	Rules 5.2 to 5.4
Placement of Citations in Sentences and Clauses	B.2	Rule 43.1
Quotations	Rule 5	Rules 47 to 49
Sections and Paragraphs (§, ¶)	Rule 3.4	Rule 6
Short Citations (*id.*, *supra*, hereinafter)	Rule 4, B5.2, B6.2, B8.2, B9.2, & B10.5	Rules 11.2 to 11.4
Signals (*e.g.*, *see*, *accord*, etc.)	Rules 1.2 to 1.5	Rules 44 to 46
String Citations	Rule 1.2	Rule 43.3(a)

Exhibit 11–2
Rule References to General Rules of Citation.

A. Typeface—*Bluebook* R-2 & B2; *ALWD*-1.1

Bluebook rule 2 requires different typeface conventions and the use of large and small capital letters for citations in law reviews and other writings such as books. Bluepages note 2 covers the use of italics/underscores in court documents and legal memoranda. *ALWD* Rule 1.1 does not distinguish between types of documents and states that ordinary type and italics or underscores should be used in all legal writing. The use of italics or underscores is discussed in the next subsection.

B. Italics and Underscoring—*Bluebook* B2; *ALWD*-1.3

These rules present a summary of the items that should be underscored or italicized. The rules governing each type of item should be checked for other provisions that may govern the use of underscoring or italics.

> **FOR EXAMPLE** When citing cases, in addition to these rules, the separate rules governing case names should be checked for other requirements, such as what names are used.

The rules are referenced next to the subject in the following list.
Items that should be *italicized* or <u>underscored</u>:

1. Case names—*Bluebook* R-10.2; *ALWD*-12.2 and 12.21
2. Titles of publications and most documents—*Bluebook* R-13, 15, and 16; *ALWD*-15.7(c), 22.1(b), 23.1(b) and 26.1(c)
3. Introductory signals such as *See* or *Contra*—*Bluebook* R-1.2; *ALWD*-45
4. Internal cross-references and short forms such as *supra*—*Bluebook* R-4; *ALWD*-10 and 11
5. Phrases indicating subsequent or prior history such as *aff'd* or *rev'd*—*Bluebook* R-10.7.1; *ALWD*-12.8 and 12.9
6. Words or phrases introducing related authority such as *available at*—*Bluebook* R-1.6, 15.5, 18.2, 18.6, and 20.1.5
7. Names of Internet sites—*ALWD*-40.1(b)
8. Words used for emphasis, words italicized in the matter quoted, or foreign words that are not common—*Bluebook* R-5 and 7

C. Citation Placement in Sentences and Clauses—*Bluebook* B2; *ALWD*-43.1

Citations are placed in legal documents as either separate citation sentences or clauses, or by incorporation within a sentence.

1. Citation Sentence

If a statement about the law is a complete sentence, the citation immediately follows the statement as a separate sentence that begins with a capital letter and ends with a period. In this situation, the placement of the citation indicates that the citation supports the entire statement about the law included in the sentence.

> **FOR EXAMPLE** It is well established that a defendant has a right to counsel at a preliminary hearing. *Coleman v. Alabama*, 399 U.S. 1 (1970).

2. Citation Clause

When the citation supports only part of a sentence, the citation is placed as a clause immediately after the statement it supports and set off by commas.

> **FOR EXAMPLE** Although the "good faith" exception to the exclusionary rule has been adopted by the United States Supreme Court, *United States v. Leon*, 468 U.S. 897 (1984), it has not been adopted by all the states, *State v. Gutierrez*, 116 N.M. 431, 863 P.2d 1052 (1993).

In this example, the first citation supports the first clause of the sentence and the second citation supports the second clause.

3. Embedded Citations

If the authority is mentioned in the sentence, the citation may be incorporated within the sentence.

> **FOR EXAMPLE** In the case of *Coleman v. Alabama*, 399 U.S. 1 (1970), the Supreme Court held that a defendant has a right to counsel at a preliminary hearing.

Placing the citation in the sentence allows you to add variety to your writing. Note that the citation is not repeated at the end of the sentence.

D. Abbreviations—*Bluebook* R-6 & Tables T.5 to T.16 & BT.1 & BT.2; *ALWD*-2 & Appendices 3 to 5

1. In General

Various terms and sources such as court names, legal periodicals, and case names, are abbreviated in legal citations.

> **FOR EXAMPLE**
>
> | Term | Abbreviation |
> | --- | --- |
> | Southern Reporter | So. |
> | United States Supreme Court | U.S. |
> | Cumberland Law Review | Cumb. L. Rev. |
> | Case name—Corporation | Corp. |

The lists of abbreviations are included in the *Bluebook* tables and the *ALWD* appendices referenced at the beginning of this subsection.

2. Spacing

In the Typical Legal Citations Analyzed section of the *Bluebook* (pp. 5–9), dots (•) are inserted in the example to indicate a single space in the citation. In the *ALWD*, a green triangle (▲) indicates a single space. Following is a summary of the rules governing spacing.

a. Single Capital Letters and Ordinals

Do not place a space between single capital letters or single capital letters and an ordinal. An ordinal is a number used to designate a position in a series such as 10th Circuit. Ordinals such as 2d or 10th are treated as a single capital letter.

> **FOR EXAMPLE** F.R.D.—Federal Rules Decisions; P.2d—Pacific Reporter Second Series. There are no spaces between the single capital letters.

b. Single Capital Letters and Multiple Capital Letters

When the abbreviation includes a capital letter or letters and an abbreviation that does not include a single capital letter, include a space between the single capital letter and the other abbreviation.

> **FOR EXAMPLE** F. Supp.—Federal Supplement. There is a space between "F." and "Supp." because "Supp." is not a single capital letter.

N.D. Miss.—Northern District of Mississippi. There is a space between "D." and "Miss." because "Miss." is not a single capital letter. There is no space between "N." and "D." because they are single capital letters.

c. Abbreviated and Nonabbreviated Words

When an abbreviated word is combined with a nonabbreviated word, place a space on each side of the nonabbreviated word.

> **FOR EXAMPLE** J. Real Est. Taxn.—Journal of Real Estate Taxation. There is a space on each side of "Real" because it is a nonabbreviated word combined with an abbreviated word.

d. Legal Periodicals

In a legal periodical, separate the institutional or geographic abbreviation from the other parts of the abbreviation with a space.

> **FOR EXAMPLE** U.S.F. L. Rev.—University of San Francisco Law Review. The "U.S.F." is separated with a space from the "L." because it is the institutional abbreviation. The "L." is set off by a space from "Rev." because "Rev." is not a single capital letter.

e. Section Symbol (§), Paragraph Symbol (¶), and Ampersand (&)

Place a space after each of these symbols.

> **FOR EXAMPLE** 18 U.S.C. § 2113—A space is placed on each side of the symbol.

f. Authorities Included in the Text of a Sentence

The name of an authority is not abbreviated when it is incorporated in a sentence. According to *Bluebook* Rule 10.2.1, widely known acronyms such as Co. and Inc. continue to be abbreviated.

> **FOR EXAMPLE** The case citation is *Bachman Chocolate Mktg. Co. v. Leigh Warehouse & Transp. Co.*, 1 N.J.239, 62 A.2d 806 (1949). When used in a sentence, Marketing, Transportation, and "and" are not abbreviated: The court ruled against the manufacturer in *Bachman Chocolate Marketing Co. v. Leigh Warehouse and Transportation Co.*, 1 N.J.239, 62 A.2d 806 (1949).

E. Capitalization—*Bluebook* R-8 & B10.6; *ALWD*-3

1. General Rule

In a heading, title, or subtitle, capitalize the initial letter of the first word, the first word following a colon or dash, and all other words except articles, prepositions, and conjunctions.

> **FOR EXAMPLE** | Michael Asimov, *Bad Lawyers in the Movies*. 24 Nova L. Rev. 533 (2000).

2. Court and Party Designations

Bluepages note 10.6 provides that in addition to capitalizing the word "Court" when referring to a specific court such as the California Supreme Court, also capitalize "Court" when the court receiving the document is referred to in the document.

> **FOR EXAMPLE** | This Court has already denied defendant's petition on two previous occasions.

Bluepages note 10.6 also provides that the party designations (Plaintiff, Defendant, Appellant, and so on) should be capitalized when referring to the parties in a matter before the court.

> **FOR EXAMPLE** | It is claimed by the Appellant that the letter should not have been admitted at trial.

On six occasions, Plaintiff attempted to contact Defendant regarding Defendant's failure to answer the interrogatories.

3. Specific Words

Rule 8 of the *Bluebook* includes a page-and-a-half list of specific words and rules governing their capitalization.

> **FOR EXAMPLE** | Capitalize "Act" only when referring to a specific act; capitalize "Code" only when referring to a specific code such as the 1990 Code; capitalize "Judge" only when it is the name of a specific judge or a justice of the U.S. Supreme Court.

4. All Other Capitalizations

Both manuals refer to the *United States Government Printing Office Style Manual* for the capitalization of other words. The *ALWD* also refers to *The Chicago Manual of Style*.

F. Quotations—*Bluebook* R-5; *ALWD*-47 to 49

Quotations are stronger than summaries or paraphrases. Too many quotations, however, may cause the writing to be disjointed and lead the reader to question whether the writer has analyzed the material at all or understands the material well enough to analyze it. Use quotations for emphasis. Use quotations primarily for statutory language, the law or legal principle presented by a court, or key portions of a court's reasoning.

1. Quotation Marks

Quotations of less than 50 words should be placed in quotation marks (" "); they are not indented. The citation is usually placed after the sentence that contains the quotation.

> **FOR EXAMPLE** The U.S. Supreme Court gave the following guidance when interpreting treaties: "In construing a treaty, as in construing a statute, we first look to its terms to determine its meaning." *United States v. Alvarez-Machain*, 504 U.S. 655, 663 (1992).
>
> The court noted that the text of the treaty must be "interpreted in good faith in accordance with the ordinary meaning to be given to the terms of the treaty in their context in light of its object and purpose." *Kreimerman v. Casa Veerkamp, S.A. de C.V.*, 22 F.3d 634, 638 (5th Cir. 1994).

Place periods and commas inside the quotation marks. Other punctuation, such as semicolons, colons, question marks, and exclamation marks, are placed outside the quotation marks unless they are a part of the quotation.

> **FOR EXAMPLE** The court defined publication as "communication to a third party"; therefore. . . .
>
> The victim then shouted, "I've been hit!" The exclamation mark is part of the quote; therefore, it is placed within the quotation marks.

2. Indented Quotations

Quotations of 50 words or more (called block quotations) are set off from the rest of the text by a 5-space indentation (one tab) from the left and right margins and are single-spaced. They are not set off by quotation marks. Place the citation at the left margin of the next line of the text following the quotation. Do not place the citation with the block quotation. The block quotation should be set off from the rest of the text with a double space.

> **FOR EXAMPLE** In regard to the individual rights of tenants in common, the court noted the following:
>
> > However, numerous other elements of control do follow the percentage of ownership. For example, if a co-tenant obtains a loan and mortgages the property, he is only able to mortgage his percentage ownership interest. If one co-tenant rents the whole property to a third party, he must share the proceeds with his co-tenants in accordance with their respective percentages of ownership. . . .
> >
> > *Garcia v. Andrus*, 692 F.2d 89, 92 (9th Cir. 1982).

Block quotations are punctuated as they appear in the original quote.

3. Quotations within a Quotation

Enclose quotations within a block quotation in double quotation marks (" "). As mentioned in the previous subsection, block quotations are punctuated as they appear in the original quotation.

Enclose quotations that appear within a short quotation in single quotation marks.

> **FOR EXAMPLE** "The statute requires that the annual statement 'must be filed within thirty (30) days of the end of the fiscal year.'"

4. Citing a Quotation within a Quotation

If the source of a Quotation within a quotation is included within the quotation, do not repeat it in the citation.

> **FOR EXAMPLE** "The state corporation statute, section 57-9-21, requires that the annual statement 'must be filed within thirty (30) days of the end of the fiscal year.'" In this situation, you do not cite section 57-9-21 again at the end of the quotation.

If the source of the quotation within a quotation is not cited within the quotation, place the citation in a parenthetical that follows the citation for the entire quotation.

> **FOR EXAMPLE** In discussing the time limits for appeal, the court in El Dorado noted "'[j]urisdiction of the matters in dispute does not lie in the courts until the statutorily required administrative procedures are fully complied with.'" *El Dorado Utils., Inc. v. Gallisteo Domestic Water Users Ass'n*, 120 N.M. 165, 167, 899 P.2d 608, 610 (Ct. App. 1995) (quoting *In re Application of Angel Fire Corp.*, 96 N.M. 651, 652, 634 P.2d 202, 203 (1981).

5. Altering Quotations

The reader must be alerted to any changes made to a quotation. The following are the rules governing alterations:

a. Altering a Letter Case

When you change the case of a letter from either uppercase to lowercase or vice versa, enclose the letter in brackets.

> **FOR EXAMPLE** Original quotation: The court does not have jurisdiction until the administrative procedures are complied with.

Alteration: The Supreme Court noted that "[t]he court does not have jurisdiction until the administrative procedures are complied with."

b. Adding, Deleting, or Changing Letters

Enclose the added, deleted, or changed letter or letters in brackets.

> **FOR EXAMPLE** Original quotation: Jurisdiction of the matter in dispute does not lie in the court.

Alteration: Jurisdiction of the matter[s] in dispute does not lie in the court.

c. Substituting or Adding Words

Place substituted or added words in brackets.

> **FOR EXAMPLE** Original quotation: Jurisdiction of the matters in dispute does not lie in the courts until the administrative procedures are fully complied with.

Alteration: Jurisdiction of the matters in dispute does not lie in the courts until the [statutorily required] administrative procedures are fully complied with.

d. Mistakes in Original Quotation

Indicate a mistake in the quoted material by placing "[sic]" after the mistake.

> **FOR EXAMPLE** The preliminary hearing is a stage at which the defendant have [sic] a right to counsel.

e. Adding Emphasis

Any change in the typeface of the quotation, such as adding emphasis, should be placed in parentheses following the citation.

> **FOR EXAMPLE** Original quotation: "If one co-tenant rents the whole property to a third party, he must share the proceeds . . . ." *Garcia v. Andrus*, 692 F.2d 89, 92 (9th Cir. 1982).

Alteration: "If one co-tenant rents the whole property to a third party, *he must share* the proceeds . . . ." *Garcia v. Andrus*, 692 F.2d 89, 92 (9th Cir. 1982) (emphasis added).

6. Omitting Words or Citations

On occasion, you may want to quote only the parts of a quoted passage relevant to the issue being discussed rather than the entire passage. When you are omitting one or more words, the following rules apply:

a. Omission of One or More Words—Ellipsis (. . .)

An ellipsis is three periods with a space between each period and a space before and after the periods. Use an ellipsis to indicate the omission of material from the middle of a quotation.

> **FOR EXAMPLE** "No will . . . shall be revoked, unless . . . by subsequent will or codicil."

To indicate the omission or words at the end of a quotation, use an ellipsis and the final punctuation of the quotation.

> **FOR EXAMPLE** The statute provides that a will may be revoked by "cutting, tearing, burning, obliterating, canceling. . . ."

Do not use an ellipsis to indicate the omission of words at the beginning of a quotation when the quotation is part of a sentence.

> **FOR EXAMPLE** Correct omission: The court noted that a testator may revoke a will by "cutting, tearing, or cancellation with the intent to revoke."

Incorrect omission: The court noted that a testator may revoke a will by ". . . cutting, tearing, or cancellation with the intent to revoke."

When language at the beginning of a quotation is omitted, capitalize the first letter and place it in brackets.

> **FOR EXAMPLE** Original quotation: "This court has held in several cases that a defendant need not brandish the firearm in a threatening manner."

Correct omission: "[D]efendant need not brandish the firearm in a threatening manner."

To indicate the omission of one or more paragraphs from a block quotation, place an ellipsis on its own line. Also, to indicate the omission of language from the beginning of a subsequent paragraph, use an ellipsis.

> **FOR EXAMPLE** However, numerous other elements of control do follow the percentage of ownership. For example, if a co-tenant obtains a loan and mortgages the property, he is only able to mortgage his percentage ownership interest.
>
> .   .   .   .
>
> . . . . If one co-tenant rents the whole property to a third party, he must share the proceeds with his co-tenants in accordance with their respective percentages of ownership.

In this example, the ellipsis on a separate line indicates the omission of a paragraph from the block quotation. The ellipsis at the beginning of the second paragraph indicates the omission of language from the beginning of the second paragraph.

b. Omission of Citations or Footnotes

A quotation may contain numerous citations or footnotes that you do not want to include in the quotation. Indicate the omission of a citation or footnote in a parenthetical.

> **FOR EXAMPLE** "It is clear, however, that in the United States, civil liability for assault and battery is not limited to the direct perpetrator, but extends to any person who by any means aids or encourages the act." *Rael v. Cadena*, 934 N.M. 684, 684, 604 P.2d 822, 823 (Ct. App. 1979) (citations omitted).

7. Paragraph Structure

If a quotation of less than 50 words is the first sentence of a paragraph from the quoted text, the paragraph is enclosed in quotation marks but is not indented. If the quotation is 50 words or more (a block quotation) and the quotation begins with the first sentence of a paragraph from the quoted text, indent a second tab on the left side of the block quotation. All subsequent paragraphs are likewise indented as they appear in the quoted text. In other words, indent the block quote like the paragraph or paragraphs from the quoted text.

> **FOR EXAMPLE** In regard to the individual rights of tenants in common, the court noted the following:
>
> However, numerous other elements of control do follow the percentage of ownership. For example, if a co-tenant obtains a loan and mortgages the property, he is only able to mortgage his percentage ownership interest. If one co-tenant rents the whole property to a third party, he must share the proceeds with his co-tenants in accordance with their respective percentages of ownership. . . .

In this example, "However" is indented in the block quote because it is the beginning of a paragraph in the quoted text.

G. Page Numbers (Pinpoint Citations)—*Bluebook* R-3.3 to 3.5; *ALWD*-5.2 to 5.4

Whenever you quote material from a source, you must include a reference to the exact page or location of the information. Also, when you paraphrase or otherwise refer to specific information rather than quote it, you should include a reference to the exact page or location. This is referred to as a *pinpoint cite* or *jump citation*. It allows the reader to refer to the exact page of the quotation rather than search through the entire source is to find a quote. This applies to all reference sources, and information on how to cite specific sources is scattered throughout the rules that discuss primary and secondary sources. The rules covering pinpoint citations in general are discussed here.

Place the page number on which the quotation or reference appears immediately after the page on which the source begins.

> **FOR EXAMPLE** "[I]t is not a search by a federal officer if evidence secured by state authorities is turned over to federal authorities on a silver platter." *Lustig v. United States*, 338 U.S. 74, 79 (1949). Page 79 is the page of the quote.
>
> The Eighth Circuit addressed the derivative nature of proceedings brought on behalf of limited partnerships. *Allright Mo., Inc. v. Billeter*, 829 F.2d 631, 638 (8th Cir. 1987). Page 638 is the page where the Eighth Circuit addressed the matter.
>
> It has been noted that that those trained in the law are confused by the topic. Terry Christlieb, Note, *Why Superseding Cause Analysis Should Be Abandoned*, 72 Tex. L. Rev. 161, 162. Page 162 is the reference page.

If the citation includes a parallel citation, then a reference to the page in the parallel citation must be included. Parallel citations are discussed in section II A3f State Court and Parallel Citations earlier.

> **FOR EXAMPLE** *Commonwealth v. Appleby*, 380 Mass. 296, 300, 402 N.E.2d 1051, 1054 (1980).

If the quotation or reference is from the first page of the reference source, repeat the initial page number.

> **FOR EXAMPLE** *Lustig v. United States*, 338 U.S. 74, 74 (1949)

If the quotation or reference covers more than one page, separate the pages by a dash or "to."

> **FOR EXAMPLE** *Lustig v. United States*, 338 U.S. 74, 74-79 (1949)

Always retain at least the last two digits of the second number.

> **FOR EXAMPLE** Correct: 74-79; Incorrect: 74-9
>
> Correct: 104-09; Incorrect 104-9

If the quotation or reference is from multiple pages that are not consecutive, list each page separated by a comma and one space. Do not use "and" or "&" before the final page.

> **FOR EXAMPLE** *Lustig v. United States*, 338 U.S. 74, 74, 76, 79 (1949)

If the quotation or reference is from a public domain format (also referred to as vendor neutral), the pinpoint citation may be to a specific paragraph rather than a page.

> **FOR EXAMPLE** *State v. Anaya*, 1997-NMSC-010, ¶ 28, 123 N.M. 14, 20, 933 P.2d 223, 229.
> The page of the quote is paragraph 28.

Consult the rule of the jurisdiction governing neutral citations. Both the *Bluebook* and the *ALWD* have tables/appendices that set out each state's citation rules and formats.

H. String Citations—*Bluebook* R-1.1 & 1.2; *ALWD*-43.3(a)

When a proposition is supported by more than one authority in a citation clause or sentence, the citation is referred to as a *string citation*. Separate each authority cited with a semicolon.

> **FOR EXAMPLE** The sudden emergency doctrine tends to elevate its principles above what is required to be proven in a negligence action. *Knapp v. Stanford*, 392 So.2d 196 (Miss. 1980); *Simonson v. White*, 220 Mont. 14, 713 P.2d 938 (1986).

The use of string citations in court documents and legal memoranda is generally disfavored, but not prohibited. The preference is to present the strongest authority in support of a proposition. String citations are more frequently seen in periodical publications such as law review articles.

I. Short Citation Forms (*Id.*, *Supra*, and Hereinafter)— *Bluebook* R-4, B5.2, B6.2, B8.2, B9.2, & B10.5; *ALWD*-11.2 to 11.4

After the full citation to an authority is presented in a document, subsequent citations to the authority may be shortened. These shortened citations are usually referred to as short citations or short-form citations. Short citations are used primarily because they save space and are less disruptive to the flow of the text. Bluepages note 5.2 of the *Bluebook* provides that short citations may be used when it is clear from the short form what is being referenced, the earlier full citation is in the same general discussion, and the reader can easily locate the full citation.

The rules included in the title to this subsection are the general rules governing short citations. The rules for each type of citation have sections on short citations; e.g., the rule governing case citations has a section on short citations, the rule governing book citation has a section on short citations, and so on. The discussion of each type of citation in Sections II and III of this chapter includes a discussion of the short citation format. This subsection addresses general rules governing all short citations and some examples of short citations.

1. *Id.* as a Short Citation

Id. means "the same" and is used in the same way as *ibid.* You use *id.* and not *ibid.* in legal writing. It is italicized or underlined; if it is underlined the period is underlined (<u>id.</u>). *Id.* is used in court documents and legal memorandum when you are referring the reader to the immediately preceding citation. In other words you must be referring to the same citation as the last citation presented.

> **FOR EXAMPLE** Numerous other elements of control do follow the percentage of ownership. *Garcia v. Andrus*, 692 F.2d 89, 92 (9th Cir. 1982). For example, if a co-tenant obtains a loan and mortgages the property, he is only able to mortgage his percentage ownership interest. If one co-tenant rents the whole property to a third party, he must share the proceeds with his co-tenants in accordance with their respective percentages of ownership. *Id.* at 94.

The use of *id.* indicates that the source of the statement is the preceding citation, *Garcia v. Andrus*. If the source was on the same page as the previous citation (page 92), then "*Id.*" alone would be used rather than "*Id.* at 94." If another citation follows *Garcia v. Andrus*, then using *id.* following that citation to refer to *Garcia v. Andrus* would be improper.

> **FOR EXAMPLE** Numerous other elements of control do follow the percentage of ownership. *Garcia v. Andrus*, 692 F.2d 89, 92 (9th Cir. 1982). For example, if a co-tenant obtains a loan and mortgages the property, he is only able to mortgage his percentage ownership interest. *Appeal of Schramm*, 414 N.W.2d. 31, 32 (S.D. 1987). If one co-tenant rents the whole property to a third party, he must share the proceeds with his co-tenants in accordance with their respective percentages of ownership. *Id*. at 94.

The use of "*Id.* at 94" to refer to *Garcia v. Andrus* is improper.

Note: When *Id.* is used with statutory or paragraph citations, the word "at" is not included when referring to a different statutory section.

> **FOR EXAMPLE** The full citation of the statute referred to is 18 U.S.C. § 1112 (1994); when the reference is to § 1113, the short citation is *Id*. § 1113, not *Id*. at § 1113.

Id. may be used for any legal authority except internal cross-references. Internal cross-references are discussed in subsection IV J Internal Cross-References later.

2. *Supra* as a Short Citation

Supra as a short citation means "above" and is used to refer to a reference source previously fully cited in a document. It cannot be used in place of *id.* In other words, it is not used when referring to an immediately preceding cited source. It is used to refer to a previously cited source in a document when there have been other intervening cited sources. *Supra* cannot be used to refer to cases, statutes, session laws, ordinances, legislative materials (other than hearings), constitutions, and administrative regulations. It is italicized or underlined; if it is underlined, do not underline any accompanying punctuation. When using *supra*, put the author's last name first (or the title if the name is not available) followed by a comma, and then *supra*. If the reference is to a page other than the page in the earlier citation, follow *supra* with a comma, then "at" and the page number.

> **FOR EXAMPLE** It is clear that a mixed motive does not invalidate zoning restrictions on adult entertainment as long as the predominate concern of the zoning body is legitimate. *See* Alfred C. Yen, *Judicial Review of the Zoning of Adult Entertainment: A Search for the Purposeful Suppression of Protected Speech*, 12 Pepp. L. Rev. 651, 655 (1985). Courts have noted that respect must be given to the community's need to preserve the quality of life. *Las Vegas v. Nevada Industries, Inc.*, 105 Nev. 174, 772 P.2d 1275 (1989). The key question is what is the predominate concern of the zoning body. Yen, *supra* at 657.

In this example, *supra* is used because there is a different citation between the Yen citation and the second reference to the Yen article. If the second Yen reference immediately followed the first full citation, *Id.* would be used.

> **FOR EXAMPLE** It is clear that a mixed motive does not invalidate zoning restrictions on adult entertainment as long as the predominate concern of the zoning body is legitimate. *See* Alfred C. Yen, *Judicial Review of the Zoning of Adult Entertainment: A Search for the Purposeful Suppression of Protected Speech*, 12 Pepp. L. Rev. 651, 655 (1985). The key question is what is the predominate concern of the zoning body. *Id*. at 657.

3. Hereinafter as a Short Citation

"Hereinafter" may be used in certain circumstances to shorten a long title that is cumbersome to cite repeatedly, such as when the source has no author and the title is long. It is also used when two or more authorities appear in a footnote and the use of *supra* would be confusing. Place the "hereinafter" designation in ordinary type in brackets ([ ]) immediately following the end of the first full citation to the authority. The shortened form should clearly identify the authority.

> **FOR EXAMPLE** Assume here the article in the previous example does not have an author: It is clear that a mixed motive does not invalidate zoning restrictions on adult entertainment as long as the predominate concern of the zoning body is legitimate. *See Judicial Review of the Zoning of Adult Entertainment: A Search for the Purposeful Suppression of Protected Speech*, 12 Pepp. L. Rev. 651 (1985), [hereinafter *Adult Entertainment Zoning*].

J. Internal Cross-References (*Supra* and *Infra*)— *Bluebook* R-3.5; *ALWD*-10

Often, especially when a document is long or includes many footnotes, you may want to refer the reader to source material on a specific page, section, or footnote of the document. For this purpose, *supra* is used to refer to material that appears earlier in the document and *infra* is used to refer to material that appears later. When used in this context, *supra* has a different function from its use as a short citation. When used as a short citation, it refers to a specific source such as a law review article. As internal cross-references, *supra* and *infra* refer to parts of the document, not specific sources. The terms are either italicized or underlined, and it may be necessary to add an explanatory parenthetical to identify the reference.

> **FOR EXAMPLE** *See supra* pp. 9-11 (discussing the rights of third parties).
>
> *Supra* n. 7 (cases supporting third party claims).
>
> *Supra* Section III. B—F.
>
> *Infra* notes 8—9 and accompanying text.
>
> *Infra* pp. 23-25 and note 16.
>
> *Infra* Part II. A and B (discussing interrogatory questions).

K. Signals—*Bluebook* R-1.2 to 1.5; *ALWD*-44 to 46

Signals are terms or words used to indicate the manner in which the cited authority supports or contradicts the text. A signal is not used if the citation identifies the source of a quotation, directly supports a statement, or identifies the authority referred to.

> **FOR EXAMPLE** The U.S. Supreme Court has adopted the "good faith" exception to the exclusionary rule. Unite*d States v. Leon*, 468 U.S. 897 (1984).

1. Types of Signals

Following is a list of citation signals followed by some examples of their use:

- *E.g.*—Indicates that the cited authority is representative of, or an example of, many other authorities that stand for the same proposition. It may be used with other signals such as *see e.g.* or *but see, e.g.*

✦ *See*—Used to indicate that the cited authority clearly supports a proposition, but does not directly state the proposition.

✦ *See Also*—Used to show additional authority that supports a proposition.

✦ *See Generally*—Used to identify authority that presents helpful background information related to the stated proposition.

✦ *Accord*—Used to indicate other cases that state or support a proposition. It is placed after the citation given in support of the proposition.

✦ *Cf*—Indicates authority that supports a proposition different from the proposition stated, but is analogous.

✦ *Compare . . . with*—Used to compare authorities that may illustrate or reach a different result from the stated proposition. Note that the *Bluebook* and the *ALWD* differ somewhat in their use of "compare."

✦ *But see*—Used to identify authority that contradicts the stated proposition.

✦ *But cf*—Identifies authority that supports a proposition analogous to the contrary of the stated proposition.

✦ *Contra*—Used to identify authority that directly contradicts the stated proposition.

2. Presentation

Capitalize the first letter of a signal that begins a sentence. Italicize or underscore signals and separate them from the rest of the citation with a space. Separate each authority within a signal with a semicolon. Both the *Bluebook* and the *ALWD* strongly urge the use of parenthetical explanations to describe the relevance of the cited authority. Some examples of the use of signals are presented here.

FOR EXAMPLE See, e.g. *Renton v. Playtime Theatres, Inc.*, 475 U.S. 41, 55 (1986); *Young v. American Mini Theatres, Inc.*, 427 U.S. 50, 59 (1976)

Goldstar (Panama) S.A. v. Unitted States, 967 F.2d 965, 968 (4th Cir 1992)

Accord Argentine Republic v. Amerada Hess Shipping Corp., 488 U.S. 428. 442 (1989) (Supreme Court determining that the convention only set forth substantive rules of conduct and did not create a private right)

Contra Knapp v. Stanford, 392 So.2d 196, 198 (Miss. 1981) (the sudden emergency doctrine confuses the principle of comparative negligence).

---

3. Order of Presentation

The following is a summary of the order of presentation of authorities. For a detailed list, refer to the *Bluebook* and the *ALWD*. Present citations in the following order.

a. Constitutions

Federal Constitution, followed by state constitutions (alphabetically by state), then foreign constitutions (alphabetically by country).

b. Statutes

Federal statutes (chronologically by title number), followed by state statutes (alphabetically by state), and then foreign statutes (alphabetically by country).

c. Cases

Federal cases (starting with the highest court to the lowest court), followed by state cases (alphabetically by state from the highest to the lowest courts), and then foreign cases (alphabetically by country).

d. Administrative and Executive Materials

Such as the *Code of Federal Regulations* or executive orders.

e. Legislative Materials

Such as bills and legislative history.

f. Secondary Authority

See *Bluebook* R-1.3 or *ALWD*-46.4(c) for the order of presentation of secondary authority.

L. Sections and Paragraphs (§ ¶)—*Bluebook* R-3.4; *ALWD*-6

The following is a summary of citation rules when an authority is organized by sections or paragraphs:

- ✦ Insert a space before and after the section or paragraph symbol—18 U.S.C. § 2111 (1994).
- ✦ Do not use "at" when referring to a paragraph or section.

FOR EXAMPLE	Correct: *Id.* § 2111
	Incorrect: *Id.* at § 2111

If the authority is divided into subsections or subparagraphs, use the punctuation of the original source to separate sections and subsections. If the source does not have any punctuation, place the subdivisions in parentheses—18 U.S.C. 842(a)(1). Note that there is no space between the main section "842" and the subsections "(a)(1)".

A section may include a letter as part of the designation. In this case, the letter does not refer to a subsection; therefore, do not separate it with punctuation, e.g., 42 U.S.C. 2000e-1(a) (1994) not 42 U.S.C. 2000(e)(1)(a) (1994). The "e" is part of the section designation and does not refer to a subsection.

When citing consecutive sections or paragraphs, include the first and last sections and separate the sections with a hyphen, a long dash, or "to." Retain all digits on both sides of the span. Use consecutive section or paragraph symbols to reference multiple sections or paragraphs.

FOR EXAMPLE	Correct: ¶¶ 115-123; §§ 15 to 17
	Incorrect: ¶¶ 115-23; §§ 15 to 7

When citing multiple sections or paragraphs that are not consecutive, place a comma between the sections or paragraphs and do not place "and" or an ampersand (&) before the final section or paragraph.

FOR EXAMPLE	Correct: ¶¶ 115, 123, 129; §§ 15, 17, 19
	Incorrect: ¶¶ 115, 123, and 129; §§ 15, 17, & 19

When citing multiple subsections or subparagraphs of a single section or paragraph, use one section or paragraph symbol.

> **FOR EXAMPLE** § 231(a)–(f); ¶ 22(g)–(k) Multiple consecutive subsections and subparagraphs.
>
> § 231(a), (f), (k); ¶ 22(a), (g), (k) Multiple nonconsecutive subsections and subparagraphs.

M. Electronic Sources—*Bluebook* R-18; *ALWD*-38 to 42

Both the *Bluebook* and the *ALWD* provide that if the authority is readily available in print, the citation should be to the print source; it is not necessary to reference the electronic source such as Westlaw or LexisNexis. This rule applies unless the documents are not available in a printed source or are difficult to obtain such as unpublished cases. The *Bluebook* and the *ALWD* differ in some electronic citation details; therefore, it is recommended that the rules be checked when citing these sources. For example, in the *ALWD*, citations to Westlaw or LexisNexis are placed in parentheses with the words "available in WL or LexisNexis", for example, (available in LexisNexis in the Legal News database). In the *Bluebook*, Westlaw and LexisNexis citations are not placed in parentheses and not preceded by "available in." The examples in this subsection follow the *Bluebook* format.

In general, a citation to an authority should include information that clearly indicates the source. The rules governing electronic sources are detailed and beyond the scope of this text. Therefore, this section contains a brief summary of the key points for citing electronic sources.

1. Commercial Sources

Due to their reliability, the *Bluebook* in Rule 18.1 prefers the use of commercial electronic databases over other Internet sources. In addition to the usual information given in a citation, such as a case name or statute number, the database identifier must be included in the citation. The identifier usually includes the database name (LexisNexis and WL for Westlaw), the year, and document number. Some examples of citations to Westlaw and LexisNexis are presented here:

> **FOR EXAMPLE** Unpublished Cases: *Christians v. Stafford*, No. 14-99-00038-CV, 2000 Tex. App. LEXIS 6423 (Tex. Ct. App. Oct. 26, 2000)
>
> *Devji v. Keller*, No. 03-99-00436-CV, 2000 Tex. App. WL 1862819, at * 2 (Tex. Ct. App. Dec. 21, 2000).

Note when you are referring to a specific screen or page number, place an asterisk before the number ("at *2" in the above example). If the reference is to a specific paragraph number, precede the number with the paragraph symbol and do not use "at" (¶ 15). In the preceding example, a specific screen page number is referenced.

Congressional Bills: H. R. 1167, 106th Cong. (1999) WL1999 CQ US HR 1167; H. R. 301, 107th Cong. (2001) LEXIS Archived Bill Text and Tracking Library, 106th Congress file.

Newsletter: Kim Biello, Susan Beck, Andrew Longstreth, *Bar Talk*, The American Lawyer, Sept. 2001, available in LEXIS Legal News Library, The American Lawyer file.

Law Review: Alfred C. Yen, *Judicial Review of the Zoning of Adult Entertainment: A Search for the Purposeful Suppression of Protected Speech*, 12 Pepp. L. Rev. 651 (1985), WL 12 PEPLR 651.

2. World Wide Web Sources

An on-line citation should include the following: the full name of the author or owner; the title in italics, pinpoint references such as paragraph numbers (if any); the URL (Web address); and the date enclosed in parentheses.

> **FOR EXAMPLE**   MSNBC, *MSNBC Home News, Oil Prices Sink after OPEC Dithers*, <http://www.msnbc.com/news/657546.asp> (Nov 15, 2001).

ALWD Rule 12.5 provides that if a case is available in a reporter or through an on-line database such as Westlaw, the Internet should not be cited.

V. KEY POINTS CHECKLIST: *Citation Checklist*

- When checking citations, always consult an authority such as the *Bluebook* or the *ALWD Citation Manual.*
- Make sure the appropriate words in a citation, such as case names, article and titles are properly italicized or underlined.
- Check case citations to ensure all the elements are present—case name, reporter volume and page, pinpoint page if the citation is to a specific page, parallel citation (if any), court abbreviation if necessary, year of the decision in parentheses, and subsequent history, if any.
- Make sure all the elements of statutory citations are present. Statutory citations usually include the name of the code or code abbreviation, the section symbol (§), title, chapter or section numbers, and in parentheses the publisher if it is a commercial publication and the year the volume was published.
- For any other citation, such as a secondary citation, check the rules to ensure that all the elements of the citation are present and properly used.
- Check the rules and tables or appendices to ensure that words such as "Incorporated" and "South Eastern Reporter" are properly capitalized, abbreviated, and spaced.
- When signals, such as *"See Also,"* are included in a citation, check to ensure their use is proper.
- Check the use of *id.* and other short citations. Is the use of a short citation proper? If so, is the citation format proper?

VI. APPLICATION

This section applies the information presented in the chapter to the hypotheticals presented at the beginning of this chapter and Chapters 1 and 2.

A. Chapter Hypothetical

Mike's research memo is based on two cases and a Georgia statute. As he researched, he wrote them down as follows: *In the Interest of M.N.L.* vol. 221 Georgia Appeals Court page 123 and volume 470 South Eastern Reporter 2d page 753, 1996; *In the Interest of G.L.H.* vol. 209 Georgia Appeals Court page 146 and volume 433 South Eastern Reporter 2d page 357, 1993; Section 15-11-94 of the Georgia Code Annotated 2000. By referring either to *Bluebook* Rule 10, Bluepages and Table T.1 or to *ALWD* Rule 12 and Appendix 1, Mike would convert his case notes to the following citations: *In the Interest of M.N.L.,* 221 Ga. App. 123, 470 S.E.2d 753 (1996); *In the Interest of G.L.H.,* 209 Ga. App.146,

433 S.E.2d 357 (1993). By consulting *Bluebook* Rule 12 and Table T.1 or *ALWD* Rule 14 and Appendix 1, he would cite the statute as Ga. Code Ann. § 15- 11-94 (2000).

B. Chapter 1 Hypothetical *Reins v. Stewart*

As discussed in Chapter 5, Vanessa located a case on point, *Rael v. Cadena*, 93 N.M. 684, 604 P.2d 822 (Ct. App. 1979). Vanessa would find the rules concerning case citation by referring to *Bluebook* Rule 10, Bluepages and Table T.1 or to *ALWD* Rule 12 and Appendix 1.

C. Chapter 2 Hypothetical *United States v. Canter*

In this case, the applicable statute is identified in the assignment as the bank robbery statute, 18 U.S.C. § 2113. Dustin will find the rules governing the citation of federal statutes by referring to *Bluebook* Rule 12 or to *ALWD* Rule 14.2.

The case Dustin located is *United States v. Martinez-Jimenez*, 864 F.2d 664 (9th Cir. 1989). The applicable case citation rules are *Bluebook* Rule 10, Bluepages and Table T.1 or to *ALWD* Rule 12 and Appendix 1.

SUMMARY

Whenever a reference is made in legal writing to a primary or secondary legal authority, the source of the reference must be identified. This reference is called a citation. A citation provides the information necessary to allow the reader to locate the reference, thus allowing the reader to check its content. Citations are usually required in most legal writing, such as office legal memoranda, and may be included in general legal correspondence or other documents when there is reference to a legal authority.

It is essential that the information included in a citation is correct. It is useless to refer a reader to a source of information and incorrectly identify the location of the source.

The main guides and sources of authority on legal citations are *The Bluebook: A Uniform System of Citation* (*Bluebook*) and the *ALWD Citation Manual: A Professional System of Citation*. The chapter presented a brief review of the main rules of citation.

The chapter began with an overview of the numerous rules of citation used when citing primary authority, that is, case, constitutional, and enacted (statutory) law. The next section summarized the citation format for major secondary sources such as legal encyclopedia, *Annotated Law Reports* (ALR), law reviews, Restatements, and treatises.

The chapter concluded with an overview of basic rules of citation to be followed when citing most legal sources. Among other topics, the section covered the use of italics, abbreviations, capitalization, quotations, pinpoint citations, short citations, signals, and citations to electronic sources.

Inasmuch as both the *Bluebook* and the *ALWD* consist of hundreds of pages, a detailed discussion of the citation rules of either text is beyond the scope of this chapter. The chapter included references to rules from both the *ALWD* and the *Bluebook* with the goal of providing quick access to the main rules of citation in either authority.

CHAPTER REFERENCES

INTERNET RESOURCES

<http://www.alwd.org>

The Web site for the *ALWD Citation Manual*. The site includes many features such as additional material, examples, and updates.

<http://www.legal*Bluebook*.com>

This Web site includes information on the 17th edition of The *Bluebook*.

 For additional materials, please go to the CD accompanying this book

 For additional resources, visit our Web site at www.paralegal.delmar.cengage.com

EXERCISES

Additional exercises are located on the Student CD-ROM accompanying the text and Online Companion.

For the following exercises, use either the *Bluebook* or the *ALWD Citation Manual*.

ASSIGNMENT 1

Provide the correct citation name for the following cases:

The United States of America v. Thomas Terry

Mary Kay Kraft, Mark Johnson, and Vanessa Hays v. Joseph Beazley and the City of Chicago

Kerry Handle et al v. The Jamestown Cooperative

Kalley Institute v. Carrington Insurance Company, Incorporated

The American Civil Liberties Union v. Micron Management Corporation dba Taylor Management

ASSIGNMENT 2

Give the correct citation for the following case, include the parallel citations: *The United States of America versus Matlock*, volume 94, page 988 of the *Supreme Court Reporter*, volume 39, page 242 of the *United States Supreme Court Reports, Lawyer's Edition*, volume 415, page 164 of the *United States Reports*, decided February 20, 1974.

ASSIGNMENT 3

Give the correct citation for the following case, include the parallel citations: *Douglas D. Robberts versus*

Carroll E. Swain, volume 487 *South Eastern Reporter* page 760, North Carolina Appeals Court 1997. The citation is to page 766.

ASSIGNMENT 4

Correct the following citation: Hoang Nguyen v. Fasano 84 F. Supp.2d 1099, (S.D.Cal.2000).

ASSIGNMENT 5

Correct the following citation: Lynda Herndon v. Jackie Barrell, 101 N.C.App. 636; 400 S.E. 2d 769 (N.C.App. 1991).

ASSIGNMENT 6

Give the correct citation for the following statutes: Title eighteen of the *United States Code* section 1112 the 1999 edition. Title eighteen of the *United States Code Annotated* section 1111 by West, a Thomson business 2000 and title eighteen of the *United States Code Service* by LexisNexis 2000.

ASSIGNMENT 7

Give the correct citation for the following: the fifth Amendment to the United States Constitution; article four section three of the United States Constitution.

ASSIGNMENT 8

Correct the following citations: 26 U. S. C. §112; U. S. Const. Amend 4.

ASSIGNMENT 9

Correct the following citation: Vol. 6 American Jur. (second), *Assault and Battery*, §2(1999).

ASSIGNMENT 10

Give the correct citation to section 40 of the treatise *The Law of Torts* by Dan B. Dobbs published by West, a Thomson business in 2000.

ASSIGNMENT 11

Give the correct citation for the following law journal article: An article by Douglas J. Gunn entitled Torts—Negligence—The Sudden Emergency Doctrine is abolished in Mississippi, volume 51, page 301 of the Mississippi Law Journal published in 1980.

     What is the short citation?

ASSIGNMENT 12

Give the citation to the Restatement of the Law of Torts Third, Apportionment of Liability Sections 8 through 10, 1999.

ASSIGNMENT 13

Give the citation to an *American Law Reports Federal* annotation published in 1999 in the 155 volume at page 535. The annotation is entitled "Effect of Use, or Alleged Use, of Internet on Personal Jurisdiction in, or Venue of, Federal Court Case" by Jason H. Eaton.

ASSIGNMENT 14

What is the short citation format for Assignments 12 and 13?

CHAPTER 12

Counteranalysis

Outline

Learning Objectives

After completing this chapter, you should understand:

✦ What counteranalysis is

✦ Why counteranalysis is important

✦ Research sources for counteranalysis

✦ The techniques of counteranalysis

On a frigid Saturday in December, Mr. Henry "Hot Dog" Thomas, an inexperienced skier, was skiing an expert run at a local resort. As he came over a hill, he encountered a patch of ice, lost control, crashed into a tree, and was severely injured. The ski resort had not posted a warning sign indicating the presence of the ice patch. Mr. Thomas consulted with Ms. Booth, a local attorney, and retained her to represent him. Shortly thereafter, Ms. Booth filed a negligence suit against the resort. She sent her paralegal a memo indicating that the resort's attorney had filed a rule 12(b)(6) motion to dismiss for failure to state a claim. The memo directed the paralegal to prepare a legal research memo assessing the likelihood of the motion being granted.

The Ski Safety Act, which governs the rights and liabilities of skiers and ski resorts, provides that:

✦ The resort has a duty to warn of hazardous conditions.

✦ The skier has the duty to be aware of and the responsibility for snow and ice conditions.

The act also provides that skiers have a duty to refrain from skiing beyond the range of their ability.

One of the questions to be addressed by the paralegal is which of the duties apply in the client's case.

The memo prepared by the paralegal focused on the resort's duty to warn and the skier's duty in regard to snow and ice conditions. Based on this focus and the relevant case law, the paralegal concluded that the resort had the duty to warn of the ice patch that the client encountered. Therefore, the 12(b)(6) motion would probably not be granted.

At the motion hearing, the resort's counsel did not focus on the issue of the resort's duty to warn, but rather argued the issue in the context of probable cause. The resort's counsel contended that the cause of the accident was the skier's admitted violation of his statutory duty to refrain from skiing beyond the range of his ability. As an admitted inexperienced skier, his skiing an expert run violated the statute and, therefore, was the cause of the accident as a matter of law. The skier's attorney, relying on the paralegal's memo, which did not address the proximate cause question, was unprepared to counter this argument. Consequently, the motion was granted and the case dismissed.

I. INTRODUCTION

What went wrong in the preceding hypothetical? Of course, the supervising attorney should have more carefully reviewed the paralegal's memo, noticed that the assistant had not addressed the proximate cause issue, and engaged in additional research. Often an attorney is too busy, however, and based on past excellent and reliable performance by a paralegal, may rely fully on the individual's work product and not sufficiently review what has been submitted.

What went wrong with the paralegal's research? The paralegal failed to anticipate the legal argument the opposing side was likely to make. He failed to analyze the position from the other side's point of view. In other words, he failed to provide a complete counteranalysis in the memo. A paralegal's role in conducting legal research, or in any situation where legal analysis is required, includes determining the potential weaknesses of a legal argument and the counterarguments the other side may present.

The purpose of legal research is not only to discover how the law applies to the client's case, but also to determine the strength of that case. To accomplish this, the strength of the opponent's case must be analyzed as well. The case must be looked at in its entirety to determine its strengths and weaknesses.

The focus of this chapter is the process of identifying the strengths and weaknesses of a client's case through research and analysis of the case from the perspective of the opposition. That is, the focus is on counteranalysis.

II. COUNTERANALYSIS—DEFINITION

If analysis is the application of the law to the facts of a case, what is counteranalysis? At one level, it is an exploration of how and why a specific law does or does not apply to the facts of a case. **Counteranalysis** is the process of anticipating the argument the opponent is likely to raise in response to your analysis of an issue—the **counterargument**. In essence, it is the process of discovering and considering the counterargument to a legal position or argument. It involves identifying and objectively evaluating the strengths and weaknesses of each legal argument you intend to raise.

III. COUNTERANALYSIS—WHY?

The role of the attorney, paralegal, or law clerk is to represent the client to the best of their ability and to pursue a course of action that is in the best interest of the client. This is accomplished by engaging in research and analysis that thoroughly examines all the aspects of the case. One of those aspects, counteranalysis, is important for several reasons:

1. **(Ethics.)** Under Rule 3.3(a)(3) of the American Bar Association's Model *Rules of Professional Conduct*, an attorney has an ethical duty to disclose legal authority adverse to the position of the client that is not disclosed by the opposing counsel.

   The goal of the adversary system is that justice be served. The ends of justice require the discovery and presentation of all relevant authority in order that a just resolution of the issues may be achieved. Therefore, a legal researcher, to properly inform the attorney, must locate and provide the attorney with all relevant authority, including that which is adverse to the client.

2. **(Ethics.)** The paralegal has an ethical duty to do a complete and competent job. See Model Rule 1.1. Research and analysis are not complete unless all

sides of an issue and all legal arguments have been considered. Failure to completely analyze a problem can constitute malpractice.

To represent the client competently, you must be prepared to respond to any legal argument raised by the other side. The identification of opposing arguments allows you to consider what the other side's position is likely to be. It allows you to answer the questions:

✦ What will they do?

✦ How can we counter their arguments?

✦ What preparation is necessary to respond?

In essence, counteranalysis allows you to anticipate opposing arguments and prepare to counter them. The last thing you want is to be responsible for the supervisory attorney being unprepared to respond to an argument.

3. Counteranalysis aids in the proper evaluation of the merits of a case and can assist in the selection of the appropriate course of action to follow.

> **FOR EXAMPLE** Counteranalysis may reveal a weakness in the client's case that leads to the conclusion that settlement should be pursued. Without conducting a thorough counteranalysis, an improper course of action could be followed, such as taking the matter to trial rather than pursuing settlement options.

4. It is important to locate and disclose adverse authority to maintain credibility with your supervisor. You may not be considered reliable and the credibility of your research may be questioned if you ignore or fail to identify and disclose adverse authority. The opposition or the court, if the issue comes before the court, most likely will discover the opposing authority. Your failure to do so indicates lack of ability, sloppiness, or intentional concealment. Your credibility and trustworthiness will be enhanced if you candidly reveal and meet head on unfavorable authority.

5. When a legal brief is submitted to a court, if you identify and address adverse authority in the brief, you have an opportunity to soften its impact by discrediting or distinguishing it. You have an opportunity to provide reasons why the adverse authority does not apply, and your credibility is enhanced. This allows the reader to consider the adverse authority in the context of your response to it. This opportunity is missed if you fail to include the adverse authority.

Weaknesses in your position or analysis will not go away if you ignore them. No matter how strongly you feel you are right, you can count on the other side raising some counterargument, and if you have not considered and prepared for the counterarguments, you may very well lose in court.

IV. COUNTERANALYSIS—WHEN?

Employ counteranalysis whenever legal research is conducted or the strengths and weaknesses of a case are considered, in other words, *always*. When addressing a legal problem, look for all potential counterarguments to any position taken. Counteranalysis is required when preparing an interoffice legal memorandum or conducting any research on an issue in a case. It is certainly necessary when you are assisting in the preparation of a response to a brief filed by the opposing party. Also, you should engage in the process even when you are just thinking about the legal issues in the client's case. Counteranalysis may be required even in the initial stages of a case.

> **FOR EXAMPLE** Some paralegals conduct the initial interview with a client and provide the supervisory attorney with a summary of the interview and the applicable statutory and case law. The summary of the applicable law should include a counteranalysis section that introduces any apparent weaknesses in the client's case.

V. COUNTERANALYSIS—RESEARCH SOURCES

When conducting legal research, counteranalysis means looking for legal authority that supports the argument the opponent is likely to raise in response to your analysis of the issue. There are several things to keep in mind and sources to look to when conducting counteranalysis and legal research.

When researching statutory law, always Shepardize the statute or check the annotations for cases that analyze or interpret the statute. The cases may present counterarguments to a position you are taking in regard to the interpretation of the statute.

When researching case law, if you have found a case that supports the client's position, Shepardize the case to determine if another case or cases analyze the law differently. Cases that distinguish, criticize, or limit the case you are researching are identified in *Shepard's*. You should check all these cases.

> **FOR EXAMPLE** Under the case you are Shepardizing is the reference "c746P2d845." The *c* means that the court opinion at 746 P2d 845 disagrees with the reasoning/decision of the case you are Shepardizing. This opinion should be checked because it may present a counterargument to the legal argument in support of the client's position.

In addition to Shepardizing the case that supports the client's position, also check the digest for other cases that may analyze the law differently. *Shepard's* will identify only those cases that mention the case you are researching. There may be other cases that analyze the same question, but do not mention the same case. Check the headnote of the case you are researching, identify the key number for the issue in question, and then check the appropriate digest for other cases on the topic.

When reading a case that supports the client's position, always check for a dissent. If there is a dissent, it will present the counterargument to the position taken in the majority opinion and often include references to cases and other sources in support of the counterargument. It is possible that the facts of the client's case are sufficiently different from the facts of the court opinion that the position of the dissent may apply.

There are several other sources to check when conducting counteranalysis. A treatise usually presents an analysis of legal issues that includes arguments and counterarguments. If there is an ALR annotation on the question being researched, it will also include a thorough analysis of the issue. It will discuss the various ways the courts have decided the issue and the arguments and counterarguments in support of those decisions. The annotation will also include references to numerous cases on the question and other research sources.

Another helpful source when conducting counteranalysis is a law review article. If a law review article discusses the question being researched, it will provide a comprehensive analysis and critique of the legal position(s) the courts have taken. Like an ALR annotation, it will include reference to numerous cases that address the question and other research sources.

VI. COUNTERANALYSIS—TECHNIQUES

A. In General

Before counteranalysis can begin, a prerequisite is that you must analyze and thoroughly research the issue or legal position being addressed. You must know the law before you can respond to it. Because of its importance, this point is emphasized and repeated throughout the chapter. Thorough research should reveal the weaknesses of a legal position and the counterarguments to it.

> **FOR EXAMPLE** Mary Kay, a door-to-door sales representative for Ace Brush, sold Ella Smith a set of brushes at Ms. Smith's residence. Ms. Smith signed a contract to purchase the brushes. The contract provided for three monthly payments. Ms. Smith called two days later and canceled the contract. When Ace Brush attempted to deliver the goods, Ms. Smith refused to accept the delivery. Ace Brush sued Ms. Smith for breach of contract.
>
> Tom, a paralegal with the firm representing Ace Brush, was assigned the task of determining whether Ms. Smith could legally cancel the contract after it was signed. He determined that article II of the state Commercial Code governed the transaction. His research indicated that the code had no provision allowing a cooling-off period for door-to-door sales, and therefore, he concluded that Ms. Smith's rejection of the goods was a breach of the contract.
>
> Tom, however, committed a major error. He failed to thoroughly research the question. The state had another statute, called the Consumer Sales Act, which provided that in the event of a credit transaction involving a home solicitation sale, the buyer had a right to cancel the sale within three days of the transaction.

Had Tom's research been thorough, he would have located the weakness in his legal position based upon the Commercial Code and identified the counterargument to the conclusion that the contract was breached.

When embarking on counteranalysis, always assume that there is a counterargument to the position you have taken. Put yourself in the opponent's place and ask yourself:

- ✦ How do I respond to this argument?
- ✦ What is the argument in response to this position?

Remember, counteranalysis consists of identifying *any* possible counterargument the opponent may use to challenge your legal position or argument.

To determine what the counterarguments to an argument or position are likely to be, it is necessary and helpful to consider the ways a legal argument is attacked. After you are familiar with the techniques used to challenge an argument, use those techniques to seek out the weaknesses in your argument, anticipate the likely counterarguments, and guide your research.

A legal argument or legal position is usually based on an enacted law or case law or both. The various approaches that you may use to attack or challenge an argument based on an enacted law or case law are explored separately in the following two sections.

B. Enacted Law

Ways to challenge or attack a legal position or argument based on an enacted law are discussed here. Enacted law, as defined in Chapter 1, includes any law passed or adopted

Challenges to a Position or Argument Based on Enacted Law
1. The elements of the statute are not met.
2. The statute is sufficiently broad to permit a construction or application different from that urged by the opposition.
3. The statute has been misconstrued or does not apply.
4. The statute relied upon as a guide to interpret another statute does not apply and, therefore, cannot be used as a guide in interpreting the other statute.
5. The statute relied upon has not been adopted in your jurisdiction.
6. The interpretation of the statute urged by the opposition is unconstitutional or violates another legislative act.
7. The statute relied upon is unconstitutional.

Exhibit 12–1
Counteranalysis
Approaches to a Legal
Position Based on a
Statute.

by the people through a representative body, such as Congress, a state legislature, or a city council. The term includes constitutional provisions, statutes, codes, ordinances, regulations, rules, and so on. Throughout the remainder of the chapter, the term *statute* is used when discussing legal arguments or positions based on enacted law.

There are several approaches to consider when attacking a legal position based on a statute. Some of these approaches are listed in Exhibit 12–1. Consider all of them when researching and analyzing an argument based on a statute to ensure that you identify all possible weaknesses and counterarguments.

1. Elements of the Statute Are Not Met

Every statute is composed of elements that must be met before the statute can apply. As discussed in Chapter 4, these components are called elements. When a client's case is based on a statute, facts must be present in the case that establish or satisfy each of the elements of the statute.

> **FOR EXAMPLE** Criminal Code § 1000 defines burglary as the breaking and entering of the residence of another with the intent to commit a crime. The elements are:
> 1. Breaking and entering
> 2. The residence
> 3. Of another
> 4. With the intent to commit a crime
>
> Facts must be present that establish or satisfy each of these elements before an individual can be convicted of burglary.

One way to attack a legal position based on a statute is to argue that the elements of the statute have not been met—that is, there are not facts present in the case to establish or satisfy one or more elements of the statute.

> **FOR EXAMPLE** Mary is charged under Criminal Code § 1000 with burglary of Steve's house. Steve is a friend of Mary, and Mary often stays at Steve's house. On the date of the alleged burglary, Steve's house was unlocked. Mary came over to see Steve, entered the house, saw money on the kitchen table, took it, and left.

The counterargument to the prosecution's reliance on the statute is that there are no facts present in the case to establish two elements of the law:

1. Mary did not break into the house; it was unlocked.
2. Mary did not enter with the intent to commit a crime. She entered with the intent to visit Steve. The intent to commit a crime did not occur until after entry had taken place.

When conducting counteranalysis of an argument based on a statute, closely examine the facts relied upon to establish *each* of the required elements. Ask yourself, "Have the elements of the statute been met?" Look for any argument that can be raised that the facts do not establish or satisfy an element or elements.

2. Statute Is Sufficiently Broad—Different Construction

In many situations, a statute may be sufficiently broad to allow an interpretation or application different from that relied upon by the opposing side.

FOR EXAMPLE Section 54-9-91 of the state domestic relations statute provides that custody shall be determined in the best interest of the children. Gerald contends that he should be granted custody of the children because he lives in a small town, and his former spouse lives in a large city. He argues that a small town is a better environment because it is safer and free from the pressures of gang violence and drug use.

A counterargument can be made that the benefits of the city, such as greater access to the arts, museums, and universities, offset the alleged disadvantages of a large city. The term *best interest of the children* can be interpreted in a manner different from that urged by the opposing side.

Where the language relied upon in a statute is broadly crafted, such as in this example, look for the counterargument that a different interpretation is permissible because of the broadness of the language. Ask this question: "Is the statute sufficiently broad to permit a construction or application different from that urged by the opposition?"

3. Statute Misconstrued or Does Not Apply

This approach is related to that discussed in the preceding subsection. Explore the possibility of a counterargument that the statute is being misconstrued or misapplied.

FOR EXAMPLE Section 9(A) of the Deceptive Trade Practices Act provides a remedy in tort for "deceptive practices in negotiation or performance" of a contract for the sale of goods. Tom and Larry have a contract for the delivery of goods. Under the contract, Tom is to deliver the goods on the fifth of each month. Every month Tom comes up with some excuse for not delivering the goods on the fifth, and the goods are always delivered between the seventh and fifteenth of the month. Finally, Larry gets fed up and sues Tom for violation of the Deceptive Trade Practices Act, claiming that Tom is engaging in deceptive practices in the performance of the contract.

A review of the legislative history and case law clearly indicates that the Deceptive Trade Practices Act is not designed to apply to simple breach of contract cases. The Sale of Goods provisions of the Commercial Code statutes govern breach of contract situations. The courts have consistently held that when there is an adequate remedy in contract law, the tort remedy available under the act does not apply. Therefore, a counterargument can be raised that the statute has been misconstrued and does not apply in a simple breach of contract case such as that of Tom and Larry.

When a legal position or argument is based on a statute, engage in counteranalysis to ensure that the statute is not being misconstrued or applied in a situation to which it clearly does not apply. Always consult case law to determine if the courts have interpreted or applied the statute in a manner different from that relied upon. Ask the following questions: "Has the statute been misconstrued or does not apply? Does another statute apply?"

4. Statute Relied upon as a Guide Does Not Apply

In some situations, the statute that governs does not have a provision that addresses a specific question raised by the facts of a client's case. In such instances, there may be an argument that a different statute, which has a section that governs a similar fact situation, may be used as guidance in interpreting the applicable statute. It is usually argued that the different statute can be used as guidance because the language and functions of the statutes are similar.

When this occurs, you can make the counterargument that the statute relied upon to interpret another statute is not intended to govern or apply to the type of situation presented by the client's case and, therefore, cannot be used as a guide. The argument usually is that the statute governs or applies only to those limited fact situations covered by the language of the statute and cannot be used as a guide for the interpretation of another statute.

> **FOR EXAMPLE**   The jurisdiction has adopted the following statutes:
>
> ✦ § 59-1 provides that an individual must be a resident of the county to be eligible to run for the position of animal control officer.
>
> ✦ § 200-1 provides that an individual must be a resident of the county for three months to run for a position on the county school board.
>
> Aaron, a resident of the city for three months, wants to run for the position of animal control officer. She argues that since § 59-1 is silent on the length of residency necessary to be eligible to run for the position of animal control officer, the three-month residency requirement established in § 200-1 should be used as a guide to determine the length of residency required under § 59-1. She reasons that because both statutes are similar in language (both use the word *resident*) and because both involve county elective offices, they are sufficiently similar for the residency requirement of § 200-1 to be used as the standard for § 59-1.
>
> Because the statutes are different, however, a counterargument can be made that the duties of animal control officer are much different from those of a school board member. The duties of the animal control officer require a degree of familiarity with the geography of the county that cannot be acquired in three months. Therefore, the differences in the requirements of the positions represent a factual difference that renders § 200-1 inappropriate for use as a guide to interpret § 59-1.

In every situation where it is argued that a provision of one statute may apply or be used to interpret a provision of a different statute, a counterargument can *always* be made that no matter how similar in language and function, the statutes differ functionally in some way. Therefore, the provisions of one statute cannot be relied upon or applied to interpret or govern the other statute.

When your legal position or argument is based upon the use of one statute as a guide to interpret another statute, consider the counterargument that focuses on the differences in the statutes. Keep in mind this question: "Is it possible that the statute relied upon as a guide is so functionally different that it cannot be used as a guide to interpret the statute being analyzed?"

5. Statute Relied upon Has Not Been Adopted in Jurisdiction

The jurisdiction has no law or statute governing a fact situation, and your legal position is based upon an argument that advocates the adoption of the language of, or principles embodied in, a statute from another jurisdiction. In such situations, you are attempting to persuade the court to adopt the law, or the principles embodied in the law, of another jurisdiction.

A counterargument can be made that a statute, or principles that apply to facts in another jurisdiction, should not be adopted to apply to similar facts in your jurisdiction. It is usually possible to point out some difference between the statutes or difference in the public policy of the jurisdictions and argue that the difference precludes the adoption of the language or principles of the statute.

FOR EXAMPLE Ida, a resident of state A, borrows her next-door neighbor's lawn mower. Due to a defect in the mower, Ida is injured. Ida sues the manufacturer, a local company, for breach of warranty. The manufacturer moves for dismissal, claiming that the warranty does not extend to nonpurchasers. The commercial code adopted in state A does not address the question, nor is there any case law on point. Ida argues that the court should adopt the language of the law of state B, a neighboring state. Section 2-389 of state B's commercial code provides that warranties extend to the buyer and any person who may be reasonably expected to use the goods, which includes a neighbor.

The manufacturer's counterargument could be that the law of state B should not be looked to because of policy differences between the states. State A, to encourage and protect the growth of local industry, has traditionally adopted a policy that narrowly limits manufacturer liability. State B's position represents an expansive view that broadly extends manufacturer liability, a position contrary to state A's traditional view.

When conducting counteranalysis, look for the argument that the statute relied upon has not been adopted and should not apply. Ask the question, "Where a legal position is based upon an argument that advocates the adoption of the language or principles embodied in a statute of another jurisdiction, are there differences in the jurisdictions that preclude the adoption of the language or principles of the statute?" Note that there is always the additional counterargument that such matters are of legislative concern and should be addressed by the legislature, not the courts.

6. Interpretation of Statute Is Unconstitutional or Violates Another Legislative Act

Be alert for an argument that the *application* or *interpretation* of the statute advocated is unconstitutional or violates another statute.

FOR EXAMPLE Section 22 of the state's Secured Transaction Code allows a creditor to repossess collateral after providing the debtor with notice of default and allowing the debtor 60 days to cure the default. A car dealer, after providing notice of default and waiting more than 60 days for the customer to cure the default, repossessed the customer's car from the customer's residence while the customer was at work. The car dealer interpreted the statute to not require prior court approval and, therefore, did not seek a court order authorizing the repossession.

The customer sued the car dealer, claiming the dealer illegally seized the car because the due process clause of the state constitution requires a court order before property can be seized. The dealer claimed that the seizure was legal because he complied with the statute—that is, he provided notice of default and waited 60 days.

The counterargument is that the interpretation of the statute urged by the dealer is unconstitutional because it allows for prejudgment seizure—that is, it allows the seizure of property without prior court approval.

Always counteranalyze a legal position or argument based on an interpretation of a law for the possibility that the interpretation violates a constitutional or statutory provision. Ask yourself this question: "Is the interpretation of the statute urged by the opposition unconstitutional or does it violate another legislative act?"

7. Statute Relied upon Is Unconstitutional

Although statutes are not usually unconstitutional and, therefore, are not likely to be vulnerable to constitutional attack, you should consider the constitutionality of the statute on which a legal position is based. Has the constitutionality of the statute been questioned in scholarly journals, law reviews, and so on? Try to anticipate any argument based on a constitutional challenge.

FOR EXAMPLE Ellen is prosecuted under a local ordinance that prohibits the sale of any material that "shows genitalia or excites a prurient interest." Such a statute may be subject to challenge as being unconstitutional because the term *prurient interest* is too vague.

When working with statutes, consider a counterargument based on a challenge to the constitutionality of the statute. Ask the question, "Is the statute unconstitutional?"

Note: When a legal position or argument is based upon a statute, be sure to conduct thorough research to ensure that some other law, provision, or court decision does not apply that affects your reliance on the statute.

C. Case Law

To understand how to counteranalyze a legal position or argument based upon reliance on case law, it is necessary to understand the process involved in determining if a court opinion is on point. Therefore, it is helpful to review Chapter 6 before beginning this section. When used in this section, the terms *rule of law* and *legal principle* include any constitutional, legislative, or case law provision, act, doctrine, principle, or test relied upon by the court in reaching its decision.

There are several approaches for challenging a legal position based upon case law. Some of these approaches are listed in Exhibit 12–2. Consider each of them when conducting counteranalysis.

1. Reliance on Court Opinion Is Misplaced—Key Fact Difference

Apply the test from the Determining If a Case Is on Point section of Chapter 6: "Substitute the client's key facts for those of the court opinion. If the substitution of the key facts would result in changing the outcome of the case, the court opinion cannot be used as precedent."

Exhibit 12–2
Counteranalysis
Approaches to a Legal
Position Based upon
Case Law.

Challenges to a Position or Argument Based on Case Law
1. Reliance upon the court opinion is misplaced because the key facts in the opinion and the key facts of the client's case are different to such a nature or degree that they render the court opinion unusable as precedent.
2. Reliance on the court opinion is misplaced because the rule of law or legal principle applied in the court opinion does not apply.
3. The court opinion is subject to an interpretation different from that relied upon in support of a legal position.
4. The rule or principle adopted in the opinion relied upon is not universally followed.
5. The opinion relied upon presents several possible solutions to the problem, and the one urged by the opposition is not mandatory and is not the best choice.
6. The position relied upon no longer represents sound public policy and should not be followed.
7. There are other equally relevant cases that do not support the position adopted in the case relied upon.

FOR EXAMPLE The plaintiff requests that a psychologist's records be admitted into evidence. Plaintiff bases his argument on the holding in the case of *Smith v. Jones*, which allowed the admission of a psychologist's records into evidence. In that case, the evidence was admitted because no claim was raised that the evidence was privileged. The decision turned on the key fact that privilege was not claimed.

In the plaintiff's case, privilege is vigorously claimed. Therefore, *Jones* cannot be relied upon as precedent to support the argument for the admission of the records because it is not on point. There is such a significant difference in the key facts that the case cannot be relied upon as precedent. In *Jones*, privilege was not claimed, but in the plaintiff's case, it is claimed.

Be cautious when your legal argument relies upon a court opinion that has key facts that are different from your case. Conduct counteranalysis to identify a possible counterargument that the court opinion relied upon does not apply because of differences in the key facts. Ask the question, "Is the opinion relied upon not on point because of key fact differences?"

2. Reliance on Court Opinion Is Misplaced—Rule of Law or Legal Principle Does Not Apply

When conducting counteranalysis, look for the counterargument that the legal principle applied in the court opinion does not apply in the case at hand.

FOR EXAMPLE In the case of *Davis v. Davis*, Ms. Davis had sole custody of her two daughters. Ms. Davis' boyfriend occasionally stayed overnight at her home, and the daughters were aware of the overnight visits. Mr. Davis, her former husband, filed a motion with the court asking for a change of custody. He based his claim solely upon his wife's alleged "immoral conduct." He presented no evidence indicating how the overnight visits impacted the children.

The trial court granted a change of custody. In overturning the trial court, the court of appeals ruled that "mere allegations of immoral conduct are not sufficient grounds to award a change of custody." The court stated that evidence must be presented showing that the alleged immoral conduct harmed the children.

In the client's case, the facts are the same as those in *Davis v. Davis* except that instead of occasional overnight visits, the custodial spouse is cohabiting with another person. Also assume a statute in the jurisdiction provides that cohabitation is per se harmful to the children—that is, in cohabitation cases, evidence of harm to the children need not be presented because cohabitation is presumed to be harmful to them.

If the custodial spouse relies on *Davis* for the proposition that the noncustodial spouse's request for change of custody must be denied because he has failed to present evidence of harm to the children, the reliance is misplaced. The reliance is misplaced because the cohabitation statute does not require the presentation of evidence of harm to the children. Therefore, the rule of law presented in *Davis* is not applicable in the client's case, and the case is not on point.

When a court opinion is used to support a legal position, ask the question, "Is reliance on the opinion misplaced because the principle applied does not apply to the case at hand?"

3. Court Opinion Is Subject to a Different Interpretation

The court may have interpreted a term in a manner that is subject to an interpretation different from that relied upon in support of a legal position.

FOR EXAMPLE Mr. Johns is charged with violating Municipal Code § 982, which prohibits nude dancing. Mr. Johns was dancing in see-through bikini briefs. In prosecuting Mr. Johns, the city relied upon the court opinion of *City v. Dew*. In that case, the court, in interpreting the term *nude dancing*, ruled that a dancer is nude when the breast or genitalia are exposed. In *Dew*, the dancer was completely nude.

In Mr. Johns' case, the city contends that Mr. Johns was nude dancing because his genitalia were exposed when he wore see-through bikini briefs. A counterargument could be made that the term *exposed*, as used in the opinion, should be interpreted to mean uncovered. Therefore, a dancer is not nude under the definition adopted in *Dew* when he is covered by any fabric, no matter how sheer. The counterargument is that the language of the opinion is subject to an interpretation different from that relied upon by the opposition.

Closely scrutinize the language of the court opinion to determine if it is subject to another interpretation. Be aware that the interpretation you adopt may not be the only possible interpretation. Ask the question, "Is the court opinion subject to a different interpretation from that relied upon?"

4. Rule or Principle Adopted in Opinion Relied upon Is Not Universally Followed

This should be a consideration when the opinion relied upon is not mandatory precedent—that is, when there is no court opinion directly on point, and a party is urging the court to follow a rule or principle adopted by another court ruling in a similar case in either the same or a different jurisdiction.

| FOR EXAMPLE | The counterargument could be, "Although the plaintiff relies upon and urges the adoption of the principle presented in *Smith v. Jones*, and that |

opinion is followed by the Ninth, Fifth, and Seventh circuits, several other circuits have chosen not to follow it. The better position, presented in the case of *Grape v. Vine*, is followed by the Fourth, Sixth, and Eleventh circuits. The principle adopted in *Vine* more accurately reflects the policies of this jurisdiction."

Identify the other rules or legal principles that may apply by reading the opinions of courts that have adopted other positions in similar cases. Keep in mind the question, "Is the rule or principle of the case relied upon universally followed?"

5. Opinion Presents Several Possible Solutions; One Urged by Opposition Is Not Mandatory and Is Not Best Choice

Check the court opinion relied upon in support of a legal position to determine if the opinion includes other solutions in addition to the one relied upon. Also, check other court opinions to identify different solutions that may have been adopted in other cases. If it is not mandatory to follow a single solution or position, conduct counteranalysis to identify the other possible solutions and anticipate counterarguments that may be based upon one of the other solutions. Ask yourself, "If the opinion relied upon is not mandatory precedent, does the opinion or another court opinion allow for other possible positions?"

| FOR EXAMPLE | A counterargument could be, "In the case of *Smith v. Harris*, the court stated that the plaintiff could pursue several avenues of relief, including |

injunction and damages. The defendant argues that *Harris* mandates the pursuit of injunctive relief when, in fact, the court allowed the pursuit of several avenues of relief in addition to injunction."

6. Position Relied upon No Longer Represents Sound Public Policy and Should Not Be Followed

If the court opinion is mandatory precedent and, therefore, must be followed, explore the possibility that it no longer represents sound public policy and should be overruled. This approach is available only if the court considering the question has the authority to overrule the precedent. A trial court does not have the power to overrule a higher court decision. If an intermediary court of appeal set the precedent, that court has the power to overturn it. If the highest court in the jurisdiction set the precedent, only that court has the power to overturn it. Note, however, that lower courts may have questioned the precedent, and those opinions may be cited to persuade the higher court that the court's position should change.

This approach is always risky because a court will not lightly choose to ignore precedent. A court usually requires a strong argument to support a decision to abandon or not follow precedent. When a position, however, is based upon a court opinion, consider the possibility that the rule or principle adopted in the opinion should no longer be followed due to some policy or other change. In such situations, it can be argued that fairness demands that the court reexamine the law.

| FOR EXAMPLE | Mr. Clark wants to move into an apartment complex that has restrictions based on parental status. The restrictions provide that no individual or |

couple may rent an apartment if they have children. The restrictions also provide that if tenants have children after they rent an apartment, they must vacate the premises within three months of the birth of a child. The only case on point is the 1935 case of *Edwards v. Frank*. In that case, the court ruled that restrictions based on parental status did not violate the Constitution and, therefore, were enforceable.

A counterargument is that current public policy strongly favors families with children, that current policy dictates that rental restrictions based upon parental status are no longer acceptable or desirable, and that, therefore, *Frank* should no longer be followed.

Always consider the question, "Does the court opinion relied upon no longer represent sound public policy and, therefore, should not be followed?"

7. Other Equally Relevant Cases Do Not Support Position Adopted in Case Relied Upon

In some instances, a matter has not been clearly settled by the highest court in the jurisdiction, or the opinions of the highest court appear to conflict. Look for other opinions that may take a position different from the one taken in the court opinion relied upon to support a legal position or argument. Ask yourself, "Are there equally relevant cases that do not support the position adopted in the case relied upon?"

FOR EXAMPLE The client is seeking punitive damages in a negligence case. There are three court opinions from the highest court in the jurisdiction. In the case of *Yaws v. Allen*, the court held that punitive damages may be recovered in a negligence case when there is a showing of gross negligence on the part of the tortfeasor. In the case of *X-ray v. Carrie*, the court ruled that before punitive damages can be awarded in a negligence case, there must be some demonstration that the tortfeasor had a culpable state of mind. In the case of *Casy v. Cox*, the court held that the establishment of gross negligence by itself does not indicate the existence of a culpable state of mind; it is also necessary to demonstrate willful and wanton misconduct by the tortfeasor.

Reliance on *Yaws v. Allen*, in support of a legal position that the establishment of gross negligence on the part of the tortfeasor is sufficient to obtain punitive damages, is subject to challenge. A counterargument is that the *Carrie* and *Cox* cases, also from the highest court in the jurisdiction, require more than gross negligence.

Note: When a legal position or argument is based upon a court opinion, always be sure that thorough research is conducted to find any other law, provision, or court decision that may affect your reliance upon the opinion. The research should identify all court opinions that present possible solutions and approaches to the problem being analyzed.

VII. COUNTERANALYSIS TECHNIQUES—COMMENTS

When engaging in legal research or analysis, review all the approaches presented in the preceding sections and determine if the legal position or argument may be challenged through any of them. Be aware, however, that the techniques and considerations presented here are not inclusive of all the available ways to attack or challenge a legal position or argument based upon a legislative act or case law. In addition to using the techniques listed, use any other approach that comes to mind. Also, combinations of methods may be used. The particular circumstances of the case will determine which, if any, of the suggested approaches are applicable. It is important to remember that when your position or argument is based upon a legislative act or case law, you must engage in thorough counteranalysis to locate any weaknesses, anticipate any counterarguments, and prepare a response.

VIII. KEY POINTS CHECKLIST: *Conducting Counteranalysis*

- For every issue presented in a legal research memorandum, consider how the other side is likely to respond.

- Put yourself in your opponent's position. Assume you are the opponent and consider all possible counterarguments, no matter how ridiculous—be ruthless.

- The more strongly you believe in the correctness of your analysis, the greater the likelihood that you will miss or overlook the counteranalysis to that analysis. Beware, when you feel extremely confident or sure, take extra precautions. Overconfidence can seriously mislead you.

- A weakness in an argument will not go away if you ignore it. You can count on either the other side or the court to bring it to light. It is much better for you to raise the counterargument and diffuse it.

- Do not let your emotions, preconceived notions, or stubbornness interfere with an objective counteranalysis of your position.

- Shepardize the case you are relying on to locate other opinions that distinguish, criticize, or limit it. These cases may present counterarguments.

- Check the digest for other cases that may analyze the law differently. *Shepard's* will identify only those cases that mention the case you are researching. There may be other cases that discuss counterarguments, but do not mention the case you are relying on.

- Counterarguments may be found by consulting a treatise or locating a law review article or ALR annotation on the topic.

- When analyzing court opinions, a counteranalysis of the majority opinion may be found in the dissenting opinion or other opinions that criticize or distinguish the majority opinion.

- When conducting counteranalysis, always consider each of the approaches listed in this chapter. Remember, more than one approach may apply, and approaches other than those listed may be available.

- Even if you find a case on point, always research thoroughly. Look for other laws or court opinions that may apply.

IX. APPLICATION

This section explores the application of the principles discussed in this chapter to the hypotheticals presented at the beginning of this chapter and Chapters 1 and 2.

A. Chapter Hypothetical

Review the example presented at the beginning of this chapter. In the hypothetical, the paralegal failed to conduct a thorough counteranalysis. The assignment was to assess the likelihood that a rule 12(b)(6) motion to dismiss for failure to state a claim would be granted. In a 12(b)(6) motion, the movant is basically claiming that under the facts of the case, the plaintiff cannot state a claim. To state a claim in a negligence case, there must be facts present that establish each of the elements of negligence: duty, breach of duty, proximate cause, and damages. In the example, the paralegal's attention was focused on duty, that is, on which duty applied. In light of the provisions of the applicable statute, the Ski Safety Act, and the facts of the case, there appeared to be a conflict of duties. The paralegal focused on which of the following two duties applied:

✦ The resort's duty to warn of hazards

✦ The skier's duty to know of and be responsible for snow and ice conditions

The paralegal's mistake was the failure to conduct a complete counteranalysis. A proper counteranalysis would have led the paralegal to consider the opponent's possible challenge involving the other areas of negligence—breach of duty, proximate cause, and damages. Had this been done, the paralegal would have recognized that the opposing side could raise a proximate cause argument: the cause of the accident was the skier's breach of duty by skiing beyond the range of his ability, not the resort's failure to warn. Had the paralegal considered this argument, a response could have been prepared, and the motion may not have been granted.

This example illustrates one of the most important considerations in counteranalysis: *when analyzing a legal position, always conduct thorough and complete research that considers every possible attack, no matter how remote.*

B. Chapter 1 Hypothetical *Reins v. Stewart*

As discussed in Chapter 5, Vanessa located a case on point, *Rael v. Cadena*, 93 N.M. 684, 604 P.2d 822 (Ct. App. 1979). When conducting counteranalysis, Vanessa's first step is to Shepardize the case to determine if another case or cases analyze the law differently. A check of the Shepard's for the *Pacific Reporter* shows that the case is distinguished at 75 P3d 417. Vanessa reads this opinion to see if it presents a counterargument to the legal argument that a bystander may be liable for verbally encouraging the perpetrator of a battery.

Vanessa also checks the *Pacific Digest* for other cases that may analyze the law differently. Shepard's will identify only those cases that mention *Rael v. Cadena*. There may be other cases that analyze the question of bystander liability, but do not mention the case.

Vanessa may also find counterarguments by consulting a tort law treatise or locating a law review article or ALR annotation on the topic. As mentioned in the Application section of Chapter 7, there is an annotation on point, *Civil Liability of One Instigating or Inciting an Assault or Assault and Battery Notwithstanding Primary or Active Participant Therein Has Been Absolved of Liability*, 72 A.L.R. 2nd 1229, an annotation on the topic by H. C. Hind. The annotation discusses the counterarguments to the position that the bystander is liable.

C. Chapter 2 Hypothetical *United States v. Canter*

The case Dustin has located is *United States v. Martinez-Jimenez*, 864 F.2d 664 (9th Cir. 1989). Dustin's first step in identifying counterarguments to the position that a fake gun may be considered a deadly weapon is to Shepardize the case. A check of the *Shepard's Federal Reporter, Second Series* shows that the case is distinguished at 21 F.3d 1139 and 305 ADC 391. Dustin reads these opinions for counterarguments.

The *Shepard's* citation also shows an ALR annotation on the topic at A.L.R. 3d 1006. Dustin reads this annotation for counterarguments.

In addition, Dustin looks for a law review article on the topic. As mentioned in the Application section of Chapter 8, there is a law review on point: Gary Garrigues, *United States v. Martinez-Jimenez* [864 F.2d 664]; *use a toy gun, go to prison*, 20 Golden Gate U. L. Rev. 167. This article provides Dustin with an exhaustive analysis of the topic.

SUMMARY

Counteranalysis is the process of discovering and presenting the counterarguments to a legal position or argument. It is important because to be able to adequately address a legal problem, all aspects of the problem must be considered. This includes identifying all the potential weaknesses in a legal position and being prepared to respond to all challenges to the position.

Employ counteranalysis whenever you are researching a legal issue or addressing a legal problem. Always be alert and look for counterarguments.

A prerequisite to engaging in counteranalysis is thorough research of the question or legal argument. When conducting legal research, counteranalysis means looking for legal authority that supports the argument the opponent is likely to raise in response to your analysis of the issue. After the research is complete, you can employ many approaches to assist you in counteranalysis.

Because most legal arguments are based upon enacted law or case law, this chapter focuses on various counterarguments that may be raised when attacking reliance on an enacted law or case law. The list of approaches presented in this chapter is by no means inclusive of all the available ways to challenge a legal argument or position. It is important to make sure that you engage in counteranalysis using *all* the avenues listed (and any other approach) when looking for potential weaknesses in or counterarguments to a legal position. You can count on the opposing side to discover weaknesses in your position and use them against you. Remember, whenever you are reviewing your client's case, you are negligent if you fail to engage in counteranalysis.

CHAPTER REFERENCES

Case Law   361
Counteranalysis   353
Counteranalysis—Definition   353
Counteranalysis—Techniques   356

Counterargument   353
Enacted Law   356
Ethics   353

INTERNET RESOURCES

At the date of the publication of this text, there are no Web sites dedicated specifically to counteranalysis. However, using a search engine and "law counteranalysis" as a topic, a limited range of sites may be found (21 when this text was drafted), which address some aspect of law and counteranalysis. Some sites involve counteranalysis in specific areas of the law, such as military law, whereas others discuss the topic in relation to taking law school exams. Although some sites briefly mention the role of counteranalysis in the analysis process, no site addresses the topic in depth.

When "law counterargument" is used as the topic, a much larger range of sites may be found (more than 2,000 when this text was drafted). Most of these sites involve counterarguments in specific cases or do not discuss the role of counterargument in the legal analysis process.

For additional materials, please go to the CD accompanying this book

For additional resources, visit our Web site at www.paralegal.delmar.cengage.com

EXERCISES

Additional exercises are located on the Student CD-ROM accompanying the text and Online Companion.

ASSIGNMENT 1

What is counteranalysis? When should counteranalysis be conducted?

ASSIGNMENT 2

Why is counteranalysis important?

ASSIGNMENT 3

Counteranalysis—Legal Position or Argument Based on a Statute

Legislative Acts: Section 359-23A of the state statutes provides that to be eligible to run for the state senate, an individual must be a resident of the state for three years.

Local ordinance section 2231 provides that an individual must be a resident of the municipality to run for a position on the city council. The ordinance does not define residency.

Facts: Jerrie wants to run for the city council. She has been a resident of the state for two years and nine months. The city clerk informs her that she is not eligible to run for city council because she has not been a resident of the state for three years. The clerk states that the city relies on the residency requirement established in section 359-23A.

Assignment: What is the counterargument to the clerk's position?

ASSIGNMENT 4

Counteranalysis—Legal Position or Argument Based on Case Law

Case Law: In the case of *Baldonado v. State*, the plaintiff sued the state for false arrest. In *Baldonado*, a police officer received information from the dispatcher concerning a violent domestic dispute and specifically describing the plaintiff and his vehicle. The dispatcher reported that the plaintiff had been drinking and was leaving the residence with his two minor children. When he arrived at the residence, the officer saw the plaintiff and his two children in the described car. At the scene, the plaintiff's spouse and neighbors corroborated the dispatcher's information that a violent dispute had taken place. When the officer requested plaintiff to shut off the engine and stay at the scene, the plaintiff attempted to leave. The officer stopped the plaintiff from leaving. The court noted that detention by a police officer is allowable only when there is reasonable suspicion that a crime has been committed. The court concluded that there was reasonable suspicion that a crime had been committed and the officer's detention of the defendant was lawful.

Facts: Officer was dispatched to plaintiff's residence to investigate a domestic dispute. When he arrived, he saw a red vehicle driving away from the residence. A neighbor was standing on the sidewalk. He informed the officer that he thought a domestic dispute had taken place at his neighbor's house and plaintiff had just left in the red vehicle. The officer pursued plaintiff and required him to return to the residence. Plaintiff is suing the officer for illegally detaining him.

Assignment: The state argues that *Baldonado v. State* supports the position that the detention was proper. What is the counterargument?

ASSIGNMENT 5

List seven ways to challenge an argument based on an enacted law.

ASSIGNMENT 6

List seven ways to challenge an argument based on case law.

ASSIGNMENT 7

Counteranalysis—Legal Position or Argument Based upon a Statute

Legislative Act: Section 40-3-6-9A of the state criminal code provides that a noncustodial parent can be convicted of custodial interference when the noncustodial parent "maliciously takes, detains, conceals, entices away, or fails to return the child, without good cause, for a protracted period of time."

Assume there is no case law on point in the jurisdiction relevant to the following fact situation.

Facts: Mary has primary custody of her son. The father, Tom, has legal custody for two months in the summer. Tom takes the son for two months in the summer, but fails to tell Mary where the son is and does not allow her to communicate with him. Before he leaves with the son, Tom tells Mary, "I'm going to punish you for the way you've treated me."

Assignment: The following are arguments presented by Mary in support of her claim that Tom is in violation of the statute. What are the counterarguments to each argument?

Part A

Tom's actions constitute concealment within the meaning of the statute.

Part B

Same facts as above, but when Tom is leaving, he says, "Because you wouldn't allow me to communicate with him when you had custody, I'm going to do the same." Mary argues that Tom's actions constitute concealment.

Part C

Same facts except that Tom says nothing when he picks up the son.

Part D

Tom allows the son to communicate with Mary, but he returns the son one day late. Mary argues that this constitutes failing to return the child without good cause for a protracted period of time.

Part E

Same facts as in part D except that Tom returns the son two weeks late.

Part F

Same facts as in part E except that Tom explains that he was unable to return the son on time because his car engine blew up, and it took two weeks to fix it.

ASSIGNMENT 8

Counteranalysis—Legal Position or Argument Based upon Case Law

In the following example, assume that the only court opinion on point is *United States v. Leon* (see Appendix C).

Facts: Officer Jones submits to Judge Bean a request for a search warrant for the search of Steve's apartment. Officer Jones knows that there is not sufficient probable cause for the issuance of the warrant, but he also knows that Judge Bean is very pro–law enforcement and will most likely issue the warrant anyway. Judge Bean issues the warrant. Officer Jones gives the warrant to other officers and instructs them to execute it. He does not tell them that he knows it is defective because of the lack of probable cause for its issuance. The other officers execute the warrant in the good faith belief that it is valid. Drugs are found, and Steve is charged with possession.

Steve moves for suppression of the evidence, claiming that the search was illegal and the evidence must be excluded under the exclusionary rule. What is the counterargument to the prosecution's position in each of the following situations?

Part A

The prosecution argues that because the officers executing the warrant were acting in the good faith belief that the warrant was valid, *United States v. Leon* governs the case. The good faith exception to the exclusionary rule applies and, therefore, the evidence should not be suppressed.

Part B

Same facts except that officer Jones delivers the warrant to members of the Citizens Protection Association, a private group of citizens trained by the police to assist in the performance of minor police functions. The group volunteers its services and is not employed by the police. They execute the warrant and make a citizen's arrest of Steve. The prosecution argues that *United States v. Leon* governs, and the case holds that the exclusionary rule is designed only to protect against police misconduct, not misconduct by private citizens.

ASSIGNMENT 9

Legislative Act: Section 41-1-6-9 of the state statutes defines defamation as the intentional publication of a false statement about a person. The statute defines publication as communication to a third person.

Case Law: *Ender v. Gault* is an opinion of the highest court in the state. In the case, Gault wrote a letter to Ender accusing Ender of defrauding his clients. Gault intended to hand-deliver the letter to Ender at a party at Ender's house. Gault became intoxicated at the party and left the letter on Ender's kitchen table. The letter was in an unsealed envelope with Ender's name on it. A business competitor of Ender who was at the party opened and read the letter.

Ender sued Gault for defamation. In its ruling in favor of Ender, the court stated that "intentional publication" as used in the statute includes "publication that occurs as a result of the gross negligence of the defendant." The court held that Gault's act of leaving the envelope unsealed on the kitchen table during a party constituted gross negligence.

Facts: Tom is a business associate of Allen. He believes Allen is stealing from their clients. Tom writes a letter to Allen stating that he knows Allen is stealing and that he intends to file criminal charges.

Tom, intending to hand-deliver the letter to Allen, goes to a restaurant where Allen usually has lunch. After waiting an hour for Allen, one of Allen's friends enters the restaurant. Tom folds the letter and seals it with scotch tape. He gives the letter to the friend and asks him to deliver it to Allen. He does not tell the friend not to open the letter. The friend peels back the tape, reads the letter, reseals it, and delivers it to Allen. Allen finds out that the friend read the letter and sues Tom for defamation under section 41-1-6-9.

Assignment: Take into consideration the statute, the court opinion, and the facts when doing the following:

Part A

Prepare an argument in support of the position that Tom defamed Allen.

Part B

Prepare a counterargument to the argument prepared in part A.

CHAPTER 13

The Research Process for Effective Legal Research

Outline

Learning Objectives

After completing this chapter, you should understand:

✦ The goal of legal research

✦ What a legal research process is and its importance

✦ The two parts of the legal research process

✦ The importance and use of an expanded outline in the legal writing process

✦ When to stop researching

✦ The importance of focus and intellectual honesty

For the past five years, Rick Strong has been the paralegal for Sara Fletcher, a criminal defense attorney. He performs a wide range of paralegal tasks for Sara. He interviews clients and witnesses, conducts investigations, arranges and maintains client files, performs legal research, and occasionally prepares legal memoranda. Rick enjoys legal research and finding the answers to legal questions.

Carol Beck recently retained Sara to represent her in the case of *State v. Carol Beck*. In the case, police officers obtained a search warrant from a magistrate court judge authorizing a search of Ms. Beck's house for drugs. On the bottom of the warrant, the judge wrote, "Unannounced entry is authorized to ensure officer safety." The officers' affidavit in support of the warrant stated that in other drug search cases, if the officers announced their presence prior to entry, the persons occupying the premises being searched often posed a threat to the officers. The affidavit did not include any particular information about Ms. Beck being a threat. Based on this affidavit, the judge authorized the officers to enter Ms. Beck's house unannounced. When the officers executed the warrant, they did not announce their presence and purpose prior to entry. Their search recovered a plastic bag containing an ounce of cocaine. Carol Beck was charged with possession with intent to distribute.

Sara and Rick have just begun the preliminary stages of preparing Ms. Beck's defense. Rick's assignment is to prepare a legal memorandum addressing the possibility of obtaining suppression of the evidence on the basis that the search was illegal. Sara tells Rick that any suppression motion must be filed in 30 days. What is the process Rick should follow when preparing the memorandum? The legal research process is presented in this chapter. The answer to Rick's question is discussed in the Application section of the chapter.

I. INTRODUCTION

The legal issue(s) in a client's case must be researched and analyzed and the results communicated, usually in written form. Legal research, analysis, and writing are all related. Each is a step in a process designed to answer legal questions and lead to the resolution of disputes. Legal research is part of the legal analysis process. It is that part of the legal analysis process that involves finding the law that applies to the legal question raised by the facts of a client's case.

For various reasons, many people believe that most legal communication is oral and takes place either in the courtroom or in a law office. This is not the case, however. The bulk of legal communication is written. The vast majority of cases never go to trial. They are settled, and the settlements are reduced to writing. When cases do go to trial, much of the trial work involves research and writing: written motions, trial briefs, jury instructions, and so on. In many instances, the practice of law engaged in by law firms rarely involves litigation, but instead focuses on the preparation of contracts, wills, corporation instruments, and other legal documents. A great deal of time is spent in research and in communicating that research in the form of legal memoranda and legal instruments.

There are many approaches to conducting legal research; there is no magic formula. This chapter presents a discussion of the legal research process, including a two-part approach to legal research and guidelines to follow when engaging in legal research.

II. GOAL OF LEGAL RESEARCH

Before addressing the considerations involved in the legal research process, it is important to identify the goal of legal research. The primary goal of legal research is to identify the law that answers the question raised by the facts of a client's case. This includes locating the applicable statutory and case law and the authority that interprets how the law applies, including secondary authority if necessary.

You may believe that you do not possess good legal research skills. Research may be a struggle for you. Research skills can be developed and research made easier through practice and the use of a *research process*.

III. LEGAL RESEARCH PROCESS

A legal research process is a systematic approach to legal research. It is an organized approach to legal research and analysis that helps you develop research skills. It makes legal research easier and is necessary for the following:

✦ Legal writing is highly organized and structured. An organized research structure helps ensure that complex subject matter is clearly communicated.

> **FOR EXAMPLE** The IRAC (Issue, Rule, Analysis, Conclusion) analytical method discussed in Chapter 1 is a structured approach to problem solving. The IRAC format, when followed in the research and preparation of a legal memorandum, helps ensure the clear communication of the complex subject matter of legal issue analysis.

The use of a legal research process helps you conduct research and analysis within the structure and format of the type of legal writing assigned. A research process saves time by providing the means for organizing your legal analysis and research material as it is gathered.

✦ If you do not have a research process and merely gather research material, you will waste a great deal of time. Most research assignments require that the results be communicated to someone in written form, such as an office legal

The Two Parts of the Legal Research Process	
Part A—Analyze the Assignment	The part of the research process where the assignment is analyzed, constraints are identified, and a research outline is prepared.
Part B—Conduct Research	The part of the research process where preliminary research is preformed if necessary, key facts and the issue(s) are identified, and the law that governs the issue is located.

Exhibit 13–1
The Parts of the Legal Research Process.

memorandum. If you begin to write without having organized your research and analysis, or without having thought through what you are going to write, you will flounder. If you gather a mountain of research that requires a great deal of analysis, time will be wasted in the struggle to determine what goes where and how. *A research process forces you to think before you write.* It forces you to follow an organized structure from the beginning. When you sit down to write, you will be ready. The assignment will have been thought through and organized.

✦ When you are researching or analyzing an assignment or engaging in legal writing, a research process helps you capture ideas as they come to you. A process provides a framework to capture ideas and record them in their proper place as they occur. Without a process, ideas may be lost. This is discussed in the Use of an Outline subsection of this chapter.

✦ A research process also helps you overcome the difficult areas of legal research and writing. You may get stuck in a difficult research area or encounter writer's block. A research process helps you avoid these problems by providing a stepped approach.

Often you become stuck or blocked because you have missed a step or left something out. A process is a guide that includes all the steps and helps ensure that nothing is left out. There are many processes and combinations of processes that you may adopt when engaging in legal research. What works for one person may not work for another. You may ultimately adopt a process that includes steps from various approaches to legal research, including some of those presented in this chapter. It does not matter what process you ultimately adopt, but it is essential that you adopt some process.

This section presents a two-part legal research process and discusses matters that you should consider at each stage of the process (see Exhibit 13–1). The first part involves analyzing the assignment; the second part is conducting research.

IV. PART A—ANALYZE THE ASSIGNMENT

Novice researchers often begin to research without adequate preparation. One of the most important aspects of the research process is performing the steps necessary to become adequately prepared to begin researching. Research is much easier if you are fully prepared when you begin. This stage of the research process may be divided into the three sections presented in Exhibit 13–2.

A. Assignment

The research process begins with identifying the type and purpose of the assignment. You must consider two questions when reviewing the assignment:

✦ Is the assignment clearly understood?
✦ If writing a document is part of the assignment, what type of document is required?

Exhibit 13–2
Sections of
Part A—Analyze
the Assignment.

The Three Sections of Part A of the Research Process	
1. Assignment	Identify the type and purpose of the research assignment.
2. Constraints	Consider any constraints placed on the assignment.
3. Organization	Organize the research assignment.

1. Is the Assignment Clearly Understood?

You may receive the assignment in the form of a written memorandum or through oral instructions from the supervising attorney. An early and important step is to be sure that you understand the task you have been assigned. If you have any questions concerning the general nature or specifics of the assignment, ask.

A misunderstanding of the assignment can result in a great deal of time being wasted in the performance of the wrong task. Most attorneys welcome inquiries and prefer that a paralegal or law clerk ask questions rather than proceed in a wrong direction. In this regard, if the assignment is unclear in any way, summarize the assignment orally with the attorney. Another approach is to draft a brief recapitulation of the assignment and submit it for the attorney's review.

2. What Type of Legal Writing (Document) Is Required?

Most legal research is communicated in written form such as a case brief, office legal memorandum, and correspondence. The next step when considering the assignment is to determine the type of legal writing the assignment requires. This is important because each type of legal writing has a different function and different requirements. Before you begin, you must know what form of legal writing is required.

There are various types of legal writing and numerous ways to categorize the types.

a. Law Office Legal Research and Analysis Memoranda

A researcher may be assigned the task of researching and analyzing the law that applies to a client's case. The law office legal memorandum is designed to inform the reader of the results of the research and analysis. The assignment may be as simple as identifying the statutory or case law that applies to a legal issue, or as complex as identifying the issues in a case and analyzing the law that applies.

b. Correspondence

There are several types of correspondence that a paralegal or law clerk may be required to draft: demand letters, settlement proposals, and notices of events such as hearing dates. The assignment may require research and preparation of the draft of a letter to be sent to the client informing the client of the law that applies in the client's case and how the law applies. Neither a paralegal nor a law clerk may give legal advice to the client, but they may prepare the draft of the correspondence that the attorney will send to the client.

c. Court Briefs

A court brief is a document filed with a court that contains an attorney's legal argument and the legal authority in support of that argument. There are primarily two categories of court briefs: trial court briefs and appellate court briefs.

✦ *Trial Court Briefs*—A court may require an attorney to submit a brief in support of a position taken by an attorney in regard to a legal issue in the case.

A trial court brief is usually submitted in support of or in opposition to a motion filed with the court.

> **FOR EXAMPLE** An attorney files a motion to dismiss a complaint, claiming that the statute of limitations has run. In support of the motion, the attorney files a legal brief that contains the legal and factual reasons why the court should grant the motion. The opposing side will also file a brief in opposition to the granting of the motion.

✦ ***Appellate Court Briefs***—An appellate brief is a document filed with an appellate court. It presents the legal arguments and authorities in support of the client's position on appeal. It is designed to persuade the appellate court to rule in the client's favor.

Each of these types of legal writing is structured differently. If legal writing is part of the assignment, you will organize your research using an outline based upon the organizational format your employer uses when drafting these documents (see subsection C Organization—Research Outline later in this chapter). The research process is governed by the type of legal writing the assignment requires. Therefore, an early step is the identification of the type of writing required.

B. Constraints

The next step in part A of the research process is to consider any possible constraints that may affect the performance of the assignment. Three major constraints that should be considered are presented in Exhibit 13–3.

1. Time

A time constraint may govern the performance of an assignment. Most assignments have a deadline. You must determine what the deadline is. After this is done, allocate a specific amount of time to each stage of the writing process.

If you fail to allocate your time or fail to stick to the allocation, you may become absorbed or stuck in one stage and fail to leave enough time to properly complete the assignment. It does no good to completely research and analyze an issue if you do not have time to translate the research and analysis into a written form.

> **FOR EXAMPLE** You have 15 days to prepare an office memorandum. You become absorbed in the intricacies of the research and leave only two days to write the memo. This is not sufficient time to prepare a well-crafted product. The memorandum will either not be turned in on time, or be poorly written. In either event, your professional reputation is negatively affected.

Major Constraints on the Research Process	
Time	If the performance of the assignment is governed by a deadline, you should allocate a specific amount of time to each part of the research process.
Length	If the assignment is limited to a set number of pages, you should organize research to ensure each section is allotted sufficient space.
Format/Organization	If the assignment is governed by a specific format or style established by office guidelines or court rule, identify the format.

Exhibit 13–3
Constraints on the Research Process.

2. Length

The assignment may have a length constraint. The supervising attorney may require that it not exceed a certain number of pages. If this is the case, keep the length limitation in mind from the start. The amount of research material you gather is affected by this limitation. Of course, you must gather all the applicable law. You must, however, screen the research to ensure that you do not gather excessive information such as numerous secondary authority sources. With the space limitation in mind, consider how much of the material that you are gathering can be included in the writing. Also, organize the writing to make sure that each section is allotted sufficient space.

> **FOR EXAMPLE** The assignment is to prepare a legal research memorandum that does not exceed 15 pages. The organization must allocate sufficient space for each section of the memorandum. If the research ends up consisting of 14 pages, there will not be sufficient space for the statement of the facts, the issue, or the conclusion.

3. Format/Organization

Most law offices have rules or guidelines that govern the organization and format of most types of legal writing, including the presentation of legal research through such means as case briefs, office memoranda, and correspondence. Courts have formal rules governing the format and style of briefs and other documents submitted for filing.

Inasmuch as you must draft the assignment within the constraints of the required format, you must identify that format at the beginning of the research process. The format is used as the basis for the research outline discussed in the next section.

C. Organization—Research Outline

Organization is the key to successful legal research. You must be organized when conducting research. This may be accomplished through the development and use of an outline. An **outline** is the skeletal structure and organizational framework of the legal research assignment. Three aspects of outlines are presented here:

- ✦ The value of an outline
- ✦ The creation of an outline
- ✦ The use of an outline

1. Value of an Outline

An outline makes research and writing easier by providing an organized framework for research and analysis. There are several reasons for this:

- ✦ The act of creating an outline causes you to organize ideas and prepare an approach to the assignment at the beginning of the process. This helps you think through all the aspects of the assignment and take a global view, thereby avoiding gaps and weaknesses in your approach. You focus your attention and organize your thinking before you jump into the assignment.

- ✦ The use of an outline saves time. When used properly, all the information from a research source is placed in the outline when research is being performed. Time is often wasted having to retrieve a research source for a second or subsequent time to gather information that you either thought was not important or forgot to retrieve. If an outline is used properly, no research source should be retrieved more than once.

✦ An outline provides an organized framework for the structure of the assignment and for conducting research and analysis. It provides a context within which to place ideas and research. This use is discussed in detail in the Use of an Outline subsection.

✦ An outline breaks complex problems into manageable components. It provides an organized framework from which to approach complex problems.

2. Creation of an Outline

The goal when creating an outline is to prepare the skeletal framework for the research and for any document you may be assigned to draft in conjunction with the research. The outline should provide an overall picture of how all the pieces of the assignment relate to each other and fit together. The form of the outline is not important. Whether you use Roman numerals (I and II), capital letters (A and B), narrative sentences, fragments of sentences, or single words does not matter. Use whatever form or style works for you. Use indentations to separate main topics from subtopics.

FOR EXAMPLE If the assignment is to conduct research and prepare a legal research memorandum the outline would consist of the following:

I.   Introduction

II. Issue

III. Analysis

    A. Rule of law

    B. Case law interpreting rule of law

       1. Name of case

       2. Facts of case

    C. Application of rule of law to client's case

IV. Conclusion

The outline of the legal research is governed by the type of research you are assigned. If the assignment is simply to locate a case or a statute, the outline may be as simple as

    I.   Key Facts

    II. Issue

    III. Case/Statute

If the research assignment requires the presentation of the results in a particular format, such as a research memorandum, locate the standard format used in the office for the type of legal writing you are drafting. In the case of an office legal memorandum or correspondence, the law office may have a special format that must be followed. Use that format as the basis for the outline. If the writing is to be filed in court, such as an appellate brief, follow the format set out in the court rules. Whatever the basic format is, it may be necessary to make additions and expand the outline.

> **FOR EXAMPLE** The firm's format for an office legal memorandum is
>
> 1. Description of assignment
> 2. Issue
> 3. Facts
> 4. Analysis
> 5. Conclusion

This is a broad format that needs a lot of filling in to be useful. It may be necessary to fill in details for each section.

> **FOR EXAMPLE** An expansion of the analysis section may be as follows:
>
> 4. Analysis
>   1. Introduction
>   2. Rule of law
>   3. Case interpreting the rule of law
>   a. Name of case/citation
>   b. Facts of case
>   c. Rule of law or legal principle presented in the case that applies to the client's facts
>   d. Application of rule/principle from the case to the client's facts
>   4. Counteranalysis

When developing an outline, there are several points to keep in mind:

(1) Keep the Facts and Issues of the Assignment in Mind while Developing the Outline.   It may be necessary to expand the outline to accommodate additional facts and issues.

> **FOR EXAMPLE** The standard office memo outline may have only one issue. Your assignment may involve more than one issue. Expand the outline to apply the standard office outline to each issue.

(2) Be Flexible when Creating and Working with an Outline.   Realize that it may be necessary to change the outline as you conduct research.

> **FOR EXAMPLE** The assignment involves researching a single issue and drafting a simple office legal memorandum. When research is conducted, it becomes apparent that there are two aspects of the rule of law that apply to the issue and two court opinions that need to be included in the analysis. The memo outline must now be expanded:
>
> 4. Analysis
>   1. Introduction
>   2. Rule of law—Slander
>   3. Case interpreting the meaning of "publication" as used in the rule of law

     a. Name of case/citation

     b. Facts of case

     c. Interpretation of term

     d. Application of the interpretation to the client's facts

  4. Case interpreting the meaning of "written" as used in the rule of law

     a. Name of case/citation

     b. Facts of case

     c. Interpretation of term

     d. Application of the interpretation to the client's facts

  5. Counteranalysis

(3) Do Not Be Surprised if It Is Necessary to Reorganize the Outline as a Result of Your Research. Research may provide a clearer picture of the relationship between issues and necessitate a rethinking of the organization of the outline.

> **FOR EXAMPLE** As a result of your research, you may realize that the sequence in which you plan to address the issues should be changed. The issue you thought should be discussed first should come second.

(4) If the Research Assignment Involves Presenting the Result in a Written Document Such as a Memo, the Basic Organizational Approach for Most Legal Writing Is the IRAC Format. That is, first state the question or issue, next identify the rule of law that governs the issue, then analyze how and why the rule applies, and end with a conclusion summarizing the analysis. This format may be followed when addressing each issue and subissue. If for some reason you are at a loss for a format to follow, the IRAC format can be used.

3. Use of an Outline

The value of an outline is determined by its use. If you prepare an outline and then set it aside while you are researching and analyzing the assignment, it is of limited value. Its only value when used in this manner is to help organize your thinking and provide the organizational framework for research and any writing that may follow. An outline is of greatest value when it is actively integrated into the research process. It can serve as an *invaluable guide* during the research and analysis process.

> **FOR EXAMPLE** Follow the outline format when researching and analyzing: first identify the issue, next locate the rule of law that governs the issue, then identify the case law that interprets the rule of law in a fact situation similar to the client's case, and so on.

When integrated into the research and analysis process, an outline provides an organized context within which to place research and ideas. If the research is part of a writing assignment, an outline will result in the development of a rough draft while research and analysis are being conducted. The result is a tremendous savings of time and effort. The integrated use of an outline when conducting research organizes the research and simplifies any writing that may be required.

How, then, do you integrate an outline into the research and analysis process? There are several ways to accomplish this. The practical approach suggested here is

Exhibit 13–4
Two-Step Approach for
Use of an Outline.

Use of an Outline		
Step 1	Convert the outline to a usable form—an expanded outline.	Use several sheets of three-holed or binder paper, or create separate pages if you are using a computer. Write the name of each section and subsection of the outline at the top of a separate page, for example, at the top of one page write "Issue," at the top of another page "Facts," and so on.
Step 2	Integrate all research, analysis, and ideas into the outline while conducting research and analysis.	As research is conducted and ideas occur concerning any aspect of the assignment, enter them on the appropriate page of the expanded outline.

to use an expanded outline. This approach is composed of the two steps presented in Exhibit 13–4.

a. Step 1 Convert the Outline to a Usable Form—An Expanded Outline

For illustration purposes, assume the assignment is to draft a legal research memorandum. The memorandum format used in the office is typed on one page of paper and is not very useful in this form. *The first step in the use of the outline is to convert it to a usable form—to expand the outline.* This is accomplished by taking several sheets of three-holed or binder paper, or creating separate pages if you are using a computer, and writing the name of each section and subsection of the outline at the top of a separate page.

> **FOR EXAMPLE** At the top of one sheet of paper or computer page, write the word *Issue*. At the top of another page, write *Statement of facts*. At the top of another page, write *Analysis—rule of law*. Continue with a new page for each of the following: *Analysis—case, Analysis—application of case to client's facts, Counteranalysis*, and *Conclusion*.

Some sections of the outline may require more than one page.

> **FOR EXAMPLE** The *Analysis—case* section may require two pages: one page for *Analysis—case—citation and facts of case* and one page for *Analysis—case—rule/principle/reasoning*. Two or more pages may be required for a case because, in many instances, a great deal of information may be taken from a case, such as lengthy quotes from the court's reasoning.

If more than one rule of law applies, there should be a separate page for each rule of law. If several cases apply, there are separate pages for each case. If there are separate issues, *research and analyze each issue separately*, and prepare a separate expanded outline for each issue.

When completed, there should be a separate page for each section and subsection of the outline. Place the pages in a loose-leaf binder or enter them in the computer in the order of the outline. In other words, the first page will be the Issue page, followed by the Statement of facts page, then the Analysis—rule of law page, and so on. If you are using binder paper, blank sheets of paper should be inserted between each section. This allows for the expansion of each section to accommodate additional notes, comments, ideas, and so on. The result is a greatly expanded outline that is usable for research.

b. Step 2 Integrate All Research, Analysis, and Ideas into the Outline while Conducting the Research and Analysis

As research is conducted and ideas occur concerning any aspect of the assignment, enter them on the appropriate page of the expanded outline.

(1) Ideas.   When any idea occurs concerning the case, enter it on the page of the expanded outline that relates to that idea.

> **FOR EXAMPLE** You may have a broad definition of the issue such as "Was there slander?" As you conduct research and give more thought to the case, more refined formulations of the issue will become apparent, such as: "Under § 20-2-2, does slander occur when one person orally communicates to a third party false statements of fact concerning an individual?" As soon as this formulation of the issue comes to you, write it on the issue page. When it comes time to write the memorandum, there will be multiple versions of the issue listed on the issue page. When all the ideas concerning the issue are in one place, it is easier to assemble the final statement of the issue.

The term *ideas* as used here includes all thoughts relating to the research of the assignment, such as how to compose transition sentences if the assignment requires a written memorandum.

> **FOR EXAMPLE** While researching a case, an idea may come to you about how the transition sentence linking the case to the rule of law should be written. Write the sentence in the beginning of the case section of the expanded outline or at the end of the rule of law page.

Keep the expanded outline with you at all times. Often the mind will work on an aspect of a case during sleep. You may wake up in the middle of the night or in the morning with an idea concerning the assignment or the answer to a problem. If the expanded outline is handy, you can immediately enter the idea or answer in the appropriate section. If it is not convenient to keep the outline with you, then carry a note pad. Enter ideas in the note pad as they come to you and place them in the outline later.

The value of the ability to immediately place ideas where they belong in the structure of the research cannot be overemphasized. Following are some of the benefits:

+ Ideas are not lost. When researching, you often may have an idea and say to yourself, "I'll remember to include this when I write the _____ section." Five minutes later, the idea is lost. If you can immediately write the idea down where it belongs, it will not be lost.

+ Confusion is avoided if ideas are recorded in the section where they belong in the research.

> **FOR EXAMPLE** While you are reading a case that interprets the rule of law, an idea may occur that relates to another aspect of the assignment, such as, "This gives me an idea about the counteranalysis of this issue." You may jot the idea down on a separate piece of paper or think you will remember it. You say to yourself, "I'll remember to include this when I write the counteranalysis."
>
> By the time you get down to writing, time has passed, and you cannot remember what the idea was or, if you jotted it down, where the idea fits into the assignment. There are several pieces of paper with notes and ideas, many of which you have forgotten what they relate to or why.

If you keep the binder with the expanded outline with you throughout the research process, and you place all ideas where they belong as they come to you, you will avoid confusion and time lost figuring out which ideas go where.

✦ Writing is made easier. If the research assignment is part of a writing assignment, when you sit down to write, all ideas are there, each in its proper place. Time is not wasted in performing the additional step of organizing ideas. Ideas are automatically organized as they come to you.

> **FOR EXAMPLE**   If the issue page of the expanded outline contains all the ideas concerning the ways the issue may be stated, it is easier to craft the final draft of the issue. Visually before you in one place are all the possible variations. Drafting the issue is just a matter of assembling the issue from the best of the variations.

(2) Research.   Just as ideas are placed in the proper place in the expanded outline as they occur, enter all the relevant research on the appropriate page as research is conducted. This makes research easier because the research is organized and in one place. The use of an outline when conducting research is discussed in the next section.

If you use an expanded outline as suggested here, all your research and ideas are assembled and organized and you are ready to write if writing is required. In effect, you have prepared a rough draft, and the writing task is made much simpler: the organization is done, ideas are captured, research is assembled in the proper place, and many transition sentences are already crafted and in place. The writing task is reduced to simply converting the outline to paragraph and sentence form.

V. PART B—CONDUCT RESEARCH

A five-step approach for conducting research and analysis is recommended. The approach is designed to help you quickly and efficiently conduct research and analysis without leaving out any critical information. The five steps are the following:

1. *Preliminary Preparation.* Gather all information necessary to research and analyze the assignment.

2. ***I****ssue.* Identify the issue (legal question) or issues raised by the facts of the client's case.

3. ***R****ule.* Identify the law that governs the issue, including the authority that interprets how the law applies to the issue.

4. ***A****nalysis/Application.* Determine how the rule of law applies to the issue.

5. ***C****onclusion.* Summarize the results of the legal analysis.

An acronym commonly used in reference to steps 2 through 5 is IRAC. IRAC is an easy way to remember the process—issue, rule, analysis/application, and conclusion.

Note: In some situations it may not be necessary to follow all the research steps.

> **FOR EXAMPLE**   1. The assignment may list specific cases that the researcher is to locate and brief. In this situation, it may not be necessary to perform step 1.
>
> 2. If the assignment specifically identifies the issue to be researched, then it may not be necessary to perform step 2.
>
> 3. If the question is how many shareholders are required for a quorum at a corporate shareholder meeting, you would go directly to the corporation statutes and steps 1 and 2 would not be necessary.

Step 1 Preliminary Preparation	Gather all information necessary to research and analyze the assignment.
	Part 1 Gather information about the case.
	Part 2 Identify the key terms and key facts.
	Part 3 Conduct preliminary research.
Step 2 Issue	Identify the issue (legal question) or issues raised by the facts of the client's case.
Step 3 Rule	Identify the law that governs the issue.
	Part 1 Locate the general law that governs the issue.
	Part 2 Locate the law that interprets how the general law applies to the specific fact situation of the issue.
	Part 3 Update research.

Exhibit 13–5
Steps of Part B of the Legal Research Process.

The research component of this process involves steps 1 through 3. Steps 4 and 5 of the process are not concerned with research, rather the analysis of the research after the research is complete. How to conduct the research steps (steps 1 through 3) in conjunction with the use of a research outline is discussed here (see Exhibit 13–5).

A. Step 1 Preliminary Preparation

Gather all information necessary to research and analyze the assignment. This step is broken down into three parts: gathering information about the case, identifying key facts and terms, and performing preliminary legal research if necessary.

Part 1 Gather Information About the Case

At the outset, it is essential to gather and review all the information about the case, that is, the facts. In every case, the legal research and analysis process involves a determination of how the law applies to the facts. As discussed in Chapter 2, facts of the client's case play a crucial role in legal research and analysis: The key facts are included in the issue; a determination of which law governs the issue is largely governed by the facts; how the law applies is governed by the facts. Without the facts, the law stands in a vacuum.

With this in mind, the analysis process should begin with a consideration of the facts of the client's case. The facts should be identified and reviewed at the outset. This preliminary step includes the following:

1. Be sure you have all the facts. Ask yourself if you have all the interviews, files, statements, and other information that have been gathered concerning the case.

2. Study the available facts to see if additional information should be gathered before legal analysis can properly begin.

3. Organize the facts. Group all related facts. Place the facts in a logical order, such as in the sequence in which they occurred (chronological) or according to topic (topical).

4. Weigh the facts. The value of some factual information, such as hearsay, may be questionable.

List all the facts on the facts page of the research outline.

Part 2 Identify the Key Terms and Key Facts

After the information has been gathered, the next step is to identify the key terms and the key facts that appear to be critical to the outcome of the case. *List the key facts on the facts page of the research outline.*

Part 3 Conduct Preliminary Research

Before conducting any research, check the office research files for previous memos or research that may have addressed the issue(s) you are researching. This may obviate the need for further research.

It may, however, be necessary to conduct some basic research in the area(s) of law that govern the issue(s) in the case. You may be unfamiliar with the area of law in general or with the specific aspect of the area that applies in the client's case. A general overview may be obtained from reference to a legal encyclopedia or a single-volume treatise. If the specific question or area is known at the outset, an ALR reference or a multivolume treatise may be appropriate. Identifying key terms helps guide you to which areas to conduct research.

If preliminary research is necessary, create a "Preliminary research" page in the outline. Include the results of the research on this page. Add all the relevant information, including the official citation of the source. If the material is lengthy, copy it, and attach it to the page. The goal is to have all the information relevant to the source in the outline so that you do not have to waste time looking up the material another time.

B. Step 2 Issue

Identify the issue (legal question) or issues raised by the facts of the client's case. The issue is the precise legal question raised by the facts of the dispute. After the preliminary preparation, identifying the issue is the second and probably most important step in the research and analysis process. You must identify the problem before you can solve it. The issue is the starting point. If it is misidentified, each subsequent step in the process is a step in the wrong direction. Time is wasted, and malpractice may result.

Place the issue or issues being researched on the issue page of the outline. If, while you are conducting research, such as reading a case, you realize the issue can be stated better, write the restated issue on the issue page.

Analyze and research each issue separately and thoroughly. If you are trying to research and analyze several issues at once, it is easy to get confused and frustrated. If you find information relevant to another issue in the case, make a reference note on a separate page in the outline for that other issue.

C. Step 3 Rule

Identify the law that governs the issue (legal research). The third step in the research and analysis process is to identify the law that applies to the issue. That is, to solve the client's problem you must find the law that applies to the problem. This is the legal research component of legal analysis. The three-part process presented in Exhibit 13–6 is recommended for conducting legal research.

The first part is locating the general law, such as a statute, that governs the question. The second part is locating the law, such as a court opinion, that interprets how the general law applies to the specific fact situation of the issue. Separate outline pages should be created for each statute and case located. The third part is to update the research sources.

Part 1	Locate the general law that governs the issue—usually statutory or case law.
Part 2	Locate the law that interprets how the general law applies to the specific fact situation of the issue—usually case law. Reference to secondary authority is necessary if there is no primary authority that applies or if additional authority is needed to help interpret the primary authority.
Part 3	Update research to ensure that the source you are reading has not been amended, repealed, revoked, overruled, modified, or otherwise changed.

Exhibit 13–6
**Three Parts of
Step 3—Rule.**

> **FOR EXAMPLE** The client wants to sue a newspaper for libel because of an article that included negative information concerning the client. The state has a tort statute governing libel and slander. The first step of the legal research component of the legal analysis process requires locating the state statute.
>
> The statute broadly defines the term "libel." The statute does not give guidance as to what constitutes libel in specific situations. The second step requires locating a court opinion (case law) that answers the question of what constitutes libel in a specific situation such as that encountered by the client. The third step is to check the research sources to ensure they are current.

A summary of the three-part research process follows.

Part 1 Locate the General Law (Primary Authority) That Governs the Issue

Identify the terms that you will use to search for the law that governs the issue. Ask yourself, "What type of law applies to the question raised by the facts of the case?" This may be enacted law or case law.

a. Enacted Law

When researching primary authority, look first for the enacted law, constitutional provision, statute, and so on, that governs the issue. There are two reasons for this. First, the constitutional or statutory provision may answer the question so that reference to case law is not required. Second, the annotations (summary of court opinions and other references that interpret the law) that follow the constitutional or statutory provision may reference a court opinion or secondary authority source that interprets the law in a fact situation similar to the facts of the issue. Therefore, you will not need to spend time researching other sources for relevant case law.

Ask yourself, "What terms will I use to search a statutory index or computer database to locate the law that applies to this issue?" List all the possible terms that might encompass the relevant law. Search the enacted law index or database using the search terms you have identified.

Review the annotations to the statute for cases that interpret the statute in fact situations similar to your case. Also, check the annotations for secondary sources, such as encyclopedia, ALR annotations, and law review articles sources which discuss the statute. Enter all the relevant research concerning the statute in the rule of law page of the outline as research is conducted. This should include the proper statutory citation, a copy of the relevant portions of statute, case citations (if any), and references to secondary sources. This avoids having to look up the statute more than once.

b. Case Law

Rules or principles established by the courts may govern the issue. In such cases there may be no statutory law that applies. Include all the relevant information from the case on the rule of law page of the outline.

Part 2 Locate the Law (Primary Authority if Possible) That Interprets How the General Law Applies to the Specific Fact Situation of the Issue

The rule of law that governs the issue may be written in such broad terms that it is necessary to look to another source, such as case law or secondary authority, to determine how the law applies to the specific fact situation of the issue. Ask yourself, "What terms will I use to search a case law digest or computer database to locate the court opinion that interprets how the general law applies to the specific fact situation raised by the issue?"

Note: Chapter 6 discusses how to determine when a court opinion applies to a specific fact situation.

When researching case law or secondary source material, retrieve everything you may need from the source and include it in the expanded outline as you read the material. Why waste time looking up and reviewing the same source twice? Place a copy of the material in the outline if necessary.

> **FOR EXAMPLE** You have found a case on point. First, read through the entire case. Then, on the second reading, as you come upon a statement of the legal principle or legal reasoning that may apply to the client's case, stop reading. Enter the information from the case in the case law page of the expanded outline. Indicate the page of the case from which it was taken and, if appropriate, quote the information. Also include the full citation, pertinent quotations concerning the rule of law or legal principle applied by the court, and the legal reasoning. Then continue your second reading and include on your outline page any additional information that may pertain to the client's case.

All too often the tendency when reading a case or other source for the second time is to tell yourself that you will come back later and note the pertinent information. If there is any possibility that you will use information from a case or other source, *retrieve it as you find it and place it* on the appropriate case or source page of the outline. You will save time by not having to reread portions of the retrieved material. Often the reasoning, rule, or principle you want to use is not where you remembered, and time is wasted wading through the material trying to relocate it. If it turns out that information retrieved is not relevant, it is simply not used. It is much better to have everything concerning the source in your expanded outline than to have to stop, retrieve, and reread it.

When looking for primary authority, always conduct counteranalysis. That is, always look for authority that may present a counterargument in response to your analysis of an issue. If you find a case on point in support of your position, look for other cases that have a different holding. Include the research in the counteranalysis page of the outline.

Role of Secondary Authority

Although it is essential to locate the primary authority that governs an issue, it is important not to overlook the importance of secondary authority. Secondary authority may be relied on by the court if there is no primary authority or if it is unclear how the primary authority applies. Sources such as ALR annotations, legal encyclopedias, and treatises often discuss and list all the statutes and cases related to a topic. Reference to such sources ensures that you have found all the laws related to the issue being researched. Also, secondary authority sources such as ALR annotations are helpful in locating counterarguments when performing counteranalysis.

Note: Refer to Appendix B for a chart listing the primary and secondary sources and their primary use as research tools.

Part 3 Update Research

You must update all research to ensure that the source you are reading has not been changed. Statutes must be checked to determine if they have been repealed or amended, cases checked to ensure they have not been reversed or modified by later cases, and secondary sources checked for additions and amendments.

VI. WHEN TO STOP

One of the more difficult problems is to determine when to stop researching. This involves two situations. The first is when to quit researching a specific source when you find nothing. The second and more common situation is when to stop researching after finding several legal sources that address the research topic. In other words, when is your research complete? Both of these situations are discussed in this section.

A. When to Stop Researching When You Find Nothing

One of the more difficult problems is when to stop looking when your research fails to produce any results.

> **FOR EXAMPLE** The assignment is to locate law identifying the elements of the tort of emotional distress. The first step is to locate the statute governing emotional distress. In many jurisdictions, torts such as this are not governed by statutory law, but instead are governed by case law. How do you know when to quit looking in the state statutes for the statutory law? There are several different approaches to take in this situation.

1. Look to Another Source of Law

In the preceding example, there may simply be no statutory law that governs the question. After you have conducted research using all the possible terms the statute may be categorized under, it's time to look to another source such as case law. It may be that the subject is covered by federal rather than state law. If after exhausting all possible avenues of research under a specific source, look to another source.

2. Reconsider the Issue and Search Terms

It may be possible that the issue or search terms are stated so broadly or narrowly that you are not finding anything.

> **FOR EXAMPLE** The issue is stated as "Is a will valid when the testator wrote 'invalid' on the title page of the will?" The researcher finds nothing when looking in the statutory index under wills, testator, and validity. A simple rephrasing of the issue to "Is a will validly revoked when the testator wrote 'invalid' on the title page of the will?" might improve your research results. Expanding the search terms to include revoked or revocation may lead to the answer.

In this regard, it may be necessary to consult the person who gave you the assignment for guidance or to make sure the assignment is clear. In addition, reference to a secondary source, such as a treatise, may help you reframe the issue or identify additional search terms.

3. Reconsider the Legal Theory

It may be that you have incorrectly analyzed the question and are searching in the wrong area of law. Review the question to see if another area of law may be involved. It may be necessary to consult a secondary source such as a legal encyclopedia for an overview of the law that compiles all the ways a topic may be addressed.

> **FOR EXAMPLE** The client runs a small business and a competitor induced a customer of the client to breach a contract with the client. Because the matter involves the breach of contract, the researcher looks to state contract law for remedies that may be available against the competitor and finds nothing. The matter, however, is governed by the state's tort law—the tort of interference with contractual relations. Reference to contract law in a legal encyclopedia will reveal that third-party interference with a contract is often governed by tort law.

4. Matters of First Impression

It may be that the issue you are researching has not been addressed in your state. That is, it is a matter of first impression with no law on the subject in your jurisdiction. If this is the case, refer to a secondary source such as a legal encyclopedia, treatise, or ALR annotation to identify how other jurisdictions have answered the question. The results of your research should not simply inform the supervising attorney that the state has not decided the matter. It should include the various ways other states have addressed the question.

B. When to Stop Researching After Finding Several Legal Sources

One of the more difficult problems is to know when to stop researching after finding several sources. There may be an endless variety of sources that address a specific question you are researching. There may be a statute, case law, encyclopedia references, ALR annotations, law review articles, and so on. There is no simple answer to the question of when to stop. Learning when to stop becomes intuitive with experience. Following are some considerations that may help you to determine when to stop.

1. Stop When You Have Found the Answer

The first research step is to find the primary authority that answers the question. If the authority clearly answers the question, stop researching. There are some questions that are simply answered.

> **FOR EXAMPLE** If the question is "What is the statute of limitations for filing a claim for breach of a written contract?" the statute will clearly provide the answer. Reference to case law or secondary authority is not necessary. The only task remaining is to update and Shepardize the statute to determine if it has been amended or repealed.

There may be case law directly on point that answers the question being researched. If this is the situation, then you must Shepardize the case to determine if it is good law and identify any cases that may criticize or affect its application. In addition, check the appropriate digest for other cases that may analyze the issue differently. Also, check a secondary source such as an ALR annotation on the topic for authority that may provide a different analysis. Include in the research any cases that are on point.

2. Several Authorities on the Research Topic

Here are some factors to keep in mind if you locate several authorities that address the research issue.

a. Primary Authority (Constitutions, Statutes, Cases)

You should always try to find a mandatory primary authority source(s) for each issue. If you have several cases that address the topic, use the mandatory authority cases. If you have case law that is mandatory authority, you do not need persuasive authority such as cases from other jurisdictions.

If you have several mandatory authority cases, select the case that is most on point, that most clearly analyzes the law, and is most recent. Courts, or the person reading your research, do not have time to read through numerous cases that address the same legal arguments. Select only the lead case or cases.

b. Secondary Authority

You do not need to include secondary sources in your research if the primary authority clearly provides the answer to the issue. However, you might want to include secondary authority sources to support your research if they specifically address the research topic. A reference to an ALR annotation or law review article on the issue allows the reader to review a comprehensive analysis of the topic if additional reference is desired.

If there is no primary authority on a topic, then reference to secondary authority is necessary. The more specific the secondary authority source, the better.

> **FOR EXAMPLE** If you have a legal encyclopedia citation that generally addresses the question being researched and an ALR annotation that specifically addresses the question, the ALR annotation is preferable.

Courts often refer to *Restatements of the Law*, ALR annotations, law review articles, and treatises when relying on secondary authority.

3. Other Factors Governing When to Stop

Time and economic factors may govern how thorough your research should be and when to stop. The assignment may be governed by a short time constraint, or you may be informed to not spend too much time on the project because the potential claim is small. The assignment may be to draft a three-page legal memorandum. Each of these situations limits the amount of research to be performed.

When this occurs, first locate the primary authority that answers or addresses the question. That is, the enacted law (statute, etc.) that applies and the case law that is on point. Follow the research sequence presented in section VC Step 3 Rule until you run out of time.

Discuss the amount of research time you should spend on the project when it is assigned. If you find that you are running out of time or the project is more complex than you anticipated, consult your supervisor.

VII. GENERAL CONSIDERATIONS

The process of analyzing a legal problem can at times be difficult, especially for a beginner. In addition to the steps addressed in the previous section, the following general considerations and guidelines will prove helpful when researching and analyzing a legal issue.

A. Focus

Focus is critical when performing the steps of the analytical process. Focus has several meanings, depending upon what part of the process is being performed.

At the broadest level, it means to keep focused on the specific task assigned. Analyze only the issue or issues assigned.

> **FOR EXAMPLE** The assignment is to analyze the question of whether a cause of action is present for civil assault. Keep focused on that issue. Answer only that question. If you come across information relevant to another issue, note it, but do not pursue it. When you have a break or at the end of the day, give your notes to the person assigned to analyze that issue. Valuable time may be lost in researching and analyzing the other issue or in interrupting your work to discuss the information with the other person.

When identifying the issue, focus on the facts of the client's case. Ask yourself, "What must be decided about which of the facts of the client's case?"

When identifying the rule of law, focus on the facts of the case and the elements of the rule of law. This will help you quickly eliminate rules of law that may not apply.

> **FOR EXAMPLE** The fact situation involves a credit purchase by the client. There may be several rules of law that govern the transaction, such as the state's usury laws, the state sale of goods statutes, and the federal truth-in-lending laws.
>
> The interest charged in the transaction in question was 10 percent and the usury statute provides that interest rates in excess of 20 percent are void. If this fact is kept in mind when locating the possible laws that apply to the transaction, the usury statute can be immediately eliminated from consideration. The interest charged does not violate the usury statute, and the statute clearly does not apply.

When analyzing and applying the rule of law in step 4, focus on the client's facts and the issue or question being analyzed. It is easy to get sidetracked, especially when reading case law. There may be interesting issues addressed in a court opinion that are close but not directly related to the issues in the client's case. Stay focused. Ask yourself, "Is the issue being addressed in this opinion really related to the issue in my case? Is it on point?" The guidelines and principles addressed in Chapter 6 are helpful in this regard.

If you do not stay focused, after you have completed your research, you may have several cases in front of you that are only marginally related to the specific issue you are analyzing. A lot of time can be wasted reading cases that are not really on point.

Focus on the work. Avoidance and procrastination are deadly. When you are stuck or having a difficult time analyzing or researching an issue, it is sometimes easy to procrastinate, to avoid working on the problem. You may find excuses for not working on the problem, such as working on an easier project. The way to overcome this is to *start*. Do not put it off. If you are at the research stage, *start researching*. If you are at the writing stage, *start writing*. Do not be discouraged if the results seem poor at first. Focus on the problem and begin. Often the barrier is beginning.

B. Ethics—Intellectual Honesty

Rule 1.1 of the American Bar Association's *Model Rules of Professional Conduct* requires that a client be represented competently. This means that it is your ethical duty to possess and exercise that degree of knowledge and skill ordinarily possessed by others in the profession. One aspect of competency requires that a legal problem be researched with intellectual honesty. **Intellectual honesty** means to research and analyze a problem objectively. Do not let emotions, preconceived notions, personal views, or stubbornness interfere with an objective analysis of the client's case. Do not assume you know the law. Check your resources. Just because you "feel" a certain outcome should occur, do not let that feeling prevent you from objectively researching and analyzing the issue.

FOR EXAMPLE The person who interviews clients in a law office has a personal history of domestic violence. When he was a child, there was domestic violence in the home. He has a strong aversion to domestic violence and harbors a prejudice against perpetrators of domestic violence. He interviews a client who complains that, the night before the interview, her husband hit her in the face with his fist. She states that he has beaten her frequently and savagely throughout their 10-year marriage. The client appears to have been severely beaten. She has two black eyes, and her face is swollen around the eyes.

The interviewer is outraged and upset by what happened to the client. As a result of his outrage, he fails to conduct a thorough and objective interview. He does not ask questions to elicit the details of the events of the previous night. He assumes the battery was unprovoked and does not ask questions concerning the reasons the client's husband hit her. His emotions and personal feelings cause him to focus on punishing the husband.

The interviewer knows that in addition to the remedies available under the criminal law, there is also a civil cause of action for domestic battery available under the state's recently passed domestic violence statute. He recommends that the supervising attorney file a civil complaint for domestic battery under the domestic violence statute. Relying on the paralegal's record for thoroughness, the supervising attorney directs that a complaint be drafted and filed. A few weeks later, the husband's counsel, a friend of the supervising attorney, calls concerning the case. "Why did you file this complaint?" she asks. "My client was acting in self-defense. He hit his wife after she stabbed him." As it turns out, the client decided to kill her husband rather than face a future of beatings. She took a kitchen knife and stabbed him in the chest. In self-defense, he hit her once, and the blow caught her between the eyes, causing the two black eyes and facial swelling.

Had the interviewer not lost his objectivity, he would have conducted a thorough interview. Probing questions concerning the events of the night in question would have revealed the true facts, and the lawsuit may not have been filed.

This is an extreme example, but it occurs in varying degrees. Personal prejudices, personal beliefs, or sympathy for the client can combine to affect objectivity, which may lead to a failure to conduct an objective, critical analysis of the case, to not vigorously pursue potential opposing arguments, or to discount opposing authority.

Remember, the client may not be telling the whole truth. This may not be intentional. It may be the result of forgetfulness or a personal tendency to discount or downplay the importance of adverse facts. In this example, the client may have been so focused upon the years of abuse and the desire to escape from further abuse that she truly considered the stabbing insignificant when weighed against what she had gone through.

Pursue the analysis of all legal issues with intellectual honesty. Identify all the facts affecting the case. Pursue all legal authority concerning the issues, including any authority that may negatively affect the client's position. Ignoring adverse authority will not make it go away. It must be addressed.

VIII. KEY POINTS CHECKLIST AND RESEARCH SUGGESTIONS

■ Adopt a research process. An organized approach is essential for legal research. Develop a process that works for you. Follow the process recommended in this chapter or create your own.

■ Consider time, length, and format constraints. Identify any constraints that affect the assignment, and design the approach to the assignment with these constraints in mind.

■ Break large assignments into manageable sections. Do not become overwhelmed by the complexity of an assignment.

■ Establish a timetable. Break the project into logical units and allocate your time accordingly. This helps you avoid spending too much time on one section of the research and running out of time. Do not become fanatical about the time schedule, however. You created the timetable, and you can break it. It is there as a guide to keep you on track and alert you to the overall time constraints.

■ Prepare and use an expanded outline when conducting research. An expanded outline provides a framework for organizing your research and capturing your ideas.

■ Always pay attention to the facts. Keep them in mind when performing each step of the research and analysis process. The process involves determining how the law applies to the facts. Make sure you have all the *facts* at the outset.

■ Become familiar with the area of law. If you are unfamiliar with the area of law that applies to the issue, obtain a general overview. Legal encyclopedias and treatises are examples of sources to consult to obtain an overview of an area of law.

■ Identify the issue first. The first step should be to identify the issue, as you cannot begin to look for an answer until you know the question. The preliminary identification of the issue may be very broad, such as "Did negligence occur?" or "Was there a breach of contract when the goods were delivered 10 days late?" This preliminary identification of the issue will usually identify the general area of law to be researched, such as contracts, and negligence.

■ Research issues one at a time. Thoroughly research to its conclusion one issue before proceeding to the next issue. If you find material on another issue, note a reference to it on the page in the expanded outline for that issue. Frustration and confusion can result from an attempt to research several issues at once.

■ Locate the enacted law that governs the question. Look first for any enacted law that governs the question, such as a statute or constitutional provision. Check the annotations for cases or secondary sources that may give guidance as to how the law applies in a fact situation such as the client's.

■ Locate the case law that may apply. Locate the relevant case law if there is no enacted law that governs or if the enacted law is so broadly drafted that case law is required to interpret the enacted law. Locate mandatory precedent first, then persuasive precedent, and secondary authority.

■ Make sure that the research is current. Check supplements and Shepardize cases to be sure that the authority located is current.

■ If you reach a dead end, reanalyze the issue. If you cannot find any authority, either primary or secondary, chances are the issue is too broadly or too narrowly stated. Restate the issue. If the issue is too broadly stated, restate it in narrower terms. Return to a basic research source for guidance, such as a legal encyclopedia. If the issue is too narrowly framed, restate it in broader terms. Chapter 3 provides help in regard to identifying and stating issues.

▪ Use common sense. If the answer to a question can be answered by a person rather than by conducting research, contact that person. For example, for a question concerning unemployment compensation eligibility, an employee at the state unemployment compensation agency may be able to provide the answer.

▪ Consult office files. Some offices keep legal research files. Check the files to determine if the issue you are researching or a similar issue has already been researched.

▪ If you become stuck, move to another part of the assignment. If you are stuck on a particular section, leave it. The mind continues to work on a problem when you are unaware of it. That is why solutions to problems often seem to appear in the morning. Let the subconscious work on the problem while you move on. The solution to the difficulty may become apparent when you return to the problem.

IX. APPLICATION

This section explores the application of the principles discussed in this chapter to the hypotheticals presented at the beginning of this chapter and Chapters 1 and 2.

A. Chapter Hypothetical

After gathering and reviewing all the information available in the office concerning Ms. Beck's case, Rick follows the process recommended in this chapter. An outline of Rick's application of the process is as follows:

    I. *Assignment.* Rick first reviews the assignment.

        A. *Is the assignment clear?* He reviews the assignment to be sure he understands what is required. Rick has no question in this regard. The assignment is to research and analyze the question of whether the evidence seized in the case can be suppressed.

        B. *What type of legal writing is required?* The assignment is to draft an office legal memorandum. Rick retrieves the office memorandum outline form used by the firm. The body of the outline is presented here.

          I. Issue

         II. Statement of facts

        III. Analysis/application

             1. Rule of law—the rule of law that governs the issue—enacted/ case law

             2. Case(s)—court interpretation of the rule of law if necessary

                A. Name and citation

                B. Brief summary of facts showing case is on point

                C. Rule/principle/reasoning applied by the court that applies to client's case

                D. Application—discussion of how the rule of law presented in the court decision applies in the client's case

             3. Counteranalysis

        IV. Conclusion—a summary of the analysis

II. *Constraints.* What are the constraints on the assignment? Rick has a time constraint. Any motion to suppress the evidence must be filed in 30 days. He must finish the memorandum sufficiently in advance of the 30 days to allow Ms. Fletcher time to review it and prepare the appropriate motion. Based on past experience, he knows Ms. Fletcher prefers to have 10 days to review the memorandum and prepare the motion. This leaves him 20 days to complete the assignment.

Rick also knows that Ms. Fletcher prefers shorter memos. She has told him that a single issue memo should not exceed seven pages. He knows he must budget his time and research to meet these constraints.

III. *Organization.* Rick organizes the assignment around the outline.

A. *Creation of expanded outline.* Rick expands the outline as suggested in the Organization—Research Outline section of this chapter. The initial expanded outline is composed of eight pages of paper or computer pages. The pages are labeled as follows: Issue; Facts; Analysis—rule of law; Analysis—case name, facts, and citation; Analysis—case rule/principle and reasoning; Analysis—application of case to facts; Counteranalysis; and Conclusion.

B. *Use of expanded outline.* Rick begins his research with the expanded outline at hand. He studies the facts and begins to formulate the issue. Every time he thinks of a way to state the issue, he writes it on the issue page.

FOR EXAMPLE The first formulation of the issue is "Can the evidence be suppressed?" Later formulations are "Can evidence be suppressed when officers execute a warrant unannounced based on the warrant's authorization of unannounced entry?" and "Under the state's exclusionary rule, can evidence be suppressed when officers conduct a search unannounced, pursuant to a warrant authorizing unannounced entry to ensure officer safety, and the authorization is based upon an affidavit that gives no particularized facts regarding threats to officer safety?"

As he researches, Rick finds article II, section 5, of the state constitution which prohibits illegal searches and seizures. He copies article II, section 5, and places it on the Analysis—rule of law page. He realizes this provision is so broadly formulated that he must locate case law for an interpretation of how it applies in an unannounced entry situation.

While looking for a case on point, he thinks of a transitional sentence that will connect the rule of law section of the memo to the case law section.

FOR EXAMPLE Article II, section 5, does not provide guidance as to what constitutes an illegal search when law enforcement officers enter into a residence unannounced; therefore, he must consult case law.

Rick immediately writes this sentence at the end of the Analysis—rule of law page of the outline.

Rick locates the court opinion of *State v. Brick.* Addressing a fact situation almost identical to Ms. Beck's, the court held that a warrant may authorize unannounced entry. The court went on to state, however, that the authorization must be based on a "particularized showing that the individuals whose residence is being searched have in the past represented a threat to officer safety. Any authorization based upon a generalized statement, such as 'Drug offenders often present a threat to officers' safety during the execution of search warrants,' violates article II, section 5, and the exclusionary rule requires the suppression of any evidence seized."

Rick enters all the relevant information from the case in the appropriate Analysis—case pages of the outline. He includes the full citation, any relevant quotations from the case, and the page number references for the quotations. He will not have to reread the case when he writes the memorandum. All the key information is in the expanded outline.

While analyzing the case, he thinks of a sentence he will use when discussing how the case applies to the client's facts. He enters this sentence in the Analysis—application of case to facts page of the outline.

> **FOR EXAMPLE** "In our case, just as in *State v. Brick*, the officers executed a warrant unannounced, based on the authorization contained in the warrant. In our case, as in *Brick*, the authorization was based upon a generalized statement that drug offenders often pose a threat to officer safety when the officers announce their presence prior to entry. In *Brick*, the court ruled that such searches violate the state constitution and the evidence seized must be suppressed. If the trial court follows the rule of law presented in *State v. Brick*, the evidence should be suppressed."

If more cases need to be included in the memo, Rick adds additional pages to the outline for each case and enters the pertinent information on the appropriate page.

Rick identifies any counterargument, such as that contained in conflicting case law, and enters it in the counteranalysis section of the outline. If Rick has any thoughts concerning the conclusion while conducting the research and analysis, he enters them in the conclusion section of the outline.

While working on the assignment, Rick keeps the outline or a notepad with him. He takes it home after work. He writes any ideas concerning the assignment on the appropriate page when the idea occurs. Nothing is lost, and all his ideas and research are organized in the outline. Transitional sentences and other parts of the writing, such as how the issue should be written, are already drafted and in the proper place. If more than one issue needs to be addressed, Rick prepares a separate section of the outline for that issue and the rule of law and case law that apply to it.

B. Chapter 1 Hypothetical *Reins v. Stewart*

Vanessa's assignment is to locate the law governing the liability, if any, of Mr. Stewart for civil battery and prepare a summary of her research.

    I. *Assignment.* Vanessa first reviews the assignment.

        A. *Is the assignment clear?* Vanessa reviews the assignment to be sure she understands what is required.

        B. *What type of legal writing is required?* The assignment is to draft a summary of the law. She retrieves the research summary outline form used by the firm.

    II. *Constraints.* What are the constraints on the assignment? No time or length constraints were mentioned when Vanessa was given the assignment. She should contact the supervising attorney to identify to determine the constraints.

    III. *Organization.* Vanessa organizes the assignment around the research summary outline.

        A. *Creation of expanded outline.* Vanessa expands the outline as suggested in the Organization—Research Outline section of this chapter. The initial expanded outline consists of pages labeled as follows: Issue; Facts; Analysis—rule of law; Analysis—case name, facts, and citation; Analysis—case rule/principle and reasoning, Analysis—secondary authority.

B. *Use of expanded outline.* How Vanessa identifies the key facts, frames the issue and locates the statutory, case law, and secondary authority is discussed in the application sections of Chapters 2 through 8.

Vanessa enters all the relevant information from her research and analysis on the appropriate page of the outline: key facts on the key facts page, statements of the issue on the issue page, statutory law material on the statute pages, case law material on the case law pages, and secondary authority source material on the secondary authority pages. There is a separate page or pages for each statute, case, and secondary source. Vanessa includes on each page all the relevant information from the source: the full citation, a copy of any relevant portions or quotations from a source, and the page number references for the quotations.

C. Chapter 2 Hypothetical *United States v. Canter*

See Assignment 11 at the end of the chapter.

SUMMARY

Contrary to popular belief, the bulk of the practice of law involves research and writing. Legal research is often complex, requiring in-depth research and detailed analysis. The complexities of an assignment, time constraints, and heavy workloads dictate the necessity of following a process when engaging in legal research. There is no established standard research process. Each individual should adopt or create a process that works. This chapter recommends a two-part legal research process and guidelines to follow when engaging in legal research. The first part involves analyzing the assignment; the second part is conducting research.

The first part of the process, analyzing the assignment, is composed of three sections: the assignment, constraints affecting the assignment, and organization of the assignment. When approaching an assignment, you should first review the assignment and consider any constraints that affect the assignment, such as time, length, and format.

After these matters are addressed, prepare an expanded outline and use it when engaging in the research and analysis of the assignment. An expanded outline consists of a separate notebook page or computer generated page for each topic and subtopic of the outline.

The second part of the research process is the research component of the research process. This part is composed of three steps: preliminary preparation, identification of the issue, and locating the law that answers the question raised by the issue. Research and analysis are entered in the expanded outline as material is gathered and analysis conducted. The result is that a rough draft of any writing that may be required is developed while research is being conducted.

Next, the chapter presents guidelines to follow for determining when to stop researching. This involves two situations. The first is when to quit researching a specific source when you find nothing. The second is when to stop researching after finding several legal sources that address the research topic.

The chapter concludes with a key points and research suggestions checklist.

CHAPTER REFERENCES

INTERNET RESOURCES

Using "legal research," "legal research memorandum," or "IRAC legal analysis" as a topic, you will find thousands of Web sites that refer to legal research. Some sites refer to legal research textbooks, some focus on legal research and analysis, some advertise research and writing services, some are Web sites for specific classes taught at schools, some advertise courses and seminars on legal research and writing, and some sites discuss legal memoranda in specific areas such as environmental law. A Chicago-Kent College of Law site, <http://www.kentlaw.edu>, presents a sample legal memorandum. In the Search box on the site, type "sample memo." The Georgetown University Law Library Web site, <http://www.ll.georgetown.edu>, provides links to research and writing resources and related materials useful to legal writers.

As with most topics on the Web, the problem is not the lack of sites, but too many sites. Probably the best strategy is to narrow your search to a specific type of legal writing and topic, such as "legal research memorandum, public service contracts." The following sites may provide useful support information when engaged in projects requiring legal research.

<http://www.nala.org>

This is the site for the National Association for Legal Assistants (NALA). The Association site provides a wealth of information ranging from articles on the profession to education and certification programs for paralegals. It includes information on court decisions affecting paralegals and links to other related sites.

<http://www.paralegals.org>

This is the Web page for the National Federation of Paralegal Associations (NFPA), another national paralegal organization. The Web page provides links to a wide range of sites of interest to paralegals such as research sources, publications, and products.

<http://www.legalassistanttoday.com>

Legal Assistant Today is a magazine geared toward the needs of paralegals. It often includes helpful articles on legal research and writing.

For additional materials, please go to the CD accompanying this book

For additional resources, visit our Web site at www.paralegal.delmar.cengage.com

EXERCISES

Additional exercises are located on the Student CD-ROM accompanying the text and Online Companion.

The following exercises may be helpful in developing an understanding of and familiarity with the use of a writing process.

ASSIGNMENT 1
Describe the parts of the legal research process.

ASSIGNMENT 2
Describe the three sections of Part A—Analyze the Assignment part of the legal research process.

ASSIGNMENT 3
Describe the types of legal writing discussed in this chapter.

ASSIGNMENT 4
What are some of the constraints that may affect your performance of an assignment? How do they affect your performance of an assignment?

ASSIGNMENT 5
What is an expanded outline? Describe the creation and elements of the body of an expanded outline for an office legal memorandum.

ASSIGNMENT 6
Describe the use of an expanded outline in the preparation of an office legal memorandum.

ASSIGNMENT 7
Describe the three steps of Part B—Conduct Research part of the research process.

ASSIGNMENT 8
Describe the recommended sequence for conducting research.

ASSIGNMENT 9
Describe the key points to be kept in mind when engaging in research.

ASSIGNMENT 10
The paralegal is assigned the task of conducting research and preparing an office legal memorandum. The memorandum is due in 10 days, and there is a five-page limit. Tom is the client. The facts and law are as follows:

Facts: Mary was Tom's stockbroker and financial advisor. Tom owned five acres of property. Mary advised Tom to sell the property to Ana at a price slightly below the market price. She recommended that Tom buy stock with the proceeds. Tom sold the property to Ana and now wants to have the transaction set aside because he believes Mary unduly and improperly influenced his decision. Mary and Ana are very close friends.

Law: *Statutory law*—section 96-4-4-1 of the state statutes provides that a contract for the sale of land may be set aside if it is entered into under undue influence.

Case law—*Lorn v. Bell.* In a fact situation similar to Tom's, the court ruled that under § 96-4-4-1, undue influence occurs when:

1. The person influenced is susceptible to undue influence.
2. The person influenced is influenced to enter the contract.
3. The opportunity to influence is present.
4. Undue influence is present.
5. The person exercising the undue influence benefits from the undue influence.

Part A
Describe in detail the application of the three sections of Part A—Analyze the Assignment of the research process.

Part B
For the Organization section of Part A of the research process, prepare an expanded outline based on the outline presented in the Use of an Outline subsection.

Part C
Based only on the information presented previously, fill in the expanded outline. Include a statement of the issue, analysis, counteranalysis, conclusion, and recommendations.

ASSIGNMENT 11
The following assignment is based on the hypothetical presented at the beginning of Chapter 2. Use the statutory law presented in the Application section of Chapter 2 and the case law presented in the Application section of Chapter 5. The memo is due in seven days and there is a five-page limit.

1. Describe in detail the application of the three sections of Part A—Analyze the Assignment of the research process.
2. For the Organization section of Part A of the research process, prepare an expanded outline based on the outline presented in the Use of an Outline subsection, under the Organization section of the chapter. Fill in the expanded outline using the information presented in the assignment. Include in the Issue section of the outline a broad statement of the issue and at least one narrow statement of the issue.

Legal Research Memorandum

In the hypothetical presented at the beginning of Chapter 2, the paralegal, Dustin, is assigned the task of preparing a legal research memorandum. The memo addresses the question of whether there is sufficient evidence to support the charge that the client, Mr. Canter, used a dangerous weapon when he robbed a bank. The hypothetical is discussed in the Application section of each chapter to illustrate how the principles and guidelines presented throughout the text apply to Dustin's assignment. The memo he drafts is presented here.

To: Supervisory Attorney

From: Paralegal

Re: *United States v. Eldon Canter*

   Armed bank robbery with a deadly weapon

STATEMENT OF ASSIGNMENT

   I have been assigned the task of determining—within the meaning of the federal bank robbery statute—whether a crudely carved wooden replica of a handgun can be considered a "dangerous weapon" when it is used in a bank robbery, and the teller who was approached believed the replica was real.

ISSUE

   Under the federal bank robbery statute, 18 U.S.C. § 2113 (a) and (d), is there sufficient evidence to support charges of bank robbery with a dangerous weapon when the weapon is a crudely carved wooden replica of a 9mm Beretta handgun, and the teller approached by the robber believed it was a real handgun, but the only other witness did not believe it was real?

BRIEF ANSWER

   Qualified yes. In the case of *U.S. v. Martinez-Jimenez*, the court held that a dangerous weapon includes a replica if it appears to be a genuine weapon to those present at the scene. In our case, the teller being robbed believed the replica was real and another teller, the only other witness, did not believe it was real. If the case is interpreted to provide that it is sufficient if any witness present believed that the replica was a real weapon, then the carved wooden replica was a dangerous weapon within the meaning of the statute.

FACTS

On January 5 of this year, Mr. Eldon Canter robbed the First State Bank. He entered the bank, approached a teller, pulled out a crudely carved wooden replica of a 9mm Beretta handgun, and robbed the bank. The replica was carved from pine, stained with dark walnut wood stain, and a hole was drilled in the "barrel" to make it look real. The teller Mr. Canter approached believed it was a real Beretta. The teller at the next window was fairly certain that it was fake. No one else observed the replica.

ANALYSIS

Mr. Canter is charged with armed bank robbery with a dangerous weapon in violation of 18 U.S.C. § 2113(a) and (d). The relevant portions of the statute provide:

> (a) Whoever, . . . by intimidation, . . . takes . . . any property or money or any other thing of value belonging to . . . a bank . . .
> Shall be fined not more than $5,000 or imprisoned not more than twenty years, or both.
> (d) Whoever, in committing . . . any offense defined in subsections (a) . . . assaults any person, or puts in jeopardy the life of any person by use of a dangerous weapon or device, shall be fined not more than $10,000 or imprisoned not more than twenty-five years, or both.

The statute does not define what constitutes a "dangerous weapon." Therefore, it is necessary to consult case law to determine how the courts have defined the term in cases where the alleged "dangerous weapon" is not in fact an actual weapon.

A case on point is *U.S. v. Martinez-Jimenez*, 864 F.2d 664 (9th Cir. 1989). In this case, the defendant robbed a bank with a toy gun that eyewitnesses identified as a dark revolver. The defendant was convicted of armed bank robbery under Section 2113(d).

On appeal, the court addressed the question of whether a toy gun is a "dangerous weapon" within the meaning of Section 2113(d). The court noted that "The toy gun did not fit the statutory definition of a firearm under 18 U.S.C. § 921(a)(3). However, it did fall within

the meaning of a 'dangerous weapon or device' under Section 2113(d)."
Id. at 666. In support of this conclusion, the court referred to other
cases where unloaded or inoperable guns were held to be dangerous
weapons and stated, "These cases reflect a policy that the robber's
creation of even the appearance of dangerousness is sufficient
to subject him to enhanced punishment." *Id.* at 666. The court went
on to note that "A robber who carries a toy gun during the commission of a bank robbery creates some of the same risk as those created by one who carries an unloaded or inoperable genuine gun." *Id.*
at 666. The court concluded that:

> The values of justice, administrability, and de-
> terrence require the rule that a robber's use of
> a replica or simulated weapon that appears to be
> a genuine weapon to those present at the scene
> of the crime, or to those charged with responsi-
> bility for responding to the crime, carries the
> same penalty as the use of a genuine weapon.

Id. at 668.

In applying the *U.S. v. Martinez-Jimenez* holding to our
facts, it appears that there is sufficient evidence to support
the charge of bank robbery with a dangerous weapon. Even though
in our case the instrumentality was a wooden replica of a handgun
rather than a toy replica, the result is the same: in both cases
the instrumentality was so sufficiently similar to a real handgun that a witness believed it was real, creating the appearance
of dangerousness and the consequent risks. As the court noted in
its conclusion, the use of a replica or simulated weapon that appears to be genuine subjects the robber to the penalty imposed by
Section 2113(d) for use of a dangerous weapon.

A possible counterargument, however, is that the instrumentality cannot be considered a dangerous weapon if some of
the witnesses believe that it is not a dangerous weapon. In *U.S.
v. Martinez-Jimenez*, all the witnesses believed the toy gun was
a real handgun. The court did not address the question of whether all the witnesses must believe the instrumentality is a real

weapon in order for it to be considered a dangerous weapon. It should not, however, make a difference if some of the witnesses do not believe the instrumentality is real. In *U.S. v. Martinez-Jimenez*, the court focused upon the increased risk to the physical security of those present at the scene created by the appearance of dangerousness. *Id.* at 667. As long as some of the witnesses believe the instrumentality is real, that risk is created. The goal of the court's holding was to eliminate or reduce that risk, and, therefore, the holding should apply whenever the risk is created, even if all the witnesses do not believe the risk is present. See the recommendation section below.

CONCLUSION

The federal bank robbery statute, 18 U.S.C. § 2113(a) and (d), establishes a criminal penalty for bank robbery with a "dangerous weapon." In *U.S. v. Martinez-Jimenez*, the Ninth Circuit Court of Appeals concluded that a replica that appears to be a genuine weapon to those present at the scene of the crime constitutes a "dangerous weapon" within the meaning of 18 U.S.C. Section 2113(d). In our case, Mr. Cantor used a carved wooden replica of a handgun when he robbed the bank, and the teller he robbed believed it was a real handgun. In light of the holding in *U.S. v. Martinez-Jimenez*, it appears that there is a sufficient basis to support the charge that he committed bank robbery by use of a "dangerous weapon" in violation of Section 2113(d).

RECOMMENDATION

Additional case law should be researched to determine if there are any cases which hold that all the witnesses must believe the instrumentality is real in order for 18 U.S.C. Section 2113(d) to apply.

APPENDIX B

Research Source Chart

RESEARCH SOURCE	PRIMARY USE AS A RESEARCH TOOL
American Law Reports Examples: *ALR Federal;* *ALR 5th*	Use to obtain a comprehensive analysis of specific legal issues. ALRs provide a greater in-depth discussion of specific legal issues than is available in a treatise. Legal issues are analyzed through synthesis and discussion of cases from every jurisdiction. They are valuable in identifying legal arguments on both sides of an issue and key cases from every jurisdiction that have addressed the issue.
Dictionaries Examples: *Black's Law Dictionary;* *Ballentine's Law Dictionary;* *Words and Phrases*	Use to obtain the spelling, pronunciation, and legal meaning of terms used in the law. *Words and Phrases* includes terms that have been defined in court opinions. It is a valuable case finder, especially in situations where you are looking for a unique definition of a term.
Digests Examples: *American Digest;* *West's Federal Practice Digest 4th;* *Atlantic Digest*	Use to locate case law that addresses specific point(s) of law. Digests are helpful in two situations: • You know the name of a case that addresses the point of law being researched and are looking for other cases that address the same point. • You do not know of any cases that address the point of law being researched.
Legal Encyclopedias Examples: *American Jurisprudence Second* (Am. Jur. 2d); *Corpus Juris Secundum* (CJS)	Use to obtain an overview of a specific area of the law and to locate case law in that area. Encyclopedias do not criticize or analyze the law. Refer to other sources such as treatises, ALR, or law review articles for an analysis or critique of legal topic.
Legislative History Sources: *United States Code Congressional and Administrative News Service* (USCCAN); *Congressional Information Service* (CIS)	Use to determine the meaning or application of a law. Legislative history may be helpful when the meaning of a law that governs a fact situation is unclear or when the law is written so broadly that its application to a specific fact situation is unclear. The legislative history includes committee reports, transcripts of hearings, statements of legislators concerning the legislation, and any other material published for legislative use in regard to the legislation.
Loose-leaf Services Examples: Commerce Clearing House (CCH); Bureau of National Affairs (BNA)	Use loose-leaf services to locate in-depth information on specific areas of law such as labor law, environmental law, family law, and tax law. The services include primary authority such as statutes, regulations, and summaries of court and administrative decisions. Also, they usually include an analysis of the law and references to secondary sources.

RESEARCH SOURCE

Periodicals
Examples:
Law Reviews; State Bar Association Journals; Legal Newspapers

Practice and Form Books
Examples:
West's Federal Forms; Am. Jur. Pleading and Practice Forms; Am. Jur. Proof of Facts

Reporters
Examples:
United States Reports, Federal Reporter; Regional Reporters

Restatements of the Law
Examples:
Restatement (Third) of Torts; Restatement of Contracts

Shepard's Citators
Examples:
Shepard's United States Citations; Shepard's Federal Statute Citations; Shepard's Code of Federal Regulations Citations

Statutes/Codes Annotated
Examples: *United States Code Annotated* (U.S.C.A.); *United States Code Service* (U.S.C.S.), State Statutes Annotated

Treatises
Examples:
First Amendment Law Handbook; O'Neal's Oppression of Minority Shareholders

Uniform Laws and Model Acts
Model Penal Code; Model Business Corporations Act

PRIMARY USE AS A RESEARCH TOOL

Use when you are seeking an analysis and critique of a specific legal topic that is more in-depth or narrower in focus than that provided by a legal encyclopedia or treatise. You may also refer to a periodical when seeking information on a recently emerging legal issue that is not yet addressed in treatises or other sources. Periodical articles are valuable for their depth of research; citation to numerous primary and secondary sources; and in-depth analysis of current legal issues, recently emerging areas of the law, or very specific topics.

Use a practice or form book if you are looking for a sample of a legal document such as a contract or a practice form such as a motion for summary judgment. Such books also include litigation guides and strategy. Model jury instructions are included in some form books such as *Am. Jur. Pleading* and *Practice Forms.*

Use reporters to read the full text of court opinions. A reporter is used after you have located the citation of a case and want to read the text of the court opinion. Which reporter you refer to is discussed in Chapter 5.

Use a *Restatement* to locate a standardized definition or statement of the law; reasons in support of the definition or statement of the law; guidance as to how the law should be defined or stated; and citations to related cases, treatises, and other secondary authority.

Use to determine whether a case, statute, regulation, or other authority is "good law." *Shepard's* indicates whether an authority has been repealed, amended, reversed, overruled, or in any way modified by a subsequent law or court decision.

Shepard's also lists any case law or secondary sources, such as ALR annotations, that have discussed the primary authority being researched and is therefore useful in locating other cases and other sources that have discussed or critiqued that authority.

Use to locate the law enacted by a legislative body. The statutory code usually includes the constitution that governs the jurisdiction, the legislative acts, and the court rules. For example, the *United States Code Annotated* includes the U.S. Constitution, laws enacted by Congress, and the Rules that govern the federal courts. Jury instructions are often published with the annotated statutes. The annotations include references to related statutes; references to other research sources such as ALR sites; law review articles; digest key numbers; and the names, citation, and summaries of key court decisions that have interpreted/analyzed the law.

Use when you are seeking more than the general summary of the law available in a legal encyclopedia. Treatises provide in-depth discussion of legal topics and explain, analyze, and criticize the law. The analysis may prove useful when seeking information on how to counter an opponent's interpretation of the law.

Treatises are also valuable in identifying key cases on the topic being researched.

Use to locate a model text from which a law may be crafted; arguments in support of the law; and citations to cases, treatises, and articles interpreting the law.

APPENDIX C

Court Opinions Referred to in the Text

INTRODUCTION

The court opinions in this appendix are presented in alphabetical order and not in the order in which they are referred in the text. To save space, portions of some cases that are not relevant to specific assignments or the discussion presented in the text have been omitted. A series of asterisks indicates that a portion of the opinion has been omitted.

ATLANTIC BEACH CASINO, INC.
d/b/a the Windjammer,
et al., Plaintiffs,

v.

EDWARD T. MARENZONI,
et al., Defendants.
Civ. A. No. 90-0471.

United States District Court,
D. Rhode Island.
Sept. 28, 1990.
749 F. Supp. 38 (D.R.I. 1990)
OPINION AND ORDER

PETTINE, Senior District Judge.

In the last few years legislators and citizens have paid increasing attention to the lyrical content of popular music. The interest if not entirely new, for "rulers have long known [music's] capacity to appeal to the intellect and to the emotions and have censored musical compositions to serve the needs of the state." *Ward v. Rock Against Racism,* _____ U.S. _____, 109 S. Ct. 2746, 2753, 105 L.Ed.2d 661 (1989). The controversy some groups have ignited is not, in itself, any reason to take such speech outside the First Amendment. Indeed, expression may "best serve its high purpose when it induces a condition of unrest, creates dissatisfaction with conditions as they are, or even stirs people to anger." *Terminiello v. Chicago,* 337 U.S. 1, 4, 69 S.Ct. 894, 96, 893 L.Ed. 1131 (1949). The message and reputation of the rap music group 2 Live Crew evidently came to the attention of the Westerly

Town Council, for they have taken steps toward possibly preventing the group from playing a scheduled concert. It is in this way that 2 Live Crew became the subject of, though not a party to, the present litigation.

On September 19, 1990, plaintiffs, who have contracted to present the 2 Live Crew concert, moved for a temporary restraining order prohibiting the defendants, members of the Westerly Town Council, from holding a show cause hearing on September 24, 1990, concerning the revocation of plaintiffs' entertainment license; from revoking the plaintiffs' entertainment license; from prohibiting the 2 Live Crew concert scheduled for October 6, 1990; and from imposing any special requirements on plaintiffs relative to the October 6 presentation. On September 21, 1990, the parties and this Court agreed that the matter would be considered as an application for a preliminary injunction and that the show cause hearing would be continued until October 1, 1990, subject to and dependent upon this Court's ruling. Based on the September 21 conference and my review of the parties' briefs, this Court has determined that the central issue in this case is plaintiffs' facial challenge to the town of Westerly's licensing ordinances on First Amendment grounds. Because I find, for the reasons set out below, that the ordinances as written are unconstitutional under the First and Fourteenth Amendments, defendants are enjoined from conducting a show cause hearing and from revoking plaintiff's entertainment license. I also enjoin the defendants from prohibiting the concert for failing to allege sufficient harm to overcome plaintiffs' First Amendment rights.

****

III. INJUNCTIVE RELIEF

In order for plaintiffs to prevail in their request for a preliminary injunction, they must meet the following standards: the plaintiff must demonstrate a likelihood of success on the merits, immediate and irreparable harm, that the injury outweighs any harm engendered by the grant of injunctive relief and that the public interest will not be adversely affected by such grant. *LeBeau v. Spirito*, 703 F.2d 639, 642 (1st Cir. 1983). I shall address each of these standards in turn.

A. Likelihood of Success on the Merits

Rather than allow 2 Live Crew to perform and then prosecute for any illegal activity that could occur, the Town Council wishes to review and decide in advance whether to allow the performance to go forward. This is a prior restraint. See *Southeastern Promotions, Ltd. v. Conrad*, 420 U.S. 546, 554–55, 95 S.Ct. 1239, 1244–45, 43 L.Ed.2d 448 (1975). "Any system of prior restraints of expression comes to this Court bearing a heavy presumption against its constitutional validity." *Bantam Books, Inc. v. Sullivan*, 372 U.S. 58, 70, 83 S.Ct. 631, 639, 9 L.Ed.2d 584 (1963). A licensing scheme involving such prior restraint survives constitutional scrutiny only when the law contains "narrow, objective and definite standards to guide the licensing authority." *Shuttlesworth v. Birmingham*, 394 U.S. 147, 150–51, 89 S.Ct. 935, 938–39, 22 L.Ed.2d 162 (1969), see *Lakewood*, 486 U.S. 760, *Southeastern Promotions*, 420 U.S. at 553, 95 S.Ct. at 1243–44, *Cox v. State of Louisiana*, 379 U.S. 536, 557–58, 85 S.Ct. 453, 465–66, 13 L.Ed.2d 471 (1965), *Irish Subcommittee v. R.I. Heritage Commission*, 646 F. Supp. 347, 359 (D.R.I. 1986).

The Westerly Ordinance, see *supra* note 3, provides even less guidance than the law struck down in *Shuttlesworth*. *Id.* 394 U.S. at 149, 89 S.Ct. at 937–38 (permit could be denied if demanded by the "public welfare, peace, safety, health, decency, good order, morals or convenience"). For example, Section 17-87 merely states, "Any license granted under Section 17-84 and 17-88 may be revoked by the Town Council after public hearing for cause shown." As in *Venuti*, the Westerly ordinance is utterly devoid of standards. See 521 F.Supp. at 1030–31 (striking down entertainment license ordinance). It leaves the issuance and revocation of licenses to the unbridled discretion of the Town Council. Our cases have long noted that "the

danger of censorship and of abridgement of our precious First Amendment freedoms is too great where officials have unbridled discretion over a forum's use." *Toward a Gayer Bicentennial Committee v. Rhode Island Bicentennial Foundation*, 417 F.Supp. 632, 641 (D.R.I. 1976) (quoting *Southeastern Promotions*, 420 U.S. at 553, 95 S.Ct. at 1242–44).

The defendants assert that they are guided by specific concerns for public safety, as outlined in their notice to plaintiffs, and not by the message of 2 Live Crew's lyrics.

When dealing with the First Amendment, however, the law does not allow us to presume good intentions on the part of the reviewing body. *Lakewood*, 486 U.S. at 770, 108 S.Ct. at 1243–44. The standards must be explicitly set out in the ordinance itself, a judicial construction or a well-established practice. *Id.* Without standards, there is a grave danger that a licensing scheme "will serve only as a mask behind which the government hides as it excludes speakers from the . . . forum solely because of what they intend to say." *Irish Subcommittee*, 646 F.Supp. at 357. Such exclusion is repugnant to the First Amendment.

This Court recognizes that the Westerly Town Council has a valid interest in regulating entertainment establishments. It is well established that time, place, and manner restrictions on expressive activity are permissible, but even then the regulations must be "narrowly and precisely tailored to their legitimate objectives." *Toward a Gayer Bicentennial*, 427 F.Supp. at 638, see Shuttlesworth, 394 U.S. at 153, 89 S.Ct. at 940; *Cox*, 379 U.S. at 558, 85 S.Ct. at 466. The Westerly licensing ordinances do not even approach the necessary level of specificity constitutionally mandated. Given the complete lack of standards in the ordinances and the long and clear line of precedent, plaintiffs' likelihood of success is overwhelming.

****

ORDER

Because Westerly Code of Ordinances, Sections 17-84 and 17-87 are facially unconstitutional, because the plaintiffs have met the other requirements for a preliminary injunction, and because defendants have failed to allege sufficient harm. IT IS ORDERED that defendants are enjoined from conducting a show cause hearing, revoking plaintiffs' license pursuant to these ordinances or from otherwise prohibiting the scheduled concert.

Dwonna Gayle Gwaltney
CARDWELL Appellant,

v.

Kenneth Wayne GWALTNEY, Appellee.

No. 87A01–9002–CV–80.
Court of Appeals of Indiana,

First District.
July 17, 1990.
556 N.E.2D 953 (IND. CT. APP. 1990)

ROBERTSON, Judge.

The sole issue raised in this appeal is whether an individual should be absolved from paying child support because of his incarceration.

(continues)

The underlying material facts show that the appellant Cardwell and the appellee Gwaltney were divorced with Gwaltney ordered to pay child support. About a year and one half later, Gwaltney filed a petition to modify the support order based upon the reason that he had spent a year in jail. Gwaltney sought to be absolved from the support which had accrued during that year and to have future support reduced. Cardwell and Gwaltney reached an agreement that, among other things, excused Gwaltney from paying support for the year he was imprisoned. The trial court approved the agreement; however, that agreement was challenged when the county prosecuting attorney appeared in the matter and sought to set aside the agreement because Cardwell had been a recipient of AFDC funds through the State and had assigned her support rights. The trial court refused to set aside the earlier agreements with this appeal resulting.

Even though the trial judge was prompted by equitable concerns when Gwaltney was excused from paying support, the law is that any modification of a support order must act prospectively:

> In *Biedron v. Biedron* (1958), 128 Ind. App. 299, 148 N.E.2d 209, the Appellate Court of Indiana said, "in this state after support installments have accrued, the court is without power to reduce, annul, or vacate such orders retrospectively, and therefore, the court committed error in attempting to do so." (Citations omitted.) Therefore, payments must be made in the manner, amount, and at the times required by the support order embodied in the divorce decree until such order is modified or set aside. *Stitle v. Stitle* (1964), 245 Ind. 168, 197 N.E.2d 174, Indiana does permit cancellation or modification of support orders as to future payments; but, all modifications operate prospectively. *Kniffen v. Courtney* (1971), 148 Ind.App. 358, 266 N.E.2d 72; *Haycraft v. Haycraft* (1978), Ind.App. [176 Ind.App. 211], 375 N.E.2d 252.

Jahn v. Jahn (1979), 179 Ind.App. 368, 385 N.E.2d 488, 490. See also *O'Neil v. O'Neil* (1988), Ind.App., 517 N.E.2d 433 (transfer granted on other grounds).

Additionally, I.C. 31–2–11–12 provides:
Modification of delinquent support payment.

(a) Except as provided in subsection (b), *a court may not retroactively modify* an obligor's duty to pay a delinquent support payment.

(b) A court with jurisdiction over a support order may modify an obligor's duty to pay a support payment that becomes due:

> (1) After notice of a petition to modify the support order has been given to each obligee; and

> (2) Before a final order concerning the petition for modification is entered. (Emphasis added.)

Although the Indiana Child Support Guidelines, effective October 1, 1989, were not officially in use at the time of the trial court's decision in this appeal, we are of the opinion that a part of the commentary to Ind. Child Support Guideline 2 takes into consideration existing statutes and case law as heretofore cited. That part of the commentary reads:

> Even in situations where the noncustodial parent has no income, Courts have routinely established a child support obligation at some minimum level. An obligor cannot be held in contempt for failure to pay support when he does not have the means to pay, but the obligation accrues and serves as a reimbursement to the custodial parent, or, more likely, to the welfare department if he later acquires the ability to meet his obligation.

We conclude that the trial court erred in retroactively excusing Gwaltney's support obligation for the time he was incarcerated.

Cause reversed and remanded for further action not inconsistent with this opinion.

Reversed and remanded.

RATLIFF, C.J., and CONOVER, J., concur.

COMMONWEALTH

v.

John J. SHEA.

No. 93–P–1066.

Appeals Court of Massachusetts, Plymouth.

Argued Sept. 12, 1994.
Decided Jan. 5, 1995.
Further Appellate Review
Denied Feb. 28, 1995.
38 Mass. App. Ct. 7, 644 N.E.2d 244 (1995)

PERRETTA, Justice.

On the afternoon of June 15, 1991, the defendant and his friend invited two women who were sun bathing on the banks of the Charles River to board the defendant's boat and go for a ride. Once the women were aboard, the defendant headed out to the open sea. An hour later and about five miles off shore from Boston, he stopped the boat, disrobed, and made sexual remarks and advances toward the women. He ignored all requests that he dress and stop his offensive behavior. When the women demanded that he return them to Boston, he threw them overboard and drove away without a backward glance. The women were rescued after managing to swim within shouting distance of a sailboat. On evidence of these acts, a jury found the defendant guilty, as to each woman, of kidnapping, attempted murder, assault and battery by means of a dangerous weapon (the ocean), and indecent assault and battery. The defendant argues on appeal that the trial judge erroneously denied (1) his request for a continuance of the trial; (2) his motion in limine by which he sought to preclude the Commonwealth's use of a videotape showing the ocean from the perspective of the women in the water and the defendant on his boat; and (3) his motion for required findings of not guilty on all the indictments. Although we conclude that the ocean is not a dangerous weapon within the meaning of G.L. c. 265, § 15A, we affirm the kidnapping and attempted murder convictions.[1]

1. *The motion for a continuance.* Trial counsel was appointed to represent the defendant on August 29, 1991.[2] On February 21, 1992, he filed a motion seeking funds for a psychiatric evaluation of the defendant. The motion was allowed that same day, and the case was continued to April 21, 1992, "for trial." One week before the scheduled trial date, counsel sought a continuance of at least two months. The Commonwealth opposed the motion on numerous grounds, not the least of which was the fact that the victims had been receiving threatening mail and telephone calls. The judge denied the request and the defendant claims error. "[A] motion for continuance . . . lies within the sound discretion of the judge, whose action will not be disturbed unless there is a patent abuse of that discretion, which is to be determined in the circumstances of each case." *Commonwealth v. Bettencourt*, 361 Mass. 515, 517–518, 281 N.E.2d 220 (1972). We relate the circumstances of the denial of the defendant's motion.

An affidavit and a letter from a psychiatrist, dated March 17, 1992, were attached to the motion for a continuance. It appears from these documents that the defendant's medical history indicated that he had suffered a series of head injuries from which he might have sustained brain trauma and that, according to the psychiatrist, the "charges now pending against him may reflect behavior caused by those head injuries." As further stated by the psychiatrist: "For a more conclusive answer to the question of the effect of Mr. Shea's head traumas to his alleged criminal acts, it would be necessary for him to undergo independent extensive neuropsychological testing and, in addition, have a BEAM study of the electrical activity of his brain."

As of April 14, 1992, the date of the hearing on the motion for a continuance, the BEAM study had been completed and the results reported to the psychiatrist. A copy of the report which had been submitted to the psychiatrist was also attached to the motion. The report recited the following conclusion of the BEAM study: "Overall this study is quite compatible with a history of multiple head injuries and suggests a generalized encephalopathy with irritable qualities falling just short of being a seizure disorder. The latter diagnosis, of course, should be made on clinical grounds."

It was not until the psychiatrist was called to testify at trial that the defendant's theory of defense took on a clarity: on the afternoon of June 15, 1991, he was experiencing a temporal lobe seizure, which prevented him from formulating the specific intent necessary for criminal liability for his actions. At the time of the hearing on the motion, however, the trial judge was informed only that a continuance of two months was necessary so that in addition to the psychiatrist, various other named medical professionals could also review the results of the BEAM study and conduct psychoneurological testing of the defendant. Even were we to conclude that an adequate case for granting the motion had been made at that time, but see *Commonwealth v. Bettencourt*, 361 Mass. at 517–518, 281 N.E.2d 220, the defendant has failed to show that his defense was prejudiced by the denial of his request.

Although the defendant argues that the denial of the continuance prevented psychoneurological testing which would have allowed the psychiatrist to opine whether, at the time in question, the defendant was experiencing a temporal lobe seizure, the psychiatrist's testimony does not support the claim. The psychiatrist testified on voir dire that had additional psychoneurological testing been available, he could be more "definitive" or "conclusive" in his opinion concerning the defendant's potential for temporal lobe seizures.[3] The psychiatrist nonetheless could, and did, relate to the jury that it was his opinion, to the requisite degree of medical certainty, that the defendant's "history, test results, and behavior is consistent with a temporal lobe disorder."

As for the more immediate question of whether the defendant was experiencing a seizure at the time of the incident, the psychiatrist testified, on voir dire, that he could not say "with [a] high degree of certainty that at that moment on that boat, that type of episode occurred."

---

1. The defendant was also found guilty on two counts of indecent assault and battery. Because he assented to those convictions being placed on file, they are not before us. See *Commonwealth v. Delgado*, 367 Mass. 432, 438, 326 N.E.2d 716 (1975).

2. Appellate counsel was not trial counsel.

---

3. The psychiatrist had reviewed some psychoneurological test results which were in the defendant's medical records. When asked by defense counsel whether he could be more conclusive in his opinion had "more extensive psychoneurological testing" been done, the psychiatrist responded, "[Y]es, everything that enhances helps becomes more definitive until ultimately, hopefully, you can become almost conclusive about it. I'm only saying I can't be conclusive, I can only render an opinion at this time."

(continues)

Rather, he could state only that "this individual, with his condition, has a high potential for things like that happening." At no time was the psychiatrist asked whether psychoneurological testing could reveal to a reasonable degree of medical certainty whether a person who suffered from temporal lobe disorder had in fact experienced a seizure at a specific time in the past.

In sum, the defendant's temporal lobe disorder was fully presented to the jury. Although the defendant's expert and the expert for the Commonwealth agreed that the defendant's BEAM study indicated a temporal lobe abnormality, they sharply disagreed on the issue of whether the defendant's actions were consistent or inconsistent with a temporal lobe seizure. However, any weaknesses that the jury might have found in the testimony of the defendant's psychiatrist cannot, on the record before us, be attributed to a lack of psychoneurological testing and the denial of the continuance.

2. *The videotapes.* At trial, the Commonwealth was allowed to use two chalks, i.e., videotapes, to illustrate to the jury the victims' testimony concerning the condition of the ocean when the defendant threw them into the water and abandoned them. The first videotape depicted the victims' view from the water as they watched the defendant drive away, and the second showed how two people in the water would appear from the vantage point of the back of the boat as it drove away from them. The Commonwealth argued that the tapes were relevant to the defendant's murderous intent. After an in camera viewing of the tapes, the trial judge ruled that the videos could be used as chalks. Immediately before the jury viewed the tapes, the trial judge instructed: "This is not offered for your consideration as evidence in this case. It is offered in the nature of what we refer to as a chalk to the extent that it may be of assistance to you in understanding the evidence that you have heard in view of the similarities, if any, and it's for you to determine if there are any similarities in the circumstances of the events of June 15, 1991." See generally Liacos, Massachusetts Evidence § 11.13.2 (6th ed. 1994) ("Chalks are used to illustrate testimony . . . they are not evidence in the ordinary sense of the word").

> The defendant complains that the tapes were a prejudicial recreation of the crime, that they were not based upon the evidence, and that they were inflammatory. We see no abuse of discretion or other error in the trial judge's decision to allow the Commonwealth to use the videotapes as chalks.

"Whether the conditions were sufficiently similar to make the observation [offered by the demonstration] of any value in aiding the jury to pass upon the issue submitted to them [is] primarily for the trial judge to determine as a matter of discretion. [The judge's] decision in this respect will not be interfered with unless plainly wrong." *Commonwealth v. Chipman,* 418 Mass. 262, 270–271,

635 N.E.2d 1204 (1994), quoting from *Field v. Gowdy,* 199 Mass. 568, 574, 85 N.E. 884 (1908). See also *Terrio v. McDonough,* 16 Mass.App.Ct. 163, 173, 450 N.E.2d 190 (1983). To the extent the videotapes do not depict anyone being thrown from the boat into the ocean, they are not a recreation of the crime. The tapes otherwise essentially track the victims' testimony.

State police officers Earle S. Sterling and Leonard Coppengrath testified that at 9:30 A.M. on April 15, 1992, they and a number of their associates boarded a boat and proceeded to the point five miles off shore from Boston where the women had been pulled from the water. They described the weather conditions that day as well as the height of the waves and the temperature of the water. They had video cameras and other equipment with them. When they reached their destination, Sterling and another man, who was holding a camera, jumped overboard. Once in the water, the other man held the camera about two inches (the eye level of the victims) above the water, and filmed the boat as it drove off. Meanwhile, Coppengrath, who remained on the boat, focused a camera on the two men in the water as another one of the men slowly drove away.[4] After proceeding about one-half mile, the men in the water were no longer visible from the boat. Coppengrath then panned the "area from where we had come and to where we were heading and circled across the skyline of Boston towards the point in Hull which is the closest point of land to where we were."

There is no persuasive force to the defendant's argument that the Commonwealth's use of the videotapes was no more than a disguised inflammatory appeal to the jurors to put themselves in the place of the victims. See, *e.g., Commonwealth v. Sevieri,* 21 Mass.App.Ct. 745, 753–754, 490 N.E.2d 481 (1986). The Commonwealth was entitled to dispel any notion that the defendant's actions were no more than a sunny-day prank gone too far and that he returned for the victims but again departed when he saw them being pulled aboard the sailboat. When the defendant first threw one of the women into the water, she screamed that she did not know how to swim. He then jumped overboard, held her head under the water, and reboarded the boat for the second woman. Before he threw her into the water, she too told him that she could not swim. Having experienced the frigid temperature of

---

4. Although the victims testified that the defendant sped away in the boat, that testimony did not require preclusion of the use of the videotapes, see *Commonwealth v. Chipman,* 418 Mass, at 270–271, 635 N.E.2d 1204 (1994), especially in light of the trial judge's instructions to the jury prior to the viewing of the films. We also think it inconsequential that there was no evidence to show that the defendant turned to watch the victims as he drove off. The information being illustrated pertained to the water conditions and surroundings, which remained the same irrespective of any particular vantage point, and the defendant's awareness of them.

the water and the height of the waves and having been told that the victims could not swim, the defendant drove away leaving the women in great peril. The videotapes show what that defendant saw and experienced, and they were relevant to the issue of whether he "did an act designed to result in death with the specific intent that death result." *Commonwealth v. Beattie*, 409 Mass. 458, 459, 567 N.E.2d 206 (1991). See also *Commonwealth v. Hebert*, 373 Mass. 535, 537, 368 N.E.2d 1204 (1977) ("An attempt to commit a crime necessarily involves an intent to commit that crime").[5] We have viewed the videotapes and conclude that the trial judge neither abused his discretion nor committed other error of law in allowing them to be seen by the jury. See *Commonwealth v. Chipman*, 418 Mass. at 271, 635 N.E.2d 1204; *Terrio v. McDonough*, 16 Mass.App.Ct. at 173, 450 N.E.2d 190.

3. *Attempted murder and kidnapping.* It is the defendant's argument that the Commonwealth failed to prove that when he threw the women into the water and drove away, he specifically intended their death. Taking the evidence in the light most favorable to the Commonwealth, we see no error in the trial judge's denial of the defendant's motion for a required finding of not guilty on the indictments charging him with attempted murder by drowning. There was evidence to show that the defendant was five miles offshore with no boats in sight when he threw the women overboard. The water was fifty-two degrees, and the waves were one to two feet high. Because the defendant had jumped into the water to hold one of the woman under, he knew that it was cold and choppy. For all he knew, they could not swim.

This evidence of the defendant's conduct was sufficient to warrant the reasonable inference that he intended that the victims drown. See *Commonwealth v. Henson*, 394 Mass. 584, 591, 476 N.E.2d 947 (1985) ("[An] intent to kill may be inferred from the defendant's conduct"); *Commonwealth v. Dixon*, 34 Mass.App.Ct. 653, 656, 614 N.E.2d 1027 (1993) (attempted murder statute reaches act of throwing someone who cannot swim from a boat into water).[6]

In arguing that there was no evidence of kidnappings apart from the conduct incidental to the attempted murders, i.e., picking the women up and throwing them into the water, the defendant ignores the testimony of the victims. Both women related that after the defendant disrobed and made sexual advances towards them, they demanded that he return them to shore. He refused, continued with his offensive behavior, became angry over their reaction, and then threw them overboard. Moreover, the conduct which the jury reasonably could find as the basis for kidnapping, forcing the women to remain at sea while the defendant committed an indecent assault and battery upon them (see note one, *supra*), would not necessarily be based on the acts that constituted the attempted murders. See *Commonwealth v. Rivera*, 397 Mass. 244, 253–254, 490 N.E.2d 1160 (1986); *Commonwealth v. Sumner*, 18 Mass.App.Ct. 349, 352–353, 465 N.E.2d 1213 (1984).

4. *The dangerous weapon.* General Laws c. 265, § 15A, reads, in pertinent part: "Whoever commits assault and battery upon another by means of a dangerous weapon shall be punished . . . ." The sole argument made by the defendant in respect to the indictments charging him with assault and battery by means of a dangerous weapon is that the ocean is not a dangerous weapon within the meaning of § 15A.

We need not consider whether the specified weapon, the ocean, is dangerous per se or dangerous as used. See *Commonwealth v. Tarrant*, 367 Mass. 411, 416–417, 326 N.E.2d 710 (1975); *Commonwealth v. Appleby*, 380 Mass. 296, 303, 402 N.E.2d 1051 (1980). Although the ocean can be and often is dangerous, it cannot be regarded in its natural state as a weapon within the meaning of § 15A. See *Commonwealth v. Farrell*, 322 Mass. 606, 614–615, 78 N.E.2d 697 (1948), stating that the term "dangerous weapon" comprehends "*any instrument or instrumentality so constructed or so used* as to be likely to produce death or great bodily harm" (emphasis added); *Commonwealth v. Tarrant*, 367 Mass. at 417 n. 6, 326 N.E.2d 710, noting with approval the definition of dangerous weapon adopted in the Proposed Criminal Code of Massachusetts c. 263, § 3(i): "'any firearm or other weapon, device, instrument, material or substance, *whether animate or inanimate*, which in the matter [in] which it is used *or is intended to be used* is capable of producing death or serious bodily injury' (emphasis added)";[7] *Commonwealth v. Appleby*, 380 Mass. at 308, 402 N.E.2d 1051, concluding that the "offense of assault and battery by means of a dangerous weapon under G.L. c. 265, § 15A, requires that the elements of assault be present . . . that there be a touching, however

---

5. As the videotapes were illustrative on the issue of the defendant's intent, we need not consider whether, as the Commonwealth argues, they were also helpful to an understanding of the victims' state of mind, an issue of questionable relevancy. See *Commonwealth v. Zagranski*, 408 Mass. 278, 282–283, 558 N.E.2d 933 (1990).

6. In deciding this issue, we need not, contrary to the defendant's argument, consider the testimony of his friend, that he was "eventually" able to persuade the defendant to turn back for the women and that with the aid of binoculars they were able to see the women about three-quarters of a mile away being pulled aboard a sailboat. See *Commonwealth v. Lydon*, 413 Mass. 309 312, 597 N.E.2d 36 (1992).

---

7. This definition tracks that of "deadly weapon" set out in § 210 of the Model Penal Code (1980), which, as noted in comment 5, was "designed to take account of the ingenuity of those who desire to hurt their fellows without encompassing every use of an ordinary object that could cause death or serious injury."

(continues)

slight . . . that the touching be by means of the weapon . . . and that the battery be accomplished by use of an inherently dangerous weapon, or by use of *some other object* as a weapon, with the intent to use *that object* in a dangerous or potentially dangerous fashion" (emphasis added).

All the cases collected and cited in the discussion of dangerous weapons, per se and as used, in *Commonwealth v. Appleby*, 380 Mass. at 303–304, 402 N.E.2d 1051, share a common fact that is consistent with the definitions of "dangerous weapons" which speak in terms of "objects" or "instrumentalities." The commonality found in those cases is that the object in issue, whether dangerous per se or as used, was an instrumentality which the batterer controlled, either through possession of or authority over it, for use of it in the intentional application of force. Because the ocean in its natural state cannot be possessed or controlled, it is not an object or instrumentality capable of use as a weapon for purposes of § 15A.

Our conclusion should not be construed to mean that there can never be criminal liability for causing physical harm to someone by subjecting them to a force of nature. We conclude only that for purposes of § 15A, the ocean, not being subject to human control, was not, in the instant case, an object or instrumentality which could be found by the jury to be a dangerous weapon. Accordingly, the defendant's motion for required findings of not guilty on the indictments charging him with assault and battery by means of a dangerous weapon should have been allowed.

5. *Conclusion.* It follows from what we have said that the judgments entered on the indictments charging kidnapping and attempted murder are affirmed. The judgments entered on the indictments charging assault and battery by means of a dangerous weapon are reversed, the verdicts are set aside and judgments for the defendant are to enter on those indictments.[8]

SO ORDERED.

---

8. The Commonwealth has not argued that the defendant should, in any event, be resentenced on the lesser offense of assault and battery, presumably for the reason, if no other, that it would make no practical difference. The sentence imposed on the conviction for assault and battery by means of a dangerous weapon was to be served concurrently with that imposed on the attempted murder conviction.

Philip J. Cooper, Administrator Pendente Lite of The Estate of W.A. Bisson, Deceased, Plaintiff-Appellant,

v.

Charles AUSTIN, Defendant-Appellant.

Court of Appeals of Tennessee, Western Section, at Jackson.

Feb. 18, 1992.

Application for Permission to Appeal Denied by Supreme Court May 26, 1992.

837 S.W.2d 606 (Tenn. Ct. App. 1992)

CRAWFORD, Judge.

This is a will contest case involving a codicil to the Last Will and Testament of Wheelock A. Bisson, M.D., deceased. Phillip Cooper, Administrator *pendente lite* of the estate, is a nominal party only; the real parties in interest are the proponent of the codicil, Alois B. Greer, and the contestant, Charles Austin.

Dr. Bisson's will, which is not contested, was executed June 18, 1982. Dr. Bisson died in 1985, and shortly thereafter Greer filed a petition in probate court to admit the June 18, 1982, will and two codicils thereto dated August 20, 1984, and August 6, 1985, respectively, to probate as and for the Last Will and Testament of Wheelock A. Bisson, M.D. By order entered November 26, 1985, the probate court admitted the paper writings to probate as the Last Will and Testament of Dr. Bisson.

On May 20, 1986, Austin filed a petition in probate court to contest the two codicils,[1] and, after answer to the petition by Greer, the probate court certified the contest to circuit court by order entered August 13, 1986.

No action was taken in circuit court until the administrator pendente lite filed a "Complaint to Establish Will and Codicil" on November 9, 1988. Austin's answer to the complaint, inter alia, denied that either codicil had been properly executed by the decedent or properly witnessed and further denied that the codicils had any legal validity or effect.

Greer filed a motion for summary judgment in October, 1990, seeking to have Austin's case dismissed on the grounds that it was barred by T.C.A. § 32–4–108 (1986), because it was brought more than two years from the entry of the order admitting the will to probate. The trial court denied this motion.

On March 26, 1991, a jury trial was held on the issue of devisavit vel non as to the 1984 codicil. The 1982 will was introduced into evidence by stipulation, and Greer offered the 1984 codicil through the attesting witnesses.

---

1. The codicil dated August 6, 1985, made no property disposition, but merely appointed Greer as executrix of the estate. During the course of the circuit court trial, the proponent withdrew this codicil from evidence. Since it is not involved in this appeal we will omit further reference to it in this Opinion.

In his 1982 will, Dr. Bisson left everything to his wife and if she predeceased him he left the majority of his estate to Austin. This disposition was changed by the 1984 codicil which provides:

CODICIL TO MY LAST WILL
AND TESTAMENT

I, Wheelock Alexander Bisson, M.D., of 2312 Park Avenue, Memphis, Shelby County, Tennessee, this August 20th, 1984. Bequeath that my adopted daughter, Alois B. Greer, receive a child's share of my estate which will consist of all real property, personal property, household furniture and any and all savings which I might have at the time of my demise.

/s/ Wheelock A. Bisson, M.D.
WHEELOCK ALEXANDER BISSON, M.D.

/s/ Michael E. Harrison
WITNESS

3907 Kerwin Dr. Memphis, Tenn. 38138
ADDRESS

/s/ Charles L. Harrison
WITNESS
4905 Sagewood, Mphs., TN. 38116
ADDRESS

Sworn to and subscribed before me this 20th day of August, 1984.

/s/ Lillie M. Thomas
NOTARY PUBLIC
My Commission Expires:
Jan. 5, 1987

On direct examination, Michael Harrison stated that he signed the codicil in the presence of Dr. Bisson. He then gave the following testimony regarding that signing:

Q. All right. When you got ready to sign did Dr. Bisson indicate to you what you were signing as a witness?
A. Yes. At the time I had no idea what a codicil was.
Q. All right.
A. But I did—I did witness it.

On cross examination, Michael Harrison gave the following testimony:

Q. All right. You didn't know what this document was now you've got in front of you at the time you signed it. Correct? This is one dated August, 1984.
A. I didn't understand your question.
Q. Well, Dr. Bisson didn't tell you what it was, he just said he needed a paper signed and notarized. Right?
A. He didn't tell me anything. I was asked to witness the document. He told Ms. Thomas. She notarized it, I was asked to witness it.

Q. At the time did you know what the document was—
A. No, sir.
Q. . . . that you were witnessing? Pardon me?
A. No, sir.
Q. And Dr. Bisson didn't tell you what it was?
A. No, sir.
Q. You didn't ask anybody what it was?
A. No, sir.

Charles Harrison, the other witness appearing on the 1984 codicil, testified on direct examination pertinent to the issue before us:

Q. All right. Do you recall the occasion when you signed this document?
A. Yes, sir.
Q. Okay. Will you give us the background as to how you came to be involved with this document at all?
A. On this particular day, the 20th of August, 1984, we were on our way back from Memorial Park— the rotunda at the Memorial Park Cemetery, and Dr. Bisson was seated on the front seat of the limousine with me.

And he said, when you get back, you know, to my place—which he referred that was his home—he said, when you get back to my place, he said, I have something I want you all to do for me. And so I said, well, okay, Doc. And that was that. And so the rest of the people that was in the limousine they were just carrying on casual conversation. So when we got back to his residence on Park Avenue we were letting them out of the limousines and he said, don't leave, come on in, I have something, you know, I want you to take care of for me. And so he asked me where was Ms. Thomas. I said, well, she's at the funeral home. He said, well, call her and tell her to come down here, I need her—you know, I need her here, you know, on this too. And so when we got inside—We came through the side entrance and we went up to his front office. And he said, I have this codicil that I want you all to notarize for me and witness, and that's how I came in contact with him.
Q. All right, sir. Now, at the time that this document was signed were you present?
A. Yes, sir.
Q. And did you see Dr. Bisson sign this document?
A. Yes, sir.
Q. Was your brother Michael also present?
A. Yes, sir.
Q. And all three of you were together at the time; is that correct?
A. Yes, sir.
Q. Ms. Thomas is on there as a notary. Was she also in the room or was she not?

(continues)

A. No, she was in the room. Yes, sir.

Q. All right. And Dr. Bisson asked you all to sign this; is that correct?

A. Yes, sir.

Q. And all three of you signed it in each other's presence?

A. That's correct.

* * * * * *

The pertinent testimony from Charles Harrison on cross examination is:

Q. Now, Dr. Bisson didn't tell you what was in the document that you were signing. Correct?

A. No, he did not.

Q. And he didn't tell you what the document was?

A. Yes, sir, he did.

Q. Well, let me ask you. Do you recall giving a deposition, meaning when you came to my conference room up at my office January 14, 1987 and you swore to tell the truth, and there was a court reporter—it wasn't this woman, but another woman with a machine like that that took down your testimony? Do you recall that?

A. January the 14th of '87?

Q. Yes, sir.

A. I remember coming to your office, yes, sir.

Q. All right.

A. I don't remember the exact date, but I do remember coming to your office.

Q. Have you had a chance to look over this document—this deposition transcript?

A. No, sir.

Q. I asked you on page 40 at that time when you were under oath, I said—At line 3 you said, I just glanced over it. I didn't stop, I just glanced over it.

Q. (Line 5) Did Dr. Bisson tell you what was in it?

A. No, sir.

Q. Did he tell you what it was?

A. No, sir.

Q. Was that your testimony at that time? Would you agree with me that your memory was probably better about this in January of 1987, which would be, what, four years ago?

A. I'm not playing with my memory, but I'd say that—well, you know, I—

Q. Would you accept that as the truth if that's what you said then?

A. Yes, sir.

Q. So Dr. Bisson didn't elaborate as to what the document was, he said I want you to witness a document. He had the document already. Right?

A. Right.

Q. You didn't give it to him?

A. No.

Q. Okay. And then he signed it and he said, okay, now you sign it, and that was it. Correct?

A. Yes, sir, basically. He didn't say sign it, he said witness it.

Q. Witness it. And then there wasn't any more conversation about it after you witnessed it, y'all got up and left. Correct?

A. Right.

On re-direct examination, Charles Harrison testified as follows:

Q. Mr. Harrison, be very careful now and think regarding both what you said previously and what you just said.
   Are you absolutely certain that Dr. Bisson told you what it was he wanted you to witness?

A. Mr. MITCHELL: Note my objection to the leading, Your Honor. He never testified he knew what it was.
   THE COURT: He did testify, I believe, in his direct-examination. He said that Dr. Bisson said he had a codicil that he wanted witnessing.
   Mr. MITCHELL: Yes, sir, that's all he said.

Q. (BY Mr. BEATY) Is that what you recall today as to what he said?

A. Yes, sir.

Mr. BEATY: That's all I have.

Charles Harrison's re-cross examination is:

Q. But that was before you ever went in the room?

A. I beg your pardon.

Q. That was before you ever went into the room, that was when you were out in the car?

A. Right.

Q. When you went in the room he didn't say what it was or what was in it, just like you testified four years ago. Right?

A. Right.

Lillie Thomas, who appears as a notary public on the 1984 codicil, testified that all Dr. Bisson said in her presence was that he had a paper that he wanted her to notarize and that he said nothing in her presence about the paper being a will, a codicil or anything of that sort. We quote from the testimony:

Q. All right. And what did Dr. Bisson say about it in your presence?

A. He said I have a—he said a paper that I want you to notarize for me.

Q. All right. Did he use any language: will, codicil, anything of that sort?

A. No. He said a paper.

Q. All right. Did he sign it in your presence?

A. Yes, sir.

Q. Did he sign it in the presence of the other witnesses?

A. Yes, sir.

Q. Now Michael Harrison was present?

A. Yes, sir.

Q. And Charles Harrison, also; is that correct?

A. Yes, sir.

Following the testimony of these witnesses, counsel for Austin moved the court to disallow submission of the codicil to the jury on the grounds that the codicil's proponent, Mrs. Greer, had not met her burden of proof pursuant to T.C.A. § 32–1–104, regarding the manner in which a will must be executed.

The trial court granted Austin's motion and directed a verdict on the grounds that Ms. Greer had not proved the proper execution of the codicil. Accordingly, judgment was entered declaring that the last will and testament of Wheelock A. Bisson dated June 18, 1982, be admitted to probate without any codicils.

Greer has appealed and presents two issues for review. The first issue is whether the trial court erred in denying Greer's motion for summary judgment on the grounds that Mr. Austin's will contest was barred by T.C.A. § 32–4–108 (Supp. 1991) which provides:

> All **actions** or **proceedings** to set aside the probate of any will, or petitions to certify such will for an issue of **devisavit vel non**, must be brought within two (2) years from entry of the order admitting the will to probate, or be forever barred, saving, however, to persons under the age of eighteen (18) years or of unsound mind at the time the cause of action accrues, the rights conferred by § 28–1–106. (Emphasis added.)

Greer contends that this statute bars Austin's action, because the 1984 codicil was admitted to probate by order entered November 26, 1985, and Austin filed no pleading in circuit court until he filed an answer to the complaint on December 2, 1988. Greer argues that the filing of the complaint in circuit court was the commencement of the action pursuant to Rule 3, Tennessee Rules of Civil Procedure, and because it was filed more than two years from the order of probate court admitting the will to probate, the action is barred by the two year statute of limitations in T.C.A. § 32–4–108.

We must respectfully disagree with Greer for several reasons. The statute itself is clear and unambiguous. It is confined to actions to set aside the probate of a will or to petitions to certify a will for an issue of devisavit vel non. Obviously, the proceedings contemplated by this statute are proceedings that take place in the probate court. It is equally clear that the proceeding in the circuit court on the issue of devisavit vel non after the case is certified from the probate court to the circuit court is in substance an original proceeding to probate the will, separate and distinct from any proceedings held in probate court. *Bearman v. Camatsos*, 215 Tenn. 231, 385 S.W.2d 91

(1964); *Arnold v. Marcom*, 49 Tenn.App. 161, 352 S.W.2d 936 (1961). In a proceeding of this nature, no particular form of pleading is required. All that is required is that the proponent shall offer it as a will and the contesting party shall deny it. See *Bowman v. Helton*, 7 Tenn.App. 325 (1928).

Finally, it has long been held in this state that the right of a contestant to resist the probate of a will is a preliminary matter and presents a separate and distinct issue from the issue of devisavit vel non, and that the order of the probate court sustaining or denying the right to contest the will in an appealable order. See *Winters v. American Trust Co.*, 158 Tenn. 479, 14 S.W.2d 740 (1929). T.C.A. § 32–4–108 clearly applies only to this separate action.

We hold that the statute of limitations set out in T.C.A. § 32–4–108 applies only to the proceeding filed in the probate court seeking to set aside the probate of a will or a certification for a will contest.

The second issue for review is whether the trial court erred in directing a verdict for the contestant Austin by refusing to allow the 1984 codicil to be submitted to the jury.

The rule for determining a motion for directed verdict requires the trial judge and the reviewing court on appeal to look to all of the evidence, taking the strongest legitimate view of it in favor of the opponent of the motion and allowing all reasonable inferences from it in his favor. The court must discard all countervailing evidence, and if there is then any dispute as to any material determinative evidence or any doubt as to the conclusion to be drawn from the whole evidence, the motion must be denied. *Tennessee Farmers Mut. Ins. Co. v. Hinson*, 651 S.W.2d 235 (Tenn. App. 1983).

The court should not direct a verdict if there is any material evidence in the record that would support a verdict for the plaintiff under any of the theories he had advanced. *See Wharton Transport Corp. v. Bridges*, 606 S.W.2d 521 (Tenn. 1980).

The formal requirements for the execution of a will are set out in T.C.A. § 32–1–104 (1984), which provides:

> **Will other than holographic or nuncupative**—The execution of a will, other than a holographic or nuncupative will, must be by the signature of the testator and of at least two (2) witnesses as follows:
>
> (1) The testator shall signify to the attesting witnesses that the instrument is his will and either:
>
> (A) Himself sign;
>
> (B) Acknowledge his signature already made; or
>
> (C) At his direction and in his presence have someone else sign his name for him; and
>
> (D) In any of the above cases the act must be done in the presence of two (2) or more attesting witnesses.
>
> (2) The attesting witness must sign:

(continues)

(A) In the presence of the testator; and

(B) In the presence of each other.

Austin contended, and the trial court agreed, that Greer's proof failed to established that Dr. Bisson did "signify to the attesting witnesses that the [1984 codicil] is his will . . ." as required by the statute. Greer argues that the testimony of the attesting witnesses was sufficient to create an issue of fact for the jury as to whether Dr. Bisson so signified.

Austin relies primarily upon the case of *Lawrence v. Lawrence*, 35 Tenn.App. 648, 250 S.W.2d 781 (1951), which involved a will without an attestation clause and where the only surviving attesting witness testified both that the testatrix informed her that the instrument to be witnessed was the testatrix's will and also testified to the contrary by stating that she did not know that the instrument was a will. The Court of Appeals, in directing a verdict against the will, said:

> The meaning of this statute is clear, plain and unambiguous. When a testator calls upon persons to witness his will, "'the testator shall signify to the attesting witnesses that the instrument in [sic] his will'." Surely it cannot be contended that this provision of the statute is doubtful of meaning. It simply means that the testator must state to the witnesses in substance that the paper writing is his will and that he wants them to sign it as witnesses.

> By the uncontradicted evidence before us that essential requisite of the execution of a valid will is lacking. The testatrix did not signify to the attesting witnesses that the instrument was the will of testatrix.

250 S.W.2d at 784.

Austin contends that the cases relied upon by Greer—*Whitlow v. Weaver*, 63 Tenn.App. 651, 478 S.W.2d 57 (Tenn. App. 1970); *Needham v. Doyle*, 39 Tenn.App. 597, 286 S.W.2d 601 (1955); and *Miller v. Thrasher*, 38 Tenn.App. 88, 251 S.W.2d 446 (1952), and *In re Estate of Bradley*, 817 S.W.2d 320 (Tenn.App.1991)—all involve wills which contained an attestation clause. He concedes that an attestation clause raises a strong presumption that the recitals therein contained are true and that contrary evidence raises a question for the jury. *Needham*, 286 S.W.2d at 601. We agree that these cases are distinguishable on their facts.

Greer also relies upon *Leathers v. Binkley*, 196 Tenn. 80, 264 S.W.2d 561 (1954). In *Leathers*, the will did not contain an attestation clause and the two attesting witnesses testified that they had signed the will in the presence of the testatrix and in the presence of each other. Neither witness testified specifically that the will had been declared by the testatrix to be her will at the time of the signing. In holding in favor of the will, the Court said:

While it is true that neither Mr. Morrison nor Mrs. Gilmer remembered every detail of the signature and attestation of the will, the important fact in the record is that there was neither from Morrison, Mrs. Gilmer, nor the Notary Public, *a line of positive affirmative testimony that would support the allegations of the petition of contest, nor the verdict of the jury, that the will had not been regularly and legally executed in strict accordance with the requirements of Code, sec. 8089.4.*

"Where, for instance, the subscribing witnesses testify that they do not recollect the circumstances, but do recognize their signatures, and declare that they would not have placed them to the instrument unless they had seen the testator sign it, or heard him acknowledge his signature, the due execution may be presumed." Sizer's Pritchard on Wills, sec. 336, p. 380.

"In establishing the facts essential to the validity of the will by a preponderance of the evidence, proponents are, however, not obliged in all cases to prove each fact by direct evidence; but they may rely upon presumptions. There is, at the outset, no presumption that the alleged testator executed the will in question or any will; but when a paper propounded as a will is shown to have been signed by the alleged testator and the requisite number of witnesses, **in the absence of any satisfactory evidence to the contrary** the presumption is that all the formalities have been complied with." (Our Emphasis.) Page on Wills, Vol 2, sec. 755, p. 462.

The forgoing statement is supported by cases from many jurisdictions, including Georgia, Illinois, Iowa, Missouri, Montana, New Jersey, New Mexico and South Carolina. Compare: Annotations, 47 L.R.A., N.S., 722; 76 A.L.R. 604; 14 L.R.A., N.S., 255; Ann.Cas. 426.

264 S.W.2d at 563. (Emphasis added.)

Austin asserts that *Leathers* is not controlling authority for the case at bar because in *Leathers* there was no positive affirmative testimony that the will had not been regularly and legally executed. We agree with Austin the *Leathers* turned on that point, so we must examine the testimony in the case at bar to determine if there is uncontroverted positive testimony that Dr. Bisson did not "signify to the attesting witnesses" that the 1984 instrument was his will or codicil.

In examining the testimony of the witnesses, we must look at the testimony in the best light and afford to it all legitimate inferences. With that direction in mind, we will examine the testimony.

Charles Harrison's testimony is to the effect that prior to the gathering of attesting witnesses, notary public and testator, testator told him that he, the testator, had "this codicil that I want you all to notarize for me and witness." He specifically pointed out that this statement by Dr. Bisson was made before the gathering for the signing of the instrument.

Michael Harrison's testimony indicates both that he was told by Dr. Bisson that it was a codicil to be witnessed and that Dr. Bisson did not tell him what it was that he was witnessing. He specifically testified that he did not know what the document was. These contradictory statements effectively eliminate any testimony from this witness on that fact. *Taylor v. Nashville Banner Pub. Co.*, 573 S.W.2d 476 (Tenn.App.1978) cert. den. 441 U.S. 923, 99 S.Ct. 2032, 60 L.Ed.2d 396 (1979); *Donaho v. Large*, 25 Tenn.App. 433, 158 S.W.2d 447 (1941).

Lillie Thomas, the notary public, testified that Dr. Bisson said he had a paper to be witnessed and he did not use any language such as will, codicil or anything of that sort. Dr. Bisson's statement was made at the time the parties gathered for the signing.

An examination of the witness' testimony indicates that there is uncontroverted affirmative proof that Dr. Bisson did not signify to at least one attesting witness that the instrument to be witnessed was his will or a codicil thereto. Therefore, the trial court correctly directed a verdict against the admission of the will.

The judgment of the trial court is affirmed and this case is remanded to the trial court for such further proceedings as may be necessary.

Costs of the appeal are assessed against the appellant.

TOMLIN, P.J. (W.S.), and HIGHERS, J., concur.

DEAN et al. v. DICKEY et al.

No. 4662.

Court of Civil Appeals of Texas. El Paso.
Sept. 28, 1949.

Rehearing Denied Oct. 26, 1949.
225 S.W.2d 999 (Tex. Civ. App. 1949)

McGILL, Justice.

The sole question presented by this appeal is whether a typewritten instrument of testamentary character typed wholly by Trollis Dell Dickey on June 12, 1945, and intended by him to be his last will and testament, and signed by him and one witness in ink, is entitled to probate as the holographic will of the said Trollis Dell Dickey, Deceased. The trial court affirmed the order of the County Court denying probate of the instrument, and this appeal has been duly perfected.

The Statutes applicable on June 12, 1945, are the following: Vernon's Texas Civil Statutes:

> Art. 8283: "Every last will and testament except where otherwise provided by law, shall be in writing and signed by the testator or by some other person by his direction and in his presence, and shall, if not wholly written by himself, be attested by two or more credible witnesses above the age of fourteen years, subscribing their names thereto in the presence of the testator."

> Art. 8284: "Where the will is wholly written by the testator the attestation of the subscribing witnesses may be dispensed with."

> Art. 3344: Sec. 4: "If the will was wholly written by the testator, by two witnesses to his handwriting, which may be made by affidavit taken in open court and subscribed to by the witnesses, or by deposition."

These Statutes construed together leave no room for doubt that the language employed in Art. 8283 "if not wholly written by himself"; in Art. 8284 "wholly written by the testator" and in Art. 3344, Sec. 4 "if the will was wholly written by the testator, by two witnesses to his handwriting," require that the words "wholly written" used in these Articles be construed to mean wholly written in the handwriting of the testator. Art. 8283 prescribes the requisites of a holographic will. Art. 8284 provides that when those requisites have been complied with, attestation by subscribing witnesses may be dispensed with, while Art. 3344, Sec. 4 prescribes the character of proof necessary to prove such will. To give the identical language "wholly written" used in these Statutes the meaning for which appellants contend would render Art. 8283 and Art. 3344, Sec. 4, inconsistent and repugnant, since such interpretation would make it impossible to prove a typewritten will in the manner prescribed by Art. 3344, Sec. 4, i.e., by two witnesses to the handwriting of the testator.

Appellants concede that this case is one of first impression in this State, and that the construction for which they contend is contrary to the overwhelming weight of authority in other jurisdictions where similar Statutes have been construed, citing 68 C.J., p. 719, Sec. 402, and 57 Am.Jur. p. 433, Sec. 634. The reason for the rule laid down by these authorities is ably stated in *Re Dreyfus' Estate*, 175 Cal. 417, 165 P. 941, L.R.A. 1917F, 391:

> "From time immemorial, letters and words have been written with the hand by means of pen and ink or pencil of some description, and it has been a well-known fact that each individual who writes in this manner acquires a style of forming, placing, and spacing the letters and words which is peculiar to himself and which in most cases renders his writing easily distinguishable from that of others by those familiar with it or by experts in chirography who make a study of the subject and who are afforded an opportunity of comparing a disputed specimen with those admitted to be genuine. The provision that a will should be valid if entirely 'written, dated, and signed

(continues)

by the hand of the testator,' is the ancient rule on the subject. There can be no doubt that it owes its origin to the fact that a successful counterfeit of another's handwriting is exceedingly difficult, and that therefore the requirement that it should be in the testator's handwriting would afford protection against a forgery of this character."

See also: *Adams'Ex'x v. Beaumont,* 226 Ky. 311, 10 S.W.2d 1106; and *McNeill v. McNeill,* 261 Ky. 240, 87 S.W.2d 367, where the statutory language "wholly written" under construction is identical with that of ours. However, appellants contend that a different interpretation should be given to Articles 8283 and 8284, supra, for two reasons: First, because of Sec. 3, Art. 23:

"Definitions" of Title 1: "General Provisions" R.C.S., which provides:

"'Written' or 'in writing' includes any representation of words, letters or figures, 'whether *by writing, printing or otherwise.*'" (Emphasis ours.)

Secondly: Because of the emergency clause of S.B. 328, enacted by the 50th Legislature, Acts of 1947, 50th Leg., Reg. Sess., Ch. 170, p. 275, which amended Articles 8283 and 8284 by substituting for the words "wholly written by himself" in Art. 8283, the words "wholly in the handwriting of the testator" and for the words "wholly written by the testator" in Art. 8284, the words "wholly written in the handwriting of the testator." The relevant portion of the emergency clause is "that under the present interpretation of the statute any form of writing including typewriting, or *printing or otherwise* (emphasis

ours) is sufficient to constitute a will which leaves a dangerous and unsafe condition not properly protecting widows and orphans of this state." Section 3.

By the very terms of Art. 23, the meaning given the words "written or in writing" by Section 3 has no application where "a different meaning is apparent from the context." As above pointed out, Art. 8283–8284 and Art. 3344, Sec. 4, construed together leave no room for doubt as to the meaning of the words "wholly written" therein employed. Therefore, Art. 23, Sec. 3 has no application. For like reason, without application is the rule enunciated in *Stanford et al. v. Butler,* 142 Tex. 692, 181 S.W.2d 269, loc. cit. 274(8, 9), 153 A.L.R. 1054:

"* * * where a later act implies a particular construction of an existing law, and particularly where the existing law is ambiguous or its meaning uncertain, interpretation of the prior act by the Legislature as contained in the later act is persuasive when a court is called upon to interpret the prior law."

Articles 8283 and 8284, when construed with Art. 3344, Sec. 4, are not ambiguous, nor is their meaning uncertain. Furthermore, when S.B. 328 was enacted there had been no decision by any appellate court of this State construing Articles 8283 and 8284 as declared in the emergency clause. From the similarity of the language emphasized it is probable that the Legislature erroneously assumed that Art. 23, Sec. 3 was applicable and controlling in its construction of Articles 8283 and 8284. For this additional reason, the above quoted rule is inapplicable.

The judgment of the trial court is affirmed.

McCLAIN et al. v. ADAMS.

In re DOUGLASS' ESTATE.
No. 2340—7579.

Commission of Appeals of Texas, Section A.
Jan. 15, 1941.
146 S.W.2d 373 (Tex. Civ. App. 1941)

HICKMAN, Commissioner.

The subject matter of this litigation is an alleged nuncupative will. Annie Douglass, deceased, was the alleged testator; Willie Adams, defendant in error, was the proponent in the probate court; and Eliza McClain and others, plaintiffs in error, the next of kin of the deceased, were the contestants. The county court of Jefferson county sustained the contest and denied the probate. On appeal the district court of that county entered judgment admitting the alleged will to probate, which judgment was affirmed by the Court of Civil Appeals. 126 S.W.2d 61.

One of the requisites of a nuncupative will, as prescribed by article 3346, R.C.S., is that, "it be made in the time of the last sickness of the deceased." As we understand the position of plaintiffs in error, they concede that the trial court was warranted in finding that all other statutory requisites of a nuncupative will were met and complied with. Their sole contention here is that, as a matter of law, the words uttered by the deceased which are claimed to constitute her will were not uttered during her "last sickness" within the meaning of those words as used in the article above referred to. The case turns upon our decision of that single question and our statement will therefore be limited to such facts as are thought to be relevant thereto.

Annie Douglass, the alleged testator, died on September 8, 1934, at the age of more than sixty years. During the four years next preceding her death she had "spells."

Dr. R. N. Miller, a witness for the proponent, began attending her professionally in June, 1934. In his opinion the original cause of her condition was malaria, but the immediate cause of her death was "aortic insufficiency," which he explained to be a weakened condition of the heart and aorta. The "spells" about which the other witnesses testified were in the nature of fainting spells brought about, according to the evidence as we understand it, by the general weakened condition of her heart. The words claimed to constitute a nuncupative will were spoken by the deceased at about 4:30 P.M. on Thursday, September 6, 1934. The proponent and four other witnesses were present in her bedroom at that time. One of the witnesses, Berttrue McDaniel, went to the home of the deceased to pay her some rent. He testified that he stayed there about two hours, and that while he was there she said to him:

> " 'Mr. McDaniels, I am feeling not very well at this time, and I know that I am going to die,' and says 'I want Willie Adams to have everything that I possess, and land and money.' She says 'She is the only one stood to me in my sick hour at my bedside.' Says, 'I haven't any relatives at all.'"
> "She called your name and said that?
> "Yes, sir, said 'Mr. McDaniels.'"
> Thereafter, on September 12, 1934, the witness committed the substance of the testimony to writing, his written memorandum being as follows:
> "'Beaumont, Texas, Sept. 12, 1934.
> "'On the 6 day of September, 1934, I was at Annie duglas home and she told me and others beside that at her death she wanted Willie Adams to have all that she had land and money and every thing else that she new she was going to die that she had no kin and she was the only one that sat at her bed side and waited on her and she wanted her to have all her estate at her death
> "'Berttrue McDaniel.'"

He testified that when he went to the home of the deceased he found her in bed; that when he paid her the rent she handed him a receipt therefor which she had theretofore written. His testimony with regard to what occurred on the occasion is, in the main, corroborated by the other witnesses who were present at that time. There is practically no testimony concerning the condition of the deceased from Thursday afternoon until about noon on Saturday. The proponent testified that "she had taken the bed on a Thursday. Friday she was in and Thursday she taken the bed and stayed in bed from Thursday up to Friday." That testimony probably means that deceased did not leave her home on Friday but was in bed at least a part of that day. Shortly before noon on Saturday morning the deceased went to the home of a neighbor, Julia Keegans, to get Julia to pay a water bill for her which amounted to $1. Deceased had only a $5 bill with her and Julia was unable to change it. Deceased next went to a grocery store near by and purchased some bacon and a small sack of flour. She then returned to Julia's home and gave her $1

with which to pay the water bill. At that time she discovered that she had failed to bring the bill with her, whereupon Julia accompanied her home to get it. The deceased carried the bacon and Julia carried the flour. Shortly after reaching home the deceased became sick. Dr. Miller was later called and he came to see her about 6 o'clock that evening. She died some two hours or more thereafter.

All text-writers and opinions on the subject of what constitutes "last sickness" within the meaning of statutes relating to nuncupative wills seem to agree that the leading authority upon the question is *Prince v. Hazleton*, 20 Johns., N.Y., 502, 11 Am.Dec. 307. Of that case the author of Red- field On The Law of Wills, 4th Ed., in Vol. 1, ch. VI, Sec.17a wrote: "* * * This subject came before the Court of Errors in New York, at an early day, * * * and is most exhaustively discussed by Chancellor Kent, and by Mr. Justice Woodworth. These opinions contain the substance of all the learning upon the subject of nuncupative wills, from the earliest days to that date and very little has occurred since, which could add much to the very full discussion which the subject there receives."

Our investigation has lead [sic] us to the conclusion that the foregoing is still an accurate statement of the situation. Nothing has been written to date, within our knowledge, which adds materially to the discussion contained in the majority and minority opinions in that case. In fact, there have been relatively few cases before the appellate courts in this generation in which a nuncupative will was offered for probate.

In the majority opinion Chancellor Kent announced this conclusion: "Upon the strength of so much authority, I feel myself warranted in concluding, that a nuncupative will is not good, unless it be made by a testator when he is in extremis, or overtaken by sudden and violent sickness, and has not time or opportunity to make a written will."

That has become known generally as the in extremis rule. The minority opinion in that case announced a somewhat more liberal rule of construction. From that decision two lines of decisions have emerged, one based upon the doctrine that the testator must be in extremis, as announced by Chancellor Kent in the majority opinion, and the other based upon the more liberal rule announced by Justice Woodworth in the dissenting opinion, that the testator need not actually be in extremis. The majority of the courts have adopted the Chancellor Kent doctrine. *Schmitz v. Summers*, 179 Miss. 260, 174 So. 569; *O'Neill v. Smith*, 33 Md. 569; *Bellamy v. Peeler*, 96 Ga. 467, 23 S.E. 387; *Page v. Page*, 2 Rob., Va., 424; *Reese v. Hawthorn*, 10 Grat., Va., 548. Annotations: 20 Am.Dec. 45; 9 A.L.R. 464; 13 L.R.A., N.S., 1092; 67 Am.St.Rep. 572.

The Court of Civil Appeals in its opinion in this case recognized the existence of both the rules above referred to, but concluded that Texas had not adopted the majority rule, and upon the theory that the minority rule was

(continues)

the more reasonable, it adopted and applied that rule. We cannot agree with its conclusions.

In the first place, this court has approved the rule of strict construction. While the facts in the cases below cited were not like those before us, still they presented situations calling upon the court to declare the rule of construction which should govern in cases like the instant one, and the court declared it in very clear language.

In *Jones v. Norton*, 10 Tex. 120, will be found the following: "* * * Nuncupative wills had their origin in the suddenness and urgency of the occasion, where there were present no means of making a formal written will, and no time for delay. And, among all civilized nations, where the necessity has been apparent, nuncupative wills have, under some regulations, been allowed. But the danger of fraud, in setting up such wills, has always exacted full and satisfactory proof of the existence of the necessity; and, where we have a statute regulating such wills, there is the same reason why we should require its conditions and requisites to be satisfactorily made out. * * *"

In *Mitchell v. Vickers*, 20 Tex. 377, it is stated: "Nuncupative wills are not favorites of the law. But as they are authorized by the statute, they must, when duly proved, be allowed and established. They are hedged round with numerous restrictions, to guard against the frauds for which oral wills offer so many facilities; and it is a well established rule, that strict proof is required of all the requisites prescribed by the law. ([Parsons v. Parsons] 2 Greenl. [Me.], 298; [In re Yarnall's Will] 4 Rawle [Pa.], 46 [26 Am.Dec. 115]; 20 Johns. 502; 1 Jarman on Wills, 89; Modern Probate of Wills, 304.) The provision of the statute (Hart.Dig. Art. 1113) is essentially a copy from the statute of frauds of the 29 Ch. 2, Sect. 19–21; and in substance the same provision is found in the codes of most of the other States; and everywhere a strict construction has been applied."

One of the authorities cited above, 20 Johns. 502, is the *Prince-Hazleton* case.

And in *Watts v. Holland*, 56 Tex. 54, Chancellor Kent's opinion in the *Prince-Hazleton* case, was cited in support of the following conclusion announced in the opinion:

"* * * Wills of this kind, by the law, are allowed to exist, on its bare toleration, and under the shadow of its jealously; and the establishment of them is allowed, subject to exacting restrictions and conditions which correspond in degree with its fears of their dangerous qualities. * * *"

From the foregoing we conclude that early in the jurisprudence of this state the majority rule that the testator must be in extremis was approved by this court.

METROPOLITAN LIFE INSURANCE
Company, Petitioner

v.

SYNTEK FINANCE CORPORATION,
Respondent.

881 S.W.2d 319 (Tex. 1994)

PER CURIAM.

This case turns on the application of the "substantial relationship" test for attorney disqualification based on prior representation of the same or a related client. Following a lengthy hearing, the trial court overruled a motion to disqualify counsel filed by Syntek Finance Corporation. After a jury trial, a judgment for approximately $6.7 million was rendered in favor of Metropolitan Life Insurance Company. The court of appeals reversed that judgment and remanded the case for a new trial, holding that the trial court abused its discretion when it denied Syntek's motion for disqualification of counsel. 880 S.W.2d 26. We reverse the judgment of the court of appeals and remand the case to that court for consideration of points of error not previously addressed.

Gene Phillips owns a controlling interest in Syntek and several other related companies. In 1986, the law firm of Hughes & Luce represented Phillips in a divorce and subsequently drafted a prenuptial agreement. In the course of that representation, Phillips disclosed his personal financial status to Hughes&Luce, including the intricate structure of his various companies. This suit, filed by Syntek in April 1989, arises out of a hotel Syntek purchased from Metropolitan. Hughes & Luce attorney Richard Nelson represented Metropolitan. Nelson made an initial conflicts check and determined to his satisfaction that there was no conflict of interest due to the firm's previous representation of Phillips.

After nearly two years of pretrial activity, Nelson acquired information about Phillips' possible involvement in Syntek's decision to stop loan payments to Metropolitan. Nelson again reviewed the circumstances of his firm's former representation of Phillips and once more satisfied himself that there was no substantial relationship between the two representations. Nelson then amended Metropolitan's pleadings to include new allegations concerning Phillips' involvement. In response, Syntek and Phillips filed a motion to disqualify Hughes & Luce. The trial court denied the motion.

[1] Rule 1.09 of the Texas Disciplinary Rules of Professional Conduct provides that a lawyer shall not take a representation that is adverse to a former client if the new matter "is the same or a substantially related matter." Tex. Disciplinary R. Prof. Conduct 1.09(a)(3) (1989), *reprinted in* Tex.Gov't Code Ann., tit. 2, subtit. G. app. (Vernon

Supp. 1993) (State Bar Rules art. X, § 9). In *NCNB Tex. Nat'l Bank v. Coker,* 765 S.W.2d 398, 400 (Tex.1989), we stated that to satisfy the substantial relationship test as a basis for disqualification a movant must prove that the facts of the previous representation ***321** are so related to the facts in the pending litigation that a genuine threat exists that confidences revealed to former counsel will be divulged to a present adversary. *Id.*

[2] The disqualification hearing consumed five days. The trial court heard live and deposition testimony from fourteen fact witnesses concerning the previous and pending representations, and from five expert witnesses concerning the *Coker* standard. There was testimony that the information at issue was both available in the public domain and provided to Metropolitan by Syntek through discovery. There was also testimony that the information used in the amended pleadings was available to the public through an examiners' report from a bankruptcy proceeding against one of the companies controlled by Phillips. The trial court also conducted an in-camera review of documents from the former representation.

The test for abuse of discretion is whether the trial court acted without reference to any guiding rules or principles, or acted in an arbitrary or unreasonable manner. *See Downer v. Aquamarine Operators, Inc.,* 701 S.W.2d 238, 241-42 (Tex.1985), *cert. denied,* 476 U.S. 1159, 106 S.Ct. 2279, 90 L.Ed.2d 721 (1986). We hold that on the evidence presented, based on the *Coker* standard, it was not an abuse of discretion for the trial court to conclude that no substantial relationship existed between the former and current representations and to deny the motion to disqualify.

We therefore conclude that the court of appeals improperly substituted its judgment for that of the trial court. *See Flores v. Fourth Court of Appeals,* 777 S.W.2d 38, 41- 42 (Tex.1989).

Accordingly, a majority of the court grants Metropolitan's application for writ of error, and without hearing oral argument, reverses the judgment of the court of appeals and remands the case to that court for consideration of Syntek's other points of error which it did not previously address. Tex.R.App.P. 170.

MORGAN

v.

GREENWALDT

786 So.2d 1037 (Miss. 2001)

SMITH, Justice, for the Court:

§ 1. Genia A. Morgan ("Morgan") sued St. Dominic-Jackson Memorial Hospital ("Hospital"), and two of the Hospital's nurses, Brenda Greenwaldt and Susan Brotherton, and a psychiatric technician, Melinda Leah Lewis, over an incident that occurred in June 1996. Morgan alleged that she had been assaulted and battered, falsely imprisoned, and treated negligently while she was a patient. She also sued for intentional infliction of emotional distress. The trial court granted a directed verdict for all the defendants on the issues of assault and battery, false imprisonment, gross negligence, and intentional infliction of emotional distress, but allowed the jury ***1040** to determine if the defendants were negligent in their treatment of Morgan. After four days of trial, the jury returned a verdict in favor of the defendants, and the trial court entered judgment accordingly.

Morgan's motion for a new trial was denied January 4, 2000, and thereafter she appealed to this Court. We find no reversible error and affirm the judgment of the trial court.

FACTS

§ 2. Genia Morgan started seeing a psychiatrist in 1990 for depression. In early June 1996, Morgan's psychiatrist,

Dr. Barbara Goff, suggested that Morgan voluntarily check into the psychiatric unit of the Hospital due to her severe depression and sleep disorder. Dr. Goff wanted Morgan in a monitored environment while she worked on adjusting Morgan's medication. At the time of her admission, Morgan was having suicidal thoughts, and her depression had advanced to the stage where she had given up her job. Also, Morgan was experiencing hallucinations and trances that required an adjustment in her antipsychotic medication. During her admission assessment, Morgan reported having a metaphysical experience. Morgan described this experience to the admitting nurse as one where "[she] was lying in bed when something grabbed [her] neck and then it let go when [she] started to pray." Upon her admittance into the Hospital, Morgan signed a Consent to Treatment Form authorizing the Hospital to treat her for illness. She was placed on the intermediate ward where patients were free to walk around the floor and mingle with other patients.

§ 3. On June 18, 1996, Morgan went to the nurses' station and asked for a bottle of hydrogen peroxide that she said she had brought to the Hospital with her. She claimed that it was her practice to brush her teeth with hydrogen peroxide. Nurse Susan Brotherton looked for the hydrogen peroxide, but could not locate it. Melinda Leah Lewis, a psychiatric technician, and Brotherton checked Morgan's personal belongings checklist, which is filled out upon a patient's admittance to the Hospital. The hydrogen peroxide was not listed on the sheet as one of the items brought in by Morgan. Brotherton told Morgan that she would call Dr. Goff to get an order for the hydrogen peroxide. Brotherton called Dr. Goff's office and left a message regarding the peroxide

(continues)

and its intended use by Morgan as a mouth rinse. Dr. Goff stated that Morgan could not have the peroxide, but could have Cepacol mouthwash instead. Brotherton informed Morgan of the doctor's orders. Morgan became upset and left the unit. Thereafter, she retreated to her room crying.

§ 4. Brotherton, Lewis, and technician Jeannie Smith walked toward Morgan's room to see what was wrong. Brotherton and Lewis entered Morgan's room. Morgan was lying across the bed crying. In an effort to calm her down, Brotherton told Morgan that even though there was no record of her bringing the hydrogen peroxide into the Hospital, the Hospital could reimburse her if she believed the Hospital was responsible for the loss. According to Brotherton's testimony, Morgan began yelling profanity and ordered the nurses out of her room. The nurses returned to their station.

§ 5. Shortly thereafter, Morgan came out of her room and approached the nurses' station. According to Brotherton and Lewis, Morgan yelled, used profanity, and demanded her hydrogen peroxide. She walked to the nurse manager's door and began pounding her fist on the door. At this point, Dr. Goff was again called, and Brotherton left a message with the doctor's secretary that Morgan was out of *1041 control and was acting in a hostile manner. Due to the escalating situation, Brotherton called the nursing supervisor, Brenda Greenwaldt. When Greenwaldt arrived and introduced herself, Morgan started ranting and raving that she demanded an apology. Morgan then proceeded to pound her fist on the nurses' station desk and point her finger in nurse Greenwaldt's face. According to Greenwaldt, Brotherton, and Lewis, the patient appeared totally out of control and became a threat to the safety of herself and others.

§ 6. . . . . [G]reenwaldt wrote an order that stated "[p]lace in seclusion for threatening staff for four to six hours until calm and nonthreatening."

§ 7. Several witnesses testified that Morgan was escorted, without any physical contact, to the seclusion area. Even Morgan stated in her testimony that she walked to seclusion on her own accord. According to Morgan, she was strip searched and forced to change into a hospital gown in front of several people. However, various staff members of the Hospital testified that it was standard procedure for someone in seclusion to be searched for dangerous instrumentalities and to change into a hospital gown. Further, according to Hospital personnel, Leah Lewis stood in front of the window to the seclusion door so there would be privacy. Morgan was left in seclusion for about two hours, from 4:30 p.m. until 6:45 p.m.

§ 8. Morgan raises the following issues on appeal:

I. WHETHER THE TRIAL COURT PROPERLY DIRECTED A VERDICT ON ALL COUNTS OF INTENTIONAL INFLICTION OF EMOTIONAL DISTRESS,

FALSE IMPRISONMENT, GROSS NEGLIGENCE, AND ASSAULT AND BATTERY?

***

ANALYSIS
I.

§ 9. At the close of the testimony, the defendants moved for a directed verdict on all counts except the medical malpractice negligence claim. The trial court granted the motion, thereby taking from the jury the claims of intentional infliction of emotional distress, false imprisonment, gross negligence, and assault and battery. Morgan argues that there was sufficient evidence to make out a jury question on all of these claims, and thus, the directed verdict for the defendants was reversible error.

[1][2][3] § 10. This Court conducts a de novo review of a motion for directed verdict. *Northern Elec. Co. v. Phillips*, 600 So.2d 1278, 1281 (Miss. 1995). If we find that the evidence favorable to the nonmoving party and the reasonable inferences drawn therefrom present a question for the jury, the motion should not be *1042 granted. *Id.* (citing *Pittman v. Home Indem. Co.*, 411 So.2d 87, 89 (Miss. 1982)). This Court has also held that an issue should only be presented to the jury when the evidence creates a question of fact on which reasonable jurors could disagree. *Herrington v. Spell*, 692 So.2d 93, 97 (Miss. 1997).

A. *False Imprisonment*

[4] § 11. False imprisonment has only two elements: "detention of the plaintiff and the unlawfulness of such detention." *Lee v. Alexander*, 607 So.2d 30, 35 (Miss. 1992) (citing *Page v. Wiggins*, 595 So.2d 1291 (Miss. 1922); *Thornhill v. Wilson*, 504 So.2d 1205, 1208 (Miss. 1987) (citing *State ex rel. Powell v. Moore*, 252 Miss. 471, 174 So.2d 352, 354 (1965); *Hart v. Walker*, 720 F.2d 1436, 1439 (5th Cir.1983))).

[5] § 12. Morgan contends that the trial court erred in granting a directed verdict because she was locked up against her will, and the determination of whether her detainment was a reasonable one should have been a question of fact for the jury. This Court finds that such an argument lacks merit. Morgan consented to the treatment at the Hospital, and such treatment includes placing patients who are out of control in a secure environment for the protection of both the patient and the others at the Hospital.

§ 13. The evidence indicates that prior to the 1996 incident in question, Morgan had undergone a psychological evaluation that concluded she was suffering from personality disorders. She had a history of mental illness dating back to 1990 and was diagnosed as having been severely depressed upon her admittance to the Hospital in

June of 1996. She also suffered from hallucinations and crying episodes. Moreover, on the morning of the alleged incident, Morgan's doctor noted in the medical records that she was experiencing trances that lasted up to fifteen minutes.

§ 14. Morgan argues that the mere fact that she was undergoing treatment in a Hospital does not mean that the Hospital is justified in performing any medical procedures it deems warranted. Although such an argument is a valid one, it is not warranted in the case sub judice. The cases Morgan cites as support for such an argument are not applicable to the case at bar. Such cases deal with situations where the appellant did not consent to the treatment or was detained upon a request or attempt of the patient to leave the Hospital. *Felton v. Coyle*, 95 Ill.App.2d 202, 238 N.E.2d 191 (1968); *Fox v. Smith*, 594 So.2d 596 (Miss. 1992). Genia Morgan voluntarily signed an Authorization for Treatment form when she was admitted to the Hospital. Moreover, there was substantial testimony to support the fact that Morgan was out of control and was posing a threat to the environment, including herself. Confinement in a secured environment is a common method of treatment in psychiatric wards and Hospitals. The Hospital is charged with the duty of maintaining a safe and secure environment for all patients. The evidence showed that Morgan was acting in a way that clearly conveyed the possibility of violence.

§ 15. Morgan relies on *Fox v. Smith*, 594 So.2d 596 (Miss.1992), to bolster her argument that the mere fact that she was undergoing treatment in a Hospital does not mean that the Hospital is justified in performing any medical procedure it deems warranted. In *Fox*, the patient was admitted to the Hospital for a laparoscopy and alleged that the removal of an intrauterine device was done without her consent. *Id.* at 596. This case can clearly be distinguished from the case at bar because the patient in *Fox* initially refused to sign the consent form because she objected to a *1043 clause in the form which authorized the Hospital to dispose of severed tissues or specimens. *Id.* at 599. The Court stated that *Fox* turned on the issue of consent, or not, for the removal of the patient's intrauterine device. *Id.* at 597. This Court made clear that a patient's informed consent to treatment is a prerequisite to treatment, and because a material dispute existed on important facts concerning the patient's consent, the question should have been presented to the jury. *Id.* at 604.

§ 16. In comparison, Morgan clearly consented to treatment by the doctors and personnel at the Hospital by signing the consent form. Moreover, Morgan never retracted her consent to receive treatment. She never

informed the nurses that she refused their treatment or that she wanted to leave the Hospital. Indeed, she even voluntarily walked to the isolation room.

§ 17. Morgan also relies upon *Felton v. Coyle*, 95 Ill. App.2d 202, 238 N.E.2d 191 (1968), for her argument that she was falsely imprisoned. This case is not only factually distinguishable from the case at bar, but is also from another jurisdiction and, therefore, not controlling on this Court. In *Felton*, the patient suffered a broken clavicle and was taken to a Chicago Hospital for treatment. *Id.* at 192. After an altercation between the patient and Hospital personnel, patient's doctor ordered him out of the Hospital. *Id.* When the patient attempted to leave the Hospital, the doctor grabbed the patient by the shoulders and told him he was going to call the police. *Id.* at 193. The doctor then sent the patient to a psychiatric Hospital. *Id.* The trial court issued a directed verdict in favor of the defendant, and on appeal the patient argued that he was entitled to a directed verdict. *Id.* at 194. The appellate court disagreed, holding that under the facts and circumstances of the case, it was properly presented to the trier of fact to determine whether the patient was improperly detained. *Id.*

§ 18. Unlike *Felton*, here there were no efforts by the Hospital to prevent Morgan from leaving the Hospital at her will. Morgan did not leave the Hospital until two days after the alleged incident. Even after that time, she continued to attend classes at the Hospital.

§ 19. The trial court properly directed a verdict on the issue of false imprisonment. There is simply no proof in the record of the unlawfulness of Morgan's detention. She voluntarily signed an Authorization for Treatment form. She had a history of psychological problems, and there was substantial testimony to support the fact that she was out of control and was posing a threat to herself and to others.

***

CONCLUSION

§ 29. In sum, the trial court did not err in granting a directed verdict on the issues of assault and battery, false imprisonment, gross negligence and intentional infliction of emotional distress. Genia A. Morgan simply failed to meet her burden of proof in showing the necessary elements of these causes of action . . . . For these reasons, we affirm the judgment of the Hinds County circuit Court.

§ 30. Affirmed.

PITTMAN, C.J., BANKS, P.J., MILLS, WALLER, COBB AND DIAZ, JJ., CONCUR. MCRAE, P.J., CONCURS IN RESULT ONLY. EASLEY, J., DISSENTS WITHOUT SEPARATE WRITTEN OPINION.

The PEOPLE of the State of
Illinois, Appellant,

v.

Robert SANDERS, Appellee.
No. 57801.
Supreme Court of Illinois.
Dec. 16, 1983.
99 Ill. 2d 262, 457 N.E.2d 1241 (1983)

SIMON, Justice:

The principal issue raised by this appeal is the construction and application to be given to the Illinois statute which prohibits husband and wife from testifying in criminal trials as to any communication or admission made one to the other or as to any conversation between them (Ill.Rev.Stat. 1981, ch. 38, par. 155–1). More precisely, the question is whether the privilege established by the statute is destroyed when the communication, admission or conversation in question is in the presence of children of the spouses (including a child of one of the spouses who is not the child of defendant) who are old enough to understand the content of the conversation. A secondary issue is whether the plain error rule (87 Ill.2d R. 615) should be applied to the admission of testimony about two conversations between spouses which may not have occurred in the presence of children but where no objection was advanced when all that was said in them was repeated in a third conversation which took place a few hours later and concerning which testimony was admissible.

A murder conviction of the defendant, Robert Sanders, in a jury trial in the circuit court of Cook County based in part upon the testimony of his wife was reversed by the appellate court (111 Ill.App.3d 1, 66 Ill.Dec. 761, 443 N.E.2d 687). We allowed the State's petition for leave to appeal (87 Ill.2d R. 315(a)).

During pretrial discovery, the defense filed a motion *in limine* to prevent the defendant's wife, Beverly Sanders, from testifying about conversations she had with her husband, the defendant. Shortly after it was filed, the public defender's office, which had been representing the defendant, was replaced by other appointed counsel, who represented the defendant at trial. Defendant's new attorney did not seek a ruling on the motion in limine, and that motion was never ruled upon. Neither did defendant's attorney object at trial to the wife's testimony.

She testified to three conversations with her husband which implicated him in the murder of which he was convicted. In the first conversation, which occurred the day before the murder, she testified the defendant told her while one or more of her children was present that he was going to rob the murder victim. The second conversation occurred in their bedroom in the early morning hours of the next day. During this conversation, at which no one else was present, the defendant gave his wife a ring and a watch which the woman who lived with the murder victim identified at trial as the victim's. The third conversation took place later that day. The defendant told her, she testified, that he had robbed the murder victim after striking him with a brick and tying him up. He also told her that he got the watch and ring during the robbery. This conversation, she said, was in the presence of their children.

The State argues that communications between spouses are privileged only when intended to be confidential. In this case the State contends the confidentiality of the first and third conversations was destroyed by the presence of their children. It contends that the second conversation was not confidential because the defendant must have expected that his wife would display the watch and ring he gave her by wearing them in public, and that he did not therefore intend his act to be confidential. The defendant argues that the record does not clearly show that their children were in the immediate presence of his wife and himself in a position to hear their first and third conversations, and that during the second communication he acted in reliance upon the expectation that what transpired would be confidential.

The starting point for our decision is the interpretation given in *People v. Palumbo* (1955), 5 Ill.2d 409, 125 N.E.2d 518, to the statute relating to the admissibility of interspousal communications (Ill.Rev.Stat.1981, ch. 38, par. 155–1). This court, in *Palumbo*, rejected the argument advanced by the defendant there that the statute covered all conversations between spouses, holding instead that the statutory privilege, like the similar common law privilege, applied only to conversations which were of a confidential character. The problem is to determine under what circumstances conversations between spouses are to be regarded as confidential in character. This court, in *Palumbo*, adopted the standards announced by the Supreme Court in *Wolfle v. United States* (1934), 291 U.S. 7, 14, 54 S.Ct. 279, 280, 78 L.Ed. 617, 620, a holding which the court 41 years later in *Trammel v. United States* (1980), 445 U.S. 40, 100 S.Ct. 906, 63 L.Ed.2d 186, said remained undisturbed, by adopting language from *Wolfle* which teaches the following: There is a presumption that interspousal communications are intended to be confidential. But if, because of the circumstances under which the communication took place, it appears that confidentiality was not intended, the communication is not to be regarded as privileged. In this regard, communications made in the presence of third persons are usually not regarded as privileged because they are not made in confidence. In *Palumbo* the communication testified to by the wife was regarded as not privileged because the entire conversation took place in the presence of a third person who, according to the wife, was trying to purchase narcotics from the husband, who was the defendant in the case.

We agree with the appellate court's conclusion that the evidence establishes that the third conversation took place in the presence of her sons, Robert who was 13, and two others who were 10 and 8 at the time. On cross-examination the wife repeated her direct testimony, which is quoted at length in the appellate court opinion, that the three children were present during the third conversation when the following exchange took place:

"Q. Did you know anything about Curtiss Lovelace?
A. Only what my husband had told me.
Q. You say he was bragging when he told you this?
A. Yes.
Q. He wasn't nervous, was he?
A. Not until he found out the man was dead.
Q. When he first told you was he nervous or bragging?
A. Not nervous.
Q. Pacing around the room?
A. No, he wasn't.
Q. Excited?
A. No.
Q. Who was present when this conversation occurred?
A. Robert, Albert and Pee Wee.
Q. They were all there?
A. Yes."

Following this exchange there was another reference during her cross-examination to the presence of the wife's oldest son:

"Q. And that day of the events that you have testified to, October the 14th, that day you had just finished a fight with your husband, right?
A. Yes.
Q. Did he threaten your son, Robert, in any way at that time?
A. No.
Q. But during all of these conversations, Robert, your son, was present, right?
A. Yes, he was."

The question presented in this case is whether the communications fell outside the ambit of the statute's protection because of the presence of the children. We have found no Illinois case holding that the confidentiality of a conversation between a husband and wife is preserved when it takes place in the presence of children. The appellate court appears to have exhaustively researched the subject and concluded, as we do, that the great weight of authority is that the presence of children of the spouses destroys confidentiality unless they are too young to understand what is being said. (See, e.g., *Master v. Master* (1960), 223 Md. 618, 166 A.2d 251; *Freeman v. Freeman* (1921), 238 Mass. 150, 130 N.E. 220; *Fuller v. Fuller* (1925), 100 W.Va. 309, 130 S.E. 270; McCormick, *Evidence* sec. 80, at 166 (2d ed. 1972); 97 C.J.S. *Witnesses* sec. 271, at 777 (1957).) Nothing in the record indicates that Robert, then 13 years old, was not old enough or sufficiently bright to understand the conversation at which he was present, particularly inasmuch as the wife's testimony indicates that some of it was directed to him. In these circumstances, under the rule followed in this State, his presence rendered the conversation ineligible for the protection of the statutory privilege.

The defendant argues that this court should recognize a privilege, which he concedes does not presently exist in Illinois, between parents and children which would include conversations between spouses at which their children are present. Courts in a few other jurisdictions have cloaked communications between parent and child with a privilege. (*In re Agosto* (D.Nev.1983), 553 F.Supp. 1298; *People v. Fitzgerald* (1979), 101 Misc.2d 712, 422 N.Y.S.2d 309.) The source of all privileges currently applicable in Illinois, with the exception of the attorney-client privilege which has a long-standing common law existence, is statutory. (See Ill.Rev.Stat. 1981, ch. 51, par. 5.1, Ill.Rev.Stat.1981, ch. 38, par. 104–14 (physician-patient); Ill.Rev.Stat.1981, ch. 51, par. 48.1 (clergymen); Ill.Rev.Stat.1981, ch. 91fi, par. 810 (therapist-client); Ill.Rev.Stat.1981, ch. 111, par. 5533 (accountants); Ill. Rev.Stat.1981, ch. 51, par. 5.2 (rape crisis personnel-victims); Ill.Rev.Stat.1981, ch. 48, par. 640 (public officers, regarding unemployment compensation).) We decline, therefore, to introduce an additional privilege by judicial authority which would be applicable to communications between parents and children. Even if we were to initiate this type of privilege, to assist the defendant here we would have to extend it to children of only one spouse, for Robert, the oldest and presumably the most discerning of the children and who was privy at least to the third conversation, was the son of the wife and not the defendant. The statute by its terms does not contemplate such a stretch. Were we to recognize such a privilege under our judicial authority, it would be impossible to contain it logically from spreading to conversations with other relatives in whom a person might normally confide, or even to close friends.

Moreover, we are constrained not only by the legislature's lack of interest in extending an interspousal communications privilege to communications between parent

(continues)

and child, but also by the fact that evidentiary privileges of this sort exclude relevant evidence and thus work against the truthseeking function of legal proceedings. In this they are distinct from evidentiary rules, such as the prohibition against hearsay testimony, which promote this function by insuring the quality of the evidence which is presented. The privilege at issue here results not from a policy of safeguarding the quality of evidence at trial but from a policy of promoting family harmony independent of what might occur in a trial at some future date. The Supreme Court in *Trammel v. United States* (1980), 445 U.S. 40, 50, 100 S.Ct. 906, 912, 63 L.Ed.2d 186, 195, has stated:

> "Testimonial exclusionary rules and privileges contravene the fundamental principle that '"the public . . . has a right to every man's evidence."' *United States v. Bryan* [(1950), 339 U.S. 323, 331, 70 S.Ct. 724, 730, 94 L.Ed. 884, 891.] As such, they must be strictly construed and accepted 'only to the very limited extent that permitting a refusal to testify or excluding relevant evidences has a public good transcending the normally predominant principle of utilizing all rational means for ascertaining truth.' *Elkins v. United States* [(1960), 364 U.S. 206, 234, 80 S.Ct. 1437, 1454, 4 L.Ed.2d 1669, 1695] (Frankfurter, J., dissenting)."

See also 8 J. Wigmore, *Evidence* sec. 2285, at 527–28 (1961).

The expansion of existing testimonial privileges and acceptance of new ones involves a balancing of public policies which should be left to the legislature. A compelling reason is that while courts, as institutions, find it easy to perceive value in public policies such as those favoring the admission of all relevant and reliable evidence which directly assist the judicial function of ascertaining the truth, it is not their primary function to promote policies aimed at broader social goals more distantly related to the judiciary. This is primarily the responsibility of the legislature. To the extent that such policies conflict with truth seeking or other values central to the judicial task, the balance that courts draw might not reflect the choice the legislature would make.

The defendant argues, however, that inasmuch as the Federal courts have recognized the right of privacy to be of constitutional dimension in the context of certain functions which are intimately associated with the family, we should hold that communications of a confidential nature between a parent and his child enjoy an evidentiary privilege under the Constitution which did not exist under the common law. The defendant points out that in *In re Agosto* (D.Nev.1983), 553 F.Supp. 1298, and *People v. Fitzgerald* (1979), 101 Misc.2d 712, 422 N.Y.S.2d 309, courts have recognized the sort of constitutionally based privilege sought to be invoked here.

We need not decide here, and we do not decide, whether the decisions in In *re Agosto* or *People v. Fitzgerald* were sound, for the question in both of these cases was whether a parent or a child could be compelled against his will to testify against the other. (See also *In re A & M* (1978), 61 A.D.2d 426, 403 N.Y.S.2d 375 (same).) The testimony in the instant case, by contrast, was given by the defendant's wife, without protest and apparently of her own free will, after she was approached and requested to give it by an assistant State's Attorney.

We find this difference to be significant. Both *Agosto* and the New York courts, in holding that a constitutional privilege protected the communications there at issue, relied heavily on conjecture that a family member who is forced to testify against her will would face the unpleasant choice of aiding the criminal conviction of a loved one, perjuring herself on the stand, or risking a citation for contempt of court for refusing to testify, and the belief that the harshness of this choice has the effect of sundering the family relationship. (*In re Agosto* (D.Nev.1983), 553 F.Supp. 1298, 1309–10, 1326; *In re A & M* (1978), 61 A.D.2d 426, 432–33, 403 N.Y.S.2d 375, 380.) Such a fear is without foundation where, as in this case, the witness who is a family member volunteers her testimony; the voluntariness of the act is strong evidence that the choice the witness faced was an easy one for her to make. We conclude that even if the Constitution bestows a privilege on communications between a parent and a child, an issue which we do not decide here, that privilege may be waived by the testifying witness acting alone. Compare *United States v. Penn* (9th Cir. 1980), 647 F.2d 876, 882 (rejecting a challenge to a child's voluntary testimony based on due process, on which the right to privacy depends).

Although they were the subject of the motion *in limine* which was never ruled upon, no objection was advanced at trial when the wife testified about the first and second conversations. Under *Palumbo* the Illinois statute preventing testimony by either spouse concerning confidential communications between them creates only a privilege, and a privilege may be waived by the holder of it, in this case the husband. (See Comment, *Marital Privileges*, 46 Chi.-Kent L.Rev. 71, 82–83 (1969).) Therefore, in order to affirm the appellate court's reversal of the conviction, we would have to conclude that the court properly applied the plain error doctrine (87 Ill.2d R. 615) in holding that testimony regarding the first two conversations was improperly admitted. We believe the appellate court erred in reaching that conclusion.

The plain error doctrine is properly applied only when the question of guilt is close and the evidence in question might have significantly affected the outcome of the case (*People v. Jackson* (1981), 84 Ill.2d 350, 359, 49 Ill.

Dec. 719, 418 N.E.2d 739; *People v. Pickett* (1973), 54 Ill.2d 280, 283, 296 N.E.2d 856), or where the error alleged is so substantial as to reflect on the fairness or impartiality of the trial regardless of how closely balanced the evidence is (*People v. Baynes* (1981), 88 Ill.2d 225, 233–34, 244, 58 Ill.Dec. 819, 430 N.E.2d 1070; *People v. Roberts* (1979), 75 Ill.2d 1, 14, 25 Ill.Dec. 675, 387 N.E.2d 331). The third conversation which we conclude, as the appellate court did, was properly admitted, incorporated substantially all of what was said in the first two conversations. The defendant, in the third conversation, discussed the robbery of the murder victim, said he hit him over the head with a brick, displayed several items of clothing taken from the victim, and referred to the watch and ring he had given his wife earlier that day. Thus, even conceding that no one overheard the first two conversations and that they were privileged and should have been excluded had timely objections been made, in practical effect they did no more than duplicate the incriminating content of the third conversation which was properly admitted. For that reason, the testimony which narrated the defendant's conversation and conduct during the first two conversations was not prejudicial. It added nothing to the third conversation that was needed by the prosecutor to implicate the defendant, and after the third conversation was in evidence, the evidence as to the defendant's guilt was no longer closely balanced.

Nor do we regard any errors that might have been made concerning the admissibility of the first and second conversations as depriving the accused of the substantial means of enjoying a fair and impartial trial (*People v. Roberts* (1979), 75 Ill.2d 1, 14, 25 Ill.Dec. 675, 387 N.E.2d 331; citing *People v. Burson* (1957), 11 Ill.2d 360, 370–71, 143 N.E.2d 237, see *People v. Whitlow* (1982), 89 Ill.2d 322, 342, 60 Ill. Dec. 587, 433 N.E.2d 629), as the admission of polygraph evidence does (see *People v. Baynes* (1981), 88 Ill.2d 225, 244, 58 Ill.Dec. 819, 430 N.E.2d 1070). As we have noted, the husband-wife testimonial privilege operates not to purge a trial of unreliable evidence but to withhold relevant and often highly reliable evidence from the trier of fact. The decision whether to apply the plain error doctrine where the evidence is not close is one of grace. (*People v. Roberts* (1979), 75 Ill.2d 1, 14, 25 Ill. Dec. 675, 387 N.E.2d 331; *People v. Burson* (1957), 11 Ill.2d 360, 370–71.) We believe it should not have been applied here, for the fairness and impartiality of the trial was not substantially compromised by the errors, if any took place. See *People v. Roberts* (1979), 75 Ill.2d 1, 14–15, 25 Ill.Dec. 675, 387 N.E.2d 331.

The defendant has raised a number of other issues, none of which were considered by the appellate court because of its erroneous reversal of the conviction on the ground of improper use of privileged communications. The judgment of the appellate court is reversed and the cause is remanded to that court for disposition of the issues raised by the defendant but not reached by its original decision. See *People v. Simpson* (1977), 68 Ill.2d 276, 284, 12 Ill.Dec. 234, 369 N.E.2d 1248.

Reversed and remanded, with directions.

STATE of Maine
v.
David BENNER.
Supreme Judicial Court of Maine.
Submitted on Briefs Jan. 3, 1995.
Decided Feb. 10, 1995.
654 A.2d 435 (Me. 1995)

CLIFFORD, Justice.

David Benner appeals from a conviction for assault, 17–A M.R.S.A. § 207 (1983 & Supp.1994),[1] following a jury trial in Superior Court (Washington County, *Mills*, J.). On appeal Benner contends, *inter alia*, that the trial court erred in giving a cautionary instruction on how the jury should consider the hearsay testimony of the investigating state trooper, and that there was insufficient evidence to support the jury's verdict. Finding no error, we affirm the conviction.

The evidence at trial revealed the following. The victim testified that Benner is her boyfriend, and at the time of the alleged assault, she was living with him. On the night of September 11, 1993, she was home alone with Benner; they were arguing and she wanted him out of the house. The victim stated that she called the state police and complained that Benner had hit her. She also testified that she told the investigating trooper that Benner had struck her on the hand with either an ax handle or a broom stick. She testified that she had said that Benner had hit her only because she wanted him out of her house and not because he had actually hit her. She further testified that the injury to the back of her hand occurred because she was drunk and had fallen.

State Trooper Raymond Bessette testified that while on patrol on the night of September 11, 1993, he received a call from the dispatcher that the victim called to complain that Benner had struck her. When Bessette arrived at the home, he observed the victim to be visibly distraught,

[1]. 17-A M.R.S.A. § 207(1) (1983) provides that "[a] person is guilty of assault if he intentionally, knowingly, or recklessly causes bodily injury or offensive physical contact to another."

(continues)

scared, and quite nervous, and that she had an injury to the back of her hand. She also had watery eyes. He did not, however, observe her to be under the influence.

In order to impeach her credibility, and without objection by the defendant,[2] Bessette further testified as to what the victim had told him that night. Before Bessette did so, however, Benner requested the jury be instructed that the statements "can be used for impeachment value, but not as substantive evidence." The court cautioned the jury as follows:

> [T]he Trooper is now going to testify about statements that were made to him by [the victim], and that testimony is offered to impeach her testimony, the statements that she has testified about. It is not offered for the truth of the matter asserted.

The defendant did not object to the instruction. The jury returned a verdict of guilty and the court accordingly entered a judgment of conviction.

I.

Benner contends that the trial court's cautionary instruction to the jury prior to Trooper Bessette's testimony was inadequate. Although he concedes that the court's instruction is a correct statement of the law, and that he failed to object, he avers that the trial court committed reversible error by failing to give a full explanation of the instructions. We disagree.

Because Benner did not object to the instruction when it was given, we review the charge only for obvious error affecting his substantial rights. *State v. McCluskie*, 611 A.2d 975, 978 (Me.1992); see M.R.Crim.P. 30(b). Giving an instruction that is a correct statement of the law does not rise to the level of obvious error. Jurors are presumed to understand the instruction. *See State v. Naoum*, 548 A.2d 120, 123 (Me.1988). While it would have been more helpful for the trial court to have given a more detailed instruction on the limited purposes for which the hearsay testimony was admitted, see D. Alexander, *Maine Jury Instruction Manual* § 6–24 (2d ed. 1990), the cautionary instruction actually given was not obvious error.

II.

Benner further contends that the evidence presented at trial was insufficient to support a judgment of conviction.

The standard to determine if evidence at trial was sufficient to support the jury's verdict is "whether, based on the evidence viewed in the light most favorable to the prosecution, any trier of fact rationally could find beyond a reasonable doubt every element of the offense charged." *State v. Barry*, 495 A.2d 825, 826 (Me.1985).

The affirmative evidence supporting a guilty verdict includes the following. The victim was home alone with Benner; the two were having an argument; the victim made a complaint; when the trooper arrived, the victim was distraught, scared, and nervous; the trooper observed the back of the victim's hand to be swollen; Benner was intoxicated; the trooper testified that the victim was sober.

Although the victim testified at the trial that Benner had not hit her and that she sustained her injuries while drunk by falling into a wall, her testimony was substantially impeached by her own testimony[3] and that of Trooper Bessette. It was reasonable for the jury to disregard her denials. As we have previously stated, "the weight of the evidence and the determination of witness credibility are the exclusive province of the jury." *State v. Glover*, 594 A.2d 1086, 1088 (Me.1991). Therefore, her testimony alone does not mandate a conclusion that the evidence was insufficient.

Although the conviction in this case was based substantially on circumstantial evidence, a conviction may be grounded on such evidence. *State v. Ingalls*, 554 A.2d 1272, 1276 (Me.1988). Indeed, a conviction based solely on circumstantial evidence is not for that reason less conclusive. *State v. LeClair*, 425 A.2d 182, 184 (Me.1981). The factfinder is allowed to draw all reasonable inferences from the circumstantial evidence. *State v. Crosby*, 456 A.2d 369, 370 (Me.1983). Viewing the evidence in the light most favorable to the State, the jury could have rationally inferred that Benner had assaulted the victim.[4]

The entry is:
Judgment affirmed.
All concurring.

---

2. Benner did not argue for the exclusion of the statements because the probative value of Bessette's testimony as to the victim's statement was substantially outweighed by the danger of unfair prejudice. *See* M.R. Evid. 403.

3. The victim's trial testimony that she told police that Benner hit her was hearsay. It normally would not be admissible for the truth of the matter asserted, but would be admissible to impeach the victim's trial testimony that Benner did not strike her. M.R.Evid. 801, 802. In this case, however, because there was no objection to the victim's statement that she told the police that Benner had hit her, there was no instruction that the testimony could be considered for impeachment only. It is not wholly unreliable and its admission was not obvious error.

4. Benner also contends that the court's instruction on the elements of assault constituted error. Our *review* of the instructions, to which Benner did not object, reveals no error. See *State v. Griffin*, 459 A.2d 1086, 1091–92 (Me. 1983); 17–A M.R.S.A. § 2(5) (1983).

UNITED STATES, Petitioner

v.

Alberto Antonio LEON et al.

No. 82–1771.

Argued Jan. 17, 1984.
Decided July 5, 1984.
Rehearing Denied Sept. 18, 1984.
468 U.S. 897 (1984)

Justice WHITE delivered the opinion of the Court.

This case presents the question whether the Fourth Amendment exclusionary rule should be modified so as not to bar the use in the prosecution's case in chief of evidence obtained by officers acting in reasonable reliance on a search warrant issued by a detached and neutral magistrate but ultimately found to be unsupported by probable cause. To resolve this question, we must consider once again the tension between the sometimes competing goals of, on the one hand, deterring official misconduct and removing inducements to unreasonable invasions of privacy and, on the other, establishing procedures under which criminal defendants are "acquitted or convicted on the basis of all the evidence which exposes the truth." *Alderman v. United States,* 394 U.S. 165, 175, 89 S.Ct. 961, 967, 22 L.Ed.2d 176 (1969).

I

In August 1981, a confidential informant of unproven reliability informed an officer of the Burbank Police Department that two persons known to him as "Armando" and "Patsy" were selling large quantities of cocaine and methaqualone from their residence at 620 Price Drive in Burbank, Cal. The informant also indicated that he had witnessed a sale of methaqualone by "Patsy" at the residence approximately five months earlier and had observed at that time a shoebox containing a large amount of cash that belong to "Patsy." He further declared that "Armando" and "Patsy" generally kept only small quantities of drugs at their residence and stored the remainder at another location in Burbank.

On the basis of this information, the Burbank police initiated an extensive investigation focusing first on the Price Drive residence and later on two other residences as well. Cars parked at the Price Drive residence were determined to belong to respondents Armando Sanchez, who had previously been arrested for possession of marihuana, and Patsy Stewart, who had no criminal record. During the course of the investigation, officers observed an automobile belonging to respondent Richardo Del Castillo, who had previously been arrested for possession of 50 pounds of marihuana, arrive at the Price Drive

residence. The driver of that car entered the house, exited shortly thereafter carrying a small paper sack, and drove away. A check of Del Castillo's probation records led the officers to respondent Alberto Leon, whose telephone number Del Castillo had listed as his employer's. Leon had been arrested in 1980 on drug charges, and a companion had informed the police at the time that Leon was heavily involved in the importation of drugs into this country. Before the current investigation began, the Burbank officers had learned that an informant had told a Glendale police officer that Leon stored a large quantity of methaqualone at his residence in Glendale. During the course of this investigation, the Burbank officers learned that Leon was living at 716 South Sunset Canyon in Burbank.

Subsequently, the officers observed several persons, at least one of whom had prior drug involvement, arriving at the Price Drive residence and leaving with small packages; observed a variety of other material activity at the two residences as well as at a condominium at 7902 Via Magdalena; and witnessed a variety of relevant activity involving respondents' automobiles. The officers also observed respondents Sanchez and Stewart board separate flights for Miami. The pair later returned to Los Angeles together, consented to a search of their luggage that revealed only a small amount of marihuana, and left the airport. Based on these and other observations summarized in the affidavit, App. 34, Office Cyril Rombach of the Burbank Police Department, an experienced and well-trained narcotics investigator, prepared an application for a warrant to search 620 Price Drive, 716 South Sunset Canyon, 7902 Via Magdalena, and automobiles registered to each of the respondents for an extensive list of items believed to be related to respondents' drug-trafficking activities. Officer Rombach's extensive application was reviewed by several Deputy District Attorneys.

A facially valid search warrant was issued in September 1981 by a State Superior Court Judge. The ensuing searches produced large quantities of drugs at the Via Magdalena and Sunset Canyon addresses and a small quantity at the Price Drive residence. Other evidence was discovered at each of the residences and in Stewart's and Del Castillo's automobiles. Respondents were indicted by a grand jury in the District Court for the Central District of California and charged with conspiracy to possess and distribute cocaine and a variety of substantive counts.

The respondents then filed motions to suppress the evidence seized pursuant to the warrant.[1] The District

---

1. Respondent Leon moved to suppress the evidence found on his person at the time of his arrest and the evidence seized from his residence at 716 South Sunset Canyon. Respondent Stewart's motion covered the fruits of searches of her residence at 620 Price Drive and the condominium at 7902 Via Magdalena and statements she made during the search of her residence.

(continues)

Court held an evidentiary hearing and, while recognizing that the case was a close one, see *id.*, at 131, granted the motions to suppress in part. It concluded that the affidavit was insufficient to establish probable cause,[2] but did not suppress all of the evidence as to all of the respondents because none of the respondents had standing to challenge all of the searches.[3] In response to a request from the Government, the court made clear that Officer Rombach had acted in good faith, but it rejected the Government's suggestion that the Fourth Amendment exclusionary rule should not apply where evidence is seized in reasonable good-faith reliance on a search warrant.[4]

The District Court denied the Government's motion for reconsideration, *id.*, at 147, and a divided panel of the Court of Appeals for the Ninth Circuit affirmed, judgt. order reported at 701 F.2d 187 (1983). The Court of Appeals first concluded that Officer Rombach's affidavit could not establish probable cause to search the Price Drive residence. To the extent that the affidavit set forth facts demonstrating the basis of the informant's knowledge of criminal activity, the information included was fatally stale. The affidavit, moreover, failed to establish the

---

Respondent Sanchez sought to suppress the evidence discovered during the search of his residence at 620 Price Drive and statements he made shortly thereafter. He also joined Stewart's motion to suppress evidence seized from the condominium. Respondent Del Castillo apparently sought to suppress all of the evidence seized in the searches. App. 78–80. The respondents also moved to suppress evidence seized in the searches of their automobiles.

2. "I just cannot find this warrant sufficient for a showing of probable cause.

* * *

"There is no question of the reliability and credibility of the informant as not being established.

"Some details given tended to corroborate, maybe, the reliability of [the informant's] information about the previous transaction, but if it is not a stale transaction, it comes awfully close to it; and all the other material I think is as consistent with innocence as it is with guilt.

"So I just do not think this affidavit can withstand the test. I find, then, that there is no probable cause in this case for the issuance of the search warrant . . ." *Id.*, at 127.

3. The District Court concluded that Sanchez and Stewart had standing to challenge the search of 620 Price Drive; that Leon had standing to contest the legality of the search of 716 South Sunset Canyon; that none of the respondents has established a legitimate expectation of privacy in the condominium at 7902 Via Magdalena; and that Stewart and Del Castillo each had standing to challenge the searches of their automobiles. The Government indicated that it did not intend to introduce evidence seized from the other respondents' vehicles. *Id.*, at 127–129. Finally, the court suppressed statements given by Sanchez and Stewart. *Id.*, at 129–130.

4. "On the issue of good faith, obviously that is not the law of the Circuit, and I am not going to apply that law.

"I will say certainly in my view, there is not any question about good faith. [Officer Rombach] went to a Superior Court judge and got a warrant; obviously laid a meticulous trail. Had surveilled for a long period of time, and I believe his testimony—I think he said he consulted with three Deputy District Attorneys before proceeding himself, and I certainly have no doubt about the fact that that is true." *Id.*, at 140.

---

informant's credibility. According, the Court of Appeals concluded that the information provided by the informant was inadequate under both prongs of the two-part test established in *Aguilar v. Texas*, 378 U.S. 108, 84 S.Ct. 1509, 12 L.Ed.2d 723 (1964), and *Spinelli v. United States*, 393 U.S. 410, 89 S.Ct. 584, 21 L.Ed.2d 637 (1969).[5]

* * *

We have concluded that, in the Fourth Amendment context, the exclusionary rule can be modified somewhat without jeopardizing its ability to perform its intended functions. Accordingly, we reverse the judgment of the Court of Appeals.

II

Language in opinions of this Court and of individual Justices has sometimes implied that the exclusionary rule is a necessary corollary of the Fourth Amendment, *Mapp v. Ohio*, 367 U.S. 643, 651, 655–657, 81 S.Ct. 1684, 1689, 1691–1692, 6 L.Ed.2d 1081 (1961); *Olmstead v. United States*, 277 U.S. 488, 462–463, 48 S.Ct. 564, 567, 72 L.Ed. 944 (1928), or that the rule is required by the conjunction of the Fourth and Fifth Amendments. *Mapp v. Ohio, supra*, 367 U.S., at 661–662, 81 S.Ct., at 1694–1695 (Black, J., concurring); *Agnello v. United States*, 269 U.S. 20, 33–34, 46 S.Ct. 4, 6–7, 70 L.Ed. 145 (1925). These implications need not detain us long. The Fifth Amendment theory has not withstood critical analysis or the test of time, see *Andresen v. Maryland*, 427 U.S. 463, 96 S.Ct. 2737, 49 L.Ed.2d 627 (1976), and the Fourth Amendment "has never been interpreted to proscribe the introduction of illegally seized evidence in all proceedings or against all persons." *Stone v. Powell*, 428 U.S. 465, 486, 96 S.Ct. 3037, 3048, 49 L.Ed.2d 1067 (1976).

A

The Fourth Amendment contains no provisions expressly precluding the use of evidence obtained in violation of its commands, and an examination of its origin and purposes makes clear that the use of fruits of a part unlawful search or seizure "work[s] no new Fourth Amendment wrong." *United States v. Calandra*, 414 U.S. 338, 354, 94 S.Ct. 613, 623, 38 L.Ed.2d 561 (1974). The wrong condemned by the Amendment is "fully accomplished" by the unlawful search or seizure itself, ibid., and the exclusionary rule is neither intended nor able to "cure the invasion of the defendant's rights which he has already suffered." *Stone v. Powell, supra*, 428 U.S., at 540,

---

5. In *Illinois v. Gates*, 462 U.S. 213, 103 S.Ct. 2317, 76 L.Ed.2d 527 (1983), decided last Term, the Court abandoned the two-pronged *Aguilar- Spinelli* test for determining whether an informant's tip suffices to establish probable cause for the issuance of a warrant and substituted in its place a "totality of the circumstances" approach.

96 S.Ct., at 3073 (WHITE, J., dissenting). The rule thus operates as "a judicially created remedy designed to safeguard Fourth Amendment rights generally through its deterrent effect, rather than a personal constitutional right of the party aggrieved." *United States v. Calandra, supra,* 414 U.S., at 348, 94 S.Ct., at 620.

* * *

The substantial social costs exacted by the exclusionary rule for the vindication of Fourth Amendment rights have long been a source of concern. "Our cases have consistently recognized that unbending application of the exclusionary sanction to enforce ideals of governmental rectitude would impede unacceptably the truth-finding functions of judge and jury." *United States v. Payner,* 447 U.S. 727, 734, 100 S.Ct. 2439, 2445, 65 L.Ed.2d 468 (1980). An objectionable collateral consequence of this interference with the criminal justice system's truth-finding function is that some guilty defendants may go free or receive reduced sentences as a result of favorable plea bargains.[6] Particularly when law enforcement officers have acted in objective good faith or their transgressions have been minor, the magnitude of the benefit conferred on such guilty defendants offends basic concepts of the criminal justice system. *Stone v. Powell,* 428 U.S., at 490, 96 S.Ct., at 3050. Indiscriminate application of the exclusionary rule, therefore, may well "generat[e] disrespect for the law and administration of justice." *Id.,* at 491, 96 S.Ct., at 3051. Accordingly, "[a]s with any remedial device, the application of the rule has been restricted to those areas where its remedial objectives are thought most efficaciously served." *United States v. Calandra, supra,* 414 U.S., at 348, 94 S.Ct., at 670; see *Stone v. Powell, supra,* 428 U.S., at 486–487, 97 S.Ct., at 3048–3049; *United States v. Janis,* 428 U.S. 433, 447, 96 S.Ct. 3021, 3028, 49 L.Ed.2d 1046 (1976).

* * *

III

A

Because a search warrant "provides the detached scrutiny of a neutral magistrate, which is a more reliable safeguard against improper searches than the hurried judgment of a law enforcement officer 'engaged in the often competitive enterprise of ferreting out crime,'" *United States v. Chadwick,* 433 U.S. 1, 9, 97 S.Ct. 2476, 2482, 53 L.Ed.2d 538 (1977) (quoting *Johnson v. United States,* 333 U.S. 10, 14, 68 S.Ct. 367, 369, 92 L.Ed. 436 (1948)), we have expressed a strong preference for warrants and declared that "in a doubtful or marginal case a search under a warrant may be sustainable where without one it would fall." *United States v. Ventresca,* 380 U.S. 102, 106, 85 S.Ct., 741, 744, 13 L.Ed.2d 687 (1965). See *Aguilar v. Texas,* 378 U.S., at 111, 84 S.Ct., at 1512. Reasonable minds frequently may differ on the question whether a particular affidavit establishes probable cause, and we have thus concluded that the preference for warrants is most appropriately effectuated by according "great deference" to a magistrate's determination. *Spinelli v. United States,* 393 U.S., at 419, 89 S.Ct., at 590. See *Illinois v. Gates,* 462 U.S., at 236, 103 S.Ct., at 2331; *United States v. Ventresca, supra,* 380 U.S., at 108–109, 85 S.Ct., at 745–746.

Deference to the magistrate, however, is not boundless. It is clear, first, that the deference accorded to a magistrate's finding of probable cause does not preclude inquiry into the knowing or reckless falsity of the affidavit on which that determination was based. *Franks v. Delaware,* 438 U.S. 154, 98 S.Ct. 2674, 57 L.Ed.2d 667 (1978).[12]

---

6. Researchers have only recently begun to study extensively the effects of the exclusionary rule on the disposition of felony arrests. One study suggests that the rule results in the nonprosecution or nonconviction of between 0.6% and 2.35% of individuals arrested for felonies. Davies, A Hard Look at What We Know (and Still Need to Learn) About the "Costs" of the Exclusionary Rule: The NIJ Study and Other Studies of "Lost" Arrests, 1983 A.B.F.Res.J. 611, 621. The estimates are higher for particular crimes the prosecution of which depends heavily on physical evidence. Thus, the cumulative loss due to non-prosecution or nonconviction of individuals arrested on felony drug charges is probably in the range of 2.8% to 7.1%. *Id.,* at 680. Davies' analysis of California data suggests that screening by police and prosecutors results in the release because of illegal searches or seizures of as many as 1.4% of all felony arrestees, *id.,* at 650, that 0.9% of felony arrestees are released, because of illegal searches or seizures, at the preliminary hearing or after trial, id., at 653, and that roughly 0.5% of all felony arrestees benefit from reversals on appeal because of illegal searches. *Id.,* at 654. See also K. Brosi, ACross-City Comparison of Felony Case Processing 16, 18–19 (1979); U.S. General Accounting Office, Report of the Comptroller General of the United States, Impact of the Exclusionary Rule on Federal Criminal Prosecutions 10–11, 14 (1979); F. Feeney, F Dill, & AWeir, Arrests Without Convictions: How Often They Occur and Why 203–206 (National Institute of Justice 1983); National Institute of Justice, The Effects of the Exclusionary Rule: AStudy in California 1–2 (1982); Nardulli, The Societal Cost of the Exclusionary Rule: An Empirical Assessment, 1983 A.B.F.Res.J. 585, 600. The exclusionary rule also has been found to affect the plea-bargaining process. S. Schlesinger, Exclusionary Injustice: The Problem of Illegally Obtained Evidence 63 (1977). But see *Davies, supra,* at 668-669; *Nardsulli, supra,* at 604–606.

Many of these researchers have concluded that the impact of the exclusionary rule is insubstantial, but the small percentages with which they deal mask a large absolute number of felons who are released because the cases against them were based in part on illegal searches or seizures. "[A]ny rule of evidence that denies the jury access to clearly probative and reliable evidence must bear a heavy burden of justification, and must be carefully limited to the circumstances in which it will pay its way by deterring official unlawlessness." *Illinois v. Gates,* 462 U.S., at 257–258, 103 S.Ct., at 2342 (WHITE, J., concurring in judgment). Because we find that the rule can have no substantial deterrent effect in the sorts of situations under consideration in this case, see *infra,* at 3417–3419, we conclude that it cannot pay its way in those situations.

* * *

---

12. Indeed, "it would be an unthinkable imposition upon [the magistrate's] authority if a warrant affidavit, revealed after the fact to contain a deliberately or recklessly false statement, were to stand beyond impeachment." 438 U.S., at 165, 98 S.Ct., at 2681.

(continues)

Second, the courts must also insist the magistrate purport to "perform his 'neutral and detached' function and not serve merely as a rubber stamp for the police." *Aguilar v. Texas, supra,* 378 U.S., at 111, 84 S.Ct., at 1512. See *Illinois v. Gates, supra,* 462 U.S., at 239, 103 S.Ct., at 2332. A magistrate failing to "manifest that neutrality and detachment demanded of a judicial officer when presented with a warrant application" and who acts instead as "an adjunct law enforcement officer" cannot provide valid authorization for an otherwise unconstitutional search. *Lo-Ji Sales, Inc. v. New York,* 442 U.S. 319, 326–327, 99 S.Ct. 2319, 2324–2325, 60 L.Ed.2d 920 (1979).

Third, reviewing courts will not defer to a warrant based on an affidavit that does not "provide the magistrate with a substantial basis for determining the existence of probable cause." *Illinois v. Gates,* 462 U.S., at 239, 103 S.Ct., at 2332. "Sufficient information must be presented to the magistrate to allow that official to determine probable cause; his action cannot be a mere ratification of the bare conclusions of others." *Ibid.* See *Aguilar v. Texas, supra* 378 U.S., at 114–115, 84 S.Ct., at 1513–1514; *Giordenello v. United States,* 357 U.S. 480, 78 S.Ct. 1245, 2 L.Ed.2d 1503 (1958); *Nathanson v. United States,* 290 U.S. 41, 54 S.Ct. 11, 78 L.Ed.159 (1933).[13] Even if the warrant application was supported by more than a "bare bones" affidavit, a reviewing court may properly conclude that, notwithstanding the deference that magistrates deserve, the warrant was invalid because the magistrate's probable-cause determination reflected an improper analysis of the totality of the circumstances, *Illinois v. Gates, supra,* 462 U.S., at 238–239, 103 S.Ct., at 2332–2333, or because the form of the warrant was improper in some respect.

Only in the first of these three situations, however, has the Court set forth a rationale for suppressing evidence obtained pursuant to a search warrant; in the other areas, it has simply excluded such evidence without considering whether Fourth Amendment interests will be advanced. To the extent that proponents of exclusion rely on its behavioral effects on judges and magistrates in these areas,

their reliance is misplaced. First, the exclusionary rule is designed to deter police misconduct rather than to punish the errors of judges and magistrates. Second, there exists no evidence suggesting that judges and magistrates are inclined to ignore or subvert the Fourth Amendment or that lawlessness among these actors requires application of the extreme sanction of exclusion.[14]

Third, and most important, we discern no basis, and are offered none, for believing that exclusion of evidence seized pursuant to a warrant will have a significant deterrent effect on the issuing judge or magistrate.[15] Many of the factors that indicate that the exclusionary rule cannot provide an effective "special" or "general" deterrent for individual offending law enforcement officers[16] apply as well to judges or magistrates. And, to the extent that the rule is thought to operate as a "systemic" deterrent on a wider audience,[17] it clearly can have no such effect on individuals empowered to issue search warrants. Judges and magistrates are not adjuncts to the law enforcement team; as neutral judicial

---

13. See also *Beck v. Ohio,* 379 U.S. 89 85 S.Ct. 223, 13 L.Ed.2d 142 (1964), in which the Court concluded that "the record . . . does not contain a single objective fact to support a belief by the officers that the petitioner was engaged in criminal activity at the time they arrested him." *Id.,* at 95, 85 S.Ct., at 227. Although the Court was willing to assume that the arresting officers acted in good faith, it concluded that:

"'[G]ood faith on the part of the arresting officers is not enough,' *Henry v. United States,* 361 U.S. 98, 102, 80 S.Ct. 168, 171, 4 L.Ed.2d 134. If subjective good faith alone were the test, the protections of the Fourth Amendment would evaporate, and the people would be 'secure in their persons, houses, papers, and effects,' only in the discretion of the police." (*Id.,* at 97, 85 S.Ct., at 228.)

We adhere to this view and emphasize that nothing in this opinion is intended to suggest a lowering of the probable-cause standard. On the contrary, we deal here with the remedy to be applied to a concededly unconstitutional search.

14. Although there are assertions that some magistrates become rubber stamps for the police and others may be unable effectively to screen police conduct, see, *e.g.,* 2 W. LaFave, Search and Seizure § 4.1 (1978); Kamisar, Does (Did) (Should) The Exclusionary Rule Rest on a "Principled Basis" Rather than an "Empirical Proposition"?, 16 Creighton L.Rev.565, 569–571 (1983); Schroeder, Deterring Fourth Amendment Violations: Alternatives to the Exclusionary Rule, 69 Geo.L.J. 1361, 1412 (1981), we are not convinced that this is a problem of major proportions. See L. Tiffany, D. McIntyre, & D. Rotenberg, Detection of Crime 119 (1967); Israel, Criminal Procedure, the Burger Court, and the Legacy of the Warren Court, 75 Mich.L.Rev. 1319, 1414, n. 396 (1977); P. Johnson, New Approaches to Enforcing the Fourth Amendment 8–10 (Working Paper, Sept. 1978), quoted in Y. Kamisar, W. LaFave, & J. Israel, Modern Criminal Procedure 229–230 (5th ed. 1980); R. Van Duizend, L. Sutton, & C. Carter, The Search Warrant Process, ch. 7 (Review Draft, National Center for State Courts, 1983).

15. As the Supreme Judicial Court of Massachusetts recognized in *Commonwealth v. Sheppard,* 387 Mass. 488, 506, 441 N.E.2d 725, 735 (1982):

"The exclusionary rule may not be well tailored to deterring judicial misconduct. If applied to judicial misconduct, the rule would be just as costly as it is when it is applied to police misconduct, but it may be ill-fitted to the job-created motivations of judges . . . [I]deally a judge is impartial as to whether a particular piece of evidence is admitted or a particular defendant convicted. Hence, in the abstract, suppression of a particular piece of evidence may not be as effective a disincentive to a neutral judge as it would be to the police. It may be that a ruling by an appellate court that a search warrant was unconstitutional would be sufficient to deter similar conduct in the future by magistrates."

But see *United States v. Karathanos,* 531 F.2d 26, 33–34 (CA2), cert. denied, 428 U.S. 910, 96 S.Ct. 3221, 49 L.Ed.2d 1217 (1976).

16. See, *e.g., Stone v. Powell,* 428 U.S., at 498, 96 S.Ct., at 3054 (BURGER, C.J., concurring); Oaks, studying the Exclusionary Rule in Search and Seizure, 37 U. Chi.I.Rev. 665, 709–710 (1970).

17. See, *e.g., Dunaway v. New York,* 442 U.S. 200, 221, 99 S.Ct. 2248, 2261, 60 L.Ed.2d 824 (1979) (STEVENS, J., concurring); Mertens & Wasserstrom, The Good Faith Exception to the Exclusionary Rule: Deregulating the Police and Derailing the Law, 70 Geo.L.J. 365, 399–401 (1981).

officers, they have no stake in the outcome of particular criminal prosecutions. The threat of exclusion thus cannot be expected significantly to deter them. Imposition of the exclusionary sanction is not necessary meaningfully to inform judicial officers of their errors, and we cannot conclude that admitting evidence obtained pursuant to a warrant while at the same time declaring that the warrant was somehow defective will in any way reduce judicial officers' professional incentives to comply with the Fourth Amendment, encourage them to repeat their mistakes, or lead to the granting of all colorable warrant requests.[18]

B

If exclusion of evidence obtained pursuant to a subsequently invalidated warrant is to have any deterrent effect, therefore, it must alter the behavior of individual law enforcement officers or the policies of their departments. One could argue that applying the exclusionary rule in cases where the police failed to demonstrate probable cause in the warrant application deters future inadequate presentations or "magistrate shopping" and thus promotes the end of the Fourth Amendment. Suppressing evidence obtained pursuant to a technically defective warrant supported by a probable cause also might encourage officers to scrutinize more closely the form of the warrant and to point out suspected judicial errors. We find such arguments speculative and conclude that suppression of evidence obtained pursuant to a warrant should be ordered only on a case-by-case basis and only in those unusual cases in which exclusion will further the purposes of the exclusionary rule.[19]

We have frequently questioned whether the exclusionary rule can have any deterrent effect when the offending officers acted in the objectively reasonable belief that their conduct did not violate the Fourth Amendment. "No empirical researcher, proponent or opponent of the rule,

has yet been able to establish with any assurance whether the rule has a deterrent effect . . ." *United States v. Janis,* 428 U.S., at 452, n. 22, 96 S.Ct., at 3031, n. 22. But even assuming that the rule effectively deters some police misconduct and provides incentives for the law enforcement profession as a whole to conduct itself in accord with the Fourth Amendment, it cannot be expected, and should not be applied, to deter objectively reasonable law enforcement activity.

As we observed in *Michigan v. Tucker,* 417 U.S. 433, 447, 94 S.Ct. 2357, 2365, 41 L.Ed.2d 182 (1974), and reiterated in *United States v. Peltier,* 422 U.S., at 539, 95 S.Ct., at 2318:

> "The deterrent purpose of the exclusionary rule necessarily assumes that the police have engaged in wilful, or at the very least negligent, conduct which has deprived the defendant of some right. By refusing to admit evidence gained as a result of such conduct, the courts hope to instill in those particular investigating officers, or in their future counterparts, a greater deal of care toward the rights of an accused. Where the official action was pursued in complete good faith, however, the deterrence rationale loses much of its force."

The *Peltier* Court continued, *id.,* at 542, 95 S.Ct., at 2320:

> "If the purpose of the exclusionary rule is to deter unlawful police conduct, then evidence obtained from a search should be suppressed only if it can be said that the law enforcement officer had knowledge, or may properly be charged with knowledge, that the search was unconstitutional under the Fourth Amendment."

See also *Illinois v. Gates,* 462 U.S., at 260–261, 103 S.Ct., at 2344 (WHITE, J., concurring in judgment); *United States v. Janis, supra,* 428 U.S., at 459, 96 S.Ct., at 3034; *Brown v. Illinois,* 422 U.S., at 610–611, 95 S.Ct., at 2265–2266 (POWELL, J., concurring in part).[20] In short, where the of-ficer's conduct is objectively reasonable,

---

18. Limiting the application of the exclusionary sanction may well increase the care with which magistrates scrutinize warrant applications. We doubt that magistrates are more desirous of avoiding the exclusion of evidence obtained pursuant to warrants they have issued than of avoiding invasions of privacy.

Federal magistrates, moreover, are subject to the direct supervision of district courts. They may be removed for "incompetency, misconduct, neglect of duty, or physical or mental disability." 28 U.S.C. § 631(i). If a magistrate serves merely as a "rubber stamp" for the police or is unable to exercise mature judgment, closer supervision or removal provides a more effective remedy than the exclusionary rule.

19. Our discussion of the deterrent effect of excluding evidence obtained in reasonable reliance on a subsequently invalidated warrant assumes, of course, that the officers properly executed the warrant and searched only those places and for those objects that it was reasonable to believe were covered by the warrant. Cf. *Massachusetts v. Sheppard,* 468 U.S. 981, 989, n. 6, 104 S.Ct. 3424, 3429, n. 6, 82 L.Ed. 2d 737 ("[I]t was not unreasonable for the police in this case to rely on the judge's assurances that the warrant authorized the search they had requested").

20. We emphasize that the standard of reasonableness we adopt is an objective one. Many objections to a good-faith exception assume that the exception will turn on the subjective good faith of individual officers. "Grounding the modification in objective reasonableness, however, retains the value of the exclusionary rule as an incentive for the law enforcement profession as a whole to conduct themselves in accord with the Fourth Amendment." *Illinois v. Gates,* 462 U.S., at 261, n. 15, 103 S.Ct., at 2344, n. 15 (WHITE, J., concurring in judgment); see *Dunaway v. New York,* 442 U.S., at 221, 99 S.Ct., at 2261 (STEVENS, J., concurring). The objective standard we adopted, moreover, requires officers to have a reasonable knowledge of what the law prohibits. *United States v. Peltier,* 442 U.S. 531, 542, 95 S.Ct. 2313, 2320, 45 L.Ed.2d 374 (1975). As Professor Jerold Israel has observed:

> "The key to the [exclusionary] rule's effectiveness as a deterrent lies, I believe, in the impetus it has provided to police training programs that make officers aware of the limits imposed by the fourth amendment and emphasize the need to operate within those limits. [An objective good-faith exception] is not likely to result in the

(continues)

"excluding the evidence will not further the ends of the exclusionary rule in any appreciable way; for it is painfully apparent . . . the officer is acting as a reasonable officer would and should act in similar circumstances. Excluding the evidence can in no way affect his future conduct unless it is to make him less willing to do his duty." *Stone v. Powell*, 428 U.S., at 539–540, 96 S.Ct., at 3073–3074 (WHITE, J., dissenting).

This is particularly true, we believe, when an officer acting with objective good faith has obtained a search warrant from a judge or magistrate and acted within its scope.[21] In most such cases, there is no police illegality and thus nothing to deter. It is the magistrate's responsibility to determine whether the officer's allegations establish probable cause and, if so, to issue a warrant comporting in form with the requirements of the Fourth Amendment. In the ordinary case, an officer cannot be expected to question the magistrate's probable-cause determination or his judgment that the form of the warrant is technically sufficient. "[O]nce the warrant issues, there is literally nothing more the policeman can do in seeking to comply with the law." *Id.*, 428 U.S., at 498, 96 S.Ct., at 3054 (BURGER, C.J., concurring). Penalizing the officer for the magistrate's error, rather than his own, cannot logically contribute to the deterrence of Fourth Amendment violations.[22]

——————

elimination of such programs, which are now viewed as an important aspect of police professionalism. Neither is it likely to alter the tenor of those programs; the possibility that illegally obtained evidence may be admitted in borderline cases is unlikely to encourage police instructors to pay less attention to fourth amendment limitations. Finally, [it] should not encourage officers to pay less attention to what they are taught, as the requirement that the officer act in 'good faith' is inconsistent with closing one's mind to the possibility of illegality."

Israel, *supra* n. 14, at 1412–1413 (footnotes omitted).

21. According to the Attorney General's Task Force on Violent Crime, Final Report (1981), the situation in which an officer relies on a duly authorized warrant

"is a particularly compelling example of good faith. A warrant is a judicial mandate to an officer to conduct a search or make an arrest, and the officer has a sworn duty to carry out its provisions. Accordingly, we believe that there should be a rule which states that evidence obtained pursuant to and within the scope of a warrant is prima facie the result of good faith on the part of the officer seizing the evidence." *Id.*, at 55.

22. To the extent that Justice STEVENS' conclusions concerning the integrity of the courts, *post*, at 3454–3455, rest on a foundation other than his judgment, which we reject, concerning the effects of our decision on the deterrence of police illegality, we find his argument unpersuasive. "Judicial integrity clearly does not mean that the courts must never admit evidence obtained in violation of the Fourth Amendment." *United States v. Janis*, 428 U.S. 433, 458, n. 35, 96 S.Ct. 3021, 3034, n. 35, 49 L.Ed.2d 1046 (1976). "While courts, of course, must ever be concerned with preserving the integrity of the judicial process, this concern has limited force as a justification for the exclusion of highly probative evidence." *Stone v. Powell*, 428 U.S., at 485,

We conclude that the marginal or nonexistent benefits produced by suppressing evidence obtained in objectively reasonable reliance on a subsequently invalidated search warrant cannot justify the substantial costs of exclusion. We do not suggest, however, that exclusion is always inappropriate in cases where an officer has obtained a warrant and abided by its terms. "[S]earches pursuant to a warrant will rarely require any deep inquiry into reasonableness," *Illinois v. Gates*, 462 U.S., at 267, 103 S.Ct., at 2347 (WHITE, J., concurring in judgment), for "a warrant issued by a magistrate normally suffices to establish" that a law enforcement officer has "acted in good faith in conducting the search." *United States v. Ross*, 456 U.S. 798, 823, n. 32, 102 S.Ct. 2157, 2172, n. 32, 72 L.Ed.2d 572 (1982). Nevertheless, the officer's reliance on the magistrate's probable-cause determination and on the technical sufficiency of the warrant he issues must be objectively reasonable, cf. *Harlow v. Fitzgerald*, 457 U.S. 800, 815–819, 102 S.Ct., 2727, 2737–2739, 73 L.Ed.2d 396 (1982),[23] and it is clear that in some circumstances the

——————

96 S.Ct., at 3048. Our cases establish that the question whether the use of illegally obtained evidence in judicial proceedings represents judicial participation in a Fourth Amendment violation and offends the integrity of the courts

"is essentially the same as the inquiry into whether exclusion would serve a deterrent purpose . . . The analysis showing that exclusion in this case has no demonstrated deterrent effect and is unlikely to have any significant such effect shows, by the same reasoning, that the admission of the evidence is unlikely to encourage violations of the Fourth Amendment."

United States v. Janis, supra, 429 U.S., at 459, n. 35, 96 S.Ct., at 3034, n. 35.

Absent unusual circumstances, when a Fourth Amendment violation has occurred because the police have reasonably relied on a warrant issued by a detached and neutral magistrate but ultimately found to be defective, "the integrity of the courts is not implicated." *Illinois v. Gates, supra*, 462 U.S., at 259, n. 14, 103 S.Ct., at 2343, n. 14 (WHITE, J., concurring in judgment). See *Stone v. Powell*, 428 U.S., at 485, n. 23, 96 S. Ct., at 3048, n. 23; *id.*, at 540, 96 S.Ct., at 3073 (WHITE, J., dissenting); *United States v. Peltier*, 442 U.S. 531, 536–539, 95 S.Ct. 2313, 2317–2318, 45 L.Ed.2d 374 (1975).

23. In *Harlow*, we eliminated the subjective component of the qualified immunity public officials enjoy in suits seeking damages for alleged deprivations of constitutional rights. The situations are not perfectly analogous, but we also eschew inquiries into the subjective beliefs of law enforcement officers who seize evidence pursuant to a subsequently invalidated warrant. Although we have suggested that, "[o]n occasion, the motive with which the officer conducts an illegal search may have some relevance in determining the propriety of applying the exclusionary rule," *Scott v. United States*, 436 U.S. 128, 139, n. 13, 98 S.Ct. 1717, 1724, n. 13, 56 L.Ed.2d 168 (1978), we believe that "sending state and federal courts on an expedition into the minds of police officers would produce a grave and fruitless misallocation of judicial resources." *Massachusetts v. Painten*, 389 U.S. 560, 565, 88 S.Ct. 660, 663, 19 L.Ed.2d 770 (1968) (WHITE, J., dissenting). Accordingly, our good-faith inquiry is confined to the objectively ascertainable question whether a reasonably well trained officer would have known that the search was illegal despite the magistrate's authorization. In making this determination, all of the circumstances—including whether the warrant application had previously been rejected by a different magistrate—may be considered.

officer[24] will have no reasonable grounds for believing that the warrant was properly issued.

Suppression therefore remains an appropriate remedy if the magistrate or judge in issuing a warrant was misled by information in an affidavit that the affiant knew was false or would have known was false except for his reckless disregard of the truth. *Franks v. Delaware,* 438 U.S. 154, 98 S.Ct. 2674, 57 L.Ed.2d 667 (1978). The exception we recognize today will also not apply in cases where the issuing magistrate wholly abandoned his judicial role in the manner condemned in *Lo-Ji Sales, Inc. v. New York,* 442 U.S. 319, 99 S.Ct. 2319, 60 L.Ed.2d 920 (1979); in such circumstances, no reasonably well-trained officer should rely on the warrant. Nor would an officer manifest objective good faith in relying on a warrant based on an affidavit "so lacking in indicia of probable cause as to render official belief in its existence entirely unreasonable." *Brown v. Illinois,* 422 U.S., at 610–611, 95 S.Ct., at 2265–2266 (POWELL, J., concurring in part); see *Illinois v. Gates, supra,* 462 U.S., at 263–264, 103 S.Ct., at 2345–2346 (WHITE, J., concurring in the judgment). Finally, depending on the circumstances of the particular case, a warrant may be so facially deficient—i.e., in failing to particularize the place to be searched or the things to be seized—that the executing officers cannot reasonably presume it to be valid. Cf. *Massachusetts v. Sheppard,* 468 U.S., at 988–991, 104 S.Ct. at 3428–3430.

In so limiting the suppression remedy, we leave untouched the probable-cause standard and the various requirements for a valid warrant. Other objections to the modification of the Fourth Amendment exclusionary rule we consider to be insubstantial. The good-faith exception for searches conducted pursuant to warrants is not intended to signal our willingness strictly to enforce the requirements of the Fourth Amendment, and we do not believe that it will have this effect. As we have already suggested, the good-faith exception, turning as it does on objective reasonableness, should not be difficult to apply in practice. When officers have acted pursuant to a warrant, the prosecution should ordinarily be able to establish objective good faith without a substantial expenditure of judicial time.

Nor are we persuaded that application of a good-faith exception to searches conducted pursuant to warrants will preclude review of the constitutionality of the search or seizure, deny needed guidance from the courts, or freeze

Fourth Amendment law in its present state.[25] There is no need for courts to adopt the inflexible practice of always deciding whether the officers' conduct manifested objective good faith before turning to the question whether the Fourth Amendment has been violated. Defendants seeking suppression of the fruits of allegedly unconstitutional searches or seizures undoubtedly raise live controversies which Art. III empowers federal courts to adjudicate. As cases addressing questions of good-faith immunity under 42 U.S.C. § 1983, compare *O'Connor v. Donaldson,* 422 U.S. 563, 95 S.Ct. 2486, 45 L.Ed.2d 396 (1975), with *Procunier v. Navarette,* 434 U.S. 555, 566, n. 14, 98 S.Ct. 855, 862, n. 14, 55 L.Ed.2d 24 (1978), and cases involving the harmless-error doctrine, compare *Milton v. Wainwright,* 407 U.S.371, 372, 92 S.Ct. 2174, 2175, 33 L.Ed.2d 1 (1972), with *Coleman v. Alabama,* 399 U.S. 1, 90 S.Ct. 1999, 26 L.Ed.2d 387 (1970), make clear, courts have considerable discretion in conforming their decision-making processes to the exigencies of particular cases.

If the resolution of a particular Fourth Amendment question is necessary to guide future action by law enforcement officers and magistrates, nothing will prevent reviewing courts from deciding that question before turning to the good-faith issue.[26] Indeed, it frequently will be difficult to determine whether the officers acted reasonably without resolving the Fourth Amendment issue. Even if the Fourth Amendment question is not one of broad import, reviewing courts could decide in particular cases that magistrates under their supervision need to be informed of their errors and so evaluate the officers' good faith only after finding a violation. In other circumstances, those courts could reject suppression motions posing no important Fourth Amendment questions by turning immediately to a consideration of the officers' good faith. We have no reason to believe that our Fourth Amendment jurisprudence would suffer by allowing reviewing courts to exercise an informed discretion in making this choice.

IV

When the principles we have enunciated today are applied to the facts of this case, it is apparent that the

---

24. References to "officer" throughout this opinion should not be read too narrowly It is necessary to consider the objective reasonableness, not only of the officers who eventually executed a warrant, but also of the officers who originally obtained it or who provided information material to the probable-cause determination. Nothing in our opinion suggests, for example, that an officer could obtain a warrant on the basis of a "bare bones" affidavit and then rely on colleagues who are ignorant of the circumstances under which the warrant was obtained to conduct the search. See *Whiteley v. Warden,* 401 U.S. 560, 568, 91 S.Ct. 1031, 1037, 28 L.Ed.2d 306 (1971).

25. The argument that defendants will lose their incentive to litigate meritorious Fourth Amendment claims as a result of the good-faith exception we adopt today is unpersuasive. Although the exception might discourage presentation of insubstantial suppression motions, the magnitude of the benefit conferred on defendants by a successful motion makes it unlikely that litigation of colorable claims will be substantially diminished.

26. It has been suggested, in fact, that "the recognition of a 'penumbral zone,' within which an inadvertent mistake would not call for exclusion, . . . will make it less tempting for judges to bend fourth amendment standards to avoid releasing a possibly dangerous criminal because of a minor and unintentional miscalculation by the police." Schroeder, *supra* n. 14, at 1420–1421 (footnote omitted); see Ashdown, Good Faith, the Exclusionary Remedy, and Rule-Oriented Adjudication in the Criminal Process, 24 Wm. & Mary L.Rev. 335, 383–384 (1983).

(continues)

judgment of the Court of Appeals cannot stand. The Court of Appeals applied the prevailing legal standards to Officer Rombach's warrant application and concluded that the application could not support the magistrate's probable-cause determination. In so doing, the court clearly informed the magistrate that he had erred in issuing the challenged warrant. This aspect of the court's judgment is not under attack in this proceeding.

Having determined that the warrant should not have issued, the Court of Appeals understandably declined to adopt a modification of the Fourth Amendment exclusionary rule that this Court had not previously sanctioned. Although the modification finds strong support in our previous cases, the Court of Appeals' commendable self-restraint is not to be criticized. We have now reexamined the purposes of the exclusionary rule and the propriety of its application in cases where officers have relied on a subsequently invalidated search warrant. Our conclusion is that the rule's purposes will only rarely be served by applying it in such circumstances.

In the absence of an allegation that the magistrate abandoned his detached and neutral role, suppression is appropriate only if the officers were dishonest or reckless in preparing their affidavit or could not have harbored an objectively reasonable belief in the existence of probable cause. Only respondent Leon has contended that no reasonably well trained police officer could have believed that there existed probable cause to search his house; significantly, the other respondents advance no comparable argument. Officer Rombach's application for a warrant clearly was supported by much more than a "bare bones" affidavit. The affidavit related the results of an extensive investigation and, as the opinions of the divided panel of the Court of Appeals make clear, provided evidence sufficient to create disagreement among thoughtful and competent judges as to the existence of probable cause. Under these circumstances, the officers' reliance on the magistrate's determination of probable cause was objectively reasonable, and application of the extreme sanction of exclusion is inappropriate.

Accordingly, the judgment of the Court of Appeals is Reversed.

Justice BLACKMUN, concurring.

The Court today holds that evidence obtained in violation of the Fourth Amendment by officers acting in objectively reasonable reliance on a search warrant issued by a neutral and detached magistrate need not be excluded, as a matter of federal law, from the case in chief of federal and state criminal prosecutions. In so doing, the Court writes another chapter in the volume of Fourth Amendment law opened by *Weeks v. United States*, 232 U.S. 383, 34 S.Ct. 341, 58 L.Ed. 652 (1914). I join the Court's opinion in this case and the one in *Massachusetts v. Sheppard*,

468 U.S. 981, 104 S.Ct. 3424, 82 L.Ed.2d 737 (1984), because I believe that the rule announced today advances the legitimate interests of the criminal justice system without sacrificing the individual rights protected by the Fourth Amendment. I write separately, however, to underscore what I regard as the unavoidably provisional nature of today's decision.

As the Court's opinion in this case makes clear, the Court has narrowed the scope of the exclusionary rule because of an empirical judgment that the rule has little appreciable effect in cases where officers act in objectively reasonable reliance on search warrants. See *ante*, at 3419–3420. Because I share the view that the exclusionary rule is not a constitutionally compelled corollary of the Fourth Amendment itself, see *ante*, at 3412, I see no way to avoid making an empirical judgment of this sort, and I am satisfied that the Court has made the correct one on the information before it. Like all courts, we face institutional limitations on our ability to gather information about "legislative facts," and the exclusionary rule itself has exacerbated the shortage of hard data concerning the behavior of police officers in the absence of such a rule. See *United States v. Janis*, 428 U.S. 433, 448–453, 96 S.Ct. 3021, 3029–3031, 49 L.Ed.2d 1046 (1976). Nonetheless, we cannot escape the responsibility to decide the question before us, however imperfect our information may be, and I am prepared to join the Court on the information now at hand.

What must be stressed, however, is that any empirical judgment about the effect of the exclusionary rule in a particular class of cases necessarily in a provisional one. By their very nature, the assumptions on which we proceed today cannot be cast in stone. To the contrary, they now will be tested in the real world of state and federal law enforcement, and this Court will attend to the results. If it should emerge from experience that, contrary to our expectations, the good-faith exception to the exclusionary rule results in a material change in police compliance with the Fourth Amendment, we shall have to reconsider what we have undertaken here. The logic of a decision that rests on untested predictions about police conduct demands no less.

If a single principle may be drawn from this Court's exclusionary rule decisions, from *Weeks* through *Mapp v. Ohio*, 367 U.S. 643, 81 S.Ct. 1684, 6 L.Ed.2d 1081 (1961), to the decisions handed down today, it is that the scope of the exclusionary rule is subject to change in light of changing judicial understanding about the effects of the rule outside the confines of the courtroom. It is incumbent on the Nation's law enforcement officers, who must continue to observe the Fourth Amendment in the wake of today's decisions, to recognize the double-edged nature of that principle.

UNITED STATES of America.
Plaintiff-Appellee,

v.

Gilbert MARTINEZ–JIMENEZ,

Defendant-Appellant.
No. 87–5305.

United States Court of Appeals,
Ninth Circuit.

Submitted Oct. 4, 1988.
Decided Jan. 3, 1989.
864 F.2d 664 (9th Cir. 1989).

NELSON, Circuit Judge.

Gilbert Martinez–Jimenez appeals his conviction following a bench trial on one count of armed bank robbery in violation of 18 U.S.C. § 2113(a) & (d). He contends that the trial court erred in concluding that the toy gun that he held during the bank robbery was a "dangerous weapon" as defined by 18 U.S.C. § 2113(d). We affirm the judgment of the district court.

PROCEDURAL BACKGROUND

On July 14, 1987 a federal grand jury in the Central District of California returned a three-count indictment that charged the appellant and an accomplice, Joe Anthony De La Torre, with armed bank robbery in violation of 18 U.S.C. § 2113(a) & (d) and with carrying a firearm during a crime of violence in violation of 18 U.S.C. § 924(c). At a bench trial the appellant and his accomplice were found guilty of armed bank robbery as charged in count one and not guilty of carrying a firearm during a crime of violence, as charged in counts two and three.

FACTS

On June 19, 1987, at approximately 12:55 P.M., Martinez–Jimenez and De La Torre entered a bank in Bell-flower, California. While De La Torre took cash from a customer and two bank drawers, Martinez–Jimenez remained in the lobby and ordered that the people in the bank lie "face down on the floor." During this time Martinez–Jimenez was holding an object that eyewitnesses thought was a handgun. These persons included two bank employees and a customer who was familiar with guns because he owned handguns, had handled weapons while in military service, and occasionally used weapons at firing ranges. The three witnesses testified that the object was a dark revolver about eight or nine inches long and that it caused them to fear for the safety of themselves and of those around them.

At trial, De La Torre testified that neither he nor Martinez–Jimenez had operable firearms when they entered the bank. He testified that Martinez–Jimenez had a toy gun that he and Martinez–Jimenez had purchased at a department store a few hours prior to the robbery. De La Torre also testified that he hid the toy gun in his closet after the robbery, that neither he nor Martinez–Jimenez wanted the bank employees to believe that they had a real gun, and that they did not want the bank employees to be in fear for their lives. Martinez–Jimenez testified that he had carried the toy gun because he felt secure with it and that during the robbery he held it down toward his leg in order to hide it so that people would not see it. The defense introduced into evidence a toy gun. Martinez–Jimenez testified that the gun used in the robbery was the toy gun introduced into evidence. It was stipulated that De La Torre's attorney had received the toy gun offered as the gun used in the robbery from De La Torre's mother.

Based upon observation of the bank robbery photographs and the toy gun, the court concluded that Martinez–Jimenez possessed a toy gun during the course of the bank robbery and that he had kept the toy gun pointed downwards by his side during the course of the bank robbery. On the basis of his display of the toy gun in the course of the robbery, Martinez–Jimenez was convicted under section 2113(d) which provides an enhanced penalty for use of a "dangerous weapon" during a bank robbery.

STANDARD OF REVIEW

The question presented is whether a toy gun is a "dangerous weapon" within the meaning of the federal bank robbery statute. Interpretation of a statute presents a question of law reviewable de novo. *United States v. Wilson*, 720 F.2d 608, 609 n. 2 (9th Cir.1983), *cert. denied*, 465 U.S. 1034, 104 S.Ct. 1304, 79 L.Ed.2d 703 (1984); *United States v. Moreno–Pulido*, 695 F.2d 1141, 1143 (9th Cir.1983).

DISCUSSION

A robber may be guilty of an armed bank robbery under section 2113(d) if he uses a dangerous weapon or device in the commission of the crime. The instrumentality does not have to be a firearm. The use, or unlawful carrying, of a firearm in a bank robbery is a more serious offense punishable separately under section 924(c). In this case, the appellant carried a toy replica of a firearm that simulated the appearance but not the weight of a genuine firearm. The toy gun did not fit the statutory definition of a firearm under 18 U.S.C. § 921(a)(3). However, it did fall within the meaning of a "dangerous weapon or device" under section 2113(d). Section 2113(d) states that

(continues)

Whoever, in committing, or in attempting to commit, any offense defined in subsections (a) and (b) of this section, assaults any person, or puts in jeopardy the life of any person by the use of a dangerous weapon or device, shall be fined not more than $10,000 or imprisoned not more than twenty-five years, or both.

In *McLaughlin v. United States,* 476 U.S. 16, 106 S.Ct. 1677, 90 L.Ed.2d 15 (1986), the Supreme Court found that a defendant who used an unloaded handgun was convicted properly under section 2113(d) because the unloaded handgun was a dangerous weapon under the statute. *Id.* at 17, 106 S.Ct. at 1677–78. Prior to *McLaughlin* this circuit, and other circuits, had assumed that section 2113(d) was violated only by the use of a loaded operable gun. *United States v. Terry,* 760 F.2d 939, 942 (9th Cir.1985); see also *Parker v. United States,* 801 F.2d 1382, 1384 n. 2 (D.C.Cir.1986), *cert. denied,* 479 U.S. 1070, 107 S.Ct. 964, 93 L.Ed.2d 1011 (1987).

The *McLaughlin* opinion stated:

Three reasons, each independently sufficient, support the conclusion that an unloaded gun is a "dangerous weapon." First, a gun is an article that is typically and characteristically dangerous; the use for which it is manufactured and sold is a dangerous one, and the law reasonably may presume that such an article is always dangerous even though it may not be armed at a particular time or place. *In addition, the display of a gun instills fear in the average citizen; as a consequence, it creates an immediate danger that a violent response will ensue.*

Finally, a gun can cause harm when used as a bludgeon. *McLaughlin,* 476 U.S. at 17–18, 106 S.Ct. at 1677–78 (footnote omitted) (emphasis added).

The *McLaughlin* opinion recognizes that the dangerousness of a device used in a bank robbery is not simply a function of its potential to injure people directly. Its dangerousness results from the greater burdens that it imposes upon victims and law enforcement officers. Therefore an unloaded gun that only simulates the threat of a loaded gun is a dangerous weapon. The use of a gun that is inoperable and incapable of firing also will support a conviction under section 921(a)(3) and section 2113(d). *United States v. York,* 830 F.2d 885, 891 (8th Cir.1987), *cert. denied,* __ U.S. __, 108 S.Ct. 1047, 98 L.Ed.2d 1010 (1988); see also *United States v. Goodheim,* 686 F.2d 776, 778 (9th Cir.1982).

These cases reflect a policy that the robber's creation of even the appearance of dangerousness is sufficient to subject him to enhanced punishment. Other cases have given effect to this policy by holding that the trier of fact may infer that the instrument carried by a bank robber was a firearm based only on witness testimony that it appeared to be genuine. *Parker,* 801 F.2d at 1283–84; *United States v. Harris,* 792 F.2d 866, 868 (9th Cir.1986). *McLaughlin*

validates this policy but eliminates the inefficiencies associated with the inference process.

A robber who carries a toy gun during the commission of a bank robbery creates some of the same risks as those created by one who carries an unloaded or inoperable genuine gun. First, the robber subjects victims to greater apprehension. Second, the robber requires law enforcement agencies to formulate a more deliberate, and less efficient, response in light of the need to counter the apparent direct and immediate threat to human life. Third, the robber creates a likelihood that the reasonable response of police and guards will include the use of deadly force. The increased chance of an armed response creates a greater risk to the physical security of victims, bystanders, and even the perpetrators. Therefore the greater harm that a robber creates by deciding to carry a toy gun is similar to the harm that he creates by deciding to carry an unloaded gun.

The *McLaughlin* opinion examined the floor debate on the provision that became section 2113(d) and concluded that Congress was concerned with the potential of an apparently dangerous article to incite fear. *McLaughlin,* 476 U.S. at 18 n. 3, 106 S.Ct. at 1678 n. 3. The House debate on the provision that became section 2113(d) indicates that an ersatz wooden gun used in a bank robbery would satisfy the statutory meaning of a dangerous weapon or device. See 78 Cong.Rec. 8132 (1934). If Congress intended that an ersatz wooden gun would fall within the statute, by analogy an ersatz plastic gun should fall within the statute. Congress' intent focused on the nature of the effect that the robber creates, not the specific nature of the instruments that he utilizes.

Appellant concedes that *McLaughlin* applies to the use of an inherently dangerous weapon such as an unloaded firearm but argues that it does not apply to a harmless instrumentality of a crime, such as a toy gun, unless the defendant used the instrumentality in an assaultive manner. The trial court found that the replica was a "totally plastic and extremely light" toy gun, and that Martinez–Jimenez had held it downward by his side and not towards any of the bank employees or customers. Therefore the defendant urges that his manner of displaying this particular toy gun avoids *McLaughlin's* definition of a dangerous weapon because it would not have instilled fear in an average citizen and would not have created a danger of a violent response.

We disagree. A bank robber's use of a firearm during the commission of the crime is punishable even if he does not make assaultive use of the device. He need not brandish the firearm in a threatening manner. *United States v. Mason,* 658 F.2d 1263, 1270–71 (9th Cir.1981). His possession of the weapon is an integral part of the crime. *United States v. Moore,* 580 F.2d 360, 362 (9th Cir.), *cert. denied,* 439 U.S. 970, 99 S.Ct. 463, 58 L.Ed.2d 430 (1978). By analogy, a bank robber's use of a replica or simulated weapon violates section 2113(d) even if he does not make assaultive use of the device. His possession of the instrument during the commission of the crime evidences his apparent ability to commit an assault. The appellant's possession of the toy gun facilitated the crime and increased its likelihood of success. The appellant testified that he carried the toy gun because he "felt secure with it." This suggests that he may not have begun the robbery without it.

Section 2113(d) is not concerned with the way that a robber displays a simulated or replica weapon. The statute focuses on the harms created, not the manner of creating the harm. The record shows substantial evidence that the appellant's possession of the toy gun created fear and apprehension in the victims. Appellant argues that we should put aside this testimony because it was based upon the witnesses' mistaken assessment of the apparent threat. Appellant's argument fails because, during a robbery, people confronted with what they believe is a deadly weapon cannot be expected to maintain a high level of critical perception.[1]

---

1. The recent trend in toy and replica manufacturing to duplicate precisely the outward appearance of genuine weaponry compounds the difficulty and risk of making any distinction. *See* N.Y. Times, Oct. 16, 1988, § 4, at 7, col. 1. This trend has led some state and local governments to enact bans on realistic toy guns. *See* N.Y. Times, Aug. 5, 1988, § A, at col. 1; L.A. Times, Apr. 29, 1988, § 1, at 2, col. 6 (home ed.). Congress has held hearings on a federal ban. 134 Cong.Rec. D 1084 (daily ed. Aug. 11, 1988).

By extension, appellant also argues that the toy gun did not jeopardize the life of any person because it did not increase the police's burden to interdict the crime during its commission or aftermath and could not have provoked the police's use of a deadly response that could have endangered others. This argument fails because the police must formulate a response to an apparently armed robber during the course of the crime, not after it. They must confront the risk that a replica or simulated gun creates before knowing that it presents no actual threat. These confrontations often lead to gunfire and casualties. *See, e.g.,* L.A. Times, Oct. 18, 1988, § 2, at 3, col. 1 (San Diego County ed.); *id.,* May 13, 1988, § 2, at 2, col. 5 (home ed.).

CONCLUSION

The values of justice, administrability, and deterrence require the rule that a robber's use of a replica or simulated weapon that appears to be a genuine weapon to those present at the scene of the crime, or to those charged with responsibility for responding to the crime, carries the same penalty as the use of a genuine weapon. In this case appellant avoided the harsher penalties associated with use of a firearm in violation of section 924(c) by proving that he only had simulated the use of a firearm. However, the appellant's decision to bluff did not eliminate the harms that Congress intended to address in section 2113(d).

AFFIRMED.

Stephen Alan WOLCOTT,
Petitioner-Appellant,

v.

Sandra Lee WOLCOTT,
Respondent-Appellee.
No. 9308.

Court of Appeals of New Mexico
March 5, 1987.

Certiorari Denied April 9, 1987.
105 N.M. 608, 735 P.2d 326 (Ct. App. 1987)

OPINION

FRUMAN, Judge.

Our opinion, previously filed on February 3, 1987, is withdrawn and the following opinion is substituted therefor.

Husband appeals from the denial of his post-divorce motions to reduce or abate his child support obligations and to terminate or abate his alimony obligation. Husband relied upon his voluntary change of employment,

which resulted in a major reduction of his income, as the substantial change of circumstances justifying his motions. In denying these motions, the trial court found that husband had not acted in good faith with regard to his support obligations when he changed employment.

Husband's issues on appeal are: "1. Whether the voluntary career change of a professional never justifies modification of his support obligation, even if undertaken in good faith." and 2. Whether there is substantial evidence to support the trial court's finding that husband was not acting in good faith when he changed specialty.

As the first issue is presented in the abstract, it would require an advisory opinion on review. This court does not give advisory opinions. *In re Bunnell,* 100 N.M. 242, 668 P.2d 1119 (Ct.App.1983). Although the first issue will not be directly addressed, it will be generally considered in our review of the second issue. We affirm the trial court on the second issue.

FACTS

Following their marriage of thirteen years, the parties were divorced in December 1983. Pursuant to the marital settlement agreement incorporated into the decree of

(continues)

dissolution, husband was to pay $1,500 monthly for the support of the three minor children, and $300 monthly for alimony for a period of five years. At the time of the divorce, husband was a physician specializing in obstetrics and gynecology in Albuquerque.

For a number of years husband had considered changing his specialty to psychiatry. In March 1985, he was accepted in a psychiatric residency program in Washington, D.C. Husband closed his Albuquerque office in June 1985 and commenced his residency the following month. The duration of the program is three to four years, and during this period, husband's annual gross income will range from approximately $21,000 to $24,000. This salary is approximately one-fourth of his annual gross income during the several years prior to and the year following the divorce.

In June 1985, husband unilaterally reduced his combined monthly child support and alimony payment from $1,800 to $550, contrary to the terms of the marital settlement agreement and without judicial approval or forewarning his former spouse.

DISCUSSION

Husband contends that the denial of his motion for reduction of support payments was erroneously based on the trial court's finding of a lack of good faith in changing his speciality and that there was not substantial evidence to support this finding.

To justify modification in the amount of child support already awarded, there must be evidence of a "substantial change of circumstances which materially affects the existing welfare of the child and which must have occurred since the prior adjudication where child support was originally awarded." *Henderson v. Lekvold*, 95 N.M. 288, 291, 621 P.2d 505, 508 (1980). See *Spingola v. Spingola*, 91 N.M. 737, 580 P.2d 958 (1978). A similar change in circumstances of the supported spouse must be shown before the request may be granted as to alimony. See *Brister v. Brister*, 92 N.M. 711, 594 P.2d 1167 (1979). The recipient's actual need for support is the essential criterion. See *Weaver v. Weaver*, 100 N.M. 165, 667 P.2d 970 (1983); *Brister v. Brister*.

Husband, as the petitioner for the modification, had the burden of proving to the trial court's satisfaction that circumstances had substantially changed and, thereby, justified his requests. See *Smith v. Smith*, 98 N.M. 468, 649 P.2d 1381 (1982); *Spingola v. Spingola*. Any change in support obligations is a matter within the discretion of the trial court, and appellate review is limited to a determination of whether that discretion has been abused. *Henderson v. Lekvold*. If substantial evidence exists to support the trial court's findings, they will be upheld. See *Chavez v. Chavez*, 98 N.M. 678, 652 P.2d 228 (1982). Cf. *Pitcher v. Pitcher*, 91 N.M. 504, 576 P.2d 1135 (1978).

The common trend in various jurisdictions is that a good faith career change, resulting in a decreased income, may constitute a material change in circumstances that warrants a reduction in a spouse's support obligation. See *Thomas v. Thomas*, 281 Ala. 397, 203 So.2d 118 (1967); *Graham v. Graham*, 21 Ill.App.3d 1032, 316 N.E.2d 143 (1974); *Schuler v. Schuler*, 382 Mass. 366, 416 N.E.2d 197 (1981); *Giesner v. Giesner*, 319 N.W.2d 718 (Minn.1982); *Fogel v. Fogel*, 184 Neb. 425, 168 N.W.2d 275 (1969); *Nelson v. Nelson*, 225 Or. 257, 357 P.2d 536 (1960); *Anderson v. Anderson*, 503 S.W.2d 124 (Tex.Civ. App. 1973); *Lambert v. Lambert*, 66 Wash.2d 503, 403 P.2d 664 (1965). Likewise, where the career change is not made in good faith, a reduction in one's support obligations will not be warranted. See *In re Marriage of Ebert*, 81 Ill.App.3d 44, 36 Ill.Dec. 415, 400 N.E.2d 995 (1980) (evidence of a desire to evade support responsibilities); *Moncada v. Moncada*, 81 Mich. App. 26, 264 N.W.2d 104 (1978) (no evidence that husband acted in bad faith or with willful disregard for the welfare of his dependents); *Bedford v. Bedford*, 49 Mich. App. 424, 212 N.W.2d 260 (1973) (husband voluntarily avoided re-employment opportunities); *Nelson v. Nelson* (no evidence that the sale of a medical practice and assumption of clinic duties, resulting in a decrease in income, was made to jeopardize the interests of the children); *Commonwealth v. Saul*, 175 Pa.Super. 540, 107 A.2d 182 (1954) (husband literally gave away assets available for support payments). *See generally* Annot., 89 A.L.R.2d 1 at 54 (1963).

Husband challenges the trial court's findings that: (1) at the time husband entered the marital settlement agreement, he had planned to terminate his private practice and return to school, but did not so advise wife; (2) although wife may have had prior knowledge of husband's future employment desires, she had no reason to believe that he would effect a career change upon entering the settlement agreement, if it interfered with the support obligations he was assuming; and (3) husband was not acting in good faith with regard to his child support and alimony obligations when he voluntarily made his career change.

The record contains both direct and reasonably inferred evidence from the testimony of the parties to support the first two challenged findings. The third finding is supported by evidence of husband's disregard for several financial obligations undertaken by him in the marital settlement agreement, by his failure or inability to make a full disclosure of his income and assets to wife and the court, and by his self-indulgence with regard to his own lifestyle and personal necessities without regard to the necessities of his children and his former spouse. We find this evidence sufficient to support the trial court's decision to deny husband's petition for a modification of his child support obligation.

Husband also argues that, during their marriage, wife was willing to make changes in the family's lifestyle as would be necessary to accommodate his career change. Because of this, husband contends that his career change following the divorce does not indicate a lack of good faith. Husband did not, however, request a finding as to this contention, and his failure to do so waives any merit the argument may have. See *Worland v. Worland,* 89 N.M. 291, 551 P.2d 981 (1976).

In the determination of alimony, the recipient's actual need for support is the focal point. See *Brister v. Brister.* While husband did request a finding as to wife's employment and there was testimony as to her employment, there was also testimony indicating her continued need for alimony. We find this evidence sufficient to support the trial court's decision to continue wife's alimony.

Although husband asserts that his voluntary career change was made entirely in good faith, without a disregard of the welfare of his children and former spouse, this change does not automatically mandate a reduction in his support obligation. See *Spingola v. Spingola.* The decision as to reducing or maintaining the support obligation rests within the trial court's discretion. *Id.*

We recognize that the "responsibilities of begetting a family many times raise havoc with dreams. Nevertheless, the duty [to support] persists, with full authority in the State to enforce it." *Romano v. Romano,* 133 Vt. 314, 316, 340 A.2d 63, 63 (1975).

Based upon our review of the record we conclude that the decision of the trial court does not constitute an abuse of its discretion. Its decision is affirmed.

IT IS SO ORDERED.

DONNELLY, C.J., and ALARID, J., concur.

Glossary

A

administrative law Rules, regulations, orders, and decisions adopted by administrative agencies that have the authority of law.

advocacy To support or urge the adoption of a position through the use of an argument.

affirm A decision of an appellate court that upholds the decision of the trial court.

appeals court A court that reviews the decision of a trial court or other lower court to determine and correct any error that may have been made.

appellant The party who files an appeal. On appeal, the appellant argues that the lower court made an error that entitles the appellant to relief.

appellate court brief A memorandum of law submitted to a court of appeals. It presents the legal analysis, authority, and argument in support of a position that the lower court's decision or ruling was either correct or incorrect. It is often referred to as an appellate brief.

appellee The party who opposes the appeal. On appeal, the appellee usually argues that the lower court did not make an error that entitles the appellant to relief.

authority Anything a court may rely on when deciding an issue. It includes the law, such as constitutions, statutes, and so on, and nonlaw sources, such as encyclopedia cites.

B

background facts Facts presented in a court opinion, case brief, or legal memorandum that put the key facts in context. They give an overview of a factual event and provide the reader with the overall context within which the key facts occurred.

brief See appellate court brief, case brief, and trial court brief.

C

canons of construction The rules and guidelines courts use when interpreting statutes.

caption In an opinion, the caption consists of the names of the parties to a lawsuit and their court status (e.g., Eddie RAEL, Plaintiff-Appellee, v. Emillio CADENA and Manuel Cadena, Defendants-Appellants).

case brief A written summary identifying the essential components of a court opinion.

case law See common law/case law.

case law analysis The analytical process engaged in to determine if and how a decision in a court opinion either governs or affects the outcome of a client's case.

cause of action The legal basis upon which a lawsuit is based (e.g., negligence). To state a claim in a lawsuit means to allege facts in support of each element of the cause of action (e.g., in a negligence case there must be facts alleged in support of each of the elements of negligence—duty, breach of duty, proximate cause, and damages).

certiorari See Writ of Certiorari.

citation Information that allows the reader to locate where a reference can be found. In case law, the term refers to the volume number, page number, and name of the reporter where a case may be found.

cite See citation.

common law/case law The body of law created by courts. It is composed of the general legal rules, doctrines, and principles adopted by courts when interpreting existing law or when creating law in the absence of controlling enacted law.

concurring opinion A judicial opinion that agrees with the majority holding in a case, but for different or additional reasons than those presented by the majority.

constitution A governing document adopted by the people that establishes the framework for the operation of the government, defines the powers of the government, and guarantees the fundamental rights of the people.

counteranalysis The process of discovering and considering the counterargument to a legal position or argument; the process of anticipating the argument the opponent is likely to raise in response to the analysis of an issue. It is the identification and objective evaluation of the strengths and weaknesses of a legal argument.

counterargument The argument in opposition to a legal argument or position. The argument the opponent is likely to raise in response to the analysis of an issue.

court opinion The statement of a court of its decision reached in a case, the rule that applies, and the reasons for the court's decision.

court rules Procedural rules adopted by a court which govern the litigation process. Court rules often govern the format and style of documents submitted to the court.

D

defendant The party against whom a lawsuit is brought.

dissenting opinion A judicial opinion in a case that disagrees with the majority opinion.

district court In many states, the district court is the trial court of general jurisdiction. See also U.S. District Court.

E

ejusdem generis A cannon of construction which provides that whenever a statute contains a specific list followed by a general term, the general term is interpreted to be limited to other things of the same class or kind as the list.

element An essential component of a law, rule, principle, or doctrine. For a law, rule, etc., to apply, the requirements of each element must be met. (The elements of negligence are duty, breach of duty, proximate cause, and damages. For a claim of negligence to prevail, the plaintiff must establish that the defendant had a duty, the defendant breached the duty, the breach of duty was the cause of the incident, and the plaintiff was damaged as a result of the breach.)

enacted law The body of law adopted by the people or legislative bodies including constitutions, statutes, ordinances, and administrative rules and regulations.

expanded outline See outline—expanded.

expressio unius A canon of construction which provides that if a statute contains a list of items covered by the statute, everything else is excluded.

F

fact Information concerning some thing, action, event, or circumstance.

federalism In the U.S. Constitution the powers to govern are separated between the federal and state governments. This separation of powers is called federalism.

G

general jurisdiction A court of general jurisdiction has the power, with few exceptions, to hear and decide any matter brought before it.

H

headnotes Summaries of the points of law discussed in a court opinion prepared by the publisher of the opinion.

holding The court's application of the rule of law to the legal question raised by the facts of a case. The court's answer to the legal issue in a case.

I

in personam jurisdiction See jurisdiction.

intellectual honesty In the context of legal analysis, intellectual honesty means to research and analyze a problem objectively. This includes analyzing all aspects of a problem free of preconceived notions, personal views, and emotions.

IRAC An acronym commonly used in reference to the legal analysis process. It is composed of the first letter of the descriptive term for each step of the process—**I**ssue, **R**ule, **A**nalysis/Application, **C**onclusion. The standard legal analysis process is the identification of the issue, followed by the presentation of the governing rule of law, the analysis/application of the rule of law, and the conclusion.

irrelevant facts Those facts that are coincidental to an event, but are not of significant legal importance in a case.

issue The precise legal question raised by the specific facts of a dispute.

issue—narrow/specific statement A complete statement of the issue, which includes the specific law, legal question, and key facts.

issue—short/broad statement A broad formulation of the issue that usually does not include reference to the specific facts of the case or the applicable law.

J

jurisdiction The court's authority to hear and resolve specific disputes. Jurisdiction is usually composed of **personal jurisdiction** (authority over persons) and **subject matter jurisdiction** (authority over the types of cases a court may hear and decide).

K

key fact(s) The legally significant facts of a case that raise the legal question of how or whether the law governing the dispute applies. The facts upon which the outcome of the case is determined. They are the facts that establish or satisfy the elements of a cause of action and are necessary to prove or disprove a claim. A key fact is so essential that if it were changed, the outcome of the case would probably change.

key facts—groups Individual facts which, when considered as a group, are key facts that may determine the outcome or a case.

key facts—individual A key fact that, if changed, the outcome of the case would be affected or changed.

key numbers West, a Thomson business, has divided all areas of American law into various topics and subtopics. Each area is identified by a topic name and each specific topic or subtopic is assigned a number called a key number.

L

law The enforceable rules that govern individual and group conduct in a society. The law establishes standards of conduct, the procedures governing standards of conduct, and the remedies available when the standards are not adhered to.

legal analysis Legal analysis is the process of determining how the law applies to the client's problem. It is an exploration of how and why a specific law does or does not apply.

legal issue See issue.

legal research Legal research is the process of finding the law that applies to a client's problem.

legal research process A legal research process is a systematic approach to legal research. It is an organized approach that simplifies research and helps develop research skills.

legislative history The record of legislation during the enactment process. It is composed of committee reports, transcripts of hearings, statements of legislators concerning the legislation, and any other material published for legislative use in regard to the legislation.

limited jurisdiction A court of limited jurisdiction is limited in the types of cases it may hear and decide.

M

majority opinion The opinion in a court decision of the majority of judges.

mandatory authority Any authority or source of law that a court must rely on or follow when reaching a decision (e.g., a decision of a higher court in the jurisdiction on the same or similar issue).

memorandum of law A written analysis of a legal problem. It is an informative document that summarizes the research and analysis of the legal issue or issues raised by the facts of a case. It contains a summary of the law and how the law applies in the case.

N

natural language search A natural language search method allows you to perform a computer search by stating the search query (the issue) using plain English.

O

office legal memorandum A legal memorandum prepared for office use. It presents an objective legal analysis of the issue(s) raised by the facts of the client's case and usually includes the arguments in favor and in opposition to the client's position. It is often referred to by different names: interoffice legal research memorandum, office legal memorandum, office research memorandum, interoffice memorandum of law, and so on.

on all fours A prior court opinion in which the key facts and applicable rule of law are identical or nearly identical with those of the client's case or the case before a court.

on point A term used to refer to a prior court opinion that is sufficiently similar to the facts of the client's case or the case before the court for the prior court opinion to apply as precedent. A case is on point if the similarity between the key facts and rule of law or legal principle of the court opinion and the client's case is sufficient for the court opinion to govern or provide guidance to a later court in deciding the outcome of the client's case.

opinion The written statement by the court expressing how it ruled in a case and the reasons for its ruling.

outline The skeletal structure and organizational framework of writing. An outline is the skeletal structure and organizational framework of the legal research assignment.

outline—expanded An outline that has been expanded so that it may be used when conducting research. The use of an expanded outline allows the integration of all research, analysis, and ideas into an organized outline structure while research and analysis are being conducted.

P

parallel citation When a court opinion is printed in more than one reporter, each citation is a parallel citation to the other citation or citations (e.g., "*Britton v. Britton,* **100 N.M. 424, 671 P.2d 1135** (1983)"—the parallel citations are in bold).

pari materia A canon of construction that provides that statutes dealing with the same subject should be interpreted consistently.

party A plaintiff or defendant in a lawsuit.

personal jurisdiction The authority of the court over the parties to resolve a legal dispute involving the parties.

persuasive authority Any authority a court is not bound to consider or follow but may consider or follow when reaching a decision (e.g., a decision of a court in another state on the same or similar issue, secondary authority, and so on).

plain meaning rule A canon of construction that provides that if the meaning of a statute is clear on its face, it will be interpreted according to its plain meaning and the other canons of construction will not be applied by the court.

plaintiff The party who starts (files) a lawsuit.

precedent An earlier court decision on an issue that applies to govern or guide a subsequent court in its determination of an identical or similar issue based upon identical or similar facts. A court opinion is precedent if there is a sufficient similarity between the key facts and rule of law or legal principle of the court opinion and the matter before the subsequent court.

primary authority Authority that is composed of the law (e.g., constitution, statutes, court opinions).

prior proceedings The events that occurred in the litigation in a lower court or administrative hearing.

purpose clause A statutory section that includes the purpose the legislative body intended to accomplish when drafting the statute.

Q

questions of fact In a jury trial, questions of fact such as whether a person performed a certain act are decided by the jury.

questions of law In a jury trial, questions of law such as what the law is or how it applies are decided by the judge.

R

remand A decision of an appellate court that sends the case back to the trial court for further action.

reverse A decision of an appellate court that disagrees with the decision of the trial court.

S

scope A statutory section that states what is specifically covered and not covered by the statute.

secondary authority Any source of law a court may rely on that is not the law (e.g., legal treatise, restatement of the law, legal encyclopedia).

short title The name by which a statute is known (e.g., Uniform Commercial Code—Sales).

stare decisis A basic principle of the common law system that requires a court to follow a previous decision of that court or a higher court when the current decision involves issues and facts similar to those involved in the previous decision. The doctrine that provides that precedent should be followed.

statement of facts The section of a memorandum of law that presents the factual context of the issue(s) addressed in the memorandum.

statutes Laws passed by legislative bodies that declare rights and duties, or command or prohibit certain conduct.

statutory analysis The interpretation and application of statutory law. The process of determining if a statute applies to a specific fact situation, how it applies, and the effect of that application.

statutory elements The specific conditions or components of a statute that must be met for the statute to apply.

statutory law The body of law composed of laws passed by legislative bodies. The term includes laws or ordinances passed by any legislative body.

subject matter jurisdiction The types or kinds of cases the court has the authority to hear and decide.

supremacy clause The supremacy clause of the U.S. Constitution (Article VI) provides that between federal and state law, federal law is supreme. If an enacted law or court decision of a state conflicts with a federal law or court decision, the state law or decision is invalid to the extent it conflicts with the federal law or decision.

T

terms and connectors search A terms and connectors search (often referred to as Boolean searching) is a search method that allows you to conduct a computer search using key words of the issue and symbols (connectors).

trial court The court where the matter is heard and decided. Testimony is taken, the evidence presented, and the decision is reached in the trial court.

trial court brief An external memorandum of law submitted to a trial court. It presents the legal authority and argument in support of a position advocated by an attorney, usually in regard to a motion or issue being addressed by the court. It is often referred to as a trial brief.

U

URL The address of a Web site is referred to as a Uniform Resource Locator or **URL**.

U.S. District Court The trial court of general jurisdiction in the federal judicial system.

U.S. Supreme Court The final court of appeals in the federal system and the highest court in the United States.

W

Writ of Certiorari A writ from a higher court asking a lower court for the record of a case. A petition for a Writ of Certiorari is a request filed by a party in a lawsuit that a higher court review the decision of a lower court.

Index